THE LETTERS TO PHILEMON,
THE COLOSSIANS, AND
THE EPHESIANS

The Letters to Philemon, the Colossians, and the Ephesians

A Socio-Rhetorical Commentary
on the Captivity Epistles

Ben Witherington III

WILLIAM B. EERDMANS PUBLISHING COMPANY
GRAND RAPIDS, MICHIGAN / CAMBRIDGE, U.K.

Published 2007 by
Wm. B. Eerdmans Publishing Co.
2140 Oak Industrial Drive N.E., Grand Rapids, Michigan 49505 /
P.O. Box 163, Cambridge CB3 9PU U.K.

Printed in the United States of America

12 11 10 09 08 07   7 6 5 4 3 2 1

Library of Congress Cataloging-in-Publication Data

Witherington, Ben, 1951-
    The letters to Philemon, the Colossians, and the Ephesians:
    a socio-rhetorical commentary on the captivity Epistles /
    Ben Witherington III.
        p.   cm.
    Includes bibliographical references.
    ISBN 978-0-8028-2488-2 (pbk.: alk. paper)
    1. Bible. N.T. Philemon — Commentaries. 2. Bible. N.T. Philemon —
Socio-rhetorical criticism. 3. Bible. N.T. Colossians — Commentaries.
4. Bible. N.T. Colossians — Socio-rhetorical criticism. 5. Bible. N.T. Ephesians —
Commentaries. 6. Bible. N.T. Ephesians — Socio-rhetorical criticism.   I. Title.

BS2765.53.W58   2007
227'.07 — dc22

                                                        2007035450

www.eerdmans.com

To Jeff and Beth Greenway and Bill and Susan Arnold
who exemplify many of the virtues spoken of in these captivity epistles.
To John, Loren, Walter, David, Tom, and Kingsley, my Durham friends.
Christmas 2006

Contents

Abbreviations

ABD	*Anchor Bible Dictionary* (New York: Doubleday, 1992)
BI	*Biblical Illustrator*
Bib	*Biblica*
BJRL	*Bulletin of the John Rylands Library*
CBQ	*Catholic Biblical Quarterly*
CIG	*Corpus Inscriptionum Graecarum*
CIJ	*Corpus Inscriptionum Judaicarum*
CIL	*Corpus Inscriptionum Latinarum*
ETL	*Ephemerides theologicae lovanienses*
EvQ	*Evangelical Quarterly*
ExpT	*Expository Times*
GTJ	*Grace Theological Journal*
HTR	*Harvard Theological Review*
IBS	*Irish Biblical Studies*
ICC	International Critical Commentary
Inst. Or.	Quintilian, *Institutio Oratio*
JBL	*Journal of Biblical Literature*
JETS	*Journal of the Evangelical Theological Society*
JSNT	*Journal for the Study of the New Testament*
JSNTS	*Journal for the Study of the New Testament* Supplements
JTS	*Journal of Theological Studies*
JTSA	*Journal of Theology for Southern Africa*
LTP	*Laval théologique et philosophique*
New Docs	*New Documents Illustrating Early Christianity* (North Ryde: Macquarie University/Grand Rapids: Eerdmans, 1976-)
NovT	*Novum Testamentum*

NT	New Testament
NTS	*New Testament Studies*
OT	Old Testament
P. Oxy.	Oxyrhynchus Papyri
RevExp	*Review and Expositor*
Rhet.	Aristotle, *Rhetoric*
Rhet. ad Her.	*Rhetorica ad Herennium*
RHR	*Revue de l'histoire des religions*
RTR	*Reformed Theological Review*
SCH	*Studies in Church History*
SEG	*Supplementum Epigraphicum Graecum*
SUNT	Studien zur Umwelt des Neuen Testaments
TC	Bruce M. Metzger, *A Textual Commentary on the Greek New Testament* (New York: United Bible Societies, 1971)
TZ	*Theologische Zeitschrift*
WBC	Word Biblical Commentary
ZNW	*Zeitschrift für die Neutestamentliche Wissenschaft*

Introduction

The study of Paul's captivity epistles, by which I mean Philippians, Philemon, Colossians, and Ephesians, has often been done piecemeal or in small clusters. Philemon is usually paired with Colossians, or occasionally with Philippians, or sometimes we find Colossians and Ephesians studied together. More rare is the study of Colossians, Ephesians, and Philemon together. It has always been realized, however, that there are some intertextual connections between Philemon, Colossians, and Ephesians, though there is debate on how these issues should be adjudicated. Which document was written first? Is Ephesians somehow literarily dependent on Colossians? Were Colossians and Philemon sent to the same destination at the same time or perhaps in sequence (Philemon first, then Colossians)? It seems high time that these three documents were assessed together and in relationship to each other. The question of authorship is of course tangled up in this discussion.

Generally speaking, the vast majority of scholars are quite convinced that Philemon is from Paul's hand, probably a majority of scholars think Colossians is also by Paul, but only about half or less of commentators think Paul himself penned Ephesians.[1] I am particularly concerned about how the issue of style affects this entire discussion, and it is my view that style cannot in this case provide

---

1. H. Hoehner's *Ephesians: An Exegetical Commentary* (Grand Rapids: Baker, 2002), pp. 9-20, presents us with exact totals of how many commentators have been for or against Pauline authorship of Ephesians. It is interesting that he is able to show that between 1971 and 1990 a slight majority of commentators said Ephesians was not Pauline (54%, 1971-80; 58%, 1981-90). However, of those commenting on Ephesians from 1991 to 2001 (some 40 commentators) there is a 50-50 split. But my sense of the literature is that a majority, though not an overwhelming majority, of scholars who have not written a commentary on Ephesians think it was not written by Paul.

any decisive reasons to dispute the Pauline character of any of these three documents, precisely because ancient writers who were rhetorically adept, as Paul was,
adopted different styles for different audiences.[2] This is not a matter of the development of style but rather of the adopting of a style to suit one's audience.[3]

Among the captivity epistles Philemon, Colossians, and Ephesians are
most similar in style and in various ways in content.[4] It is my conviction that
something of great importance has been missing in the study of these documents, namely their rhetorical character, especially in light of the locale to
which these documents were directed. They are the only letters attributed to
Paul that were written to destinations in Asia. One of the keys, though by no
means the only one, to understanding these documents, especially Ephesians, is
recognition that they reflect a deliberate attempt at Asiatic rhetoric. In the case
of Ephesians we are also dealing with epideictic rhetoric, which further explains
why it stands out to some degree from Colossians and Philemon.[5] B. Reicke,
over three decades ago, made a very astute observation without demonstrating
his point. He argued that the captivity epistles in "their vocabulary and theology were adapted to audiences living in these countries. *Therefore their style
took over elements of Asianist rhetoric.*"[6] I intend to show that he was correct. In
writing these documents to Asian Christians, Paul made them words on target,
partly by adopting and adapting an Asiatic style of Greek rhetoric. Ephesians
most reflects this style precisely because it is basically a circular epideictic homily with only the bare minimum of epistolary elements added so that it could be
sent as a written document.[7] As a document meant to be declaimed, Ephesians
partakes of the full gamut of Asiatic epideictic rhetoric.

---

2. See rightly, L. T. Johnson, *The Writings of the New Testament* (Minneapolis: Fortress,
1999), p. 409: "One factor often left out in this discussion is that ancient rhetorical training
cultivated using and adapting a wide range of styles to match particular rhetorical occasions
. . . the style and character of a text is determined mostly by the occasion that gives rise to it,
the type of material treated, the particular persona the writer chooses to adopt, and the
writer's specific relationship with the reader."

3. In other words, one could not draw conclusions about the chronological relationship between these letters and other Pauline letters purely on the basis of style. Style depended on the audience one was addressing, one's subject matter, and to some degree the
species of rhetoric one was employing.

4. I have already written a commentary on Philippians — *Friendship and Finances in
Philippi* (Valley Forge: Trinity, 1994).

5. Of necessity, because Ephesians raises more questions and problems, more space
must be given to discussion of it in this Introduction than to the other two letters we are examining. For further discussion on them see pp. 12-14 below and the introductions to each
book on p. 51 and pp. 99-114.

6. B. Reicke, "The Historical Setting of Colossians," *Review and Expositor* 70 (1973):
429-38, here p. 438, emphasis added.

7. One of the usual bases for rejecting the Pauline authorship of Ephesians is the im-

Ephesians is not a letter in any real sense, nor was it written particularly to Ephesus in all probability. The textual evidence in Eph. 1.1 slightly favors the conclusion that the words "in Ephesus" were not an original part of the document.[8] But it is believable that that city's name was later appended because that is where the document finally ended up, whatever other cities it circulated in. In other words, the reference to Ephesus does let us know, in general, the region in which this document circulated.[9]

Colossians and Philemon are letters, but they are rhetorically shaped letters, being basically oral in character. Both of them reflect deliberative rhetoric.[10] This is another reason that Ephesians differs from Colossians and Philemon in some respects. Ephesians, unlike Colossians and Philemon, is not a problem-solving document and is not focused on the future, but rather offers a series of praises and testimonies about the nature of salvation, the unity of the church, the character of Christian marriage, and the like.[11] All three documents have a concern for Christian unity, which necessarily entails a break from and with the non-Christian values of those outside the community. The pagan ways of the past must be left in the past, including the pagan way of treating slaves as less than human.

---

personal nature of the document. But of course Paul was as capable of composing a homily meant for several groups of Christians as he was of composing a particularistic letter to a single congregation. See Hoehner, *Ephesians*, pp. 21-24.

8. See pp. 215-24 below on Eph. 1.1. The words are absent from the following important manuscripts — ℗46, ℵ*, B*, 424c, 1739, the manuscripts used by Origen, and apparently also those used by Tertullian and Ephraem. Marcion identifies this document as "to the Laodiceans," not to Ephesus, which may support the theory this was indeed an encyclical that acquired city names when a copy was left in one or another city. See B. M. Metzger, *A Textual Commentary on the Greek New Testament* (New York: United Bible Societies, 1998), p. 532.

9. As will be seen (pp. 217-19 below), this means that attempts to see Ephesians as addressing some particular crisis or situation in Ephesus are probably misguided.

10. Philemon, though not a private letter, is clearly the most intentionally personal of the three, reflecting third order moral discourse (on which see pp. 99-120 below). 90.9% of the use of first person in Philemon is of the first person singular (some 40 occurrences), as opposed, for instance, to Colossians, which uses the first person singular only a slight majority of the time, and Ephesians, which uses the first person plural (to identify with the audience) some 62.4% of the time and thus uses the first person singular 37.6% of the time. See the chart by S. R. Llewelyn in *New Docs* 6, p. 171.

11. See K. Snodgrass, *The NIV Application Bible Commentary: Ephesians* (Grand Rapids: Zondervan, 1996), pp. 18-20.

Differences in Rhetorical Style

Asianism in Ephesians

There were in fact three different approaches to Greek style in the first century A.D. There was first of all Koine, or common, Greek. This basic style could be called the lowest common denominator, and it was used as a "medium of communication throughout the Near East by persons without deep roots in Greek culture."[12] It is often assumed, too often in fact, that the NT reflects only this unvarnished approach to Greek. How often have we been told that the NT is simply written in Koine Greek? That is not entirely true, as should have been realized once it was admitted that some NT authors' Greek style and ability go well beyond ordinary or basic communication Greek (e.g. Hebrews, 1 Peter, to mention but two non-Pauline examples). In other words, some portions of the NT reflect a more self-conscious and literary quality of Greek.

When it comes to the self-conscious adaptation of a style of Greek that goes beyond Koine, there were basically two options: to take up an Asiatic style or to take up an Atticizing style of Greek. Atticizing style was a deliberate attempt to emulate Classical Greek style, and it is not a surprise that some Christian writers of the second century A.D. did strive to do this. When they attempted to do apologetics in a Greek vein, they did sometimes adopt such a style. This is not what we find in the Pauline Captivity Epistles. Instead what we find, particularly in Ephesians, is Asiatic style. Asianism was "a highly artificial, self-conscious search for striking expression in diction, sentence structure and rhythm. It deliberately goes to almost any possible extreme."[13]

But in fact there seem to have been two kinds of Asianism. Cicero (*Brutus* 325) says that one kind of Asian style is epigrammatic and brilliant (called smooth, sententious, and euphonious) with a focus on utterances that are neat and charming. This was generally the less substantive form of Asiatic rhetoric. The other form of Asiatic rhetoric was noted for a torrent of speech full of ornamentation, redundancy, and fine language. This style was called swift and impetuous. Cicero says that the latter was especially prevalent in his day. He cites two first-century B.C. orators from Asia, Aeschylus from Cnidus and

---

12. G. A. Kennedy, *New Testament Interpretation through Rhetorical Criticism* (Chapel Hill: University of North Carolina Press, 1984), p. 32. Kennedy in fact calls Koine a simplified form of Attic Greek. See his *Classical Rhetoric and Its Christian and Secular Tradition from Ancient to Modern Times* (Chapel Hill: University of North Carolina Press, 1980), p. 86.

13. Kennedy, *New Testament Interpretation,* p. 32. Philemon is such a short document that it betrays this style of writing the least, though there are some hints, especially in the repetition of a limited number of terms, wordplay, and a very high degree of emotional expression throughout. See pp. 57-60 below.

Aeschines of Miletus, who modeled this style.[14] Asiatic style was noted for a particular kind of sing-song rhythm — the dichoree or double trochee was regarded as the favorite Asianist rhythm (Cicero, *Orator* 212). Cicero himself, it seems, adopted this second Asiatic style, while his detractors favored a more Attic style of Greek and rhetorical delivery.[15]

> The hallmarks of Ciceronian style, most of which have been identified with "Asianism," appear in [Cicero's] speeches of all periods, early and late. Among these we might mention: complex periodicity, often making elaborate use of parallelism; the presence of rhythm, both in the sense of the employment of clauses within periods that are carefully balanced in length and sound, as well as the employment of favored combination of long and short syllables at the end of periods . . . ; constant use of a wide variety of *ornamenta,* involving both word and phrase, aimed at artistic expression and often privileging sound and general impression over precision of meaning; recourse to wit, irony, wordplay, and humor; employment of *variatio* at all levels, including within the period, between periods, between parts of speech, as well as in the styles employed in different types of speech; and the constant appeal to the emotions, especially in the opening and closing sections of the speech.[16]

Asiatic rhetoric was noted for its emotion and even affectation:

> The styles of Asiatic oratory are two, one epigrammatic and pointed, full of fine ideas which are not so weighty and serious as neat and graceful, the other with not so many sententious ideas, but voluble and hurried in its flow of language, and marked by an ornamented and elegant diction. (*Brutus* 95, 325)

We see Asiatic style quite clearly in Asian Christian writers of a slightly later period — for example, Melito of Sardis.

So many of these stylistic features and techniques occur in Ephesians that

---

14. See the analysis in G. A. Kennedy, *The Art of Rhetoric in the Roman World 300 B.C.–A.D. 300* (Princeton: Princeton University Press, 1972), pp. 97-100. Kennedy points out that many Romans like Cicero went to Asia to study rhetoric because there were so many famous rhetoricians and schools in the region.

15. The first of these two styles strives for sophisticated sentences full of wordplay and metaphors, arranged in artificial rhythmic patterns. The second is characterized as less flamboyant but still involving a flow of colorful words, often involving redundancy (e.g., "the strength of his might"), alliteration, assonance, and digressions, all of which we find in Ephesians.

16. A. Vasaly, "Cicero's Early Speeches," in *Brill's Companion to Cicero,* ed. J. M. May (Leiden: Brill, 2002), pp. 71-111, here p. 86. I am indebted to Professor Christopher McDonough of Sewanee for pointing me to some of this material.

it is hard to understand why Ephesians has not more readily been recognized as an exercise in an Asiatic style of rhetoric. It is however unfortunate that we have no recording of the "sound" of the Asiatic style because the oral dimensions of this sort of rhetoric were important — pitch, volume, speed, intonation, voice modulation, and the like (not to mention the visual dimensions such as facial contortions and gestures) all contributed to this style.[17]

It appears that Asiatic oratory was a development of the highly ornamental style cultivated by Isocrates (436-338 B.C.). It thus had a long history prior to NT times. It was especially prized and often practiced in western Asia Minor by sophists and rhetors of various sorts.[18] This thoroughly Hellenized region of the Empire had long been a haven for the rhetoric of praise and blame, a trend only exacerbated with the rise of the emperor cult. It is entirely believable that in Ephesians Paul is striving to speak of Christ and the church in the same sort of laudatory and effusive terms often used of the emperor, his virtues, his accomplishments, and the like as well as of various religious cults, including the cult of Artemis. Indeed, Paul is seeking to show how God in Christ eclipses the glory and accomplishments of the emperor and other such pagan figures (and deities).

Does Philemon also reflect the style characteristic of Asiatic rhetoric? We do find some redundancy: "I appeal to you for my son Onesmius, who became my son. . . ." (v. 10), "no longer as a slave but more than a slave" (v. 16), "he is very dear to me, but even dearer to you" (v. 16). There is also the ornamentation through wordplay in vv. 11 and 20 on Onesimus's name (which is really a nickname meaning "useful"). Furthermore, as we have seen there was lots of pathos and emotion in Asiatic rhetoric, and this is perhaps why in Philemon we find Paul playing the pathos card well before the end of his little speech: "I appeal to you on the basis of love, I Paul, an old man and now also a prisoner . . ." (v. 9). This may be a short document but it is a heart-wrenching plea for the freedom of Onesimus ("he is my very heart," v. 12) using not so subtle attempts at arm-twisting. Philemon is a miniature rhetorical masterpiece in an Asiatic vein.

---

17. See A.D. Leeman, *Orationis Ratio: The Stylistic Theories and Practice of the Roman Orators, Historians, and Philosophers* I (Amsterdam: Hakkert, 1963), pp. 93-94. As Leeman says, reading Cicero's orations is but a poor shadow of hearing them properly delivered, particularly because of the histrionic Asiatic style of the material and its delivery.

18. On the many sophists and rhetors in western Asia, especially in Ephesus, Pergamum, Smyrna, and in the Lycus valley in Hierapolis, see G. W. Bowersock, *Greek Sophists in the Roman Empire* (Oxford: Clarendon, 1969), pp. 17-29.

Epideictic Rhetoric in Ephesians

Epideictic rhetoric was the rhetoric of display and demonstration, of praise and blame in dramatic tones. It was also especially appropriate for a document that was intended to be a part of worship and to inculcate worship. "Epideictic is perhaps best regarded as including any discourse, oral or written, that does not aim at a specific action or decision but seeks to enhance knowledge, understanding, or belief, often through praise or blame, whether of persons, things, or values. It is thus an important feature of cultural or group cohesion. Most religious preaching . . . can be viewed as epideictic."[19] This description aptly delineates the character of the homily we know as Ephesians.[20]

Epideictic rhetoric celebrates what is already true or exists and attempts to inculcate an attitude of awe, respect, even wonder in the listener in regard to these realities. Effusive language is in part the tool used to inculcate this attitude of awe or reverence. Epideictic is the language of someone bearing witness to a reality or truth that the audience is meant to take to heart and commit to memory (as Parmenides, Fragment 6, says quite clearly). This sort of rhetoric, if done well, creates in the audience "a beholding wonder, an overwhelming sense of exultation that sweeps over us when we catch a glimmer of excellence abiding in a familiar object or event. This jubilation is on the order of an admiring gratitude. . . . And it is this re-creation of aesthetic revelation that the Greek orator sought to achieve through *em-phasis,* a sharing with the community of his wonder-at-invisibles, an act of testimony that took precedent over simple persuasion."[21] Epideictic rhetoric is primarily about testimony and appreciation, not primarily about argumentation and proofs. But the audience is not just to appreciate. They are being reminded of what is true, things they already know or ought to know. They are being urged to embrace these truths or virtues. Epideictic rhetoric triggers remembrance of fundamental things. Thus toward the end of Ephesians Paul rehearses again with amplification what he has already taught the audience in Colossians about household codes and the like.

While in the Roman setting this sort of rhetoric could have practical functions (e.g., at funerals),[22] in the Greek setting it was far more often used for

---

19. G. A. Kennedy, "The Genres of Rhetoric," in *Handbook of Classical Rhetoric in the Hellenistic Period 330 B.C.–A.D. 400,* ed. S. E. Porter (Leiden: Brill, 1997), pp. 43-50, here p. 45.

20. Of recent commentators W. F. Taylor is the first to have noticed that Ephesians appears to be an epideictic discourse. His treatment differs from that of A. T. Lincoln in seeing the whole of Ephesians as fitting this rhetorical species, whereas Lincoln sees the second half of Ephesians as deliberative rhetoric. See W. F. Taylor and J. Reumann, *Ephesians, Colossians* (Augsburg Commentary on the New Testament; Minneapolis: Augsburg, 1985), pp. 22-23.

21. L. Rosenfield, "The Practical Celebration of Epideictic," in *A Synoptic History of Classical Rhetoric,* ed. J. J. Murphy (Davis: Hermagoras, 1983), pp. 131-55, here p. 138.

22. In fact, in a Roman setting epideictic rhetoric was primarily, and sometimes almost

offering a panegyric to a god, a hero of the past, or some great virtue or the like (see Quintilian, *Inst. Or.* 3.7.3). As Quintilian reminds us, epideictic rhetoric is not the rhetoric that seeks to deal with an issue or a problem. The arguments in an epideictic piece may bear a semblance of a proof, but, since display and exposition is the function of this rhetoric, it is not noted for syllogistic logic or proofs. "The proper function of panegyric is to amplify and embellish its themes" (3.7.6). Amplification and embellishment usually take the form of dramatic hyperbole, long sentences, the use of big words and ornate language, and a good deal of repetition for emphasis. Epideictic is

> directed in the main to the praise of gods and men, but may occasionally be applied to the praise of animals or even inanimate objects. In praising the gods our first step will be to express our veneration of the majesty of their nature in general terms, next we shall proceed to praise the special power of the individual god and the "inventions" by which he has benefited the human race. . . . Next we must record their exploits as handed down from antiquity. . . . Some again may be praised because they were born immortal, others because they won immortality by their valor. (3.7.6-9)

It is hard not to notice how apt a description this is of Eph. 1.3-14 (and beyond), which focuses on praising God and what he has accomplished in Christ for his people. In general epideictic rhetoric is highly emotional in character meant to inspire the audience to appreciate something or someone, or at the other end of the spectrum, despise something or someone. It seeks to charm or to cast odium. Aristotle says that one of the first aims of such rhetoric is to excite admiration of someone or something (*Rhet.* 3.2.5).

Quintilian reminds us that the same form of ornamentation will not suit the three different species of rhetoric:

> For the oratory of display aims solely at delighting the audience, and therefore develops all the resources of eloquence and deploys all its ornament, since it seeks not to steal its way into the mind nor to wrest the victory from its opponent, but aims solely at honor and glory. Consequently the orator, like the hawker who displays his wares, will set forth before his audience for

---

exclusively used for encomiums or funeral oratory. See Kennedy, *The Art of Rhetoric*, pp. 21-23. This is perhaps why Paul does not really use epideictic rhetoric when he is addressing the Christians in Rome. See B. Witherington and D. Hyatt, *The Epistle to the Romans* (Grand Rapids: Eerdmans, 2004), pp. 1ff. It should also be added that since Asiatic rhetoric was not in vogue in Rome in the first century A.D., in fact was already waning in popularity during the latter part of the first century B.C. in Cicero's last days, it is no surprise that Paul does not use it in Romans. Those who lived in Rome and partook of Roman culture on the whole wanted a rhetoric that had more *gravitas* and was less florid and ornamental. See rightly Leeman, *Orationis*, p. 111.

their inspection, no, almost for their handling, all his most attractive reflections, all the brilliance that language and the charm that figures can supply,
together with all the magnificence of metaphor and the elaborate art of
composition that is at his disposal. (*Inst. Or.* 8.3.11-12).

In general what one would expect from epideictic rhetoric is more use of metaphor, use of the more elaborate, euphonious, elegant, or attractive words when
choosing among synonyms, and the arrangement of words that "sounds"
better.

Ephesians contains eight very long sentences (1.3-14; 1.15-23; 2.1-7; 3.2-13;
3.14-19; 4.1-6; 4.11-16; 6.14-20). They are spread evenly throughout the work and
are a regular feature of the work. They are not confined to prayers, doxologies,
or complex theological material, but are even found in mere parenthetical remarks (4.1-6, 11-16). How do we best account for this? By noting that 1) this is an
oral document, 2) this is a rhetorical document, and especially 3) this is an
epideictic and Asiatic document, and long-winded sentences are common in
the rhetoric of praise and blame, of commendation and condemnation, especially in the region which especially favored such expansive rhetoric — Asia. In
other words, various stylistic mysteries of Ephesians would not have been seen
as mysterious, never mind beyond the realm of Pauline possibility, if the rhetorical dimensions of the document had been considered.

Let us consider one other distinctive feature of the style of Ephesians. Five
times we find the phrase "in the heavenlies" rather than the normal "in the
heaven(s)." The phrase does not occur in Colossians or Philemon even though
there are other similarities in style among these documents.[23] This is because
epideictic rhetoric by nature focuses on what is true on earth and in heaven *in
the present,* particularly in regard to the deceased. Thus Christ is praised like a
hero who has achieved apotheosis and enthronement beyond death. Asiatic redundant language is particularly seen in "That power is like the working of his
mighty strength which he exerted in Christ when he raised him from the dead
and seated him at his right hand in the heavenlies" (1.19-20). 2.6 then applies
this language indirectly to the audience: in the person of their representative Jesus they are now seated in the heavenlies as well. This makes good sense in the
Greco-Roman environment, where it was believed that there was an integral
connection between the living and the dead, especially with one's own ances-
tors, whose spirit or "genius" could inform and inspire one to good deeds. The
point is that Jesus is in the afterlife, and because believers are "in him" they also
already have a provisional and glorious place in heaven. Indeed they already
have, in him who is in the heavens, the condition of being blessed with every

---

23. This is because deliberative rhetoric does not focus on what is now the case,
whether here or in heaven. It focuses on the future.

spiritual blessing in the present, but in the heavenlies (1.3). The author speaks of this in the present tense, as is appropriate in epideictic rhetoric.

Epideictic rhetoric is not that of debate, discussion, dialogue, or diatribe and is thus unlike forensic and deliberative rhetoric. It is the rhetoric of a monologue, speech, lecture, or sermon that does not expect a direct response. Therefore, Ephesians does not have the conversational, epistolary, or diatribal character of other Pauline letters. It is not intended to be a part of a conversation. It is an official pronouncement or homily, meant to be received, believed, appreciated, and appropriated, but not responded to in the form of correspondence or debate.

One of the major social settings where one would find epideictic rhetoric was at the games in speeches of exhortation to the athletes or sometimes to the audiences. A similar social setting is seen where a commander exhorts his troops before they go into battle, praising their fine qualities and urging them to be strong and brave and to fight the good fight. This is exactly what we find in the *peroratio* at the end of Ephesians, where Christians are exhorted to stand, having put on the full armor of Christ (6.10-20).[24]

The Different Rhetorical Situations

The rhetorical situations which Paul addressed in these three documents are varied. While Philemon was apparently a convert of Paul's, the church at Colossae was not one that Paul had founded (see Col. 2.1). Rather it was apparently founded by one of his coworkers or understudies. This did not put him in the same position when writing to Colossae as he was with Romans, where he did not even have an indirect connection with the founding of the church.[25] But still, in Colossians and probably Ephesians as well, he had to take into account this indirect relationship if his rhetoric was to be effective. In Philemon he is able to exercise direct authority as Philemon's spiritual father, but this was not the case with the Colossians in general, it would appear. He had to deal with the people of the church in Colossae as he found them, starting with them where they were and attempting to persuade them to adopt some new positions, as we shall see. It is clear that there were problems at both cognitive and behavioral levels and that Paul feels he must address both in Colossians.

It was a poor rhetor indeed who did not at least attempt to address the audience in a manner that reflected the sort of relationship he had with them

---

24. Here I follow A. T. Lincoln, "'Stand, Therefore . . .': Ephesians 6:10-20 as Peroratio," *BI* 3 (1995): 99-114.

25. See Witherington and Hyatt, *Romans,* pp. 1-40.

and the level of rapport that he had with them. There are at least three levels of moral discourse:

1. the level of discourse one feels free to use with an audience one is familiar with but has not personally addressed before — what can be called the opening gambit,
2. the level of discourse that builds on what has been heard and believed by the audience before, of which they must be reminded in a way that is generally applicable to all in the audience, with elaborations on these commonly held beliefs, and
3. the level of discourse one offers as if to an intimate with whom one can fully and truly speak freely, directly, and personally, without great fear of alienating the audience.

1. represents what we find in Colossians, 2. represents what we find in Ephesians, and 3. represents what we find in Philemon.

Other Stylistic Objections to the Pauline Character of Ephesians and Colossians

We have already suggested some very good reasons that militate against the conclusion that Ephesians, and Colossians as well, should be seen as un-Pauline on stylistic grounds. But it will be well to deal with some of the arguments that ignore the rhetorical dimensions to the question of style at this juncture.

The Vocabulary of Ephesians

It has sometimes been urged that Ephesians has too many unique words to be Pauline. This argument ignores the need for "invention" and stylistic variation in both Asiatic rhetoric in general and epideictic rhetoric specifically. But even excluding rhetorical considerations, Ephesians has no more distinctive or unique vocabulary than Galatians:

	Galatians	Ephesians
total words	2220	2429
different words used	526	530
words appearing nowhere else in the NT	35	41
words found elsewhere in the NT, but not in Paul	90	84[26]

26. Hoehner, *Ephesians,* p. 24.

Furthermore, the number of hapax legomena (words appearing nowhere else in the NT) per page in Ephesians is about the same as in other Pauline letters. H. J. Cadbury once summed up the matter aptly when he said: "Which is more likely — that an imitator of Paul in the first century composed a writing ninety or ninety-five percent in accordance with Paul's style or that Paul himself wrote a letter diverging five or ten percent from his usual style?"[27] While I would want to urge that the percentages are not quite that imbalanced (i.e. Asiatic style makes more than a 5% difference in what we find in these Captivity Epistles), nonetheless his basic point is well taken.

The Relationship between Colossians and Ephesians

But what about the issues of intertextuality between Ephesians and Colossians? What do we make of the fact that while there are echoes of various earlier Pauline letters in Ephesians, there appears to be a literary relationship between Colossians and Ephesians? A. T. Lincoln regards the literary dependence of Ephesians on Colossians and its use of earlier Pauline material, especially from Romans, as what most decisively tells against Pauline authorship of Ephesians.[28] There are several problems with this conclusion, especially from a rhetorical point of view. If Ephesians is indeed a homily meant to distill and sum up the essence of Paulinism, the heart of his message and ministry to Gentiles, it is hardly a surprise that it has echoes of his earlier letters, especially where he most clearly expressed himself on the heart of the matter when it came to the relationship of Jews and Gentiles, namely in Romans. Paul could have done this summing up as easily as some anonymous coworker or later tradent. Indeed, I would suggest that he would be more likely to do so and would do it better than an imitator, especially as he reached the end of his period of house arrest in Rome and was thinking of moving on to further ministry. But let us consider the specific intertextual issues between Colossians and Ephesians.

It is my judgment that the degree and nature of this intertextuality is similar to what we find between Jude and 2 Peter and does establish the literary dependence of Ephesians on Colossians. But we are also probably dealing with common authorship, which is not the case with Jude and 2 Peter. Looking first at word usage: 26.5% of Ephesians is paralleled verbally in Colossians. A total of 246 words are shared by these two letters, many of which are used multiple

27. H. J. Cadbury, "The Dilemma of Ephesians," *NTS* 5 (1958-59): 95-101, here p. 101. The importance of Cadbury's conclusion should not be underestimated since Cadbury, as his work on Acts also shows, was meticulous in his analysis of the style of an author.

28. A. T. Lincoln and A. J. M. Wedderburn, *The Theology of the Later Pauline Letters* (Cambridge: Cambridge University Press, 1993), p. 84.

times, and "when accounting for the multiple use of these 246 words, they make up 2057 words (out of 2429 words) in Ephesians and 1362 (out of 1574 words) in Colossians."[29] 13 shared words occur 25 times or more in Ephesians, and 9 shared words occur 25 times or more in Colossians, making up 46% of Ephesians and 43% of Colossians. Even allowing for the multiple uses of common conjunctions, articles, and names, this is still significant. 21 words are found in both Ephesians and Colossians but not elsewhere in Paul's letters, 11 of them occurring nowhere else in the NT.

There are also parallel passages. Three times we have 7 words in the same order in both Colossians and Ephesians (Eph. 1.1-2 = Col. 1.1-2; Eph. 3.2 = Col. 1.25; Eph. 3.9 = Col. 1.26). Twice 5 consecutive words are identical (Eph. 1.7 = Col. 1.14; Eph. 4.16 = Col. 2.9). Perhaps the clearest proof of at least some literary dependence is the information regarding Tychicus. Here we find 29 words in a row that are identical in these two documents (Eph. 6.21-22 = Col. 4.7-8). The order of similar material is also paralleled (Eph. 1.15-23 = Col. 1.3-14; Eph. 2.11-22 = Col. 1.21-23; Eph. 3.1-13 = Col. 1.24–2.3; Eph. 4.17-32 = Col. 3.5-11; Eph. 5.1-6 = Col. 3.12-15; Eph. 5.15-21 = Col. 3.16-17; Eph. 5.22–6.9 = Col. 3.18–4.1; Eph. 6.18-20 = Col. 4.2-4; Eph. 6.23-24 = Col. 4.18).[30] The sheer volume of similar content and content arranged in the same order again strongly supports the case for dependence of one of these documents on the other. Yet Lincoln is clearly correct in concluding that "this is free and creative dependence, not a slavish imitation or copying."[31] Of the two, Ephesians is certainly the fuller and more expansive exposition, particularly of the household codes. In my view this means that Ephesians was written either by Paul or by a Paulinist sufficiently confident that he understood and could represent Paul well, that he had the authority to represent Paul's views for a later audience, and that he did not need to be a mere copier or slavish imitator of Paul.

If Colossians is deemed authentic, as most scholars still think, then we must imagine a pseudepigrapher lifting some parts of Colossians verbatim and changing others, adding to the discussion, varying the word-use and style and writing in a more expansive epideictic mode.[32] It seems far more likely that the original author would have felt free to do this, not a later copier striving hard to make Ephesians look like an authentic Pauline document in both style and content. "[I]t is difficult to believe that a later writer who followed Colossians so

---

29. Hoehner, *Ephesians*, p. 31. Hoehner unfortunately does not allow these facts to have their full weight in his assessment of the matter.

30. See further Hoehner, *Ephesians*, p. 34.

31. Lincoln, *Ephesians* (Waco: Word; 1990), p. lv.

32. On Colossians as a pseudepigraph see A. Standhartinger, *Studien zur Entstehungsgeschichte und Intention des Kolosserbriefs* (Leiden: Brill, 1999). Standhartinger relies on the dubious and unprovable hypothesis that the author of Colossians relied on oral traditions, including oral reports about Paul's ministry, to make the letter appear sufficiently Pauline.

assiduously would use the shared vocabulary in such different ways. The whole idea behind pseudepigraphy is to replicate the thought and style of the exemplar as closely as possible."[33] Perhaps, with T. Moritz, we could see Ephesians as drawing on Colossians and enriching those traditions with OT traditions presumably because the audience for Ephesians includes more Jewish Christians than Colossians does.[34] But this is not a sufficient explanation of the differences between Colossians and Ephesians, not least because Ephesians offers more of a detailed Christian perspective on matters treated in Colossians, such as marriage.[35]

Theological Differences between Ephesians and Earlier Letters of Paul

The theological differences between Ephesians and earlier unquestioned Pauline letters are often considered the decisive proof that Paul did not write Ephesians.[36] Some of these complaints do not take into account the necessary "present tense" focus of epideictic rhetoric. For example, it is pointed out that the death of Christ and the theology of the cross is less prominent in Ephesians than in the earlier letters and that salvation itself is referred to as an accomplished act (the perfect tense of *sōzō* in 2.8). The future dimension of salvation, while not entirely absent, is also less in evidence in Ephesians. Christ's resurrection, exaltation, and cosmic lordship are more prominent, noticeably more than even in Colossians.

But when one knows the time frame of epideictic rhetoric, which affects the way one presents one's theological ideas, this is precisely what we would expect in Ephesians. It is what is *now* the case, what is now true about Christ, that we would expect Paul to concentrate on in Ephesians. Christ is now the risen Lord, he is now the exalted one sitting beside God, he is now the cosmic lord of the universe. There is furthermore the social factor that Paul seems keen in this letter to establish that Jesus is now Lord over powers, principalities, and world rulers, so that Caesar is therefore not. So some of what was predicated of Nero Caesar, the son of the deified Claudius, is instead predicated of Christ. This

---

33. Johnson, *Writings*, p. 409.

34. T. Moritz, *A Profound Mystery: The Use of the Old Testament in Ephesians* (Leiden: Brill, 1996), p. 220.

35. Moritz, p. 220, is right that there is a difference in contextualization of the material in these two documents, but there is also a profound difference in the character of the rhetoric as well, which he overlooks.

36. See, e.g., W. G. Kümmel, *Introduction to the New Testament* (London: SCM, 1975), p. 360, who states overconfidently that the theology of Ephesians makes it impossible for the letter to be from Paul.

could be, to some extent, seen as revolutionary rhetoric opposing the emperor cult in Asia.[37]

Another frequent complaint about Ephesians is that it contradicts Paul's earlier teachings about the Law. Eph. 2.15 says that Christ's death has nullified the Law. This judgment actually depends on a dubious reading of both Galatians and Romans. I have elsewhere argued at length that Paul is indeed saying as early as Galatians that Christ came to redeem those under the Law out from under the Law and that in and by Christ's death the Law came to an end for those who are in Christ (cf. Rom. 10.4 to Gal. 3.25).[38] Paul believes that the eschatological situation is such that the turn of the era happened by means of Christ's death and resurrection, and that now we must speak of a new covenant, not merely a renewed old one.[39]

Yet another complaint is that Ephesians does not use the Pauline language of justification when it speaks about redemption. Of course there are other undisputed Pauline letters which have little or no such language even though they discuss salvation. Of the some 85 occurrences of this sort of forensic language in Paul's letters, 61 are in either Galatians or Romans. Justification language is the language of the law court, forensic rhetoric, and this is precisely not the sort of rhetoric one finds in Ephesians. Justification language could also be used in deliberative rhetoric, but this too is not what we find in Ephesians. Ephesians is all about testimonies to what is now true: we are saved by grace through faith. It is also about exhortations based on those present and abiding truths.

Another complaint about Ephesians is its more developed ecclesiology. We may grant that the body image, for example, is more developed in both Colossians and Ephesians than we find in 1 Corinthians 12. Christ is now said clearly to be the head of the body. But this is hardly a development against the flow of Pauline thought or away from Paul's original metaphor. It is in fact an especially important development in any piece of rhetoric critiquing the emperor cult, for the emperor was the one who was said to be the head of the body, of, that is, the empire. Here the head is clearly counter-identified as the exalted Christ. Ephesians uses *ekklēsia* exclusively of the church universal. Of course

---

37. See the discussion of C. E. Arnold, pp. 109-10 below.

38. See my more detailed arguments in *Grace in Galatia* (Grand Rapids: Eerdmans, 1998), pp. 341-56, and in Witherington and Hyatt, *Romans,* the extended treatment of Romans 2–5.

39. Here is where I would part company with my good friend N. T. Wright and others. The nature of ancient acts of covenanting and treaty-making in the ancient Near East makes it clear that a sovereign's enactment of a new covenant makes an old one null and void, even if there is some overlap between the stipulations or promises of the two. Paul is actually arguing that neither Jew nor Gentile in Christ is any longer beholden to the Mosaic Law or obliged to keep the Mosaic covenant.

this more generic usage is what one might expect in an encyclical addressed to a variety of churches. Furthermore, Paul shows some signs of using the terminology in this very way in Gal. 1.13; 1 Cor. 10.32; 15.9; and, more proximately to the time of Ephesians' writing, Phil. 3.6. In none of those texts is Paul using the singular noun to refer to a particular congregation.

What, however, about the issue of Paul referring to the church being built on the foundation of the prophets and apostles in Eph. 2.20? What of the discussion of Paul's ministry in 3.1-13 which seems to see it as something in the past? Several considerations need to be kept in mind, one of the most important of which is that epideictic rhetoric is supposed to remind the audience of the essential truths or virtues or foundational assumptions on which they presently stand and because of which they are willing to praise persons who model such qualities. This simply comes with the nature of epideictic rhetoric. If it is offering present praise about a deceased person it will praise the enduring virtues and positive qualities he modeled. If it is offering praise about some present matter or quality, it will highlight how that stands in continuity with the enduring values of that society.

If Ephesians is regarded as having been written during an Ephesian imprisonment,[40] then a retrospective account of Paul's ministry, which is in part what we find in ch. 3, is a bit premature to say the least. But this would not be the case if Ephesians was written near the end of Paul's career, say in 61-62 while he was still under house arrest in Rome and uncertain of the outcome of his trial.[41] Indeed, it would be quite apt for him under those circumstances to write a homily to some converts in Asia for whom he and his coworkers had labored long, summing up his message and ministry. According to Acts 19.10 Paul spent over two years in Ephesus and its environs, longer than he spent in any other place among his largely Gentile churches. It is highly likely that he spent considerable time there teaching the things he shared with other audiences in his earlier letters, and indeed it is likely that he may have written one or more of those letters from Ephesus (e.g., 1 Corinthians). In any case, if he wrote to Asia in the 60s, there is no reason that he might not refer back to the foundational work of apostles and prophets, many of whom had already paid for their faithfulness with their lives. Ephesians is a sermon about the Pauline and Christian legacy and about the nature and unity of the church, but this sermon is a living legacy because the author, while under duress and no longer young, is still alive.

Sometimes it is complained that Ephesians presents us with a unified church, not a church in turmoil with Jews and Gentiles at odds with one another (in contrast to, for example, Galatians or Romans). In epideictic rhetoric,

---

40. About which I am quite dubious since neither Paul's letters nor Acts says so, but see pp. 72-73 below.

41. On this matter see my *Friendship and Finances in Philippi*, pp. 1-29.

however, it is important to emphasize the qualities and truths that unify the community in the midst of loss or uncertainty of direction. To some degree epideictic rhetoric attempts to paint the picture of the community or the individual at its or his ideal best. While not ignoring problems, an epideictic speech is not the occasion to dwell on them. Paul is stressing in Ephesians what believers already are in Christ and in the heavenlies and what the Christian community is in part but must also continue to become. The "church must become what it already is in Christ through knowing, filling, growing and building."[42] Unity exists but must be enacted and expressed.

Epideictic rhetoric both celebrates and inculcates such unity. It is no accident that this homily focuses on what is true in "this present age" but also looks to (and is the only Pauline letter to mention) "the age to come" (1.21). Epideictic rhetoric builds community in the present for the future, recognizing there is more yet to come, without inspecting or dissecting that future. Paul has not forgotten about the "not yet," but in an epideictic homily it is not appropriate to dwell on the future. Paul uses the clear two-ages language here and not elsewhere because epideictic rhetoric makes a clear delineation between the present and the future, and Paul does not offer us any other large-scale epideictic pieces among his letters (1 Corinthians 13 being a small-scale example).

K. Snodgrass puts his finger on some of the major difficulties in asserting that Ephesians is a pseudepigraph: What would motivate a pseudonymous author to write this sort of general material for an unspecified audience? Why would it have been important to remind the audience of their debt to Paul years after his death? Furthermore, the admonitions offered in Ephesians hardly seem to be addressed to any sort of spiritual crisis. As Snodgrass asks in critiquing R. Schnackenburg — would one really offer muted and general admonitions if one was really dealing with some specific crisis? It seems most unlikely. Snodgrass is right that this document reads more like a general exhortation to be encouraged and united in love and better understand their heritage.[43] But then that is precisely the nature of epideictic exhortations.

Stylistic Arguments against Pauline Authorship of Colossians

The stylistic features in Colossians sometimes thought to indicate that it was not written by Paul include expansive expressions that seem redundant through the use of synonyms or words based on the same stem: strengthened with all power (1.11), praying and asking (1.9), "holy . . . without blemish . . . free from accusation" (1.22), "if you continue in your faith, established and firm, not moved"

---

42. Hoehner, *Ephesians*, p. 53.
43. K. Snodgrass, *Ephesians* (Grand Rapids: Zondervan, 1996), pp. 22-23.

(1.23), "kept hidden for ages and generations" (1.26), "in him you were circumcised with a circumcision made without hands in the putting off of the sinful inclinations in the circumcision of Christ" (2.11), and "from whom the whole body, supported and held together by its ligaments and sinews, grows as God causes it to grow" (2.19). "Whereas Paul uses repetition to develop his argument in a logical direction, the repetitions in Colossians mostly function to build rhetorical effect." Furthermore, "Colossians lacks the adversative, causal, consecutive, recitative, copulative, and disjunctive conjunctions that are characteristic of Paul's style. Instead it is characterized by long sentences with relative clauses, nouns linked in genitive constructions, and the piling up of synonyms." "It also lacks completely the articular infinitive, a construction frequently employed by Paul to represent a dependent clause. Colossians employs 'which is' (*ho estin . . .*) as a special idiom five times (1:24, 27; 2:10, 17; 3:14)."[44]

But the expansive and redundant nature of the style of Colossians is, as we have seen, characteristic of Asiatic rhetoric, which was characterized by long lugubrious sentences, piling up of synonyms for rhetorical effect, and the absence of conjunctions so that the sentences keep flowing in the torrent of eloquence.[45] This stylistic feature cannot be accounted for simply on the basis of the letter's content. Leaner prose could have been used to speak of the difficulties Paul addresses in this letter. Rather, the style reflects a deliberate attempt to make this document a word on target for an audience adept in and familiar with Asiatic rhetoric. It is not likely evidence of an author other than Paul. Johnson rightly says in regard to the illogical nature of much of the argument for Colossians and Ephesians being pseudepigraphical: "First, Colossians must be viewed as a deliberate forgery, using the information derived only from Philemon to certify its authenticity, even though Philemon is a private note. Then, Ephesians must be thought of as written by the same pseudepigrapher in a style very similar, but not identical to that of Colossians — except that the impulse to certify authenticity by using personal references would have been mysteriously neglected."[46]

---

44. A. T. Lincoln, "Colossians," in *The New Interpreter's Bible* XI (Nashville: Abingdon, 2000), p. 578, following the stylistic observations of W. Bujard, *Stilanalytische Untersuchungen zum Kolosserbrief als Beitrag zur Methodik von Sprachvergleichen* (Göttingen: Vandenhoeck und Ruprecht, 1973), and cf. M. Kiley, *Colossians as Pseudepigraphy* (Sheffield: JSOT, 1973).

45. Lincoln is well aware of the rhetorical character of Colossians, but his failure to coordinate this fact with the possibility of Paul's use of an Asiatic style of rhetoric in these letters is unfortunate as it skews some of his conclusions, including his conclusion about authorship.

46. Johnson, *Writings*, p. 409. On the more general difficulties with talking about these letters as Pauline pseudepigraphs (something of an oxymoron) see Hoehner, *Ephesians*, pp. 38-49.

If then there are not solid reasons on the grounds of style (or substance for that matter) in Colossians for regarding this epistle as non-Pauline or post-Pauline, it is worthwhile to briefly point out that already in the early second century A.D. and continuing on through that century, there is strong attestation to Paul being the author of this document (Ignatius, *Ephesians* 2; *Magnesians* 2; *Philadelphians* 4; *Smyrnaeans* 1.2, 12; *Trallians* 5.2; Irenaeus, *Adversus Haereses* 3.14.1; Tertullian *De Praescriptione Haereticorum* 7; Clement of Alexandria, *Stromateis* 1.1; the Muratorian Canon). Sometimes one also hears the argument that Paul could not have written to Colossae from Rome as late as A.D. 62 because the city of Colossae was destroyed by an earthquake in that year. This is confusing the earthquake which struck Laodicea in A.D. 60-61 with the earthquake which hit Colossae in A.D. 64. It is unfortunate that while Laodicea has undergone a good deal of archaeological work in recent years, Colossae still remains one of the NT sites which has never been excavated. Work would need to be done there before we could begin to assess the effects of the earthquake on that small town.

We have seen thus far that the usual reasons for doubting the Pauline character of Ephesians or even Colossians on grounds of form and formal presentation of content appear to be in some cases clearly invalid and in others inadequate to support the conclusion. It is our contention that he did write them and did so during his house arrest in Rome in the early 60s A.D.

Epistolary and Rhetorical Structures

Philemon

Prescript and Greeting (vv. 1-3)

Thanksgiving Prayer/Exordium (vv. 4-7)

Propositio — An Appeal in and on the Basis of Love (vv. 8-11)

Probatio — The Rationale for the Return (vv. 12-16)

Peroratio (vv. 17-21)

    1) Welcome, Repay (vv. 17-19)[47]

    2) Final Plea for Benefit, Refreshment, Obedience (vv. 20-21)

Travel Plans (v. 22)

Final Greetings/ Benediction (vv. 23-25)[48]

---

47. Including the mention of Paul's signature, v. 19.

48. On the rhetorical analysis of Philemon see S. S. Bartchy, "Philemon, Epistle to," in *ABD* V, pp. 305-10, here pp. 306-7; F. F. Church, "Rhetorical Structure and Design in Paul's Letter to Philemon," *HTR* 71 (1978): 17-33.

*   *   *

Colossians

Prescript and Greetings (1.1-2)

Exordium/Thanksgiving Prayer (1.3-14)

Narratio — The Pattern of Christ (1.15-20)

Propositio (1.21-23)[49]

Probatio — The Knowledge and Work of Paul (1.24–2.5)

Exhortatio (2.6–4.1)

    1) Continue to Live in Christ, Forsaking Other Knowledge, Philosophies, Principles, Rituals (2.6-23)

    2) Forsaking Other Lifestyles, Filled with the Word and Wisdom of
Christ (3.1-17)

    3) Submission and Obedience in the Christian Household (3.18–4.1)

Peroratio — A Call to Prayer and Other Forms of Wise Speech and Action (4.2-6)

Closing Greetings and Instructions (4.7-18)

*   *   *

Ephesians

Prescript and Greetings (1.1-2)

Exordium (1.3-23)

    1) Eulogy/Encomium (1.3-14)[50]

    2) Thanksgiving Prayer (1.15-23)

Narratio — The Account of Then and Now/Before and After of Gentile
Converts and of Paul's Role in Their Lives (2.1–3.21)

    1) Dead in Trespasses, Then Alive in Christ (2.1-10)

    2) Excluded and Separated, Now Citizens Unified and at Peace (2.11-22)

---

49. Two treatments of the rhetoric of Colossians in commentaries, those of A. T. Lincoln and J. N. Aletti, whom Lincoln is to some extent following, find 1.21-23 to be the multifaceted propositio or partitio. I concur, and their conclusion about the peroratio being in 4.2-
6 is also correct. See Lincoln, "Colossians," pp. 557-60, and J. N. Aletti, *St. Paul. Épître aux
Colossians* (Paris: Gabalda, 1993), p. 39.

50. Vv. 9-10 serve as a sort of propositio, the theme and thesis being that God has a
plan in Christ to unite all things and that this plan is revealed in the present through the
speaker.

3) Paul's Ministry and Life as Exemplum of God's Plan (3.2-13)[51]

4) Concluding Prayer and Benediction (3.1, 14-21).

Exhortatio (4.1–6.9)

1) Maintenance of Church's Unity (4.1-16)

2) Live No Longer as Gentiles, but as New Creatures (4.17-24)

3) Putting Off and Putting On (4.25-32)

4) The Imitation of God and the Image of Holiness (5.1-20)

5) Mutual Submission in Christ and in Marriage; Setting the House in Order (5.21-6.9)

Peroratio (6.10-20)

Postscript (6.21-24)[52]

The Social Settings of Paul and of His Audiences

There are many dimensions to the social settings out of which these documents are written and into which they are spoken. Our first issue must be to consider the social setting of Paul himself. Is he in prison, or is he under house arrest? What do these letters suggest about the matter?[53] It is of course possible that they were not all written at the same time and in the same place, but both the

---

51. While R. Jeal, *Integrating Theology and Ethics in Ephesians: The Ethos of Communication* (Lewiston: Mellen, 2000), pp. 163-64, is right that Paul begins the concluding prayer at 3.1 and then picks it up again at 3.14, this does not really make 3.2-13 a digression. It is rather that Paul is using a rhetorical technique he uses elsewhere of interlocking construction in which one introduces the next stage of the discourse before finishing the present stage or argument. On Paul's use of this technique see Witherington and Hyatt, *Romans*, pp. 193-206, and see now the detailed study by Bruce Longenecker, *Rhetoric at the Boundaries: The Art and Theology of New Testament Chain-Link Transitions* (Waco: Baylor University Press, 2005). Eph. 3.2-14 is the third and final stage of the narratio.

52. In this rhetorical and epistolary analysis I am mostly following Lincoln, *Ephesians*, pp. xliii-xliv, with some refinements. It is noteworthy how the rhetorical analysis of Ephesians has largely been neglected even by those who have engaged in rhetorical analysis of Paul's letters. E.g., *Rhetoric and the New Testament: Essays from the 1992 Heidelberg Conference*, ed. T. H. Olbricht and S. E. Porter (Sheffield: Sheffield Academic, 1993). It was only after I had already done this analysis that I discovered that Roy Jeal deals with the rhetoric of Ephesians and also argues that it is a rhetorically adept homily. See R. Jeal, *Integrating Theology and Ethics in Ephesians: The Ethos of Communication* (Lewiston: Mellen, 2000), pp. 66-67.

53. This matter has of course been canvassed many times. One of the more helpful recent treatments is P. Rapske, *The Book of Acts and Paul in Roman Custody* (Grand Rapids: Eerdmans, 1994).

shared personal names in and the substantive connections of both Philemon and Ephesians with Colossians suggest that they were. Let us then consider what all three letters tell us about Paul's situation.

Where Was Paul?

The letter of Philemon has Paul calling himself a prisoner of Christ, not of Rome (vv, 1, 9), and he speaks of having a fellow prisoner with him — Epaphras (v. 23). He is a bit more specific in v. 10, which speaks of Onesimus who was "begotten in chains," which presumably means that Onesimus became a Christian while Paul was in chains. Now this could mean that Paul was in a prison, but it is perhaps more likely to mean he was chained to a guard and under house arrest as described in Acts 28. This is likely because Paul seems to have the freedom to have quite a good deal of company and the freedom to write and converse with others. Roman citizens were not all that often thrown in prison in any case.[54] Several factors favoring the Roman location as the social setting from which Paul wrote these documents must now be mentioned.

The subscription to Colossians found in K, L, and other manuscripts states "written from Rome by Tychicus and Onesimus." This same sort of subscript is found in various manuscripts of Philemon as well. We also have a subscript to Ephesians in several manuscripts, including B, that says it, too, came from Rome.[55] These assertions represent a rather unanimous testimony on this matter from the time of the early church until well into the modern era.

Ephesus and Caesarea Maritima have been proposed only in the modern era as locations from which these documents were written. It is argued that the distance between Rome and Colossae (some 1200 miles) is thought to be too great for Paul to have meaningfully told Philemon to prepare him a guest room (Phlm. 22) and for Onesimus to have run to when he fled Colossae. Modern doubts about the historical accuracy of Acts have contributed to these alternate suggestions. None of these reasons are sufficient to overturn the earlier universal testimony and opinion.

Ancient persons like Paul were highly mobile, and he may have believed that his release was imminent and so he would be following the letters to

---

54. See M. Barth and H. Blanke, *Colossians* (New York: Doubleday, 1994), pp. 126-34. "Only the theory of a return of Paul to the east after his (first) Roman captivity, and of an imprisonment at Ephesus at that occasion, could place the origin of Colossians in an Ephesian prison" (p. 128). They also point out the lack of logic to the suggestion that Paul wrote to the Ephesians from prison in Ephesus, when he was able to converse with people on the spot when he wrote any or all of these three documents.

55. See Metzger, *Textual Commentary*, pp. 589, 543.

Colossae and to Philemon by only a little time, hence the valid request for a guest room. Rome was the slave capital of the empire, and it would certainly have been safer for Onesimus to flee there and blend in with the millions there, including thousands upon thousands of slaves, rather than to simply flee to Ephesus, a city only 110 miles from Colossae.

There is no hard evidence whatever in the NT of an Ephesian imprisonment.[56] One is loathe to take the word of Marcion, who in his prologue to Colossians says that "the apostle, already in chains, writes to them from Ephesus."[57] One may also note that the portrayal in Acts of Paul's relationship to authority figures in Ephesus is positive. Acts 19.31 suggests that he was on friendly terms with provincial officials, including the Asiarchs (which is not unbelievable since he was a well-educated Roman citizen of some status), and we should note the defense of Paul by the town clerk of Ephesus (19.35-40) even in the midst of a riot. "Wrestling with wild beasts" metaphorically in Ephesus (1 Cor. 15.32) aptly describes dealing with an angry mob, but it provides no basis for the theory of an Ephesian imprisonment or other official action against Paul.[58]

I have written in detail elsewhere about the historical accuracy of the latter part of Acts, and simply point out here that there is still good reason to trust the idea that the "we" there includes Luke, which in turn means that Luke was present with Paul in both Caesarea Maritima and then on the journey to Rome, where Paul ended up under house arrest.[59] Col. 4.14 and Phlm. 24 mention Luke's presence with Paul. Acts 27.2 suggests that Aristarchus accompanied Paul to Rome, and he, too, is mentioned in Col. 4.10 and Phlm. 24.

One can add that in all these documents, but particularly in Colossians and Ephesians, there is an element of retrospective and distance that suggests a considerable period of time since Paul has been in the region of Asia. This sense of retrospective also applies to the way Paul talks about his own ministry in both Colossians and Ephesians. The arguments that this sense of distance favors a post-Pauline origin for these documents actually work just as well if there is simply a late Pauline character to these documents. Paul calls himself an "old man" in Phlm. 9, which must have been true, however much he says it to create pathos and sympathy in the audience.

Caesarea was hardly any closer to Colossae than Rome was and so pro-

---

56. Barth and Blanke, *Colossians,* pp. 126-34. Barth and Blanke also use the argument that dating these letters in the 60s allows enough time for Paul's style to develop. Style, however, can be chosen, and it is the development of thought which points more strongly to these letters being written at a later period than the Corinthian correspondence or Romans.

57. See P. O'Brien, *Colossians, Philemon* (Waco: Word, 1982), p. lii.

58. See rightly, Hoehner, *Ephesians,* p. 96.

59. See my *The Acts of the Apostles* (Grand Rapids: Eerdmans, 1997), pp. 480-85.

vides no advantage of distance in regard to Phlm. 22. Paul could always appeal to Rome from Caesarea, so the sense of finality and resolution of the matter in Philippians, which was likely written from the same time period and location, suggests Rome as the location, as do the references to the household of Caesar and the praetorian guard in Philippians. To this we may add that Phlm. 22 also implies a release not too long in the future. Putting all these considerations together, no locale better suits the composition of these documents than Rome, and no time in his career better suits than late in his apostolic ministry.

Paul's Imprisonment, Tychicus, and Timothy

In Ephesians Paul calls himself a "prisoner of Christ" (3.1; 4.1). In Colossians Paul, though he does not call himself a prisoner, speaks of his fellow prisoner Aristarchus (4.10) and asks that the audience remember his chains (4.18). Col. 4.7-9 also suggests that Colossians and Philemon were written and sent together. So Paul was likely under house arrest with others when these documents were composed, and this included his being in chains. This did not hinder him from continuing some forms of ministry, including letter writing. He anticipates, according to Phlm. 22, being released from house arrest and returning to visit Philemon. This suggests, and nothing in the other two letters contradicts it, that Paul did not see his situation as severe, or likely to end in death. Philippians, while reckoning with death, nonetheless indicates that Paul is also confident that he will continue to live (Phil. 1.19-26).[60]

Tychicus is going to Colossae with Onesimus and is to update everyone about what is happening with Paul (Col. 4:7). This makes it plausible that he was given both Colossians and Philemon to carry with him and was charged with orally delivering and presenting these documents in a rhetorically effective way and with adding personal information not contained in the letters. Eph. 6.21-22 is basically a rerun of Col. 4.7-8. Tychicus is thus connected with both documents and with their audiences, which in turn suggests that the two letters were sent to the same vicinity. But the letter written to Laodicea which the Colossians are to get and read (Col. 4.16) is probably not what we know as Ephesians, especially since Ephesians does not really seem to be a personal letter, though the conclusion is not impossible.[61]

Both Colossians and Philemon mention Timothy, perhaps as a coauthor

---

60. On these verses see my *Friendship and Finances in Philippi*, pp. 42-49.

61. Paul does not seem to have been the one to convert the audience being addressed in Ephesians. He speaks in Eph. 1.15 of having *heard* of their faith in Christ. This does not fit Christians in Ephesus very well, but it could fit Christians in Colossae, Laodicea, and Hierapolis, who had been converted not by Paul but by one of Paul's coworkers.

of these documents, but at least as a co-authority addressing these audiences. Perhaps Timothy was Paul's scribe. According to Acts 16.1, when Paul first encountered Timothy he lived in Lystra, his mother was a Jew, and his father Greek. His father was not a believer, but his mother was, a fact confirmed by 2 Tim. 1.5. We are also told in Acts that Paul had Timothy circumcised, presumably so he could work among Jews and Gentiles as Paul did. Since Timothy's father was Greek, Timothy probably learned Greek at an early age and could well have been able to compose documents that were rhetorically apt, including documents reflecting the Asiatic style.[62] In fact, it may not be Paul himself that should be praised for the rhetorically impressive style of these documents. Perhaps not Paul but Timothy knew this style, having grown up near Asia, and Paul was content to have him compose these documents accordingly to make them more nearly words on target.[63] Since we have already shown good reasons why Ephesians was likely composed on the basis of Colossians and probably at or near the same time, it may be, though Ephesians does not mention him, that Timothy was involved in the composition of that document as well.[64]

Col. 4.18 says that Paul wrote the greeting in that verse in his own hand, which suggests that someone else wrote down the rest of the document. The similar remark about promising repayment in his own handwriting at Philemon v. 19 suggests that Paul is using a scribe for that letter as well. Philippians, which also mentions Timothy in the prescript, was likely the latest of the captivity letters to be written. Philemon, Colossians, and Ephesians were written earlier, perhaps in A.D. 61 or 62. It seems likely Timothy was involved in all these documents, and Tychicus is connected with two of them. Either or both of these two men may have helped Paul in the composition of these documents so that they bore an effective Asiatic rhetorical form.[65]

---

62. For much more on Timothy see B. Witherington, *Letters and Homilies for Hellenized Christians* I (Downers Grove: InterVarsity, 2006).

63. S. R. Llewelyn, *New Docs* VII, p. 56, makes the interesting suggestion that Paul's coworker letter-bearers were like the couriers for Augustus. Augustus had changed the postal system so that one messenger carried the message the whole way from the sender to the emperor or vice versa. This allowed the emperor to question the messenger for explication of what the sender meant. Llewelyn points out that Paul's coworkers were no mere secretaries or couriers (cf. 1 Cor. 4.17; 1 Thess. 3.2-6). It was one of their functions to remind, encourage, and strengthen the Pauline churches. It is thus possible not only that Timothy was an active helper in the composition of this letter, but also that Epaphras was an active interpreter and oral "deliverer" of the letter in a rhetorically effective manner.

64. On the other hand, the differing meanings of common terminology such as "mystery" in these two documents may suggest that they had different scribes.

65. Onesimus is called "one of you" in Col. 4.9, while Tychicus must be introduced to the audience as a fellow Christian and coworker in 4.7 (so also Eph. 6.21).

Slavery

In these letters Paul gives advice to slave owners, and in Philemon is even boldly asking for the emancipation of a slave. This means that at least some of the audience of these letters had slaves. We have addressed the issue of slavery previously at some length, but here we must consider it again and ask how it sheds light on our understanding of these particular letters.[66] One principle that is important in dealing with this issue is that the trajectory of Paul's remarks is as important as the exhortation he gives.

Our concern in this commentary is not with slavery in general in the Roman Empire but with domestic slaves in particular, which are all Paul refers to in all three of these letters. There seems to have been a marked difference in the way domestic slaves (and government slaves) were usually treated from how agricultural slaves and mine-working slaves were treated. Domestic slaves were part of the household, as Colossians 3–4 and Ephesians 5–6 make clear.[67] When a domestic slave was manumitted, not only would he obtain restricted citizenship status but he could even inherit his patron's (his former owner's) estate. "There is evidence that the feeling that a loyal domestic servant ought automatically to be granted freedom and civic rights after a number of years was so widespread that the 'model' of slavery as a process of integration may be useful here. . . . On the other hand . . . those slaves working on agricultural estates, received very different treatment and had virtually no opportunity to benefit from this ideal."[68]

Paul then may be said to be drawing on some recognition in Greco-Roman culture that it was important to treat at least domestic slaves well, but he is swimming upstream at various points as we shall see when we compare his

---

66. See my *Conflict and Community in Corinth* (Grand Rapids: Eerdmans, 1994), pp. 181-85. I regret that J. A. Harrill's fine study *Slaves in the New Testament: Literary, Social and Moral Dimensions* (Minneapolis: Augsburg Fortress, 2005) arrived too late on my desk to be integrated into this work. The work does however provide some further support for various of the conclusions reached here. His work from a decade earlier on this subject has been drawn on.

67. I leave aside here the totally unconvincing argument of A. D. Callahan, *Embassy of Onesimus: The Letter of Paul to Philemon* (Valley Forge: Trinity, 1997) that Philemon was not a slave, even though vv. 15-16 make it quite clear he was, and that Paul is not really arguing for emancipation of a slave. The use of *doulos* in this document comports with the use in Colossians and Ephesians, where there is no dispute that the term means "slave." Callahan's argument seems to be grounded in his drawing on nineteenth-century American abolitionist arguments about and studies of these texts.

68. T. Wiedemann, *Greek and Roman Slavery* (Baltimore: Johns Hopkins University Press, 1981), p. 3. The best survey of slavery in the first three centuries of the Christian era remains H. Guzlow, *Christentum und Sklaverei in den ersten drei Jahrhunderten* (Bonn: Habelt, 1969).

household codes to Greco-Roman household codes (pp. 70-73 and 181-96 below). No ancient government ever sought to abolish slavery in general, no former slaves ever wrote treatises attacking the institution, and even when slaves revolted it was not in an attempt to abolish slavery in general but rather an attempt to rectify abuses of the system.[69] Though it may seem a mystery to us, there were inscriptions on some slaves' graves which read "Slavery was never unkind to me" (CIL 13.7119).

Slaves in the Greco-Roman world were legally property, not persons, and Roman law reinforced this concept. As far back as the time of Aristotle slaves were called property with a soul (*Politics* 1.2). Even in NT times the law allowed an owner to mistreat or even kill his slave without real repercussions. The law also allowed, however, by means of a legal fiction and a third party (usually a priest in a temple), for a slave to buy his or her way out of bondage, saving up his *peculium,* a Roman expedient that allowed living property (slaves) to own property such as land or money. But the owner of a slave had to consent to a process of manumission. Slaves could not obtain their own freedom otherwise.

There were certainly laws in regard to runaway slaves. A runaway was called "fugitivus," and the owner could take out a warrant for his arrest. A second-century B.C. document containing such a warrant has survived to our time. It describes in detail the appearance of the slave, what he was wearing, and what he was carrying with him. It also contains promise of reward if the slave is returned.[70]

It is not absolutely certain that Onesimus was a runaway slave, although all the ancient commentators who wrote while slavery was still an institution in the region thought so. Perhaps he simply went to Paul because of some disagreement between himself and Philemon that needed to be adjudicated. Paul would then be writing this letter in the role of the "friend of the master" *(amicus domini)* pleading Onesimus's cause and case.[71] I am, however, unconvinced by this suggestion.

The parallel usually cited to prove that Paul is playing the role of a "friend of the master" and intervening in a domestic dispute is not apt. Pliny's letter to Sabinianus is certainly an *amicus domini* letter but is rhetorically very different from Philemon and in any case deals not with a slave-master relationship but with a patron-client relationship (in this case a former slave, apparently of the patron). Pliny follows the rhetorical conventions in regard to

69. See S. Bartchy, *First Century Slavery and the Interpretation of 1 Cor. 7.21* (Missoula: Scholars, 1973), p. 63.

70. See J. Fitzmyer, *The Letter to Philemon* (New York: Doubleday, 2000), pp. 26-27, for citation and discussion.

71. So Fitzmyer, *Philemon,* pp. 17-24, and J. D. G. Dunn, *The Epistles to the Colossians and to Philemon* (Grand Rapids: Eerdmans, 1996), pp. 301-8.

deprecatio, a plea for mercy. Not only do we not have a plea for mercy in Paul's letter, we also have no mention of repentance so that there could be forgiveness. On the contrary there is the language of commerce and legal harm. The parallels between these two letters are not sufficient to overcome these significant differences of rhetorical tone and strategy. They address very different social situations calling for different rhetoric (see further pp. 53-60 below). Pliny's letter is a private appeal to a master, while Philemon, though it is a personal letter, is not private at all.

Onesimus seems to have been in more trouble than would be presumed by an *amicus domini* situation. Paul's letter says nothing about Onesimus seeking Paul's legal intervention on his behalf in regard to some relatively minor matter, with which, at any rate, other Christians more local could have helped Onesimus. Why did Onesimus flee so far, to the very slave capital of the empire, unless he was very afraid? Paul writes as if Onesimus owes Philemon something important. At the very least he owed him the time of service he has been away from Colossae, but in addition he owed him himself: he was Philemon's property, not free to go off on his own without his master's permission. He may also have taken some money with him when he fled. The legal language of wronging Philemon (v. 18) seems to suggest a more serious situation than just a domestic dispute over something (e.g., that the slave has been indolent or useless).[72]

Paul seems quite aware of the urgent need to return Onesimus to his owner lest he, Paul, be accused of illegally harboring a fugitive (a crime of theft according to P. Oxy. 12.1422; *Digest* 11.4.1). He is asking for more than forgiveness of Onesimus. The not so subtle appeal that Philemon treat Onesimus "no longer as a slave," indeed that he treat him as if he were Paul himself visiting Philemon, shows that Paul is pushing for liberation, not merely trying to solve a domestic dispute. In fact, when Paul asks to profit from Philemon and be refreshed by him he is probably implicitly asking for Onesimus to be sent back to him as a freedman. This is probably the "more" referred to (beyond emancipation) in v. 21.

Though Onesimus's repentance is not mentioned, his conversion while Paul is in chains is. Why would Onesimus, as a non-Christian, come to Paul? It is hard to believe it was a chance encounter. It seems more likely that the slave came to Paul because he feared the worst, having left Philemon's service without permission. He knew Paul to be someone whom Philemon respected, and indeed even was indebted to. In other words, Onesimus knew how the reciprocity networks of the empire worked. It was not just "Philemon's character as a Christian which Onesimus saw as likely to work most effectively in his favor."[73]

---

72. Phrygian slaves had a reputation for being unsatisfactory or even useless, which is a term Paul uses here, and in fact the name Onesimus was used of Phrygian slaves.

73. So Dunn, *Colossians and Philemon,* p. 305.

It was rather Philemon's indebtedness to Paul for the gospel, a fact Paul stresses in the letter, which provided muscle to the request for liberation.

Onesimus fears for his life, but wants to return home to Colossae, which explains why Paul goes out of his way to tell Philemon that Onesimus is now spiritually his child,[74] the heart of his own heart, and is to be treated as if he were Paul himself when he shows up in Colossae. This is no timid rhetoric. It is a bold attempt to make sure that Onesimus is not in any way harmed when he returns with this document in hand. Onesimus has come under the protection of the apostle himself, and Paul makes clear that if Onesimus is harmed it will definitely harm Philemon's relationship with Paul and partnership with him in the gospel. There is an issue of honor and shame here, and if Philemon does not wish to be shamed in the eyes of his house church he must acquiesce to the powerful persuasion in this letter and do both what Paul asks and what he hints at.

A runaway could be resold to a harsher master, scourged, branded, cut, made to wear an iron collar, crucified, thrown to beasts, or killed by some other means (see P. Oxy. 14.1643). There were those who traded in runaway slaves and in fact helped them either to obtain their freedom or to be resold to a better master.[75] Still, Paul would have been in violation of the law had he long harbored Onesimus or failed to send him back to his owner, and the last thing Paul needed was to give his own captors another reason to prosecute and possibly execute him.[76]

In this setting it is notable what Paul actually says in 1 Corinthians 7 and Philemon about slaves and their being freed. His view is that a believing slave is already the Lord's freedman and should be treated as a brother or sister in Christ. Paul is also opposed to persons selling themselves into slavery, and he gives theological rationale for this (1 Cor. 7.23: "You were bought at a price. Do not become slaves of people"). He did not just baptize the institutions of Greco-Roman culture and call them good, nor did he simply support the status quo or Christianize existing situations, whether we think of patriarchy or slavery. He says clearly enough in 1 Cor. 7.21, speaking to domestic slaves, if you can obtain your freedom, do so. We find further proof of Paul's basic attitude to slavery in Philemon when he pulls out all the rhetorical stops not only to protect the life of a runaway slave but to obtain both the slave's freedom and the slave's recognition by his former owner as a brother in Christ to be treated as if he were Paul himself.

---

74. One wonders how·old Onesimus was when he met Paul in Rome. A very substantial number of slaves in the Roman Empire were freed by their masters before their thirtieth birthdays. See Wiedemann, *Greek and Roman Slavery*, p. 51.

75. See D. Daube, "Dodges and Rackets in Roman Law," *Proceedings of the Classical Association* 61 (1964): 28-30.

76. It is also unlikely that Paul's domicile in Rome would have been seen by Roman officials as a place and situation where the rules of sanctuary and "friend of the master" might apply.

Nothing in Colossians or Ephesians negates these conclusions. To the contrary, in these letters he works hard to ameliorate the harsher aspects of existing institutions. He must start with society as he finds it. Then he attempts not to attack the problem in the public sphere but rather to put the leaven of the gospel into the structures of the Christian community and let it do its work over the course of time, all the while advocating Christian treatment of all members of the household, involving the sort of respect all "persons" deserve even if they play subordinate roles in the structure of the family.

Paul believes in living a true Christian life and letting that life bring transformation within the community to patriarchal and slave structures. The Christian community was to live out the new freedom they had in Christ, and that always had social implications. This commentary will dispute the assertion found not infrequently that the household codes reflect a post-Pauline retrenchment or going back on the radical social implications of Paul's gospel. On the contrary, these codes show how Paul was diligently working for change within the Christian community. As C. F. D. Moule long ago noted, Paul's principle that all Christians are created in the image of God and renewed in the image of Christ and are brothers and sisters in Christ led eventually to a situation where it became clear that slavery and Christianity, with the latter's views about human dignity and freedom and total availability to only one Master, were incompatible.[77] The changes Paul made in the household codes reflect these principles, and in this case it is indeed the trajectory of the argument that is as crucial as the actual advice he gives. Perhaps most telling is what Paul says in Gal. 3.28 but also in Col. 3.11 — that in Christ there is no such thing as slave or free, but rather all are one, all are persons of sacred worth in Christ. It has been often pointed out that Ephesians states that the barrier between Jew and Gentile has been abolished by the death of Jesus, and that clearly had social and cultural implications. Some of the texts that we will be examining in this commentary that deal with slavery show how Paul was trying to implement his fundamental beliefs about equality in Christ, which did indeed involve changing the social situation of the slave where possible, and especially within the context of the church (see pp. 183-90 below).

Opponents and Opposing Philosophy?

Another issue to be dealt with in regard to Colossians is whether Paul is countering actual opponents in what he says, or only aberrant ideas. There is no hint of opponents in Philemon, and it would be hard to find them in Ephesians as

---

77. C. F. D. Moule, *The Epistles of Paul to the Colossians and to Philemon* (Cambridge: Cambridge University Press, 1957), pp. 11-12.

well. This is not to say that Paul is not opposing aberrant and unhelpful ideas in Ephesians. Syncretism was indeed likely to be an issue in Asia, as was Jewish opposition (cf. Revelation 2–3). An amalgam of long extant pagan philosophies and religious ideas coupled with the rise of the ideology of the imperial cult, the prominence and importance of the cult of Artemis, and long-standing Jewish ideology and ideas could well have served up a socioreligious soup that many in Paul's audience had imbibed. There is probably a reason that Paul says a good deal about powers and principalities in Ephesians, but there is no evidence that he is opposing some particular group of pagans who are disturbing the Christians he is writing to with such ideas. "[I]t is clear that Ephesians was not sent to deal with some particular false teaching in a specific congregation. The general contents and relative lack of personal details prevent us from coming to this conclusion."[78] Ephesians was, after all, meant to be a sermon of general application to several groups of Christians in Asia.

There may, however, be an issue of astral thinking or religion in Colossians, where the matter seems a little more clear than in Ephesians. But he uses expressions like "so that no one may deceive you" (2.4), "see to it that no one takes you captive" (2.8), "do not let anyone judge you" (2.16), or "do not let anyone who delights in . . ." (2.18). He refers to these deceivers or misleaders as "such people" (2.18). A little more light is shed on the matter when he adds that such people have "lost connection with the head" (2.19). This suggests that he is referring to members of the Colossian Christian community who are offering up false teaching and ideas. Yet he does not stigmatize or single out a particular category of persons ("super-apostles," "false teachers," Judaizers, as in other letters). Indeed, what he says is that *anyone* who suggests such teaching should not be heard or heeded. This suggests not a divided house with factions in Colossae or a particular group of opponents known to Paul but that he is attempting to combat a sort of false teaching that might affect and infect anyone, or indeed everyone, due to the prevailing religious and philosophical pluralism of the milieu.

It is not really helpful to speak of Gnosticism in connection with any of these documents. While some of the ideas which were to become prominent in Gnostic philosophy in the second century were already floating around in Asia when Paul wrote these documents, there is no good historical evidence that there was such a thing as full-blown Gnosticism in the mid-first century. Gnosticism was in any case a system of thought that collected and combined various older ideas, recycling them in new permutations. In fact, it is perhaps more possible that Paul is opposing the influence of some sort of mystical Jewish thinking that involved some kind of ascetic piety thought to lead to higher knowledge and also to "the worship of angels," which may mean worshiping with the heavenly angels (see pp. 160-64 below). J. D. G. Dunn's summary is judicious:

78. P. T. O'Brien, *The Letter to the Ephesians* (Grand Rapids: Eerdmans, 1999).

None of the features of the teaching alluded to in 2:8-23 resist being understood in Jewish terms, and several can only or most plausibly be understood in Jewish terms. . . . To be more precise the division of the world into
"circumcision and uncircumcision" (2:11-13; 3:11) and the observance of the
Sabbath (2:16) would generally be recognized in the ancient world as distinctively Jewish, as indeed also food and purity rules (2:16, 21) . . . calendar
piety, food laws, and circumcision can not be regarded as random elements
of some syncretistic cult, but the very norms that provide and confirm the
identity of Israel.[79]

Dunn envisions the trouble emanating from the synagogue, though it seems
more likely that it came from Jewish Christians in the church at Colossae.
Dunn also argues that there is no clear persuasive evidence of Jewish syncretism
in Asia. Whatever else one may say, the Jewishness of the ideas suggests a time
before A.D. 70 when the church in Asia, though predominantly Gentile, was still
in close contact with Jews, Jewish ideas, and perhaps even the synagogue.[80]

Social Nexus: Paul and His Audiences in and near Colossae

In his landmark study N. Petersen points out that there was a difference between how Paul perceived the social reality of Christian communities and how
his audiences seem to have perceived it.[81] Paul sees them as *ekklesiae,* like the
democratic assemblies of old, subject to persuasion and dissuasion and sometimes properly subject to command *in extremis,* whereas his audience seems to
see the church as something like a collegium or voluntary association. For Paul
participation in the community is mandatory and necessary: "the hand cannot
say to the body, I have no need of you." This difference in perception of the
church's social reality affects the nature of Paul's rhetoric. He is, by rights, authorized by Christ to command, especially when it comes to his own converts,
such as Philemon, but he truly would rather persuade. The problem with per-

---

79. Dunn, *Colossians and Philemon,* p. 34. See his detailed treatment of the matter in
"The Colossians Philosophy: A Confident Jewish Apologia," *Biblica* 76 (1995): 153-81.

80. Very different is the sort of argument we find in W. T. Wilson, *The Hope of Glory:
Education and Exhortation in the Epistles to the Colossians* (Leiden: Brill, 1997), who wants to
argue that what we have in Colossians is moral philosophy/parenesis that would be familiar
to the largely Gentile audience and that the author is largely using Hellenistic pedagogical
techniques. There is some merit in these arguments, because clearly there is some overlap
with the larger cultural values in Asia (household advice, vice and virtue lists, and rhetorical
techniques), but in regard to the substance of Paul's discourse Dunn is right that it has a profoundly Jewish character, and many of the values he inculcates (e.g., humility) were counterintuitive to the way of thinking in the dominant Greco-Roman culture.

81. N. Petersen, *Rediscovering Paul* (Philadelphia: Fortress, 1985), p. 83.

suading in a non-democratic world such as the Roman Empire is that it leaves the impression that obedience and community involvement are optional, not obligatory.

It is fair to say, as Petersen does, that "the rhetoric, the style, the tone of a letter correspond to the addresser's perception of his or her status in relation to the addressee."[82] So then, is Paul really using gentle rhetoric in Colossians because his social relationship with the audience is as tenuous as in Romans since they are not his converts? Probably not, but it is true that deciphering rhetorical tone is crucial to determining meaning. In Philemon we have a letter full of pathos as Paul pulls out all the emotional stops to make sure that Onesimus is emancipated. As Petersen aptly points out, though, Paul in Philemon (and in Colossians and Ephesians as well) prefers to appeal to his audience to change or act in a certain way. "Paul's 'appeals' are a convention, also employed by royalty, which replaces a command when used with those who know that he has the power to command. Thus the appeal, which on the face of it would appear to come from an inferior or an equal, has the force of a command because it comes from someone who claims and is recognized to be a superior, that is, who claims, or has, the power to command."[83] As it turns out, then, the social nexus in which Paul is operating in these documents is one in which he is addressing Christians who are part of the larger circle of Pauline churches, even if he himself did not convert various of the Colossians and others that he is addressing.

The degree to which Paul is prepared to risk losing his relationship with Philemon is clear from the degree to which he is prepared to insist on a social change in relationship between Philemon and Onesimus. Here again Petersen is perceptive and helpful. He points out that too often the interpretation of Philemon has concentrated on the description of Onesimus as a brother and the need for him to be received as such. This is true enough, but in theory a person could remain a slave and still be recognized as a fellow believer in Christ.

> The usual interpretation of vv. 15-16 rightly points both to Paul's primary orientation to brotherly relations and to the fact that Philemon and Onesimus are related as master and slave. However, its concentration on "as a brother" fails to do justice to "no longer as a slave." The interpretation properly emphasizes Paul's expectations about Philemon's new *relations* with his slave, but it too hastily dismisses the idea that these relations entail a *structural* change in their relationship as master and slave.[84]

In fact, Paul even goes so far as to tell Philemon to treat Onesimus as an equal, indeed treat him as he would treat Paul himself! Paul is pushing the envelope

82. Petersen, p. 64.
83. Petersen, p. 65.
84. Petersen, p. 96.

here and seeking to change the social nexus of relating even as he sends the slave back to his master as the law requires. This makes clear an important point. While Paul, for example in Colossians and Ephesians, adopts various ameliorating tactics to deal with slave-master relationships within Christian households in general, when he is dealing with someone who is directly his convert and coworker and something of a social equal, as well as being a close friend, then he is prepared to press the matter rhetorically to the point of urging emancipation. Here he shows his true colors in regard to the issue of slavery, but this tactic also shows that Paul is wise enough to know when and with whom to push the matter to its desired fully Christian conclusion and when to work gradually for the deconstruction and reconstruction of fallen human structures within the Christian community.

Colossae and Its Social Milieu

Colossae was perhaps the least important or influential city to which Paul ever directed a letter.[85] Located some 110 miles east of Ephesus in the Lycus Valley, its neighbor cities of Laodicea and Hierapolis were both more important at the time. Being near the Meander River, Colossae was noted for its water supply, even though its major industry (the dark red dyed wool that the Romans called *colossinus*) had seen better days by the time Paul was writing these documents. Colossae had once been a famous and great city in ancient Phrygia, as Herodotus attests (7.30.1). Xenophon also spoke of it as a populous and wealthy city (*Anabasis* 1.21.6). The entire Lycus Valley region was bequeathed to the Romans in 133 B.C. and so had long been under Roman control by the time Paul wrote. We have no significant archaeological data to help us understand Colossae at this juncture.[86] The city was destroyed by an earthquake in A.D. 63-64 and was apparently not rebuilt for some time.[87] This provides something of

---

85. It is truly unfortunate that this site still, as of July 2007, has never been dug, though I was able to see a small odeum or theater protruding from the tell when doing a survey of the mound in May of 2005, and also evidence of attempts to ransack the tell for artifacts. The Turkish government is very willing to have the site dug, but there is a fee of $50,000 and one will have to work with the local Turkish archaeologists on the dig, with the requisite government permissions in hand. Hopefully this long-standing problem can be remedied soon.

86. The sheer spread of the mounds and ruins at Hierapolis and Laodicea compared to the small tell at Colossae suggests how much smaller Colossae must have been when Paul was writing these documents.

87. Eusebius, *Chronicle* 1.21-22 refers to this earthquake which destroyed all three of the major towns in the Lycus Valley. Tacitus speaks of an earlier earthquake which destroyed Laodicea in A.D. 60-61 (*Annals* 14.27). Lincoln, "Colossians," p. 580 notes that there is no evidence of habitation at Colossae after A.D. 63-64 until coins reappear in the late second cen-

a *terminus* after which Colossians probably could not have been written, especially if it is a genuine Pauline letter, or even if it was written by one of his close coworkers shortly after his death.

Jews appear to have first settled in Colossae in the second century B.C., and it was not by choice, as exiled Jews from Babylon were brought to the region to be settled (Josephus, *Antiquities* 12.147-53). There may have been as many as 11,000 Jews living in the region of Colossae and Hierapolis and Laodicea in Paul's day.[88] Christians were apparently in Colossae in the 50s, probably due to some missionary work by a Pauline coworker, perhaps Epaphras (Col. 1.7; 4.12-13). While Philemon was a convert of Paul himself, we are not told that this took place in Colossae, and the character of the letters to Philemon and the Colossians does not suggest that Paul had taken the lead in evangelizing the city. Indeed, Col. 2.1 probably rules this out. This is not an inconsequential point. While Paul is able to argue directly with Philemon and exhibit and draw upon his apostolic authority as well as his spiritual parenthood of Philemon to persuade him to release Onesimus, in Colossians Paul uses more generic arguments, not on the whole appealing to his apostolic authority over the audience, though he does appeal to himself as an example of proper Christian living.

Philemon was a slave owner and had a house large enough to host a house church. We may also assume that he could appreciate a good rhetorical address when he heard one, since Paul's letter to him is something of a masterpiece in that category. So at least some of those addressed by these letters were of reasonably high social status, both economically and probably also educationally. This is confirmed by the extended exhortations in Colossians and Ephesians of the slave owner/head of household unlike what we find in household codes outside the NT. Colossians and Ephesians also seem to presuppose an audience capable of a rather high degree of abstract and profoundly theological and philosophical thinking.

In Colossians Paul expects a fair degree of familiarity with Judaism and its practices, as well as a thirst for knowledge and understanding of the mystery of salvation unveiled and enacted in Christ. These letters do not suggest Paul is promulgating a religion that mainly caters to slaves, the illiterate, the uneducated — the low-status members of society. In his recent landmark sociological

---

tury. Col. 2.1 and 4.15 speak of a Christian presence at Laodicea when Paul writes. It is possible either that Paul is writing just before or during the Laodicean earthquake (and does not know of it yet), or that the earthquake was not totally devastating and the church in Laodicea survived it.

88. On all the above cf. L. MacDonald and S. E. Porter, *Early Christianity and Its Sacred Literature* (Peabody: Hendrickson, 2000), p. 471, to my *New Testament History* (Grand Rapids: Baker, 2001), pp. 326-29.

study of early Christianity, R. Stark concludes that Christianity had its largest appeal to what he calls "the solid citizens of the Empire." "If as is now believed, the Christians were not a mass of degraded outsiders but from the early days had members, friends, and relatives in high places — often within the Imperial family — this would have greatly mitigated repression and persecution."[89] Stark stresses that it seems to have been in the Greek cities of Asia Minor that Christianity made its greatest early headway. This would explain not only these three letters but also why Paul stayed such a long time in that general vicinity. It was fertile soil where one could speak of even the deeper mysteries of the faith and hope to be understood.

Why did Christianity have such success there? One reason is that it offered a cohesive community removed from the realm of honor challenges and the worst features of an agonistic culture. The call for humility, compassion, forgiveness, and love (Col. 3.12-14) was a call to virtues which the dominant culture did not often model and indeed in various cases did not endorse. This was not just because of the agonistic nature of Greco-Roman culture but also because various Greek philosophers had taught that mercy and pity were pathological emotions that violated the reciprocity cycle. They led to undeserved benefit, grace, unearned help, or relief, which was seen as contrary to justice. "Pity was a defect of character unworthy of the wise and excusable only in those who have not yet grown up. It was an impulsive response based on ignorance."[90] Yet, of course, it was precisely these sorts of virtues that could help communities and families stay together. Forgiveness and compassion certainly build community, and they appear to have done so in these cities in and near the Lycus Valley. Even the letter to Philemon can be seen as an exercise in inculcating these peculiar Christian virtues in order to patch up human relationships.

---

89. R. Stark, *The Rise of Christianity* (Princeton: Princeton University Press, 1996), pp. 45-46.

90. E. A. Judge, "The Quest for Mercy in Late Antiquity," in *God Who Is Rich in Mercy: Essays Presented to D. B. Knox,* ed. P. T. O'Brien and D. G. Peterson (Sydney: Macquarie University Press, 1986), pp. 107-21, here pp. 107-8.

An Annotated Bibliography

This bibliography is not intended to be exhaustive, only representative of the resources available on these three letters. Of the shorter commentaries in English available on two or more of these letters several can be commended. C. F. D. Moule's *The Epistles to the Colossians and Philemon* (Cambridge: Cambridge University Press, 1968) has helped several generations of students, but it requires some knowledge of Greek. More accessible and covering all the letters also covered in this commentary is G. B. Caird's *Paul's Letters from Prison* (Oxford: Oxford University Press, 1976). Another brief commentary that deals with all three of these captivity documents is R. P. Martin, *Ephesians, Colossians, and Philemon* (Atlanta: John Knox, 1991). Martin, unlike Caird, thinks Colossians and Ephesians are post-Pauline. Caird's little gem is a good place to start with these documents for the Bible student. At a somewhat more popular and definitely readable level is N. T. Wright's *Colossians and Philemon* (Grand Rapids: Eerdmans, 1986). More recent and up to date is R. W. Wall's *Colossians and Philemon* (Downers Grove: InterVarsity, 1993). From a fine Catholic scholar we have even more recently D. J. Harrington's *Paul's Prison Letters* (Hyde Park: New City, 1997), which does not treat Ephesians, but does also deal with Philippians. The best of these is still Caird's volume.

There are numerous detailed commentaries that deal with Colossians and Philemon together. One of the more enduring and still useful is E. Lohse's *Colossians and Philemon* (Philadelphia: Fortress, 1971). Another which gives considerable attention to grammatical and semantic issues is M. J. Harris, *Colossians and Philemon* (Grand Rapids: Eerdmans, 1991). Detailed interaction with the recent scholarly discussion of these letters from a traditional point of view can be found in P. T. O'Brien's *Colossians, Philemon* (Waco: Word, 1982), though this volume, like Lohse's, is somewhat dated now. Equally helpful and with the best interaction with recent scholarly discussion of these letters is J. D. G. Dunn's *The Epistles to the Colossians and to Philemon* (Grand Rapids: Eerdmans, 1996).

Of treatments only of Colossians, we have M. Barth and H. Blanke's *Colossians* (New York: Doubleday, 1994) which is useful but a pale shadow of Barth's landmark Ephesians commentary (see below). Now, however, we also have the helpful and rhetorically sensitive treatment of Colossians by A. T. Lincoln in *The New Interpreter's Bible* XI (Nashville: Abingdon, 2000), pp. 553-669. This commentary is a must for those who want to understand the persuasive art of Colossians.

The best of the detailed commentaries that deal only with Philemon is M. Barth and H. Blanke, *The Letter to Philemon* (Grand Rapids: Eerdmans, 2000). Also helpful, though brief, and with more up to date bibliography is J. Fitzmyer's *The Letter to Philemon* (New York: Doubleday, 2000). C. Hope Felder, "The Letter to Philemon," *The New Interpreter's Bible* XI (Nashville: Abingdon, 2000), pp. 898-99, should also be consulted for a brief treatment. Cf. Mary Ann Getty, *Philippians and Philemon* (Wilmington: Glazier, 1980). Arguing against the traditional reading of Philemon is A. D. Callahan, *Embassy of Onesimus: The Letter to Philemon* (Valley Forge: Trinity, 1997).

Of the full-scale commentaries on Ephesians, for many years M. Barth's two-volume magnum opus, *Ephesians 1–3* and *Ephesians 4–6* (Garden City: Doubleday, 1974), was the gold standard. We now have the new ICC volume from E. Best, *Ephesians* (Edinburgh: Clark, 1998), which is only outdone in its thoroughness in attention to traditional grammatico-linguistic concerns by the mammoth treatment of H. Hoehner, *Ephesians* (Grand Rapids: Baker, 2002). Neither of these commentaries really treats the rhetoric of Ephesians, but they also do not disparage such treatments. Like Hoehner and Barth, P. T. O'Brien, *The Letter to the Ephesians* (Grand Rapids: Eerdmans, 1999) takes the traditional position on the Pauline authorship of this document, but unfortunately has an allergic reaction to rhetorical analysis of Ephesians. Nonetheless, there is much helpful traditional exegetical discussion in his commentary and helpful critique of those who view Ephesians as post-Pauline. The best full-length treatment of the rhetoric of Ephesians is still A. T. Lincoln, *Ephesians* (Waco: Word, 1990), although the discussion has since moved beyond some of his insights in fresh directions (e.g., analyzing the rhetoric more particularly in light of Asiatic conventions).

A more recent treatment of Ephesians which is rhetorically informed is that of P. Perkins, "The Letter to the Ephesians," in *The New Interpreter's Bible* XI. M. Y. MacDonald, *Colossians, Ephesians* (Collegeville: Liturgical, 2000) pursues a post-Pauline sociological analysis of these letters, arguing that Ephesians in particular reflects an isolationist sect mentality. Her social analysis however relies too heavily on B. Malina and later cultural anthropological concepts and too little on actual social history tied to the period. It is very doubtful that

Ephesians was written to or for an isolationist sect. There are, however, many stimulating and fresh insights in her commentary. W. F. Taylor's commentary in Taylor and J. Reumann, *Ephesians, Colossians* (Minneapolis: Augsburg, 1985), is one of the few on Ephesians that is rhetorically informed. Reumann's Colossians commentary in the same volume does not deal with Paul's rhetoric. Another shorter but very helpful treatment of Ephesians is K. Snodgrass, *Ephesians* (Grand Rapids: Zondervan, 1996).

Of the shorter continental commentaries now available in English on Ephesians, the best is clearly R. Schnackenburg, *The Epistle to the Ephesians: A Commentary*, trans. H. Heron (Edinburgh: Clark, 1991). On Colossians we have P. Pokorný, *Colossians: A Commentary* (Peabody: Hendrickson, 1991).

There are numerous fine continental commentaries on one or more of these three Pauline letters that have not been translated but must not be overlooked. For example, in French we have J. N. Aletti's *Saint Paul. Épître aux Colossiens* (Paris: Gabalda, 1993) and this commentary does interact with the rhetorical analysis of discussion of Colossians. It is therefore surprising that Aletti's *Saint Paul. Épître aux Éphésiens* (Paris: Gabalda, 2001) does not really take the measure of the rhetoric of Ephesians in any detailed way. Also to be commended among the commentaries in French is M. Bouttier's *L'Épître de Saint Paul aux Éphésiens* (Geneva: Labor et Fides, 1991). Also interesting though dated is C. Masson, *L'Épître de Saint Paul aux Colossiens* (Neuchâtel: Delachaux, 1950).

Some of the most helpful commentaries in German are J. Gnilka, *Der Epheserbrief* (Freiburg: Herder, 1971), *Der Kolosserbrief* (Freiburg: Herder, 1980), and *Philemonbrief* (Freiburg: Herder, 1982). Of the commentaries now a generation old H. Schlier's *Der Brief an die Epheser* (Düsseldorf: Patmos, 1957) is still a standard reference work, as is M. Dibelius, *An die Kolosser, Epheser, an Philemon,* revised by H. Greeven (Tübingen: Mohr, 1953). More helpful and abreast of current discussion is M. Wolter's *Der Brief an die Kolosser. Der Brief an Philemon* (Gütersloh: Mohn/Würzburg: Echter, 1993). See also, P. Stuhlmacher, *Der Brief an Philemon* (Neukirchen: Neukirchener Verlag, 1975).

Of classic commentaries and commentating one can still learn a lot from J. B. Lighfoot's *St. Paul's Epistles to the Colossians and to Philemon* (London: Macmillan, 1879), and more recently we have the very illuminating volume in the Ancient Christian Commentary on Scripture, *Colossians, 1-2 Thessalonians, 1-2 Timothy, Titus, Philemon,* ed. P. Gorday (Downers Grove: InterVarsity, 2000).

Rhetorical Resources

We now have numerous resources on the use of rhetoric in Paul's letters, but one of the most helpful recent studies that demonstrates how Paul definitely uses the ancient Greco-Roman rhetorical conventions and patterns of argument and persuasion (and so his use of rhetoric cannot be confined to figures of style, or micro-rhetoric) is J. S. Vos, *Die Kunst der Argumentation bei Paulus. Studien zu antiken Rhetorik* (Tübingen: Mohr, 2002). Vos sticks to the capital Paulines to make his case, but he makes it effectively and it has clear implications for how we should read the later Paulines.

For a general introduction to the genres of rhetoric see G. A. Kennedy, *New Testament Interpretation through Rhetorical Criticism* (Chapel Hill: University of North Carolina Press, 1984). See also his *Classical Rhetoric and Its Christian and Secular Tradition from Ancient to Modern Times* (Chapel Hill: University of North Carolina Press, 1980); "The Genres of Rhetoric," in *Handbook of Classical Rhetoric in the Hellenistic Period* (Leiden: Brill, 1997), pp. 43-50; and *The Art of Rhetoric in the Roman World 300 B.C.–A.D. 300* (Princeton: Princeton University Press, 1972); and A. Vasaly, "Cicero's Early Speeches," in *Brill's Companion to Cicero,* ed. J. M. May (Leiden: Brill, 2002), pp. 71-111, A. D. Leeman, *Orationis Ratio: The Stylistic Theories and Practice of the Roman Orators, Historians and Philosophers* I (Amsterdam: Hakkert, 1963); G. W. Bowersock, *Greek Sophists in the Roman Empire* (Oxford: Clarendon, 1969); and on epideictic rhetoric in particular T. C. Burgess, "Epideictic Literature," *Studies in Classical Philology* 3 (1902): 209-14, 231-33, and L. Rosenfield, "The Practical Celebration of Epideictic," in *A Synoptic History of Classical Rhetoric,* ed. J. J. Murphy (Davis: Hermagoras, 1983), pp. 131-55.

On rhetoric in the Pauline corpus and among Paul's coworkers see my *Grace in Galatia* (Grand Rapids: Eerdmans, 1998); B. Witherington and D. Hyatt, *The Letter to the Romans* (Grand Rapids: Eerdmans, 2004); my *Friendship and Finances in Philippi* (Valley Forge: Trinity, 1994); and my *The Acts of the Apostles* (Grand Rapids: Eerdmans, 1998). On the use of the rhetorical device of interlocking arguments see now Bruce Longenecker, *Rhetoric at the Boundaries: The Art and Theology of New Testament Chain-Link Transitions* (Waco: Baylor University Press, 2005). On the even later Pastoral Epistles and the issue of pseudepigraphy see my *Letters and Homilies for Hellenized Christians* I: *The Pastoral and Johannine Epistles* (Downers Grove: InterVarsity, 2006).

Ephesians

Chrysostom, John, "Homilies on Colossians, Ephesians, Philemon." Pride of
place should go to Chrysostom, who understood well both the Greek and
the rhetoric of Paul, being one of the last Greek Fathers to be in the same
sort of ethos and operating with the same sort of rhetorical assumptions as
the apostle.

Dahl, N., "Adresse und Proömium des Epheser-briefes," *TZ* 7 (1951): 241-64.

Jeal, Roy R., *Integrating Theology and Ethics in Ephesians: The Ethos of Communication* (Lewiston: Mellen, 2000). Perhaps the most important monograph on the rhetoric of any of these letters.

Lincoln, A. T., *Ephesians* (WBC 42; Waco: Word, 1990).

————, "'Stand, Therefore . . .': Ephesians 6:10-20 as Peroratio," *BI* 3 (1995): 99-114.

Martin, W. W., "The Hebrew Symmetry in the Greek Sentences of Paul the Apostle: A Study," *The Quarterly Review of the Methodist Episcopal Church, South* 37/1 (April, 1893): 20-28.

Moutin, E., "The Communicative Power of the Epistle to the Ephesians," in *Rhetoric, Scripture and Theology: Essays from the 1994 Pretoria Conference,* ed. S. E. Porter and T. H. Olbricht (JSNTS 131; Sheffield: Sheffield Academic, 1996): 280-307.

Robbins, C. J., "The Composition of Eph 1:3-14," *JBL* 105 (1986): 677-87.

Colossians

Aletti, J.-N., *Saint Paul: Épître aux Colossiens* (Études bibliques 20; Paris: Gabalda, 1993).

Basevi, C., "Las características literarias de texto de Col 1,15-20 y su doctrina cristológica," in *Biblia exegesis y cultura: Estudios en honor del Prof. D. José María Casciaro,* ed. G. Aranda, C. Basevi, and J. Chapa (Facultad de Teologia Universidad de Navarra: Coleccion Teologica 83; Pamplona: Ediciones Universidad de Navarra, 1994), pp. 349-62.

Botha, J., "A Stylistic Analysis of the Christ Hymn (Colossians 1:15-20)," in *A South African Perspective on the New Testament,* ed. J. H. Petzer and P. J. Hartin (Leiden: Brill, 1986), pp. 238-51.

Bujard, W., Stilanalytische Untersuchungen zum Kolosser-brief als Beitrag zur Methodik von Sprachvergleichen (SUNT 11; Göttingen: Vandenhoeck und Ruprecht, 1973).

Cahill, M., "The Neglected Parallelism in Colossians 1,24-25," *ETL* 68 (1992): 142-47.

Christopher, G. T., "A Discourse Analysis of Colossians 2:16–3:17," *GTJ* 11 (1990): 205-20.

Collins, M., "Rhetoric, Household and Cosmos: A Rhetorical and Sociological Analysis of the Letter to the Colossians with Particular Focus on Col. 3:18–4:1" (Ph.D. dissertation, Vanderbilt University, 1995).

Drake, A. E., "The Riddle of Colossians: Quaerendo Invenietis," *NTS* 41 (1995): 123-44.

Legare, C., "Figural et figuratif dans l'Épître aux Colossiens," *LTP* 48 (1992): 31-42.

Melanchthon, P., *Paul's Letter to the Colossians* (trans. D. C. Parker; Historic Texts and Interpreters in Biblical Scholarship; Sheffield: Sheffield Academic, 1989).

Neesley, J. W., "A Rhetorical Analysis of the Epistle to the Colossians" (Ph.D. dissertation, New Orleans Baptist Theological Seminary, 1994).

Olbricht, T. H., "The Stoicheia and the Rhetoric of Colossians: Then and Now," in *Rhetoric, Scripture and Theology: Essays from the 1994 Pretoria Conference,* ed. S. E. Porter and T. H. Olbricht (JSNTS 131; Sheffield: Sheffield Academic, 1996), pp. 308-28.

Pokorný, P., *Colossians: A Commentary* (trans. S. S. Schatzmann; Peabody: Hendrickson, 1991). Offers a rhetorical outline on pp. 23-26.

Van der Watt, J. G., "Colossians 1:3-12 Considered as an Exordium," *JTSA* 57 (1986): 32-42.

Philemon

Allen, D. L., "The Discourse Structure of Philemon: A Study in Textlinguistics," in *Scribes and Scripture: New Testament Essays in Honor of J. Harold Greenlee,* ed. D. A. Black (Winona Lake: Eisenbrauns, 1992), pp. 77-96.

Church, F. F., "Rhetorical Structure and Design in Paul's Letter to Philemon," *HTR* 71 (1978): 17-33.

Couchoud, P. L., "Le style rythmé dans l'Épître de Saint Paul à Philémon," *RHR* 96 (1927): 129-46.

Martin, C. J., "The Rhetorical Function of Commercial Language in Paul's Letter to Philemon (Verse 18)," in *Persuasive Artistry: Studies in New Testament Rhetoric in Honor of George A. Kennedy,* ed. D. F. Watson (JSNTS 50; Sheffield: Sheffield Academic, 1991), pp. 321-37.

Reyes, L. C., "The Structure and Rhetoric of Colossians 1.15-20," *Filologia Neotestamentaria* 23-24 (1999): 139-54.

Snyman, A. H., "A Semantic Discourse Analysis of the Letter to Philemon," in *Text and Interpretation: New Approaches in the Criticism of the New Testament,* ed. P. J. Hartin and J. H. Petzer (Leiden: Brill, 1991), pp. 83-99.

Steyn, G. J., "Some Figures of Style in the Epistle to Philemon: Their Contribution Towards the Persuasive Nature of the Epistle," *Ekklesiastikos Pharos* n.s. 77 (1995): 64-80.

Monographs and Other Resources

Certainly one of the most important series to deal with papyri of relevance to the study of the NT is *New Documents Illustrating Early Christianity,* now in nine volumes, with more on the horizon. These documents have been produced by a series of historians and classics scholars at Macquarie University in Sydney, Australia (G. H. R. Horsley, editor of volumes 1-5, 1981-89, and S. R. Llewelyn of volumes 6-9, 1992-2002). The first six volumes were published by Macquarie University itself, but now Eerdmans has taken over the publication of the whole series. Particularly important for the study of these three Pauline letters are the discussions of slavery in vol. 6, pp. 48-81, vol. 7, pp. 163-96, and vol. 8, pp. 1-46. Also very helpful is the discussion of marriage in the NT era in vol. 6, pp. 1-47.

To my knowledge there are no detailed annotated bibliographical works on Colossians or Philemon in English, but we now have such a monograph for Ephesians that is very helpful — W. W. Klein's *The Book of Ephesians: An Annotated Bibliography* (New York: Garland, 1996). This work has two oversights. It does not really deal with rhetorical resources on Ephesians, and of course it only canvasses resources up to about 1994.

Arnold C. E., *The Colossians Syncretism* (Tübingen: Mohr, 1995).

————, *Ephesians: Power and Magic: The Concept of Power in Ephesians in Light of Its Historical Setting* (Cambridge: Cambridge University Press, 1989). This work attempts to see Ephesians as a response to a particular social issue, especially the worship of the goddess Artemis, but also to the magical and astrological approach to the "powers and principalities." While he is right that Paul does sometimes refer to evil supernatural powers, it is simply pushing the argument too far to urge that Ephesians especially addresses predilections in the audience to continue to be involved in magic and with the powers. Ephesians is an encyclical, not an argument targeting a problem in the Ephesian church.

Balch, D. L. *Let Wives Be Submissive* (Chico: Scholars, 1981).

Barclay, J. M. G., *Colossians and Philemon* (Sheffield: Sheffield Academic, 1997). This is certainly one of the best brief guides to these two complex documents, and it is accessible even for those just beginning serious study of Paul's letters.

Bartchy, S. S., *First Century Slavery and 1 Corinthians 7.21* (Missoula: Scholars, 1973). Very helpful in framing the right questions about what a slave could and could not do in Paul's world.

Barth, M., *The Broken Wall: A Study of the Epistle to the Ephesians* (Chicago: Judson, 1959). This is a very helpful study as one approaches the hermeneutical questions about the relevance of Ephesians for modern Jewish-Christian dialogues and the like.

Bassler, J. M., *Divine Impartiality: Paul and a Theological Axiom* (Chico: Scholars, 1982).

Bevere, A. R., *Sharing in the Inheritance: Identity and the Moral Life in Colossians* (Sheffield: Sheffield Academic, 2003). This is the most helpful monograph in refuting the syncretistic theory or the predominantly non-Jewish theory about the nature of the Colossian philosophy Paul is opposing.

Bujard, W., *Stilanalytische Untersuchungen zum Kolosserbrief als Beitrag zur Methodik von Sprachvergleichen* (Göttingen: Vandenhoeck und Ruprecht, 1973).

Burtchaell, J. T., *Philemon's Problem* (Chicago: ACTA, 1973).

Cannon, G. E., *The Use of Traditional Materials in Colossians* (Macon: Mercer University Press, 1983).

Caragounis, C. C., *The Ephesian Mysterion: Meaning and Content* (Lund: Gleerup, 1977).

Carr, W., *Angels and Principalities: The Background, Meaning, and Development of the Pauline Phrase* hai archai kai hai exousiai (Cambridge: Cambridge University Press, 1981). A tour de force argument that Paul does not use the phrase in question to refer to any beings that were malevolent or evil. His extreme conclusion is no more convincing on one end of the spectrum than Arnold's is on the other.

Collins, J. J., *Diakonia: Re-Interpreting the Ancient Sources* (Oxford: Oxford University Press, 1990).

Dawes, Gregory W., *The Body in Question: Metaphor and Meaning in the Interpretation of Ephesians 5.21-33* (Leiden: Brill, 1998).

DeMaris, R. E., *The Colossians Controversy: Wisdom in Dispute at Colossae* (Sheffield: JSOT Press, 1994).

Deming, W., *Paul on Marriage and Celibacy: The Hellenistic Background of 1 Corinthians 7* (Cambridge: Cambridge University Press, 1995). This study seeks to find points of contact with Stoic and Cynic discussions on marriage and asceticism. But the background of Paul's thinking about these matters lies elsewhere than in Stoicism or Cynicism.

Elliott, N., *Liberating Paul: The Justice of God and the Politics of the Apostle* (Sheffield: Sheffield Academic, 1995). A helpful study in pinpointing the political character of some of Paul's rhetoric.

Fee, G. D., *God's Empowering Presence* (Peabody: Hendrickson, 1994). The single most important treatment of the Holy Spirit in Paul's Letters, full of exegetical insights.

Francis, F., and W. A. Meeks, *Conflict at Colossae* (Missoula: Scholars, 1975). A helpful collection of older essays trying to pinpoint just what the Colossian error or false teaching was.

Gunther, J. J., *St. Paul's Opponents and Their Background* (Leiden: Brill, 1973).

Guzlow, H., *Christentum und Sklaverei in den ersten drei Jahrhunderten* (Bonn: Habelt, 1969).

Harrill, J. A., *The Manumission of Slaves in Early Christianity* (Tübingen: Mohr, 1995).

————, *Slaves in the New Testament: Literary, Social and Moral Dimensions* (Minneapolis: Augsburg Fortress, 2005).

Harris, W. H., *The Descent of Christ: Ephesians 4.7-11 and Traditional Hebrew Imagery* (Leiden: Brill, 1996).

Kiley, M., *Colossians as Pseudepigraphy* (Sheffield: JSOT, 1973).

Lincoln, A. T., *Paradise Now and Not Yet: Studies in the Role of the Heavenly Dimension in Paul's Thought with Special Reference to Eschatology* (Cambridge: Cambridge University Press, 1981). Still one of the most helpful studies in dealing with the "other world" language in Colossians and Ephesians.

Lyall, F., *Slaves, Citizens, Sons: Legal Metaphors in the Epistles* (Grand Rapids: Zondervan, 1984). Though dated, this is still a helpful discussion of the metaphorical use of such language. It needs to be compared to D. B. Martin's work.

MacDonald, M. Y., *The Pauline Churches: A Socio-Historical Study of Institutionalization in the Pauline and Deutero-Pauline Churches* (Cambridge: Cambridge University Press, 1988). This is a helpful monograph dealing with sociological factors in assessing Paul's churches. But the attempt to see the depiction of the church in these captivity epistles as reflecting a post-Pauline rather than late Pauline situation is not convincing.

Martin, D. B., *Slavery as Salvation: The Metaphor of Slavery in Pauline Christianity* (New Haven: Yale University Press, 1990). The best study of its sort, even though it mainly focuses on the Corinthian material.

Martin, R. P., *Reconciliation: A Study of Paul's Theology* (Atlanta: John Knox, 1981).

Martin, T. W., *By Philosophy and Empty Deceit: Colossians as Response to a Cynic Critique* (Sheffield: Sheffield Academic, 1996).

Miletic, S. F., *"One Flesh": Eph. 5.21-22, 31: Marriage and the New Creation* (Rome: Biblical Institute Press, 1988).

Mitchell, M., *The Heavenly Trumpet: John Chrysostom and the Art of Pauline Interpretation* (Louisville: Westminster/John Knox, 2002).

Moritz, T., *A Profound Mystery: The Use of the Old Testament in Ephesians* (Leiden: Brill, 1996).

Neufeld, T. R. Yoder, *"Put on the Armour of God": The Divine Warrior from Isaiah to Ephesians* (Sheffield: Sheffield Academic, 1997).

Panikulam, G., *Koinonia in the New Testament: A Dynamic Expression of Christian Life* (Rome: Biblical Institute Press, 1979).

Percy, E., *Die Probleme der Kolosser- und Epheserbriefe* (Lund: Gleerup, 1946).

Petersen, N. R., *Rediscovering Paul: Philemon and the Sociology of Paul's Narrative World* (Philadelphia: Fortress, 1985). A groundbreaking work in sociological study of Paul's letters, and still very useful today in understanding Philemon and Paul's symbolic universe.

Rapske, B., *Paul in Roman Custody* (The Book of Acts in Its First Century Setting, 3; Grand Rapids: Eerdmans, 1994).

Reynolds, J., and R. Tannenbaum, *Jews and Godfearers at Aphrodisias* (Cambridge: Cambridge University Press, 1987).

Richards, E. R., *The Secretary in the Letters of Paul* (Tübingen: Mohr, 1991).

Sampley, J. P., *And the Two Shall Become One Flesh: A Study of Traditions in Ephesians 5.21-33* (Cambridge: Cambridge University Press, 1971).

————, *Pauline Partnership in Christ* (Philadelphia: Fortress, 1980).

Sanders, J. T., *Schismatics, Sectarians, Dissidents, Deviants: The First One Hundred Years of Jewish-Christian Relations* (London: SCM, 1993).

Sappington, T. J., *Revelation and Redemption at Colossae* (Sheffield: JSOT, 1991). In some ways this is the most helpful monograph in coming to grips with the Colossian error and its character.

Seesemann, H., *Der Begriff* KOINONIA *im Neuen Testament* (Giessen: Töpelmann, 1933).

Standhartinger, A., *Studien zur Entstehungs-geschichte und Intention des Kolosserbriefs* (Leiden: Brill, 1999).

Stark, R., *The Rise of Christianity* (Princeton: Princeton University Press, 1996).

Sumney, J., *Identifying Paul's Oppnents* (Sheffield: Sheffield Academic, 1990).

Tachau, P., *"Einst" und "Jetzt" im Neuen Testament* (Göttingen: Vandenhoeck und Ruprecht, 1972).

Trebilco, P., *Jewish Communities in Asia Minor* (Cambridge: Cambridge University Press, 1991).

Van Roon, A., *The Authenticity of Ephesians* (Leiden: Brill, 1974). This is a large and detailed defense of the Pauline authorship of Ephesians, but it is now dated and it is not rhetorically informed.

Verner, D. C., *The Household of God: The Social World of the Pastoral Epistles* (Chico: Scholars, 1983).

Walsh, B. J., and S. C. Keesmaat, *Colossians Remixed: Subverting the Empire* (Downers Grove: InterVarsity, 2004).

Watson, A., *Roman Slave Law* (Baltimore: Johns Hopkins University Press, 1987).

White, J., *The Form and the Function of the Body of the Greek Letter* (Missoula: Scholars, 1972).

Wink, W., *Naming the Powers* (Philadelphia: Fortress, 1984).

Wedderburn, A. J. M., and A. T. Lincoln, *The Theology of the Later Pauline Letters* (Cambridge: Cambridge University Press, 1993).

Wiedemann, T., *Greek and Roman Slavery* (Baltimore: Johns Hopkins University Press, 1981).

Wilson, W. T., *The Hope of Glory: Education and Exhortation in the Epistle to the Colossians* (Leiden: Brill, 1997).

Witherington, B., *Women in the Earliest Churches* (Cambridge: Cambridge University Press, 1988).

Witherington, B., and L. Ice, *The Shadow of the Almighty* (Grand Rapids: Eerdmans, 2000).

Woyke, J., *Die neutestamentliche Haustafeln. Ein kritischer und konstruktiver Forschungsüberblick* (Stuttgart: Katholisches Bibelwerk, 2000).

Wright, J. E., *The Early History of Heaven* (Oxford: Oxford University Press, 2000).

Articles of Note

Achtemeier, P. J., "*Omne verbum sonat:* The New Testament and the Oral Environment of Late Western Antiquity," *JBL* 109 (1990): 3-27.

Arzt-Grabner, P., "The Case of Onesimos: An Interpretation of Paul's Letter to Philemon Based on Documentary Papyri and Ostraca," *Annali di storia dell'esegesi* 18 (2001): 589-614.

Balge, R. D., "Exegetical Brief: Ephesians 5:21B A Transitional Verse," *Wisconsin Lutheran Quarterly* 95 (1998): 41-43.

Barclay, J. M. G., "Mirror-Reading a Polemical Letter: Galatians as a Test Case," *JSNT* 31 (1987): 73-93.

————, "Paul, Philemon and Christian Slave-Ownership," *NTS* 37 (1991): 161-86.

Batey, R., "The *mia sarx* Union of Christ and the Church," *NTS* 13 (1967): 270-81.

Bauckham, R. J., "Colossians 1:24 Again: The Apocalyptic Motif," *EvQ* 47 (1975): 168-70.

————, "Pseudo-Apostolic Letters," *JBL* 107 (1988): 469-94.

Bedale, S., "The Meaning of *kephalē* in the Pauline Epistles," *JTS* 5 (1954): 211-15.

Best, E., "Who Used Whom? The Relationship of Ephesians and Colossians," *NTS* 43 (1997): 72-96.

————, "Thieves in the Church: Ephesians 4:28," *IBS* 14 (1992): 2-9.

Birdsall, J. N., "*Presbutēs* in Philemon 9: A Study in Conjectural Emendation," *NTS* 39 (1993): 625-30.

Bouttier, M., "Remarques sur la conscience apostolique de St. Paul," in *OIKONOMIA. Heilsgeschichte al Thema der Theologie,* ed. F. Christ (Hamburg–Bergstadt: Reich, 1967), pp. 100-108.

Briggs, S., "Paul on Bondage and Freedom in Imperial Roman Society," in *Paul and Politics,* ed. R. A. Horsley (Harrisburg: Trinity, 2000), pp. 110-23.

Cadbury, H. J., "The Dilemma of Ephesians," *NTS* 5 (1958-59): 95-101.

Cambier, J., "Le grande mystère concernant le Christ et son Eglise. Ephésiens 5,22-33," *Bib* 47 (1966): 43-90, 223-42.

Clark, E. A., "Comment: Chrysostom and Pauline Social Ethics," in *Paul and the Legacies of Paul*, ed. W. S. Babcock (Dallas: Southern Methodist University Press, 1990), pp. 193-99.

Dahl, N. A., "Cosmic Dimensions and Religious Knowledge (Eph. 3:18)," in *Jesus und Paulus*, ed. E. E. Ellis and E. Grasser (Göttingen: Vandenhoeck und Ruprecht, 1975).

Daube, D., "Dodges and Rackets in Roman Law," *Proceedings of the Classical Association* 61 (1964): 28-30.

Davis, J. J., "Ephesians 4:12 Once More: Equipping the Saints for the Work of Ministry," *Evangelical Review of Theology* 24 (2000): 161-76.

de Sainte Croix, G. E. M., "Early Christian Attitudes to Property and Slavery," *SCH* 12 (1975): 1-38.

Drake, A. E., "The Riddle of Colossians: *Quaerendo invenietis*," *NTS* 41 (1995): 123-44.

Dudrey, R., "'Submit Yourselves to One Another': A Socio-Historical Look at the Household Code of Ephesians 5:15–6:9," *Restoration Quarterly* 41 (1999): 27-44.

Dunn, J. D. G., "The Colossian Philosophy: A Confident Jewish Apologia," *Bib* 76 (1995): 153-81.

Evans, C. A., "The Colossian Mystics," *Bib* 63 (1982): 188-205.

Glasson, T. F., "Col. 1:18 and Sirach 24," *NovT* 11 (1969): 154-56.

Gordon, T. D., "Equipping Ministry in Ephesians 4?" *JETS* 37 (1994): 69-78.

Gudorf, M. E., "The use of *palē* in Ephesians 6:12," *JBL* 117 (1998): 334.

Harrill, J. A., "Using the Roman Jurists to Interpret Philemon," *ZNW* 90 (1999): 135-38.

Jenson, J., "Does *Porneia* Mean Fornication? A Critique of Bruce Malina," *NovT* 20 (1978): 161-84.

Jeremias, J., "Eckstein-Schlußstein," *ZNW* 36 (1937): 154-57.

Kea, P. V., "Paul's Letter to Philemon," *Perspectives in Religious Studies* 23 (1996): 223-32.

Köstenberger, A. J., "What Does It Mean to Be Filled with the Spirit? A Biblical Investigation," *JETS* 40 (1997): 229-40.

Kreitzer, L., "Crude Language and 'Shameful Things Done in Secret' (Ephesians 5:4,12): Allusions to the Cult of Demeter/Cybele in Hierapolis," *JSNT* 71 (1998): 51-77.

———, "The Plutonium of Hierapolis and the Descent of Christ into the 'Lowermost Parts of the Earth' (Ephesians 4,9)," *Bib* 79 (1998): 381-93.

Lewis, L., "An African-American Appraisal of the Philemon-Paul-Onesimus Triangle," in *Stony the Road We Trod: African American Biblical Interpretation*, ed. C. H. Felder (Minneapolis: Fortress, 1991), pp. 240-48.

Lincoln, A. T., "The Church and Israel in Ephesians 2," *CBQ* 49 (1987): 605-24.

―――, "The Household Code and Wisdom Mode of Colossians," *JSNT* 74 (1999): 93-112.

―――, "The Use of the Old Testament in Ephesians," *JSNT* 14 (1982): 16-57.

Maier, H. O., "Purity and Danger in Polycarp's Epistle to the Philippians: The Sin of Valens in a Social Perspective," *Journal for Early Christian Studies* 1 (1993): 229-37.

Marrow, S. B., "*Parrhēsia* and the New Testament," *NTS* 44 (1982): 431-46.

Marshall, I. H., "Incarnational Christology in the New Testament," in *Christ the Lord: Studies in Christology Presented to Donald Guthrie,* ed. H. H. Rowdon (Downers Grove: InterVarsity, 1982), pp. 1-16.

―――, "The Theology of Philemon," in *The Theology of the Shorter Pauline Letters,* ed. K. P. Donfried and I. H. Marshall (Cambridge: Cambridge University Press, 1993), pp. 177-91.

Martin, C. J., "Commercial Language in Philemon," in *Persuasive Artistry,* ed. D. F. Watson (Sheffield: Sheffield University Press, 1991), pp. 321-37.

Meeks, W. A., "In One Body: The Unity of Humankind in Colossians and Ephesians," in *God's Christ and His People,* ed. J. Jervell and W. A. Meeks (Oslo: Universitetforlaget, 1977), pp. 209-17.

Malina, B., "Does *Porneia* Mean Fornication?" *NovT* 14 (1972): 10-17.

Moule, C. F. D., "A Note on *opthalmodoulia,*" *ExpT* 59 (1947-48): 250.

Mullins, T. Y., "The Thanksgivings of Philemon and Colossians," *NTS* 30 (1984): 288-93.

Newman, C. C., "Election and Predestination in Ephesians 1:4-6a: An Exegetical-Theological Study of the Historical, Christological Realization of God's Purpose," *RevExp* 93 (1996): 237-47.

O'Brien, P. T., "Principalities and Powers and Their Relationship to Structures," *RTR* 40 (1981): 1-10.

―――, "Principalities and Powers," in *Biblical Interpretation and the Church,* ed. D. A. Carson (Exeter: Paternoster, 1984), pp. 110-50.

―――, "Romans 8:26, 27: A Revolutionary Approach to Prayer?" *RTR* 46 (1987): 65-73.

O'Neill, J. C., "The Source of Christology in Colossians," *NTS* 26 (1979): 87-100.

―――, "The Work of Ministry in Ephesians 4:12 and the New Testament," *ExpT* 112 (2001): 338-40.

Osiek, C., "The Ephesian Household Code," *The Bible Today* 36 (1998): 360-64.

Polhill, J. B., "The Relationship between Ephesians and Colossians," *RevExp* 70 (1973): 439-50.

Porter, S., and K. Clarke, "A Canonical-Critical Perspective on the Relationship of Colossians and Ephesians," *Bib* 78 (1997): 76-83.

Qualls, P., and J. D. W. Watts, "Isaiah in Ephesians," *RevExp* 93 (1996): 249-57.

Rapske, B., "The Prisoner Paul in the Eyes of Onesimus," in *NTS* 37 (1991): 187-203.

Reumann, J. A, "OIKONOMIA: Terms in Paul in Comparison with Lucan *Heilsgeschichte*," *NTS* 13 (1966-67): 147-67.

———, "'Stewards of God': Pre-Christian Religious Application of OIKONOMOS in Greek," *JBL* 77 (1958): 339-49.

Reyes, L. C., "The Structure and Rhetoric of Colossians 1:15-20," *Filologia Neotestamentaria* 23-24 (1999): 139-54.

Ritter, A. M., "John Chrysostom as an Interpreter of Pauline Social Ethics," in *Paul and the Legacies of Paul*, ed. W. S. Babcock (Dallas: Southern Methodist University Press, 1990), pp. 183-92.

Robbins, C. J., "The Composition of Ephesians 1:3-14," *JBL* 105 (1986): 677-87.

Roberts, J. H., "Jewish Mystical Experience in the Early Christian Era as Background to Understanding Colossians," *Neotestamentica* 32 (1998): 161-87.

Rowland, C., "Apocalyptic Visions and the Exaltation of Christ in the Letter to the Colossians," *JSNT* 19 (1983): 78-83.

Schweizer, E., "The Church as the Missionary Body of Christ," *NTS* 8 (1961): 1-11.

———, "Slaves of the Elements and Worshippers of Angels: Gal. 4:3, 9 and Col. 2:8, 18-20," *JBL* 107 (1988): 455-68.

Sumney, J., "Those Who 'Pass Judgment': The Identity of the Opponents in Colossians," *Bib* 74 (1993): 366-88.

Thurston, B., "Paul's Associates in Colossians 4:7-17," *Restoration Quarterly* 41 (1999): 45-53.

Van Broekhoven, H., "The Social Profiles in the Colossian Debate," *JSNT* 66 (1997): 73-90.

Van Dyke, R. H. "Paul's Letter to Philemon," *Sewanee Theological Review* 41 (1998): 384-98.

Van Unnik, W. C., "The Christian's Freedom of Speech in the New Testament," *BJRL* 44 (1962): 466-88.

Wall, R. W., "Wifely Submission in the Context of Ephesians," *Christian Scholars Review* 17 (1988): 272-85.

Wallace, D. B., "*Orgizesthe* in Ephes. 4:26: Command or Condition?" *Criswell Theological Review* 3 (1989): 353-72.

Wild, R. A., "'Put on the Armor of God,'" *The Bible Today* 36 (1998): 365-70.

———, "The Warrior and the Prisoner: Some Reflections on Ephesians 6:10-20," *CBQ* 46 (1984): 284-98.

Wink, W., "Hymn of the Cosmic Christ," in *The Conversation Continues: Studies in Paul and John in Honor of J. L. Martyn* (Nashville: Abingdon, 1990), pp. 235-44.

Winter, S. C., "Paul's Letter to Philemon," *NTS* 33 (1987): 1-15.

Wright, N. T., "Poetry and Theology in Colossians 1:15-20," *NTS* 36 (1990): 444-68.

THE LETTER TO PHILEMON

We have spoken in the Introduction about the rhetoric of Philemon and will be discussing it in some detail as the commentary proceeds. But at the outset we must emphasize that understanding what Paul is saying and trying to accomplish in this letter depends to some degree on recognizing how he is using the art of persuasion. Throughout Philemon Paul uses various rhetorical figures of style, as has been more than amply demonstrated by G. J. Steyn. "The style of writing in this epistle contributes towards its persuasive nature," or to put it the other way around, the letter's "persuasive nature is established and confirmed, inter alia, by the application of the stylistic features."[1] In other words, the micro-rhetoric of Philemon contributes to and is in service of the macro-rhetoric, such that it is inadequate simply to recognize the rhetoric devices *within* Philemon. One must ask how they serve the larger rhetorical purposes of the discourse. The major purpose of this discourse is to get Philemon to do what Paul judges to be the right thing, and to that end Paul pulls out all the emotive stops, rhetorical devices, and Asiatic style he can muster in this deliberative discourse.[2]

1. G. J. Steyn, "Some Figures of Style in the Epistle to Philemon: Their Contribution Towards the Persuasive Nature of the Epistle," *Ekklesiastikos Pharos* 77 (1995): 64-80, here pp. 78-79.

2. If we ask why Paul did not take a more vigorous and direct method of opposing slavery, the answer R. P. Martin gives (*Ephesians, Colossians, and Philemon* [Atlanta: John Knox, 1991], p. 138) is the correct one: that would have required revolution, which in turn would have been a violation of the teaching of Jesus in regard to nonviolence. In other words, it was not a legitimate moral option, never mind an effective or practical option for a tiny minority sect. See also R. H. Van Dyke, "Paul's Letter to Philemon," *Sewanee Theological Review* 41 (1998): 384-98, here p. 393: "Paul did attack slavery — the one place where he could effectively elicit a change, the church. He did so in this letter to Philemon." Paul encourages Philemon to make a decision outside of the customs and norms that were regulating his life.

51

The Epistolary Prescript — vv. 1-3

Paul, a prisoner of Jesus Christ, and Timothy, the brother: to Philemon, the beloved and our coworker, to Apphia the sister[1] and Archippus our fellow soldier, and to the assembly in your house. Grace to you and peace from God our Father and the Lord Jesus Christ.

This epistolary prescript, including the initial greeting, follows the familiar pattern found in other Pauline letters (cf. Col. 1.1-2; 1 Cor. 1.1-3). First Paul names himself and his co-sender Timothy (who may be his scribe on this occasion). Notice the contrast between what Paul says about himself (a prisoner), and what he says about his addressees (the beloved, our coworker, the sister, our fellow soldier).[2] Rhetorically this is an effective tactic in that it already generates sympathy for Paul. He is in a disadvantaged social condition and position compared to his audience. He does not mention his superior status as apostle. As

---

1. There are really no major textual problems in this letter. The text is found whole and complete in twelve of the major uncial manuscripts. *Adelphē* is supported by most of the major early witnesses and should be read here, as opposed to *agapētē*, which is found in D and most minuscules. See Metzger, *TC*, p. 588.

2. Calling Philemon both "beloved" and "coworker" is part of Paul's attempt to establish rapport and not a mere formulaic expression, as shown by the fact that it is found nowhere else in the Pauline corpus. See M. Barth and H. Blanke, *The Letter to Philemon* (Grand Rapids: Eerdmans, 2000), pp. 250-51. These two authors are also right that this way of putting things already exerts some emotional pressure on Philemon. "Actually, by calling Philemon 'our dear fellow worker' Paul lays on the man a hand that is warm and heavy at the same time. Its warmth will be felt when it turns out that love is the main theme of the epistle; its pressure when Paul appeals to Philemon: May he, by receiving Onesimus as a brother, continue and crown the praiseworthy work carried out thus far!" (p. 253).

Dunn rightly points out, the particular form of self-identification here, leaving out his apostolic status or any other epithet (including servant), is unique.[3] Paul's rhetorical aims have dictated this way of beginning which immediately generates emotion and concern for him.[4]

All the audience is addressed in Christian terms and Paul stresses the co-laborer aspect of his relationship with Philemon. As G. B. Caird and others have rightly stressed, this is most certainly not a private letter, even though its message is directed at Philemon.[5] Nor is it written simply to a family, though it is likely that Apphia is either Philemon's wife or less possibly his sister.[6] She is said to be "our sister," which reminds us that in early Christianity every adult female was seen as one's sister and every adult male Christian as one's brother.[7] The reference to the church at or in Philemon's house rules out the notion that this is a letter written just to a family, and as S. C. Winter remarks this reference cannot be reduced to the idea of the household at worship. Non-household members are among the addressees of this letter.[8]

It is not clear what Archippus's relationship is to Philemon or Apphia. Is he Philemon's son? Whoever he is, he is called a "fellow soldier." He is probably the Archippus mentioned at Col. 4.17, where he is seen as a follower of Epaphras, who seems to have been the one who planted the churches in the Lycus Valley, and is clearly a minister of some sort.[9] In this light, the use of military terminology here probably means no more than "our comrade in arms," though it may suggest that Archippus has been through some battles for the sake of Christ, just as Paul has. It is interesting that Paul does not speak of Christians in general as soldiers, reserving the term for himself and his coworkers, but we do have the soldier analogy in Ephesians 6.[10]

The name Philemon was common enough, and we find it in inscriptions

---

3. J. D. G. Dunn, *The Epistles to the Colossians and to Philemon* (Grand Rapids: Eerdmans, 1996), p. 310.

4. Dunn, *Colossians and Philemon*, p. 311: "he evidently wishes to introduce a theme on which he will play several times in the letter, no doubt because of its emotive and persuasive power (vv. 9, 10, 13, 23 . . . .)."

5. See G. B. Caird, *Paul's Letters from Prison* (Oxford: Oxford University Press, 1981), p. 218. Contrast P. T. O'Brien, *Colossians, Philemon* (Waco: Word, 1982), p. 273.

6. The name Apphia is Phrygian. There is a grave inscription from Colossae which refers to a woman of this name who is said to have been born in the city (CIG III, 1168n, 4380k3; cf. O'Brien, *Colossians and Philemon*, p. 273).

7. See Barth and Blanke, *Philemon*, p. 254.

8. S. C. Winter, "Paul's Letter to Philemon," *NTS* 33 (1987): 1-15, here p. 1. She also properly points out (p. 2) that the language of philosophical and ethical discourse ("according to what is fitting," "free speech," "the good," "what you ought to do") points to a public speech as well. This observation also applies to the commercial and legal language in the document.

9. Barth and Blanke, *Philemon*, pp. 258-59.

10. O'Brien, *Colossians and Philemon*, p. 273.

referring to a Roman citizen in Lycaonia, though the vast majority of occurrences seem to refer to slaves.[11] Our Philemon is clearly a higher status person who owns slaves. Paul uses "the beloved one" elsewhere for fellow Christians and particularly fellow Christian workers or converts who are dear to him (1 Cor. 10.14; 15.58; 2 Cor. 7.1; 12.19; Phil. 2.12; 4.1; Rom. 1.7; 16.5, 8, 9, 12).[12] Here he is establishing rapport with Philemon and making clear how much he cares for him at the very outset of this document. This perhaps puts some subtle pressure on Philemon to remain in Paul's favor and good graces. Philemon is also said to be Paul's and Timothy's coworker. The term *synergos* here as elsewhere in Paul refers to someone involved in some way in ministry with Paul, though we do not learn the specifics of how Philemon serves other than as the host of a house church. Paul uses the term elsewhere of church leaders, both women and men, who share in the spread of the gospel (cf. 1 Thess. 3.2; Rom. 16.3, 9, 21; 2 Cor. 8.23; Phil. 4.2-3). Here it establishes Philemon's responsibility as a leader to continue to act in ways that are Christian, setting an example for those in his house church. His honor rating is currently high, and he will want to do nothing to besmirch it.[13]

The reference to the assembly meeting in Philemon's house is in line with the pattern of groups of Christians elsewhere in the empire (cf. 1 Cor. 16.19; Rom. 16.5), but only here is the house church mentioned in the greeting.[14] This turns what might have been a private letter into a public appeal and perhaps democratizes to some degree the way the Onesimus matter is to be handled if Philemon is not to lose face with his fellow house-church members. Since the members are addressed here, they are meant to hear this document when Philemon and his family hear it. This is probably important to the intended outcome of this matter, for it means that Philemon will be unable to keep this a private matter involving just himself or himself and his immediate family.[15]

---

11. See *New Docs* 3, p. 91.

12. On the theology of this discourse see I. H. Marshall, "The Theology of Philemon," in K. P. Donfried and I. H. Marshall, *The Theology of the Shorter Pauline Letters* (Cambridge: Cambridge University Press, 1993), pp. 177-91.

13. Notice how in v. 5 Paul is concerned about Philemon's faith being or becoming effective. Could it be that Paul is suggesting that since Onesimus was converted by Paul and not by Philemon there had been some ineffectiveness in the case of Philemon in regard to his own household? See R. H. Van Dyke, "Paul's Letter to Philemon," *Sewanee Theological Review* 41 (1998): 384-98, here pp. 396-98.

14. This intimates that there was more than one house church in Colossae, as Col. 4.15 seems to suggest there was in Laodicea as well. See Barth and Blanke, *Philemon*, p. 261.

15. J. T. Burtchaell, *Philemon's Problem* (Chicago: ACTA, 1973), pp. 3-4, makes this interesting observation: "With Paul afoul of the law for preaching publicly the Jesus who was being worshiped at private gatherings beneath Philemon's own roof, the gentleman at Colossae was not in a position to be scrupulous over the civil statutes." In other words, Philemon was unlikely to go to court or stand on the civil law in regard to what he would do about Onesimus.

The eyes of his church will be on him, watching how he responds to Paul's appeal. There may also be the effect of putting pressure on the community in regard to their Christian commitment so that they will not simply side with Philemon, who is their friend and high status host.[16]

The term *ekklēsia* refers to an assembly of persons, in this case believing Christian persons, not to a building in which they meet. It is not a technical term for a Christian meeting or congregation. It has, rather, a long history of reference in Greek settings to political and even democratic assemblies.[17] Is this one reason Paul chooses to appeal and persuade rather than simply command Philemon? Perhaps so.

The greeting in v. 3 is the standard Pauline greeting and involves both a Greek and a Jewish way of greeting (cf. 1 Thess. 1.1; Gal. 1.3; 1 Cor. 1.3), with the modified Greek form of greeting coming first. Paul substitutes *charis* for the standard Greek *chairein*. "Grace" of course refers to the undeserved or unmerited benefit or favor God bestows in Christ, and "peace" or *shalom* refers to the wholeness and rest that comes from being in right relationship with God in Christ. In Rom. 5.1 we see Paul's theological reflection on the source of this peace. Here we are told that this "grace and peace" come from both God the Father and from Jesus Christ, who is the risen Lord. "Calling Jesus Christ *kyrios* in this letter is particularly significant, because as a common noun the word denotes 'lord, master' and was particularly used in the contrast of *kyrios* and *doulos,* 'master' and 'slave' in the social world of the time."[18] This takes on added significance in this letter because Philemon himself has a Master, who provides him with a model as to how he should behave in this situation.

16. See N. R. Petersen, *Rediscovering Paul: Philemon and the Sociology of Paul's Narrative World* (Philadelphia: Fortress, 1985), pp. 99-100. Not only was this a public, though personal, letter from the start, it was also to continue to be a public letter when it was accepted as part of the corpus of Paul's letters.

17. See my *Conflict and Community in Corinth: A Socio-Rhetorical Commentary on 1 and 2 Corinthians* (Grand Rapids: Eerdmans, 1995), pp. 90-93.

18. J. Fitzmyer, *The Letter to Philemon* (New York: Doubleday, 2000), p. 91.

Thanksgiving/Exordium —
A Refresher Course — vv. 4-7

I give thanks to my God always, making remembrance of you in my prayers, hearing of your love and faith, which you have toward the Lord Jesus and unto all the saints, in order that the sharing in common of your faith might be effective in realization of all the good which is in you[1] in Christ, for I have derived much joy and encouragement from your love, for the very depths of the beings[2] of the saints are refreshed through you, brother.

This is the shortest of all the Pauline exordia.[3] Like other Pauline thanksgiving/exordium sections it gives a preview of matters that will come into play later in the letter. Some eight themes are mentioned in this section, and four of them come up later in the letter (love, the Lord Jesus, koinonia, and "the good").[4] Since this previewing is not a regular feature of opening health wishes or thanksgiving prayers in the epistolary literature of the era, it can hardly be called an epistolary feature. In fact, the so-called thanksgiving period is not a regular epistolary feature of the time. It is best to recognize that this section of the discourse is more beholden to rhetorical than to epistolary conventions, for

1. The reading "in you" is marginally better supported than "in us" (supported by Aleph, P61, G, P, the *Textus Receptus,* and a host of other mss.). Since the driving force of the argument is about Philemon and his character and conduct, this reading is to be preferred. But see Metzger *TC,* p. 588.

2. The refreshment is said to happen in the deepest part of the human being, literally the "bowels" or entrails. This is a vivid way to speak of refreshment at the deepest emotional level. See M. J. Harris, *Colossians and Philemon* (Grand Rapids: Eerdmans, 1991), p. 254.

3. On the scope of this thanksgiving period see M. Dibelius, *An die Kolosser, Epheser, an Philemon,* revised by H. Greeven (Tübingen: Mohr, 1953), p. 101.

4. See J. Fitzmyer, *The Letter to Philemon* (New York: Doubleday, 2000), pp. 93-94.

in Greco-Roman rhetoric the exordium does indeed seek both to establish rapport with the audience, establish the author's ethos, and provide a preview of what is to follow.

From a rhetorical point of view, Paul is lauding Philemon and thanking God for his virtues in preparation for giving Philemon an opportunity to further demonstrate his love and generosity and so realize his potential for doing "the good." The structure of this section is somewhat prolix, as ideas are started in one place and then finished later, being interrupted by other thoughts, as is not uncommon in Asiatic rhetoric.[5] What in fact seems to be happening is that the ideas which carry the most emotive freight at the moment (love, generosity, joy, fellowship, etc.) are mentioned, and then they are mentioned again later in one way or another for the sake of reinforcement. In fact vv. 4-7 is one long Asiatic style sentence. The style comports with what the audience would be used to hearing.[6]

From a rhetorical point of view, however, something more is going on here. As Aristotle says, the attempt to appeal to the deeper emotions such as love and so to create pathos in the hearer is an attempt to put the hearer into a certain kind of receptive frame of mind (Aristotle, *Rhet.* 1.2.3). The appeal to the emotions may well reach a person at a level that pure logic will not. Normally in deliberative rhetoric, such as we find here, the two primary motives for action will be honor and advantage (cf. Quintilian, *Inst. Or.* 3.8.1; *Rhet. ad Her.* 3.2.3). Paul certainly does use these motivations to reach Philemon. Philemon currently has a high honor rating in the Christian community as one who has been a big blessing to various of the saints. It will certainly be to his advantage in the community if he continues down this track. Furthermore, Paul will explain how it will be to Philemon's advantage to accept Onesimus back: Onesimus will become useful to Philemon and others now that he is a Christian.

But despite Paul's use of these motivating factors, there is no missing the fact that *adfectus,* the stirring appeal to the heart and to love, is the prime motivator Paul is using here. As Aristotle says, the key is to demonstrate friendship

---

5. See the analysis of J. B. Lightfoot, *St. Paul's Epistles to the Colossians and to Philemon* (London: Macmillan, 1879), p. 334: "all established principles of arrangement are defied in the anxiety to give expression to the thought which is uppermost for the moment. [For example,] The clause *akouōn k.t.l.* is separated from *eucharistō k.t.l.,* on which it depends, by the intervening clause *mneian sou k.t.l.,* which introduces another thought." This rush of thoughts and ideas pressing for expression in an emotive way and leading to lengthy periods is typical of Asiatic rhetoric. Lightfoot, however, does not realize that we are dealing with a deliberately chosen style, suited to the audience.

6. M. Barth and H. Blanke, *The Letter to Philemon* (Grand Rapids: Eerdmans, 2000), pp. 271-72, note the duplication of "you" in v. 5 and the deliberate choice of an "ungraceful" (read Asiatic) style here in this long sentence.

and love for the hearer so as to induce good will in the hearer and make him in-clined to act as requested (*Rhet.* 2.4-7). In short, the appeal to the emotions in Philemon is found especially at the beginning and end of the speech, which is where one would expect them in a rhetorical discourse, with the appeal to honor and advantage coming in the middle. As we shall see, the peroratio in Philemon both sums up the arguments and makes a final emotional appeal for Paul's inner being to be "refreshed" by Philemon. Paul would rather not use the command mode or the reciprocity mode of discourse, even though Philemon is said to owe Paul his spiritual life. Paul would also rather not shame Philemon, although the potential is already set up for that to happen if Philemon denies Paul's request in the presence of his own house-church.

In the exordium we are clearly dealing with a *captatio benevolentiae*. Paul is preparing Philemon for a request by reminding him of his previous generos-ity. About this rhetorical tactic John Chyrsostom says "nothing so shames us into giving as to bring forward the kindnesses we have bestowed on others" (*Homilia in Philemon* 2.1.7). The careful rhetorical structure and the way Paul builds to a rhetorically effective climax has been demonstrated by F. F. Church:

Exordium	*Proof*	*Peroratio*
my prayer (v. 4)		your prayers (v. 22)
your love (vv. 5, 7)	through love (v. 9)	
all the good (v. 6)	the good (v. 9)	
the sharing in common of your faith (v. 6)		sharing in common with me (v. 17)
the inner being of the saints has been refreshed through you (v. 7)	Onesimus my inner being, a beloved brother (vv. 10, 12, 16)	I desire some "benefit" *(onaimēn)* in the Lord, refresh my inner being (v. 20)[7]

The care and effectiveness of this structure is evident, especially the way the peroratio draws out the hints and themes of the exordium. The term *splanchna*, "bowels, depths," is found in all three rhetorical sections of the discourse. It re-fers to the deepest innermost part of the person where his or her emotions may be healed, ministered to, renewed, and refreshed. The deep inner selves of both the saints and of Paul are at stake here. Paul could hardly have made his request on a more emotive basis and foundation. "If Philemon refreshes the very hearts of the saints (v. 7); and Onesimus is St. Paul's very heart (v. 12); then to refresh

---

7. F. F. Church, "Rhetorical Structure and Design in Paul's Letter to Philemon," *HTR* 71 (1978): 17-33, here p. 23.

Paul's very heart, Philemon must refresh Onesimus."[8] Indeed he must emancipate Onesimus.

The use of "saints" twice in this section raises the question of the referent. Does it refer to all Christians or to a particular group of Christians, namely Jewish Christians? While either is theoretically possible, in this letter it seems likely that the reference is to all Christians, as the phrase "all the saints" may suggest. V. 5 indicates that Paul "is hearing"[9] a good report about Philemon. But from whom? It might have come from another member of the church in Colossae or perhaps Epaphras, but it could have come from Onesimus. One gets the sense that Philemon is a kind and generous person who has been sharing both from his faith and his substance, but in Paul's view has yet to fully realize his potential. Yet oddly, whatever sharing of his faith he has done, Philemon apparently has not shared the faith with his own slave Onesimus, who was converted by Paul in Rome.

Paul has received much joy and comfort from the exercise of Philemon's faith on behalf of the saints and prepares now to give Philemon another chance to produce such joy and comfort.[10] The term *koinōnia* refers to a sharing or participation in common with others that can result in fellowship or partnership.[11] Here it has to do with the sharing of faith in common (cf. Tit. 1.3). "Refreshment" will come up again at the end of the speech in reference to Paul himself in particular. The verbal form here is in the perfect tense, which perhaps points to a particular act of kindness completed in the past (cf. 1 Cor. 16.18 on the refreshing of Paul's spirit). Here Paul is referring to a deep inner satisfaction and renewal. Both the saints and Paul are objects of refreshment from Philemon (cf. v. 20).

Paul is dealing with a difficult and possibly dangerous situation, dangerous for Onesimus and for Paul, and in another sense dangerous for Philemon since he could lose face if he does not respond properly to Paul's appeal. Cicero and others speak of such a case as difficult or even scandalous, not least because the audience's affections and sympathies will not be naturally in line with the appeal (*De Inventione* 1.15.20; cf. *Rhet. ad Her.* 1.3-6). Philemon will not be natu-

---

8. Church, "Rhetorical Structure," p. 24.

9. Present participle, unlike the aorist "have heard" in Eph. 1.15 and Col. 1.4.

10. Commentators have conjectured that this may be a reference to some particular act of benevolence such as aiding Christians in the region after the earthquake in A.D. 60-61. This is possible but unprovable.

11. See my discussion of the term in *Conflict and Community in Corinth: A Socio-Rhetorical Commentary on 1 and 2 Corinthians* (Grand Rapids: Eerdmans, 1995), pp. 224-25, and on its use in this verse see N. T. Wright, *Colossians and Philemon* (Leicester: InterVarsity, 1986), p. 176, and G. Panikulam, *Koinonia in the New Testament: A Dynamic Expression of Christian Life* (Rome: Biblical Institute Press, 1979), pp. 86-90, and H. Seesemann, *Der Begriff KOINONIA im Neuen Testament* (Giessen: Töpelmann, 1933), pp. 79-83.

rally predisposed to respond favorably to Paul's request. The natural reaction of a slave owner to seeing Onesimus again would be anger, perhaps even rage, even if Onesimus fled taking only the clothes on his back with him. At the very least there was a serious breach of trust as well as of law.[12]

Considering the rhetorically delicate way Paul works his way up to his request, withholding even the name of Onesimus for as long as possible in the discourse, there is little likelihood that Onesimus had permission to leave home or left a note on the kitchen counter saying he was going to consult with Paul and would be back in due course. No, there has been a real breakdown in this relationship between master and slave, and so Paul must be very cautious. Thus Paul chooses to follow the indirect rhetorical method known as *insinuatio*. He does not attack the problem head on, but rather builds rapport with Philemon, praises his character and previous behavior, appeals to the deeper emotions, and then shows how the requested action gives Philemon an opportunity to continue to behave in such gracious Christian ways. Cicero points out the path that Paul must tread in a difficult case: "we shall derive our greatest supply of openings designed either to conciliate or to stimulate the judge from topics contained in the case that are calculated to produce emotions . . . though it will not be proper to develop these fully at the start, but only to give a slight preliminary nudge to the judge, from topics contained in the case that are calculated to produce emotions" (*De Oratore* 2.79.324). Paul really must pull out all the emotional stops to win this appeal because the case is so difficult and dangerous.[13]

12. See rightly, Church, "Rhetorical Structure," pp. 19-20. The attempt by S. C. Winter, "Paul's Letter to Philemon," *NTS* 33 (1987): 1-15, to argue that the thanksgiving prayer does not fit the runaway slave hypothesis is unconvincing, not least because she does not recognize the delicacy of the situation and the need to follow the procedure called *insinuatio*. Of course Paul is not going to mention this delicate problem immediately while he is trying to establish rapport with Philemon so that he then can make a difficult request.

13. Perhaps it does not need to be said, but I am not suggesting that Paul resorts to artifice. Paul really feels the emotions described here and believes in Philemon's good character and generosity in the past. But as a pastor he knows perfectly well that even good Christians do sin from time to time and act inconsistently, and he seeks to head off such a possibility by using the rhetorical approach he does. J. D. G. Dunn, *The Epistles to the Colossians and to Philemon* (Grand Rapids: Eerdmans, 1996), p. 323, puts the matter well: "Paul's rhetoric here, as elsewhere, should not be denigrated as manipulative and contrived. It is typical of a leader with a strong personality that he should sincerely want to encourage and leave it open to his audience to respond of their own free will, while at the same time being so convinced of the rightness of his own opinion that he naturally seeks to persuade them to share it."

A Closer Look: When Rhetoric Is Not Mere Rhetoric

Sometimes, even when scholars are attuned to the way Paul uses rhetoric, they fail to recognize the nuances of his approach and style and so misgauge the actual situation he is addressing. Such has happened in regard to the rhetoric found in Paul's discourse to Philemon. The particular cause of the misreading is a failure to pick up the signals that Paul is taking the more subtle line of approach called *insinuatio*. Thus, he avoids use of certain potentially inflammatory or offensive language, including direct reference to the fact that Onesimus has run away or that he may have taken some money or resources with him. He offers, instead, one of his usual exordia in order to establish rapport with Philemon and withholds his actual request and indeed even the mention of Onesimus until well into the argument. He appeals to Philemon, but only implies he could command him, he uses wordplay to defuse the tension and real danger of the situation, and only gets to direct speech and a clear request in the peroratio.

Failure to recognize these rhetorical nuances signaling *insinuatio* has misled several interpreters and has even led to arguments that Onesimus was not a runaway and that Paul is not even arguing for his emancipation. For example, we have the careful rhetorical argument of C. J. Martin in dealing in particular with the peroratio in vv. 17-22 but she comes to the conclusion that the commercial language used in Paul's discourse is merely for the sake of rhetorical effect. It does not connote that Onesimus was really indebted or indentured to Philemon and that Paul was really seeking to pay the bill.[14]

A. Callahan, both in articles and in his commentary,[15] has argued that the notion that Onesimus was actually a runaway slave can be traced back to the ingenious rhetoric of John Chrysostom. This argument however has been shown to be a misreading of the evidence both in Chrysostom and in the earlier church fathers. As M. Mitchell has made clear, before Chrysostom, Athanasius, Basil of Caesarea, the author of the Marcionite prologues to the Pauline Epistles, Ambrosiaster, and the author of the *Apostolic Constitutions* all assumed or argued that Onesimus was indeed a runaway slave, as did many of Chrysostom's contemporaries (e.g., Theodore of Mopsuestia, Gregory of Nyssa, and Jerome).[16] As Mitchell also points out, the use of

---

14. C. J. Martin, "The Rhetorical Function of Commercial Language in Paul's Letter to Philemon (Verse 18)," in *Persuasive Artistry: Studies in New Testament Rhetoric in Honor of George A. Kennedy*, ed. D. F. Watson (Sheffield: Sheffield Academic, 1991), pp. 321-37, particularly pp. 334-35. There is also the further problem with both her argument and A. Callahan's (see below) that v. 18 is not taken to be a real condition (i.e., they do not assume that Onesimus really did some harm or commercial damage to Philemon). This is probably a mistake, as M. M. Mitchell, "John Chrysostom on Philemon: A Second Look," *HTR* 88 (1995): 135-48, here p. 147 n. 47, points out.

15. A. D. Callahan, *Embassy of Onesimus: The Letter to Philemon* (Valley Forge: Trinity, 1997).

16. See Mitchell, "John Chrysostom," pp. 145-46.

hōs in v. 16 need not, in fact probably does not, point to a virtual rather than a real state of affairs.[17] Callahan has been beguiled by the subtle and indirect way not only of how Chrysostom puts things, but also of how Paul puts things in some cases. For example, when Paul gets to direct speech in the peroratio at v. 16 and says "no longer as a slave," he does not mean "no longer as if he were a slave" but precisely what he says. The nature of *insinuatio* is to begin indirectly so as not to offend or anger the audience and then in the peroratio to pull out all the emotional stops and make one's appeal boldly and directly. Knowing where Paul is in the argument must dictate how one weighs what he says (for example contrasting the diction in the exordium with the peroratio).

In some cases the failure to take into account the rhetorical force of Chrysostom's argument has also led to a failure to properly read Paul's rhetoric in Philemon. A good example of this problem is found in the debate about whether Chrysostom, in commenting on Philemon and other Pauline literature, did or did not oppose slavery and favor the manumission of Onesimus.[18] Chrysostom understood perfectly well the radical nature of some of Paul's rhetoric and sometimes, and sometimes not, follows the implications of what Paul says about slavery in this example of third-order moral discourse.

The failure to take the measure of Paul's rhetoric also leads to some skewed conclusions about whether Paul was trying to create a countercultural community or merely a subculture within the Roman Empire. For example, in an otherwise helpful study, P. V. Kea argues that Paul is simply trying to carve out a niche for the Christian community within the empire and its values without upsetting any of the fundamental assumptions about slavery and the like.[19] For example, he argues that when Paul says he could have commanded Philemon to do the right thing but refrains from doing so he is thereby avoiding confrontation with the cultural values in regard to slavery.

But this is failing to take the measure of what extreme emotional pressure Paul does bring to bear in this discourse, and how in fact he brings in the reciprocity conventions ("not to mention that you owe me your very spiritual life") to achieve his aims of having Onesimus not only freed but returned. Furthermore, Paul inverts the usual sense of honor and shame. He is actually arguing that it would be shameful for an honorable person like Philemon to continue to view, treat, or require Onesimus to be a slave any longer, when in fact he has become his brother in Christ. The usual cultural argument was that there was no shame in treating a slave as a slave. The fact that

17. Mitchell, "John Chrysostom," p. 147.

18. Cf. A. M. Ritter, "John Chrysostom as an Interpreter of Pauline Social Ethics," in *Paul and the Legacies of Paul,* ed. W. S. Babcock (Dallas: Southern Methodist University Press, 1990), pp. 183-92, and the response in the same volume by E. A. Clark, "Comment: Chrysostom and Pauline Social Ethics," pp. 193-99. I agree with Clark that Chrysostom is in fact more socially conservative than Paul on some matters, though he does see slavery as an evil effect of human sin.

19. P. V. Kea, "Paul's Letter to Philemon," *Perspectives in Religious Studies* 23 (1996): 223-32.

there are some cultural values (e.g., "friendship") that Paul can endorse in some ways does not change the fact that some of his teaching had socially radical implications. But much of the problem here in reading Philemon comes not merely from managing to ignore the rhetorical signals in the discourse, but also failing to recognize *what kind of rhetorical strategy* Paul is pursuing here — namely *insinuatio* — because of the delicacy of the matter and precisely because he does want to urge a course of action that was counterintuitive in that culture, and even countercultural.[20]

---

20. Manumitting slaves was indeed a regular part of the Roman Empire and in fact was a means of propping up the institution by offering the prospect and carrot of release (under limited terms usually). But arguing that because one became a member of a fledgling minority religious sect one *ought not* to be any longer, or be considered, a slave even by one's owner was certainly not a part of the regular cultural assumptions. Within the context of the Christian community, Paul was indeed constructing a new vision of social reality.

An Appeal for a Useful Servant — vv. 8-16

There is no narratio in this brief discourse, but then such was not required in deliberative rhetoric. Whether there is actually a propositio followed by the argument, or simply the one argument which expounds the singular thesis can also be debated. In any case, vv. 8-16 are indeed the appeal or main act of persuasion in deliberative form, which will quickly be followed by a classic example of a brief peroratio, which will not only sum up and amplify what has gone before but also end with an emotional appeal, as was appropriate, reiterating the term "refresh."

So it is that, having enough boldness in Christ to command you about what is your duty, because of love I would rather make an appeal, being such as I am now, Paul the old man,[1] but also a prisoner of Christ Jesus. I appeal to you concerning my child, whom I have begotten in chains, Onesimus, the one who was once useless to you, but now to you and to me useful, whom I have sent back to you, he himself, that is, my very inner being, whom I myself wish to hold on to so that on behalf of you there is service to me in the imprisonment of the gospel. But without your consent I wish to do nothing lest your good [deed] be by compulsion rather than voluntary. For perhaps because of this he was separated from you for an hour so that you might receive him back for an eternity, no longer as a slave, but as more than a slave, a beloved brother, supremely so to me, but how much more to you both in the flesh and in the Lord.

V. 8 makes quite clear from a rhetorical point of view how serious Paul thinks the situation is. In what is supposed to be an act of persuasion, one does

---

1. There is no good textual basis for the frequent conjecture that *presbeutēs* ("ambassador") should be read here rather than *presbytēs* ("old man"). See Metzger, *TC*, p. 588.

not boldly trot out the heavy artillery of command and obedience up front except perhaps to warn that it might have to come to that if the appeal is resisted. Paul indicates that he has the clout and authority and indeed "boldness" (parrēsia) in Christ to command Philemon to do his duty.[2] This noun often conveys a note of unexpected boldness in Paul and elsewhere (cf. 2 Cor. 3.12; Phil. 1.20; Eph. 6.19; Acts 4.13). In fact, the term literally means "free speech" and was used originally in the Greek context to signify the democratic right of a Greek citizen to speak his opinion, to be candid, to speak openly and boldly the truth (cf. Euripides, Hippolytus 420-23; Aristotle, Nichomachean Ethics 9.2.9; as the frank language one uses with an intimate friend, Plutarch, Adulat. 51C; Pss. 93.1; 11.5 LXX).[3] It is possible that parrēsia still carried some of this nuance since Paul saw the ekklēsia as a place where one would speak freely and honestly, as in the ancient Greek assemblies from which the term ekklēsia came. In Paul's immediate milieu parrēsia had come to refer to the kind of speech that was characteristic between true friends — they spoke openly and candidly without flattery (cf. 2 Cor. 7.4).[4]

Epitassein, "command," is a very strong term used of a superior's authority over an inferior. Paul could act like a general and pull rank on Philemon. But then he speaks of Philemon's duty or what is proper. As Dunn rightly says, Paul is not talking about Philemon's civic duty, for that could entail punishing Onesimus the runaway slave. Paul is, rather, talking about Philemon's Christian duty.[5] Paul would certainly rather take the high road and attempt to appeal to Philemon's own growing sense of Christian responsibility, but that the first words out of his mouth when he gets to the appeal are words about command and obedience makes clear how potentially grave Paul views the situation. To miss the rhetorical tone here and underplay the reference to command and obedience, especially when it is always Paul's preference to use the art of persuasion, is to misread the seriousness of the situation Paul is dealing with here.

It is no accident that Paul serves up v. 9 just prior to v. 10. He will try to generate as much pathos as he can before mentioning Onesimus.[6] Indeed all of

---

2. See S. B. Marrow, "Parrhēsia and the New Testament," NTS 44 (1982): 431-46, here p. 446: "When Christians pray for this gift of parrhēsia they pray not for the freedom of speech in some putatively democratic institution, nor for the frankness of friendship's affection and concern. . . . Parrhēsia is a gift granted the Christian for direct access to God in prayer and for the untrammeled freedom to proclaim 'in season and out of season,' the gospel of his Son."

3. See Marrow, "Parrhēsia and the New Testament"; P. T. O'Brien, Colossians, Philemon (Waco: Word, 1982), p. 287.

4. See W. C. Van Unnik, "The Christian's Freedom of Speech in the New Testament," BJRL 44 (1962): 466-88.

5. J. D. G. Dunn, The Epistles to the Colossians and to Philemon (Grand Rapids: Eerdmans, 1996), p. 325; O'Brien, Colossians, Philemon, p. 288.

6. This name, like Apphia, is Phrygian, and it was a common slave nickname. Phrygian

vv. 9 and 10, leading up to the last word of v. 10, is intended to serve that function. Paul has not only delayed mentioning Onesimus until v. 10, he also delays making his full request until v. 17. Such is the delicacy of the matter. V. 9 begins with a reference to love, then to Paul being an old man, then to him being a prisoner, then to his child who was "begotten in chains." If Philemon was not moved by the initial prayer, he would have been a really hard-hearted person not to be moved by the stirring of the deeper emotions including both love and sympathy. What could be more pathetic than a beloved apostle who was old and a prisoner, or a child born in chains?

There is no good textual reason to substitute *presbeutēs*, "ambassador," for *presbytēs*, "old man." That this conjecture is without textual or phonetic merit has now been demonstrated by J. N. Birdsall.[7] This letter is not an ambassadorial letter but an emotive appeal using Asiatic rhetoric. Paul calls himself an old man to provoke sympathy in Philemon and the rest of the audience. According to Philo, *presbytēs* refers to a person who is in the range of 50 to 56 years old (*De Opificio Mundi* 105), though it could also be used of the oldest class of men, those 60 and older. Paul was probably born in the first decade of the first century A.D. *Presbytēs* would have been inappropriate if Paul were writing from Ephesus in the 50s and Paul was not even in his 50s yet. There are then good rhetorical reasons why Paul uses this term here. He wants to be sure to excite as much sympathetic feeling as he can before he mentions Onesimus and then makes his request. Such tugging on the heartstrings in long sentences is typical of Asiatic rhetoric.[8] Paul says "I appeal" in v. 9, then apparently gets carried away with emotion and must say again at the beginning of v. 10 "I appeal to you."

From the outset of v. 10 Paul lays his own personal claim on Onesimus. Onesimus is his child, whom Paul begat in chains. The image of a slave and a high status Roman citizen who was nonetheless a prisoner in chains becoming spiritual father and child is meant to both surprise and move the audience. The name Onesimus was indeed a common slave name in that region and era.[9]

---

slaves had a reputation for not being useful, so it is possible that Paul is actually playing on a common cliché about such slaves.

7. M. Barth and H. Blanke, *The Letter to Philemon* (Grand Rapids: Eerdmans, 2000), pp. 321-24, try to argue the two terms are near synonyms, but in the end they choose the translation "ambassador" because they think the alternative would suggest Paul is resorting to emotional extortion. In short, they fail to realize how the rhetorical conventions in such a situation work. See now the definitive refutation of J. B. Lightfoot's conjecture in J. N. Birdsall, "*Presbytēs* in Philemon 9: A Study in Conjectural Emendation," *NTS* 39 (1993): 625-30. He shows not only that we have no examples of such a transcription error but also that there is no likelihood of a mishearing of the one word for the other in the NT era. He is also correct that the use of "old man" favors the Roman house arrest theory in terms of a date for Philemon.

8. See pp. 4-9 above.

9. See *New Docs* 3, pp. 128-29 on its use in nearby Phrygia.

More importantly, Paul is here laying claim to Onesimus belonging to him in the Lord.[10] Paul elsewhere refers to his motherhood when he is discussing those who have been converted through his ministry (cf. 1 Thess. 2.7-9; Gal. 4.19).

A Closer Look: Paul in Chains, Onesimus in Bondage

The reference to chains is important as it speaks to the nature of Paul's confinement. One must assume, since Paul in both Philemon and Colossians refers to a variety of associates and friends with whom he is able to have regular conversation and dealings, that his confinement cannot have been too severe. Indeed, that Onesimus somehow came across Paul speaks to this reality as well. As B. Rapske points out, there is always difficulty deciding the exact nature of confinement. A "prisoner" was not necessarily in a prison cell, the terms "chains" and "prison" could be virtually interchangeable, and one could be in chains and not in prison (*Digest* 50.16.216).[11] Roman imprisonment without chains was a concession given sometimes to a high status prisoner and one could be chained without imprisonment while awaiting trial.

During the imperial period, when the Roman armies extended the scope of the empire, it was not uncommon for persons to be taken prisoner by the military rather than by a governing official. Military custody in fact became increasingly common during the first century A.D., and sometimes a governing official would simply turn over a prisoner to the military. Military custody is indeed what is depicted in Acts from 22.22 through Paul's time in Rome: from the outset Paul is chained, and he is escorted to Rome by a soldier or group of soldiers. One could be in military custody in a barracks or a military camp, such as on the Campus Martius in Rome, in the camp of the Praetorian Guard in Rome (see Phil. 1.13),[12] or in one's own apartment, which presumably would need to be near the military camp. "Military custody in a private house was much less severe than in the military camp. . . . The level of creature comfort was apparently limited only by the prisoner's own resources and the constraints of security."[13] Paul was in military custody to assure his appearance at trial. Under house arrest a prisoner would normally have his right hand chained to the left hand of his guard, which gave the advantage to the right-handed guard if there were a struggle or an attempt at escape (see Seneca, *Epistle* 5.7).

Since a prisoner had to have permission to approach or be approached by others, we must conclude that Paul's confinement was one of the lightest possible, for he

---

10. See Barth and Blanke, *Philemon*, p. 328.

11. That is, one could say one was in chains and mean one was in prison, but one could mean one was chained and under house arrest as well. See B. Rapske, *Paul in Roman Custody* (The Book of Acts in Its First Century Setting, 3; Grand Rapids: Eerdmans, 1994), pp. 25-26.

12. See my *Friendship and Finances in Philippi* (Valley Forge: Trinity, 1994), pp. 44-45 on this verse.

13. Rapske, *Paul in Roman Custody*, p. 29.

seems to continue to have ongoing dealings with a variety of people, even non-high status people like Onesimus, and of course Paul suggests in Phlm. 22 that he expects to be released. It was regular practice to allow Roman citizens to be placed in the custody of their families or in their own chosen apartment, which is likely to have been Paul's situation when he wrote these documents.[14] Winter is however right to point out that it is unlikely that a runaway slave would be able to seek asylum in a place of Roman incarceration! By this I mean the theory that Onesimus is not really a runaway but is simply a wanderer seeking intervention for some sort of minor squabble or concern, really does not work.[15] But what of Onesimus, the man who was still a slave? Was he actually in a more perilous situation than Paul? I think the answer to this is yes, not least because he was a slave.

Too often when NT scholars have debated the status and situation of Onesimus, it has been done in the context of previous NT scholarship on the matter without adequate attention to the state of play of Roman Law in the first century, whether it was relevant to the situation in Colossae, and the differences between American slavery before 1865 and slavery in the Greco-Roman world.[16] Fortunately now, we have the careful work of S. R. Llewelyn, a scholar not only conversant with the NT and the Greek and Roman classics, but also one who has worked through all the relevant sources, including the evidence in the papyri.[17]

As Llewelyn points out, Paul's description of what Onesimus has done is vague. Col. 4.1 and Eph. 6.9 exhort masters to give up threatening their slaves and instead to treat them justly and fairly. This bespeaks a milieu in which Onesimus and others might well expect that their masters' Christianity would not necessarily change the way they would treat their slaves, else why would such a Pauline exhortation be needed? Llewelyn, rightly in my view, assumes that Onesimus has fled from Philemon's house. Since there is no mention of Onesimus fleeing with others, we must assume that he undertook this risky venture alone, which speaks to the degree of fear of punishment he felt. We may also rightly assume that Philemon, in light of the circumstances of his absence, assumed Onesimus was a fugitive, and this normally meant he would face punishment when returning (at least whipping, perhaps branding, attachment of a metal collar, or worse).[18] As Barth and Blanke point out, it was only the acceptance of a letter of intercession that might exempt a slave like Onesimus

---

14. Even in chains, Paul is free both to have a scribe write the letter and to write a line in the letter himself. On house arrest for Roman citizens see Rapske, *Paul in Roman Custody*, p. 33. It is improbable that Paul was shackled on both arms and legs. See Rapske, pp. 206-9.

15. S. C. Winter, "Paul's Letter to Philemon," *NTS* 33 (1987): 2-3.

16. It is an interesting exercise to compare and contrast Paul's views on slavery and property with that of other early Christian figures and writers. See G. E. M. de Ste. Croix, "Early Christian Attitudes to Property and Slavery," *SCH* 12 (1975): 1-38.

17. His study of slavery in *New Docs* 8, pp. 1-46, is now indispensable reading for this entire discussion.

18. See B. Rapske, "The Prisoner Paul in the Eyes of Onesimus," in *NTS* 37 (1991): 187-203, here p. 189.

from punishment or prosecution, hence the urgency of this discourse. Onesimus could not assume that simply because Paul was prepared to intervene, he would not be treated as a fugitive.[19]

As Llewelyn shows, the arguments of P. Lampe and others that Onesimus was not a fugitive are not cogent.[20] Whether Onesimus fled to Rome or to Ephesus (if Paul was there), he is not merely hiding, as is clear from his meetings with Paul. As such he does not fall under the purview of the Roman law that distinguishes between hiding temporally while a problem is solved and actually running away (*Digest* 21.1.17.4). If the intention of the slave was to stay in the service of his master, then he would not be deemed a runaway. But if this was Onesimus's intent it is hard to understand why Paul is the one said to be sending Onesimus back to Philemon. It sounds as if Paul insisted that it had to be done this way.[21]

A letter from Pliny (*Epistle* 9.21, 24) is often cited as a parallel:

> The freedman of yours with whom you said you were angry has been with me, flung himself at my feet, and clung to me as if I were you. He begged my help with many tears, though he left a good deal unsaid; in short, he convinced me of his genuine penitence. I believe he has reformed, because he realizes he did wrong. You are angry, I know, and I know too that your anger was deserved, but mercy wins more praise when there is just cause for anger. You loved the man once, and I hope you will love him again, but it is sufficient for the moment if you allow yourself to be placated.[22] You can always be angry again if he deserves it, and will have more excuse if you were once placated. Make some concession to his youth, his tears, and your own kind heart, and do not torment him or yourself any longer — anger can only be a torment to your gentle self.
>
> I am afraid you will think I am using pressure, not persuasion, if I add my prayers to his — but this is what I shall do, and all the more freely and fully because I have given the man a severe scolding and warned him firmly that I will never make such a request again. This was because he deserved a fright, and it is not intended for your ears; for maybe I shall make another request and obtain it, as long as it is nothing unsuitable for me to ask and you to grant (*Epistle* 9.21).

---

19. Barth and Blanke, *Philemon*, p. 228; cf. pp. 141-42.

20. Arguments repeated in P. Artz-Grabner, "The Case of Onesimos: An Interpretation of Paul's Letter to Philemon Based on Documentary Papyri and Ostraca," *Annali di storia dell'esegesi* 18 (2001): 589-614.

21. As Artz-Grabner, "The Case of Onesimos," p. 605, notes, the appeal to receive Onesimus as Paul would be utterly senseless if Philemon in fact had sent Onesimus to Paul on some errand. There would be no need for an appeal to receive him back if something was not wrong, and it involved Onesimus being gone from home. As Artz-Grabner says: "it does not seem logical, that he should have pleaded for a slave who had been trustworthy enough to be sent to him and bring him a letter or some food or something else."

22. I am following the helpful translation of F. F. Church, "Rhetorical Structure and Design in Paul's Letter to Philemon," *HTR* 71 (1978): 17-33, here p. 31, with minor modifications.

Pliny's description of the remorse and repentance of the slave for what he has done "seems a necessary element in any attempt to restore a harmonious relationship between unequals where the blame was perceived to lie with the weaker party. It is also consistent with the definition of who is a fugitive and who is not, for if a person is defined as a fugitive by his intention, then the letter, one expects, will demonstrate that his actions and thoughts are consistent with an intention not to escape."[23]

But we find nothing like this in Paul's letter. Paul is entirely silent on why Onesimus has fled or what his intentions are. Paul would have had to discuss these matters if he were writing a "friend of the master" sort of letter like that of Pliny and if Onesimus were intending to go back home. Nor do we find any pleas for mercy and indulgence of the slave in Paul's letter, unlike what we find in Pliny. Nor is there any mention of Philemon's anger with the slave.

Instead of indications of remorse and pleas for mercy, what we have in Philemon is Paul's IOU for anything owed to Philemon by Onesimus and mention of Onesimus having wronged Philemon. This sounds as if Onesimus may have taken some money, along with depriving his master of himself. It seems to me likely that when Paul says to Philemon "not to mention you owe me your very self" he is alluding to the fact that a slave owes his very self to his master, and if he flees he has deprived his master of vital property.

> However unclear his language might seem to us, it was not so to Philemon, who being fully aware of the wrong might have expected an expression of remorse from the slave. Also it is difficult to see how the two areas of difference [i.e., the wrong done and the debt owed] can be properly omitted, if Paul's letter to Philemon is to be construed as a mediation between a slave and his wronged master. It seems almost essential to the genre to include some overt expression of or allusion to remorse.[24]

Just so, and Paul would know perfectly well that mere remorse or pleas for mercy would be insufficient when dealing with a case of a runaway. This is why he avoids mentioning such things. He is dealing with a more severe problem that requires a more miraculous remedy than just forgiveness — namely manumission.

Furthermore, as Llewelyn stresses, whether a slave intended to escape from slavery must be judged by actions. If a slave did not flee first to a temple, to a friend of the master, or to a family member, then he was a runaway. If a slave did not approach the mediator first when he left, then he was a runaway. "It did not count, if the fleeing fugitive had a change of heart and sought the intervention of a mediator."[25] Paul notes that Onesimus has been separated from Philemon for a while (v. 15). This "hour," as the text says literally, included not only enough time for Paul to meet and convert Onesimus, but also enough time for the slave to have become useful to Paul in Rome (vv. 10-11). Paul would hardly mention a time interval, and try to minimize it by

23. Llewelyn, *New Docs* 8, p. 41.
24. Llewelyn, *New Docs* 8, p. 42.
25. Llewelyn, *New Docs* 8, pp. 42-43.

contrasting it with eternity (!) if some considerable period of time had not gone by, and in fact if Paul himself had not been reluctant to part with Onesimus. This means that Paul did not, unlike the situation in the letter of Pliny, immediately write a letter of intercession on Onesimus's behalf and send him packing.

Paul was probably not in a prison cell (see above), so the assumption of Lampe and others that Onesimus, if a runaway, would hardly have sought refuge in such a place does not apply. Furthermore, at the mid-first century Roman authorities did not have a bureau actively looking out for and pursuing cases of runaway slaves. It is not even clear that the case of Onesimus would fall under Roman Law since Philemon lived in Colossae, unless Philemon himself was a Roman citizen.

Other considerations also lead to the likely conclusion that Onesimus was a runaway. J. M. G. Barclay summarizes some of them aptly:

> A tactful letter of appeal written on behalf of a runaway might well avoid referring directly to the offending facts, and in this light it is easy to see why Paul should use the vague expression *echōristhē* in v. 15. . . . Indeed, the extraordinarily tactful approach that Paul adopts throughout this letter is a clear indication that he is dealing with a delicate situation in which Philemon could well react awkwardly.

Paul would not make negative remarks about Onesimus, as he does in vv. 11 and 18, "unless they were a major obstacle in the relationship between Philemon and Onesimus." Philemon, regarding Onesimus as "useless," would not have sent him away to help Paul or to fulfill some other task. That Onesimus was a runaway is therefore the best conclusion.[26]

A third to a half of the population of the city of Rome was slaves. It is not at all unbelievable that a runaway slave would flee to the one place where he could best blend in without notice. Ephesus, though a big city, was both too close to Colossae and too accessible to a high status person like Philemon for Onesimus to be sure he would not be followed or discovered. There were even persons whose trade was to catch runaway slaves.[27] At the same time, the Christian community in Rome was surely small enough that Onesimus would eventually have been able to track down Paul, whom, we must assume, Onesimus had heard of from his master or had even met, recognizing how beholden his master was to Paul. The supposition that Onesimus fortuitously found Paul in jail because he was captured and put there is unlikely in the extreme because a slave would hardly be put in the same place as a high status Roman citizen. There was a slave prison for the likes of Onesimus, and Paul could hardly have been free to send Onesimus back to Philemon if Onesimus were in Roman custody.[28]

26. J. M. G. Barclay, "Paul, Philemon and Christian Slave-Ownership," *NTS* 37 (1991): 161-86, here p. 164.

27. See G. B. Caird's *Paul's Letters from Prison* (Oxford: Oxford University Press, 1976), p. 214: "Rome might seem a long way from Colossae, yet its cosmopolitan populace offered better cover for the fugitive than anywhere else in the world."

28. See Rapske, "The Prisoner Paul," p. 191.

There might well have been a warrant out for Onesimus's capture and arrest. We have a sample of such a warrant from the eastern part of the empire (Alexandria, second century B.C.):

> On the 16 Epeiph (year) 25, a slave . . . by name of Hermon, also called Neilos, Syrian by birth from Bambyke, about 18 years of age, medium height, beardless, with strong calves, dimple in chin, mole on nose on the left, scar above corner of mouth on the left, tattooed on the right wrist with two foreign letters, having of coined gold 3 minae, 10 pearls, an iron ring on which an oil bottle and strigils [are represented] and about his body a cloak and loin cloth. Whoever brings this [slave] back will receive 3 bronze talents. . . .[29]

To sum up, it does not appear Paul was in prison, nor does it appear that Onesimus's case involved something less than his being a *fugitivus*.[30] This being so, Onesimus was probably in a far greater pickle than Paul, and Paul is trying to help him out of it by the bold gesture of having Onesimus be granted a change in social status — no longer a slave, but now a dearly beloved Christian brother. Paul expected to be freed from his chains soon. He sought to help Onesimus be freed of his bondage even sooner.

While it is hard to convey in English, there are various attempts in this discourse to attend to the aural dimensions of rhetoric, one good example being found in v. 11 in the contrast between *achrēston* and *euchrēston,* "useless" and "useful."[31] There are numerous instances of this wordplay outside the NT, going all the way back to Plato (*Republic* 411A), and in later Christian sources as well (Hermas, *Vision* 3.6.7). In Paul's letter the contrast also plays on the name Onesimus ("advantageous, profitable"), which appears at the end of the preceding verse. This is not just an attempt to play word games in the middle of a

29. See *New Docs* 8, pp. 11-12.
30. See now J. A. Harrill, "Using the Roman Jurists to Interpret Philemon," *ZNW* 90 (1999): 135-38, who rightly critiques P. Lampe's view that Onesimus does not meet the criteria under Roman law to be seen as a fugitive. It is unlikely that in Colossae, which was not in any case a Roman colony, Roman law alone would be at issue in this matter. The local magistrates were not Romans and would be dealing with a grab-bag of local, Greek, and Roman ways of handling the matter, while from Paul's end there would be more urgency to follow Roman rules. As Harrill stresses, ancient slavery needs to be evaluated in light of social, economic, and familial as well as legal considerations, and not just Roman legal considerations either.
31. There may even be a further level to the wordplay in terms of pronunciation since as Winter, "The Letter to Philemon," pp. 4-5 points out, *achrēston* would have been pronounced as *achriston* and so heard as "without Christ." Onesimus was useless while he was without Christ but now is in Christ *(euchrēstos)* and so useful.

difficult and tense situation. That would be like telling inappropriate jokes at a funeral. The wordplay is meant to indicate Onesimus's change of status in his conversion so that his change of social status will be more easy to effect. God has already transformed his condition.[32] Now he will be Philemon's brother forever in Christ. Why should his inferior social status be perpetuated any longer if he is already a brother spiritually? The far more radical change had already happened. Furthermore, when Paul says that Onesimus has been useless to Philemon, it is not clear if he is referring only to the time Onesimus has been away from home or making a general assessment, but either way, he is now suggesting that Onesimus is prepared to live up to his moniker or nickname. The wordplay is more than just clever verbal pyrotechnics. It helps the argument along. "Paul establishes the motive of *utilitas* and a secondary motive as well, *affectio,* defined as 'change in the aspect of things due to time, so it seems that things should not be regarded in the same light as they have been' (Cicero, *De inv.* 2.58.176)."[33]

What could Paul do about this difficult situation?[34] He gives his answer as quickly as possible after mentioning the name of Onesimus. In vv. 12-14 he will explain that he is sending[35] Onesimus back to Philemon as the law requires,[36] but at great cost to himself because Onesimus is Paul's very heart and has served Paul in Philemon's stead and can continue doing so if he stays in Rome. Paul ratchets up the emotional intensity yet again by calling Onesimus "my very inner being." The word *splanchna,* "inner being," was used to describe one's relationship with one's children. "The children are said to be inward" (*hoi paides splanchna,* Artemidorus, *Oneirocriticus* 1.44). Just how intimate a term this is is also shown in Eusebius, who uses it to identify the self (*Historia Ecclesiastica* 7.21.3). Paul therefore means that the slave has become a profound part of himself, taken into his heart, life, and ministry. Sending him away is very

---

32. As Barth and Blanke, *Philemon,* pp. 340-42, mention, this verse has been used to suggest that Onesimus was a bad or lazy slave previously. Paul, however, might simply mean that Onesimus was of no use to Philemon since he had fled and was not serving in the house, or it might reflect how the slave owner had felt about Onesimus because he was not adept at what he was expected to do. In any case, nothing is said here about him being sinful or wicked.

33. Church, "Rhetorical Structure," pp. 26-27.

34. Winter, "Letter to Philemon," pp. 6-7, notes that Paul seems to be putting his request in vv. 8-14 in proper legal form, using the right sort of phrasing and terms. However, it is unlikely that the verb "send back" actually should be rendered "send up."

35. The epistolary aorist is used here because of course when this document is read out in Colossae Onesimus has long since been sent. It is a dilemma whether to translate this from the posture of the writer ("I am sending") or that of the recipient ("I have sent").

36. On Roman slave law on harboring fugitives see A. Watson, *Roman Slave Law* (Baltimore: Johns Hopkins University Press, 1987), pp. 49-60.

difficult. How Philemon treats Onesimus will be how he treats Paul's heart, or very self.[37] One needs to take note of the rhetorically effective and Asiatic way Paul has intensified the way he expresses things here. There is first a relative clause (introduced by the pronoun "whom," *hon*), which is then resumed by the redundant *auton* ("him") which intensifies the relative pronoun so that the text reads "*whom* I am sending to you, *him, that is, the one* who is my inner self."[38] This is not a Semitism, it is typical Asiatic rhetoric using redundancy like a pile driver to force the point home. This rhetoric is meant to prepare for the exhortation "treat him as me" (v. 17). Philemon is to show Onesimus the same love and respect he would show Paul himself. Onesimus is now to be seen as an extension of Paul.

Cicero reminds us that "if the scandalous nature of the case occasions offense, it is necessary to substitute for the person at whom offense is taken another who is favored . . . in order that the attention of the auditor may be shifted from what he hates to what he loves" (*De Inventione* 1.17.24). Quintilian likewise says that an advocate may sometimes assume close intimacy with his client so that an attack on the client is an attack on the advocate, and by the same token so that a good deed done for the client is a good deed done for the advocate (*Inst. Or.* 6.1.24). Furthermore, Paul is doing what Quintilian commends in regard to modeling for his audience the qualities one wants them to exhibit (*Inst. Or.* 2.6.18). He self-sacrificially sends Onesimus back to Philemon, hoping that Philemon will do the same thing in reverse. Thus, while there is an element of truth that Paul has sent the slave back so that Philemon can do the right thing without compulsion, there is still a very heavy onus laid on Philemon to do the right thing because of both the moral suasion Paul is unleashing and the example he has now set in regard to Onesimus himself. In other words, Paul has actually set up a reciprocity cycle. God providentially sent Onesimus Paul's way. Paul has in turn self-sacrificially sent him back to Philemon. The ball is now in Philemon's court from a set of events which God set in motion.

V. 13 has sometimes been read to intimate that Onesimus was anxious to go home, but this is not at all a necessary implication. What is compelling Paul to return Onesimus home is not Onesimus's anxiousness to leave, but rather both the legal situation and Paul's desire to have Onesimus available to help him and others on the best of terms, without a legal sword of Damocles hanging over his (and Paul's) head.[39] The imperfect tense of "I was wanting" sug-

---

37. See Barth and Blanke, *Philemon*, pp. 360-61.

38. See J. Fitzmyer, *The Letter to Philemon* (New York: Doubleday, 2000), p. 110.

39. It is clear from this verse that Paul does not feel bound by what Deut. 23.15-16 says should apply within Israel, but then it is clear that Paul did not think Christians were obligated to keep the Mosaic Law. See my discussion in *Grace in Galatia* (Grand Rapids: Eerd-

gests that Paul has deliberated for some time before deciding what to do.[40] He would like to have kept Onesimus for himself. "To me service in the chains of the gospel" might portray the gospel as something Paul is bound to and to which Onesimus has become bound as well. It probably also refers to the fact that it was the gospel that has landed Paul in chains. Paul intimates in a rather direct manner that by sending Onesimus away he is now being deprived of his coworker Philemon's help. This not only conveys the sacrificial nature of Paul's action but also places a debit on Philemon's side of the ledger. The service that Onesimus might render is called *diakonia,* which covers a wide range of practical service. It might have been anything from bringing food to running errands or sharing the gospel. The verb "I was wanting" likely implies a period in which Paul deliberated what to do.

In v. 14 Paul probably uses legal terminology. The noun *gnōmē,* translated "consent" in this sort of context, means previous knowledge and/or legal consent. This is the meaning of the term in a variety of sources (2 Macc. 4.39; Josephus, *Antiquities* 7.2.2; Ignatius, *Polycarp* 4.1; 5.2; so also the papyri).[41] Paul does not want the good that he is expecting Philemon to do to be done as a result of force or a direct and stern command, but he certainly is not above resorting to all sorts of rhetorical pressure. Paul intimates that he could force the issue, but does not want to do so.

In fact Paul wants a series of things from Philemon:

1. that Onesimus be received in a friendly manner, as if it were Paul showing up;
2. that Onesimus, Paul's "very heart," not be tormented or harmed in any way;
3. that Onesimus be freed; and
4. that he be sent back to Paul so that Paul may be assisted by him, courtesy of Philemon.

---

mans, 1998), pp. 341-56. One could say that Paul let Onesimus take refuge for a while, as some time must have elapsed after his arrival for his conversion and his serving Paul. But ultimately Paul returns Onesimus to his owner, which Deuteronomy says not to do. Paul may be following the customs of the eastern empire here, which Philemon might expect. O'Brien, *Colossians, Philemon,* p. 292, reminds us that in "the Eastern part of the Roman Empire during this period, fugitive slaves who sought sanctuary in a household were likely to be given temporary protection by the householder until either a reconciliation with the master had been effected or else the slave had been put up for sale in the market and the resulting price paid to the owner." Nothing in Jewish Law corresponded to the freedman in Roman law. See F. Lyall, *Slaves, Citizens, Sons* (Grand Rapids: Zondervan, 1984), p. 41.

40. See Dunn, *Colossians and Philemon,* p. 330.

41. See Fitzmyer, *Philemon,* p. 111.

This is of course a tall order, and it explains why Paul's rhetoric is so bold and emotive and indeed pushy at points. Paul feels he must not fail in his advocacy for Onesimus. There is too much riding on it. There is a sense in which the very character and miracle of the gospel is riding on it because of the freedom in Christ that is supposed to exist among brothers and sisters in the Lord. Paul sees a window of opportunity to flesh out faith statements like Gal. 3.28 and Col. 3.11, and he is seizing the moment to turn rhetoric into reality.

Paul contrasts acting according to constraint to acting according to a free-will offering (see Num. 15.3).[42] Philemon must be free to set Onesimus free; otherwise the kind of constraint imposed on a slave would be imposed on a reluctant and unwilling Philemon. Paul does not wish to enslave Philemon to his own will in order to free Onesimus. "Paul touches here on a delicate human problem: that the good that humans do must come from them spontaneously and of their own free will, and not because of any necessity or constraint. This is the essence of being human. In his *Homilies on Jeremiah*, Origen cites this verse to show how even God rules and seeks to get human subjects to do what is right not by force but by their own good will."[43] Origen believes that Paul's use of persuasion reflects Paul's view of the character and modus operandi of God:

> God does not tyrannize but rules, and when he rules, he does not coerce but encourages and he wishes that those under him yield themselves willingly to his direction so that the good of someone may not be according to compulsion but according to his free will. This is what Paul with understanding was saying to Philemon in the letter to Philemon. . . . Thus the God of the universe hypothetically might have produced a supposed good in us so that we give alms from "compulsion" and we would be temperate from "compulsion" but he has not wished to do so. (*Homilies on Jeremiah* 20.2)[44]

To put it in the words of Barth and Blanke, "when counseling a Christian, and in view of the communal life and order of the Christian congregation, he trusts the power of persuasion, the conscience, and the Spirit."[45]

The reference to Philemon's "good deed" picks up on what was said in v. 6. I suspect that this is a reference to one or all of the things listed above which Paul is desiring from Philemon, but Paul wants to leave things on the moral high ground, trusting to Philemon's best instincts and Christian charac-

---

42. On the nature of free will in Greek philosophical discussions see Barth and Blanke, *Philemon*, pp. 389-92. They point out the awkwardness of the phrase here which involves a noun and then an adjective — "not according to necessity but according to voluntary. . . ."

43. Fitzmyer, *Philemon*, p. 112.

44. See P. Gorday, ed., *Colossians, 1-2 Thessalonians, 1-2 Timothy, Titus, Philemon* (Ancient Christian Commentary on Scripture IX; Downers Grove: InterVarsity, 2000), pp. 314-15.

45. Barth and Blanke, *Philemon*, p. 393.

ter, indeed his character as a coworker with Paul and leader of a house church. It may even be that here and elsewhere in this short discourse Paul is presupposing that there exists already a limited partnership, a kind of *societas* relationship between Paul and Philemon, in which Paul now wants to include Onesimus since he has become truly useful.[46] "In the social relationships of a church existing in an unequal society there is a particular responsibility on the part of the powerful to act toward others in a spirit of goodness rather than standing on their rights."[47] Paul is appealing not to the Stoic virtue of clemency or mercy but to the Christian virtues of love and generosity.[48]

The argument from advantage is of course a deliberative argument, and Paul makes it with some style here, using the gradual *insinuatio* approach. Chrysostom, well attuned to the rhetorical dimensions of Paul's letters, aptly sums up what Paul has accomplished thus far:

> Be careful to observe how much groundwork is necessary before Paul honorably brought Onesimus before his master. Observe how wisely he has done this. See for how much he makes Philemon answerable and how much he honors Onesimus. You have found, he says, a way by which you may through Onesimus repay your service to me. Here Paul shows that he has considered Philemon's advantage more than that of his slave and that he deeply respects him. (*Homilies on Philemon* 2 on v. 13)[49]

In short, Paul has shown that it will be to Philemon's advantage to receive Onesimus as a brother, set him free, and return him to Paul for service in the gospel.

In v. 15 Paul introduces an argument that supplements what he has said and provides something of a theological underpinning. This argument from providence is a more specifically Christian one, but no less rhetorically effective for that. Church calls it "the capstone of Paul's proof. It is designed to motivate Philemon, not account for Paul's actions. Not only does Philemon stand to gain by the loss that for awhile he has incurred, but by receiving Onesimus back as a beloved brother, he is completing God's designs."[50] Church goes on to argue that by using the providence argument, Paul thereby frees Onesimus from the onus of a crime. Paul carefully avoids saying "perhaps Onesimus fled because. . . ." Instead, "perhaps he was separated [by God] from you for a

---

46. See Winter, "The Letter to Philemon," pp. 11-12. Cf. J. P. Sampley, *Pauline Partnership in Christ* (Philadelphia: Fortress, 1980).

47. Dunn, *Colossians and Philemon,* p. 333.

48. E. Lohse, *Colossians and Philemon* (Philadelphia: Fortress, 1971), p. 197.

49. See the translation in Gorday, ed., *Colossians, 1-2 Thessalonians, 1-2 Timothy, Titus, Philemon,* p. 314.

50. Church, "Rhetorical Structure," p. 28.

while. . . ."[51] The verb *echōristhē* is in the passive. In its active form it means "flee" or "go away" (cf. Acts 18.1), and so we have here Paul's artful and indirect way of acknowledging that yes, Onesimus fled. But, says Paul, God's hand was in this — call it "being separated" rather than "fleeing" says Paul. The force of this final argument is that Philemon must then recognize a larger divine design beyond the surface reality, which was that Onesimus ran away. Chrysostom puts it this way: "And he has not said, 'therefore he fled' but 'therefore he was separated,' in order to elicit some tenderness on the part of Philemon" (*Homilies on Philemon* 2 on v. 15).

What does Philemon stand to gain by taking a Christian perspective on this matter?[52] "Perhaps Onesimus was separated from you for a brief time so that you may receive him back forever . . . as a brother in Christ!" (vv. 15-16).[53] "Philemon may indeed have lost the services of an unfaithful slave but in recompense he stands to receive the faithful services of one whose worth can now be measured only by hyperbole."[54] Strictly speaking we should speak of the second half of v. 16 not as hyperbole but as the rhetorical technique called amplification, as Quintilian explains the device (*Inst. Or.* 8.4.5-6). V. 16 climaxes the argument and leads directly to the peroratio in vv. 17-22.

Ouketi hōs does not mean "not only as" or "not merely as." Here it means "no longer as." The *ouketi . . . alla* ("no longer . . . but") contrast emphasizes that the former condition is to stop and that the latter condition exceeds and supersedes it. To suggest that receiving Onesimus "no longer as a slave" has no social implications and that Paul is merely saying what we hear in 1 Corinthians 7 (the Christian slave is actually the Lord's freedman) is to underestimate totally the force and content of Paul's rhetoric here. There was already a sentiment among the Stoics that all persons were created equal by God. "Please remember that he whom you call your slave sprang from the same stock, is smiled upon by the same skies, and on equal terms with yourself breathes, lives, and dies" (Seneca, *Epistle* 47.10). "All persons, if traced back to their original source, spring from the

---

51. This form of argument is called attenuatio and rhetorically speaking is the opposite of amplification. Here the crime of flight is downgraded to separation. The failure to recognize the rhetorical device has wrongly led some scholars to suggest that Onesimus was not fleeing, but if that were the case there would have been no need for the elaborate rhetorical tour de force we call the Letter to Philemon, see Barth and Blanke, *Philemon* pp. 395-96.

52. Vv. 15-16 are quoted by Ignatius of Antioch (*Polycarp* 4.3, fragment). See Fitzmyer, *Philemon*, p. 113. This demonstrates that the letter was in circulation in Asia well into the second century.

53. "Forever" probably does not refer to Onesimus remaining henceforth in the house and service of Philemon. Rather it refers to the new spiritual dimension to their relationship — brothers in Christ forever. See Fitzmyer, *Philemon*, pp. 112-13; cf. Barth and Blanke, *Philemon*, pp. 398-400.

54. Church, "Rhetorical Structure," p. 28.

gods" (*Epistle* 44.1).[55] Paul certainly believes that all persons in Christ are new creatures and of equal sacred worth. This clearly has implications for the way he treats Jews and Gentiles and men and women, and there is no reason to doubt it would have social implications for his views about relationships between Christian slaves and masters. Paul is perhaps here offering a statement of fact: when God sets people free, they are free indeed, no matter how people view them. Paul seeks, then, to persuade Philemon to view the matter from God's point of view. "The reality of the world as seen from within the world is replaced by the reality seen from within the church. For Paul there is only one reality."[56]

If Onesimus is not to be received or treated or viewed as a slave anymore, then what is he to be viewed as? The answer is given in the second half of the sentence: "much more than a slave, a beloved brother, supremely so to me, and how much more to you both in the flesh and in the Lord." Here Paul may be drawing on the OT passages in which a Hebrew slave is called a brother (Lev. 25.39; Deut. 15.12). Nevertheless, Phlm. 16 is the only place in the NT that a slave is directly called a brother, and this fact must be allowed to have its full force.[57] If Paul had simply left the climax of the argument with the remark "how much more to you *in the Lord*," then it might be possible to contrast what Onesimus was for Philemon "in the flesh" to what he was for Philemon "in the Lord." But Paul places the two together. "Even in the flesh" builds on "no longer a slave." Onesimus is now to become a brother to Philemon, not merely in a spiritual sense ("in the Lord") but "in the flesh" as well, that is, in his physical and social condition and location. This can mean only one thing. In a masterful way Paul is telling Philemon that he surely must manumit Onesimus now that he and Onesimus are brothers in Christ.

Onesimus has become a beloved brother "especially" to Paul, and Paul wants the same to be the case between Onesimus and Philemon, "even more so." Most commentators say that since *malista* ("especially"), which normally has a superlative meaning ("most of all"), is followed by "even more so," it must have an elative sense ("exceedingly so"). This overlooks the hyperbolic nature of Asiatic rhetoric. In this sort of rhetoric it is possible to be redundant and say something like "supremely so to me and even more so to you."

It would appear Paul is suggesting a social arrangement in which Philemon would become not merely Onesimus's patron, as was often the case with freed slaves, but welcome him back as a different sort of member of his

---

55. I owe these references to Professor Peter O'Brien and thank him for his kind hospitality while I lectured at Moore College in Sydney Australia in August of 2001.

56. N. R. Petersen, *Rediscovering Paul: Philemon and the Sociology of Paul's Narrative World* (Philadelphia: Fortress, 1985), p. 188 n. 111; cf. Barth and Blanke, *Philemon*, pp. 418-20.

57. See the helpful excursus on the use of brother language in antiquity and in the church in Barth and Blanke, *Philemon*, pp. 423-46.

larger *familia,* as a long-lost brother or a partner in business in the same way that Paul is already a partner with Philemon.[58] The social location of Onesimus in Philemon's home would then be "no longer a slave, but now a brother" in the house, treated as if he were a flesh and blood brother as well as a spiritual brother in Christ. This way of concluding the main proof or argument can only be called stunning.

Quintilian talks about how to exceed even normal hyperbole by means of amplification. He calls it *supra summum adiectio,* which literally means passing beyond the highest degree (*Inst. Or.* 8.4.5-6). Onesimus is a Christian brother to Paul — "exceedingly so" — but he will not thereby become a brother within the household of Paul, who has no household. But he will become "much more" to Philemon by returning to him and being welcomed back into Philemon's *familia,* not as a shamed slave, but as an honored brother (not to mention becoming a freedman), and even as a partner in ministry. Unless Onesimus becomes at least a freedman, he cannot legally or socially be regarded as Philemon's brother. Manumission, then, is the key that opens many doors here.[59]

---

58. It is important to stress that a freedman was not necessarily completely free in the full sense of the term. In fact the freedman could be saddled with various responsibilities and continuing obligations to his former master. In the Greek world, such as in Asia, manumission documents could have riders such as a provision that the former slave not move far away or seek employment with someone other than his master. See Barclay, "Paul, Philemon," p. 169. Lyall, *Slaves, Citizens, Sons,* p. 43, adds: "a fundamental difference existed between the freed and the freeborn. The former was still to a degree subject to his former owner — his patron. . . . it was usual for the *libertinus,* the freedman, to agree to render certain services to his master *(operae).* These, enforceable by civil action, normally consisted of a certain number of days of work per week, month, or year geared to his abilities and former employment in the household of the master." Under these sorts of circumstances, it is clear that Paul is not simply asking Philemon to make Onesimus a freedman in the limited sense of the term, with entangling obligations of various sorts. He may be suggesting that Onesimus as a freedman could continue to serve Philemon in the extended sense of helping with Paul's ministry, just as Philemon also did as Paul's coworker. On the possibility of a *societas* relationship being set up here, see Winter, "Paul's Letter to Philemon," pp. 1-15; Barth and Blanke, *Philemon,* pp. 473-75.

59. S. S. Bartchy, "Slavery," *ABD* VI, p. 71, rightly points out that freedom for a freedman could have several components: freedom to represent himself in legal matters (which is not the case with a slave, which is also in part why Paul must act for Onesimus); security from seizure as a piece of "living property"; freedom to earn one's living as one chooses; and freedom to live where one wants. Practically speaking, however, the last two freedoms were limited in nature unless one had a trade that could be practiced almost anywhere or was already in business, as was sometimes the case when generous owners set up their slaves in business and then manumitted them. Normally a slave would continue to be a client of his master after he became a freedman. But this was not always the case. Paul then is asking Philemon to go a step beyond the usual procedures which normally followed freeing a slave, particularly when he intimates that he wants Onesimus back.

Peroratio — Summing Up and Touching the Heart of the Matter — vv. 17-22

If then you have any sharing in common with me, welcome him as me. But if he has wronged you in anything or owes anything, put it down to my account. I Paul write this with my own hand, I will pay it back, not to mention to you that you owe me even your very self. Yes brother, I ask some benefit of you in the Lord. Refresh my inner being in Christ.

Being persuaded of your obedience I write to you, knowing that you will do even above and beyond what I ask. But at the same time, also prepare me a guest room, for I hope that through your prayers I will be granted to you.

Vv. 17-22 are the conclusion of the rhetorical argument in this document. What follows v. 22 falls into the category of an epistolary conclusion, since Paul had to offer this discourse in the context of a letter. It is interesting to see how epistolary theorists have had difficulty explaining how this document winds down, purely on the basis of epistolary parallels and theory. For example, John White can find no adequate parallels from private letters of request or in the papyri or in actual petitions for the lengthy oblique request found in Philemon.[1] Typical epistolary elements are also missing. For example, in a normal letter, including those found in the papyri, one expects a straightforward stating of the problem followed by a request, not the sort of roundabout approach we have in Philemon. What we find in Philemon is far more shaped by rhetorical conventions than by epistolary conventions, except at the beginning and close of the document. These Pauline letters are not just surrogates for the presence of Paul (so-called "apostolic parousia"), they are ways that Paul can speak to an audi-

1. J. White, *The Form and the Function of the Body of the Greek Letter* (Missoula: Scholars, 1972), p. 78.

ence in a rhetorically effective manner while he is absent. This likely required that the person delivering the letter could "deliver" it orally in an effective Pauline manner.

While they may be something of a puzzle from an epistolary point of view, vv. 17-22 are not difficult to explain once one knows of the form and function of a peroratio in a speech (see Aristotle, *Rhet.* 3.14-19). The four usual elements in a good peroratio are: restatement (in this case of the request), amplification, emotional appeal, and sealing of the bargain, making sure one has secured the hearer's favor. The first can be found in v. 17, the second in vv. 18-19, the third in v. 20, and the fourth in vv. 21-22.[2] All of the peroratio was also to be permeated with pathos. Quintilian stresses: "It is in the peroration . . . that we must let loose the whole torrent of our eloquence. For if we have spoken well in the rest of the speech, we shall now have the judges on our side, and shall be in position, now that we have emerged from the reefs and shoals, to spread out all our sail" (*Inst. Or.* 6.1.52). It was appropriate in a deliberative peroratio to exercise a maximum of pathos, and doubly so in a speech drawing on Asiatic rhetoric.[3] Philemon is about to be put on the spot: "the return of Onesimus as a Christian, with Paul's strong support, presented Philemon with a major and pressing decision: would he deny his Christian identity by acting first of all with the prerogatives of an angry slave owner, or would he strengthen it by doing all in his power as Onesimus' patron to make him his 'beloved brother'. . . . His house church was watching, and Paul hoped to be there soon to see for himself."[4]

V. 17 speaks of a real condition and one could almost translate it "Since therefore you have a share in me . . . ," that is, "since then you have me as a partner," by which Paul would mean Philemon had a share in Paul's ministry. This same sort of language about a partner in ministry is found in 2 Cor. 8.23 (using *koinōnos*). Philemon could hardly deny that this was the case. The request that follows is built on the fact of this existing partnership in ministry: "welcome him as me." Hospitality is to be extended to the runaway slave, indeed extended as if he were the apostle present in the flesh.[5] The papyri have similar requests: "look upon him as if he were myself" (P. Oxy. 1.32.6).[6] Paul has a deep connec-

---

2. See S. S. Bartchy, "Philemon," *ABD* V, p. 307.

3. See F. F. Church, "Rhetorical Structure and Design in Paul's Letter to Philemon," *HTR* 71 (1978): 28.

4. Bartchy, "Philemon," p. 309.

5. Many commentators take "as me" to be a truncated form of "as you would me." I doubt this. Paul is talking about living relationships in which there is a spiritual connection between the people. Onesimus is Paul's spiritual child. Even if Onesimus were only Paul's biological child, Paul would expect the son to be treated as the father was treated. But here Paul is actually indicating that Onesimus, his very inner being, is in a sense an extension of himself, such that to reject him is to reject Paul.

6. P. Artz-Grabner, "The Case of Onesimos: An Interpretation of Paul's Letter to

tion with Philemon, and also with Onesimus, so that if Philemon refuses to properly receive Onesimus he will be violating his relationship and partnership with Paul.[7]

As with v. 17, v. 18 is dealing with a real, not just a possible condition. The verb *ēdikēsen* refers to a wrong or injury or unjust treatment. It can refer to a financial wrong such as theft (2 Pet. 2.13). The aorist tense here suggests a particular event in the past. The second verb *(opheilei)* refers to owing something and is in the present tense, indicating an outstanding debt of some kind. Paul is not dealing with a hypothetical situation here. The form of the conditional statement indicates a real condition, not just a possible one. The third verb presents us with a second commercial term: "put it down," "charge it," to Paul's account.[8] Paul uses here the rhetorical device called "anticipation" by which one forestalls possible objections to the appeal in advance (*Rhetorica ad Alexandrum* 36).

Paul knows, at a minimum, that Onesimus has deprived his master of his service for a period of time, but he also speaks of a wrong, not merely of a debt. We do not know specifically the nature of this injury or wrong (was there also a theft of funds involved, or is this just a reference to Onesimus' decision to run away?).[9] C. J. Martin has tried to minimize the likelihood that actual theft is involved and wishes to treat these conditional remarks as if a simple conditional statement as we find here with present tense verbs does not have to imply the reality of the condition, indeed that it may be said simply for the sake of argument.[10] But Paul does not just assume that Onesimus has done something wrong. He knows he has, precisely because he is not where he is supposed to be, and the very nature of Paul's indirect rhetoric and careful appeal shows that Onesimus does not have his master's permission to be where he is. Even if he stole nothing else from his master, he took himself out of his master's service. This was considered a form of theft.

The first half of v. 19 provides Philemon with an IOU in Paul's own hand,

---

Philemon Based on Documentary Papyri and Ostraca," *Annali di storia dell'esegesi* 18 (2001): 589-614, here p. 608, takes this to mean that Paul is asking Philemon to accept Onesimus as his business partner. This is not impossible, but it is not the language of partnership that Paul applies to Onesimus but the language of agency ("accept him as me" means either as you would treat me or as my agent, not as Philemon's agent). Artz-Grabner is of course right that there is plenty of evidence in the papyri for the use of *koinōnos* of business partners.

7. See the echo of this verse in Ignatius, *Ephesians* 6.1.

8. See M. Barth and H. Blanke, *The Letter to Philemon* (Grand Rapids: Eerdmans, 2000), pp. 482-83.

9. See P. Stuhlmacher, *Der Brief an Philemon* (Neukirchen: Neukirchener Verlag, 1975), p. 49, who suggests that the terms refer both to running away and to pilfering some funds to finance the flight.

10. C. J. Martin, "Commercial Language in Philemon," in *Persuasive Artistry,* ed. D. F. Watson (Sheffield: Sheffield University Press, 1991), pp. 321-37.

and probably we are meant to sense some pathos here. A man in chains who is not well-to-do is promising to pay off a high status convert. A. Deissmann long ago was right to see here a stereotypical memorandum of debt.[11] It was the writing of the sentence in one's own hand that gave it a validity as a legal receipt. "My own hand" also probably suggests that the previous part of the letter was not written by Paul's hand, but perhaps by Timothy.[12]

The second half of v. 19 provides us with a fine example of praeteritio or paraleipsis, a rhetorical device in which "we say we are passing by, or do not know, or refuse to say that which precisely now we are saying" (Cicero, *ad Herennium* 4.27.37). Paul says he will not mention the very thing that he does mention, namely that Philemon owes him his very spiritual life (cf. 2 Cor. 9.4). This use of commercial language to talk about a spiritual debt can also be found at Rom. 15.27. We thus are meant to deduce that Philemon is Paul's convert, just as Onesimus is. What this phrase does is turn the tables of debt around. Now Philemon is the debtor.[13]

All this rhetorical finesse[14] prepares for the final reiteration of the appeal in v. 20 with a further and even more transparent wordplay. Though Paul has used terms for "useful" and "useless" before (see pp. 73-75 above), here he deliberately uses a form, *onaimēn*, that most closely approximates Onesimus's name. Paul equates this "benefit" with the refreshing of his very "inner being," and so he returns full circle to the theme he mentioned for the first time in the exordium. It may also be the case that Paul has deliberately resorted again to wordplay to lighten the mood here at the end of the discourse since the matter is such a serious one.[15]

Vv. 21-22 serve as a sort of epilogue or transition to the epistolary closing. Paul not only has confidence in and is fully persuaded[16] by his own rhetoric and its likely effect, he also has confidence and is fully persuaded that Philemon

11. A. Deissmann, *Light from the Ancient East* (reprint, Grand Rapids: Baker, 1978), pp. 331-32, and see the adjoining picture of such a receipt.

12. See M. Dibelius, *An die Kolosser, Epheser, an Philemon*, revised by H. Greeven (Tübingen: Mohr, 1953), pp. 106-7.

13. See J. M. G. Barclay, "Paul, Philemon and the Dilemma of Christian Slave-Ownership," *NTS* 37 (1991): 161-86.

14. And one may say that this letter at the very least, unlike some of his others, should have demonstrated beyond reasonable doubt even to the skeptical just how much rhetorical skill Paul in fact had. The Corinthians were quite right to note that his letters were rhetorically powerful and adept (2 Cor. 10.10).

15. See J. D. G. Dunn, *The Epistles to the Colossians and to Philemon* (Grand Rapids: Eerdmans, 1996), p. 341.

16. *Peithō*, a verb used most often to refer to rhetoric. It means "persuade" and here in the perfect indicates that the act of persuasion is already complete for Paul. It is a neat way to signal the end of a deliberative discourse of this nature.

will obey,[17] indeed that he will do even more than Paul asks. The "even more" presumably is that Philemon will not only welcome Onesimus and not only treat him no longer as a slave, but that he will actually send Onesimus back to Paul as a freedman.[18] V. 22 could be seen as a sort of final sanction or rhetorical tactic to make sure the right thing happens.[19] It could be rendered "But at the same time, prepare for me a guest room." With *hama de kai*, "but at the same time," Paul attempts to link the plea for Onesimus with his request for hospitality for himself.[20] He is hoping to come to town, and he intends to take advantage of Philemon's fabled generosity and hospitality. That Paul speaks of *a* rather than *the* "guest room"[21] may suggest that Philemon is a man with a considerable house. Theodoret wrote in the fifth century that Philemon's house still survived.[22] Paul says that this visit in some way hinges on the prayers of Philemon, his family, and the house church with him. He hopes "to be spared to you." This is one final reminder that Paul himself is in a situation that could cost him dearly, even cost him his life. The pathos is obvious.[23] It is clear that

17. An interesting and often overlooked point is that "obey" *(hypakouō)* is in fact derived from "hear" *(akouō)*. Obedience is a matter of heedful hearing (Dunn, *Colossians and Philemon,* p. 345) or listening intently and then acting accordingly and appropriately.

18. The majority of commentators tend to entertain this option as a way to read the "something more." What especially favors this conclusion is that Paul has already directly asked for Philemon to receive Onesimus back "no longer as a slave." The question then must be: what could be more than that? The answer is hinted throughout the letter, especially at the end: Paul wants some "Onesimus," some "benefit" from Philemon. Paul wants his useful helper back.

19. See Barclay, "Paul, Philemon," p. 171: "His request that Philemon prepare a guest-room for him . . . is surely designed to make Philemon take this letter seriously: Paul will very soon be on the spot to see how Philemon has responded!"

20. Dunn, *Colossians and Philemon,* p. 343.

21. *Xenia* has as its most basic meaning "hospitality" or by extension a room where guests can be entertained or lodged. See M. Harris, *Colossians and Philemon* (Grand Rapids: Eerdmans, 1991), p. 279. The parallel in Acts 28.23 is important for establishing the word's use of a place, and indeed a place where Paul stayed in Rome.

22. See F. F. Bruce, *The Epistles to the Colossians, Philemon, and the Ephesians* (Grand Rapids: Eerdmans, 1984), p. 222 n. 100.

23. Only if one concludes that Colossians was written after Philemon might one deduce that Paul's hope to be released was not realized. This assumption is not valid if these two documents were written and sent at the same time. Col. 4.9 suggests that Onesimus traveled with Tychicus to Colossae, probably bearing at least these two documents, if not also Ephesians. Philemon and Colossians have the same authors and basically the same set of greeters at the end of each document. As we shall see, the supposition that Colossians was based on Philemon and created in a post-Pauline situation hardly makes sense of the particulars of the personalia and the activities mentioned at the end of Colossians. What needs explanation are why Colossians does not mention Philemon and why the letter to Philemon does not mention Tychicus. This is not so difficult to explain if Philemon's house church is in one place

Paul believes it will require an act of God for him to be "spared" or "released" or "graciously granted" (hence the reference to prayers and the use of the verb *charizomai*, literally "be shown favor"), but this does not imply that he thinks it would be a matter of the Roman judge being merciful. It is just that Paul is aware that even Roman justice sometimes goes awry.

What we see in this document is the limits to which Paul was prepared to go rhetorically to achieve an important aim. While of course he was not prepared to resort to dishonesty or trickery, nor would he conjure up feigned emotions, he was prepared to use all the normal rhetorical conventions, pulling out all the stops, including combining references to persuasion and command and playing the emotion card repeatedly, to give a discourse the necessary weight to achieve its goal. If this makes us uncomfortable because it seems manipulative by modern standards, it is because we do not live in the kind of social and rhetorical environment Paul did, where this kind of discourse was not only commonplace but actually relished and applauded, and where power inequities in relationships and social iniquities such as slavery presented the orator with situations requiring very strident and bold rhetoric to accomplish some purposes.

A Closer Look: The Cost of Manumission

Not too many commentators have thought through the "cost" of manumission in a world enmeshed in slavery.[24] It was of course perfectly possible that Philemon could sell Onesimus to Paul and that Onesimus would thus remain a slave. He might also manumit Onesimus on condition that he accept a continuing obligation to work for Paul (and for Philemon himself?) in the Christian enterprise. It is doubtful that Paul means that Philemon is to have Onesimus back forever as a slave or as a business associate (vv. 15-16). Paul is referring to their spiritual relationship.[25] Would in any case Philemon expect to be compensated for the loss of Onesimus and his services? As Barclay points out, what would it do for the morale of Philemon's other slaves if a

---

and the main Colossian congregation meets elsewhere, with Onesimus heading primarily to the former destination and Tychicus to the latter. See pp. 203-7 below.

24. An exception is Stuhlmacher, *Brief an Philemon*, p. 54.

25. It may also be the case that Paul is being sensitive to the embarrassing situation Philemon is in. A runaway slave might suggest that he was a cruel and unchristian master in his treatment of Onesimus. If this is a factor, Paul's praise of Philemon and his explanation that God has had a hand in Onesimus running away may help to rehabilitate Philemon in the eyes of his house church. See Llewelyn in *New Docs* 6, pp. 59-60. The usual reasons for a slave to flee were that he or she was about to be sold and sent away, the cruelty of the master, or fear of the master's reprisal for some minor infraction such as petty theft (cf. Cicero, *Ad familiares* 13.77.3).

runaway slave was promptly manumitted on return from running away?[26] Or how would they react if they knew that Onesimus was manumitted because he became a Christian? It is going too far to suggest that Philemon would stand to lose all his servants if he manumitted Onesimus, nor is it really the case that he would not be able to maintain his house if he freed all his slaves. Freedmen might well be required to stay on and tend to the house once manumitted.[27]

Fortunately, there is now a full and definitive study of manumission in Paul's era.[28] It makes the following important points: First, manumission was not opposed in the Roman world, even by social conservatives, because it was in fact a way of maintaining the ongoing existence and stability of the system. It was a carrot dangled with strings attached, which continued to be attached even when the carrot had been grasped. Second, slavery as an institution was not under any fundamental attack in the Greco-Roman world even though it was by no means a humane institution in general. It was so endemic to that world in so many of its social aspects that this is hardly surprising. "Since slavery was not under fundamental attack in the ancient world, freeing slaves was not placed in the context of a condemnation of slavery and a call for its abolition. Even if one sees Paul as a social conservative, this would not have been expressed as opposition to slaves' obtaining their freedom, since manumission underpinned rather than subverted the ancient social order."[29] Third, Paul is in fact evaluating slavery from a Christian point of view, not merely using slavery as a positive metaphor for Christian service or for following the example of Christ.[30] Briggs in fact perceptively suggests "It is possible that Onesimus, if he were a slave running away from Philemon, sought out Paul initially to have him arbitrate an agreement on manumission, which he believed Philemon was reneging on."[31] This could well be true.

N. Petersen has ably summed up the degree to and way in which Paul has put Philemon on the spot in regard to manumitting Onesimus:

> If Onesimus' conversion and return pose for Paul and the church at Philemon's house the issue of the integrity of the brotherhood and its symbolic universe, for Philemon the issue entails a decision between two symbolic universes, two social worlds, and most of all two identities. In Paul's mind Philemon has only one option, but in Philemon's mind there are two because prior to Onesimus' running away he lived in two worlds. Previously, he could be "in Christ" while still being

---

26. See Barclay, p. 176.

27. Against Barclay, p. 176. He thinks that slavery had to continue for wealthy patrons like Philemon to provide places for the churches to meet in.

28. J. A. Harrill, *The Manumission of Slaves in Early Christianity* (Tübingen: Mohr, 1995).

29. S. Briggs, "Paul on Bondage and Freedom in Imperial Roman Society," in *Paul and Politics*, ed. R. A. Horsley (Harrisburg: Trinity, 2000), pp. 110-23, here p. 113, following Harrill.

30. On the use of slavery as a positive metaphor see D. B. Martin, *Slavery as Salvation* (New Haven: Yale University Press, 1990).

31. Briggs, "Paul on Bondage," p. 121.

and acting like the master of a slave "in the world." Now he finds that "being in Christ" makes a totalistic claim upon him from which there are no exceptions. *If he is to remain in the service of Christ the Lord, he cannot be "in Christ" only when he is "in church."* . . . Because they *are* in Christ, Onesimus cannot *be* both Philemon's slave and his brother, and Philemon cannot *be* both Onesimus' master and his brother. A believer can act *as though* he were his brother's slave, but his brother can neither act like nor be his master. . . . Through his letter to Philemon, Paul therefore engineers a crisis for his fellow worker in which he has to make a decision about which of the two worlds are to be his.[32]

How did the church in the region feel about manumission? We cannot be sure of the answer during Paul's time, but we do have evidence from Ignatius, *Polycarp* 4.3 from a slightly later period that churches in the region did pay for the release of slaves, and we also have evidence of this from the church in Rome (Hermas, *Mandates* 8.10; *Similitudes* 1.8). There was in any case always a cost to manumission, and it appears that Paul was asking Philemon to bear it, though he offered to pay for Onesimus's wrongdoing and for what Onesimus owed Philemon. What Paul does not say or suggest is that he would pay for Onesimus's manumission.

It would appear that early Christians from Paul onward addressed the issue of slavery by seeking manumission of particular slaves within their Christian communities, sometimes offering a theological and ethical rationale for why the condition of slavery was neither desirable nor fully consistent with Christian living. Paul thought no Christian should seek to become a slave. There was something inherently wrong with giving up one's freedom in this way (1 Cor. 7.21-23). Paul also gives advice to ameliorate the problems for those who are already slaves. He is not unaware of the problems created when a slave is manumitted. It is just that he thinks that the problems created when someone is enslaved or refuses to take the opportunity to become free are greater. In any case, what we see in the Pauline corpus is an attempt at reformation and emancipation within the Christian community, not revolution against the institution of slavery in the culture in general. It must be remembered that manumission was quite common in Paul's day, and so it would not be even remotely unprecedented for a Roman citizen to ask another high status person to manumit a slave.[33]

It is wrong, however, to ignore the subversive potential of Paul's rhetoric in general. "A Christian community, which internally and theologically blurred the distinction between slave and free, could easily be seen by outsiders as subversive."[34] En-

---

32. N. R. Petersen, *Rediscovering Paul: Philemon and the Sociology of Paul's Narrative World* (Philadelphia: Fortress, 1985), p. 269. This summary is basically correct, but Petersen goes too far when he suggests that the church that met in Philemon's house would have to excommunicate Philemon if he did not accede to Paul's request.

33. On Paul's Roman citizenship see my *The Paul Quest: The Renewed Search for the Jew of Tarsus* (Downers Grove: InterVarsity, 1998), pp. 69-73.

34. Briggs, "Paul on Bondage," p. 123.

slavement to Christ could be seen as displacing the social institution of slavery in the Christian community. Paul's rhetoric puts all persons on equal terms before God and in Christ. The working out of the implications of this could not but be subversive. This subversive rhetoric is seen in the frequent use of family language in Paul's letter to Philemon: "brother" (vv. 1, 7, 16, 20), "sister" (v. 2), "child" and "father" (v. 10). This language shows the sort of vision of family that Paul wants to uphold in contrast to the family structure with slaves that existed and, with the phrase "no longer as a slave," shows that Paul has "an unwillingness to canonize social roles found in his environment."[35]

> Even at its most humane, the institution of slavery was in itself incompatible with the belief in the right of an individual to be treated as an end in himself and not as a mere tool or a means to an end. To claim ownership of human property is a contradiction of this belief, however tenderly the property may be used. . . . It was Christianity which first transformed the relationship between master and slave so completely as to apply an explosive charge to the whole institution. . . . The letter to Philemon gives us a close-up view of it at work. But why then was the force so portentously slow in acting? . . . It was not simply the best policy, then — it was the only policy to apply the far more subtle solvent of the transformation of character. And that is *necessarily* a slow method.[36]

One further witness on this point is worth quoting. Not long before he passed away, Raymond Brown argued that Paul urged "a Christian slave owner to defy the conventions: To forgive and receive back into the household a runaway slave; to refuse financial reparation when it is offered, mindful of what one owes to Christ as proclaimed by Paul; to go farther in generosity by freeing the servant; and most important of all from a theological viewpoint to recognize in Onesimus a beloved brother and thus acknowledge his Christian transformation."[37]

---

35. L. Lewis, "An African-American Appraisal of the Philemon-Paul-Onesimus Triangle," in *Stony the Road We Trod: African American Biblical Interpretation,* ed. C. H. Felder (Minneapolis: Fortress, 1991), pp. 232-46, here p. 246. Cf. Mary Ann Getty, *Philippians and Philemon* (Wilmington: Glazier, 1980), pp. 78-79.

36. C. F. D. Moule, *The Epistles to the Colossians and to Philemon* (Cambridge: Cambridge University Press, 1957), pp. 10-12.

37. R. E. Brown, *An Introduction to the New Testament* (New York: Doubleday, 1997), p. 506. See also the discussion by C. Hope Felder, "The Letter to Philemon," *New Interpreter's Bible* XI, pp. 898-99.

Epistolary Conclusion — vv. 23-24

Epaphras, my fellow prisoner in Christ Jesus, greets you. Mark, Aristarchus, Demas, Luke, my co-workers [greet you]. The grace of our Lord Jesus Christ be with your spirit.[1]

Vv. 23-24 provide us with the final greetings. Epaphras, called Paul's fellow prisoner, sends greetings. The fact that he is mentioned initially suggests some particular relationship he has with the church in that region, as Col. 4.12 makes clear. Indeed, Col. 1.7-8 suggests that he planted the church in Colossae (see pp. 122-24 below). His name is the shortened form of Epaphroditus (see Phil. 2.25; 4.18, though there the reference is to a different man), and it seems likely that this is the same person who later became bishop of Colossae and a martyr.[2] Mark, Aristarchus, Demas, and Luke are all called Paul's coworkers and likewise send greetings.

V. 25 provides the closing benediction for the worship service in which the document is to be orally delivered: "the grace of the Lord Jesus be with your spirits" (cf. Gal. 6.18; Phil. 4.23). Paul does not subscribe to the Greco-Roman notion of the immortal soul, but he is happy to speak of the human spirit, the

---

1. There are a wide variety of interesting subscripts at the end of the letter. For example ms. P says that the letter was written from Rome. K, 1908, and others, followed by the *Textus Receptus* say it was written from Rome "through Onesimus the household servant," which presumably means that Onesimus delivered it, though it could also mean he wrote it down for Paul. If Onesimus was a household scribe, this might explain why he had become so useful to Paul while Paul was under house arrest and immobilized in Rome. Ms. 101 says the same thing about Onesimus as do several others and calls Archippus the deacon of the Colossian church.

2. See J. Fitzmyer, *The Letter to Philemon* (New York: Doubleday, 2000), p. 123.

inner non-material part of the person. But here the term may mean persons as spiritual beings.

It is probably safe to assume that, since this letter was preserved, copied, and circulated in the early church, its appeal and request were successful.[3] It is also possible, though unprovable, that our Onesimus went on to become the bishop of Ephesus whom Ignatius of Antioch refers to in *Ephesians* 1.3 (110-15 A.D.), but the later *Apostolic Constitutions* 7.46 say someone named Onesimus was bishop of Berea in Macedonia. It was a very common name, and if Onesimus was a grown man when Paul knew him in the early 60s he would have been 70 or more in 110.

---

3. F. F. Bruce, *Paul, Apostle of the Heart Set Free* (Grand Rapids: Eerdmans, 1977), p. 406, even suggests that the letter was preserved by Onesimus as his charter of freedom.

Bridging the Horizons — Philemon

In commenting on v. 9 of this brief missive Tom Wright makes a crucial point: "Living Christianly makes people more human, not less. No Christian should grumble at the extra demands of love. They are golden opportunities to draw on the reserve of divine love, and in so doing become more fully oneself in Christ, more completely in the image of God, more authentically human."[1]

The converse of what Wright says is also true — living or acting in an unchristian manner makes one less human. I have cause to be mindful of this now because I recently watched some Christians attempt a hostile takeover of a Christian organization. I was stunned because some of the persons involved I had known and loved for years. I could never imagine them operating in such an unkind, unchristian, inhuman kind of way, for the leaders of that organization were bound to be deeply hurt and compromised in the attempt. It is always depressing when we see the church acting like the world, especially when it does so simply because it did not get its own way in the previous round of hirings or whatever. I remember one of my other friends at that institution saying that he felt used, indeed violated, because he had trusted the persons in charge. One can only imagine then how slaves in antiquity must have felt, who had little or no say in their own fates. They were just pawns on the chessboard of the masters, and one had to hope that the master played the game gracefully and with care and forethought.

Philemon brings us right to the edge of what should be attempted when a Christian is trying to change a difficult situation. Since the church is a voluntary society, and not the army, persuasion should be the chief change agent applied to a difficult situation, not back-channeling, smoke-filled-room politics,

---

1. N. T. Wright, *Colossians and Philemon* (Grand Rapids: Eerdmans, 1986), p. 180.

93

or the like. Of course there is a leadership structure and there are times when commanding things may be necessary, but even in this difficult situation Paul wants to command only as a last resort. He would much rather persuade so that the person being persuaded has a chance to embrace the vision on his own. Wright is surely correct that when we do indeed act with love and respect toward others it not only humanizes them but us as well. It makes us more authentically human. And as we have seen in a quotation from Origen (see p. 77 above), God is also one who operates with his human subjects by means of persuasion — the persuasion of the proclamation and implementation of the gospel. God is of course Lord, but he prefers to operate as Lover, wooing his people to do the right thing and be their best selves. It is an awesome thing to be created in the image of such a God.

When one actually discovers the sort of rhetoric Paul was prepared to use in Philemon, one of the normal modern reactions is that this seems quite manipulative and too emotive. This reaction is understandable from those who do not understand either the conventions of ancient rhetoric or what was within the bounds of the honorable and appropriate in such a culture, but we might not have expected such a reaction from those modern students of Paul who are better informed about such things.

It seems to me that we must assess whether Paul's style of persuasion in fact works in our own rhetorical situation. The less we live in an honor and shame culture the more we will have difficulties with this sort of rhetoric and disappointments when we try to apply it without translation into our own setting. What sort of preaching is in fact effective in our own postmodern situation? What approaches do we find that people respond to in positive ways and are persuaded by? Of course there will be those who see any sort of preaching as a form of manipulation and any sort of rhetoric as a bad thing, but those who react this way are in fact not being honest. All of us listen to and accept acts of persuasion from friends, family, advisors, teachers, counselors, even ministers, and often we accept their pleas and wisdom and persuasion gratefully. If we have a distaste for the same sort of thing coming from a pulpit, we would do well to ask why. What is it that we find offensive about passionate persuasion in regard to matters religious, and Jesus Christ in particular? This may well tell us more about ourselves than it does about the actions of the preacher being inappropriate or over the top.

Still in all, it is a wise preacher who learns how to craft his words, his tone of voice, his gestures so that the whole package will become a word on target and thereby a living Word of God for the audience in question. If there is not care in the presentation and persuasion, the audience may be turned off rather quickly or, worse still, lost altogether. There is a difference between being like John Chrysostom, called "golden mouth," and being a silver-tongued devil leading an audience down the garden path. And that difference comes in part from whether the persuader is himself or herself persuaded about what he or she is passionately urging. There is a difference between an eloquent orator who knows but does not believe or embrace his subject and someone who is eloquent, passionate, and himself persuaded. Such a person was Paul, and when we reread Philemon we must remember that he saw the situation he was addressing as grave and urgent. A life was potentially at stake. In such a situation, the rhetoric we find in this little document was appropriate then, and I would argue that with very little modification it is appropriate now.

Burtchaell in his powerful study of Philemon has some telling remarks:

> All societies rest upon inequities — some concealed, others noticed — that make brotherhood impossible. Every age and locale has its particular and familiar slaveries. What heightens injustice is that all believers — exploiters or exploited — are equally nearsighted about the oppressions we have unwittingly learned to live with. No one cries out: the strong because they need not, the weak for they dare not. Or perhaps this is unfair: it might seem that slaves would sense injustice that owners ignore. But even slaves must have their eyes and their feelings dulled; you cannot long entertain hope for what is unattainable. So, rather than live in perpetual frustration, the enslaved man generally will not allow his conscience to become too sensitive. . . . Yet there is no social order, no revision of the economy, no advance in politics, no possible world situation that adequately conforms to the gospel or even makes room for its full realization, no revolution that does not eventually redistribute injustice.[2]

Yet, God is not limited in the way human attempts at justice and equity are. God can make a way when there seems to be no way.

I have had the privilege and pleasure of lecturing some in South Africa at former Afrikaans Universities like the ones at Pretoria or Bloemfontein or Stellenbosch. I have made friends with persons on both sides of the apartheid struggle. One of the more surprising things I have learned is just how blind devout Christians could be to the systematic inequities of their own culture. As the quotation from Burtchaell suggests, those who are the oppressed in certain situations find ways to anesthetize their consciences since real change does not seem to be coming. But this is not true of all such persons. It was not true of Desmond Tutu or Bishop Storey, who stood with the blacks on their side of the struggle. God showed them a way where there seemed to be none. There came a day outside Johannesburg when these two men were taken off into the woods in order to be shot. One of them on impulse just before the end shouted at the Afrikaans young men "Are you Christians?" When the answer came back "Yes," then came the words from those about to be executed: "Then you cannot do

2. J. T. Burtchaell, *Philemon's Problem* (Chicago: ACTA, 1973), pp. 7-9.

this! You cannot do this!" And they stood down. The blinders had finally fallen from their eyes, and they could see the evil they were doing supposedly in the name of a Christian form of government.

All of us have blind spots, some moral, some of other sorts. Yes, even Christians can have huge blind spots and bouts with selective conscience. Before we too quickly condemn a Paul for not being more strident in his condemnation of slavery, we need to bear in mind that he was seeking a way to remedy an existing evil, not endorsing an oppressive situation. The letter to Philemon raises in an acute way the whole question of what sort of means can and will achieve great and good ends, and what sort will amount to raging against the machine without effect. The answer actually lies in part in the art of effective persuasion, and of course also in the grace of God. It requires that the persuader know his own limits, know his audience, and also know his God and what God is capable of.

Bishop William Cannon was a remarkable man — a celibate Methodist bishop who was also a great scholar in Wesley studies and other fields. He certainly had the gift of persuasion in many respects, but on one occasion when he was dealing with a Methodist church in Georgia that was about to split, he had reached his limits. He could not slow down the freight train of division that was bearing down on that congregation. In desperation he called up one of his local preachers — a simple man of no great education whose most notable attribute was that he was a powerful man of prayer. The bishop called him, as he knew he served in a nearby church, and asked him to come over at once.

The man arrived looking just the opposite of a bishop — unkempt, disheveled, poorly dressed. His ethos did not immediately convey the image of a great statesman or healer of divisions like Henry Clay for instance. The Bishop simply asked the man to begin to pray, and pray he did. Beginning slowly he took his lament to the highest court of appeal, and it seemed that God was about to have his own arm twisted. "Bill," as the man was called, spoke as if he knew the Almighty personally and was used to persuading him about many things. He brought before the throne of grace the concerns of this divided congregation with passion, with power, with urgency. After about five minutes of this sort of crisis intervention there was a notable change in the tenor of the congregation — it went from tense to repentant. After about ten minutes of this sort of praying pretty much everyone in the room was weeping and asking God to personally forgive them for their pride and stubbornness. By the time Bill finished his prayerful persuasion the congregation had been brought to the beginning place of healing the fissure. And Bishop Cannon took it from there.

The church today, as in Paul's day, is a voluntary society. And as such, it must live and die by persuasion, freely offered and freely received, if we are to treat each other with respect and dignity and love. Persuasion is just a sort of prayer or faith act turned toward our fellow believers and offered up in the sight of the one who is capable of things that mere mortals are not capable of. Before we disparage rhetoric, we would do well to realize that it is the main weapon in our arsenal, for it is the divinely ordained means of evangelizing the world, discipling the saints, and leading congregations in the paths of righteousness. Rhetoric, as it turns out, is not the real manipulation. That comes when people try to bypass or circumvent persuasion and attempt to accomplish things by strong-arm tactics, secret meetings, and other sorts of passive-aggressive behavior. And as we shall see when we turn to Colossians, rhetoric can even be used to uncover all sorts of bad religion and false philosophies.

THE LETTER TO THE COLOSSIANS

Colossians is a theologically and ethically powerful discourse and has had its effect on various church controversies through the ages (unlike Philemon, which seems to have received little attention in theological discussions). For example, the description of Christ as "the image of God and the firstborn of all creation" led in part to the Arian controversy because Arius used Col. 1.15 as one of his major prooftexts to demonstrate that Christ was himself a creature. Athanasius countered that Christ was in a different category from the creatures, being "begotten, not made." The two-natures doctrine of Christ developed in part out of the dueling interpretations of the Christ hymn in Colossians 1.[1]

Colossians has also had an ongoing life in combating other sorts of atypical interpretations of Christian life. For example, John Chrysostom used it to combat the notion of "angel cults." It was also used to combat extreme Christian asceticism, Judaizing practices, and indeed Judaism itself.[2]

Controversy has dogged the interpretation of Colossians in the modern era as well. On the one hand, it has been the battlefield for heated discussion of the cosmic Christ, and on the other hand it has been taken as endorsing patriarchy and the institution of slavery. This latter conclusion has also helped fuel the arguments that Colossians must be post-Pauline, especially if Philemon is Pauline.[3]

Our concern in this commentary is not with the modern theological con-

---

1. See J. M. G. Barclay, *Colossians and Philemon* (Sheffield: Sheffield Academic, 1997), pp. 11-12.

2. Barclay, *Colossians and Philemon*, p. 12.

3. See, e.g., N. Elliott, *Liberating Paul: The Justice of God and the Politics of the Apostle* (Sheffield: Sheffield Academic, 1995).

troversies that Colossians has been used to engender except insofar as they are grounded in and involve the exegesis of particular Colossian texts. Thus, we will have an occasion to say some things about the implications of the household code in chs. 3–4 in due course, but the modern and often esoteric discussions of the cosmic Christ are beyond the scope of this study. Equally, since we find the case for the Pauline authorship of Colossians more persuasive than the suggestion it is by a later Paulinist, we will not be engaging in the debate about what this letter tells us about the post-Pauline situation of the Pauline churches. But a bit more needs to be said on that subject here.

The Authorship of Colossians[4]

Here is where the remark of Barclay, who suggests that it is a close call to determine whether this is a letter by Paul or not, has some force:

> It turns out . . . that the differences are not large between Paul himself writing this letter, Paul writing with the aid of a secretary, Paul authorizing an associate to write it, and the letter being composed by a knowledgeable imitator or pupil of Paul. Perhaps with our intense concern to demarcate "Paul" from "non-Paul" we are working with an artificial or anachronistic notion of individual uniqueness: was Paul completely different from his contemporaries and associates, or did he typically work with others, influencing them and being influenced by them? Have we created a Paul of utter uniqueness in line with the peculiarly modern cult of the individual? Whether by Paul, by a secretary, by an associate or by a pupil, Colossians is clearly a "Pauline" letter.[5]

---

4. For the traditional objections to the Pauline authorship of both Colossians and Ephesians see E. Percy, *Die Probleme der Kolosser- und Epheserbriefe* (Lund: Gleerup, 1946).

5. Barclay, *Colossians and Philemon*, p. 35. Note Barclay's conclusion (pp. 24-25) in regard to alleged internal evidence that Colossians must be post-Pauline: "Thus it cannot be said that there is anything in this letter that argues against its composition in Paul's lifetime: indeed Schweizer and Dunn, who both take the stylistic arguments to rule out Pauline authorship, nonetheless hold that Colossians was written in Paul's lifetime, but by an associate." Neither Schweizer nor Dunn, however, takes the measure of the rhetorical dimensions and style of Colossians. Barclay, p. 33, also makes the good point that "We can judge that Colossians is a little unlike Paul in certain respects, but not that it is like any 'Paulinist' whom we know independently." In other words, to posit an unknown author is to posit someone whose style or agenda we have no independent evidence of. And if one argues that the author of Ephesians must have written Colossians (or vice versa, in either case a circular argument), that still does not provide us with evidence outside the Pauline corpus to judge the matter.

These are helpful remarks, but they require several qualifications. If Colossians was written by a pupil of Paul, there was no reason not to have gone the route of anonymity that we find another Pauline associate taking in Hebrews. In other words, there was no need for pseudonymity. And yes, there is a problem with pseudonymity in this particular document because it presents itself as a word on target dealing with a specific Colossian problem and dealing with it within the context of Paul's own life and living ministry as though it existed while Paul was alive and thus as *he* dealt with it. It is understandable that one can argue that a homily like Ephesians, a circular document with no personalia of any consequence and no attempt to deal with specific problems, could possibly be by a later Paulinist seeking to "epitomize" the Pauline gospel, not seeking to usurp the role and voice and authority of the apostle to deal with an urgent matter. But this is far less plausible in the case of Colossians. There seems to be a living connection between the living voice of Paul and the person who wrote this down or composed this for the apostle. Epaphras, for example, had no need to claim to be Paul to address his own converts and their problems. He could have spoken in his own voice and had authority over the audience. The plausibility structure used to support the notion that Colossians can viably be seen as a pseudonymous document collapses when one starts probing this matter deeply and examining what other alternatives, such as anonymity or speaking in one's own voice to deal with a particular time and problem, were available.

While Barclay is quite right that we moderns too often evaluate Paul anachronistically as if he were a late Western individual,[6] nevertheless when we are dealing with Paul we are dealing with a towering and influential figure who even put most of his associates and coworkers in the shade and was prepared to take on and confront so august and apostolic a figure as Peter (Galatians 2). The author of Acts was not making it up as he was going along when he presented Paul as, humanly speaking, the dominant figure in the Gentile mission and the expansion of the church throughout the northern part of the eastern Mediterranean. Apart from the author of Hebrews (who feels no need to claim to be Paul), we have no viable historical evidence of another Pauline coworker or associate capable of thinking and writing rhetorically and theologically at the same level as Paul. This being so, the burden of proof must be on those who want to argue Colossians is not by Paul and to suggest that the theological acumen it reflects is from a later imitator of Paul.

The major conclusions of Lohse's detailed study are that there are clearly both similarities and differences between Colossians and the earlier Pauline letters, that the real problem with Colossians lies in the area of style, and that Colossians "is marked by a liturgical-hymnic style. In its long sentences in which parts are occasionally interlocked with each other, a seemingly endless

6. See my *The Paul Quest* (Downers Grove: InterVarsity, 1997), pp. 1ff.

chain of verbose expression is arranged into a pleonastic unit."[7] Yet the truth is that once one gets beyond the hymn, one cannot really call the following material hymnic or liturgical for that matter. Lohse rightly points out that the special content of parts of Colossians is insufficient to explain the peculiar style of Colossians, since the style is manifested throughout, not just in sections like 2.6–3.4. He also admits that after a century of investigation the jury is still out on the question of the language and style of Colossians.[8]

But the jury could have reached a verdict by now if Colossians had been adequately studied in the light of Asiatic rhetoric and its characteristic features of style. Lohse concludes that "the voice is Jacob's voice but the hands are the hands of Esau": Paul is speaking but Timothy is writing.[9] But as several have pointed out, this description of the situation is inadequate not least because Timothy may well have been involved in some of the earlier Paulines (e.g., 1 Thessalonians), and those letters do not manifest the style Colossians does. Rather the explanation must be that the voice is indeed Paul's and that the secretary is likely Timothy, but the decisive consideration is that Colossians is written in a style effective for reaching the audience in the Lycus Valley, namely the style of Asiatic rhetoric. The style is deliberately chosen and probably reflects the skill of the composer, not merely his unreflected "natural" style.

To some extent the special vocabulary we find in Colossians (34 NT hapax legomena and 28 other words not found elsewhere in Paul's letters) comes to us by way of the discussion of the Colossian philosophy, which is not replicated in Ephesians, and some of the rest of it is a result of Asiatic rhetorical tendency toward using special vocabulary. Most of the remainder comes when Paul quotes traditional material, as in the Christ hymn in ch. 1. When one takes into account these three factors, it becomes clear why an assessment of the entire document

7. E. Lohse, *Colossians and Philemon* (Philadelphia: Fortress, 1971), p. 89.

8. Lohse, *Colossians*, p. 90.

9. Lohse, *Colossians*, p. 91. G. E. Cannon, *The Use of Traditional Material in Colossians* (Macon: Mercer University Press, 1983) argues that Colossians is Pauline but looks a bit different because of the use of traditional material. While this may explain some of the differences between Colossians and the earlier undisputed Paulines, it is not sufficient in itself to explain the letter's distinctive traits. For example, the use of traditional material does not adequately explain the lack of connectives (e.g., adversative, causal, consecutive, copulative, and disjunctive conjunctions), the lack of the articular infinitive, the amassing of synonyms, and very long sentences. See the most thorough study of the grammatical style of Colossians by W. Bujard, *Stilanalytische Untersuchungen zum Kolosserbrief als Beitrag zur Methodik von Sprachvergleichen* (Göttingen: Vandenhoeck und Ruprecht, 1973). Unfortunately, Bujard did not take rhetoric into account adequately (he does attempt to assess how the author advances and argues his case), particularly the influence of the Asiatic style of rhetoric on the very traits mentioned above. It is fair to say that the great majority of distinctive traits Bujard finds in Colossians are normal traits of Greek in the Asiatic rhetorical style.

and its character is necessary before one can make pronouncements about the issue of authorship based on vocabulary. If the subject matter or the rhetorical style or the source material demands such vocabulary, we learn nothing of a negative sort about the Pauline authorship of the document from its special language.

Further Thoughts on the Relationship of Colossians and Ephesians

Before we can actually consider Colossians itself there are several other issues of prolegomena that need to be attended to first, not the least of which is to consider in more detail the nature of the relationship between Colossians and Ephesians. Even the most conservative commentators on these documents have to admit that Col. 4.7-9 and Eph. 6.21-22 seem to indicate some sort of literary relationship between these two documents. Few would dispute that these two documents are more similar than any other two documents in the Pauline corpus, and perhaps in the NT. Most scholars too quickly conclude that Ephesians must be based on and be an expansion of Colossians, though in fact there is a long tradition that has suggested that any dependence must go the other direction (or at least in both directions), a view already presented in T. K. Abbott's 1897 commentary and found as recently as E. Best's 1998 commentary on Ephesians.[10] While the dependence of Colossians on Ephesians is a minority opinion, nonetheless it makes clear that the issue is far more complex than it is sometimes made out to be.

In my view, the least problematic conclusion involves the recognition that

Colossians is the chronologically earlier document;
Ephesians was written later, though perhaps not long thereafter;
there is some literary borrowing from Colossians in Ephesians, particularly at the end of Ephesians, and influence of ideas, phrases and the like from Colossians throughout Ephesians;
in fact the very best explanation for all the creative combinations and permutations of ideas, phrases, words that seem to be shared by these documents is that they come from the same mind and author, namely the mind of Paul, even though he may well have had Timothy or others to help him compose these documents[11]; and

10. See also E. Best, "Who Used Whom? The Relationship of Ephesians and Colossians," *NTS* 43 (1997): 72-96. See also M. Barth and H. Blanke, *Colossians* (New York: Doubleday, 1994), pp. 74-104, especially pp. 101-4.

11. G. D. Fee, *God's Empowering Presence* (Peabody: Hendrickson, 1994), p. 659 n. 5,

the epistolary elements in Ephesians were added after that sermon or
homily was composed, by the scribe copying from Colossians with minor changes to reflect a somewhat later situation.

Both Colossians and Ephesians reflect the style of Asiatic rhetoric, which
partly accounts for their similarity and their difference from all the other Pauline documents (with the partial exception of Philemon, which is too short and
too non-theological to give much room for the real display element in Asiatic
rhetoric, though it certainly does reflect the emotive character and redundancy
of the Asiatic style; see pp. 1-11 above). But within this sharing of a style of rhetoric there is a deliberate difference in the species of rhetoric. Colossians, like
Philemon, is deliberative rhetoric, whereas Ephesians is epideictic rhetoric.
This explains, for example, why we have a eulogy at the beginning of Ephesians
but not in Colossians. It also explains other features such as the differences between the peroratios in these two documents. Furthermore it explains why
Colossians contains actual arguments dealing with specific problems of false
teaching, while Ephesians does not. Ephesians is an epideictic homily of a general nature meant to circulate through several churches and so does not seek to
address a particular problem or issue, nor does it offer arguments or proofs. Indeed it would have been inappropriate to do so in a piece of epideictic rhetoric
(see pp. 4-11 above).

Among other similarities between Colossians and Ephesians (see pp. 12-13
above), they share various short sequences of words and ideas that do not appear elsewhere in the Pauline corpus. For example, "redeeming the time" (Col.
4.5; Eph. 5.16), covetousness described as idolatry (Col. 3:5; Eph. 5:5), and the
exhortation to forbear one another (Col. 3.13; Eph. 4.2).[12] Of the 155 verses in
Ephesians roughly half (73) have verbal parallels in Colossians. But there does
not seem to be evidence of imitation. Sometimes the Colossians version of a

---

rightly in my judgment argues that Colossians and Ephesians are both from the mind of
Paul. It is not very credible that the author of Ephesians so thoroughly imbibed the Paul of
the earlier letters, including Colossians, that he could seem to write in a recognizably Pauline
manner but without being a slavish imitator. To the contrary the author of Ephesians develops in a consistent trajectory Pauline ideas in various subtle and creative ways and chooses to
launch out in an entirely new direction, writing a homily (something Paul never attempts in
his earlier letters) drawing especially on Colossians and expecting his audience to assume
that it is by Paul without meticulously imitating Paul's earlier style or presentation of thinking. The function of a pseudepigraph is not to raise questions about the claimed authorship
of the document but rather to be unobtrusively in line with earlier presentations of the author's style and content to effectively address later audiences in the same manner and with
the same authority.

12. On what follows here see J. B. Polhill, "The Relationship between Ephesians and
Colossians," *RevExp* 70 (1973): 439-50.

phrase seems more creative and compelling than the parallel in Ephesians, and sometimes it is the other way around. For example, the discussion of being transferred from the old realm to the new by conversion is more developed in Eph. 2.1-10 than in Col. 1.13-14, but the personal greetings in Col. 4.7-17 are more expansive than the near verbatim parallel of some of this material in Eph. 6.21-22. Or again certain key terms such as "body," "mystery," and "fullness" are used with slightly different, though not incompatible, semantic ranges in these two documents.

Both Colossians and Ephesians include newly coined words. This could come under the category of rhetorical "invention" and was especially likely to be trotted out in Greek oratory in general and Asiatic oratory in particular. Quintilian says this is more permissible in Greek than in Latin, because there was a long history of Greeks coining words (*Inst. Or.* 8.3.30). Asia Minor had been Hellenized for centuries and was thoroughly Greek in character, though with an increasing Roman overlay. One reason Asiatic rhetoric was so popular in its own region and not in Rome was precisely because Asia was such a thoroughly Greek region. Both the major cities and smaller cities such as Ephesus or Hierapolis or even Colossae were far more likely to reflect Greek culture and a love of things Greek than many other places in the empire. This is where the Hellenistic revolution of Alexander came to full flower.

Both Colossians and Ephesians contain a coined word for reconciliation (*apokatallassō*), but they use it in slightly differing ways and contexts (Col. 1.20, 22; Eph. 2.16). S. Porter and K. Clarke see this sort of creativity and willingness to modify the nuance in the later document as an argument in favor of the Pauline nature of both documents. A pseudepigrapher would tend to eschew such invention and stick with tried and true Pauline phrases and ideas from the earlier letters since the goal would be verisimilitude, making the document look convincingly Pauline on the basis of previous Pauline examples.[13] This kind of complex evidence must count against the idea that one of these documents is the product of a slavish imitator of a Pauline document, but the question is whether it is easier to conceive of *one* author feeling free to make these sorts of shifts from one document to the other, or is it easier to believe one is by Paul and the other by some unknown author who is capable of not merely thinking Paul's thoughts after him but intuiting how Paul would develop them in new ways for a different audience. The supposition of common authorship makes much better sense of this conundrum than positing some unknown Paulinist who can produce Ephesians, a document that has been called by various evaluators the quintessence of Paulinism. But that is not the end to the complexity of this issue.

13. S. Porter and K. Clarke, "Canonical-Critical Perspective and the Relationship of Colossians and Ephesians," *Bib* 78 (1997): 76-83.

Lincoln is right that there are echoes in Ephesians of Paul's earlier letters, particularly Romans and the Corinthian correspondence, and not of the Pastoral Epistles, which tells us something of the location of Ephesians in the chronology of Pauline letters.[14] But these echoes also tell us that the author of Ephesians certainly thinks Colossians is a Pauline letter, for he echoes it far more than any other Pauline letter, while also drawing on Romans and other Pauline letters, but not on other early Christian documents.

So perhaps Ephesians is a homiletical reworking of much of the substance of Colossians, one that follows rhetorical rules about the reuse of common terms, ideas, phrases, and the like. In general terms, Ephesians is an example of rhetorical re-audiencing and *amplificatio.* Epideictic is naturally more expansive than deliberative rhetoric because it is the rhetoric of display and ornamentation. If an author takes a deliberative speech and uses it as the basis for an epideictic one for a more general audience, we may expect the sort of thing we find in Ephesians when compared to Colossians.

Quintilian reminds us that the same sort of ornament will not suit the various differing sorts of rhetoric (*Inst. Or.* 8.3.11). The oratory of display (epideictic) aims at the honor and glory of its subject matter while deliberative rhetoric, while it is to be lofty and should have a certain impetuosity of eloquence, is nonetheless more reserved in its use of metaphor, ornament, and the like than epideictic speech (8.3.14). A careful comparison of Colossians and Ephesians shows that this describes some of the differences between Colossians and Ephesians. Both reflect Asiatic rhetoric, but Ephesians is Asiatic rhetoric with the volume turned up and with the Sunday best clothes on display. For example, Col. 1.9-20 is indeed one long Asiatic style sentence, but it pales in comparison to the length and magnitude of Eph. 1.3-14 followed by 1.15-23.

One feature particularly found in epideictic rhetoric is euphony, concern with how a word or a series of words sounds. Quintilian stresses "But as several words may often have the same meaning (they are called synonyms) some will be more distinguished, sublime, brilliant, attractive or euphonious than others. For as those syllables are the most pleasing to the ear which are composed of the more euphonious letters, thus words composed of such syllables will sound better than others, and the more vowel sounds they contain the more attractive they will be to hear" (8.3.16). All other things being equal, we would expect more euphonious ways of putting things in Ephesians than in Colossians because of the type of rhetoric it is — the rhetoric of display.

This is in fact what one finds by reading both Ephesians and Colossians aloud. The longer periods in Ephesians with the piling up of words with similar endings are notable. For example, at the beginning of the exhortatio in Eph. 4.1 we have words ending with *-ios, -iōs,* and *eōs,* v. 4 contains two nouns ending

---

14. A. T. Lincoln, *Ephesians* (Waco: Word, 1990), pp. lvii-lviii.

with -*ma*, and v. 6 has *pantōn* three times in quick succession. In 1.21 we have the sibilant endings -*ēs, -ēs, -as, -eōs* followed by the euphonious *kuriotētos kai pantos onomatos onomazomenou*. This is clearly a document meant to be heard and to make an effect on the audience by the sound of the words. Consider also 1.23: *hētis estin to sōma autou, to plērōma tou ta panta en pasin plēroumenou*. Colossians uses euphony more on the scale of what is in Paul's other delibera-tive discourses (e.g. Philippians or 1 Corinthians), and Ephesians often looks like a deliberate amplification, modification, and modulation of Colossians to make the proclamation "sound" more convincing.

Another good example of *amplificatio* is the use in Ephesians alone in the Pauline corpus of both a eulogy (1.3-14) and a thanksgiving and prayer period (1.15-23). This amplification and expansion of the praise section of the homily is perfectly acceptable in an epideictic homily dedicated to praise and honor, es-pecially so in Asiatic rhetoric, where the more effusive the better.

One form of amplification or augmentation that Quintilian refers to is the accumulation of words and sentences identical or very close in meaning. Climax or emphasis is achieved by the piling up of words, in particular synonyms (*Inst. Or.* 8.4.27). We find much of this in Ephesians, and it is typical of the rhetoric of display. For example, Eph. 1.17 contains a twofold reference to God the Father (with appropriate variation "the God of our Lord Jesus Christ, the Father of glory"), then we are told that God bequeathed to believers "the spirit of wisdom and revelation in the knowledge of him." This is especially characteristic of Asi-atic rhetoric. Col. 1.9 has a somewhat less effusive use of the same language: "in order that you might be filled with the knowledge of his will in all wisdom and spiritual understanding." The difference is striking. In Ephesians, the sense is that we have three synonyms, "wisdom," "revelation," and "knowledge." In Colossians, being filled with the knowledge of God's will is accompanied by all wisdom and understanding. The author is talking about two things, not one.

Other excellent examples of rhetorical "accumulation" are found in the ex-amples cited above from Eph. 1.21 and 23, and many more could be trotted out from Ephesians. For example, 2.2: "according to the aeon of this world, according to the ruler of the power/authority of the air, of the spirit which is now at work in the sons of disobedience." While this is probably an example not of straight redu-plication of ideas but of one idea built on another, it is still a collection of similar ideas and serves as an example of amplification and accumulation.

The False Teaching/Philosophy in Colossae

Study of the so-called opponents and "heresy" in Colossae has led to a wide range of opinions: Paul is combating some sort of gnosticizing or pre-Gnostic syncretism, Jewish ideas, or some combination of Hellenistic, Jewish, and Christian ideas.[15] The tone of Colossians is by no means the same as that of Galatians. If there actually were false teachers in Colossae, Paul seems much less exercised about it than he was in dealing with the Judaizing Jewish Christians in Galatians. It is certainly a mistake to lump all of Paul's letters together as if they were broadsides against one sort of heresy or false teaching.[16]

Only in Col. 2.8-23, a section that stands out when comparing the parallel document Ephesians, does Paul seem to be addressing some sort of aberrant theology, and only Col. 2.19 seems to suggest that some of Paul's audience may have embraced such a belief and the praxis which arose out of it. But *stoicheia tou kosmou* (2.8, 20) may well refer to "elementary principles or teachings of the universe" (cf. Hebrews 6) rather than to elementary beings or cosmic spirits, not least because *stoicheia* never means "beings" in earlier Greek literature and because Colossians 2 clearly argues against elementary teachings such as "don't taste, don't touch" (v. 21). Furthermore, "worship of angels" (v. 18) could mean worship with angels rather than worshiping angels, connoting some sort of mystical worship experience. If so, then the nature of the Colossian philosophy will be considerably different from some portraits painted of it.[17] What we can say for sure is that Paul is critiquing something that affects both belief and be-

---

15. The very variety and scope of the conjectures shows how much this is a matter of reading between the lines by drawing on one or another sort of data from the larger social context. For example, R. E. DeMaris, *The Colossian Controversy: Wisdom in Dispute at Colossae* (Sheffield: JSOT, 1994) argues that middle Platonism is at the heart of the false teaching, while T. W. Martin, *By Philosophy and Empty Deceit: Colossians as a Response to a Cynic Critique* (Sheffield: Sheffield Academic, 1996) actually claims that Cynic teachers had entered the congregation in Colossae, confusing some of the Christians there.

16. I have dealt elsewhere with this problem of mirror-reading of Paul's letters, which assumes that what Paul affirms and asserts must be the counterpart of what others were denying, a very dubious assumption when one recognizes the rhetorical character of Paul's letters (see my *Conflict and Community in Corinth* [Grand Rapids: Eerdmans, 1995], pp. 343-51). Mirror-reading takes a particularly problematic form when it is assumed that there was some sort of united front of opposition against Paul which plagued him in various places and times and which justifies taking bits and pieces from a wide array of Pauline letters and reconstructing this opposition and its views. See the helpful methodological critique of such views by J. L. Sumney, *Identifying Paul's Opponents: The Question of Method in 2 Corinthians* (Sheffield: JSOT, 1990). Especially helpful are the warnings against assuming that we know the historical situation Paul is addressing better than Paul knew it and against mirror-reading. J. J. Gunther has found no less than 44 different suggestions in regard to the identity of the opponents in Colossae (*St. Paul's Opponents and Their Background* [Leiden: Brill, 1973]).

17. I take Dunn's point (*Colossians and Philemon* [Grand Rapids: Eerdmans, 1996], pp. 24-26) that it is better not to overly problematize the error we are dealing with here by calling it a "heresy," a term used later when there was a more fixed concept of the borders of orthodoxy. The Colossian "philosophy" or "false teaching" is perhaps a better term.

havior, both philosophy and praxis, ascetic praxis related to visions and doxological experiences.[18]

The weakness of the theory that the opponents held some sort of gnosticizing syncretistic view has been amply shown by Dunn. In particular there is certainly no evidence that Paul is polemicizing against dualism of some sort, which is characteristic of Gnosticism.[19] It is far more plausible that he is dealing with some sort of ascetic Jewish piety.[20] There was a substantial Jewish presence in the Lycus Valley at the time.[21] Paul's letters and Acts indicate that he sought to share the message of Christ in synagogues first wherever he went (e.g., Acts 18–19), and it is likely that his coworkers did the same. There was probably no great barrier yet between Jewish and Christian worshiping groups in this region with contact or connection between the groups being disallowed. Ignatius of Antioch would still in the early second century be warning Christians in the general vicinity against "Judaizing" (*Magnesians* 8.1; 10.3).

C. Arnold has argued that magic and folk religion mixed together with Jewish cultic observances and mystery cult initiation were served up as a gumbo that some of the converts in Colossae consumed.[22] There is evidence that the Jews of the area did not live a sort of ghettoized existence, but rather absorbed a good deal from their larger cultural milieu. P. Trebilco's study of Jewish communities within a 150-mile radius of Colossae shows Jews well integrated into the larger community.[23] But whatever notions Jews may have absorbed from the larger culture, what Paul is addressing is recognizably Jewish, with concern for circumcision (2.11-13; 3.11), observance of the Sabbath (2.16), and food rules (2.16,21). These are indeed the very elements that served as boundary markers for Jews and distinguished them from other groups.[24] Furthermore, Arnold's case rests on some very questionable assumptions: that later

18. As Barclay, *Colossians and Philemon,* p. 37, suggests, it appears that in Colossians 1 Paul is stockpiling theological weapons and arguments necessary to attack the false teaching in ch. 2. The first major salvo (2.8) leads right into a comment about Christ's fullness (2.9).

19. Contrast Lohse, *Colossians and Philemon,* pp. 114-20, with Dunn, *Colossians and Philemon,* pp. 27-28.

20. See now the thorough demonstration of the Jewish nature of the philosophy by A. R. Bevere, *Sharing in the Inheritance: Identity and the Moral Life in Colossians* (Sheffield: Sheffield Academic, 2003).

21. In 200 B.C. Antiochus III transplanted a large colony of Jews to this region, and one estimate suggests that there were at least 11,000 Jewish males in Laodicea alone in Paul's day.

22. C. E. Arnold, *The Colossian Syncretism* (Tübingen: Mohr, 1995).

23. P. Trebilco, *Jewish Communities in Asia Minor* (Cambridge: Cambridge University Press, 1991); cf. J. Reynolds and R. Tannenbaum, *Jews and Godfearers at Aphrodisias* (Cambridge: Cambridge University Press, 1987).

24. See J. T. Sanders, *Schismatics, Sectarians, Dissidents, Deviants: The First One Hundred Years of Jewish-Christian Relations* (London: SCM, 1993).

evidence of Greek magical papyri provides a key to understanding what Paul is concerned about, that "worship of angels" means invoking angels for protection from principalities and powers, and that *stoicheia tou kosmou* refers to beings rather than principles or teachings. Arnold also bases his assessment of Colossians on what he thinks went on in the rituals of the mystery cults, but we know too little about their secret rituals to be confident that Paul is somehow echoing and countering them in Colossians 2.

Thus I am inclined to agree with F. O. Francis, Dunn, and T. J. Sappington[25] that we seem to be dealing with some sort of esoteric and mystical Jewish philosophy, perhaps lightly influenced by Greek philosophy, not some sort of largely pagan philosophy to which have been added a few marginal Jewish elements.[26] These Jews were "confident in their religion (2:4, 8), above all in the access it gave them to the worship of heaven (2:18), through faithfulness to what were traditional (Jewish) observances (2:16, 21-23),"[27] plus perhaps some additional ascetic practices, and they were quite confident that one did not need to be worshiping or following Jesus Christ to obtain this access to the knowledge and presence of God. Paul then would be countering not a virulent direct attack on the Christian house churches in Colossae but an apologetic that was rhetorically powerful and persuasive and that offered some of the same benefits to some of Paul's audience without the exclusive christological features of Christianity.[28] It seems clear from 2.18-19 that Paul is indeed concerned that some Christians (or a Christian) in Colossae are actually trying to incorporate some of this other Jewish view into the Christian worldview, with deleterious

25. T. J. Sappington, *Revelation and Redemption at Colossae* (Sheffield: JSOT, 1991). I intend to deal with this matter in more detail in connection with Col. 2.6–3.4 (see pp. 151-65 below).

26. I do not deny that there may be some influence from Greek philosophy, but it certainly seems to be less of an issue than it is, for instance, in Philo's writings. I would also note that the antidote administered in the christological focus of this document, especially in chs. 1–2, draws almost exclusively on Jewish thinking about Wisdom. One sort of Jewish thinking is offered up in contradistinction to another that seems to have been enticing some Colossians. See now also J. H. Roberts, "Jewish Mystical Experience in the Early Christian Era as Background to Understanding Colossians," *Neotestamentica* 32 (1998): 161-87.

27. Dunn, *Colossians and Philemon*, p. 34.

28. See J. D. G. Dunn, "The Colossian Philosophy: A Confident Jewish Apologia," *Biblica* 76 (1995): 153-81. Cf. P. T. O'Brien, *Colossians, Philemon* (Waco: Word, 1982), pp. xxx-xli. I am not confident that Dunn is right that Paul is actually countering anything that was being said in the synagogue. The synagogue does not come up for discussion in this letter, only the lives of Christians. Thus I do not think we should be talking about a strictly non-christological synagogue apologetic. Paul is rather countering some Christian belief and practice that has been influenced in some way by mystical and apocalyptic Judaism. In other words, Paul is not necessarily countering a synagogue leader or group that is reacting to the tiny Christian community in Colossae.

results.[29] Paul combats this problem directly now that it has entered the Christian community itself and is affecting its adherents.[30]

The Theology of Colossians

There is a healthy balance of both theological and ethical material in Colossians,[31] as is typical of Paul's other letters, and it is not wrong to note that there is some development in Paul's thought in Colossians, and in Ephesians as well. In particular, in Colossians we have a cosmic christology, and the body metaphor is developed further with Christ now being called the head of the body. Christ is the sole agent of creation and of redemption and all things hold together in him, including this letter, which is held together by its christological focus. This cosmic christology quite naturally leads to a universalistic ecclesiology, as we see in 1.18, an ecclesiology which will be more fully developed in Ephesians, which is more ecclesiocentric while Colossians is certainly more christocentric.[32] Since Paul sees the church as Christ's body and Christ as Lord over both the cosmos and the church, it is no surprise that he refers to an expanded vision of the church as more than just a series of independent local congregations, each called *ekklēsia*. This broader use of the term is occasionally found in the earlier Pauline letters and should not be seen as a post-Pauline development (see pp. 53-54 above).

29. Paul is clearly concerned with how this Colossian Jewish philosophy was affecting Christians. See A. T. Lincoln, "Colossians," in *The New Interpreter's Bible* XI (Nashville: Abingdon, 2000), p. 567. Paul is not attempting apologetics in general in Colossians.

30. See the helpful conclusions of Barclay, *Colossians and Philemon*, pp. 53-54: the "heresy" probably involved the main elements of the Jewish calendar, Jewish food laws, and some regulations having to do with physical activities; it claimed visionary experiences in association with worship; it claimed to offer some sort of special wisdom; and it was sponsored by Christians (see the connection of 2.18 and 19). He also considers it possible that the heresy involved the veneration of a variety of higher powers. In sum, "Reconstructions that obliterate the Jewish element in the mixture seem to be the most precarious" (p. 54). I also agree that the view defended by Wright that the same issues are dealt with in Galatians is not likely since the polemics in the two letters are quite different. See J. Sumney, "Those Who 'Pass Judgment': The Identity of the Opponents in Colossians," *Bib* 74 (1993): 366-88, here pp. 386-88.

31. And though we do not find the clear division between the two that characterizes Ephesians 1–3 and 4–6, in general it is true that theology comes first in Colossians and the ethical section afterward.

32. This cosmic christology is not without precedent in Paul's earlier letters (cf. Rom. 8.38; 1 Cor. 2.8; 8.6; 15.20-28; 2 Cor. 4.4; Gal. 4.3-9; and, from a letter written near the same time as Colossians, Phil. 2.10).

It is also no surprise in a letter shaped by Asiatic rhetoric that we hear the bold claim that the gospel about Jesus is proclaimed "to every creature under heaven" (1.23). After Paul had reached the heart of the empire and watched the triumphant spread of the gospel across the northern half of the Mediterranean between A.D. 48 and 60, it is not surprising that he would sound such an exultant note when writing from Rome in 61-62. In Colossians the content of the "mystery" being revealed is Christ among the Gentiles or within the Gentile world (1.26-27; 2.2; 4.3). The christocentric force of the letter is also brought home by the fact that the content of "the faith" (1.23; 2.6-7) is Christ Jesus the Lord, which is the tradition the Colossian Christians learned from the beginning.[33]

The nexus between Paul as messenger and his christocentric message is close in Colossians, as he participates in the imitation of Christ while offering the invitation to accept Christ. 1.23–2.5 "underlines that, as Paul played his unique role in its missionary proclamation, he became the suffering servant of the gospel who participated in the same pattern of suffering experienced by Christ. Service of the gospel was also stewardship of the mystery on the part of Paul; just as the gospel has a teaching content and is universal in its scope, so also Paul's stewardship of it involves a teaching role that is universal in its reach, 'teaching every human being' (1:28)."[34]

There is also more focus on what is sometimes called realized eschatology in Colossians compared to the earlier Paulines, but this would be better termed *vertical* eschatology (i.e., the influence of what is above on the here and now). There is more focus on what is already true "up there" than on what will be true "out there." It is not true, however, that there is no future eschatology in Colossians, as 3.4, 6, and 24 show. The false philosophy seems to have focused on the believer's present relationship with God and on the heavenly worship. In response Paul focuses on the possession of those benefits through Christ, who is in the heavenlies and is not a mere angel. Paul corrects the errant vertical eschatology of those disseminating the Colossian Jewish philosophy. There is in fact a connection between this vertical eschatology and Paul's cosmic christology. One could say that the idea of Christ being the head of the body is something of a logical development from the notion that Christ is above, in heaven, ruling from that locus. Paul has already spoken of the church as Christ's body (1 Cor. 1.13; 12.12-13; Gal. 3.28), and so what we find here is hardly a revolutionary further step in either Pauline christology or ecclesiology. Indeed, it is a logical step.

How does this largely realized eschatological perspective affect the portrayal of Christ's relationship with the principalities and powers? Lincoln thinks that Colossians depicts these powers as having been pacified and even

33. See rightly Lincoln, "Colossians," p. 569.
34. Lincoln, "Colossians," p. 569.

reconciled back into God's order and plan by the death of Jesus.[35] I am unconvinced by this argument, at least in regard to reconciliation. Lincoln is right that the death of Jesus has dramatically changed the status of the principalities and powers, just as it has transferred believers from the realm of darkness and death into the realm of light and life, but, as 1.13 suggests, the principalities and powers are still active and malevolent. Perhaps one can say that they have been stripped of their authority over the cosmos and over humans but still have power and are still fighting a rearguard action against the world and Christians. But the Christus Victor motif is clear, not least because Christ is the image of the invisible and all-powerful God, the one in whom the fullness of God dwells bodily (2.9).

The soteriological emphasis on Christ's death and his shed blood as the means and meaning of reconciliation of humankind to God is at the very heart of the theology of this document, even though the term "salvation" never appears. While sin and the powers remain, they no longer reign in the believer's life. The believer looks forward to glory (1.27), by which is meant sharing in the resurrection that Christ experienced (1.18), since Christ is the firstborn from the dead. Paul stresses that his gospel is the wisdom his audience needs and that they need not listen to rival claims about wisdom and knowledge. The theme of wisdom appears in each major section of the letter and "features at all levels in the letter's theology. Christ embodies wisdom; Paul supremely, but also all other believers are recipients and then teachers of wisdom; and Christian living is walking in wisdom."[36] This wisdom is both exclusive (it excludes other avenues or teachings such as the Colossian philosophy) and inclusive (all can be reconciled to God through Christ, the Wisdom of God). The polemical edge of this sapiential teaching, ruling out the Colossian Jewish false teaching, is clear enough. But lest we think that this letter is purely about esoteric theology, the latter portion of the discourse is all about how to live wisely as Christians and in Christian households on the basis of the wisdom christology already enunciated.

The Occasion of Colossians

Can we pinpoint what prompted Paul to write Colossians? Epaphras (not to be confused with Epaphroditus from Philippi, mentioned in Phil. 2.25; 4.18) had apparently planted the church in Colossae (Col. 1.7-8; 4.12-13). He has sent a report about some difficulties in Colossae. It would seem that the Colossian Jewish philosophy and piety has begun to permeate the thinking of some Colossian

35. Lincoln, p. 570.
36. Lincoln, p. 576.

Christians and was affecting their behavior, and this is what prompts Paul to write on this occasion. He insists that not specific Jewish practices (calendrical, ascetic, ritual, or mystical) but rather a relationship with the one mediator between God and humankind, Jesus Christ, is what ushers one into the presence of God and the doxological center of the universe. But Paul uses this occasion to speak to other issues as well, such as the wise ordering of the Christian household, which is no surprise since the issue of slavery was uppermost in his mind since he has written Philemon only shortly before. The ethical enjoinders are not, however, merely tacked on at the end of a theological discourse. They are the logical outworking of the christocentric theology. As is so often said, the imperative is based on the indicative as Paul shows how Christian belief affects and transforms Christian behavior and relationships.

Epistolary Prescript — 1.1-2

Paul, apostle of Christ Jesus through the will of God, and Timothy the brother, to those in Colossae, saints and faithful brothers in Christ. Grace to you and peace from God our Father.[1]

This very succinct prescript should be compared with the one in Philemon. Both mention Timothy, but here Paul is called "apostle" and in Philemon he is called "prisoner." Paul presents himself in his official apostolic role from the outset of Colossians and wishes his discourse to be seen as authoritative teaching. As always, he claims to be an apostle or authorized emissary of Jesus Christ, not just of some particular church. It is striking that he is prepared to exercise

---

1. This shorter reading with no reference to Jesus is well supported by B, D, K, L, and many other manuscripts, though the elongated reading with "and the Lord Jesus Christ" also has strong support from ℵ, A, C, and other manuscripts. As Metzger *TC*, p. 552, says, it is more likely that the reference to Christ was added to conform this greeting to other Pauline greetings, rather than being deleted.

The text of Colossians presents us with some problems which are sometimes underplayed. There are more textual variants to consider than with almost any other Pauline document, no surprise given the letter's convoluted Asiatic style, which tempted later scribes to simplify or alternately to clarify by amplifying. Fortunately we have a good number of manuscripts, including P46 from about A.D. 200, P61, codices ℵ, B, C, D, G, H, and I, and various majuscles such as 048, 0198, and 0208 (see the discussion in M. Barth and H. Blanke, *Colossians* [New York: Doubleday, 1994], pp. 50-51). No two of these manuscripts represent the text of Colossians identically, but there are certain patterns or family groupings. Few if any major exegetical issues hang on the various textual variants. The bulk of the idiosyncrasies of style that lead to textual variants are found in chs. 1 and 2 (as in the parallel material in Eph. 1.1–4.24). The person who composed these documents had a mastery over several styles of Greek prose.

authority over a church he did not found, which may be because he saw himself as the apostle of Gentiles in general, in whatever church they might be found. This would also explain why he is bold enough to address the Romans as he does.[2] In deliberative rhetoric the authority of the speaker was considered crucial to the persuasiveness of the discourse. Paul shows no hesitancy to exhort the Colossian Christians, which suggests that he saw churches founded by his coworkers as extensions of his own ministry. The distinctive reference to the will of God, a theme which will come up again at v. 9, should be noted.

It was not the usual practice to mention a second sender in the prescript unless that person was actually involved in the composition of a letter.[3] Timothy might then be a coauthor of Colossians. But as Lincoln points out, this factor alone probably cannot account for the style of this document, since it differs from Philippians and 2 Corinthians in style, which include Timothy's name as well. Nonetheless, Timothy was from the region just beyond Asia and his father was a Greek. It could well be that he took a more active role in composing this document in Asiatic style since he was familiar with it, while he played less of a role in the letters that do not reflect this style.[4] As Dunn points out, that Timothy is mentioned here though he seems to have had no direct connection with the Colossian church, may favor the suggestion that he had more to do with the writing of this letter than with some other Pauline letters in which he is named, letters directed to congregations he had something to do with.[5] In any case, Timothy is mentioned more frequently than any other Pauline coworker and clearly was a trusted emissary and helper of Paul (1 Cor. 4.17; 16.10; Phil. 2.19; 1 Thess. 3.2, 6; in greetings: Rom. 16.21; in prescripts: 2 Cor. 1.1; Phil. 1.1; 1 Thess. 1.1; Phlm. 1).

Here, as consistently in Colossians, Jesus is called "Christ Jesus" with the words in that order, which may suggest that "Christ" was recognized in Colossae as a title ("Messiah, anointed one") and Jesus as a personal name. This might mean that the Colossians were aware that Jesus was a Jewish messianic figure.[6]

"Saints" here might be a reference to Jewish Christians in Colossae and

---

2. See J. D. G. Dunn, *Colossians and Philemon* (Grand Rapids: Eerdmans, 1996), pp. 44-45. On Romans see B. Witherington and D. Hyatt, *Paul's Letter to the Romans* (Grand Rapids: Eerdmans, 2004), pp. 29-32.

3. See E. R. Richards, *The Secretary in the Letters of Paul* (Tübingen: Mohr, 1991), p. 47, n. 138.

4. But see A. T. Lincoln, "Colossians," in *The New Interpreter's Bible* XI (Nashville: Abingdon, 2000), p. 587.

5. See Dunn, *Colossians and Philemon*, p. 47; cf. J. Gnilka, *Der Kolosserbrief* (Freiburg: Herder, 1980), p. 28.

6. See N. T. Wright, *Colossians and Philemon* (Grand Rapids: Eerdmans, 1986), pp. 46-47.

"the faithful brothers in Christ" to Gentile Christians. In Eph. 1.1 that "saints" is a reference to Jewish Christians seems quite possible, but in some of the earlier Pauline letters this seems less likely.[7] In any case, "saints" here does not distinguish a group of Christians as somehow more sanctified than others and is, indeed, probably not a comment on sanctification at all, for *hagios* is a noun rather than a qualifying adjective here. It simply refers to the "set apart" status of believers. "In Colossae" seems to qualify only "saints" and "in Christ" only "the faithful brothers." "Faithful brothers" is without parallel in Pauline greetings.

We have the standard Pauline combination greeting of "grace and peace" (Greek component first, Jewish component second; see p. 56 above). This initial greeting or "grace" is simply from God our Father, not also from Christ as in Phlm. 3 and Eph. 1.3.

7. See pp. 225-26 below. Romans 15 and 16 seem to point in this direction. See Witherington and Hyatt, *Letter to the Romans*, ad loc.

Exordium/Thanksgiving Prayer — 1.3-14

If we ask whether this section of Colossians is more influenced by epistolary or rhetorical conventions, the answer must be rhetorical. The function of any exordium is to establish the ethos of the speaker in such a way as to establish not merely contact but rapport with the audience and express the essential aim or function of the discourse (Aristotle, *Rhet.* 3.13-14). This prayer section serves to foreshadow some of the themes of the discourse, which makes evident the rhetorical character of this section, because it was not an epistolary convention to pray in advance about the things one was going to address in the letter.[1] Most often in Greco-Roman letters the prayer was just a brief health wish. This being the case we must consider carefully the rhetorical qualities of this particular exordium. Since Paul does not have a personal relationship with his audience it is all the more critical that he establish something positive with them so that they will be open to the discourse that follows. "So expressing his thankfulness for their faith and love, declaring his knowledge of the fruitfulness of the gospel in their lives, seeing them as part of the worldwide growth of the Christian movement, mentioning Epaphras as the go-between, assuring them of his constant prayers. . . . are all part of establishing a positive relationship that will make them conducive to accept what follows."[2] This exordium makes clear to the au-

---

1. T. Y. Mullins, "The Thanksgivings of Philemon and Colossians," *NTS* 30 (1984): 288-93, rightly points out that the structure and character of the thanksgiving period in Colossians are typically Pauline, foreshadowing as it does certain themes to be stressed in the rest of the discourse. This is another small point in favor of the Pauline authorship of Colossians.

2. A. T. Lincoln, "Colossians," in *The New Interpreter's Bible* XI (Nashville: Abingdon, 2000), pp. 557-58.

dience Paul's pastoral care for those he instructs and exhorts. He lifts them up before he enlightens and exhorts them.

We give thanks to God, Father of our Lord Jesus Christ, always concerning you when we pray, hearing of your faith in Christ Jesus and the love which you have toward all the saints because of the hope which is reserved for you in the heavens, about which you already heard in the word of truth [i.e., the gospel], which has come to you, just as also in all the cosmos it is bearing fruit and increasing, just as also in you from the day you heard and came to know the grace of God in truth, just as you learned from Epaphras our beloved fellow slave, who is faithful for you, a servant of Christ, the one who also told us of your love in the Spirit.

Because of this also we, from the day we heard, have not ceased praying for you and beseeching that you may be filled with the knowledge of his will in all wisdom and spiritual understanding to live worthy of the Lord pleasing unto all, in all good works bearing fruit and increasing in the knowledge of God, being strengthened in all power according to the power of his glory unto all fortitude and patience with joy, giving thanks to the Father, making you fit[3] unto the portion of the lot of the saints in light, who delivered you from the power of darkness and transferred you into the kingdom of his beloved Son, in whom we have the redemption, the forgiveness of sins —

To judge from Paul's exordium we should see this discourse as oriented toward progress rather than primarily toward solving problems. The Colossians have been, according to the reports Paul has received, faithful Christians. He wants them to continue growing and maturing in Christ, both in their beliefs and in their behavior. True, he will deal with the one major problem he knows about in ch. 2, but overall it is a mistake to see this whole letter as a broadside against this problem. Paul is concerned that the Colossians continue to go down the path they started down when they were converted and not be diverted by false teaching or philosophy which undermines the notion of the sufficiency of Christ, his grace, and their faith in Christ to enable them to reach the desired goal of glorification and perfect union with God.

To some degree it is artificial to break off the translation at v. 14, as v. 15 begins with a relative clause, but what we have here is Paul making a smooth transition into a doxological mode, drawing on an existing Christ hymn. Prayer quite naturally can lead into praise and doxology. Beginning in vv. 15, Paul will provide a bit of a narratio retelling the story of Christ from a cosmic perspective, and in ch. 2 he will similarly tell his own story. The narrative in 1.13-14 con-

---

3. Some manuscripts have here "calling you" rather than "making you fit" in v. 12, substituting a more familiar word for a less familiar one. *Hikanōsanti*, however, is well supported by P46, ℵ, A, C, K, L, and many other manuscripts. See Metzger, *TC,* p. 553.

cerns the conversion of the Colossians, which is picked up again immediately after the Christ hymn at v. 21. Christology will serve then to ground the ethical appeal, but it will also explain how and why the story of the Colossians changed as they went from the realm of darkness into the realm of light. It is Christ who has transformed them and is transforming them into his image. They do not need to look for other experiences or practices to accomplish their desired religious goals. Ethics comes after the hymn (unlike Philippians 2), but implicit in the prayer that precedes the hymn is the suggestion that the Colossians need to keep maturing in Christ, continuing in their faith, and so become increasingly like Christ.

From an epistolary point of view, it is not incidental that the form of what we find here in Colossians is closest to the form of the thanksgiving prayer in Philemon and Philippians:[4]

Colossians		Philippians	Philemon
1.3	statement of thanksgiving and prayer	1.3-4	v. 4
1.4-8	elaboration of thanksgiving	1.5-8	v. 5
1.9-14	elaboration of prayer	1.9-11	v. 6

This chart reinforces the appropriateness of identifying Col. 1.14 as the end of the prayer/exordium. It also provides a further clue that Colossians was written at about the same time as Philemon and Philippians, even though the rhetorical style of Philippians is different.

The plural "we thank" in v. 3 suggests that Paul had a coauthor, as in 1 Thess. 1.2; 2 Thess. 1.3 and unlike Rom. 1.8; 1 Cor. 1.4; Phil. 1.3; Phlm. 4. The impression here left of Paul is that he is very much a pastoral person who prays frequently not only for his own converts but also for those converted through the extension of his ministry through his coworkers. "The Father of our Lord Jesus Christ"[5] identifies the God in question as the God of Israel, but now he is known for his special relationship with Jesus, as the Father of Jesus. This is a variant of the usual Pauline form "the God and Father of our Lord Jesus Christ" (Rom. 15.6; 2 Cor. 1.3; 11.31; Eph. 1.3, 17). Perhaps there is some concern here to make clear that Christ has not replaced or eclipsed the Father in light of all the exalted language about Christ that is to come in this discourse. The Father is still the one to whom most prayers are offered. Is Paul really speaking of un-

---

4. J. D. G. Dunn, *Colossians and Philemon* (Grand Rapids: Eerdmans, 1996), p. 53.

5. That "Christ" is titular here is probably shown by the way Paul carefully avoids putting two titles together here (e.g., "Lord Christ"). The form of the name here may suggest a certain parallel with that of the emperor — Gaius Julius Caesar, with the middle name the proper personal name.

ceasing prayer, or is this just the natural effusive language of prayer used by a fervent Paul? It is probably the latter.[6]

In vv. 4-5 we see the frequent triad of faith, love, and hope. The close juxtaposition of faith, hope, and love (Gal. 5.5-6; 1 Cor. 13.13; 1 Thess. 1.3; 5.8) is a clear Pauline distinctive. Here faith and love are based on "the hope reserved for you in the heavens." "Faith" is the term Paul most often uses to describe the posture of a believer in relationship to God. Some 142 of the 243 NT occurrences of *pistis,* "faith," occur in Paul's letters. In a notable departure from his typical phrase we have here "faith in Jesus Christ" with the preposition *en*.[7] This cannot be accidental and probably reflects the fact that this document is deliberately christocentric in order to rule out the Colossian error, which sought to achieve piety's aims without going through or finding them in Christ. *Agapē,* which is said to characterize how the Colossians relate to all the saints,[8] is another characteristic Pauline term (75 of 116 NT occurrences are in Paul's letters). Dunn calls this "one of the important and far-reaching emphases marking out Christianity among other religions of the time, for of the different Greek words for 'love' *agapē* was little used at the time: it appears only rarely in non-biblical Greek before the second or third century A.D."[9]

Some 36 of the 53 NT occurrences of *elpis,* "hope," are found in Paul's letters. When Paul refers to hope, he means that Christians must act always with one eye on the ultimate goal or horizon. A proper eschatological worldview motivates proper behavior, and that worldview insists that we have a great future. Paul uses the same sort of future eschatological argument in 1 Corinthians 15 to motivate behavior. Here "the hope" refers not to subjective hoping but to the object of hope, which is being made like Christ in the future by means of resurrection. Paul tells his audience that their hope is already reserved for them in the heavens,[10] meaning that what exists already in promise in heaven will exist one day in reality on earth, because when Christ returns he will bring the

---

6. See P. T. O'Brien, *Colossians, Philemon* (Waco: Word, 1982), p. 10. It may also be true that Paul continued to maintain the usual Jewish practice of praying three times a day (cf. Dan. 6.10; Acts 3.1; 10.3; *Didache* 8.3).

7. It should be noted however that this differs little in sense from the typical Pauline phrase "believe in Christ" with the preposition *eis* (Gal. 2.16; Rom. 10.14; Phil. 1.29).

8. Is this possibly an allusion to their earlier contribution to the collection for the Jerusalem church, and if so does "all the saints" refer to the Jewish Christians in Jerusalem? This is possible. On the saints in Jerusalem see Rom. 15.25-26 and the discussion in B. Witherington and D. Hyatt, *Paul's Letter to the Romans* (Grand Rapids: Eerdmans, 2004), ad loc.

9. Dunn, *Colossians and Philemon,* p. 57. It is also rarely used in the LXX of anything other than conjugal love, but cf. Jer. 2.2 and Wis. 3.9; 6.18.

10. The plural form *ouranoi* is typically Jewish and is hardly ever found in non-biblical Greek. Jews believed in multiple layers of heaven (e.g., 2 Cor. 12.2, where Paul refers to the third level of heaven).

heavenly good things with him or will cause them to happen when he returns. In Paul's theology resurrection, eternal life, glory, and the new Jerusalem are all linked to Christ and his return rather than to dying and going to heaven.[11] Christ is the key both subjectively and objectively. He will fulfill the objective hope when he comes, but he is already the basis of the Christian's subjective hope: "Christ in us" is both the foretaste of glory and the solid basis for the hope of human glorification.

The Colossians had already heard of this hope when "the word of truth," that is, "the gospel," was preached to them. Like faith, hope, and love, *euangelion,* "gospel," is typically Pauline, with some 60 of the 76 NT occurrences found in Paul's letters. What is especially noteworthy is the singular form of the word, for almost always the term is found in the plural in extrabiblical Greek literature. Vv. 4 and 5 provide somewhat of a primer of characteristic Pauline and early Christian vocabulary — faith, hope, love, the Good News, truth. All these terms are connected with or focus on Christ in some way.

Kosmos in v. 6 refers to the inhabited world (cf., e.g., John 1.10).[12] Thus Paul is saying here that the gospel has come not only to the Colossians but to all people.[13] It is possible that we should be hearing resonances of the Hellenistic concept of the *oikoumenē,* by which was meant the civilized Greek-speaking world. Even if this is what is meant here, Paul will go on in 3.11 to make clear that the gospel is also for "barbarians" (i.e. non-Greek speakers) as well.

With two agricultural metaphors Paul says that the gospel has been making converts all over the empire. If he is thinking in the normal Jewish calendrical fashion with the year beginning with autumn, "bearing fruit" does indeed precede the sprouting of new growth. The gospel is thus a living thing that bears fruit and grows. "Just as a tree without fruit and growth would no longer be a tree, so a gospel that bore no fruit would cease to be a gospel."[14] These same two terms will be applied to the believer in v. 10. The Word must first go forth and bear fruit and grow before the believer can do so.

Paul says in v. 6b that fruit-bearing has been going on among the

---

11. To speak of something laid up or reserved in heaven was a Jewish way of referring to that which God has already designated as part of the divine plan but which has not yet come to fruition on earth (Gen. 49.10; Job 38.23; *Joseph and Aseneth* 15.10; of eschatological rewards 2 Macc. 12.45 and 2 Tim. 4.8).

12. Like most ancient commentators, including Theodore of Mopsuestia, Chrysostom says in his first homily on Colossians that Paul is referring to the world by this term. Augustine, *Letter* 199.13-51, says that Paul is referring to the eschatological growth of the church which will spread throughout the world and then adds that the end cannot come before this spread takes place.

13. I do not think that Paul is referring to a proclamation to the evil spirits or fallen angels here or to those who dwell in the heavenlies.

14. E. Schweizer, *The Letter to the Colossians* (Minneapolis: Augsburg, 1982), p. 37.

Colossians since they first heard the gospel; that is, presumably, numbers have been added to their fold and those who are Christians are maturing and doing good works. It was through Epaphras, the faithful fellow servant, who is a minister of Christ,[15] that they came into this condition. The Colossians are commended not only for their love of all the saints (v. 4) but also for their love for Paul (and Timothy? v. 8), even though they have never met Paul.[16] It becomes clearer in 2.1-2 that Epaphras has been Paul's emissary to Colossae and the cities in the Lycus Valley in general and was the one who carried the gospel to the three major cities there. The Colossian Christians have no doubt heard much about Paul from Epaphras and perhaps will again (cf. 4.12-13).[17] Perhaps Epaphras undertook this ministry during the three years Paul was in Ephesus in the mid-50s. If so, then this church has been going and growing for five or six years before Paul writes this letter. The exordium certainly supports the notion that the Colossians have been Christians for some time and are delving into some of the deeper mysteries and matters of the faith and its practice. This is why Paul is able to write about Christ and other things at the level of discourse that we find in this document. He is not addressing neophytes. He must, however, step carefully since this is the first time he has addressed them.

There is much repetition of language from vv. 4-6 in vv. 9-11 (e.g., "all," "from the day you/we heard," "came to know the grace of God/knowledge of his will/knowledge of God"),[18] which is typical of Asiatic rhetoric. Rhetorically the

---

15. *Diakonos* here probably has the sense of "minister" to slightly differentiate it from *syndoulos,* but considering the redundant nature of Asiatic rhetoric it is perfectly possible that we should translate it "fellow servant, servant of Christ" here. The name Epaphras (here and at 4.12), though it is a shortened form of Epaphroditus, refers to a different person than the man mentioned in Phil. 2.25; 4.18. There is no evidence of these two names being used of the same person. See *New Docs* 4, p. 22.

16. There is very little said about the Holy Spirit in this letter, so christocentric is its focus, but at least here the Spirit is referred to in v. 8. There are other indirect references to the Spirit's activities in 1.9, 11, 29; 3.16. As G. D. Fee, *God's Empowering Presence* (Peabody: Hendrickson, 1994), pp. 637-39, rightly points out, the person and activity of the Spirit is not at issue in Colossae and so is not more prominently featured. This is not different from the treatment of the Spirit in other genuine Pauline letters where the Spirit is not the issue (e.g., Philemon or Philippians). It is thus no argument against the Pauline nature of this document to point out that the Spirit is seldom mentioned.

17. The double commendation of Epaphras at the beginning and end of the letter may suggest that he needed some moral support from Paul and Timothy as his honor rating may have slipped in Colossae. See R. W. Wall, *Colossians and Philemon* (Downers Grove: InterVarsity, 1993), pp. 42-43. As Wall says, it appears that some of Epaphras's Pauline teaching in Colossae was coming in for some criticism or even possible replacement with the Colossian philosophy.

18. Rightly pointed out by E. Lohse, *Colossians and Philemon* (Philadelphia: Fortress, 1971), p. 24.

redundancy is a means of reinforcement and emphasis but also of building to a climax. The specific part of the prayer that goes beyond thanksgiving to petition is made known in v. 9. Paul is concerned that the Colossian Christians pursue the gospel knowledge they have received from Epaphras to its full extent and not exchange it for some false teaching or Colossian Jewish philosophy. They are to fulfill the knowledge of God's will in all wisdom and spiritual understanding. Paul is probably not talking about mere recognition of God's will, although the term in question, *epignōsis,* could be translated that way in vv. 6, 9, and 10. What we likely have in the use of this term instead of the simpler *gnōsis* is rhetorical flourish of the Asiatic sort.[19]

Knowledge is a crucial part of Christian life and growth. The Christian faith is not just about what one has experienced but also about what one knows. Paul is not, however, talking about some sort of abstract knowledge, but rather a knowledge that leads to praise and seeking to please God "in all good works." For Paul, theology and ethics are always integrally linked and should not be radically separated. The truth of the gospel is the motive for action and for worthy living, whether it is a truth about the character of God or about something God has already done or will yet do in Christ. Here Paul is referring to knowledge that comes to the believer through the Holy Spirit, which is why it is called spiritual understanding here (cf. 1 Cor. 2.9-15). Wisdom and understanding are said to come from God's Spirit in numerous Jewish texts (Exod. 31.3; 35.31; Isa. 11.2; Wis. 9.17-18; Sir. 39.6; *4 Ezra* 14.22), but it is also striking that Aristotle enumerates wisdom and understanding as two of the highest virtues (*Nichomachean Ethics* 1.13).

In the pluralistic world in which the Colossians lived, the notion that one could achieve the highest level of generally recognized civic virtue by means of aid of the Holy Spirit would be welcome news and an impetus to continue to cultivate one's Christian faith. Notice the emphasis on that which is "pleasing (*areskeia,* found only here in the NT) to all" (v. 10). In a deliberative discourse we would expect such an emphasis, for deliberative rhetoric is meant to talk about that which is pleasing and beneficial and will aid the audience in the future if they behave in a pleasing fashion. Paul is perhaps thinking of the need to be winsome as one lives out the gospel. The aim of obtaining such knowledge then was practical — so that one could live a good and virtuous life, or, in the Jewish way that Paul puts it, so that one might walk in a worthy fashion, noted for one's good deeds. Paul does not hesitate to commend good works (Rom. 3.7; 13.3; 2 Cor. 9.8; Gal. 6.10; Phil. 1.6; 2 Thess. 2.17; Eph. 2.10). He simply does not see them as a means of salvation.

---

19. See rightly, Dunn, *Colossians and Philemon,* p. 62. The Asiatic style loves polysyllabic words. Why use a two-syllable word when a four-syllable synonym that sounds more grandiose is available?

The Colossians are called to walk worthily of the Lord, which they will do by desiring to please in all good works. God provides the power (note the three words for power or strength and two for patient endurance in v. 11).[20] Were there those who were offering an alternate source of power through mystical ascent into heavenly worship? It is possible (see pp. 153-60 below). God's power will give the Christians the fortitude and patience with joy to wait for the completion of what God promised without attempting a ritual or mystical shortcut. Paul may actually be countering something of an over-realized eschatology that suggests that "the future is now" through visionary or mystical experience.

Paul then makes clear that there is a "not yet" dimension to things, which he calls the portion, lot, or inheritance of the saints in light (v. 12). This alludes to the OT notion that different tribes would receive different portions of the Promised Land. Paul says that receiving such a portion is in the future, and in the present it is God, not believers or teachers or ritual practices, that is making the Colossians fit to receive the portion.[21] Whatever claims the false philosophy might make, whatever knowledge, wisdom, or experience might be on offer, these things cannot make the Colossians fit for the inheritance. Only God in Christ can do that. There was plenty of precedent for using this sort of language to speak of the eschatological hope of a share in the resurrection and the life to come (Dan. 12.13; Wis. 5.5; 1 Enoch 48.7). At Qumran "the lot of the saints" or their "everlasting portion" refers quite specifically to such eschatological blessings (1QH 11.10-12; 1QS 11.7-8).[22]

In v. 13 Paul urges the Colossians to think back on their conversions. They, like Paul, were delivered from darkness to light, which means that they are no longer subject to the powers of darkness and have been transferred into the Son's kingdom. There are very few allusions or references in the NT to a messianic kingdom as distinguished from God's kingdom, but this seems to be one. Texts like 1 Cor. 15.24-28, however, make clear that one enters or obtains the kingdom of God only at the eschaton, only at the resurrection, because flesh

---

20. Asiatic rhetorical redundancy reaches a new height here in v. 11: "empowered with all power *(en pasē dynamei dynamoumenoi)* according to the might *(kratos)* of his glory," followed by two near synonyms that refer to patient endurance, *hypomonē* and *makrothymia*.

21. Chrysostom says in his second homily on Colossians: "But why does he call it an inheritance (a lot)? To show that by his own achievement no one obtains the kingdom. . . . For no one leads a life so good as to be counted worthy of the kingdom, but the whole is his free gift."

22. Since elsewhere Paul does not call angels *hagioi*, we should probably not see in v. 12 a reference to the issue addressed in 2.18, so this is probably not about sharing an inheritance with angels. But see T. J. Sappington, *Revelation and Redemption at Colossae* (Sheffield: JSOT, 1991), p. 199. Paul has called believers "saints" in 1.2, 4 and continues to do so here and then again at 1.26. By contrast he uses *angelos* for angel in 2.18. See Lincoln, "Colossians," p. 594.

and blood cannot inherit or obtain it now (cf. Eph. 5.5; *1 Clement* 50.3).[23] As Dunn says, the "kingdom of Christ, insofar as it is to be distinguished from the kingdom of God, is a further way of expressing the tension between what has already been accomplished (the kingdom of Christ) and what is still to be accomplished (the kingdom of God). This also means that participation in Christ's kingship will always be experienced within the contradiction of a world that does not yet own the sovereign rule of God."[24]

If we are to ask where this reigning of Christ is actually taking place, Paul would have given a twofold answer: 1) Christ has "over-ruled" the powers and principalities through his death (see pp. 156-60 below). This does not mean that they do not still have power, but it does mean that they are operating on borrowed time and that they do not reign in or over the lives of believers. 2) The reign of Christ is also evident in believers' lives as it is so vividly described in v. 13. They are no longer in thrall to darkness. They have been transferred into a realm or condition where Christ is Lord of their lives. The verbs "delivered" and "transferred" are punctiliar aorists indicating events that have transpired in the past. V. 13 is the only place in Colossians where Jesus is called "the Son," and he is described interestingly as "the Son of [God's] love," which is equivalent to "beloved Son" (cf. Eph. 1.6) and prepares the audience for what Paul will say in the Christ hymn which follows.

In v. 14 Paul defines what believers have received — redemption, which is identified as the forgiveness of sins. *Apolytrōsis,* "redemption," is rare in non-biblical Greek and occurs only once in the LXX, but the verbal cognate does appear in texts like Deut. 7.8; 9.26; 13.5; 15.15; and 24.18. It denotes the ransom or release or deliverance of a captive from either war or some sort of slavery, like release of the Israelites from bondage.[25] The believer before conversion is therefore in a form of bondage, enslaved by and in darkness. "The forgiveness of sins" stands in apposition to "redemption," further explicating what is meant. Paul does not speak often of forgiveness (see Rom. 4.7, quoting Psalm 32), but here he makes plain that he sees it as the heart of the benefits of Christ's work for us. Paul will say more about forgiveness at Col. 2.13. Forgiveness comes to believers through the death of Christ and by faith, not through other sacrifices, and not through performing acts of piety or supererogatory works. The release Paul has in mind is both from the power of sin and the guilt for having sinned.

Aletti points out the close parallel between the language of Paul in Acts

---

23. See the discussion in my *Jesus, Paul, and the End of the World* (Downers Grove: InterVarsity, 1992), pp. 51-58, on kingdom language. On the notion of a millennial kingdom before the coming of the new heaven and new earth see my *Revelation* (Cambridge: Cambridge University Press, 2003), pp. 286-91.

24. Dunn, *Colossians and Philemon* p. 79.

25. See Dunn, *Colossians and Philemon,* p. 80.

26.18 and what we find here in vv. 13-14.[26] This is very interesting and suggests that this is the sort of language Paul would and did use of conversion (including presumably his own), but he is not normally talking about that subject in his letters, since they are all addressed to Christians, whose problem is not need for conversion. Paul mentions it here only by way of reminder of the Colossian Christians' past (cf. Eph. 1.7). V. 14 is a transitional verse that smoothly leads us into v. 15 and the Christ hymn. It turns the focus specifically on Christ by the initial *en hō* clause, which prepares for the *hos* which introduces the hymn in v. 15.

26. J. N. Aletti, *Saint Paul. Épître aux Colossiens* (Paris: Gabalda, 1993), pp. 81-82.

Narratio — The Pattern of Christ — 1.15-20

It was not required in a deliberative discourse to have a narratio, but it was certainly appropriate if there was a story, a set of facts, that not only had bearing on the arguments that follow but that in some sense were the basis for the arguments (Dio Chrysostom *Oratio* 40.8-19; 41.1-6). The requirements for a narratio, particularly in a deliberative discourse, were that it be short and lucid, saying no more than was sufficient and necessary, and that it describe the problem that has generated the discourse (Quintilian, *Inst. Or.* 4.2.45). As will become evident when we examine these verses, the problem here is a deficient christology in Colossae which seems to have led some to attempt to add to the gospel religious practices and experiences to supply what they see as its deficiency. In this regard, though the problem or exigency is somewhat different in Colossae than in Galatia, Paul's rhetorical strategy for attacking the problem is much the same. He will simply say that the Colossians already have all they need in Christ and in the gospel and do not need to add the Colossian philosophy or false teaching and the praxis it involves to obtain the desired salvific or sanctifying results.

It was the mark of a good orator to make a smooth transition from one part of the discourse to the next, and certainly we find that here with the transitions from v. 14 to v. 15 and from the narratio to the partitio in vv. 20 and 21. These smooth transitions show us that the somewhat prolix style of the author is not due to his lack of facility in the language but rather due to his deliberate adoption and adaptation of the Asiatic style of discourse. Paul does not need to write in long, cumbersome sentences, offer up repeated redundant phrases, pile up clauses, or drop his usual connectives. That he does so is because it was part of the Asiatic style of rhetoric.

I   Who is the image of the invisible God,
   Firstborn of all creation,
   Because in him were created all things
   In the heavens and on the earth,
   The seen and the unseen,
   Whether thrones or dominions
   Or sovereignties or powers.
   Everything [created] through him was also created for him.
   And he is before everything and everything coheres in him.
   And he is the head of the body, the church.

II   Who is the beginning (source),
   The firstborn from the dead,
   In order that he might take precedence[1] in all things.
   Because in him is pleased to dwell all the plērōma,
   And through him[2] is reconciled everything for him,
   Making peace through the blood of his cross,
   Whether things on earth or in the heavens.

In terms of its rhetorical function in the larger discourse this hymn establishes a christocentric foundation for all of the arguments that follow, thereby undercutting the logic of the Colossian philosophy, according to which something else needed to be added to Colossian belief and praxis for them to have a fully beneficial religious or spiritual life. "All things" are repeatedly connected to Christ. Everything points to him. This hymn is also as far as one could imagine from Gnostic dualistic thought since it has a robust appreciation for creation and re-creation, and its vision of redemption includes resurrection. Furthermore, the hymn leaves no room for additional mediators between God and humankind. Christ is the be-all and end-all of all mediators. Angels and principalities need not apply. The hymn thus not only makes clear the basis on which the Colossians already have the salvific benefits they need and the reason they need not entertain supplements or replacements for what they have already believed

1. There is evidence in the papyri for use of *prōteuōn* as a title, "the first," "the preeminent one," or "of the first rank." See *New Docs* 2, p. 96; 4, p. 172.

2. There is really only one textual issue of significance in this Christ hymn. B, D*, F, G, I, L, and various other manuscripts omit "through him" at this juncture. But the inclusion is well supported by P46, ℵ, A, C, and many other manuscripts. The phrase is awkward and can even be said to interrupt the flow of the hymn. Thus Metzger, *TC*, p. 554, indicates that there was a great deal of uncertainty as to whether this phrase should be included as original or not. In my view it seems likely that Paul, adapting the hymn material here, may well have inserted a few phrases so that it would not stand out too much from the Asiatic rhetorical style surrounding the hymn. Thus I think the phrase should be seen as original.

and have been doing, but also provides a pattern or trajectory of the Christian life which involves death, resurrection, and eventual glorification. The story of Jesus, first in creation and first in redemption, flows right into the thesis statements made in vv. 21-23 about the Christian life. The philosophy Paul is confronting is thoroughly Jewish, and he opposes to it a thoroughly Jewish christology grounded in Jewish sapiential thinking, which calls for more detailed discussion.

A Closer Look: The Formation of the Christ Hymn[3]

It is hardly surprising in a discourse that exhorts believers to sing hymns (Col. 3.16) that one such hymn might be quoted, modified, or even created by the author.[4] Col. 1.15-20 is profoundly indebted to Jewish wisdom literature, in particular various passages from the Wisdom of Solomon. What is said there about the personified Wisdom of God Paul now says about Christ:

Colossians	Wisdom of Solomon
1:15a	"For she is . . . a spotless mirror of the working of God and an image of his goodness" (7.26).
1:15b	"I tell you what Wisdom is and how she came to be . . . I will trace her course *from the beginning of creation*" (6.22).
1:16a	"For he created all things so that they might exist" (1.14).
1:16d	on thrones and scepters (5.23d; 6.21; 7.8)
1:16-17, 19	"For Wisdom . . . because of her purity pervades and penetrates all things" (7.24b).
1:17b	"that which holds all things together knows what is said" (1:7); "she reaches mightily from one end of the earth to the other, and she orders all things well" (8.1b)
1:17a, 18d	on priority and superiority (7.29c)[5]

There are also some echoes of Sirach, particularly Sir. 1.4 ("Wisdom was created before all other things") and Wisdom's self-description in 24.9 ("Before the ages, in

---

3. The discussion to follow repeats what I said in *Jesus the Sage* (Minneapolis: Fortress, 1994), pp. 266-72, with some emendations and additions.

4. One of the more notable features of the context which sets off Col. 1.15-20 is that it is preceded by the direct address to the audience ("you") and use of "we" and "us" in abundance in 1.2-14 and followed by this same sort of personal language in vv. 21-23.

5. On these parallels see W. Wink, "Hymn of the Cosmic Christ," in *The Conversation Continues: Studies in Paul and John in Honor of J. L. Martyn* (Nashville: Abingdon, 1990), pp. 235-44, here p. 235.

the beginning, he created me, and for all ages I shall not cease to be"). There are also more remote echoes from Proverbs 3, 8, and 9, which also speak of personified Wisdom, but clearly the more evident and close parallels are from the later Jewish wisdom literature. This wisdom material is not the only source of the Christ hymn, for some of the clauses reflect the story of Christ's death.[6] E. Schweizer argued that the first stanza of the hymn could be explained on the basis of the wisdom material but that the second is originally Christian.[7] But in one sense the whole hymn is originally Christian, not a mere quoting of earlier material, for now it all speaks in a Christian way about the cosmic Christ. While in the earlier Jewish literature it is clear that we are talking about Wisdom being created by God, this is not so clear in this hymn when the material is applied to Christ. The only part of the second stanza of the hymn which could be called clearly a Pauline addition is the reference to the church as the body of Christ. Otherwise, the second stanza also reflects Wisdom influence.

J. C. O'Neill has argued that the hymn uses the language of public declaration, in which clauses and phrases and participles are piled up as an act of praise, leaving out proper connectives as well as proper concern for grammar.[8] What he fails to realize is that this sort of exalted or extended style also largely characterizes the entire Colossian letter, and is precisely what Asiatic rhetoric normally looks like. The Christ hymn is just a bit more poetic or liturgical use of Asiatic style,[9] and it seems quite possible that in this case Paul has either transformed an earlier hymn into this Asiatic style or has composed the hymn himself for this specific occasion and discourse, for it fits so perfectly in this discourse and in its immediate context.

There are some similarities here to the Christ hymn in Philippians 2, but the differences also stand out. There is no servant language here, and while the Philippian hymn is about personal vindication, this one in Colossians is about cosmic victory. Christ is seen here, much more clearly than in Philippians 2, as the creator, sustainer, and redeemer, all in one person. There is a strong emphasis here on the "fullness" of God, not on just a part of God being pleased to dwell in Christ, a point that will be amplified and explicated in Col. 2.9. The concept of incarnation is not as clear here as in Philippians 2, but it is surely latent here in view of the reference to the death on the cross. One must first take on flesh before one can die.

Christological hymns have V patterns, speaking of the preexistence, earthly existence, and exalted subsequent existence in heaven of the Christ. It is striking that in Colossians 1 the nadir of the V is neither the incarnation nor apparently the death of Jesus, but rather the church as the body of Christ. Paul does go on to refer to "making peace through the blood of the cross," and perhaps, if this hymn did come from someone before Paul, he has transferred this phrase to later in the hymn so that the

6. Paul seems to have added references to the death of Jesus to the hymns in both Colossians 1 and Philippians 2. On Philippians 2 see *Jesus the Sage*, pp. 257-66.

7. Schweizer, "The Church as the Missionary Body of Christ," *NTS* 8 (1961): 1-11.

8. J. C. O'Neill, "The Source of Christology in Colossians," *NTS* 26 (1979): 87-100.

9. See E. Norden, *Agnostos Theos* (Darmstadt: Wissenschaftliche Buchgesellschaft, 1956), pp. 168ff., 201ff.

"body" could be the nadir of the V. There are other clauses that perhaps Paul added to a pre-existing pattern, namely the reference to thrones in v. 16, which could be said to counter the false teaching in Colossae, and "the church" may be a Pauline addition in v. 18.[10] The church is where Christ is even now present on earth. Even if Paul did use a pre-existing pattern, he has made the material his own and adapted it to his rhetorical purposes in this discourse.

The parallelism of the two strophes of the hymn is quite evident. The use of such parallelism with language repeated but used in slightly different ways is yet another characteristic of Asiatic rhetorical style. Both strophes begin with the relative pronoun *hos* (vv. 15a, 18b) so that "he is the image" has its parallel in "he is the beginning/source." *Prōtotokos* also occurs in both verses. Each of the relative clauses is followed by a causal *hoti* clause ("because in him . . . ," vv. 16, 19). The cosmic dimension concludes each strophe, first in creation ("whether thrones . . .") then in redemption ("whether things on earth . . ."). The hymn keeps the christological focus throughout with "in him," "through him," "for him," and the emphatic *autos* ("he himself") in vv. 17 and 18.[11]

I. H. Marshall is surely correct that the language of Col. 1.15-20 refers to the personal activity of the one who is the very image or exact representation of God and participates in the acts of creation.[12] This is the reasonable conclusion when one sees Paul applying the language of Wisdom's role in creation to the Son, a person whom Paul worships. In other words, the element of personal preexistence in this hymn goes beyond the personification of Wisdom in the Jewish sapiential material.[13] The first stanza is about a person, not merely the power God exhibited in creation, for that power was exercised in person by the Son. This is an understandable development of wisdom thinking since already in Sirach 24 we have the concept of Wisdom taking a concrete historical form in the Torah. Whereas Wisdom is seen as bringing God's people together in Sirach, Christ is given this role in the christology of Colossians and Ephesians.[14] This and the other christological hymns in the NT demonstrate what a

10. On possible additions see A. T. Lincoln, "Colossians," in *The New Interpreter's Bible* XI (Nashville: Abingdon, 2000), pp. 602-3; on the background to the hymn in general see his excursus on pp. 601-5.

11. One factor that favors the view that Paul is modifying a pre-existing hymn is the fair number of words in this hymn not found elsewhere in his letters. Some, such as "thrones," could be explained by the focus of the text, but the rest ("visible," "hold together," "beginning," "be preeminent," "making peace," and "the blood of the cross") are not technical terms and could have been used by Paul elsewhere but are not. See J. D. G. Dunn, *Colossians and Philemon* (Grand Rapids: Eerdmans, 1996), p. 84. On the suggested additions see N. T. Wright, "Poetry and Theology in Colossians 1.15-20," *NTS* 36 (1990): 444-68.

12. I. H. Marshall, "Incarnational Christology in the New Testament," in *Christ the Lord: Studies in Christology Presented to Donald Guthrie,* ed. H. H. Rowdon (Downers Grove: InterVarsity, 1982), pp. 1-16.

13. See rightly L. L. Helyer, "Cosmic Christology and Col. 1.15-20," *JETS* 37 (1994): 235-46, critiquing Dunn's denial of preexistence christology here.

14. Some scholars have seen a christological hymn fragment in Eph. 2.13-18, but for

high christology existed in the church, even before and during the time of Paul. Such a christology was certainly not an invention of the author of the Gospel of John at the end of the first century.

L. C. Reyes has examined the rhetoric of this hymn in some detail.[15] He points out that v. 16, 17-18, and 20 use the rhetorical device of isocolon in that there is a near identical number of syllables in each of these pairs of two lines, meant to give the hymn an orderly meter and add to its stateliness. He also notes in v. 16 the use of inclusio *(ektisthē ta panta . . . ta panta . . . ektistai)*, antithesis (heaven and earth, things visible and things invisible), and paronomasia (similar forms, differing meanings: *orata, aorata)*, which reminds us of the oral character of this material. It was meant to be heard. There is also the use of epanaphora (the same sound or word repeated at regular intervals indicating a kind of enumeration: *eite . . . eite . . . eite . . . eite)*. There is also considerable evidence of alliteration at the end of lines, particularly the last three phrases at the end of v. 16. Reyes's discussion of possible chiasmus is more debatable, but the evidence for other devices like polysyndeton and distributio is strongly demonstrated by Reyes.[16] He has shown how these devices in the hymn serve to set Christ apart from and over all of creation.

V. 15 states from the outset that Christ is the image of the invisible God. We could tease this out to say he is the visible image of the invisible God.[17] *Eikōn* here does not mean merely "likeness," as in outward appearance, but the exact and full representation of God in character and otherwise. Whoever has seen the Son has seen the Father. *Eikōn* is used of the resurrected and exalted Christ in 1 Cor. 15.49 and 2 Cor. 4.4. "This notion was then pushed back as far as it could go. If the resurrected Christ was the supreme expression of the image of God, then he must always have been so. This creates the paradox that the one who can be described in Adamic language (cf. Gen. 1.27) can also be held to have existed before Adam and to have been on the side of the Creator as well as on the side of creation."[18]

---

formal and content reasons this appears more to be a reflection on the death of Jesus, and indeed perhaps an expansion of Col. 1.20. It seeks to make clear the ecclesiological implications of Christ's death, namely the reconciliation of Jew and Gentile.

15. L. C. Reyes, "The Structure and Rhetoric of Colossians 1.15-20," *Filologia Neotestamentaria* 23-24 (1999): 139-54.

16. Reyes, " Structure and Rhetoric," pp. 144-53.

17. It is interesting and of course expected that Jews would stress that God cannot be seen (cf. Rom. 1.20; 1 Tim. 1.17; Heb. 11.27). For a pagan, used to visible images of God, the key question then became "If God cannot be seen, how can he be known?" Paul's answer is that God has been made visible in Christ, who is the image of God. See Dunn, *Colossians, Philemon*, p. 87.

18. Lincoln, "Colossians," p. 597.

The second clause in v. 15 speaks of Christ being first of all creation. While literally *prōtotokos* can mean "firstborn," it is unlikely to have this sense here for several reasons. In the first place it is clear that *prōtotokos* is used metaphorically for temporal priority in v. 18. Secondly, Paul is indicating here that Christ is the author of creation, not merely first among many creatures. Christ stood on the creator side of the creator-creature distinction when he was the preexistent Son. It is probable that *prōtotokos* indicates Christ's relationship to creation while *eikōn* indicates his relationship to God the Father. It is possible as well that we should see the use of *prōtotokos* in light of what is said in Ps. 89.27 where God promises to make the king the firstborn, that is, preeminent or supreme in rank. So the primary sense of *prōtotokos* here in Col. 1.15 is that Christ has temporal priority over creation. He existed before creation and precisely because of that has preeminence in rank over creation, having also been the agent who helped create it all. He is the one that John of Patmos was later to call the Alpha as well as the Omega.[19]

V. 16 makes even more clear the Son's role in creation. In, or, better said, *through* him, all things were created in heaven and on earth, both seen and unseen things. Nothing at all was created apart from the Son. His work was all-encompassing. All things were created through him and indeed for him (v. 16c). In v. 16b Paul enumerates some of the things or beings that were created by the Son: "thrones, dominions, sovereignties, powers." These were common terms for supernatural beings existing in the heavens (e.g., *Testament of Levi* 3.8: "in heaven there are thrones and dominions"; *1 Enoch* 61.10: "all angels of power and all angels of principalities"; *2 Enoch* 20.1: "I saw there [in the seventh heaven] dominions, governments, cherubim . . . thrones . . ."; cf. 2 Macc. 3.24). Since the Son created them, they were apparently good, though some have fallen thereafter. Otherwise they would not need reconciling to God, and v. 20 speaks of the reconciliation of things in heaven.

V. 17 indicates that Christ is the glue, the one in whom all things cohere or are established. His present ongoing role is to sustain all things in their existence. He is thus like Wisdom in Wis. 1.7-10, the logos of Sir. 43.26, or the Stoic concept of the all-pervading divine logos.[20]

Despite the special pleading of O'Brien, it is surely the case that *ekklēsia* in v. 18 refers to the church universal.[21] We have already seen that use of *ekklēsia* in a

19. There is an interesting parallel in the old Latin version of Sir. 24.3: "I went forth out of the mouth of the Most High, firstborn before every creature. . . ." That is, Wisdom came forth before any creature and so is not the first creature or created being. See T. F. Glasson, "Col. 1.18 and Sirach 24," *NovT* 11 (1969): 154-56. Philo calls Wisdom the "firstborn Mother of all things" (*Quaestiones in Genesin* 4.97).

20. See Dunn, *Colossians, Philemon*, p. 93. Dunn rightly cautions that words in a hymn are those of poetic imagination, not clinical analysis.

21. But see P. T. O'Brien, *Colossians, Philemon* (Waco: Word, 1982), pp. 48-50, 57-61.

corporate rather than local sense is not unknown in the earlier Paulines (see p. 56 above). Here the term must simply represent the people of God rather than the assembled congregation in some locality. The metaphor of the body with a head occurs here for the first time in Paul, and clearly the body here is not just the body of believers in one place. Christ is the head of the whole church.

This can be said to be a natural christological development of the body metaphor in 1 Corinthians 12, where Paul's concern is relationships among Christians. Here in Colossae the problem is not so much body life as holding on to the head. So now Paul stresses the relationship of Christ to the body.[22] *Kephalē*, "head," denotes Christ's rule or authority over the church which is his body (cf. the use of *rō'š* in Deut. 28.13; Judg. 11.11; 2 Sam. 22.44).[23] Ideas of both authority and origin come together in this use of the word because the origin of something was thought to be determinative for what came forth or followed from it.[24] In the papyri we find the following from an epitaph of an Isis devotee: "the heavenly creation is my head."[25]

The second strophe begins in v. 18c and speaks of Christ as the beginning (rather than "source" as a translation for *archē*) of the resurrection from out of the realm of the dead. "Like both 'head' and 'firstborn' 'beginning' had two linked connotations: primacy in the temporal sense and primacy with reference to the authority or sovereignty."[26] Christ takes precedence over all of creation and over all in re-creation. He is the first in both realms.[27] The rest of this verse is another example of Asiatic redundancy: "in order that he himself might be preeminent in all things."

V. 19 says that the entire "fullness" *(plērōma)* is pleased to dwell in Christ. In later Gnostic thought *plērōma* was used of all the intermediaries between God and humankind. These "aeons" existed as a sort of buffer zone between God and the evil material universe. This way of thinking should not, however, be read back into this text, which makes perfectly clear the goodness of all creation, which was made by the good God. 2.9 is indeed the proper commentary

---

22. The Greek philosophical concept of the universe as a body (Plato, *Timaeus* 31b, 32a; *Orphic fragment* 168, where Zeus is the head and the cosmos is his body) is often thought to stand behind some of the thinking here, but Paul never calls the cosmos a body, and the relationship of Christ to the church is what he stresses here. Closer is the concept of the emperor as the head and the empire his body.

23. See Lincoln, "Colossians," p. 599.

24. S. Bedale, "The Meaning of *kephalē* in the Pauline Epistles," *JTS* 5 (1954): 211-15.

25. *New Docs* 3, p. 46.

26. Lincoln, "Colossians," p. 599.

27. It is especially striking to contrast the Philippians 2 hymn at this juncture. Its first half focuses on Christ's divine condescension and humbling of himself, whereas here both strophes stress the exalted nature and preeminence of Christ to make clear that Christ outshines the competition, so to speak.

on what is meant here: the fullness of God dwells bodily in the resurrected and exalted Christ.[28] The implication is clearly that there is no more divine nature to be found in angels or lesser supernatural beings. Union with the divine must come through Christ or not at all.

About v. 20 it is often asked whether "all" really means "all," in which case we have universalism here: all creatures of all kinds will eventually be saved. But this overlooks the differences between hostile forces that are placated and forced to recognize their Lord unwillingly and believers who are at peace with and reconciled to God. The universe will one day be at peace, but some will have that peace in them and some will simply be pacified or laid to rest.[29] But this verse does make clear that redemption is not just for those on earth, though whether that involves lost angels or not is not clear. It is in any case wrong to overpress the hyperbolic language of a passage that not only is from a hymn but is framed in hyperbolic Asiatic rhetoric. The aorist of a newly coined extended form of the verb *katallassō* is used here: *apokatallaxai* (on the coining of new words as a rhetorical practice see pp. 4-10 above). "The implication is that the purpose, means, and manner of (final) reconciliation have already been expressed by God, not that the reconciliation is already complete."[30]

Peace is said to be made through the blood Christ shed on the cross. In view of the fact that this hymn speaks of the relationship of God to his people, one must conclude that the peace referred to is between God and human beings. This in turn suggests that the author of the hymn thinks that God needed to be pacified through a blood sacrifice. This in turn suggests that what is latent here is the notion of propitiation of God's wrath through a sacrificial death, which makes possible peace and forgiveness and reconciliation. Underlying all of this are both the righteous and holy character of God on the one hand, and the loving character of God providing a substitute so that we need not endure the punishment for sin.

What is the intended rhetorical effect of this Christ hymn? Lincoln sums things up well: "It establishes a positive relationship with the readers through the citation of material that they may well have in common with the writer; it encourages them to assent to its praise as they are carried along by its rhythms and flow; and it makes them conducive to accepting the subsequent message that has made the perspective of the hymn its foundation."[31] There will be both echoes and further developments of ideas found in the Christ hymn as the largely theological portion of the discourse develops in 1.21–3.4 (cf. 1.24; 2.3, 9-10, 15, 19; 3.11).

---

28. Cf. Jer. 23.24; Seneca, *De Beneficiis* 4.8.2, where it is said that nothing is void of God, that God fills all his work. See also Philo, *Legum Allegoriae* 3.4.

29. See O'Brien, *Colossians, Philemon*, pp. 53-55.

30. Dunn, *Colossians and Philemon*, p. 103.

31. Lincoln, "Colossians," p. 601.

Propositio/Partitio — 1.21-23

When the thesis an orator is going to argue is complex, having several parts, the propositio is divided up into several parts. It is interesting that Paul enumerates the parts in reverse order from how he will treat them in the discourse:

the recognition of Paul's role in proclaiming the gospel	1.23c	1.24–2.5
the need for the addressees to continue in the faith	1.23a-b	2.6–3.4
the work of Christ to produce holiness in the believers' lives	1.21-22	3.5–4.1

The thesis statement in 1.21-23 thus begins to apply lessons learned from the Christ hymn which will be fleshed out at length in 1.24–4.1.[1] Paul raises these points in this reverse order probably because he wants, having spoken of Christ, to then set forth another example in himself before dealing with the behavior and beliefs of his audience. After all he does not know them personally, so he reserves his critique until well into the discourse.

Some rhetoricians said that one should not go beyond three propositions in a partitio (Quintilian, *Inst. Or.* 4.5.3). In his discussion of the partitio Quintilian reminds us that it is not just the duty of the orator to instruct, for

---

1. On this rhetorical analysis cf. J. N. Aletti, *Saint Paul. Épître aux Colossiens* (Paris: Gabalda, 1993), pp. 38-40, 119-22 to A. T. Lincoln, "Colossians," in *The New Interpreter's Bible* XI (Nashville: Abingdon, 2000), p. 558. J. D. G. Dunn, *Colossians and Philemon* (Grand Rapids: Eerdmans, 1996), p. 105, however, seems to have misunderstood Aletti, for he argues that the arguments are taken up in the same order as they are presented in vv. 21-23, with vv. 21-22 picked up in 1.24–2.5, v. 23a in 2.6-13, and v. 23b in 3.1-4. I agree with Lincoln that they are addressed in the reverse order to which they are mentioned in vv. 21-23.

"the power of eloquence is greatest in emotional appeals" (4.5.6). Paul has just offered an inspiring look at Christ and what Christ has accomplished for the believer, which itself followed an emotive prayer for the audience. Fervent prayer and inspiring hymn, both of which carry heavy emotional freight, lead up to the thesis statement. Perhaps what is most notable about Paul's partition of the proposition here is that it is clear and succinct in comparison to the more expansive rhetoric that precedes and follows it. "The proposition, whether single or multiple, must, on every occasion when it can be employed with profit, be clear and lucid; for what could be more discreditable than the portion of the speech whose sole purpose is to prevent obscurity elsewhere, should itself be obscure?" (*Inst. Or.* 4.5.26). Quintilian adds that brevity is important here, that no superfluous words should be used because one is not yet explaining what he is saying, but what one is going to say. It is then not a shock that vv. 21-23 are the least Asiatic in character in the whole discourse when it comes to the matter of redundancy, though they are in fact one continuous sentence.

And you, having been alienated and having hostile minds in evil works, but now you have been reconciled[2] in the body of his flesh through the death — to present you holy and unblemished and irreproachable before him. If you remain established in the faith and stable and immovable from the hope of the gospel which you heard, which was preached to all creatures under heaven, of which I Paul became a servant.

There is a sense in which one can see vv. 21-23 as commentary on the hymn, or better said application to believers of the hymn's implications. V. 21 conveys the sense that Paul is referring mainly to Gentiles, those who were once alienated[3] from God and mentally hostile to the God of Israel due to their idolatry and immorality or evil deeds.[4] Rom. 1.18-32 serves as a good commentary on what

---

2. The textual issue is between the active third person singular ("he reconciled") or the second person plural passive ("you have been reconciled"). The latter has good support from P46, B, and other manuscripts and as the more difficult reading should probably be seen as original. See Metzger, *TC*, pp. 554-55.

3. *Apallotrioō* appears only here and in Eph. 2.12; 4.18 in the Pauline corpus (on the meaning "alienate" in the papyri see *New Docs* 3, p. 62). *Dianoia* ("mental disposition") occurs only here and in Eph. 2.3; 4.18 in the Pauline corpus. The more one studies the connections between Colossians and Ephesians, the more profoundly one becomes convinced that they are the product of the same mind who can creatively reuse material and terms in slightly different ways and contexts to suit a new situation and rhetorical agenda.

4. Here only in Paul do we have the phrase "evil deeds" (John 3.19; 7.7). The text seems to suggest that doing evil deeds engenders hostility of mind against the one who resists and opposes such deeds — God. See M. Y. MacDonald, *Colossians, Ephesians* (Collegeville: Liturgical, 2000), p. 71.

Paul has in view here.[5] "It is not simply that habitual wrongdoing has turned the mind away from God. Nor is the word translated 'mind' . . . strictly the mind itself, but the way it works, the process of understanding and intellect. Thought and act are both tainted, each pushing the other into further corruption."[6] We see in this verse and the next the typical contrast between what once was the case with the audience and what is now the case. The language here will be picked up again at the beginning of Ephesians, where it is quite clear that Gentiles are the ones spoken of.

V. 22 indicates that they are no longer estranged from God, for reconciliation has been brought about once for all time through Christ's death. This way of speaking of reconciliation echoes what we find in Rom. 5.10 and 2 Cor. 5.18-20.[7] Paul stresses the concrete and historical character of that which produced reconciliation. We do not need to reconcile ourselves to God since God has already provided that through the death of Christ. "The body of his flesh" might sound redundant, but in fact since Paul has just referred to the church as Christ's body in v. 18, it is not.[8] The phrase here "stresses the physicality of Christ's death and by making clear that the physical body of Christ was the means of reconciliation,[9] may well have been meant to contrast this view of redemption with that of the philosophy and its denigration of the physical body (2:23)."[10]

The goal of this process of human transformation, which has not yet been completed, is to present the believers unblemished and irreproachable before the throne of God. The verb "present" (cf. 1 Cor. 8.8; 2 Cor. 4.14; 11.2; Eph. 5.27; 2 Tim. 2.15) has a cultic overtone, and "holy" and "unblemished" also come from the cultic sphere. What is envisioned here is much the same as what Paul talks about in Rom. 12.1-2, where he exhorts believers to present themselves as

---

5. See Dunn, *Colossians,* p. 106.

6. N. T. Wright, *Colossians and Philemon* (Grand Rapids: Eerdmans, 1986), p. 81.

7. While the attempt to make reconciliation the central metaphor of Paul for salvation is pushing things too far, nevertheless this is an important theme in Paul, as R. P. Martin, *Reconciliation: A Study of Paul's Theology* (Atlanta: John Knox, 1981), pp. 125-26, shows.

8. It is interesting that over 60% of all the uses of *sarx* and *sōma* in the NT are in Paul's letters. Basically "flesh" *(sarx)* when used literally refers to the substance of which the body is composed, while "body" *(sōma)* refers to the outward physical nature of a human being. See Dunn, *Colossians and Philemon,* p. 107.

9. E. Lohse, *Colossians and Philemon* (Philadelphia: Fortress, 1971), p. 64, stresses that "of flesh" highlights the concept of the frailty of the body, its subjection to suffering.

10. Lincoln, "Colossians," p. 606. And of course verses such as this provided a strong antidote to later Gnostic thought. Tertullian, *Adversus Marcionem* 5.19.6 says that Marcion did not include "of the flesh" in his reading of Col. 1.22 and took the reference to the "body" as referring to the church. In 1QpHab 9.2 the wicked priest suffers "vengeance on his body of flesh." See also Sir. 23.16-17; *1 Enoch* 102.5.

living sacrifices, except that here God is presenting believers to himself and that here the time in question is the eschatological final review. The third adjective used, "irreproachable" or "free from accusation," is a judicial term and provides the courtroom overtone appropriate to the final judgment scene, when believers will appear before God. Because of Christ's unblemished offering of himself as a sacrifice, believers can be presented unblemished[11] and without accusation before God at the final judgment.[12]

In v. 23 the conditional clause uses *ei* and the present tense, indicating that Paul has no serious doubt about the outcome, *provided* the Colossians stand firm and be immovable from the hope that Epaphras has offered them and not switch to some sort of ascetic, mystical, or ritual practices which cannot advance them in their sanctification.[13] The proviso here is important. Paul believes that moral effort is required of the Colossians if they are to reach the finish line and hear the benediction on their lives. Reconciliation is not some automatic process. On the contrary the Colossians need to continue steadfast in the faith,[14] unmoved from the hope that was originally offered to them. Human willing and faithfulness are involved.[15] The believers need to continue to be firmly grounded in the gospel.

11. See G. B. Caird, *Paul's Letters from Prison* (Oxford: Oxford University Press, 1976), p. 182.

12. But Paul does not mean that believers are not expected, indeed required to go on and live holy lives. Christ's unblemished sacrifice is not a substitute for the believer's sacrifice of a holy life but a means by which the believer can be sanctified and so present himself as a living sacrifice. Only Christ's sacrifice atones for human sin, and so the believer's sacrifice is not an atoning sacrifice, but it does involve holiness. Paul does not affirm the notion of purely imputed righteousness. Right standing is a gift of grace, but righteousness as a moral condition is the work of the Holy Spirit within the believer. The righteousness of Christ enables him to be the perfect sacrifice and to offer right standing to all as a gift of pure grace, but the unblemished condition of the believer which is reviewed at judgment is not a legal fiction but the product of progressive sanctification in the actual life of the believer.

13. Dunn, *Colossians and Philemon*, p. 110, puts it well: "*Ei ge* may denote confidence more than doubt (cf. its use in 2 Cor. 5:3; Eph. 3:2; 4:21), but final acceptance is nevertheless dependent on remaining in the faith. The parenetic and pastoral point is that however such persistence must be and is enabled by God through his Spirit (1:11), there must be such persistence." But cf. P. T. O'Brien, *Colossians, Philemon* (Waco: Word, 1982), p. 69.

14. Notice the definite article here before "faith." Paul occasionally speaks in his earlier letters of "the faith" as the content of what is believed, but not often. See 1 Cor. 16.13 for a very similar exhortation.

15. Chrysostom in his fourth homily on Colossians: Paul says "you that do not act against your wills, nor from compulsion, but with your wills and wishes are sprung away from him, you he has reconciled, though you were unworthy of it." See R. W. Wall, *Colossians and Philemon* (Downers Grove: InterVarsity, 1993), p. 81: "According to Paul's gospel, getting into the faith community, which has covenanted with God for salvation, requires the believer's confidence in the redemptive merit of Christ's death (as defined in vv. 21-22). And

Here is the heart of this letter's exhortation. Paul does not want those who are already believers to sell their birthright for a mess of pottage which cannot in the end draw them closer to God. In other words, he is concerned about the danger of theological infidelity and moral or spiritual apostasy, a concern brought on by the influence of the Colossian philosophy on some in the Colossian church. While earlier Paul talked about the Colossians growing and bearing fruit, here the emphasis is on standing firm and being unmoved by appeals to head in another direction, in a wrong direction. One gets the sense here, because of the emphasis on "hope," that the Colossian philosophy was offering some sort of glorification or perfection in advance of the eschaton. Paul counters this by suggesting that believers need to continue to live in hope, standing firm on the foundation of the faith they already have assented to and believe in.

Paul reminds his audience that he (not some false teacher) is the minister[16] of this true and sufficient gospel about Christ which has been preached throughout the known world. In Paul's earlier letters he has referred to apostles as ministers of God (2 Cor. 6.4), of Christ (2 Cor. 11.23), or of a new covenant (2 Cor. 3.6). He mentions here that he is a minister of the gospel to remind the Colossians that they are not alone in believing in this christocentric message and that what has been effective for others will also be effective for them. The implication may be that the false teaching they are hearing in Colossae is not a widely received teaching.

---

staying in the community requires the believer to keep the faith. Paul does not teach a 'once saved always saved' kind of religion; nor does he understand faith as a 'once for all' decision for Christ. In fact, apostasy (loss of faith) imperils one's relationship with God and with the community that has covenanted with God for salvation."

16. Paul uses *diakonos* here of himself, as in 1 Cor. 3.5, and is no indication that this is a post-Pauline usage, though the specific phrase "a minister of the Gospel" is found only here in the chief Pauline letters. See O'Brien, *Colossians,* p. 71. J. N. Collins, *Diakonia: Re-Interpreting the Ancient Sources* (Oxford: Oxford University Press, 1990), has shown that this word was often used in the Greco-Roman world to refer to an agent, messenger, or intermediary for a high ranking official, and it could certainly have that sense here. This same term is used of Epaphras (1.7) and Tychicus (4.7), and it may be doubted that it means "deacon" in any of these instances, and if Paul had wanted to say "servant," the word *doulos* would have been his normal choice (as in Rom. 1.1).

Probatio — Argument One —
Minister of the Mystery — 1.24–2.5

Here as elsewhere Paul usually leads from strength, offering the most potent and potentially effective argument, the one thought most likely to move his audience in the right direction, first after the propositio (cf. Gal. 3.1-5; 1 Cor. 1.18ff.). Paul also tends in his first "proof" to speak of deeply personal matters, about the audience and how they came to Christ, about himself and his role in their conversion, or about both (cf. Phil. 1.12-30). The assumption is that the audience cannot deny their own experience of salvation and are unlikely to dispute Paul's apostolic labors on the behalf of them and others. In an honor-shame culture, to dispute either of these things would be shameful. "The emphasis on Paul's sufferings on behalf of the church, on the energy he expends in proclaiming Christ, and on the intensity of his pastoral concern demonstrates the excellence of his character as an apostle (ethos) and at the same time arouses in the readers admiration and sympathy (pathos)."[1]

The transition from the propositio to the first "proof" is extremely smooth since Paul has already begun to speak of his own ministry in v. 23. The probatio in a deliberative discourse was not intended to prove something true or false as in forensic rhetoric, but rather to show how a certain course of conduct would be beneficial, useful, honorable, and glorious while a different course of conduct would be useless and pointless or bring strife. In other words it normally involved persuasion and dissuasion. We see persuasion in the first argument in Colossians, but the second argument (2.6–3.4) is primarily an exercise in dissuasion.[2]

---

1. A. T. Lincoln, "Colossians," in *The New Interpreter's Bible* XI (Nashville: Abingdon, 2000), p. 613.

2. On Colossians as a document meant to be heard, as well as having some visual pat-

The first argument falls under the heading of an artificial proof, much as in 1 Corinthians. Paul cannot appeal to previous authorities about this "mystery" (1.26, 27), which has only just recently been unveiled and received by many people. The wisdom he will speak of is Good News, and it is news — something new. Thus he must stress the effect of the preaching and how it was received among the Colossians. The appeal to both the audience's and the apostle's experience is crucial and full of pathos. Suffering for the cause, indeed Paul's suffering in place of the Colossians, will be mentioned. Thus Paul attempts affectively to move his audience in the first argument so that they will be willing to heed the dissuasion in the second. Isocrates says that in a deliberative speech the rhetor "who wants to change your opinions must touch on many matters and must speak at length reminding, then rebuking, then commending, and then advising you" (*Oratio* 8.27), thus laying out the order in which Paul proceeds in Colossians, reminding in argument one, rebuking and then encouraging in argument two, and advising in argument three (3.5–4.1).

As a general rule, arguments that depend on an appeal to experience or pathos are more dependent on style and even tone of delivery than arguments appealing strictly to logic. Then too, Paul must use an inductive method in dealing with the problem in Colossae, since he does not have a direct personal connection with the Christians there. In a sense Paul is still building up rapport with and empathy in the audience in this first argument before he tackles the bone of contention, the false philosophy in Colossae. In an inductive approach one first presents an argument that the audience is likely to give ready assent to, building up credibility and trust. As Cicero says this "leads the person with whom one is arguing to give assent to certain undisputed facts; through this assent it wins his approval of a proposition about which there is doubt, because this resembles the facts to which he has assented" (*De Inventione* 1.31.51). Paul has been building up momentum to deal with the problem in Colossae ever since the opening prescript. If the audience is moved by the prayers, assents to the theology of the hymn, and nods approvingly at the first argument, then they will have to take a critical look at the philosophy that some have found enticing and interesting and indeed seriously entertain rejecting it. Unlike the situation in Corinth and more like the situation in Galatia, one does not sense that there is a major problem with factions, requiring the rhetoric of concord and unity. Rather, Paul must persuade all the Colossians to avoid going the

---

terns that the oral performer of the document was meant to note and take account of see A. E. Drake, "The Riddle of Colossians: *Quaerendo invenietis*," NTS 41 (1995): 123-44. P. J. Achtemeier, "*Omne verbum sonat*: The New Testament and the Oral Environment of Late Western Antiquity," *JBL* 109 (1990): 3-27, here p. 17: "Reading was . . . oral performance *whenever* it occurred and in whatever circumstances. Late antiquity knew nothing of the 'silent, solitary reader.'"

route of adopting the Colossian philosophy, which some already seem to have been dabbling in.

Now I rejoice in the sufferings for you,[3] even filling up what is lacking of the sufferings of Christ in my flesh for his body, which is the church, of which I became a minister according to the administration of God which was given to me to fulfill the Word of God for you, the mystery which was hidden for aeons and for generations but now is revealed to his saints, to whom God willed to make known the wealth of glory of this mystery in the nations, which is Christ in you, the hope of glory, whom we proclaim, admonishing everyone and teaching everyone in all wisdom in order to present everyone perfect in Christ, for whom I also labor, striving according to his energy which is at work in me in power.[4]

For I wish you to know how greatly I have struggled for you and for those in Laodicea and for whoever has not seen my face in the flesh, in order to encourage your hearts, being brought together in love and in all wealth of conviction of understanding unto the knowledge of the mystery of God, of Christ,[5] in whom are all the treasures of wisdom and hidden knowledge. This I say to you so that you will not be deluded by plausible arguments. For even if I am absent in the flesh, nonetheless I am with you in spirit, rejoicing and seeing your discipline and the firmness of your faith in Christ.

V. 24 is a famous crux and there have been many interpretations of it.[6] Probably the one which presents the fewest difficulties is that Paul is talking about suffering the messianic woes. He does not speak here of dying for or with Christ. The issue is *thlipsis*, some sort of travail involving suffering. Paul does not use this term of Christ's death on the cross. It would have been counterproductive to suggest that he and others might complete the redemptive death of Jesus by their sufferings, since he has just stressed and will stress again that Christ's death is all-sufficient for salvation and reconciliation. The idea here then is some sort of preordained amount of suffering that the saints must go through during the eschatological age before the end can come. It is not unrelated to the

---

3. The definite article with "sufferings" makes this a reference to a specific set of sufferings. Though *mou* ("my") is not found in most manuscripts, it is surely a correct understanding of what sufferings are in view: Paul's. Eph. 3.13 correctly explicates what is referred to here.

4. N. T. Wright, *Colossians and Philemon* (Grand Rapids: Eerdmans, 1986), p. 93, captures the sense of the prolix language here: "struggling with all his energy which so powerfully works in me."

5. Though "of God, of Christ" is awkward it has strong support in P46 and B and more than adequately explains the other readings. See Metzger, *TC*, p. 555.

6. For a list of options see P. T. O'Brien, *Colossians, Philemon* (Waco: Word, 1982), pp. 76-79.

opposite notion of the wrath of God being stored up in heaven for an appointed time when sin will have presumably reached its peak (as in the story of Noah). Paul then is suggesting that he is already in the period of great tribulation and suffering that the saints must go through before the end can come (Dan. 12.1). These sufferings were sometimes seen as preceding the coming of the Messiah and the messianic age and sometimes as preceding the end of history, when God will establish the age to come (cf. *1 Enoch* 47.1-4; *2 Baruch* 30.2; *4 Ezra* 13.16-19). The phrase "the suffering/travail of the Messiah" is found in the Talmud (Shabbat 118a; Pesachim 118a; Mekilta Exod. 16.25 [58b]), but these texts likely come from a somewhat later period. The verb *antanaplērō* has a double compound prefix which suggests that Paul is suffering *instead of* the church in Colossae.[7]

Thus it appears that Paul envisions suffering in himself the messianic woes (cf. Phil. 3.10; Rom. 8.17)[8] so that the Colossians have to suffer less, since there is a definite amount to be suffered,[9] and so that obstacles to the end and the return of Christ may be removed. Paul then can be said to suffer for Christ's body, the church, and while this suffering is not redemptive it nonetheless has positive benefit for the believers.[10] There may be lurking in the background here the fact of Paul's own conversion experience, during which, it is reported, a voice from heaven asked why he was persecuting the Christ. The notion of Christ being so connected to his people that when they suffer he suffers, and therefore that their suffering can be called his, may be latent here. Paul rejoices "*in* suffering" (cf. Rom. 5.3; 2 Cor. 7.4), not *because of* the suffering itself. He is no masochist. God has given him joy in the midst of the suffering, and he is also rejoicing because his suffering lessens the suffering of others.[11]

In v. 25 Paul calls himself the church's minister[12] according to the admin-

---

7. Wright, *Colossians*, p. 90; G. B. Caird, *Paul's Letters from Prison* (Oxford: Oxford University Press, 1976), p. 184.

8. See R. J. Bauckham, "Colossians 1:24 Again: The Apocalyptic Motif," *EvQ* 47 (1975): 168-70, for confirmation that we are on the right track here.

9. See Wright, *Colossians*, p. 89: "By drawing the enemies' fire on to himself, he may allow the young church something of a respite from the fierce attacks they might otherwise be facing."

10. Caird, *Paul's Letters from Prison*, p. 183: "Wherever the gospel of reconciliation is preached there is a price to be paid in suffering. Paul has been glad to draw off on himself something of the full tally of suffering which would otherwise have been borne by the churches, and he regards this as an integral part of his ministry."

11. J. D. G. Dunn, *The Epistles to the Colossians and to Philemon* (Grand Rapids: Eerdmans, 1996), p. 114.

12. Earlier Paul called himself a minister of the gospel (1.23), here a minister of the church. In favor of "minister" as surely the proper translation, and not "servant" (for which Paul uses *doulos*), is that Paul frequently speaks of his work as ministry (*diakonia*, Rom. 11.13; 15.31; 1 Cor. 16.15; 2 Cor. 3.7-9; 4.1; 5.18; 6.3; on *diakoneō* see Rom. 15.25; 2 Cor. 3.3; 8.19-20).

istration of God. *Oikonomia* was used of household rules or the concern of the steward or administrator of a household or estate, who was usually a slave.[13] The sense here seems to be "I am a minister according to the administration (household ruling principles) of God, the execution of which has been conferred on me in that which concerns you."[14] Paul uses *oikonomia* in Eph. 1.10 of God's administration of the world and of salvation and in 1 Cor. 9.17 of Paul's administration of his apostolic office. In 1 Cor. 4.1 Paul describes himself as a steward *(oikonomos)* or administrator of the mysteries of God.[15] It is hard to escape the conclusion that Paul sees himself as the head steward in God's household, in charge of managing at least the Gentile portion of the estate (cf. 1 Cor. 3.10-15; Rom. 1.11-12; Eph. 2.19-20).[16]

V. 26 begins to speak of the apocalyptic secret, "the mystery which was hidden for ages[17] but now is revealed" in the Gospel to all the saints, not just a select few. "Mystery" was used in apocalyptic literature (Dan. 2.18-19, 27-30; 4 *Ezra* 14.5; 1 *Enoch* 51.3; 103.2) and at Qumran (1QM 3.8; 16.9; 1QS 3.21-23; 1QH 7.27; 10.4) of some secret part of God's plans that was to be disclosed.[18] This rich and glorious secret reveals God's largess to the nations, namely redemption provided for all in Christ.

Paul defines the mystery as "Christ in you" (v. 27; cf. 1 Cor. 2.7; Gal. 1.15)[19]

---

13. See D. B. Martin, *Slavery as Salvation: The Metaphor of Slavery in Pauline Christianity* (New Haven: Yale University Press, 1990), pp. 15-17.

14. O'Brien, *Colossians*, p. 81.

15. On this concept see J. Reumann, "'Stewards of God' — Pre-Christian Religious Application of OIKONOMOS in Greek," *JBL* 77 (1958): 339-49; idem, "OIKONOMIA — Terms in Paul in Comparison with Lucan *Heilsgeschichte*," *NTS* 13 (1966-67): 147-67; M. Bouttier, "Remarques sur la conscience apostolique de St. Paul," *OIKONOMIA. Heilsgeschichte al Thema der Theologie*, ed. F. Christ (Hamburg: Reich, 1967), pp. 100-108. On this term Peter Gorday, *Colossians, 1-2 Thessalonians, 1-2 Timothy, Titus, Philemon* (Ancient Christian Commentary on Scripture IX; Downers Grove: InterVarsity, 2000), p. 25 n. 9, says: "The term *dispensation*, or *economy*, is an extraordinarily rich and polyvalent one for the Fathers. Chrysostom believes that Paul in his work somehow carries forward, becomes an instrument of, embodies a new phase of all that God has been doing providentially in the whole work of creation and redemption. The notion of dispensation covers, therefore, the idea of the divine ordering, purpose and the provision in an unfolding, guiding process that is internally consistent and subject in all of its details to the wisdom of God's governance." See Chrysostom's fourth homily On Colossians.

16. See R. W. Wall, *Colossians and Philemon* (Downers Grove: InterVarsity, 1993), p. 89.

17. Notice the Asiatic redundancy: the mystery has been hidden for aeons and generations.

18. Lincoln, "Colossians," p. 615.

19. Since "you" is plural, it is possible to translate here "Christ *among* you, the hope of glory." In light of Rom. 8.10; 2 Cor. 13.5; and Eph. 3.17, however, Paul probably is referring to Christ dwelling within "each of you" here as well as in the midst of the community. The individual reference is all the more likely since the problem in Colossae was some individuals en-

and as the basis of one's hope for glory in the future.[20] So the secret is less a set of ideas than a person and what God has done, is doing, and will do through that person — Jesus Christ. Dunn is, however, right to stress "as Eph. 3.4-6 shows the two thoughts (the mystery of Jew and Gentile together as recipients of God's saving grace and the mystery of Christ) are two aspects of the same larger divine plan as Paul had come to see it. . . . And that double aspect of the mystery is still in view here in the assertion that the mystery was not only to be made known 'among the Gentiles' but precisely as the mystery of 'Christ . . . in you,' that is, in you Gentiles. . . ."[21]

This is an open secret, one that is taught "by us"[22] (v. 28) to all so that finally every person may be presented perfect in Christ. No doubt "every person" is rhetorical hyperbole, but it is meant to counter the notion that salvation is an esoteric thing for the elect and select few who are in the know.[23] "Every person" is repeated three times in v. 28. Wright takes it to mean that "every single Christian is capable of the maturity of which Paul speaks, since, though it involves 'knowledge' and 'wisdom' these are not to be weighed in the scale of ordinary human intellectual ability, but are of an altogether different order."[24] But it is not clear that every Christian is what is meant by *panta anthrōpon*. The purpose of proclamation is to lead all persons to Christ, and once in Christ to full conformity with Christ's image. "Admonishing," *noutheteō*, comes from the family of words for the mind and has the sense of straightening out muddled or immature thinking.[25] Some Colossians were apparently confused about what amounted to true wisdom and knowledge.

Teleion here can be translated "complete," "mature," or "perfect," but since Paul has already talked about believers being presented blameless and unblemished at the judgment and since *teleion* was used in non-biblical Greek of

---

gaging in attempts to draw closer to the divine by individual ascetic practices. Cf. Wright, *Colossians*, p. 92; Dunn, *Colossians*, p. 123; E. Lohse, *Colossians and Philemon* (Philadelphia: Fortress, 1971), p. 76; P. Pokorný, *Colossians: A Commentary* (Peabody: Hendrickson, 1991), p. 103. The objection that "among you" would make the phrase mean the same thing as "among the nations," which precedes it, is not valid since this Asiatic discourse is full of redundancy. See Lincoln, "Colossians," p. 615.

20. Caird, *Paul's Letters from Prison*, p. 186: "If the indwelling Christ can transcend the deepest social, political, and religious divisions which split mankind, no limits can be set to his ultimate accomplishment."

21. Dunn, *Colossians and Philemon*, pp. 121, 122; cf. C. F. D. Moule, *The Epistles to the Colossians and Philemon* (Cambridge: Cambridge University Press, 1968), pp. 82-83.

22. "We" occurs only here in v. 28 in this section. This is presumably because it was Paul's coworkers rather than Paul who did the preaching and teaching of the Colossians. See D. J. Harrington, *Paul's Prison Letters* (Hyde Park: New City, 1997), p. 100.

23. See rightly Lincoln, "Colossians," p. 615.

24. Wright, *Colossians*, p. 93.

25. Wall, *Colossians and Philemon*, p. 94.

the quality of a sacrificial victim (i.e., unblemished; cf. Exod. 12.5 LXX; of persons Gen. 6.9; Sir. 44.17), the meaning is certainly more than just "complete" or "mature." In its eschatological sense this term refers to a completely Christlike condition, the opposite of being lost, bound in sin, or alienated from God. This is the eschatological hope of the believer: to be fully conformed to Christ's image and so made perfect by means of the resurrection, which puts one beyond disease, decay, and death, beyond sin, suffering, and sorrow. Such a goal is of course not fully attainable before the return of Christ and the raising of the believing dead.

Paul says in v. 29 that he puts out a maximum effort in this regard, striving (the word for a strenuous athletic contest, from which we get the word agony) according to the powerful working or energy *(energein)* of God, which is at work in the apostle in power. "The word 'struggling' whose root can mean 'to compete in the games' carries, as often in Paul, the idea of athletic contest: Paul does not go about his work half-heartedly, hoping vaguely that grace will fill the gaps which he is too lazy to work at himself. Nor, however, does he imagine that it is 'all up to him' so that unless he burns himself out with restless, anxious toil nothing will be achieved."[26] 1 Cor. 9.25-27 uses this same language to the full effect.[27]

At 2.1 Paul continues to explain his own ministry and says that he has been struggling vigorously, like an athlete straining in a contest, for those in Colossae and Laodicea, even though they have never seen his face.[28] How then is Paul struggling for them? Perhaps we are to think of him wrestling in prayer, and certainly the exordium has already borne witness to his prayers for them. Perhaps Paul is referring to his general labor for the gospel or to the work he is putting into this letter as part of his struggle on their behalf, since he will be dealing with the false philosophy. V. 2 gives substance to this last suggestion since Paul says that he has been struggling in order to encourage their hearts, or, better said, to give their hearts courage, and in this verse he is surely referring to this letter. The goal, then, of this discourse is to bring them together or even knit them together in the bond of love[29] (false teaching is always divisive) and

26. Wall, *Colossians and Philemon*, p. 94.

27. See the discussion of this metaphorical motif and its significance in an agonistic culture in my *Conflict and Community in Corinth* (Grand Rapids: Eerdmans, 1995), pp. 214-16.

28. Notice the redundancy of "my face in the flesh." How else could they have seen his face? The Asiatic redundancy is deliberate and does not reflect a lack of literary and rhetorical skill. Notice, for example, the careful balancing in proof. This first proof can be divided into two parts, 1.24-29 and 2.1-5. As Dunn, *Colossians*, pp. 128-29, points out, key terms are repeated binding the two sections together ("rejoice," 1.24; 2.5; "knowledge," 1.27; 2.2; "riches of the mystery," 1.27; 2.2; "struggle/contest," 1.29; 2.1).

29. See Harrington, *Paul's Prison Letters*, p. 104. Notice that it is both love and knowledge that bring a group of Christians to maturity and unity in Christ. An argument for con-

to encourage them, bolstering their faith and resolve to stand firm in the gospel they have already received, and to reaffirm them in the knowledge of the mystery of God — that is, their knowledge of Christ.

It is in Christ that all the riches of wisdom and hidden knowledge are to be found,[30] not in some ascetic practices or esoteric teachings about angels (v. 3). Here Paul is ascribing to Christ the attributes of personified Wisdom. In Christ this wisdom is now accessible, and so it is now an open secret, though hidden from those who are not yet in Christ. Paul will be stressing the all-sufficiency of Christ for wisdom and for redemption throughout this section. "Christ himself is 'the mystery of God': not just a clue or key to it."[31]

"The conviction of understanding" (*plēphoria tēs syneseōs,* v. 2) likely means the conviction that comes from understanding. Paul is certainly no anti-intellectual. He believes that knowledge and understanding deepen one's confidence and conviction in faith. Knowledge is not sufficient but is necessary for a deep faith that has more than an affective "trust" side to it. When head and heart agree there is a profound faith. "Clearly verse 3 is parallel to verse 2 in thought. The idea contained in the phrase *full riches of complete understanding* is virtually repeated in the following phrase *all the treasures of wisdom and knowledge* so that the idea of *mystery* finds a parallel in the word *hidden.*"[32] The rhetorical techniques of accumulation and amplification for emphasis are used here in this Asiatic discourse (on which see pp. 4-12 above).

Paul says at v. 4 that he is saying these things so that the audience will not be deluded or deceived by plausible sounding arguments.[33] *Pithanologia,* "plausible arguments," is the antithesis of the rhetorical term *apodeixis.* The latter refers to "demonstration," that is, a convincing conclusion drawn from accepted and logical premises (Aristotle, *Nichomachean Ethics* 1.3.4; Epictetus 1.8.7; Plato, *Theaetetus* 162E). The opposite is a plausible sounding but ill-founded conclusion. So some substantial rhetoric has been used on at least some in Colossae in regard to the cogency of the Colossian philosophy. As this chapter proceeds, the

---

cord or unity is a classic form of deliberative argument, and we see it elsewhere for example in 1 Corinthians.

30. Notice the rhetorically effective alliteration and piling up of terms which in itself gives the sense of completeness: *pan ploutos tēs plērophorias,* "all the riches of full assurance." This is followed in short order by the redundant and awkward "of God, of Christ." Whether this was actually composed by Paul or Timothy we are dealing with the deliberate assuming of the expansive Asiatic style. Harrington, *Paul's Prison Letters,* p. 104, speaks of a deliberate overloading of terms to emphasize the theme of knowledge. This is what redundancy is meant to accomplish — emphasis, and so a lasting impression is left on the audience.

31. Wright, *Colosssians,* p. 95.

32. Wall, *Colossians and Philemon,* p. 97.

33. Here the connotation is arguments that "sound" good but are in the end specious. See Lincoln, "Colossians," p. 616.

nature of the false teaching becomes clearer. Someone is teaching what Paul calls a *philosophia* (v. 8) that apparently includes logical or rhetorical arguments to convince others, and a few have indeed been convinced already.

Paul is probably not whistling in the dark when he says in v. 5 that he rejoices to see the Colossians' firmness of faith and the order in their Christian belief. The impression left is that the community is basically in good shape and needs to keep maturing, going forward in the direction they began in when converted, but that there is a particular problem that needs addressing. An inclusio is formed by the repetition of "I rejoice" from 1.24 in 2.5b, thus marking off the section as a rhetorically identifiable discrete unit and "setting the tone of this section and its attempts to cement the links between the readers and the gospel originating in Paul's unique mission."[34] He also says that though he is absent in the body, he is present in spirit with them, a familiar Pauline phrase (cf. 1 Cor. 5.3; 1 Thess. 2.17). This may be more than a rhetorical flourish. Fee suggests that in these Pauline uses of the phrase Paul means that he is in some sense present, by means of the Holy Spirit, with the congregation when they gather for worship and to hear the delivery of his words.[35]

34. Lincoln, "Colossians," p. 617.
35. G. D. Fee, *God's Empowering Presence* (Peabody: Hendrickson, 1994), p. 646.

Probatio — Argument Two —
The Bone of Contention — 2.6–3.4

At the middle of the *logoi* or arguments is the discussion of the main issue in Colossae. The "positioning of this section reminds the interpreter that the danger from the opposing teaching is at the center of the letter's rhetorical situation. This teaching has provoked the writing of this letter, but the writer then uses the opportunity provided by the perceived danger to fashion a more general message of exhortation, in which the concerns and the language of the philosophy are taken up into a new framework and thereby given new content." One can also note that 2.16-23 is where the issue is really joined in detail and that this part of this argument is framed by two somewhat more general sections in 2.6-15 and 3.1-4.[1] Here Paul becomes the most polemical and strident, and here the Asiatic character of the rhetoric is dialed up a notch as well.

Asiatic rhetoric was in all circumstances highly emotive and grandiose in character. In polemics the sentences tended to flow fast and furious with the piling up of phrases, clauses, synonyms, and the like. Again, this section can best be appreciated if heard and not read. For example, the end rhyme sets the cadence in 2.16 with *brōsei, posei,* and *merei* and in vv. 18 and 19 with *thelōn, tōn angelōn, embateuōn, kratōn, tōn haphōn, syndesmōn,* and then *epichorēgoumenon* and *symbibazomenon.* The length of the terms goes from two syllables to three to seven and six. By the very sound of the rhetoric, Paul is building to a conclusion, and the most polysyllabic terms, those that make the biggest impression, are served up last. Furthermore, few connectives are used so that the words that begin or end with similar sounds can be more closely juxtaposed. This is just good Asiatic rhetorical tactics. Thus what reads and translates with some difficulty

---

1. A. T. Lincoln, "Colossians," in *The New Interpreter's Bible* XI (Nashville: Abingdon, 2000), p. 619.

nonetheless "sounds" more impressive and becomes more nearly a word on target. To a significant degree, it is the failure to examine the oral as well as rhetorical dimensions of Colossians that has caused puzzlement over its style compared to other Pauline letters.

Quintilian says about rhythm and meter: "a style which flows in a continuous stream with all the full development of its force is better than one which is rough and broken. Nothing can penetrate to the emotions that stumbles at the portals of the ears. . . . Man is naturally attracted by harmonious sounds" (*Inst. Or.* 9.4.7, 10). There is an integral connection between sound and emotion. Quintilian goes on to draw an analogy to what is moving and what is grating or off-putting in music. Asiatic rhetoric attempts to move the feelings of the audience by euphony in various forms, even at the expense of connectives and sometimes other aspects of grammar. "But if there is such secret power in rhythm and melody alone, this power is found at its strongest in eloquence, and however important the selection of words for the expression of our thoughts, the structural art which welds them together in the body of a period or rounds them off at the close, has at least an equal claim to importance" (9.4.13).

Quintilian then proceeds to give some advice about effective style. He stresses that sentences should rise and grow in force, which means among other things that the more impressive and memorable words should be used later in the sentence, rounding it off (9.4.23). He also says that it is permissible for an orator to choose a word for its euphony so long as the sense is unaffected (9.4.58). He sums up his discussion of style and structure as follows: "artistic structure must be decorous, pleasing, and varied. It consists of three parts — order, connection, and rhythm. The method of its achievement lies in addition, subtraction, and alteration of words. Its practice will depend upon the nature of our theme" (9.4.147).

As then you received Christ Jesus the Lord, walk in him, being rooted and building on him and established in the faith just as you were taught, being rich in thanksgiving. Take care lest someone carries you away through philosophy and empty deceit and according to [mere] human traditions, according to the elementary principles of the world, and not according to Christ, because in him dwells all the fullness of deity bodily/in person, and you are fulfilled, you have come to fullness in him who is the head of all sovereignties and powers, in whom also you were circumcised with a circumcision made without hands, in the divesting of the body of flesh, in the circumcision of Christ, being buried together with him in baptism,[2]

---

2. The reading *baptismos* at 2.12 is to be preferred to *baptisma* since the latter is the more common term in the NT and the former would more likely be changed to the latter. *Baptismos* is well supported by P46, Aleph, B, D*, G, and numerous other witnesses. It normally refers to dipping or even ritual washing (cf. Mark 7.4; Heb. 9.10). See M. Y. MacDonald, *Colossians, Ephesians* (Collegeville: Liturgical, 2000), p. 12.

in whom you were also raised together through faith in the effective working of God who raised him from the dead; and while you were dead in trespasses and the uncircumcision of your flesh, we have been made alive together with you with him, freely forgiving us all the wrongdoing, having wiped out the signature/manuscript of decree against us, which was against us, and he himself has removed it from the midst, having nailed it to the cross, having divested himself of the sovereignties and powers, he exposed them in openness, leading them around in triumphal procession as prisoners by it.

Let no one judge you in eating and in drinking or in the subject of festivals or new moons or Sabbaths, which are shadows of the things to come, but the substance belongs to Christ. Let no one give judgment against you wishing in humility, and the worship of angels, being initiated into what he saw,[3] making one conceited in the mind of his flesh, and not seizing the head, from whom all the body through being supplied the ligaments and sinews and uniting is caused to grow the growth which is of God.

If you died with Christ from the elementary principles of the world, why then are you living as one dictated to in the world — "Do not handle," "Do not taste," "Do not touch" — things which are for the decay of wear and tear, things according to the order and teaching of humans? These are the things having the reputation of wisdom in self-chosen worship and humility and rigor of body, but are not anything of value against the gratification of the flesh.

If you then have been raised with Christ, seek the things above, where Christ is sitting at the right hand. Give your mind to the things above and not to things on the earth; for you have died and your life has been hidden with Christ in God. When Christ appears, your life will also appear with him in glory.

While there are not many textual issues with this segment of Colossians, this argument bristles with grammatical and exegetical difficulties, and in order to convey the nature of this material we have chosen not to divide up the run-on sentences or smooth out the syntax in the translation, hoping to give the reader a sense of the prolix nature of Asiatic oratory with its seemingly endless clauses and phrases and redundancy all the while striving for euphony, accumulation, amplification, and even an orderly arrangement of the overall argument.

At 2.6 Paul begins to expound on some of the elements of faith which the Colossians have already accepted, building on things already said in ch. 1. As the Colossians have received Christ,[4] so they are to walk in him, being rooted in

---

3. Some manuscripts have "not" rather than *ha*, "the," in 2.18, i.e., "things which he has not seen," but this is likely a polemical correction. *Ha* is well supported by P46, ℵ, A, B, D. See Metzger, *TC*, pp. 556-57.

4. The verb *paralambanō* should probably be seen as a technical term here referring to the reception of sacred oral tradition, especially since the very next verse uses the phrase "just

him, and building on him. This is a classic example of mixing of metaphors, for how can one walk if one is rooted or is building on an immobile foundation?[5] Yet it is quite characteristic of Asiatic rhetoric to throw a cornucopia of images and metaphors at the audience, trusting that one or the other will lodge in their brains. The Colossians are to build on what they have already learned from the Pauline teaching, not going in some new and aberrant direction. They are to re-affirm that foundation in Christ that they are grounded in and give thanks for it. In v. 7 Paul speaks of being strengthened in "the faith," referring thus to the content of what the Colossian Christians should believe.[6]

In v. 8 Paul characterizes the false teaching not only as "philosophy," which in itself would not be a problem, but as philosophy built on merely "hu-man tradition" and on what Paul calls "empty deceit." The verb *sylagōgeō* is rare, found only here in biblical Greek, and means "kidnap" or better "carry off as booty."[7] "Here then, given the fuller description that follows, the thought is of some popular rhetorician (2:4) or philosopher captivating . . . some in his audi-ence by the power of his rhetoric or the impressiveness of his claims."[8] The message that is offered is deceptive and cannot deliver what it claims. Paul's use of *tis* here suggests that the audience should look out for one particular person as a major advocate of the philosophy in question.[9] Paul is speaking into a rhe-torically and philosophically saturated environment. When someone puts those two things together and the philosophy is false, there is a grave danger to Christians who are prone to listen to such powerful persuasion and to be influ-enced by it. Paul therefore is in the awkward position of not being able to speak directly and in person to his audience, thus losing a good portion of the rhetor-ical arsenal (gestures, tone of voice, etc.). Yet still he must offer an even more powerful and philosophically substantive act of persuasion than is given by those who are beguiling the Colossians.

The philosophy is characterized as being "according to the *stoicheia tou kosmou.*" The basic options for translation of this phrase are

---

as you were taught." See G. B. Caird, *Paul's Letters from Prison* (Oxford: Oxford University Press, 1976), p. 189.

5. See N. T. Wright, *Colossians and Philemon* (Grand Rapids: Eerdmans, 1986), p. 99: "Even he must have had difficulty imagining Christians 'walking' in Christ by being well rooted like a tree, solidly built like a house, confirmed and settled like a legal document, and overflowing like a jug full of wine."

6. See R. W. Wall, *Colossians and Philemon* (Downers Grove: InterVarsity, 1993), p. 104.

7. It seems farfetched to suggest this is a pun on the word "synagogue," but see Wright, *Colossians*, p. 100.

8. J. D. G. Dunn, *The Epistles to the Colossians and to Philemon* (Grand Rapids: Eerd-mans, 1996), p. 147.

9. See Lincoln, "Colossians," p. 622.

1. the basic elements of the world/cosmos (i.e., earth, air, fire, and water),
2. the elementary teachings or principles of the world,
3. the heavenly bodies composed of the basic elements, and
4. the elementary spirits of the universe (e.g., demons, angels, and spirits).

An immediate drawback to arguing for either 3 or 4 is that there is no lexical evidence that *stoicheia* had such a meaning before or during NT times. This would have to be the first place in all of Greek literature that *stoicheia* meant "spirits" or "beings." The earliest attestation of the meaning in 3 comes in the middle of the second century, and the earliest for the meaning in 4 comes not before the third or fourth century.[10] The meaning "elements of the world/universe" has plentiful evidence before and during the NT era (e.g., Wis. 7.17-19; 19.18; 2 Pet. 3.10, 12; *4 Maccabees* 12.13).[11] There is also plenty of evidence in sources from Aristotle to the NT for *stoicheia* meaning "elementary teachings" or basic rules and principles such as the rules of geometry or logic.[12] Examples include Heb. 5.12 and probably Gal. 4.3, 9.[13] The verbal cognate in Acts 21.24 is used of regulating a life according to a specific set of rules.

We have already noted that *kosmos* seems to refer in Colossians to the world of humanity. Paul never includes *stoicheia* in lists of angelic or supernatural beings (cf. Col. 1.16 to Rom. 8.38). In this immediate context he refers to angels with the normal term *angeloi*. He refers more than once in this context to mere human tradition *(paradosis)*, which he contrasts with what has been learned of and in Christ. The most reasonable conclusion then is that *stoicheia tou kosmou* refers to some sort of rudimentary teaching that Paul opposes, and we will learn some of the content of that teaching shortly: it has to do with asceticism, food rules, Jewish calendrical observances, and "the worship of angels."

In 2.9 Paul expands on the Christ hymn making abundantly clear that God in all his fullness dwells in Christ.[14] One need look nowhere else. "He is uniquely 'God's presence and his very self.'"[15] There is considerable debate about what *sōmatikōs,* "bodily," means. The verb "dwells" is in the continual

10. See rightly, R. Longenecker, *Galatians* (Dallas: Word, 1990), p. 165.

11. See the discussion by E. Schweizer, "Slaves of the Elements and Worshipers of Angels: Gal. 4.3,9 and Col. 2.8, 18.20," *JBL* 107 (1988): 455-68.

12. See Aristotle, *Politics* 1309b16. Plato, *Laws* 7.790C uses it of a basic assumption. Xenophon speaks of elementary instructions for youth about what to eat (*Memorabilia* 2.1.1). Philo uses the term of the letters or rules in grammar as part of elementary education (*De Opificio Mundi* 126).

13. On which see my *Grace in Galatia* (Grand Rapids: Eerdmans, 1998), pp. 284-85.

14. Lincoln, "Colossians," p. 623: "the phrase 'in Him' occurs at the beginning of v. 9 and at the end of v. 15 and 'in Him' or 'in whom' is found five times in these verses." The christological focus and point is made by means of repetition.

15. Wright, *Colossians and Philemon,* p. 103.

present tense, so the clause is probably not a reference to the event of the incarnation, but it can refer to the ongoing abiding of God's full presence in Christ.[16] It might function something like *sōma* in v. 17, referring to the reality or substance of something. In Paul's view Christ still has a body, albeit a resurrected and glorified body. The point would be, then, that God dwells in the embodied Christ in fullness or in person. This would mean that there can be nothing inherently wrong or evil about matter, which the ascetic teachers may have been suggesting, hence the rules about abstinence, and that the fullness and personal presence of God is to be found in Christ and nowhere else.[17] Some light can be shed on this subject from the papyri where *sōmatikōs* is not uncommon and seems most often to mean "in person" or "in reality."[18]

Theotēs is an abstract noun meaning the divine essence or godhead, as opposed to *theiotēs* which indicates that which is god-like or divine in quality. Paul is not claiming merely that Christ is god-like. Christ is not just another supernatural being or intermediary between humans and God but God in the flesh and God in his fullness, the full representation of God. As in the Christ hymn, Paul keeps ringing the changes on the phrase "in him." This passage focuses not on the believer but on all that the believer has in Christ. This needs to be kept in mind as the passage progresses and the subject of circumcision comes up. I will argue that by "the circumcision of Christ" Paul refers to the death of Jesus, not to the spiritual death or cutting off of the believer's old nature.

In v. 10 Paul says that as Christ is full of God, so the believer is full of Christ (and need not be filled with anyone or anything else). The perfect passive participle *peplērōmenoi* ("filled") indicates an ongoing condition that began in the past. The believer has already been filled with Christ, and since Christ is where the whole fullness of God dwells, it follows that one need not and should not look elsewhere to experience God or to be filled with the divine presence.[19] Christ is the head over all supernatural powers, and so the believer owes the powers no allegiance.

In v. 11 we are told that believers have been circumcised "in him."[20] It does

16. MacDonald, *Colossians, Ephesians*, p. 98, says it means that the whole of the fullness of God dwells in Christ: "The eternal dwelling of God in Christ is in view here."

17. Caird, *Paul's Letters from Prison*, p. 191, suggests "in organic unity," i.e., not diffused throughout a hierarchy of beings, as a translation. This captures the essence of what Paul is trying to say.

18. *New Docs* 3, p. 86.

19. MacDonald, *Colossians, Ephesians*, p. 98.

20. The redundancies in v. 11 are often not evident in English translations, which reduce the text to something less convoluted and thereby remove the evidence of the deliberate Asiatic rhetorical style. Note the comment of Dunn, *Colossians*, p. 153: "The principle difficulty for both translator and exegete is that the piling up of phrases seems excessive and unnecessarily redundant and encourages them to consider renderings which reduce the redun-

not say either that "he circumcised us" or that the circumcision took place "in us." It is quite true that the believer has undergone a transformation, the death of the old self, because of the death of Jesus, but the focus here is on what has happened "in him."[21] "The putting off/stripping off of the body of flesh" also refers to Christ's death on the cross rather than to the believer's experience: it could hardly apply literally to the living Christians Paul is addressing.[22] In v. 11 Paul is not explaining what happens to the believer in baptism.[23]

In vv. 12 and 13 Paul does use the language of circumcision and baptism, the initiatory rites for two covenants, but he does so to describe the conversion experience of believers, which may or may not coincide with the water ritual itself.[24] In v. 12b the *en hō* which follows the mention of baptism should be translated "in whom" (i.e., in Christ), not "in which" (i.e., in baptism).[25] The language of being buried with Christ has to do with the spiritual death of the old self, not with immersion, not least because being buried involves earth, not water! The death of the old self and the rising of a new creature in Christ by conversion and through faith is in view here. Believers have been buried together and raised together with Christ. What happened to Christ made possible what happens to the believer, is replicated in a spiritual manner in the believer's experience, and eventually will be physically replicated when believers are raised from the dead. This all happens through faith in Christ. Believers experience the same transforming power of God that Christ did when he was raised from the dead. The Colossians were spiritually "dead in trespasses" (i.e., willful and deliberate violations of known laws), and in the uncircumcision of their fallen

---

dancy by broadening the focus of meaning. But the key to what the authors were after is probably to recognize that the redundancy is deliberate, that is, that they were using the technique precisely to focus with greater intensity on the significance of the act of redemption and reconciliation already spoken of (1:14, 20, 22)." Precisely so, and therefore many modern translations have managed to erase the particularities of the Asiatic style used in this document, a style not found in the earlier Paulines.

21. See rightly Dunn, *Colossians*, p. 158: this is "a concise description of the death of Christ under the metaphor of circumcision. It is clearly implied, of course, from the first phrase, that conversion-initiation could consequently be understood as a sharing in the circumcision, but it is precisely a sharing in *his* circumcision-death and not an independent act of Christians' own circumcision-death."

22. See rightly, Lincoln, "Colossians," p. 624, who takes this as an objective genitive. There will be a triple stripping off: of the flesh of Jesus (2:11), of the powers (2:15), and of the believer's old nature (3.9).

23. As is made clear by the careful exposition of O'Brien, countering Caird and others. P. T. O'Brien, *Colossians, Philemon* (Waco: Word, 1982), pp. 119-21; cf. Caird, *Prison Letters*, pp. 192-94.

24. See the helpful discussion by Dunn, *Baptism in the Holy Spirit* (London: SCM, 1970), passim.

25. See rightly Lincoln, "Colossians," p. 624, and Lincoln is a Baptist!

natures. The language of dying and rising with Christ is used a bit differently in Colossians than in Romans 6, or at least with a different, more present-oriented emphasis. Here resurrection, at least in part, is said to have already happened in the believer's life, whereas in Romans 6 resurrection seems to be largely a matter of a future eschatological event. However, as Lincoln points out, even in Rom. 6.4, 10-13 there is a present dimension to new life in Christ.[26]

V. 13 makes it clear that Paul takes the majority of his audience to be uncircumcised Gentiles. But unlike in Galatians, Paul makes no direct reference to the false philosophy requiring circumcision. The circumcision language is used here only in the double metaphor of the physical death of Jesus and the spiritual death of the old nature of the convert. This internal transformation of the convert in part entails the receiving of forgiveness for all wrongdoing.[27]

V. 14 says Christ's death wiped out the IOU (a record of debts owed written by the hand of the debtor; cf. Phlm. 19; *Testament of Job* 11.11) which stood against believers.[28] While *cheirograph* is used of a receipt in Tob. 5.3 and 9.5, it is not found elsewhere in the NT. Here it seems to be a reference to the heavenly book of deeds in which a record of one's wrongdoings is kept. In fact in *Apocalypse of Zephaniah* 3.6-9; 7.1-8 the same word is used for that book (cf. *Apocalypse of Paul* 17; Rev. 5.1-5; 20.12). It should be noted that while this idea sometimes involves a recording angel, the angel is not seen as a hostile power standing over against the sinner but rather as an agent and extension of the righteousness and justice of God.

God has removed or erased the record of debt (*exaleiphō* denotes the erasing of an entry in a ledger of some kind; cf. Ps. 69.28; *1 Enoch* 108.3; Rev. 3.5), thus setting it out of the midst, nailing it to the cross, like the written indictment sometimes nailed up with a crucified person (see Mark 15.26). This is of course all metaphorical and is a way of saying that believers need not keep paying a debt to those sorts of records of sin or indebtedness or to such laws and rules that say they still owe something. Jesus paid it all. Lincoln suggests that "the thought may well be then that through the death of Christ's fleshly body any indictment of the body of flesh by the heavenly powers has already been dealt with by God."[29] But Paul says nothing directly here about hostile heavenly

---

26. Lincoln, "Colossians," p. 624.

27. This may be seen as retrospective or may be all-encompassing, including even future sins. If the latter, this might explain why there is little talk in Paul of the necessity of repentance in order for the believer to receive forgiveness for current or future sins.

28. The term *cheirograph* literally refers to a handwritten document or a bond of indebtedness while *dogmata* refers to stipulations or even regulations. In Eph. 2.15 this refers to the Mosaic Law, but it is not clear it does so here. In fact it appears more likely to refer to the regulations the false philosophy was serving up (see v. 20).

29. Lincoln, "Colossians," p. 626. However, I am not at all sure that Paul is referring to hostile heavenly powers holding something against believers or other mortals. This has to be

powers accusing the Colossians. It is the false teacher or teachers that are presented as the adversary here, and the Colossians would, in any case, be indebted to God as sinners.[30] If there are angels lurking behind the scenes here, they are the recording angels in heaven, not hostile powers. In the final analysis, the believers do not owe angels anything.

V. 15 begins with the word *apekdysamenos*, which can be taken either as a middle participle or as a deponent active participle. If one takes it in the middle sense, "having stripped/divested himself," then only Christ is said to be free of "the principalities." If the active sense is intended, which is more likely, then, as O'Brien says, God "stripped the principalities and powers, who had kept us in their grip, divesting them of their dignity and might . . . leading them in Christ in his triumphal procession."[31] God is the subject, the one who nailed the decree to the cross and then stripped the powers of their dignity and might, leading them around in a ceremonial triumph as prisoners. The verb *deigmatizō* refers to a public shaming or making an example of, which would be the ultimate humiliation in an honor and shame culture.[32] Paul also uses the image of the Roman triumph in 2 Cor. 2.14-16, but there he places himself in the role of the prisoner.[33] Christ is the conquering hero leading the triumph, but as with the Roman heroes the idea is that a god operated in or through the hero to bring about victory. But these spiritual powers are, however we translate the participle, not said to be annihilated. During the procession to their death they are still alive, visible, and potentially dangerous, though they are condemned and headed for destruction. "Nevertheless, they are powerless figures unable to harm the Christian who lives under the Lordship of Christ."[34]

An interesting alternative interpretation of this difficult verse is offered by Caird, who takes the reference to principalities and powers to refer to human rulers, in particular the Romans who were responsible for crucifying Jesus. On this reading, the logic of the passage is as follows:

> Jesus was sentenced to death as a criminal by the combined action of the highest religion and the best government the world had till then known. By crucifying him who subsequently proved to be God's own Son, the powers

---

read into Colossians. It is more likely that the indictment is coming from all too earthly ascetics. Yet the next verse could support such a reading as Lincoln's.

30. See Wall, *Colossians*, p. 118.

31. O'Brien, *Colossians, Philemon*, p. 133. Needless to say this presents a very different picture from the one in popular Christian fiction such as F. Peretti's *This Present Darkness* (Wheaton: Crossway, 2003).

32. See MacDonald, *Colossians, Ephesians*, p. 104.

33. See my *Conflict and Community in Corinth* (Grand Rapids: Eerdmans, 1995), pp. 367-70.

34. O'Brien, *Colossians, Philemon*, p. 133.

showed that they had totally misrepresented God's will. In the cross therefore, which appeared to be the exercise of their authority, God in fact *disarmed* them, stripped them of their authority. In the cross he had *made a public example of them,* exposing them as usurpers who had tried to make their limited authority absolute and had succeeded only in making it demonic. In the cross he had reduced the powers to submission, like a Roman emperor celebrating his victories in the field by leading his conquered enemies in his triumphal procession.[35]

This is a very appealing argument, but nowhere else in Colossians does Paul address the relationship of his audience with human powers or authorities. When he does so in Romans 13, he says nothing about the authorities having been stripped of power or authority. Quite to the contrary he speaks of their being empowered or authorized by God. Furthermore, what would it have meant to the Colossians (who in any case were not part of a Roman colony city or under direct Roman rule), that Christ's death had disenfranchised the Roman authorities, and how would that have helped them to deal with the false religious philosophy in Colossae, which had to do with angels? On the whole then it appears Paul is talking about supernatural powers here.

Paul appears to believe that if Christ is the Lord of the believer's life there is no room for other lordships and that one should not be paying homage to other lesser supernatural beings. The theology of Colossians enunciates real problems for some forms of Christian thought that refer to demon-possessed Christians or even the demonizing of Christians. These forces, says Paul, have been publicly shamed and exposed for what they are and are being led around by the nose in a procession which will end in their destruction.

As a consequence, Paul says in v. 16, believers should let no one judge them with food rules, festivals, or Sabbath requirements.[36] Christians are not under such OT rules. Rather they are creatures of the new covenant. It is evading the point to say that Paul meant that believers no longer keep the Sabbath in the way that the false teachers were suggesting. Rather, Paul says, "let no one cause you to submit to food laws or Sabbath regulations."[37] It would appear that he believed that Christ fulfilled or brought to an end (or both) all such rules and paid the price so that believers are no longer in their debt. We owe the rules nothing. As Paul says in v. 17, these rules, while good in their day, are but

---

35. Caird, *Paul's Letters,* p. 196.

36. There are no drink regulations for Israelites in general in the Mosaic law except for Nazirites and priests ministering in the tabernacle (Lev. 10.9; Num. 6.3). Perhaps the errorists were urging a priestly duty on all who would enlist in service of an asceticism that could lead to participation in heavenly worship. After all, the Pharisees did try to apply the priestly regulations to all Jews.

37. See 1 Chron. 23.31; 2 Chron. 2.4; 31.3; Ezek. 45.17; Hos. 2.13 in the LXX.

shadows to be left behind now that the real substance that they foreshadowed has appeared — Christ.[38]

V. 18 is one of the major problem verses of this discourse. Someone was urging self-abasement and ascetical practices. The key phrase is *thrēskeia tōn angelōn*. The major issue here is whether we are dealing with an objective or a subjective genitive. *Thrēskeia* certainly means worship (cf. Acts 26.5; Jas. 1.26-27). Does then this phrase refer to worship directed to angels or done by angels?[39] Several clues in the context help to make the decision. First, the very next phrase says literally, "which he has seen upon entering." This surely refers to some sort of visionary experience.[40] Humans worshiping or placating angels would not require a visionary experience. Second, as J. Sumney has pointed out: "Since *tōn angelōn* probably modifies both humility and worship, they most likely stand in the same relationship to it. That is, since the genitive is subjective in relationship to humility, it is subjective in relationship to worship."[41]

What are we to envision here?[42] It appears that some in Colossae were

---

38. Chrysostom, *Baptismal Instructions* 3.21 offers an interesting exposition of this passage: "Christ came once and found the certificate of our ancestral indebtedness which Adam contracted. By our subsequent sins we increased the amount owed. In this contract are written a curse and a sin and death and the condemnation of the Law. Christ took all these away and pardoned them. St. Paul cries out and says, 'The decree of our sins which was against us, he has taken it completely away, nailing it to the cross.' He did not say 'erasing the decree' or 'blotting it out' but 'nailing it to the cross' so that no trace of it might remain." He adds in his sixth homily on Colossians: "At the cross death received its wound, having met its death stroke from a dead body."

39. It is interesting that later in Christian history, the Council of Laodicea prohibited angel worship in its 35th canon. What is not usually noted is that this is part and parcel of a larger warning against Christians Judaizing. The context is not a direct critique of the synagogue any more than Colossians is.

40. See Dunn, *Colossians, Philemon*, pp. 183-84, who rightly rejects the notion that the verb *embateuō* needs to be seen as some sort of technical term for entering the mystery cult. At Qumran we hear of angels entering through the doors of heaven to see and participate in heavenly worship (4Q405 14-15.i:3-10).

41. J. Sumney, "Those Who 'Pass Judgment': The Identity of the Opponents in Colossians," *Bib* 74 (1993): 366-88, here p. 377. Cf. M. J. Harris, *Colossians and Philemon* (Grand Rapids: Eerdmans, 1991), p. 121: "The non-repetition of the prep. *en* . . . before *thrēskeia* . . . points to the close conceptual link between this self-humiliation and angel-worship. It may even be a case of hendiadys, false humility expressed in angel-worship."

42. Of course there are texts where *thrēskeia* is used with the subjective genitive where human worship is referred to (as in "the worship of the Jews"; 4 *Maccabees* 5.7; Josephus, *Antiquities* 12.5.4). But the subjective genitive could of course be used with any subordinate being or creature worshiping the creator God, and in any case we clearly have descriptions of angels worshiping in early Jewish literature and in the NT even though this phrase is not used outside Col. 2.18 of such activities. Arnold overpresses the point that he has been unable to find this phrase used for angels worshiping elsewhere in the relevant literature. The issue is

touting ascetic practices which induced an ecstatic state in which one had a vision of the worshiping angels. Perhaps we are to think of a vision of angels bowing down in heaven, which practice believers were encouraged to emulate on earth and so participate in the heavenly worship (cf., e.g., 1QH 3.21-22 and especially 1QSb 4.25-26).[43] Clearly the desire for participation in the heavenly worship of angels is a prominent motif in mystical Judaism of this period (cf. *1 Enoch* 36.4; 39–40; 61.10-12; *2 Enoch* 20–21; *Testament of Levi* 3.3-8; *Apocalypse of Abraham* 17–18). Philo warns against getting carried away in this sort of mystical experience (*De Fuga et Inventione* 212; *De Somniis* 1.232, 238). Perhaps we are to think of a scene much like we find in Isa. 6.1-4 or Rev. 5.11-13.

So then some of the Colossians have claimed to enter into such an exalted heavenly worship experience, but Paul says that this is a matter of an overheated imagination, the mind of the flesh generating visions of grandeur. Thus they enter these experiences in vain. Paradoxically the errorist insisted on self-abasement but thus became "puffed up in his fleshly mind" (v. 18c). An act of humility or self-humbling became a source of pride. *Tapeinophrosynē* here seems to have a semi-technical sense for self-humbling or self-abasement consisting in fasting and similar rigors, whereas in 3.12 it will have its more general sense of humbling oneself and will be seen in a positive light. We see the term used as here in the more specific sense in Hermas, *Vision* 3.10.6; *Similitude* 5.3.7 and also in Tertullian,[44] and even without the term in question the idea of fasting in connection with visions is clearly present in texts like Dan. 10.2-9.

What they should have been doing instead of fasting is holding fast to the

---

not whether we have this precise phrase but whether the concept of angels worshiping was common and familiar, which it was, and whether this phrase could be used to describe it, and it could. But see C. E. Arnold, *The Colossian Syncretism: The Interface between Christianity and Folk Belief at Colossae* (Tübingen: Mohr, 1995). It needs to also be said that Arnold has no direct evidence from Colossae itself to support his case, that the magical papyri evidence he uses is from a later period than Colossians, that he underplays the Jewishness of what Paul is dealing with here, and that to worship angels is not necessarily the same thing as placating hostile cosmic powers. If Paul had wanted to refer to the latter he certainly could have and should have used different terms, in particular a term other than *angelos,* which elsewhere he always uses in a positive sense. The Pauline lists of principalities and powers never includes this term *angelos.*

43. For songs that congregations sing which are viewed as songs the angels are also singing as part of the heavenly liturgy see 4Q400-405. For the helpful elaboration of Francis's original thesis see C. A. Evans, "The Colossian Mystics," *Biblica* 63 (1982): 188-205; C. Rowland, "Apocalyptic Visions and the Exaltation of Christ in the Letter to the Colossians," *JSNT* 19 (1983): 78-83; and T. J. Sappington, *Revelation and Redemption at Colossae* (Sheffield: JSOT, 1991).

44. See the discussion of F. O. Francis, "Humility and Angelic Worship in Colossae," in F. O. Francis and W. A. Meeks, *Conflict at Colossae* (Missoula: Scholars, 1975), pp. 163-95, here pp. 167-68. On the cognate verb used for fasting see Ps. 35.13; Isa. 58.3, 5; LXX Judith 4.9.

head, that is, Christ (v. 19). The practices of these ascetics reflect an inadequate christology and insufficient reliance on Christ's sufficiency to meet all their spiritual needs. It is Christ who causes the body to grow the real growth of God, not some pretentious and deceptive initiatory experiences. "By not holding firmly to the head, the philosophy's advocate is in danger of being deprived of the essential connection with the true source of fullness (see v. 10). By implication, such a person is a loose ligament out of alignment with the rest of the body, and the philosophy fails to pass the key test of contribution to the growth of the whole body."[45] Paul uses the image of sinews and ligaments a little differently than we will see in Ephesians (see pp. 252-60 below). Here the point is that all believers are bound to Christ. There it will be that they are bound to each other in the body of Christ. This reflects the major theological difference between the two discourses: Colossians is christocentric, while Ephesians is ecclesiocentric.

In v. 21 Paul may be citing the actual exhortations of the errorists: "do not handle, do not taste, do not touch." The first refers to a more substantial sort of contact, and the last may well refer to sexual touching (cf. 1 Cor. 7.1).[46] This suggests that various sorts of asceticism, including sexual asceticism, were involved. Paul asks the appropriate rhetorical question (v. 20): If with Christ they have died to or from these elementary principles or rules, why should believers live as though they are run by or dictated to by such rules? V. 22 is convoluted, but the essence is that these rules are purely human and have to do with things that decay and perish, things of no lasting value. In fact, they have no value against the gratification of the flesh (v. 23), or Paul might be saying that following this sort of ascetic practices is in a strange way a form of gratifying the flesh, not the spirit. In any case, Paul says that these are voluntary matters. A Christian is not obligated to do these things. *Ethelothrēskia* is a "self-chosen pattern of worship." We thus know that Paul is talking both about worship by angels, and also by humans in Colossae, the latter being connected to the former. Paul's message to the Colossians is to stick to what they were originally taught and to ignore this new philosophy. *Apheidia sōmatos,* "severity of the body" seems to refer to physical rigors of various sorts. Paul's verdict on such ascetic practices is that far from quenching the lusts of the flesh they actually are of no value in curbing fleshly indulgences.

45. Lincoln, "Colossians," p. 633.
46. See MacDonald, *Colossians, Ephesians,* p. 116.

A Closer Look: The Colossian "Philosophy"

Were there actual opponents in Colossae, or are we only dealing with some confused Christians who have been influenced by some false philosophy or teaching? Paul does not specifically mention non-Christian opponents in this letter, and so even if such exist they are not the target of Paul's rhetoric — rather wavering Christians are. It is especially a mistake to read Colossians as though it were addressing Judaizers, as Galatians does, or Jews in general. Paul does not attack the practice of circumcision or exhort his charges not to get themselves circumcised, in contrast to what we find in Galatians. Paul's concern in Colossians is with Christians who have not grasped the christological nettle and are not holding onto the head in both faith and praxis.[47]

The methodological issues in discerning and analyzing Paul's opponents have now been appropriately addressed by both J. L. Sumney and J. M. G. Barclay,[48] and the results are that one must be very cautious in what one asserts, especially on the basis of a mirror-reading of polemical passages in Paul's letters, including Col. 2.6–3.4. We have already seen a brief list of what Barclay deems likely about the situation in Colossae on the basis of a careful critical reading of the data (see pp. 107-11 above), and to this we may add some observations from Sumney. Unlike Barclay, who urges that one must deal primarily with the polemical passage and only bring in other passages as relevant, Sumney thinks one must look at the whole of the letter and handle the polemical passage most cautiously, having more confidence in non-polemical remarks. They both agree that reconstructions that leave out the Jewish character of the false philosophy have missed the boat. Sumney believes that the criticism of the false philosophy permeates the entire letter such that, for instance, the purpose of the hymn in ch. 1 is to assure the Colossians of their place before God in Christ without need for ascetic exercises.

Sumney's summary conclusion is worth quoting:

> We have found that Col. addresses a community troubled by ascetic visionaries. Their asceticism includes food and drink regulation and the observance of certain holy days, including sabbaths and new moons. These holy days suggest that they have drawn on Judaism for some aspects of their teachings, but there is no evidence that they demand circumcision or other commandments from Judaism beyond these holy days. In their visions the opponents observe and probably par-

---

47. In an otherwise very helpful dissertation that clearly establishes the Jewishness of both Paul's argument and the Colossian philosophy, A. Bevere makes the mistake of thinking Paul is arguing with the synagogue here, an entity nowhere mentioned in this letter. But surely 2.19a can not be a reference to non-Christian Jews. See A. Bevere, *Sharing in the Inheritance: Identity and the Moral Life in Colossians* (Sheffield: Sheffield Academic, 2003).

48. In addition to Sumney's important monograph, *Identifying Paul's Opponents* (Sheffield: Sheffield Academic, 1990) and his article on the opponents in Colossae already referred to, there is also J. M. G. Barclay, "Mirror-Reading a Polemical Letter: Galatians as a Test Case," *JSNT* 31 (1987): 73-93.

ticipate in angelic humility and angelic worship. These angelic practices are the model for their ascetical regulations, and perhaps their self-imposed worship. . . . They do not seem to have venerated spiritual beings or angels. The reference to various spiritual beings are quotations of traditional material and accusations against opponents.[49]

But what is the larger context out of which such beliefs and praxis arose? This question has been addressed by various scholars in various ways over the last half century. We have mentioned some of the options (see pp. 107-11 above). Here we can only hope to point to a particular line of approach that seems the most fruitful.

The proper context to understand the nature of what Paul is both dealing with and responding to in this central argument in Colossians is apocalyptic and mystical Judaism. This has been recognized widely since the influential study of F. O. Francis.[50] Furthering this line of thinking was also the important monograph of A. T. Lincoln,[51] in which he makes the following telling points[52]:

> *Tapeinophrosynē* is used of acts of self-abasement, in particular fasting (cf. Dan. 12.4; Exod. 5.13; Hermas, *Vision* 3.10.6).
>
> Participation with angels in heavenly worship is also referred to in other early Jewish texts (cf. 2 *Enoch* 20.3, 4; 3 *Enoch* 1.12; *Testament of Job* 48.50).
>
> Lincoln urges that the *cheirograph* in Col. 2.14 should not be seen as the Mosaic Law but as the book in heaven which registers the bad deeds one has committed and is thus the heavenly register and record against a person (cf. *Apocalypse of Elijah*).
>
> The heresy being combated in Colossae is a syncretistic mixture of apocalyptic Judaism and some speculative Hellenistic ideas.
>
> The list of heavenly powers in the Christ hymn in Colossians 1 has a clear parallel in 2 *Enoch* 20–22, where in the seventh heaven there are ten classes of angels on ten steps according to rank.
>
> "He took it out of the middle" in Col. 2.14 alludes to the position of the accusing witness standing in the middle of the courtroom. In short, Christ's death removed the accusing witness.
>
> The difference between Paul's advice to seek the things above and that of the false teachers is that Paul starts from the top down, the false teachers from the bottom up. That is, they seek to reach heavenly-mindedness by

49. Sumney, "Those Who 'Pass Judgment,'" p. 386.

50. Francis, "Humility and Angelic Worship"; idem, "The Background of EMBATEU-EIN (Col. 2:18) in Legal Papyri and Oracle Inscriptions," in F. O. Francis and W. A. Meeks, *Conflict at Colossae* (Missoula: Scholars, 1975), pp. 197-207.

51. *Paradise Now and Not Yet* (Cambridge: Cambridge University Press, 1981), pp. 110-34.

52. I find his reflections in this work more persuasive than his later views in his Colossians commentary, where he sides with those who think that veneration of angelic beings, and even placating of hostile cosmic powers, is in view in this passage.

ascetic exercises and visions, whereas Paul is talking about Christ reaching down and revealing himself to believers. Paul sees this wisdom as a free gift of God's grace, not a result of "self-chosen worship" patterns. Also, the false teachers see participating in angelic worship, rather than focusing on and holding onto Christ, as the goal. "The advocates of the philosophy take the earthly situation as their starting point from which by their own efforts and techniques they will ascend into the heavenlies. Paul moves in the reverse direction, since he sees the starting-point and source of the believer's life in the resurrected Christ in heaven, from where it works itself out into earthly life (3:5ff.) and from where it will eventually be revealed for what it is (3:4)."[53] Life, power, and spiritual vitality flow from the heavenly Christ into his body and cannot be grasped by human efforts.

Paul believes in the apocalyptic idea of future salvation being already present in heaven now. This is why he speaks of our life being hidden in Christ, or as Christ simply waiting to be revealed. If Christ is above and the believer's life is bound up with Christ, then necessarily that life is hidden until Christ returns, and believers will receive it in full only then. There are no shortcuts to this perfecting or completing of the human spiritual pilgrimage.

The heavenly life that flows into Christ's body structures that body and effects social relationships not only in worship structure but also in family structure and relationships among Christians. The revision of the household codes flows out of union with Christ and the understanding that all are one and are of equal value. Heavenly-mindedness is not an escape from worldly concerns but rather provides the basis for structuring human relations and proceeding in human affairs. It involves pursuing a certain form of heavenly behavior on earth. The reality in heaven enables the ethic on earth to be transformed.

The line that has been pursued by Francis, Lincoln, and others has now been fleshed out even more by T. J. Sappington. He confirms that Paul is dealing with the ascetic-mystical piety of Jewish apocalypticism. The particular strength of Sappington's work is to show that the direct descriptions of the error in Col. 2.16-23 suggest that the issue is not just participation in heavenly worship through visions but that the errorists are seeking information, revelation from above, wisdom from the heavenly realm. Paul then is undermining their insistence on the need for visionary ascent to receive such revelation and the felt need to participate in angelic worship in order to draw closer to God. "It is 'in Christ,' Paul argues, that 'all the treasures of wisdom and knowledge' are hidden; and since believers at Colossae are 'in him,' they can know 'the full riches of complete understanding' apart from ascetic-mystical practices and experiences."[54] In

---

53. Lincoln, *Paradise Now and Not Yet*, p. 127.
54. *Revelation and Redemption at Colossae*, p. 224.

other words, Sappington has put his finger on the cognitive side of the issue with the errorists and how Paul has combated that.

There is more, because Sappington has also shown that one should not misread the realized eschatology in Colossians. This emphasis is largely due to the rhetorical attempt to counter the errorists and show that believers already to a significant degree have now in Christ what they are looking for in the ascetic practices and experiences. Thus they need not go in a new direction to obtain such things. Nor should the references to future eschatology be underplayed. The "not yet appears several times in Colossians and its significance should not be minimized. There is simply no reason to believe that Paul would have taken over traditional eschatological formulae if they did not authentically reflect his own thoughts. And so 3:4, 24 are important for understanding the teaching of the Colossian letter."[55] In fact, on the basis of his analysis of 1.12-14, 22, 28; 2.13-15 Sappington argues that the future eschatological judgment is a central issue in this letter. Paul refers to eventually presenting everyone perfect in Christ at the last judgment (1.22). The Colossians are told that they are qualified in Christ to share in the inheritance of the saints in the kingdom but will not share in that inheritance fully until later (1.12). "Yet they must wait to receive their inheritance at the revelation of their glory, when their participation in Christ's victory over the powers is realized."[56] This is an important corrective to assertions by some who have overly dramatized the differences between the eschatological teaching in Colossians and that found in the earlier Paulines and have used this as a reason to deny that Colossians was written by Paul. One is not surprised in a piece of deliberative rhetoric to find some emphasis on future eschatology, even though the errors in Colossae called for more emphasis on what was already true for the believer in Christ. Though no school of interpretation of the Colossian error is without weaknesses, it seems clear that the one that does the best job of explaining the data we find in Colossians and the historical and social context of that church is the line of approach which sees the error arising out of ascetic and mystical Jewish apocalyptic thought and practice adapted for Christian use.[57]

3.1-4 provides the conclusion of the argument found in ch. 2. Paul urges the Colossians to set their sights higher, so to speak, above and beyond angels to the one who is seated on the throne, namely Christ.[58] V. 1 indicates that if the

55. *Revelation and Redemption at Colossae*, pp. 226-227.
56. *Revelation and Redemption at Colossae*, p. 228.
57. For a very helpful critique of T. Martin, C. Arnold, and R. DeMaris, who have tried to locate the Colossian philosophy primarily in non-Jewish or syncretistic material see Bevere, *Sharing in the Inheritance*, pp. 30-46.
58. See Lincoln, "Colossians," p. 638, who recognizes Paul's top-down argument as opposed to the errorists' bottom-up argument, reaching up into the heavenlies by ascetic practices leading to mystical or visionary ascent. Chrysostom, *Baptismal Instructions* 7.20, as so

Colossians have had their lives changed by Christ they must seek the things above, where Christ is. Christians have something of an otherworldly focus because they have an otherworldly source of life, power, and instruction and look to heaven, from which will come the final solution to the human dilemma. V. 3b alludes to Ps. 110.1 and Christ's position of power and honor at the right hand of the Father, a role he assumed after his resurrection (cf. Rom. 8.34; 1 Cor. 15.25). The Colossians are to give their minds to "the above," not to the all-too-human self-help schemes the ascetics are offering. The Colossians' lives are no longer those of the persons they used to be, who have died, but now their lives are hidden in Christ. Paul may use "hidden" here because it was used by the ascetics for the secrets they were claiming one could gain by the visionary experience of angelic worship. Paul's response is No, that all that wisdom and life and power are to be found hidden in Christ specifically, not just in heaven in general or in any other being or beings in heaven. The key is Christ and one's relationship with him. V. 4 clearly has in mind the conclusion of salvation history when believers will be made like Christ, having a similar glorious resurrection body when he returns, but not before. When he appears/returns/is revealed, then believers will be made like him (cf. 2 Thess. 1.7, 10).[59] Then the full installment of new life, even bodily life, will be received.[60]

A Closer Look: The Theological Substance of Colossians

Here at the end of the "theological" portion of Colossians is a good place to assess the contribution of this discourse to Paul's theological thought-world. To some extent of course, whether one sees Colossians as Pauline or not will to some degree determine how one assesses its theology. One can either emphasize how the thought here differs from the earlier Paulines, or emphasize the similarities and minimize the differences.[61] By and large, those who are apt to see the problem in Colossae as basically

---

often says it best: "He cuts a path through the midst of all the angels, archangels, thrones, dominions, principalities, virtues, all those invisible powers, the cherubim and seraphim and sets the thoughts of the faithful right before the very throne of the king."

59. On the eschatological nature and orientation of Col. 3.1-4 see Bevere, *Sharing the Inheritance*, pp. 148-81.

60. While this is the only direct reference to the parousia in this discourse, we have already seen various references to final judgment. See pp. 165-67 above.

61. Notice the comment of J. M. G. Barclay, *Colossians and Philemon* (Sheffield: Sheffield Academic, 1997), pp. 75-76: "When Colossians is dubbed 'deutero-Pauline' that label typically signifies an assessment that the letter is secondary not only in chronology but also in significance. Thus the tendency of scholars to emphasize contrasts between Colossians and the 'assured' Pauline letters nearly always directs attention away from Colossians to earlier, more pristine documents, which are generally treated as of greater theological weight. Correspond-

Jewish in character are more apt to favor Pauline authorship of the letter (e.g., Wright, O'Brien, Caird, Harris, Dunn, and Wall). Those who are apt to see the problem as far more Hellenistic or syncretistic or even proto-Gnostic are more apt to opt for a post-Pauline situation and author (e.g., Lohse, MacDonald, and Lincoln).

Colossians is a situation-specific discourse and thus its author does theology out of and as part of the attempt to address the philosophy that is warned against in 2.6–3.4. Yet "it is not clear that the letter is to be regarded as *wholly* absorbed by the counter-ideology; the 'direction' of its thought should not be reduced to its possible contextual motives."[62] It is important not to get so focused on what the author is opposing that we fail to ask what he is supporting and affirming. It is also well to keep in mind that strictly speaking letters do not have theologies any more than they have philosophies or political agendas.[63] The people who write such documents have theologies or other sorts of ideologies. It is therefore inappropriate to talk in a narrow way about the theology of Colossians, but we can talk about the theologizing that is being done in Colossians and what it contributes to our understanding of Paul's thought-world.

The christological hymn in Colossians 1, which has received the most theological comment of all the material in this discourse, sets up the terms of the discussion in the rest of the discourse, including the discussion of the errorists' philosophy. Paul enunciates a clear christocentric (though not christomonistic) message immediately after the exordium that undergirds all that is said both theologically and ethically in the remainder of the discourse. "In the theology of Colossians, christology is central and everything else flows from the belief that Christ is the key to understanding of reality."[64] While it is a cliché it is nonetheless true that the major theological difference in emphasis between Colossians and Ephesians is that Ephesians is far more ecclesiocentric and Colossians more christocentric.[65] In Colossians we see Paul theologizing into a particular situation, not some sort of preformed theology. Theology is the abstraction and compilation of later scholars based on the theologizing that Paul has done. This is one reason why different scholars read the theological emphases of this letter differently. How one assembles and evaluates the pieces affects the as-

---

ingly, discussions of 'Pauline theology' (a common theme) typically leave Colossians out of account."

62. Barclay, *Colossians and Philemon*, p. 76.

63. The attempt to analyze discrete theologies on a letter-by-letter basis by the Society of Biblical Literature Seminar on Pauline Theology in the 1980s and 90s was methodologically flawed to start with, but nevertheless led to some interesting and insightful discussions of the Hauptbriefe. Of some interest for this commentary are the introductory essays and the discussion of Philemon in *Pauline Theology* I: *Thessalonians, Philippians, Galatians, Philemon*, ed. J. Bassler (Minneapolis: Fortress, 1991). Unfortunately Colossians was not really discussed since its authorship was debated, nor was Ephesians for the same reason.

64. Lincoln, "Colossians," p. 569.

65. As is often noted, so christocentric is this document that there is only scant mention of the Holy Spirit (but see 1.8-9; 3.16).

sessment of the whole. Lincoln, however, is surely right when he says "Perhaps what makes Colossians distinctive is its combination of a wisdom theology with a polemical theology of grace. Both elements are a result of the confrontation with the rival philosophy."[66]

Very few scholars would deny the christocentric focus of Colossians,[67] but there are those, like Dunn, who precisely because of his views of Paul's theology and still wishing to maintain a strong connection between this letter and Paul, proceeds to deny that there is, for example, a preexistence christology in Colossians 1 or elsewhere in the letter. One suspects that Dunn thinks that had Paul affirmed such a thing it would have been a violation of the way he, Paul, viewed Jewish monotheism. Dunn does not want to talk about a full-scale "parting of the ways" with early Judaism in the person and writings of Paul when it comes to christology. But this must be called special pleading in regard to Colossians (or even 1 Cor. 8.6 or Rom. 9.5). As Lincoln says, "The claim is not that it is some rational principle or even personified Wisdom that holds the key to the created universe but that it is the *person* believers confess as Christ who does so."[68] Just so. A person is in mind, the one who is the chosen agent for the work of creation just as he is the chosen agent for the work of redemption and reconciliation. In other words, we are dealing in Paul with the christological reformulation of Jewish monotheism.[69] The thinking about Christ we find in Colossians has a precedent already in 1 Cor. 8.6 and Rom. 9.5, and we see it also well developed in the Christ hymn in Philippians 2. So far as assessing Paul's theology, it does not really much matter whether the Christ hymn in Colossians 1 has been adapted from a source or not, for Paul endorses what he has adopted and adapted and has made the material his own.[70]

This brings us to the remark in Col. 2.9. There is a reason Paul uses the term "godhead" *(theotēs),* rather than just "god-likeness" *(theiotēs).* He believes that Christ is not just one among many supernatural creatures like the angels. He believes that in Christ and Christ alone dwells the fullness of the godhead. This is most certainly a claim that Christ is himself divine, not merely that the divine presence dwells in Christ. Indeed, Paul is busily de-divinizing the angels while stressing the divinity of Christ in this discourse. In fact, Paul is claiming that the deity of God dwells exclusively in Christ and in no other person who ever had a human nature (notice the term

---

66. Lincoln, "Colossians," p. 575. This is why abstracting the theology from its exegetical and social and historical contexts is always a dangerous enterprise, because the potential for distortion of the thrust of what is being said is great.

67. See Barclay, *Colossians and Philemon,* p. 77: "The theology of Colossians is at every point christological, and it is the success of the author in disclosing Christ as the centre of all reality that integrates and energizes the letter."

68. Lincoln, p. 570, emphasis added.

69. See the careful discussion of the theology of Colossians by A. J. M. Wedderburn in *The Theology of the Later Pauline Letters* (Cambridge: Cambridge University Press, 1993), pp. 23-57, pp. 27-28 for a critique of Dunn's approach to the Christ hymn.

70. See the discussion in Barclay, *Colossians and Philemon,* pp. 59-68.

"bodily") and indeed in no other creature. This may also be a salvo against emperors who claimed to be gods in embodied form walking the earth.

Christ, as God's Wisdom before creation, God come in the flesh, the Messiah on the cross, risen from the dead, ascended to the right hand of the Father, and coming again in glory is seen as the center of all things, not merely in the church but also in the cosmos,[71] and it is the great merit of Paul's presentation in Colossians that he is able to show how Christ is related to a whole series of other theological matters so that Christ is presented as the key to the universe or, to put it another way, the now revealed secret of all reality.[72] It is no accident, for instance, that only in this letter do we hear about the kingdom of God's Son, which believers have already been transferred into (1.13-14).[73] Christ is the one through whom and by whose death the powers and principalities have already been put in their place. Christ is the one who indwells his community and thereby provides for believers the hope of glory, which turns out in the end to mean that they will eventually be made perfectly Christlike. Christ is the only redeemer believers need because by his death he deals not only with external sources of human problems (the powers and principalities) but also with internal sources as well (sin, trespasses, the need for forgiveness).

Peace has been made between God and humankind by the blood of the cross. Not only so, but the debt owed to God, the record of wrongdoing, has been expunged by the death of Christ. Believers are new creatures in Christ, as he has wrought a profound inward change in their lives (3.10). It is here in Colossians that we learn explicitly that Christ is the head of the body which is the church. Christ is Lord over the believer's life, and so believers are accountable to him and he is owed complete allegiance (cf. 1.10; 2.6; 3.17). So much is Christ Lord that even the OT phrase "fearing the Lord" refers to Jesus rather than Yahweh (3.22). The point of all this is that protology, eschatology, ecclesiology, soteriology, demonology, and anthropology, not to mention discipleship and family relationships, are all interpreted through a christological lens or related to Christ in some way in this letter. Christ is preeminent over all in the realm of creation and likewise "first" in the eschatological order of

71. Commentators have long suspected that the original Christ hymn had the cosmos as the body of Christ and the redemption of the cosmos as the focus, which Paul has narrowed down to the church as the body of Christ and redemption as the reconciliation of human beings. See Wedderburn, *Theology of the Later Paulines,* pp. 41-42. This is possible, but Paul himself does seem to be concerned about the reconciliation of all creation in and through Christ (cf. Romans 8 to Col. 1.20). I agree with Wedderburn that it is unlikely that the hymn originally just focused on angels, for this might be closer to the theology of the errorists than of Paul.

72. Barclay, *Colossians and Philemon,* p. 79.

73. The Father certainly does play an important role in this letter. Christ still has a Father (1.3) and remains the Son even though he partakes of the godhead (1.13) and is in fact the image of God (1.15), perhaps alluding to the notion that Christ is the eschatological Adam who went the right path. It is also God the Father who is at work in the cross stripping the powers and principalities.

those to be raised from the dead. So much is the believers' future bound up with Christ that their hopes are said to be located in heaven (3.1-4) because that is where Christ currently is. In fact, the believer's life is said to *be* Christ (3.4).

It is therefore no surprise, since Christ can do it all for everyone, that there is a universalistic thrust to the letter. The message about Christ has been, is being, and should be taken to all. It is a "one for all, and all for one" kind of theology. It is bearing fruit and growing in the entire world (1.5-6), and we even hear the astounding claim that it has been or is being preached to every creature in the world (1.23). The intended goal is to present everyone perfect in Christ (1.28). This reflects a remarkable confidence in the gospel and in the way it has and will spread throughout the empire, and indeed the world.[74] In 3.11 the formula of who is in Christ extends beyond the Jew-Gentile tandem to include even those regarded as the least civilized — Scythians and barbarians. "It is not merely that all these classes of people are 'one in Christ' (Gal. 3:28) . . . rather, Col. 3:11 makes the far broader claim that 'Christ is all and in all.'"[75]

The one hope for the unity of humankind is Christ. Potential universalism is offered through unrelenting exclusive christological particularism and with confidence and trust that "he who has begun a good work within you can bring it to conclusion," to borrow a phrase. Whatever else one can say, this letter makes emphatically clear that it is not God's intent to save only some. The divine plan of salvation is not just offered to all but is intended for the benefit of all. Does this then mean that Paul believes all will be saved? Certainly he believes that all need to be saved and can be saved, and even that all can be saved to the uttermost, to the point of what he calls perfection. But he stops short of saying all will definitely be saved, precisely because he has not given up his strong stress on the need for the persuasion and grace of the gospel to be allowed to work (1.5-6), on the need for humans to respond freely in faith to the christological message, and on the undoubted need for conversion.[76] Nor has he given up calling the world the "realm of darkness" out of which the Christian minority has been transferred by faith in Christ. Nonetheless, there is no mistaking the optimism about the message about Christ and grace and about its remarkable continued success throughout the world.[77] One key reason for this optimism is the enunciated truths about the cosmic Christ: the major barriers and opposition to reconciliation and unity have been overcome by Christ's death, including the overcoming of the powers and principalities.

---

74. See Barclay, *Colossians and Philemon*, p. 78.

75. Barclay, *Colossians and Philemon*, p. 79.

76. See Lincoln, "Colossians," p. 576: "Colossians does not make grace a separate theme so much as an underlying presupposition that it reinforces through both the content and the mode of its theologizing."

77. Barclay, *Colossians and Philemon*, pp. 92-93. The particularism Barclay refers to is not the exclusivity of salvation in Christ but rather the particularism of the process of salvation involving conversion and initiation.

The kerygma of the crucified and risen Messiah meant nothing less than the renewal of creation. Not merely in theological statements, but in ritual, community organization, and ethos the Pauline school labored to manifest that sense of the New. Yet the new world and the New Human must needs have a place to stand, for the old world still exists. The sectarian consciousness encapsulates the secret of the new, bearing the exhilarating secret of the new world as a growing foetus in the womb of the tiny body corporate. It could go the way of other fantastic utopian sects. But for Paul and his companions it could not be so, for as "God is one" he is the God of all persons. Hence for Paul the world was always at issue,[78]

and Christ was always the answer to the question of the travail of the cosmos and creation, to the human dilemma, to the human future, to the unity of the world, and finally to the glorification of all those who are in Christ.

If we were to choose one word that Paul might have used to sum up this breathtaking theologizing in this letter, it would have to be wisdom.

> Christ embodies wisdom; Paul supremely, but also all other believers are recipients and then teachers of wisdom; and Christian living is walking in wisdom. The wisdom christology of the hymn leads to the cosmic and universal dimensions of the letter's theology. These in turn color the depiction of believers' relation to the exalted Christ. United to this Christ, they have a genuine heavenly orientation that works itself out in their lives on earth.[79]

It is certainly possible to imagine an immobile Paul, toward the end of his life, with time on his hands, reflecting in this sort of grand way about what had already been accomplished with the message of the gospel and the work of Christ around the Mediterranean crescent and even in the Eternal City. There had been steady, indeed remarkable, growth and spread of the Christian message and community for some three decades with no sign of abating. It is more difficult to imagine Paul looking back in this sort of comprehensive way and making such all-inclusive claims about the gospel and Christ at an earlier period in the 50s while in jail in Ephesus. But whenever Paul wrote this document he reached the apex of his reflections on Christ, and all of us should be grateful that this discourse was preserved.

---

78. W. A. Meeks, "In One Body: The Unity of Humankind in Colossians and Ephesians," in *God's Christ and His People,* ed. J. Jervell and W. A. Meeks (Oslo: Universitetforlaget, 1977), pp. 209-17, here p. 216.

79. Lincoln, "Colossians," p. 576.

Probatio — Argument Three —
The Necessity Of Virtue — 3.5–4.1

For his third and final argument in this discourse, Paul not surprisingly turns to the ethical implications that arise out of the theology he has enunciated thus far in the discourse. Since the problem in Colossae had as much to do with praxis as belief, it is no surprise that Paul brings his arguments to a climax by dealing with the question of how the Colossians should live, having just argued that the ascetic lifestyle is not required. Paul wishes to make clear, among other things, that by rejecting asceticism he is not thereby endorsing a lax sexual ethic. "The focus in Col. 3:11 [and elsewhere in this argument] is on unifying the community, dispelling claims of special status, and recommending a way of life that allows each member to walk (cf. 3:7) as a new self in the world."[1] This sort of unifying rhetoric that not only argues for unity but argues against boundary markers and rituals that divide the community is clearly deliberative in character.

The Greek rhetoricians had a term for the hortatory or ethical section of a discourse — *parainetikon,* from which we get the word parenesis (see *Inst. Or.* 9.2.103). Parenesis was considered appropriate in a deliberative discourse since the goal of such a discourse was to persuade an audience to do that which is of benefit or useful or fitting. Exhortations most often belong to deliberative rhetoric, though sometimes one finds them in epideictic rhetoric as well. "One delivering an exhortation must prove that the courses to which he exhorts are just, lawful, expedient, honorable, pleasant and easily practicable. . . . One dissuading must apply hindrance by the opposite means: he must show that the action is not just, not lawful, not expedient" (*Rhetorica ad Alexandrum* 1421b.23ff.). One may divide this section into a discussion of vices and virtues in general using the language of putting off and putting on (3.5-17) and words on

1. M. Y. MacDonald, *Colossians, Ephesians* (Collegeville: Liturgical, 2000), p. 148.

the specific issue of behavior in the Christian household (3.18–4.1). The first discussion undergirds the second.

Vice and Virtue Lists — 3:5-17

Put to death therefore the members, the things upon the earth, sexual immorality, impurity, passion, evil desire, and the selfish greed which is idolatry, because of which the wrath of God is coming,[2] in which you also walked then when you lived in them. But now you have put off all these things — anger, rage, malice, slander, obscenity from your mouths. Do not lie to one another, having stripped off the old self with its deeds, and put on the new person, which is being renewed in knowledge according to the image of the one who created him, where there is not any Greek and Jew, circumcised and uncircumcised, barbarian, Scythian, free, but Christ is all and in all.

Put on then as the elect of God, holy and beloved, deep feelings of compassion, goodness, humility, gentleness, patience, putting up with one another and forgiving each other if anyone has cause for blaming about something, just as the Lord forgave you. Thus also you [must do]. But above all this love, which is the bond of perfection; and the peace of Christ rule in your hearts, to which also you were called in one body, and show yourselves thankful. May the word of Christ dwell in you richly, in all wisdom, teaching and admonishing each other [in] songs of praise, hymns, spiritual songs by grace singing in your hearts to God, and all whatever you may do in word or deed, all in the name of the Lord Jesus, give thanks to God the Father through/because of him.

This argument begins with an exhortation to kill self-centeredness (mortify "the flesh"),[3] which is to be contrasted with the following exhortation in v. 12 about putting something on.[4] There is also some rhetorically effective symmetry in-

---

2. Here at v. 6 many early manuscripts with good geographical spread have the additional phrase "upon the sons of disobedience." This may well be original, but then again it may well be an insertion based on Eph. 5.6. If it is an insertion, it is an early one. It is hard to explain why P46, B, and various other manuscripts and church fathers omit the phrase if it was original. See Metzger, *TC*, p. 557. Ephesians eclipsed Colossians in popularity. From this juncture on to the end of the letter there is more overlap between the two documents than before. Therefore, it is quite believable that the textual tradition for Colossians was influenced by that of Ephesians. See for example Col. 3.21, which is influenced by the textual tradition at Eph. 6.4 in various manuscripts. Metzger *TC*, p. 558.

3. See C. F. D. Moule, *The Epistles to the Colossians and Philemon* (Cambridge: Cambridge University Press, 1968), p. 115.

4. The force of these imperatives, which Paul does expect to be obeyed, should not be

volved: five vices will be mentioned (cf. Rom. 1.24-26, 29-31; Eph. 4.31; 5.3-5; 6.14-17) and in v. 12 five virtues. The behavior of believers is to be different from the standard behavior they exhibited before they became followers of Christ.

"The members" and "the things upon the earth" are difficult phrases, presumably two ways of referring to the earthly passions that sometimes dwell in our bodies. If so, then Paul has begun his third and final argument in good Asiatic fashion with another redundancy, both phrases indicating the habit of using one's limbs for earthly or sinful purposes.[5] It is implicitly assumed here that it is possible by God's grace to shed these deeds and desires.

The first four examples of inglorious behavior in v. 5 are all sexual — *porneia* can refer to a specific kind of sexual sin (incest or intercourse with a prostitute: a *pornē* was a prostitute), but can also be used as an omnibus term for all sorts of sexual misbehavior. "Impurity" "highlights the contamination of character effected by immoral behavior."[6] *Pathos* here means "passion" (i.e., lust; cf. 1 Thess. 4.3-5). Both improper sexual desire and sexual deeds are to be renounced, or, as Paul says here, "put off." Throughout this section Paul uses the language of putting off and putting on, perhaps drawing from the early Christian baptismal ceremony, where one would put off one's clothes, be baptized, and then put on a new robe as a symbol of new life in Christ.

---

blunted by comments like "his point is not to prescribe a code of conduct which must be obeyed if one is to be fully Christian. This would oppose Paul's core ethical conviction: that the Spirit of the Risen Christ has replaced 'written codes' in the new dispensation of God's salvation" (R. W. Wall, *Colossians and Philemon* [Downers Grove: InterVarsity, 1993], p. 139). It is clear enough that Paul is not simply describing the effect of God's work in the believer's life here. He is describing how believers must behave if they are to mirror the character of Christ. As early as Galatians it is clear that Paul does not have a problem with prescribing codes of conduct and expecting them to be obeyed. Indeed, he calls the Christian code the law of Christ (see my *Grace in Galatia* [Grand Rapids: Eerdmans, 1998], pp. 341-56). 2 Corinthians 3 is not about the replacement of all written codes with only pneumatic guidance. It is about the replacement of the Mosaic code and covenant in particular with a situation where one is guided by both Word and indwelling Spirit, not just the latter. The commandments of God do not become in Paul's hands suggestions, or even descriptions of divine actions in the believer.

5. It is interesting that when a classicist analyzed Paul she came to the conclusion that none of his letters really reflect the Attic style, and that leaves a choice between Koine and the Asiatic style of writing Greek. She urges "Paul was no Athenian. In terms of literary criticism of his day he would surely have been regarded as an *Asianus,* and not only for his disinclination to eliminate non-Attic elements from his diction." J. Fairweather, "The Epistle to the Galatians and Classical Rhetoric Part 3," *Tyndale Bulletin* 45 (1994): 213-43, here p. 229. While Galatians might well because of its emotional character be seen by some as like Asiatic rhetoric, the letters we are examining would have been more evidently of this ilk because of both their formal elements and grammar and their emotional character.

6. N. T. Wright, *Colossians and Philemon* (Grand Rapids: Eerdmans, 1986), p. 134.

The last vice listed in this verse is "selfish greed," covetousness, acquisitiveness which is idolatry (see Eph. 5.5). The root sin of all sins is ultimately self-centeredness and selfishness, and greed is one of the more obvious forms of this orientation in life. Self-centeredness is called idolatry in early Jewish and Christian contexts because it amounts to a form of self-worship, as opposed to giving God his due. *Testament of Judah* 19.1 says that greed seizes hold of persons and leads them away from God, holding them captive in idolatry (cf. Wis. 14.12). But it is appropriate to ask: What sort of Christian person would need an exhortation against greed? With that, what sort of Christian would need an exhortation about slave management? The answer must be certain relatively high status Christians in Colossae. The "exhortation against greed will have had an important role in reminding well-to-do leaders of their primary allegiance to the church, especially when business concerns would have tempted them to form close associations with outsiders."[7]

In general, Paul is trying to construct strict moral boundaries around the community while rejecting ethnic, social, and gender barriers as ways of defining the community. What is noticeably missing is any strong stress in this letter on ritual boundaries (i.e., circumcision or baptism). Paul does not argue against circumcision in any sort of direct way here, unlike in Galatians. Nor does he spend time constructing a theology or ethic of baptism. He concentrates, rather, on the realities of which circumcision and baptism are only signs or metaphors, both in the life and death of Christ and in the life of his followers. Paul is opposing a certain kind of ritualism and asceticism in the Christian community, not endorsing it. His ethic is generated out of his beliefs about Christ and how Christ transforms human lives, not out of his beliefs about the potency of rituals like baptism.

Paul adopts and adapts various early Jewish and OT vice and virtue lists and uses them for his own purposes, most often to stress the contrast between what the believer once was and ought not to be now and vice versa. It does not follow from this that these lists are meaningless and inapplicable to the Colossians, for Paul says that they as pagans had also indulged in such behavior (v. 7), though perhaps not every one of the vices listed was characteristic of them. The point is that he does not want them to slip back into the pattern of their old lives. To "walk" in Paul refers to a course of conduct pursued by someone, whereas to "live" is something more fundamental, a settled disposition or way of life. So to talk about the life one once lived is to take things a step beyond "the way you used to walk" (cf. Gal. 5.25).[8] Paul is speaking as though he is addressing Gentiles mainly, if not almost exclusively so.

7. H. O. Maier, "Purity and Danger in Polycarp's Epistle to the Philippians: The Sin of Valens in a Social Perspective," *Journal for Early Christian Studies* 1 (1993): 229-37, here p. 234.

8. See Wright, *Colossians and Philemon*, p. 136

A further list of related vices that are also to be put off appears in v. 8[9]: anger, outburst of temper, malice, slanderous speech, and obscenity.[10] These seem to be grouped together as sins of speech, for the list ends with *ek tou stomatos hymōn* ("which come out from your gut"). Words "do not merely convey information or let off steam. They change situations and relationships often irrevocably. They can wound as well as heal."[11] The danger is not so much that a member of the listening audience might become that old self again but that one might sometimes act or have attitudes like the old self. Clearly, Paul thinks the hearer has a choice about this matter, precisely because he is no longer that old person captive in the bondage of sin. He or she is a new person who, still, paradoxically is being renewed[12] according to the image[13] of the one who created him or her. It is possible even that the term "creator" here refers to Christ in light of ch. 1 (cf. Rom. 8.26-27), but perhaps more likely we have an allusion to Gen. 1.27 here. The Christian is not viewed as both the old and new person simultaneously but as solely the new person, though he or she may sometimes act and feel like the old person he or she once was.

In the creator's mind there is no Greek or Jew (an amazing claim since Paul still thinks there are some special benefits to being a Jew). Circumcision or the lack thereof does not matter in Christ, nor does one's social status, whether slave or free. Even if one is a non-Greek-speaking person (the meaning of *barbaros*) or a Scythian (tribes from around the Black Sea that were considered particularly rustic, barbaric, and crude),[14] it does not detract from one's status,

---

9. On this metaphor used in tandem with the phrase "putting on" see Rom. 13.12.

10. Chrysostom stresses in his eighth homily on Colossians that "moral choice rather than human nature is the determining factor and rather constitutes 'the human condition' than the natural determinants. . . . If then our real essence as human beings is the body, which in any case cannot be accountable, how can one say the body is evil? But what does Paul say? 'With your doings.' He means freedom of choice, with its accompanying acts."

11. Wright, *Colossians and Philemon*, p. 137.

12. A present passive participle indicating God's ongoing action in the believer's life. This is not a one-time experience or even repeated sanctifying experiences, but rather an ongoing progressive process of sanctification and inward renewal.

13. See G. B. Caird, *Paul's Letters from Prison* (Oxford: Oxford University Press, 1976), p. 206: "This is not to say that the Christian, recreated in baptism, is thereafter in constant need of repair, though there may be some truth even in that. It is rather that his transformation is a gradual change 'from one degree of glory to another' (2 Cor. 3:18; cf. 4:16). Moreover, although every man must himself take the active and deliberate step of putting on *the new nature*, it is not the product of his own moral effort, but the creative handiwork of God." It is interesting that Pyrrho said that his aim is *ekdynai ton anthrōpon*, to strip off his human nature, which parallels to some degree Col. 3.9 and Eph. 4.22, which speaks of stripping off the old human nature. See *New Docs* 4, p. 176.

14. Indeed, they were even considered wild men (cf. Aeschylus *Prometheus Vinctus* 2; Aristophanes, *Acharnenses* 704; Josephus, *Contra Apionem* 2.37; Herodotus 4.1-117). After the

standing, or honor rating in Christ (Paul is perhaps quoting a formula he has modified a bit). In Christ, whoever one is, one is a new person, because Christ is all and is in all these different kinds of people. "Christ is the measure by which everything is to be defined."[15] Therefore we are to see Christ in all these different sorts of people regardless of race, class, ethnic extraction, social status, or gender (according to Gal. 3.28).

As becomes clear from 1 Corinthians 9 and Romans 9–11, Paul does not mean that these distinctions and differences cease to exist when one becomes a Christian. Greeks are still Greeks and Jews are still Jews, of course. He means at the very least that these distinctions no longer determine who is among God's people. These distinctions no longer have any soteriological weight. And since such distinctions have been radically relativized in Christ, they should not be the basis of any sort of hierarchy or pecking order in the church. What matters is that all are equally new persons in Christ and equally in the process of being renewed. There is then a spiritual basis for real equality in Christ. The basis of any kind of ordering in the church is according to what one is called and gifted to do, a rather bold break from the way things tended to be determined in the pagan world, and also to a larger degree in the Jewish world.[16]

Beginning at v. 12 Paul gives a list of qualities believers should put on, and it is noteworthy that all of them are said somewhere in the Bible to be characteristic of God or Christ.[17] The three synonyms piled up together at the outset — the elect, the holy ones, the beloved — are again an Asiatic trait. Believers are to put on deep feelings of compassion — literally "entrails of mercy," the graphic image meant to stress the idea of deep feelings, something "heartfelt" as we would say.[18] They are to put on kindness (a way of relating to others) and humility (a way of stepping down and self-sacrificially serving others), here the

---

time of Alexander it appears that the term was used to refer to any of the peoples of northern Asia bordering the Black Sea.

15. E. Schweizer, *The Letter to the Colossians* (Minneapolis: Augsburg, 1982), p. 200.

16. See J. D. G. Dunn, *The Epistles to the Colossians and to Philemon* (Grand Rapids: Eerdmans, 1996), p. 223: "The thought is clearly that Christ makes irrelevant ethnic, cultural, and social distinctions, that is, in practical terms, in the church"; cf. J. N. Aletti, *Saint Paul. Épître aux Colossiens* (Paris: Gabalda, 1993), p. 232. Dunn is probably right that this text hints at the fact that the false teaching was Jewish in character, and Paul is countering it here and elsewhere by this whole verse, including the phrase "Christ is all and in all."

17. Again Wall, *Colossians,* p. 145 has it wrong when he says "Paul defines Christian character rather than prescribes rules to obey." In fact, Paul sees obedience to imperatives as part of the process that shapes Christian character. Paul's ethics are both descriptive and prescriptive.

18. On this term for "entrails" see p. 57 n. 2 above. As Horsley points out (*New Docs* 3, p. 84), there is no need to see a Hebraic usage here, since Hellenistic sources also use the term to refer to compassion.

term used in a positive sense whereas in ch. 2 it was used of the wrong sort of self-abasement.[19]

V. 13 says that Christians must put up with one another and learn to forgive each other freely, for Paul realizes there will be occasions when one Christian wrongs another. They are to forgive in the same free manner as they have been forgiven by the Lord.[20] It "is utterly inappropriate for one who knows the joy and release of being forgiven to refuse to share that blessing with another. Secondly, it is highly presumptuous to refuse to forgive one whom Christ himself has already forgiven."[21]

But above all these virtues is love, which is called in a beautiful turn of phrase "the bond of perfection" (v. 14). This perhaps means that love is the one quality or virtue that most perfectly unites and binds the body of Christ together. We may compare this to Epictetus's assertion that friendship is the bond of all virtues (208a). Lincoln puts it this way: "Perfection then, is not some individually gained state but a corporate one achieved in a relationship of love." Love "acts as a bond not only for the other virtues but also for the community in which they are displayed."[22] Or perhaps the idea is of a supreme virtue binding the other virtues together into a proper ethic. Or is love seen as the means by which all other virtues should be exercised, hence binding the community together by and through the loving exercise of the ethic?

V. 15 says that the peace of Christ should not merely exist in the hearts of the Colossians, but should either rule there or preside as a judge in their midst. By this Paul does not advocate some sort of passivity or calm but the concept of shalom — well-being and wholeness. Nothing should be allowed to interfere with the well-being of the body of Christ. Peace must be the ruling principle. In an agonistic culture where rivalry and competition for honor was a part of everyday life, the audience must be reminded they are called to peace. These general ethical principles of faith, love, peace and the like are enunciated first and then are applied in the household code which follows in vv. 18ff.

V. 16 indicates that the basis of sound and wise teaching and admonition is the word of Christ dwelling in the midst of the community richly. This ex-

---

19. A. R. Bevere, *Sharing in the Inheritance: Identity and the Moral Life in Colossians* (Sheffield: Sheffield Academic, 2003), pp. 182-224, demonstrates ably that some of these virtues would not be recognized as virtues by pagans and that some of these vices would not be recognized as vices either. The Jewish, or better said Jewish Christian, nature of this material is made clear by Bevere.

20. "The characteristic of Christians is not that they never do anything wrong but that they know how to deal with faults and complaints by mutual forbearance and forgiveness." Caird, *Paul's Letters*, p. 207.

21. Wright, *Colossians*, p. 142.

22. A. T. Lincoln, "Colossians," in *The New Interpreter's Bible* XI (Nashville: Abingdon, 2000), p. 648.

hortation is given to all, and the assumption is that this is as appropriate when predicated of all as when these terms are used in 1.28 of Paul's ministry. This exhortation is not directed, for instance, just to the men of the audience, any more than the next exhortation about singing is.[23] Of the three types of songs, psalms would presumably refer primarily to the OT songs we find in the Psalter, hymns to the kind of christological material we find in Colossians 1 (it certainly refers to something sung to a deity), and spiritual songs to songs prompted by the Holy Spirit, perhaps spontaneously.[24] The grammar allows the conclusion that singing is viewed as one form of teaching and admonition,[25] and certainly Eph. 5.19 mentions speaking the songs to one another. Colossians 1 revealed Paul using a hymn for just such an instructional purpose. According to v. 17 the Christian life is also to be characterized by being and showing oneself thankful for all God has done, and by doing and saying all that one does and says in the name and according to the nature of Christ. This verse should be seen as a summary of the whole first half of the third argument (vv. 5-16).[26]

The Household Code — 3:18–4:1

Wives, submit yourselves to your husbands, as is proper in the Lord. Husbands, love your wives and do not be sharp with them. Children, obey your parents in everything, for this is pleasing in the Lord. Fathers, do not provoke your children, in order that they not be despondent. Slaves, obey in everything those who are your lords according to the flesh, not in eye-service as one currying favor, but in single-mindedness of heart, fearing the Lord. But whatever you do, work wholeheartedly as to the Lord and not to humans, seeing that from the Lord you receive the reward of inheritance. To the Lord Christ you are enslaved. For the one doing wrong will be requited for the wrong he did, and it is not [a matter of] favoritism. Masters, provide to your slaves justice and equality, knowing that you also have a Lord in heaven.

For good reasons scholars have often suggested that 3.18–4.1 is a pre-existing piece which has been inserted into its present context.[27] Of course what some

---

23. A worship setting is clearly in view here, and as Lincoln, "Colossians," p. 641, suggests, this is not accidental since the errorists were offering new worship practices among other things.

24. See Dunn, *Colossians, Philemon*, pp. 237-39.

25. See G. D. Fee, *God's Empowering Presence* (Peabody: Hendrickson, 1994), pp. 649-56.

26. See MacDonald, *Colossians, Ephesians*, p. 144.

27. An earlier and somewhat different form of this material may be found in my *Women in the Earliest Churches* (Cambridge: Cambridge University Press, 1988), pp. 47-61.

scholars fail to take into account is that this is precisely how a rhetorical digression is meant to work. It is a self-contained unit after which the author returns to the subject he left behind at the outset of the digression. Indeed, 3.17 and 4.2 seem to go together, both referring to prayer. Furthermore, and very importantly from the point of view of style, the sentences in this section are terse and to the point, quite unlike the long periods with redundancies and other features of the Asiatic style.[28] This material is closer to the normal Pauline style than the rest of the discourse.[29]

While the similarities between Col. 3.18–4.1 and Eph. 5.22–6.9 may be put down to the dependence of Ephesians on Colossians or their common authorship (or both), it seems unlikely that the author of 1 Pet. 2.18–3.7 knew Colossians or Ephesians. This being the case, it would appear that what we find in Col. 3.18–4.1 is either a Pauline creation or more likely a Pauline modification of an early Christian household code, which may even have existed in some form in writing prior to the writing of Colossians.[30]

Even if this code has been adopted and adapted by Paul, he has made it his own, and it fits nicely within the context of the wisdom discussion in Colossians.[31] We of course find addresses to slaves elsewhere in the NT (1 Tim.

28. Rightly noted by Bevere, *Sharing in the Inheritance,* pp. 225-54.

29. See E. Percy, *Die Probleme der Kolosser- und Epheserbriefe* (Lund: Gleerup, 1946), p. 36.

30. See Caird, *Paul's Letters,* p. 208: "Paul is a man of the mid first century advising his contemporaries how best they may apply their new faith to the social conditions of their day, and specifically to the family as they knew it. Jew and Gentile alike assumed that the head of a household would wield authority which others were bound to obey, Paul does not openly challenge this assumption, but he modifies both the authority and its acceptance by the Christian principle of mutual love and deference, so that both are transformed."

31. A. T. Lincoln, "The Household Code and Wisdom Mode of Colossians," *JSNT* 74 (1999): 93-112. Notice in particular how the reference to wise conduct in 4.5 as part of the peroratio alludes back to the household code, and on the other hand how the exhortations to be filled with wisdom (1.9-10) and to teach each other wisdom (3.16) can be said to take a concrete form in this code. Especially important is the insight that while the false philosophy offers a wisdom from below that strives after union and unity with God through asceticism and mystical experiences, Paul offers a wisdom from the top down where God has created a union through faith in Christ and where such supererogatory works are not only not helpful but reflect a false wisdom. "The wisdom of the Christian gospel . . . is that believers are already related to the above through union with Christ and that this relationship is to be worked out on earth. . . . Having a Lord in heaven does not direct attention away from the earthly. Rather it is meant to provide the motivation for taking earthly relationships with all seriousness and living distinctively within them" (Lincoln, "Household Code," pp. 111-12). Not asceticism nor even conformity to the larger cultural norms is being advocated in this code, but we find rather a development of Jewish-Christian wisdom that has some conventional and some radical features to it, as one would expect of a monotheistic code operating in a polytheistic environment.

6.1-2), and it is instructive to look at the somewhat later Christian development of these sorts of imperatives as well (cf. *Didache* 4.9-11; *Barnabas* 19.5, 7; *1 Clement* 1.3; 21.6-8; 38.2; Polycarp, *Philippians* 4–6; Ignatius, *Polycarp* 4–6).[32] The early church met in homes, and family as well as family of faith issues needed to be addressed since there was overlap between the two groups when they shared the same social location or venue. MacDonald has suggested that the "household code reveals the strong convictions of a household transformed in the Lord even if to onlookers this household might have had a largely conventional appearance."[33] If in fact Paul's imperatives were implemented in full, the household would have had a rather different and unconventional ethos and appearance in several respects, as we shall see, and clearly the use of christological and eschatological motivating clauses distinguishes this material from any secular codes and from parallel Jewish texts as well.[34]

A Closer Look: Evaluating the Household Codes Fairly in Paul's Context

There has been no end of debate about these household codes, and since Colossians seems to contain one of the earliest forms of the code, a great deal of debate has centered on it.[35] Barclay is right that "there is no precise analogy to the form and theme of the Colossian code, although one can point to many sources that discuss the theme

32. There is rightly some debate about whether the term "household code" is appropriate if we are talking about duties to emperors and the like, or for that matter admonitions to overseers, elders, or deacons. See Bevere, *Sharing the Inheritance*, pp. 226-27.

33. MacDonald, *Colossians, Ephesians*, p. 154.

34. E. Lohse, *Colossians and Philemon* (Philadelphia: Fortress, 1971), p. 156, is on the right track in saying: "The phrase 'in the Lord' however which introduces the new motivation, is not a mere formal element whose only function is to Christianize the traditional material. Rather the entire life, thought and conduct of believers is subordinated to the lordship of the Kyrios. At the same time the words 'in the Lord' set forth a critical principle which makes it possible to determine which ethical admonitions were considered binding for the community." For Jewish treatment of the household relationships see Philo, *De Decalogo* 165-67; Josephus, *Contra Apionem* 199-210; Sir. 7.19-28. Doubtless this tradition has affected what is being done in this Christian code as well. See Lincoln, "Colossians," p. 654.

35. The debate rages on. See R. E. DeMaris, *The Colossians Controversy: Wisdom in Dispute at Colossae* (Sheffield: JSOT, 1994); C. E. Arnold, *The Colossian Syncretism* (Tübingen: Mohr, 1995); T. W. Martin, *By Philosophy and Empty Deceit: Colossians as Response to a Cynic Critique* (Sheffield: Sheffield Academic, 1996). What all these studies have in common is too much mirror-reading in trying to figure out the Colossian error. The least plausible of these three is Martin, who wants to insist that it was a purely Hellenistic philosophy Paul was opposing. This is at the other end of the spectrum from Dunn, who wants to see it as coming purely from synagogue polemics.

of household relationships and a few texts (both Jewish and non-Jewish) in which such relationships are viewed from both sides."[36]

Some scholars have suspected that this sort of code and the one in Ephesians and perhaps also the one in 1 Peter were constructed either to counter a revolutionary spirit among Hellenistic Christians, particularly slaves and women,[37] or that it was apologetic in character, countering the notion that Christians were social radicals.[38] The problem with both these suggestions is that they do not account for the exhortations to parents and children or for the fact that the Colossian code is directed to those who are already Christians in Colossae, and directed to the whole household.[39] Equally unconvincing is the suggestion that there is nothing profoundly Christian or especially radical about these household codes, that they just baptize the status quo and call it good. To the contrary, when one compares this material to either the ancient discussion of household management in Aristotle and other sources or to Stoic or other Greco-Roman codes, one is profoundly struck by not just the Christian elements but also the social engineering that is being undertaken here to limit the abuse of power by the head of the household, using Christian rationales to equalize and personalize as well as Christianize the relationship between the head and the rest of the family. We do not find the exhortation to heads of households to love their wives, not to break the spirit of their children, or to treat their slaves with some equity and justice in most of the parallel literature.[40] Thus, while what we find here may not be totally unique (most of it is found in bits and pieces elsewhere), it is certainly distinctive of a Christian approach to these relationships. As D. Horrell says, what we find here is the attempt to embed the Christian faith and its ethical values in the social structures that already exist.[41] Wright puts the matter well:

> It is . . . extremely unlikely that Paul, having warned the young Christians against conforming their lives to the present world, would now require just that of them after all. Nor does he. The Stoics (who provide some of the closest parallels to these household lists) based their teaching on the law of nature: this is the way the

36. J. M. G. Barclay, *Colossians and Philemon* (Sheffield: Sheffield Academic, 1997), p. 70. See his further remark on the same page — "It would be safer to say that the Colossian code has no exact formal antecedent. . . ."

37. J. E. Crouch, *The Origin and Intention of the Colossian Haustafel* (Göttingen: Vandenhoeck und Ruprecht, 1972).

38. D. L. Balch, *Let Wives Be Submissive* (Chico: Scholars, 1981). See also Lincoln, "Colossians," p. 653.

39. See Barclay, *Colossians and Philemon*, p. 72.

40. In fact the head of the household is rarely addressed in such codes at all. But see Seneca, *Epistulae* 94.1: the proper philosophy will "advise how a husband should conduct himself toward his wife, or how a father should bring up his children, or how a master should rule his slaves." There are no matched pairs of advice here, only a focus on the head of the household. Cf. Dionysius of Halicarnassus, *Roman Antiquities* 2.25.4–26.4.

41. D. Horrell, *The Social Ethos of the Corinthian Correspondence: Interests and Ideology from 1 Corinthians to 1 Clement* (Edinburgh: Clark, 1996).

world is, so this is how you must live in harmony with it. Paul bases his on the law of the *new* nature: Christ releases you to be truly human, and you must now learn to express your true self according to the divine pattern, not in self-assertion but in self-giving.[42]

The attempt to see this code as an effort to stabilize the Pauline community in the post-Pauline situation and demonstrate that it was a supporter of the conventional cultural household codes and traditional virtues ignores the profound Christianizing of this material and the way it goes against the flow of the culture.[43] It is also different from traditional Jewish wisdom, which did seek to repristinize patriarchy (compare the attitude toward women's roles in Sirach and Josephus, *Contra Apionem* 2.24-30).

Paul argues for the manumission of a slave in Philemon and does so on the basis of the principle that those who are brothers or sisters should not be or be treated as slaves. 1 Corinthians 7 says not only that Christians should not become slaves but also that they should avail themselves of opportunities for freedom. Why then is Colossians different? There are at least six factors of importance here: 1) Paul is addressing here an existing situation of Christian households that have slaves and is clearly trying to minimize the possibility for abusive or unchristian behavior by either master or slave (or others). He is regulating an existing condition, not endorsing the institution of slavery. Limiting rather than licensing the situation is the ethical move Paul is trying to make here. The same applies to his comments about the patriarchal family structure.

2) Paul is not addressing a personal convert or close friend here, indeed is addressing a group of Christians who are not his converts and whom, so far as we know, he has never addressed in a letter before. There are levels of moral discourse possible depending on the audience one is addressing. If the goal is damage control, such as here, and Paul believes that is all that can be accomplished on this first contact, it is understandable that he does not fire all of his guns with regard to slavery or patriarchy. This is Paul's opening gambit with the Colossians on these subjects, not his last word with them. It must be judged in that light.

3) Even in the form in which this household code appears here, it is already swimming upstream, as we shall see, going against the flow of much of the cultural assumptions about slavery and patriarchy.

4) The household code must not be abstracted from its present literary context and analyzed on its own, as is so often done, if the goal is to see what Paul is driving at in the use of this material. Not only must we take into consideration the larger social context in evaluating this material but also the immediate literary or exegetical context as well. When what comes immediately before the code is taken into account, it

---

42. Wright, *Colossians*, p. 147.

43. But see M. Y. MacDonald, *The Pauline Churches: A Socio-Historical Study of Institutionalization in the Pauline and Deutero-Pauline Letters* (Cambridge: Cambridge University Press, 1988).

becomes clear that Paul expects all household members to behave in ways that are in accord with Christian virtues and not to continue or go back to old patterns of behavior in their family relationships. The general ethic enunciated in 3.5-17 prepares for and undergirds the advice given in 3.18–4.1. If love, peace, forgiveness, respect, and a recognition that in Christ even social relationships like slave and master or husband and wife have been relativized and transformed (3.11) are the ruling principles guiding conduct, then a reforming and refashioning of the household relationships is not only possible but required. Paul is not offering up suggestions in the household code but exhorting by means of imperatives. And each exhortation is tied to the person in question's relationship with the Lord. Even the household ethic and its living-out are christocentric.

5) The trajectory of the remarks in this household code is as important as the advice actually given. This becomes clearer when we get to the parallel household code in Ephesians 5–6, where Paul has put even more Christian leaven into the dough of household relationships.

6) Understanding this material and judging it fairly is a matter of asking the right questions: How does it compare to the standard advice given in the culture about household relationships? Where is this advice heading? What would the social situation look like if all the ethical advice given in and around these codes was followed faithfully?

In regard to this last issue we now have the helpful analysis of H. Van Broekhoven.[44] Broekhoven applies the group grid form of social analysis to Colossians with telling results. He finds Paul inculcating a high group high grid situation. That is, he is trying to draw clear boundaries around the community, though without turning it into an isolationist group or sect. He also attempts to clarify the profile of role definitions (high grid). "There is both affirmation of group boundaries and a conformity to generally accepted social structures. The vice-virtue lists help define boundaries and internal cohesion while the house-table rules define structure. The writer, and his co-workers, exemplify a personal identity shaped by group loyalty *and* a strong internalized sense of role."[45]

Broekhoven rightly adds that the philosophy Paul is opposing not only is ascetic but also stresses individualism, as opposed to group bonding experiences. As Mary Douglas points out, in a high grid low group situation individuals are left to their own devices and tend to trust know-how, individualistic religious practices, the power of rules, and even magic or intermediary beings.[46] High grid low group communities try to fend off or control cosmic forces and define themselves over against the society. These descriptors certainly are reflected in the philosophy Paul seems to be criticizing.

---

44. H. Van Broekhoven, "The Social Profiles in the Colossian Debate," *JSNT* 66 (1997): 73-90.

45. Broekhoven, "Social Profiles," p. 79.

46. M. Douglas, *Natural Symbols: Explorations in Cosmology* (New York: Pantheon, 1982), p. 144.

Against introversion and individualistic tendencies Paul's task was "to socialize the church to become a harmonious, caring, stable community with some concern for the social and cultural world of his time. His own self-denial, mentioned in 1:24, serves as a counterpoint to that more self-serving asceticism of the rivals."[47] There is then some modeling as well as exhortations in Paul's attempt to form the community in Colossae. That Paul is willing to attempt this sort of moral suasion says something about the apostolic authority he assumes he has, even over those who were not directly converted by him.

In terms of the social provenance of the Colossian household code, G. E. Cannon is surely right when he suggests that it may well reflect a situation in which there were considerable expectations on the part of women and slaves that their treatment in the home would be changed by the coming of the gospel. After all, in this very letter we find Col. 3.11, which echoes Gal. 3.28.[48] But then is this code trying to dampen their enthusiasm for more freedom and less restrictions? Probably not, as what Paul actually says is not an attempt to put women or slaves or even children in their place, but rather to make sure that they behave like Christians in the social roles they are already playing. There is no evidence of a feminist or slave revolution in play in the church in Colossae that Paul is trying to stifle. Quite the contrary, Paul is trying to Christianize a difficult and possibly abusive situation on his first occasion of addressing the Colossians and so to help the subordinate members of the household not merely survive but have a more Christian environment in which to operate. What most distinguishes this household code from those of the pagan or Jewish world in general is that Paul is giving strong limiting exhortations to the superordinate person in the family, the husband/father/master. Non-Christian household codes almost always direct exhortations only to the subordinate members of the household. What is new about the code here then is the Christian limitations placed on the head of household. That is what would stand out to an ancient person hearing Paul's discourse for the first time.

Several structural elements in this household code should be kept in mind: 1) The subordinate member of a given relationship is addressed first (wives, children, slaves), but always in tandem with the head of the household. In fact the head of the household gets three sets of exhortations, whereas everyone else only gets one. 2) Each exhortation consists of an address and admonition and in some cases a motive or reason for the exhortation, sometimes a spe-

47. Broekhoven, "Social Profiles," p. 89.
48. G. E. Cannon, *The Use of Traditional Materials in Colossians* (Macon: Mercer, 1983), p. 131.

cifically Christian one. 3) The groups are arranged from most to least intimate relationships (wife-husband, children-parents, slaves-masters).

Women are addressed first in v. 18, and here the term *gynaikes* surely means "wives." Paul is not attempting to address the general issue of the relationship of all Christian women to all Christian men. Nor is he merely commenting on behavior in Christian worship. What is said to the wife applies only in her relationship to her husband.[49] Here and throughout this code, all the members of the family are addressed as morally responsible individuals capable of hearing and heeding the exhortation that is being given on their own. Furthermore, here, unlike in 1 Corinthians 7, Paul does not seem to be addressing religiously mixed marriage situations. He is addressing homes where all the members of the family are assumed to be Christians and therefore can receive Paul's exhortation.

A Closer Look: Paul on Marriage and Slavery in Context

From the papyri we have compelling evidence of how early people were married in Paul's world. From the Jewish papyri we have clear references to various women being married as early as age twelve (CIJ I.105; I.55) and only one not married by fifteen or sixteen. Non-Jewish papyri also speak of women married at twelve or thirteen (IGUR I.323; I.673), and we also find the use of the term *monandros* for women only married to one man in their lifetime (462, 579, 1205, 1311.2). Equally telling are epitaphs to girls who die unmarried: only one is over twenty. In terms of general trends the evidence suggests that Jewish and Christian girls tended to get married at fifteen to sixteen, whereas pagan girls were married at twelve or thirteen.[50]

There are various tributes on tombs to those who were seen as exemplary wives, some of whom died in childbirth and many of whom predeceased their husbands. For example, SEG 1536 reads

> Here lies Valeria, daughter of Marcus, of freeborn status from Caesarea in Mauritania. She was kind, affectionate, dignified, blameless; she loved her husband and her children, and was faithful to her marriage. Out of respect and love for what is good her husband, Lucius Dexios from Herculaneum, buried her.

---

49. See Wall, *Colossians*, pp. 155-56: "If the wife sees herself as subservient to her husband, she will allow him to dominate and even abuse her. If, however, she views herself as Christ's disciple and her husband's equal in Christ, her understanding of submission will be changed: she will submit herself to her husband in the same way that Christ submitted himself to God. . . . Being made equal in Christ will radically alter the way two disciples relate to each other as husband and wife. The result will be the woman's elevation within the Christian home and the end of her abuse there . . . and this in turn will be a witness to a misogynistic world."

50. See the discussion and charts in *New Docs* 4, pp. 221-29.

Notice in particular how the wife is said to have loved her husband, but interestingly the husband is said to love and respect that which is good.[51]

This inscription needs to be compared to the more famous Laudatio Turiae from just before the turn of the era. It is the longest Latin inscription erected by and for a private individual, which in itself says something. The rhetorical form of the inscription is of course a eulogy, and so we may expect some measure of hyperbole (it has these other rhetorical features: anaphora, chiasmus, and occultatio), but there is such a sincere tone to the whole inscription that one senses the deep feeling behind it for the deceased wife. The couple, whose names we do not know, were married for a remarkable forty-one years. The husband is older than his wife and wishes he could have died first. Clearly he loved her. He praises her for

> loyalty (to our marriage), obedience, courteousness, easy good nature, your assiduous wool-working, reverence (for the gods) without superstition [i.e., foreign cults], attire not designed for attracting attention, modest refinement . . . love for her own, your devotion to your family, since you have treated with equal honor my mother and your own parents, and provided for her the same peace (in retirement) as for your own family.

The husband also remarks not only on how uncommon such longevity in marriage was, but also how uncommon it was for it not to end in divorce. The second column praises the wife for the astonishing and striking gesture of offering to allow herself to be divorced so he could remarry or at least to allow another woman to provide him with an heir since they were childless. She only asked that she be allowed to pick for him his future partner. The text also makes clear she was in charge of managing the house, under his headship and permission. It is not clear how common such a Roman marriage was, but the author of the inscription suggests that it was uncommon both in longevity and in character, especially in view of the lack of children.[52]

What is strikingly different between these eulogies and the exhortations of Paul is that these two wives are praised for their remarkable fulfillment of the patriarchal ideal of what a wife should be like, whereas Paul is busy exhorting household members about behaving as Christians within household relationships. The inscriptions reflect the culture while Paul is seeking to revise the patriarchal situation, pushing it in a more Christian direction.[53]

Did slavery actually change much under Christianity? The answer seems to be yes, considering that the entire Roman economy depended on slave labor and that there was no chance that it would change during Paul's era. A slave owner was obli-

---

51. See the discussion in *New Docs* 3, pp. 40-41.

52. See the discussion in *New Docs* 3, pp. 33-36.

53. The things that Paul leaves out of discussion are interesting, for example the dowry, and Llewelyn suggests that this is because many Christians came from the lower social classes and unwritten marriages prevailed (*New Docs* 6, p. 16). This suggestion has some merit, but the marriages Paul is referring to are in homes that include slaves, and this argues against the conclusion that he is mainly referring to undowried marriages.

gated by law only to feed and clothe his slaves, but Paul clearly is demanding much more than this.[54] There was in Roman law a certain ambiguity about slaves. They were property when it came to the ownership issue, but they could have property and were even allowed to marry. In some ways they were treated as property, in some ways as persons. By Paul's day, slaves could refuse to commit a crime for their master (see Seneca, *De Beneficiis* 3.20), and they could also flee to a third party if mistreated and have the third party adjudicate the matter.

As Llewelyn stresses, the NT household codes do not address what would happen if obedience to the master violated the law or some widely recognized moral code.[55] Paul says absolutely nothing to encourage the continued treatment of slaves as property, but he also does not try to set up rules to deal with ethically conflicting situations. He offers a picture of a household running under normal circumstances and, it is assumed, on the basis of Christian principles. Slaves are seen as valuable members of the household and as Christians fully capable of responding to exhortations often involving delicate moral matters.

From a considerably later period (the fifth century) a bronze slave collar has survived which is inscribed "I am the slave of archdeacon Felix. Hold me so that I do not flee." This practice of "collaring" a slave as we would a dog is of course inhuman by modern standards, but it was actually an improvement over the practice prior to Constantine of branding slaves on the face.[56] It is interesting that slave names (including Onesimus) crop up in the papyri predicated of persons who are clearly free and perhaps even freeborn and of high social status.[57]

The verb *hypotassō* is critical in v. 18. We find it in the present tense, middle voice which can then be translated "wives submit yourselves . . ." Paul does not tell the husbands to subordinate their wives or to exhort their wives to be subordinate. The exhortation goes directly to the wife, and it is incumbent on her to subordinate herself. This verb was not widely used in other Greek literature on marriage, though Plutarch a little after the time of Paul does use it (*Advice to the Bride and Groom, Moralia* 142E). Since this verb is also used of Christ's relationship to God the Father (1 Cor. 15.28) and of believers to each other (Eph. 5.21), it surely does not imply the ontological inferiority of the submitter to the one submitted to. Rather it has to do with the nature of a relationship between two persons. It may also in fact have more to do with following the example of Christ, who humbled himself and took a lower place. In other words, in a Christian context the verb has to do with humility and service as modeled by

---

54. *New Docs* 7, p. 165.
55. *New Docs* 7, pp. 194-96.
56. See *New Docs* 1, pp. 140-41.
57. See *New Docs* 4, pp. 179-81.

Christ, who served the lost as well as believers. We are not told in practical terms how this submission to one's husband is to be manifested. Paul assumes that his audience knows what is implied.

The clause *hōs anēken* modifies the exhortation to wives and is in turn modified by the phrase "in the Lord." The verb *anēken* is in the imperfect and literally rendered the clause would be "as was fitting in the Lord." This form of the verb is found in neither classical nor Stoic discussions of what is fitting. The point seems to be that this action has been customary Christian behavior before and in the present. This clause is appropriate in a deliberative discourse, where one is supposed to discuss what is fitting and proper and useful and beneficial.[58] Submission is a normal and expected part of a close Christian relationship. Conformity to Christ, not to society or to what is "natural" is at issue. Here the motive for the behavior is not missionary, as in 1 Pet. 3.1, since here Paul is addressing a fully Christian household. Not only is a new reason given for this behavior but it seems to be implied that one will measure or model one's conduct by a new model — the Lord.

The parallel exhortation to the husband in v. 19 involves the characteristic Christian virtue of "love." The verb *agapaō* is not used in Hellenistic discussions of the household duties of the husband and so is by no means a conventional exhortation repeated here.[59] It is not, however, a uniquely Christian word either, though it is a term that most often characterizes the Christian ethic. It is interesting that wives are never exhorted to love their husbands in the NT household codes. It is fair to assume that Paul thinks that husbands especially need this exhortation.[60]

This is followed by a negative corollary to the positive exhortation which shows clearly that Paul is trying to limit bad behavior by the head of household. The phrase could be translated either "don't be sharp with them" or "don't be embittered against them." The husband's action and his anger must be limited by love. As a Christian he is not free to do as he pleases with his wife. It is telling to contrast what is said on this subject by Ben Sira, who always takes the side of the husband and father in these matters (cf. Sirach 25–26; 30.1-13; 42.9-14). While Ben Sira is trying to reinforce a patriarchal authority structure, Paul is not. Paul is, rather, trying to ameliorate the harm the existing structure does and can do. Chrysostom grasped the spirit of what Paul was trying to accom-

---

58. Notice that *hōs anēken* is omitted in the Ephesian parallel at this juncture, which is part of an epideictic discourse.

59. See Lohse, *Colossians*, p. 158. One has to look hard for anything remotely close to this from this whole era. See however Musonius, *Orationes* 13A.

60. While we often hear claims that *agapaō* always refers to Godlike love, in fact there are places in the NT where it is used of more self-regarding or unworthy forms of love (John 3.19; 2 Tim. 4.10; 2 Pet. 2.15; 1 John 2.15).

plish in these exhortations to husband and wife: "Observe again that Paul has exhorted husbands and wives to reciprocity. . . . From being loved, the wife too becomes loving; and from her being submissive, the husband learns to yield" (tenth homily on Colossians).

At v. 20 children (both male and female) are exhorted to obey their parents in everything. They are directly addressed, which suggests that they will be present in the worship service to hear the presentation of this discourse.[61] The difference between *hypakouō*, used here of children, and *hypotassō*, used of wives in v. 18, seems to be that while *hypakouō* always means "obey," the other term only sometimes involves or means this (see 1 Pet. 3.5-6). *Hypakouō* is in the active imperative, which suggests absolute or unquestioned obedience, by contrast with the form of the verb used of wives, which is in the middle voice. "Again here Paul mentions submission and love. And he did not say 'Love your children,' for this would have been unnecessary, seeing that nature itself causes us to do so. Rather he corrected what needed correction; that the love shown in this case should be much stronger, because the obedience commanded is greater" (Chrysostom, tenth homily on Colossians). The parallel Hellenistic codes speak of children honoring their parents rather than obeying them, which suggests that we should not see the Christian code as a mere adaptation of the Hellenistic codes.

In addition to *kata panta*, "in everything," which is comprehensive in scope and will be used again in regard to slaves in v. 22, there is the further qualification "for this is pleasing in the Lord." This is what one would expect in a deliberative exhortation, where what is "pleasing" or "proper" *(euarestos)* is a major issue. In Eph. 6.1, however, the issue is what is "right." This difference is due to the different rhetorical species of the discourse. Paul modifies the code in one way or another to suit the rhetorical species he is dealing with in a given discourse. It is well to point out, as O'Brien does, that since Paul has the Christian family here in view, he is likely assuming that the Christian parents would not demand something of their children which is contrary to Christian teaching. The same applies in the situation of husband and wife.[62] Here as in v. 18 the phrase "in the Lord" may mean in the Christian community indwelt by Christ.

V. 21 begins with the term *pateres*, which, while it could refer to both parents, probably means "fathers" here. The father then is exhorted not to provoke his children and so break their spirits or make them despondent. Notice that the stress is on the father's responsibility and duties. Unlike Eph. 6.4 there is nothing here about the positive duty to train or bring up the children. "The

---

61. See Dunn, *Colossians, Philemon,* p. 250; J. Gnilka, *Der Kolosserbrief* (Freiburg: Herder, 1980), p. 220.

62. P. T. O'Brien, *Colossians, Philemon* (Waco: Word, 1982), pp. 224-25.

sensitive understanding of children, with the realization that they might become discouraged and lose heart . . . is a striking feature in this new chapter in
social history."[63] There is a notable contrast here with the fact that the head of a
Roman household and even in some cases in Hellenistic Judaism had nearly
unlimited authority to do as he pleased with his children. Dionysius of
Halicarnassus describes how the *patria potestas* still continued when the child
was an adult: "The law-giver of the Romans gave virtually full power to the father over his son, whether he thought it proper to imprison him, to scourge
him, to put him in chains, and keep him at work in the fields, or to put him to
death; and this even though the son was already engaged in public affairs,
though he was numbered among the highest magistrates, and though he was
celebrated for his zeal for the commonwealth" (*Roman Antiquities* 2.26.4). The
father also received custody of the children if there was a divorce. This code in
Colossians certainly goes against the flow of the culture in several respects. I
have used the example from the Roman situation as it more nearly approximates the situation in Asia than does the situation under Jewish Law, as it is
clear that Paul is mainly dealing with Gentiles in this discourse. Paul then is
quite specifically limiting that authority and privilege. He does not exhort the
father to exercise his authority in relationship to the children nor does he urge
disciplining the children.[64] What we see throughout this household code is a
deliberate modification of the existing patriarchal household structure, an attempt, that is, to rein in the authority and behavior of the head of the household, making it more nearly Christian in character.

By far the longest exhortation in this code is addressed to slaves (vv. 22-
25), who like children are also treated as responsible members of the congregation. In light of 3.11 they are seen as equal members, persons of equal, sacred
worth in the church. These verses should be read in light of that earlier text.[65]
Like the exhortation to children, the imperatives here begin with the command
to obey in everything. The assumption must be, especially in light of 4.1, that
the Christian master will treat the slave fairly and properly. Masters are called
"lords according to the flesh" with an implicit distinction from the Lord. The
slave is exhorted to wholehearted labor, not just when being watched.[66] Paul is

---

63. Moule, *Colossians, Philemon*, p. 129.

64. See Lincoln, "Colossians," p. 656: "It is noticeable that the writer does not exhort
fathers to exercise their authority. Instead, he presupposes that authority and sets the bounds
for its use. He also presupposes that children are not simply their father's legal property but
are owed dignity as human beings in their own right."

65. See Dunn, *Colossians, Philemon*, p. 253.

66. *Opthalmodoulia* does not occur in earlier Greek literature (cf. Eph. 6.6) and may
have been coined by Paul. It means a service not done to please God or for its own sake but
performed for the sole purpose of attracting attention. So Lohse, *Colossians*, p. 160. One of
the rules of rhetoric was that if one was using traditional material, one needed to vary it by

apparently dealing with a trait that was assumed to be commonplace, namely laziness when not under supervision. While "fearing the l/Lord" could refer to the slave's "lord according to the flesh," it is more likely another example of the Christianizing of this material with the implication that a Christian slave should work with the recognition that the Lord is always watching, thinking of the Lord's evaluation of his conduct rather than in fear of reprisals from the master. V. 23 certainly supports this interpretation. All work should be done from the heart and "as to the Lord, not as to human beings." This removes the usual motivation for human behavior and places the conduct strictly on the basis of Christian motivation. The approval one should seek is not human but that of God, and the evaluation one should be concerned about is that of the Lord, not of lords.

The real reason and encouragement for such advice is given in v. 24. The slave in the Greco-Roman world received a *peculium,* a small amount of money, on a regular basis that they could eventually use to pay the price of manumission, if that was allowed by the master. Though technically a slave could not inherit property (being considered living property) this *peculium* was in a sense the slave's inheritance. So here Paul speaks of a different sort of inheritance, a "reward" or "repayment" that the slave will definitely receive from the Lord. Since Paul is addressing Christian slaves it is clear enough that he is not referring to initial salvation as a reward. Rather it is the same sort of reward Jesus promises to believers for good conduct during their believing lives. Paul believes there will be rewards (lesser and greater) in the eschatological state based on one's behavior in this life (cf. 1 Cor. 3.10-15).

This is followed by the intriguing remark that in fact the slave belongs to or is enslaved to the Lord Christ. The reference to Christ leads into v. 25, where the reference is not clear. Is this a promise that Christ, who does not play favorites, will deal with unfair masters in due course and so Christian slaves should not misbehave if mistreated? This is certainly possible in light of 4.1. On the other hand, the sense could be that the slave is being warned against unrighteous conduct being repaid in the eschatological age, just as righteous conduct will be rewarded. It is appropriate to ponder whether the reason for this extended exhortation to the slave is due to the Onesimus situation, attempting to head off further illegal behavior by slaves in Colossae. This is certainly possible.

The net effect of this advice is to place the conduct of slaves clearly under

---

word substitution so as to make it one's own, and if one could coin a word and put it in traditional material, one was showing one's abilities at "invention" despite the constraints of conventional material. In v. 25 we have *prosōpolēmpsia,* which also seems to have been coined by Paul or some early Christian, since it does not appear in earlier or contemporary Greek literature. We thus probably have two attempts by Paul to bring some new interest and ideas to a familiar topic of discussion.

the light of divine scrutiny and to help them think this way about it, with a special stress on working hard and wholeheartedly at what they do, knowing that their real lord to whom they are bound and even "enslaved" is Jesus, who died for them and set them free already from their sins and bad behavior. Traditional discussions of household management did not address slaves directly, but here slaves are addressed directly as both members of the household and as members of the house church. There are some five references to Christ as Lord in this section involving slaves and masters to make very clear that there has been a thorough overhaul of the way that relationship should be envisioned and of what motivates proper behavior when both parties are Christians. This contrasts drastically with the usual ways slaves were motivated to work hard (e.g. holding out rewards such as praise, food, better clothing; see Xenophon, *Oeconomicus* 13.9-12).

4.1 concludes the third argument with a word for the masters.[67] The stress is on Christian "lords" also having a Lord in heaven to whom they are answerable for their conduct. Conduct again is to be guided or modified because of the watchful eye of Christ. This reference to the masters' master sets apart this exhortation from other considerations of the master-slave relationship of the time and relativizes the position and power of the master within the Christian community.[68] The master does not represent Christ, but the relationship of slave to master represents that of all believers to the Lord. Thus the last clause of 3.24, taken as imperative (a possible rendering: "Be slaves of the Lord Jesus Christ") is for all and the position of slaves "receives the most attention as a paradigm for the motivation that should inform all members of the household."[69]

Masters are not to cheat their slaves, but rather to provide them with what is right and fair. This is diametrically opposed to what Aristotle says when he remarks that the issue of justice is not raised in regard to slaves, that there can be no injustice involved in the way one treats mere property (*Nichomachean Ethics* 5.1134b). Compared to Aristotle, what Paul is saying here is revolutionary. It would have sounded odd since it suggests that "slaves too are human beings with rights. To talk of 'justice' and 'equality'[70] in relation to slaves would sound

67. "Masters are also to be admonished that they offend God by priding themselves on his gift to them, without realizing that they who are held in subjection by reason of their state of life are their equals in virtue of their common humanity" (Gregory the Great, *Pastoral Care* 3.5). One could add that Paul also believed they were equal in Christ because of the eschatological work creating new persons.

68. See MacDonald, *Colossians, Ephesians,* p. 159.

69. Lincoln, "Colossians," p. 657.

70. *Isotēta* is a striking term which was used in earlier Greek democracy and law to speak of equality. Aristotle (*Topica* 6.5) in fact defines justice as "a state productive of equality *(isotētos)* or distributive of what is equal." So could Paul really be saying that masters should treat their slaves on the basis of "equality"? Dunn, *Colossians and Philemon,* p. 260, says that

extraordinary to most slave-owners of the ancient world."[71] Thus even if to our ears this advice sounds rather conventional or even conservative and commonplace, the truth is that it was not in that day.

Paul has already, on the first occasion of addressing the Colossians, been pushing the envelope of their thinking so that they will consider all subordinate members of the household, even slaves, as persons with rights, including the right to fair and equal treatment. The head of the household as a Christian must alter his conduct in his relationships with his wife, children, and slaves so that the Lord will be pleased. It is this curtailing and Christianizing of the head of the household's rights, privileges, and roles that especially stands out in these exhortations as Paul attempts to transform the character of Christian household relationships by ameliorating the harsh edges of the existing institutions of slavery and patriarchy.

---

the idea of equality of slave and master in law was impossible at this time. But Paul is not talking about "in law" but in the community. In light of 3.11 "equality" is precisely what Paul means, and here we have a principle that, like what we find in Philemon, would lead to the demise of slavery among Christians. Paul applied some of the democratic ideals of old Greece: he calls his community an *ekklēsia,* which is a place where free persons assemble to discuss matters of importance and make decisions, and he uses the ancient art of persuasion, which is the opposite of strong-arm tactics or dictatorial approaches. Persuasion is a form of treating others with respect as free individuals capable of making their own decisions and judgments. Equality in Christ was a precious notion to Paul and one to which he returned early and late in the Pauline corpus (cf. Gal. 3.28; 1 Cor. 12.13; Col. 3.11). See rightly Dunn, *Colossians and Philemon,* p. 223.

71. Wright, *Colossians, Philemon,* p. 151.

Peroratio — Prayer and Wisdom — 4.2-6

In the Greek tradition the *epilogos,* as the Greeks called the peroratio, had as its focus summing up the most essential points of the previous discourse. Usually there would also be an attempt to arouse the deeper emotions (love, hate, compassion, envy), and finally there could also be some amplification about some pressing matter (Aristotle, *Rhet.* 3.19.1; Cicero, *De Inventione* 1.52.98-99; *Rhet. ad Her.* 2.30). It was also often the case that the peroratio would recall or echo at least some of the propositio, which is the case here (cf. 4.2-6 to 1.22-23). There are plenty of examples of peroratios in deliberative discourse in the Greek tradition (see Demosthenes, *Oratio* 2.31; 3.36; Isocrates, *Oratio* 5.154; Aristides, *Oratio* 23.80).

Rhetorica ad Herennium 33.1439b.12ff. says that the peroratio could take five different forms: argument, enumeration, proposal of policy, interrogation, or irony. The peroratio in Colossians focuses on two themes: prayer and behavior (deeds and words) in public. This falls into the category of proposal of policy and as such is an example of amplification, repeating what has been said before, only here clearly applying it to one's conduct among non-Christians. The first part of the peroratio focuses on reiterating major themes or arguments of the discourse including especially prayer (cf. 1.12; 2.7; 3.15-17). In terms of recapitulation, 4.3c points back to 1.24–2.5. Paul being enabled to share the mystery of Christ in an appropriate way is what the second argument in 2.6–3.4 was all about. Lincoln suggests that 4.5a sums up the parenesis in 3.5–4.1. The reference to Paul being in bonds or chains is meant to arouse empathy or compassion (recalling 1.24–2.5), as is the request for prayer for the apostle. "In addition, the section appeals to the reader's emotions by conveying a sense of urgency with its call to alertness (4:2b) and to make the most of the time (4:5b)."[1]

The focus then in the peroratio is on getting the Colossians back on track with normal acts of devotion (as opposed to the ascetic suggestions of the errorists) and appropriate wisdom regarding behavior in relationship to outsiders. While praxis seems to be to the fore here, as 4.6 suggests, Paul also cares about witness, and so the Colossians' understanding of the gospel so that they can answer all comers.[2] What binds the requests for prayer for Paul and the discussion of deeds and speech together is the concern for spreading the gospel among outsiders.[3]

Remain constant in prayer, be watchful in it in thanksgiving, praying at the same time concerning us, in order that God might open to us a door for the Word to speak the mystery of Christ, through which we also are bound, in order to make it clear, as it is necessary for me to speak. Walk in wisdom before those outside, buying back/exploiting the time. Your words always gracious, seasoned with salt, know how it is necessary to respond to each one.

Typically Paul as he draws his discourse to a close urges prayer,[4] here associating watchfulness with thanksgiving. Gratitude prevents prayer from becoming just a shopping trip full of requests and pleas. Watchfulness suggests attentiveness rather than spiritual complacency.[5] It also suggests an attitude of expectancy, which can fuel a return to prayer over and over again. It is probably also true that there is an air of eschatological expectancy expressed here, as "buying back" or "exploiting the time" will suggest in v. 5.[6]

Paul's request for prayer for himself may imply that he anticipates being released.[7] "Us" here, however, might also refer to Timothy and Epaphras as well and their work for the gospel.[8] Paul has elsewhere spoken about an "open door" for the gospel (1 Cor. 16.9; 2 Cor. 2.12), so this is a characteristic way for him to

---

1. A. T. Lincoln, "Colossians," in *The New Interpreter's Bible* XI (Nashville: Abingdon, 2000), p. 661.

2. See Lincoln, "Colossians," p. 661 on this peroratio.

3. M. Y. MacDonald, *Colossians, Ephesians* (Collegeville: Liturgical, 2000), p. 174.

4. Cf. especially Eph. 6.18-20. Paul's discourses are often framed by prayers or talk about prayer (cf. Rom. 1.9-10; 15.30-32; Phil. 1.9-11; 4.6; 1 Thess. 1.2-3; 5.17, 25; Phlm. 4-6, 22).

5. See Lincoln, "Colossians," p. 661.

6. See J. D. G. Dunn, *The Epistles to the Colossians and to Philemon* (Grand Rapids: Eerdmans, 1996), p. 262.

7. See E. Lohse, *Colossians and Philemon* (Philadelphia: Fortress, 1971), p. 165. Or alternately he could be referring to praying for opportunities to witness while in prison, on which see Phil. 1.12-14. MacDonald, *Colossians, Ephesians*, p. 171.

8. See M. J. Harris, *Colossians and Philemon* (Grand Rapids: Eerdmans, 1991), p. 193.

express how God is the one who provides openings for the proclamation of the gospel in new ways and new places. But Paul does not want just to share the gospel; he wants prayer that he will do it "in the way it is necessary for me to speak." In other words, he wants to use the appropriate words for the specific occasion which will make the proclamation a revelation and rhetorically effective for those listening. Paul also reminds his audience here, as he did at the beginning of this discourse, that he is suffering for the sake of the gospel (1.24), only at this juncture he specifies that he is bound in chains.[9]

V. 5 uses the language of a close-knit religious group by referring to non-Christians as "the ones outside" the community. Christians are to "walk wisely" toward non-Christians (this echoes 1.9-10; 2.6-7). This means they are to act in a way that is cognizant of who is watching and of the impact their behavior may have for the gospel. Wisdom in the Jewish tradition involved just these sorts of practical matters in regard to the art of living well on a daily basis, as well as the sort of profound reflections on Wisdom that we find in such texts as Proverbs 8–9 and Colossians 1. The Colossians are exhorted to "buy back" or "redeem" or even "exploit" the time.[10] This might mean to take advantage of all opportunities to bear witness, but it could also mean to make up for lost time, for the time wasted before their conversion. There was definitely a tension in early Christianity between the missionary mandate and the attempt to create a tight-knit Christian community. It is difficult to create a group with clearly distinguishable identity and boundaries and yet have it include all sorts of persons and indeed recruit different sorts of people as part of its missionary agenda. On top of this, to use sociological terms, it appears that the community in Colossae was "high group, low grid." That is there was not much of a local hierarchal leadership structure that could have dealt with the false philosophy, and yet still the Colossian church was a distinguishable group. Furthermore, Paul is seeking to strengthen that sense of distinctive Christian existence.[11]

V. 6 indicates that the Christian's speech is to be "gracious and seasoned with salt" (cf. Job 6.6), which means not flat, dull, or insipid,[12] or it could mean witty[13] or winsome. Perhaps Paul is drawing on a familiar Greek saying found in Plutarch: a speaker can convey "a certain grace by means of words as with salt" (*On Talkativeness* 654F). In light of this, Paul may have winsome speech in view. However, Plutarch also has the following saying: "For wit is probably the

9. Against Dunn, *Colossians and Philemon*, p. 263, prison is not necessarily in view here since a person under house arrest might well be chained to a guard. See pp. 68-72 above.

10. See P. T. O'Brien, *Colossians, Philemon* (Waco: Word, 1982), pp. 241-42.

11. See MacDonald, *Colossians, Ephesians*, p. 174.

12. See Dunn, *Colossians and Philemon*, p. 266.

13. See J. B. Lightfoot, *Saint Paul's Epistles to the Colossians and to Philemon* (London: Macmillan, 1879), pp. 230-31.

tastiest condiment of all. Therefore, some call it 'graciousness' because it makes
the necessary chore of eating pleasant" (*Moralia* 685A). Paul is speaking about
rhetorically effective speech. "Gracious and seasoned with salt" "captures the
wisdom of ancient rhetoric: ideological substance without personal style fails
to convince people."[14] It also makes clear that Christians must engage in
friendly conversation with nonbelievers and must be prepared to know how to
respond to each and every outsider, regardless of their remarks or questions (cf.
1 Pet. 3.15).[15] "This paragraph is a reminder of how much was done by word of
mouth. A letter was a comparatively rare vehicle, and its contents and purpose
would be correspondingly specialized: the ordinary remarks would be trans-
mitted verbally, especially when there were urgent doctrinal and pastoral matters demanding such writing-space as there was."[16]

Dunn makes the important point that we do not get the sense in
Colossians that there is an atmosphere where persecution seems to be present
or imminent,[17] which contrasts with what we find in Revelation 2–3, which
deals in part with the same region. There is even some contrast with the tone of
1 Pet. 3.15 (cf. 4.12-19), which is from a slightly later time than Colossians but
not as late as Revelation.[18]

14. R. W. Wall, *Colossians and Philemon* (Downers Grove: InterVarsity, 1993), p. 167.

15. See P. Pokorný, *Colossians: A Commentary* (Peabody: Hendrickson, 1991), pp. 187-
88.

16. C. F. D. Moule, *The Epistles to the Colossians and Philemon* (Cambridge: Cambridge
University Press, 1968), p. 136.

17. Dunn, *Colossians and Philemon*, p. 267.

18. On these chronological matters see my *New Testament History* (Grand Rapids:
Baker, 2001) and *The New Testament Story* (Grand Rapids: Eerdmans, 2004).

Epistolary Closing — 4:7-18

Colossians has all the features of the end of a normal Pauline letter including mention of travel plans (4.7-9; cf. Rom. 15.22-32; 1 Cor. 16.1-18), final greetings (4.10-15; cf. Rom. 16.3-16; 1 Cor. 16.19-20), final instructions (4.16-17; cf. 1 Cor. 16.15-18; 1 Thess. 5.27), a personal note (4.18; cf. Rom. 16.17-20; 1 Cor. 16.21-24), and a final benediction (4.18; cf. Rom. 16.20; 1 Cor. 16.23).[1]

It is this section in particular which makes it difficult to imagine this letter coming from a post-Pauline situation, for it has a very personal Pauline character to it. MacDonald argues that the material is a way of strengthening the authority of some anonymous post-Pauline figure. Yet she is forced to admit that verses like 4.17, which involves a direct personal request of an urgent nature, make it difficult to accept that this material could be part of a pseudonymous fiction.[2] It must be asked, how can a pseudonymous letter strengthen the authority of an unknown or anonymous figure? And if the author is actually a Pauline coworker or disciple who is known and has some authority and name-recognition and some connection with the audience (e.g., Epaphras), why would he not either write in his own name or use the anonymous format one finds in Hebrews? Why would he take the chance of Colossians being seen as an attempt at deception or as the bolstering up of the authority of a person who lacked authority and authorization from God in Christ?

Some have suggested that the personalia in Colossians are modeled on Phlm. 23-24.[3] Yet Philemon (the person) is omitted in Colossians and Jesus

---

1. See J. D. G. Dunn, *The Epistles to the Colossians and to Philemon* (Grand Rapids: Eerdmans, 1996), p. 269.

2. M. Y. MacDonald, *Colossians, Ephesians* (Collegeville: Liturgical, 2000), pp. 184-85.

3. See E. Lohse, *Colossians and Philemon* (Philadelphia: Fortress, 1971), pp. 175-76. The

Justus, Nympha, and Tychicus cannot be found in Philemon's closing remarks. Furthermore, Colossians is much more substantive than Phlm. 23-24. It is not simply a case of copying. The difference between what we find when we compare the end of Colossians and Ephesians and what we find we compare the end of Colossians and Philemon is telling.[4]

It is true that one of the aims of this section seems to be the bolstering of the authority of some Pauline coworkers, such as Epaphras, Onesimus, or Tychicus, as they address or visit the Colossians as emissaries of Paul, or Nympha as she continues her ministry in the area. But nothing here suggests that Paul has already passed the baton to such figures and is now deceased. Indeed, if that were the case when Colossians was written it would not be Paul bolstering their authority but some other anonymous figure, which is odd. Why would genuine Pauline coworkers who already have an honor rating in the community need the endorsement of a Pauline ghost-writer? And would Paul's own coworkers themselves want or need to contrive a literary fiction like this?

It is precisely because of considerations such as these that Dunn endorses the theory that Colossians was written by Timothy but while Paul was still alive and confined, and "all we need envisage is Paul's approval in substance if not in detail and sufficient occasion for him to add 4:18 in his own hand."[5] This may well be correct, and if so it means that Timothy was much more of a theologian and Christian ethicist than anything in the NT about him would lead us to imagine. In my view, it is easier to see this document as from the mind of Paul but composed by someone well-versed in Asiatic rhetoric (its style and form), perhaps Timothy, while Paul was under house arrest and so still readily accessible to a whole host of coworkers, as the end of the letter suggests.

Those named represent quite a social mix: those financially well enough off to travel on gospel business (4.7, 10, 12), slaves (4.9), a doctor (4.14), and large estate owners (4.15).[6] Early Christianity was not merely a collection of refugees from the lower orders of society. In fact, it involved quite a few high status persons who played prominent if not dominant roles in various Christian congregations and in the Pauline mission in various places.

---

basis for this conclusion is that the list in Philemon is shorter and less substantive than the one in Colossians. But Colossians is not a personal letter to be read in the house-church but a group communication, which would explain the more extensive use of personalia. It is a mistake to conclude that Philemon is the source of the list in Colossians on the basis of length.

4. See the discussion of B. Thurston, "Paul's Associates in Colossians 4.7-17," *Restoration Quarterly* 41 (1999): 45-53.

5. Dunn, *Colossians and Philemon*, p. 269.

6. See Dunn, *Colossians and Philemon*, p. 270.

Tychicus the beloved brother and faithful minister and fellow servant in the Lord will let you know everything concerning me, whom I am sending to you for this very thing, in order that you might know the things concerning us and encourage your hearts, with Onesimus the faithful and beloved brother who is from you. He will let you know all the news from here.

Aristarchus, my fellow prisoner of war, greets you, and Mark the cousin of Barnabas (concerning whom you received instructions — if he comes to you, you must welcome him), and Jesus, the one called Justus. These fellow workers for the kingdom of God alone from the circumcision are the ones who have been a consolation to me. Epaphras, who is from you, a servant of Christ, greets you, always striving for you in prayer in order that you might stand perfect and be absolutely convinced in all the will of God. For I bear witness to you that he has labored very hard for you and those in Laodicea and those in Hierapolis. Luke the beloved doctor and Demas greet you. Greet the brothers in Laodicea and Nympha[7] and the church that meets in her house, and when the letter has been read among you, do it in order also that it be read in the Laodicean assembly, and the [letter] from Laodicea, in order also that you might read it. And tell Archippus "See to the ministry which you received in the Lord" in order that he might fulfill it. The greeting is in my hand — Paul. Remember my chains. Grace be with you.

We gather from v. 7 that Tychicus is the bearer of this letter. The letter then is but a part of Paul's total attempt to communicate, and Tychicus will fill in the gaps when he arrives in Colossae. He is not just the postman but will orally deliver the news. In good Asiatic rhetorical fashion we are told three times that he will give the Colossians the news about Paul (vv. 7-9). He is called a faithful minister (*diakonos;* see pp. 145-46 above) and a fellow slave/servant in the Lord, which indicates clearly that he is one of Paul's coworkers for the gospel. He is mentioned also in Acts 20.4 as Paul's companion in Greece, and he accompanies Paul to Jerusalem with the collection. In 2 Tim. 4.12 he is said to be sent on a mission to Ephesus. Obviously he was an important and trusted associate minister under Paul. It was conventional to write a note of commendation for the one bearing the letter, so undergirding his authority to speak and interpret it. In v. 8 we have the epistolary aorist "I sent" even though Paul is only now sending Tychicus. Onesimus the slave is sent along as well and is said to be "from you," which surely indicates that he is from Colossae (and thus so is

---

7. Is it Nympha or Nymphas? It was originally urged by J. B. Lightfoot, *Saint Paul's Epistles to the Colossians and to Philemon* (London: Macmillan, 1879), p. 241, that Paul would not use the Doric Greek form for Nympha, but as P. T. O'Brien, *Colossians, Philemon* (Waco: Word, 1982), p. 246, says, it may well be an Attic feminine with a short alpha. The feminine form was certainly more likely to be changed later to a masculine one, and the feminine form has some good support (B, 6, 1739, 1877, 1881, etc.). See Metzger, *TC*, p. 560.

Philemon), since we have learned from the letter to Philemon that he was not yet a Christian when he was living in Colossae before.[8]

Paul says that the only Jewish Christians still among his coworkers are Mark, Aristarchus, and Jesus Justus (vv. 10-11).[9] Aristarchus is called "my fellow prisoner of war," which does not mean merely fellow prisoner as a text like Rom. 16.7 probably indicates. "It is an honorific title which he accords to a small group of friends who were Christ's captives like himself (Rom. 16:7; Phlm. 23; cf. 2 Cor. 2:4)."[10] Mark is referred to as Barnabas's cousin, which explains why Barnabas wanted to take him along on various missionary journeys. His presence with Paul may indicate that things have been patched up between Paul and Mark (cf. Acts 15.37-39), as does the reference to Paul being comforted by Mark and others. 1 Pet. 5.13 also suggests that Mark was in Rome at a slightly later period of time. It could be that what Paul says about receiving Mark and about other instructions regarding him reflects the fact that he was somewhat under a cloud because of his previous failures in the Pauline mission.[11] If so, we see the graciousness of Paul to forgive and reemploy Mark.[12] "Jesus" is the Greek form of the Hebrew name Joshua, while "Justus" would be a name used in Latin-speaking environments.[13]

Paul's use of "kingdom of God" with regard to the work of these three men may suggest that he used this phrase when preaching the gospel to Jews. These Jewish Christians brought Paul some consolation,[14] which may suggest that the mission to Jews and by Jewish Christians was not faring well at that juncture. We may perhaps coordinate this with the situation Paul was already dealing with in Rome in which Jewish Christians seem to have been being marginalized or not fully accepted by the largely Gentile congregation.[15]

Epaphras is mentioned as one from Colossae who is presently with Paul,

8. See G. B. Caird, *Paul's Letters from Prison* (Oxford: Oxford University Press, 1976), p. 211.

9. This surely implies that Luke was a Gentile.

10. Caird, *Paul's Letters*, p. 211. Thus it is not a problem that Aristarchus is not said to be a fellow prisoner in Phlm. 24. If the term is metaphorical then these two letters need not have been written with much time between their compositions.

11. Cf. Dunn, *Colossians*, p. 277; M. Y. MacDonald, *Colossians, Ephesians* (Collegeville: Liturgical, 2000), p. 180.

12. See N. T. Wright, *Colossians and Philemon* (Grand Rapids: Eerdmans, 1986), p. 157.

13. See A. T. Lincoln, "Colossians," in *The New Interpreter's Bible* XI (Nashville: Abingdon, 2000), p. 667.

14. *Parēgoria*, only here in the NT, means the most profound sort of comfort, which assuages or alleviates things. It is a word often used on gravestones and in letters of condolence. See Thurston. "Paul's Associates," p. 49.

15. See B. Witherington and D. Hyatt, *Paul's Letter to the Romans* (Grand Rapids: Eerdmans, 2004), ad loc.

striving for them in prayer so that they might stand perfect (presumably at the last judgment), being completely convinced of the will of God, presumably as it pertains to them.[16] Epaphras appears likely to have been the one who founded the gospel work in the three cities of the Lycus Valley — Colossae, Hierapolis, and Laodicea. It is hard to know what "he has worked very hard for you" might mean since he is at a distance, beyond the fact that he has prayed hard for them.

Luke is called a doctor here for the only time in the NT. He may be with Paul to minister to Paul's wounds or ailments in some capacity.[17] He is also called "beloved," which suggests a close relationship between Paul and Luke and perhaps between Luke and many Christians. Mark and Luke, the probable authors of the second and third Gospels, are thus present with Paul in Rome in the early 60s. Quite a number of people have access to Paul, which strongly suggests that he is under house arrest and not in prison.

V. 15 reminds us that there were no church buildings in the first century. Indeed, little evidence of any before the third century exists. Meetings took place largely in people's homes, and so the conversion of householders became very important in the early days. Paul's letters were meant to be read aloud during house-church worship. Paul is probably referring to a house-church meeting in the home of a woman named Nympha here. The word "her" with "house" is supported by B, 5, 1739, and sy[h], whereas the Western and Byzantine witnesses (D, G, and others) have "his." We know, however, that there were anti-feminist tendencies in the Western text, especially in Acts,[18] and it is certainly more likely that "her" would have been changed to "his" than the reverse. The accusative form *Nymphan* here could refer to either the feminine name Nympha or the masculine name Nymphas. Both names are well-attested in Greek literature and in the papyri, though Nympha is a bit more common.[19] It is possible that Nympha was the head of a household because she was a widow, but whatever is the case about that, Paul knows her and picks her out from among the house-churches in Laodicea to greet, which suggests that she was a well-known church leader,

16. On future perfection and glory in Colossians see pp. 147-48 above. Another way to read this would be "that you may stand firm, mature and convinced, engaged in doing all the will of God." See C. F. D. Moule, *The Epistles to the Colossians and Philemon* (Cambridge: Cambridge University Press, 1968), p. 138.

17. Demas is mentioned with Luke both here and in Phlm. 24. He sadly is also mentioned in 2 Tim. 4.10 as someone who deserted Paul at the end of Paul's life and ran off to Thessalonike.

18. See my "The Anti-Feminist Tendencies of the Western Text of Acts," *JBL* 103 (1984): 82-84.

19. See P. Pokorný, *Colossians: A Commentary* (Peabody: Hendrickson, 1991), p. 195; M. J. Harris, *Colossians and Philemon* (Grand Rapids: Eerdmans, 1991), pp. 211-12.

for it does not appear Paul had been to Laodicea any more than he had been to Colossae.[20]

V. 16 has led to endless speculation. Where is this Laodicean letter?[21] Caird suggests that it is the circular document we know as Ephesians, and this is certainly possible.[22] This leads to the conjecture that Tychicus took with him Colossians and Ephesians and that Onesimus took the letter to Philemon, which also entails the view that these three documents were written together within a short span of time.[23] But the text here seems to suggest that the letter to Laodicea had already been sent and read by the congregation there. Furthermore a letter to Laodicea would not have been simply a circular letter any more than Colossians is, and yet these congregations are to exchange letters with each other. Ephesians does not seem to be a particularistic letter to a specific Pauline congregation.[24] What we do have a hint of here is how the process of collecting and later canonizing Paul's letters transpired. Letters were exchanged or copied and exchanged, and precisely because they were seen as of ongoing value they were kept and reused.[25]

V. 17 asks the Colossians to spur Archippus on in regard to his ministry in their midst. He is to "fulfill" it. The idea is that God has given him a commission to fulfill.

Paul closes this letter like various of his other genuine letters, with a personal touch, his signature, perhaps precisely to prevent forgery (v. 18). The wording here is exactly the same as in 1 Cor. 16.21. Paul asks that the Colossians

20. See Dunn, *Colossians*, pp. 284-85; J. N. Aletti, *Saint Paul. Épître aux Colossiens* (Paris: Gabalda, 1993), p. 269.

21. Later Christian writers attempted to fill this void. Somewhere in the fourth or fifth century someone composed a letter to the Laodiceans, perhaps in Greek though the oldest extant text is in Latin. This document was composed by taking lines from various Pauline letters and weaving them together. See the lengthy excursus in Lightfoot, *Colossians*, pp. 272-98, and MacDonald, *Colossians, Ephesians*, p. 183. Amazingly, this pseudepigraph was regarded as authentic, though not canonical, in the Western Church for almost 1,000 years.

22. See G. B. Caird, *Paul's Letters from Prison* (Oxford: Oxford University Press, 1976), p. 212: "It is odd that Paul is sending greetings via Colossae to Laodicea when he was also writing to Laodicea. The problem is resolved if the letter from Laodicea was Ephesians, a circular letter without personal greetings." See pp. 217-19 below.

23. See Wright, *Colossians*, p. 161.

24. See R. W. Wall, *Colossians and Philemon* (Downers Grove: InterVarsity, 1993), pp. 174-75.

25. See Dunn, *Colossians*, p. 286: It "is significant that a letter written for a particular church should be regarded as of sufficiently wider relevance as to be read elsewhere. That suggests an awareness on the part of the author(s) that Paul's teaching, even in specific letters, was of not merely occasional or passing significance. In other words, we see here already the beginning of the sense of the letters' importance that thereafter developed over the decades into the acknowledgment of their canonical status."

remember his chains, probably in prayer as that which is hindering his proclamation of the gospel and his coming to them. This could, however, just mean
"pray regarding my difficult condition." Thus Paul leaves his audience on a note
of pathos before wishing them, as at the beginning of the letter, the grace of
God. The subscript in A, B, P, and L all mention that this letter was written from
Rome, and both K and L say it is a letter conveyed "through Tychicus and
Onesimus."[26]

26. Chrysostom argues in his first homily on Colossians that the letter was written after Romans but at the same time as Philemon, Ephesians, and Philippians "near upon the
close of his preaching."

Bridging the Horizons — Colossians

Paul drags the false worship back down to earth where it belongs. For the "super-spirituality" of which such teachers boasted Paul substitutes "unspirituality" (literally "the mind of the flesh"). . . . This warning against confusing the supernatural with the genuinely "spiritual" remains relevant throughout the history of religion; it is perhaps particularly pertinent to Christians living in a rationalistic age, who may be tempted to regard a wide variety of paranormal or supernatural occurrences as somehow "spiritual."

Its elaborate liturgies and seemingly rigorous self-abasing asceticism give it a name for serious piety: but it is a sham. . . . What looks like rigorous discipline is in fact a subtle form of self-indulgence.[1]

One of the great dangers for the church in an age of pan-spirituality is the resort to gimmicks or even divination in its modern forms to heighten the spiritual tenor of one's congregation or to deepen its spiritual maturity or piety. The quotations above properly warn us about the difference between "the supernatural" and what can properly be called "spiritual." Let me explain. Going to a spiritual advisor in order to contact "familiar spirits" (be they human or supernatural) is something quite clearly forbidden in the Bible (see 1 Samuel 28). The Bible says not that it is impossible but that it is inappropriate. Why? For the very good reason that divination, as opposed to prayer, is the human attempt to use the divine or the supernatural to satisfy its own purposes, its pious curiosity, its desire to have inside knowledge or power of a supernatural sort. Prayer, by contrast, is a spiritual exercise which leaves the results in God's hands, not an attempt to get one's hands on the levers that control the universe.

1. N. T. Wright, *Colossians and Philemon* (Grand Rapids: Eerdmans, 1986), pp. 122-23, 127.

On a radio show I spoke with a call-in guest, a woman stuck in traffic on the Santa Monica Freeway. She said "I am sitting here holding my crystals and feeling really close to Jesus, and I am wondering what is the connection between these crystals and Jesus." I told her there was none, except that Colossians suggests he made those crystals, that he is the solid rock to which we should cling, and that those crystals are certainly not that solid rock.

Paul in Colossians is dealing with a specific sort of spiritual problem — aberrant forms of worship engaged in by Christians. Christians were striving through ascetic acts to enter the heavenly worship with the angels, perhaps to enter into a visionary or ecstatic state. Here we have the use of ascetic acts in hopes that they will trigger some specific "spiritual experience." Yet in fact genuine spiritual experiences cannot be triggered by some human "technique." They are caused by the Holy Spirit, who blows in whatever direction the Spirit chooses. If the Spirit is not moving, the experience either is not happening or is contrived and not genuine.

In addition, Paul is critical of settling for something less than the proper object of worship — namely Christ himself. It is possible that "the worship of angels" actually refers to worshiping the angels themselves rather than just participating with angels in worship. Paul has nothing but condemnation for that sort of thing, and one might expect him to say the same thing today about the wrong sort of veneration of various saints or Mary. They are not the proper objects of our worship, our devotion, or our prayers according to the NT. Veneration of them ignores the fact that Christians can boldly approach the throne of grace directly through Christ himself. One can pray directly to the head of the universe, the tri-personal God. The vision Paul holds up in Colossians is christocentric, and there is no room in it for the worship or adoration of lesser beings, even if they are angels.

Chrysostom says in *On the Priesthood* 5.2 that homileticians preaching this material in Colossians

> should not be governed by their desires. It is impossible to acquire this power except by these two qualities: contempt of praise [for oneself] and the force of eloquence. If either is lacking, the one left is made useless by the divorce from the other. If a preacher despises praise yet does not produce the kind of teaching which is "with grace, seasoned with salt," he is despised by the people, and his sublime words accomplish nothing. And if he is eloquent but a slave to the sound of applause, again an equal damage threatens both him and the people, because through his passion for praise he aims to speak more for the pleasure than the profit of his hearers.

There are many occasions in the life of the church where disaster can be, or could be, averted if the right words, carefully chosen, judicious and winsome, are spoken. The church is in large measure a community that lives on the basis of words — the preached Word, the taught Word, the word of comfort, the word of counsel, the prayed words, and so on. It is no accident that there is so much said in the NT about how one should control one's tongue, learn how to speak properly, and even become skilled in the art of persuasion. And yet, strangely, I have been in many congregations where prepared sermons were viewed skeptically as if somehow they did not leave room for the Holy Spirit to speak. A seminary student came to me groaning because of all the study and reading which was required of him: "I don't know why I need to do all this study when I can just get up in the pulpit and the Spirit will give me utterance." I answered: "Yes, you can do that, but it is a shame that you are not giving the Spirit more to work with."

Chrysostom is warning about the dangers of falling in love with being praised or with one's reviews. While a preacher's speech should be seasoned with salt, and so be gracious and preservative in character, that same preacher should take with a grain of salt most of the kudos that come her or his way. Chrysostom is all for eloquence, but not when accompanied by a tendency to be a people-pleaser or to live for applause. That leads to the skewing of the message simply in order to please and admired trying to give the people what they desire. The preacher's words should be full of grace, but the preacher should not be full of himself. To win some, one usually needs to be winsome, but God can use even reluctant and short-spoken Jonah to bring a city to repentance.

It is easy to fall into the trap of speaking in manners most likely to entertain, please, or prompt admiration in one's audience. In the course of doing so, one loses altogether the ability to speak prophetically to one's congregation. Of course all of us long to be loved and appreciated, and this can lead to precisely the problems Chrysostom warns about. I must confess that it took me some years in the parish before I realized that it was not my job to please the people and help out God. For one thing, there is no pleasing the people, for their desires and wants are ever shifting and vary from member to member. For another thing, God can do it quite nicely without me. This fact is sobering — that one is not indispensable to people's lives or to God.

And yet many ministers act as if they are indispensable to their people and to God. Chrysostom would have us know that our task is to please God, do God's will, and help the people, and sometimes that means speaking a prophetic word or taking a prophetic action in due season, which may well cause alarm or even protest and rejection by some. It is easy to forget that one is a steward of the mysteries of God, finally answerable to God, not a steward of the pocketbooks of one's members, beholden to them for one's ministerial office and role. And so Chrysostom calls ministers to that balance of eloquence and persuasion on the one hand and not allowing other people's eloquent praise of oneself to over-inflate one's fragile ego, on the other.

*   *   *

Many Christians tend to concentrate on one [vice] list or the other; one knows of Christian communities that would be appalled at the slightest sexual irregularity but which are nests of malicious intrigue, backbiting, gossip and bad temper, and conversely, of others where people are so concerned to live in untroubled harmony with each other that they tolerate flagrant immorality.[2]

It was the great American Transcendentalist Ralph Waldo Emerson who said "A foolish consistency is the hobgoblin of little minds, adored by little statesmen and philosophers and divines." Doubtless he was right, but in fact impartiality and fairness to all are not small virtues. All sin should be taken seriously, whether a sin like gluttony, greed, or egocentrism or a sexual or theological sin of some sort. The leader of the Lambda chapter at Vanderbilt asked me at a forum on homosexuality whether he would be welcome in my church. I told him that everyone is welcome to come as they are into the church, that it is meant to be a hospital for sick sinners not a museum for saints. But equally *no one* is welcome to stay as they are. As Paul says so clearly in Colossians, everyone must repent and leave behind their old selves, their old ways. This includes heterosexuals leaving behind homophobia and gay-bashing, both of which are serious sins, and homosexuals leaving behind the kind of sexual actions which are clearly condemned in the Bible — namely same-sex sexual sharing. I agree with Bishop Wright in the quotation above that neither extreme should characterize the church. But it is also true that the existence of a blind spot in one's recognition of a certain kind of sin does not mean one should stop preaching against all sin on the basis of it being unfair. Rather one's conscience should be raised so that one becomes an equal-opportunity critic of all sin, calling all persons equally to repentance.

Too often the condemnation of hypocrisy (including the straining out of small virtues while swallowing major vices), which is proper, has led to the silencing of the prophetic critique of sin altogether. All Christians should be calling all other Christians to moral accountability for their behavior. This is why, for instance, James 5 encourages us to confess our sins to one another — not merely to the priest or counselor or friend. There needs to be a community of saved sinners that is forming into an accountable body of Christ, helping each other to grow in grace. Instead of pointing fingers, we need to hold outstretched hands and help each other follow all the proper moral paths for the Lord's name's sake. Tolerance of sin is no more a virtue than hypocritical condemnation of selective sins. We are all called to accountability, and will have to render account to Christ one day as well.

2. Wright, *Colossians, Philemon*, p. 133.

We are also all called to speak the truth in love, neither merely speaking the truth nor merely indulgently loving. Paul calls for the balance that leads to what he calls "the perfection of love" (3:14). Love is a sanctifying force that leads one to be one's best self, not allowing one to settle for behaving badly. Paul's call to love is not separated from the call to holiness and sanctification. Love without holiness is mere indulgence and permissiveness. It never leads to moral rectitude. But holiness without love is mere censoriousness and leads to condemnation and guilt rather than to growth in grace and in stature.

There is much in the last two chapters of Colossians in its discussion of ethics we would do well to ponder. Jimmy Dunn comes to these conclusions in his comments on the Colossian household code:

> And as for the continuing relevance of such household rules, we need to recall how much they were conditioned by and adapted to the situation of the times. They are not timeless rules . . . and can no more be transferred directly to the different circumstances of today than can the rules of, say, Susannah Wesley (mother of John and Charles) for bringing up children. It is the orientation and motivation indicated in the repeated reference to the Lord . . . which provide the fixed points for a continuing Christian ethic.

> [In] the cities of Paul's day the great bulk of Christians would have had no possibility whatsoever of exerting any political pressure for any particular policy or reform. In such circumstances a pragmatic quietism was the most effective means of gaining room enough to develop the quality of personal relationships which would establish and build up the microcosms (churches) of transformed communities.[3]

There is truth in what he says here, but he concedes too much. Paul's words are not culturally bound, though they are certainly culturally relevant as words on target for that audience and that time. It is true of course that when Paul is dealing with a socially defunct practice like slavery there is no direct application for today. Yet there are Christian principles in operation here that are germane to our own modern situations. We have noted not only how Paul attempts to Christianize an existing fallen situation, whether it be slavery or patriarchy, but we have also pointed out the trajectory of change in his remarks — swimming upstream against the prevailing cultural current. This is both noteworthy and relevant. At the very least we learn that Paul believes that the leaven of the gospel can transform social relationships within the community of Christ itself. And it is precisely this sort of social engineering that Paul is engaging in, in the latter stages of this document. Paul believes that there are norms of conduct

---

3. J. D. G. Dunn, *The Epistles to the Colossians and to Philemon* (Grand Rapids: Eerdmans, 1996), pp. 246, 253.

and behavior that grow out of one's enduring relationship with Christ, the head of the body. He is urging the Colossian Christians not to be conformed to the patterns of this world, but rather to be new persons in Christ. This is certainly an enduring and endearing Christian principle.

And then too all the ways Paul encourages mutual service, mutual respect, and mutual love are always important and imperative for the church in any age. Paul believes the household, as well as the household of faith can behave better! He believes that it can change into a more Christlike pattern of conduct. And he believes in the broader principles implemented in these specific situations, some of which are:

> Each person in the household must be treated as a person, not as mere chattel.
> Each person is a moral agent who can respond to imperatives and should do so, even children.
> More responsibility must lie on the shoulders of the head of the household — hence the most exhortations are given to that person.
> It is especially the head of the household who should set the pattern of Christian behavior toward the other members of the household and who will be held accountable for doing so.
> Domestic behavior does not merely mean being accountable to the head of the house. There is a higher accountability to God, to whom all members of the house are answerable.
> Love and devotion are the key motivators of conduct and the key gauges of what conduct is appropriate. If something cannot be done in love, it should not be done.
> Each person must respond to the imperatives directed to him or her. It is not for another member of the household to lord it over the others demanding obedience or submission.

Much more could be said, but this is enough to show that it is not right to say that Paul is not laying down eternal rules or principles of Christian or human conduct. In fact he is, though not all the principles can be applied in the same way today because the social situations now are not identical with the social situation then. The principle of analogy must come into play.

THE HOMILY CALLED EPHESIANS

Homilies in the New Testament Era

It is hard to know precisely what a Christian sermon, spoken to other Christians, would have sounded like in the middle of the first century. Acts 20.18-35[1] is perhaps the best sample summary of a Pauline sermon directed to Christians we have, and what is interesting about it is that unlike some of the summaries of sermons preached to nonbelievers in Acts, it is not only not an exposition of one or more OT texts, it never even cites such a text. The only text cited is an otherwise unknown saying of Jesus (v. 35), which concludes the exposition rather than being its starting point. Early Christian sermons directed to Christian audiences were not necessarily based on scriptural texts. We cannot tell whether something is a sermon on the basis of whether it exposits some specific biblical text or texts. So the fact that Ephesians is not an exposition of Scripture does not disqualify it from being a sermon. Some texts from Isaiah seem to have influenced the exposition in Ephesians without being the main basis of the exposition (see pp. 247-48 below).

It is possible to see 1 John as a homily written to those who are already believers, and it, too, is not an exposition of one or more OT texts. Rather, like the sermon summary in Acts 20 it is an exposition of key Christian theological and ethical themes, though not a sort of farewell address or autobiographical sermon like the sermon in Acts 20. What we find in Ephesians is closer to 1 John than it is to Acts 20 (though 1 John lacks any epistolary elements), and Ephesians is also not that much longer than 1 John. We do not know what the stan-

---

1. On which see my *The Acts of the Apostles* (Grand Rapids: Eerdmans, 1998), pp. 610-18.

dard length of an early Christian sermon was, but Ephesians and 1 John would be considered lengthy sermons by most modern standards. To present either in an effective manner with appropriate pauses and gestures would take more than twenty to twenty-five minutes. In fact, it would have taken closer to an hour if it was rhetorically delivered. Hebrews is called a word of exhortation (13.22) and also has no epistolary opening, though it does have a brief epistolary conclusion (13.22-25). Despite the disclaimer in Heb. 13.22, it is a lengthy discourse, twice as long as Ephesians. Unlike the other previously mentioned sermons, Hebrews does deal at length with a variety of OT texts, probably because its target audience is Jewish Christians.

The author of Ephesians may well be familiar with sermonic practice in the synagogue. The Jewish sermon would often open with a benediction ("blessed be the name . . .") and close with prayer and doxology. These elements are found in the first half of the discourse in Eph. 1.3-14 and 3.14-21.[2] Yet we also seem clearly to have a proper rhetorical eulogy in ch. 1, as we shall see, and so some mixing of Jewish and Greek influences must be accounted for.

Homilia is the Greek term for conversation or an informal address, which in due course came to be used for a sermon, and the Latin term *sermo* also originally indicated a conversation, not a formal sermon. NT homilies are not formal treatises, like philosophical treatises or essays, but a more informal form of communication, like most modern sermons. R. Jeal offers a helpful definition of sermon that seems suitable for the rhetorically adept discourse we find in Ephesians:

> the sermon . . . is a speech or text that is not intended to deal with controversies or problematic issues nor to answer questions,[3] but is directed to an audience of *theoroi* [observers] who, rather than acting as *kritai* [critics] who make a decision on the basis of the argument presented to them, are encouraged to think and behave in accord with the speaker's or author's leading or persuasion. The speaker/author is concerned to stimulate the thoughts and sentiments of the audience rather than argue critically, so as to persuade the audience to take the course of action seen to be appropriate.[4]

One may say that the goal is to inspire the audience to be their best selves, or to use the language of R. Bultmann they are to "become what they already in part

---

2. See Roy R. Jeal, *Integrating Theology and Ethics in Ephesians: The Ethos of Communication* (Lewiston: Mellen, 2000), pp. 46-47.

3. Thus all of the Pauline documents are surrogates for oral communication and so have oral qualities to them, but only Ephesians appears not to be a specific word addressed to a particular set of circumstances in Paul's churches.

4. Jeal, *Integrating Theology and Ethics*, p. 49. This comports with what we noted in the Introduction about the nature of argumentation in epideictic rhetoric. See pp. 4-10 above.

are." Asiatic rhetoric in an epideictic mode appeals very strongly to the emotions to persuade the audience under the assumption that right belief and behavior will result if one wins the hearts and not just the minds.

As Kennedy points out,

> Jewish midrash and the Christian homily . . . are also forms of public address. Though often simple and unpretentious, they fall under the general rubric of epideictic, and John Chrysostom developed their artistic potentialities. The panegyrical sermon as practiced in later antiquity by Gregory Thaumaturgus, Eusebius of Caesarea, Gregory of Nazianzus, Ambrose, and others is quite consciously epideictic in form, often strongly influenced by the teaching of rhetorical schools.[5]

All these later Christian preachers, especially Chrysostom, had Paul as a model.[6] Ephesians was one of their favorite documents to expound and model their preaching on, and one reason may be that it naturally fit the pattern of epideictic oratory.[7]

Ephesians as a Letter to Ephesus?

Ephesians is a circular homily included in a document rather than a circular Pauline letter. The latter part of epistolary framework in ch. 6 is probably copied directly from Colossians, and 1.1-2 is certainly a bare minimum of an epistolary opening.

Also pointing away from the idea that Ephesians is actually a letter, much less a Pauline letter, is its general character. It does not deal with any particular problems of one or more house-churches nor does it have the personal elements of a Pauline letter. It lacks not only the opening personal prayer but also the rehearsal of relevant events and the travelogue. It mentions no other people by name except Tychicus (6.21), but that is a carry-over from Colossians and refers to the Pauline coworker carrying this document. There is no reference to any particular person in the audience. This is nearly impossible to explain if this document is addressed to the church in Ephesus in particular, since according to Acts 18–20 Paul had not only founded the church in Ephesus but he had stayed there for

---

5. G. A. Kennedy, "The Genres of Rhetoric," in *The Handbook of Classical Rhetoric in the Hellenistic Period* (Leiden: Brill, 1997), p. 47.

6. See now the detailed and helpful study of M. Mitchell, *The Heavenly Trumpet: John Chrysostom and the Art of Pauline Interpretation* (Louisville: Westminster/John Knox, 2002).

7. For further discussion on Christian homilies in the NT see my *Letters and Homilies to Hellenized Christians* I (Downers Grove: InterVarsity, 2006), Introduction.

some years. All this is because the document is not addressed to some particular audience and because the author does not know many of the recipients (cf. 1.15; 3.2; 4.21). Ephesians seems to be addressed to a whole group of Christians in a particular area — namely Asia.[8] We have no other such Pauline document.

What of the apparent reference to Ephesus in 1.1? The words "in Ephesus" are absent from some of our most important early witnesses (P46, ℵ*, B*, 424, 1739, Origen, and manuscripts mentioned by Basil). In addition Marcion designated this document in about A.D. 150 as "to the Laodiceans," and both Tertullian and Ephraem know it but never mention the words "in Ephesus" when talking about its beginning.[9] These witnesses have good geographical spread, some are quite early, and they include the original readings of two of the most important codexes, Sinaiticus and Vaticanus.

If we leave out "in Ephesus" the Greek sentence is still very awkward. Only Colossians describes its recipients as "faithful . . . in Christ," and Colossians in many ways seems to be the model for Ephesians. The phrase without the reference to Ephesus literally reads "to the saints, those being . . . and to the faithful in Christ." In the Pauline parallels in 2 Cor. 1.1 and Phil. 1.1 the present participle *ousin* is followed by geographical locations. It is then possible that the name of the particular audience in Ephesians was left blank so that the oral deliverer of the discourse could insert the name according to where he was sharing the sermon.[10] This is a plausible thesis, but there are no manuscripts that have "in" with no location, nor is there any ancient epistolary evidence for such a practice. But this document should not be compared to letters, as it really is not one.

Lincoln has conjectured that the text originally read "to the saints those being in . . . and in . . . , faithful in Christ Jesus." In other words, two destinations were originally mentioned.[11] This is certainly conjectural since we also have no manuscripts with two "in" phrases either. In my view, it is quite possible that Paul is not addressing two different destinations but two groups of people — "the saints" being Jewish Christians and "the faithful in Christ" being Gentiles.[12] Clearly still something is missing after "being" and we would expect

8. It seems to be mainly addressed to Gentiles (see 3.1), which is not surprising since Paul is mainly the apostle to the Gentiles, but not exclusively so.

9. See Metzger, *TC*, p. 532.

10. There may be a precedent for this in ancient Greek letter writing from royal courts during the Hellenistic period. See G. Zuntz, *The Text of the Epistles* (London: British Academy, 1954), p. 228. According to Zuntz, the master copy left the address blank, and then when multiple copies were made of the document, the differing addresses were filled in the different copies as they were sent out.

11. A. T. Lincoln, *Ephesians* (Waco: Word, 1990), p. 3.

12. See G. B. Caird, *Paul's Letters from Prison* (Oxford: Oxford University Press, 1976), p. 31. I disagree with Lincoln, *Ephesians*, p. 2, who says that in no other Pauline letter does he

a particular destination inserted. In my view it was originally left blank for such an insertion because it was a circular document, a homiletical encyclical of sorts.

But what finally tips the scales in favor of this being a homily is that it is a large-scale example of epideictic rhetoric in praise of the nature and unity of the church in Christ, the only one of its kind in the Pauline corpus or indeed in the "letters" section of the NT.[13] The proof of the pudding, however, is in the eating, and so this must be substantiated as we work through the discourse itself. For now, we must conclude by saying that "in Ephesus" is an early addition and probably reflects the place, or one of the places, this document first lodged and was copied, with the copyist adding the particular locale. It is not, in all likelihood, a document that was originally sent specifically to Ephesus.

Epideictic Rhetoric: The Art of Persuasive Sermon-Making

Sermons were of course not uncommon in Paul's day. They could be heard on a weekly basis in synagogues all across the empire.[14] They were a particular sort of religious oration, and since Christian sermons tended not to deal with priests, temples, and correct religious rituals (although some referred to circumcision or baptism, and some to the sacrifice of Christ), and since a good deal of the time they were not expositions of some OT text, they would not generally have been viewed as specifically "religious" as opposed to philosophical in character by Gentiles who heard them. The profound theological and ethical reflections found in Ephesians would have sounded more like a philosophical oration to Gentile ears.

Demonstrative, or epideictic, or "ceremonial" rhetoric had a long history before the time of Paul going back at least as far as Aristotle. It was celebratory rhetoric, the rhetoric of praise and blame, and its primary temporal focus was on the present. It could be heard at festivals or funerals or sometimes just in the marketplace. The audience was not a judge or an assembly but simply interested spectators of various sorts. Epideictic oratory tended to focus on the core values of a society or some subset of a society seeking to affirm, reaffirm, or

---

call Jewish Christians "the saints." Paul does this in Romans, which is also a document written to a congregation that Paul has not founded. See B. Witherington and D. Hyatt, *Paul's Letter to the Romans* (Grand Rapids: Eerdmans, 2004), Introduction.

13. 1 Corinthians 13 is a small-scale example of epideictic rhetoric imbedded in a deliberative discourse. See my *Conflict and Community in Corinth* (Grand Rapids: Eerdmans, 1995), pp. 264-73.

14. See Jeal, *Integrating Theology and Ethics*, pp. 44-45.

even inculcate such values (see Aristotle, *Rhetoric* 2.18:1391b17). Quintilian, in Paul's era, simply concurs with Aristotle about the three species of rhetoric, recognizing epideictic as an important sort of discourse (*Inst. Or.* 3.4). In summarizing what characterized epideictic rhetoric G. A. Kennedy makes these telling remarks: "Epideictic is perhaps best regarded as including any discourse, oral or written, that does not aim at a specific action or decision but seeks to enhance knowledge, understanding, or belief, often through praise or blame, whether of persons, things, or values. It is thus an important feature of cultural or group cohesion. Most religious preaching . . . can be viewed as epideictic."[15] This is an accurate summary of what we find in Ephesians, describing its character and rhetorical aims quite clearly. Ephesians wants to praise and lift up certain essential theological and ethical truths as a means of focusing on and celebrating the union of Jew and Gentile together in the Pauline community.

Epideictic rhetoric tended to get short shrift compared to judicial or deliberative rhetoric in the standard handbooks, being deemed the least important of the three species of rhetoric. Aristotle seems to have started this trend, giving epideictic only one chapter's scrutiny in his *Rhetoric* compared to deliberative, which gets four chapters, and judicial, which gets six. Cicero gives only a very brief treatment of epideictic in *De Inventione* at the end of book two, and Quintilian only devotes one chapter to the subject (*Inst. Or.* 3.7). Yet the truth is, with the rise of the empire and the demise of any sort of real democracy (except in the micro-assemblies of small groups, including churches, that were not official political bodies), epideictic oratory became an increasingly important feature of the culture, especially with the increase in Olympic-style games and the spread of the emperor cult. There were more Roman triumphs, more festivals, more religious celebrations, more games, and hence more epideictic oratory in various venues and settings. Quintilian even speaks of an annual contest in Rome which involved creating an oration in praise of Jupiter Capitolinus (*Inst. Or.* 3.7.4). Christianity had to, and did, respond to this proliferation of the rhetoric of praise and blame.

Quintilian goes on to speak about the character of epideictic and its function during the empire. He says "the proper function however of panegyric is to amplify and embellish its themes" (*Inst. Or.* 3.7.6). It is my judgment that Ephesians takes the themes of Colossians, gives them a ecclesiocentric focus, and then embellishes them insofar as they are germane to a praising form of rhetoric. Quintilian stresses that this form of rhetoric is directed in the main to the praise of gods and human beings (3.7.6-7), which suits Ephesians well since what is praised is God in Christ, the work of the Spirit, and the result of that work in the creating of community. "In praising the gods our first step will be

---

15. G. A. Kennedy, "The Genres of Rhetoric," in *Handbook of Classical Rhetoric in the Hellenistic Period* (Leiden: Brill, 1997), pp. 43-50, here p. 45.

to express our veneration of the majesty of their nature in general terms, next we shall proceed to praise the special power of the individual god and the activities by which he has benefited the human race. . . . Next we must record their exploits as handed down from antiquity. Even gods may derive honor from their descent" (3.7.7-8). We certainly see a good deal of this in the eulogy of Christ in Ephesians 1. There is a thin line between deliberative oratory and epideictic because, as Quintilian says, the same topics that are advised in deliberative oratory are praised in epideictic oratory (3.7.28). In general, humans are praised for virtues and condemned for vices, and the same applies to communities of humans as well (see also pp. 174-83 above).

At the hands of the Sophists, epideictic rhetoric was sometimes nothing more than the art of display or speaking well — eloquence for its own sake, or for the sake of flattering a governor or a group of citizens. But at its best epideictic rhetoric set out the values and ideals of conduct for a society and let the audience learn and embrace them. It was primarily a Greek phenomenon and thrived in settings where Hellenistic culture had taken deep roots and not been supplanted by the overlay of Roman culture. This was especially true in Asia, home of Asiatic rhetoric, which often took the form of panegyric or epideictic oratory. This sort of oratory was heard all the time, not just at public functions such as at weddings and funerals but even in personal encounters such as welcoming guests or bidding farewell to friends. At the *symposion* the after-dinner speaker would often serve up an epideictic dessert. It was often effusive in character and involved long periods (e.g., Eph. 1.3-14; 2.14-18; 3.14-19). The household then was often the setting for such rhetoric, the very social setting where Christians met. It is not a surprise then to find good samplings of epideictic rhetoric in the NT, namely in Ephesians and Hebrews.

In his important work on Ephesians, J. Gnilka comes to the conclusion that Ephesians should be seen as a "liturgische Homilie."[16] Lincoln as well concludes that Ephesians appears to be the written equivalent of a homily that one would deliver to a congregation in a worship service.[17] The first full-scale treatment of Ephesians as a rhetorically adept homily has now been provided by R. R. Jeal. He is particularly concerned about how a rhetorical analysis can help us understand the relationship between the theology in chs. 1–3 and the ethics in chs. 4–6. Do chs. 1–3 create a sense of awe, gratitude, and humility which then inspires and motivates a person to take on and practice what is urged in chs. 4–6? Jeal sees Ephesians as a specialized form of sermonic oratory meant to speak to the audience in a positive encouraging way and so motivate their behavior.[18] The audience of such a discourse is expected to act not as judges or

---

16. J. Gnilka, *Der Epheserbrief* (Freiburg: Herder, 1971), p. 33.
17. Lincoln, *Ephesians*, p. 28.
18. Jeal, *Integrating Theology and Ethics*, pp. 28-29.

politicians, but as critical observers who when edified are called on to respond positively.

It is Jeal's view that the first half of Ephesians should be seen as epideictic rhetoric while chs. 4–6 should be seen as deliberative rhetoric calling for specific future behavioral change in the near future.[19] This may well be correct, especially since there seems to be a clear demarcation between the two halves. But it was not inappropriate in an epideictic oration to end with some exhortations based on the praise and blame that came before. We have seen the comment above from Quintilian about how parenesis in deliberative and epideictic speeches could look very much the same. The question is: Is Ephesians 4–6 essentially an attempt to laud the proper behavior and criticize improper behavior (and so an exercise in praise and blame), or is Paul in fact trying to *change* the behavior of the audience in the near future? There is no disputing that we have imperatives in chs. 4–6, but how do they function? Is Paul saying to the audience "You are not doing this, but this is what you ought to do," or is he saying "Here is praiseworthy and blameworthy behavior which every Christian must practice or shun," without asking for a change in behavior? I think, since this document does not have one particular audience or any particular problem in mind, that it is better to regard chs. 4–6 as also hortatory and epideictic in character, though one must be open to the possibility that it is deliberative in nature. When the subject of praise becomes a community's values it is natural for imperatives to be interspersed into the discussion. The audience, especially if it is living out advice like that given in Colossians 3–4, is already in the present doing, at least in part, what is described in Ephesians 4–6 and what it already knows it ought to do. What is necessary under such circumstances is not a proposal for a change of policy or praxis, but rather a lauding of good conduct and exhortation to carry on in such fashion, as well as a blaming of bad conduct. Quintilian stresses that "praise in general terms may be awarded to noble sayings and deeds. . . . I do not agree that panegyric concerns only questions regarding what is honorable" (*Inst. Or.* 3.7.28).[20] I submit that throughout this discourse the audience is being asked to learn or remember (e.g., 1.13-14; 2.11-22; 4.17ff.; 5.8), not to change their conduct. The peroratio in Ephesians 6 makes perfectly clear that the audience is being asked to stand firm and equip themselves with armor they already have ready to hand, not change direction.[21]

If we ask why Paul has chosen to write such an epideictic masterpiece to

---

19. Jeal, *Integrating Theology and Ethics,* p. 43, following Lincoln, *Ephesians,* xlii.

20. Notice how very easily the epideictic showpiece on love in 1 Corinthians 13 leads immediately into the imperative in 14.1, "follow the way of love. . . ."

21. On Ephesians as epideictic rhetoric see W. F. Taylor, *Ephesians, Colossians* (Minneapolis: Augsburg, 1985), pp. 22-23, and also now P. Perkins, "The Letter to the Ephesians," in *The New Interpreter's Bible* XI (Nashville: Abingdon, 2000), pp. 351-55.

Christians in Asia, using the style of Asiatic rhetoric, the answer must in part be the nature of the audience. Not only are they all Asians, it appears also that they are also overwhelmingly Gentile (1.11-14; 2.11-13, 17-19; 3.1; 4.17-19; 5.8) and as such grew up in the highly Greek and rhetoric-saturated environment that characterized Hellenistic culture in the province of Asia. As we have already noted (see pp. 4-11 above), this very region was the seed bed of Asiatic rhetoric, especially in its epideictic form. Though Ephesians is a general oration, it becomes a word on target by tapping into the rhetorical culture and predilections of the area. "You persuade a man only insofar as you talk his language by speech, gesture, tonality, order, image, attitude, idea, identifying your ways with his."[22] Paul has done this in Ephesians and done it well by his choice of style, form, and species of rhetoric.

The rhetorical purpose then of this discourse is to reinforce by way of reminder what is already believed and practices already followed.[23] "The presence of anamnesis . . . indicates that the audience members had knowledge of salvation and reconciliation, but were still in need of reminders that would sharpen their consciousness of their participation in the blessings of the Christian faith, and thereby lead to growth."[24] To this it may be added that P. Perkins is probably right that the rhetorical strategies used in this discourse assume an audience that will recognize what it hears in this letter as tradition, not new instruction, hence the call to remember.[25]

Pseudonymity?

Finally, one further word about the question of the possible pseudonymity of Ephesians needs to be offered. Deciding such issues is a matter of weighing probabilities. When a theory causes more problems than it solves, it should be abandoned. Such is the theory of Ephesians being written by an imitator of Paul. Consider Snodgrass's conclusions:

> The hypothesis of an imitator of Paul creates problems. The author would be a person who had read Paul's letters, especially Colossians, so much that he (or she) became a *mirror* of Paul, not just someone who sounds a bit like Paul. Does the human mind even operate this way, particularly on the basis

22. K. A. Burke, *A Rhetoric of Motives* (Berkeley: University of California Press, 1969), p. 55.

23. See Lincoln, *Ephesians*, p. lxxxvi: "intended to reinforce its readers' identity as participants in the Church and to underline their distinctive role and conduct in the world."

24. Jeal, *Integrating Theology and Ethics*, p. 62.

25. Perkins, "Ephesians," p. 354. It is thus not a proposal of new policy.

of a letter as short as Colossians? Would a first-century imitator even attempt to adhere to the style of his source? No evidence exists that this happened. Who is this marvelous mysterious theologian who mirrors and even exceeds Paul, but has left no other known trace? Why would this person copy verbatim the instructions to Tychicus, the least important part of the letter? As G. B. Caird indicated, there are difficulties in attributing Ephesians to Paul, but these are insignificant in comparison with the difficulties of attributing it to an imitator.[26]

26. K. Snodgrass, *Ephesians* (Grand Rapids: Zondervan, 1996), p. 28. Notice too the discussion of R. J. Bauckham, "Pseudo-Apostolic Letters," *JBL* 107 (1988): 469-94. As Bauckham says, such letters were exceedingly rare even in the post-apostolic era, and in any case there is not a single known example of someone or some Christian community accepting a letter *known* to be a forgery. This becomes problematic especially in the case of a document like Ephesians which places such emphasis on truth. As Bauckham also stresses, the audience allegedly addressed in a pseudepigraph cannot be the real audience. The document must actually address another audience in an analogous situation. For a massive though now dated and not rhetorically informed defense of the Pauline authorship of Ephesians see A. Van Roon, *The Authenticity of Ephesians* (Leiden: Brill, 1974).

Epistolary Prescript — 1.1-2

This is the most perfunctory of epistolary prescripts, but even so it is recognizably Pauline. It includes the familiar Pauline "grace and peace" greeting and the Pauline "in Christ."

Paul, apostle of Christ Jesus through the will of God, to the saints, those being . . .[1] *and to the faithful in Christ Jesus. Grace to you and peace from God our Father and the Lord Jesus Christ.*

Ephesians begins much like Colossians speaking of Paul[2] as an apostle through the will of God (cf. Col. 1.1; 2 Cor. 1.1). This discourse has more references to the will of God than any other NT letter (1.1, 5, 9, 11; 5.17; 6.6), and in fact more than any other NT document except the Gospel of John. "Ephesians does not support the notion of an impersonal fate or cosmic blueprint that underlies historic events, or of an impersonal and unchangeable divine rule that determines all acts of human obedience."[3] This is an important point for a largely Gentile audience that may well have believed in "fate" and impersonal determinism when they were pagans.

In light of 1.12-14; 2.1; and several other texts it appears likely that what Paul means by *hagioi,* "saints," here is Jewish Christians, a usage also found in Romans.[4]

1. On the original text here see pp. 217-18 above.
2. Of the undisputed Paulines, only Romans names Paul alone as the author.
3. M. Barth, *Ephesians 1–3* (Garden City: Doubleday, 1974), p. 65.
4. See G. B. Caird, *Paul's Letters from Prison* (Oxford: Oxford University Press, 1976), p. 31; and on Romans see B. Witherington and D. Hyatt, *Paul's Letter to the Romans* (Grand Rapids: Eerdmans, 2004), Introduction.

The *pistoi*, "faithful," then, appear to be Gentile Christians,[5] who are mainly addressed in this discourse, not surprisingly since Paul is the apostle to the Gentiles wherever one may find them.[6] He will argue in this discourse, as he does in Romans 9–11, for the indebtedness of Gentile believers to Jewish Christianity and beyond that to pre-Christian biblical faith and its practitioners.[7] He does not use the term *christianos* to refer to Christians. He speaks of those who are "in Christ" and is one of only two NT authors to use this phrase (the other being Peter in 1 Peter). It is not surprising in an ecclesiocentric discourse that emphasizes the unity of Jew and Gentile in Christ that this phrase occurs often, for example some eleven times in 1.3-14. Only in Ephesians do we have three different variants on the more familiar "in Christ": "in Christ Jesus" (3.11), "in Jesus" (4.21), and "in the Lord" (2:21).

V. 2 reiterates the reference to God and Jesus, but here God is called "our Father" (cf. 3.14; 5.20). It is part of the rhetorical strategy here to emphasize not only the unity of Jew and Gentile in Christ but also the unity of the author and the audience, hence "*our* Father." "Father" is the normal way Paul identifies God, and "Lord" and "Christ" the normal descriptors for Jesus. Grace and peace, unmerited divine favor and wholeness or well-being, come from both of these persons (see p. 56 above on this greeting). There are similar greetings in some Jewish documents (e.g., 2 *Baruch* 78.2 has "mercy and peace"; cf. *Jubilees* 12.29; 22.8-9).

5. The one factor which may count against there being two groups referred to here is the single definite article before "saints." See E. Best, *Ephesians* (Edinburgh: Clark, 1998), p. 101. The word *kai*, however, is awkward for this theory for it then must mean something other than "and," which seems unlikely here.

6. This means for example, that in Romans, even when Paul is addressing Gentiles he did not convert and a church he did not start, nonetheless he feels free to exhort them precisely because of his distinctive calling. See Witherington and Hyatt, *The Letter to the Romans*.

7. "Ephesians, more than any other NT epistle, will press the point that Gentiles receive no salvation other than the one they share with Israel and receive through the Messiah." Barth, *Ephesians 1–3*, p. 66.

Exordium — A Blessing of a Eulogy — 1.3-14

The difference in how Ephesians begins compared to most Pauline letters is immediately apparent in 1.3. We seem on first blush to have arrived at the end of an act of worship, at the benediction, but in fact the discourse is just beginning. 1.3-14 partakes of the character of a Jewish blessing, which could begin a sermonic section of synagogue worship, but it also partakes of the character of a eulogy, as we shall see.[1] Since it comes at the beginning of a rhetorical discourse, it also serves as the exordium which establishes the ethos of the speaker and establishes rapport with the audience.

There is a certain implicit trinitarian structure to this eulogy: election by the Father, salvation through the Son, and "sealing" in the Spirit.[2] The eulogy addresses not just the theology that will be discussed in chs. 1–3, for v. 4 foreshadows the discussions in chs. 4–6 when it says that election occurs in Christ so that God will have a people that are holy and blameless. There is an ethical component or aim to this salvation. If we ask what is the point of this paean of praise, it is not merely to arouse praise in the audience, but, by so engaging their emotions, emotions of gratitude, humility, and joy, Paul hopes to arouse receptivity here within the audience so as to facilitate unity in the body and obedience to the later exhortations.[3] Paul is working his way toward the audience's

---

1. I am in agreement with the majority of scholars that this eulogy should be treated as a unified composition and that it probably does not derive from an early hymn, though that cannot be completely ruled out. See, e.g., R. Schnackenburg, *The Epistle to the Ephesians: A Commentary* (Edinburgh: Clark, 1991), p. 46.

2. Schnackenburg, *Ephesians*, p. 46.

3. See Roy R. Jeal, *Integrating Theology and Ethics in Ephesians: The Ethos of Communication* (Lewiston: Mellen, 2000), p. 79; Schnackenburg, *Ephesians*, pp. 68-69.

further understanding and embracing of the beliefs and behavior, the Christian
values and virtues they have already accepted, so that they can do an even better
job of becoming what they already are — elect in Christ, redeemed by his
blood, sealed in the Spirit, moving toward holiness and perfection.

In some ways this eulogy is much like the sort of rhetorical praises offered
to benefactors. P. Perkins puts it this way: "True to the rhetorical conventions of
such speech, Ephesians indicates that such praise is the appropriate response to
benefits conferred. In the secular sphere, speech in praise of a benefactor might
elicit future benefactions by cementing the relationship between a powerful individual and those who participate in his praise."[4]

*Blessed be the God and Father of our Lord Jesus Christ, the one blessing us in all
spiritual blessings in the heavens in Christ, just as he chose us in him before the
foundation of the cosmos, for us to be holy and unblemished in his sight in love,
predestining us to adoption through Jesus Christ unto him, according to the goodwill of his will, for the glorious praise of his grace which he graced us with in the
Beloved, in whom we have redemption through his blood, the forgiveness of transgressions according to the riches of his grace, which he caused to overflow unto us
in all wisdom and understanding, making known to us the mystery of his will, according to his goodwill which he purposed in him, unto the administration/plan of
the fullness of time, summing up under one head everything in Christ, things in
heaven and things on the earth, in him, in whom also we were chosen, being predestined according to the purpose of the carrying out of everything according to the
intention of his will unto our being for his glorious praise, which we were hoping
for before in Christ, in whom also we, hearing the word of truth, the good news of
your salvation in whom also having believed a seal was affixed — the promised
Holy Spirit, who[5] is the pledge/down payment of our inheritance unto the acquisition of redemption, for the praise of his glory.*

I have deliberately left this translation in as literal and direct a form as possible
so the repeated redundancies and reduplication of sounds and ideas throughout
the section will be evident and the sense that this is one long sentence (some 202
words) will come across even in English.[6] This is a classic example of Asiatic

---

4. P. Perkins, "The Letter to the Ephesians," in *The New Interpreter's Bible* XI (Nashville: Abingdon, 2000), p. 372.

5. There are no major textual issues in this section of the discourse, but here at v. 14
there is a question as to whether *hos* or *ho* is the original reading. Probably *ho* is the original
reading (found in numerous good witnesses: P46, A, B, F, G, L, P, and others), and it agrees
with the gender of the preceding word *pneuma* rather than the following word *arrabōn*,
which would require *hos*. See Metzger, *TC*, p. 533.

6. In an interesting rhetorical analysis, C. J. Robbins actually suggests that the eulogy's
length and structure were dictated by rhetorical precedent about periodical sentences and

rhetoric in its epideictic form, where amplification is accomplished by repetition of both content and form. *Oratio perpetua* is what Aristotle called this (*Rhetoric* 3.9), the practice of deliberately extending a sentence by using relative clauses, participles, and prepositions rather than dividing it into separate sentences. There could be little doubt left in the hearers' minds that this was epideictic rhetoric as Paul rings the changes on *eulogētos, eulogēsas,* and *eulogia* at the outset of the eulogy.[7] The eulogy begins with a stress on praise and ends that way as well, as we are repeatedly hearing about blessing, praise, or glory and as the phrase "in him" or something similar comes again and again. This "praise" passage has as part of its rhetorical aim to get the audience caught up in love, wonder, and praise of what God has done for them, to be, that is, an impetus for praise and to stir the deeper emotions of the audience right from the outset. Paul is picking a theme which should quite naturally produce a positive response, causing the audience to join in the praise of God. "The author of Ephesians is treating with esteem a theme which is esteemed by the audience members (cf. Arist. *Rhet.* 1.9.30-31). . . . The author is thus using pathos (Arist. *Rhet.* 1.2.5)."[8] It is of course a theme that has a long history since praise in response to God's acts of salvation was part of the biblical tradition (cf. Pss. 96.1-4; 118.1).[9]

In his detailed rhetorical analysis of the structuring of periods within a long rhetorical sentence, C. J. Robbins draws some important conclusions. 1) He

---

that the length of the periods within the sentence was determined by what the rhetorician could manage to say in one breath. See C. J. Robbins, "The Composition of Ephesians 1.3-14," *JBL* 105 (1986): 677-87.

7. On the device of reduplication see *Rhet. ad Her.* 4.28.38. The function is to make a deep impression on the audience, to amplify a key point, and to move the audience to deeper emotions. We see this clearly in terms of using the same stem in v. 3 and 6, with the latter verse using *charis* in various ways. See A. T. Lincoln, *Ephesians* (Waco: Word; 1990), p. 26.

8. Jeal, *Integrating Theology and Ethics*, p. 81.

9. It should also be noted that this first long sentence is followed immediately by two more (1.15-23; 2.1-7). This would have left a definite impact on the listeners, setting up an expectation of long periods and sentences. After a brief hiatus, Paul begins again with a series of long periods at 3.2-13, 14-19. The rhythm is only briefly interrupted at 3.20-21 by a benediction, and then we start again with another long period, 4.1-6. There are others at 4.11-16 and finally at 6.14-20. See P. T. O'Brien, *The Letter to the Ephesians* (Grand Rapids: Eerdmans, 1999), p. 90. Thus while these eight long sentences are spread throughout the discourse, they are mostly clustered in the first four chapters. There is then a concerted attempt by Paul to build on the momentum of the first long sentence in a fashion that is typical of epideictic rhetoric. H. Hoehner, *Ephesians* (Grand Rapids: Baker, 2002), p. 471, seeks to explain the length of three of the eight long sentences in Ephesians by noting that they are prayers (1.3-14, 15-23; 3.14-21). This however does not explain the other five long sentences in Ephesians and it is better to see this as a matter of Asiatic epideictic rhetorical style which characterizes the work as a whole.

demonstrates how sentences like Eph. 1.3-14 were not uncommon, especially in epideictic rhetoric, a classic example being found in Isocrates, *Panegyricus* 47-49. As Cicero (*Orator* 207-8) points out, "In epideictic oratory . . . it is desirable to have everything done in the periodical style of Isocrates . . . so that the language runs on as if enclosed in a circle until it comes to an end with each phrase complete and perfect." 2) Thus, it is not true that the colas and periods in this sentence are as they are because of the content of the eulogy, for we find similar substance and similar structures in other parts of the NT that are not hymnic or prayers, in, for example, the speeches in Acts. The form of this eulogy is best explained on the basis of the rhetorical conventions the author is following. 3) What determines the length of the period within the extended sentence is how much one can say in one breath. According to Cicero, "It was failure or scantiness of breath that originated periodic structure and pauses between words; but now that this has once been discovered, it is so attractive that, even if a person were endowed with breath that never failed, we should still not wish him to deliver an unbroken flow of words; for our ears are only gratified by a style of delivery which is not merely endurable but also easy for the human lungs" (*De Oratore* 3.46.181). Quintilian agrees (*Inst. Or.* 9.4.125).[10]

Jeal deals well with the aural dimensions of this eulogy and the effect it would likely have had on its listening audience. He stresses that one of the reasons for the piling up of subordinate clauses beginning with *en* or *kata* is that it gives the material a sense of rhythm which the audience can get caught up in and anticipate.[11] This repetition, in this case of prepositions or relatives, is called *epanaphora*, the repetition of the same term at the beginning or end of a phrase, creating emphasis or a sense of finality. The repetition serves to emphasize that the action, including salvation, happens *in* Christ and *according to* the plan of God. The matter was not left to chance, and there was only one agency through which salvation could and did happen for the audience.

Following the statement of praise (1.3), God's blessings are named to support the praise. This use of examples to arouse praise was recommended by the writers on rhetoric (*Rhet. ad Her.* 3.6.10-11; *Rhetorica ad Alexandrum* 1440b.5-1441b.10; Aristotle, *Rhet.* 1.9.1-30). The blessings that prompt the praise are election (1.4), predestination (1.5), redemption and forgiveness (1.7), revelation of the mystery (1.9), and being made God's portion (1.11). This progression begins in the preexistent life of Christ and ends with the eschatological inheritance of the saints. In other words, this is a comprehensive presentation of the trajectory of salvation. Aristotle says that it is important that the audience participate and see that they have a stake in the praise, that the benefits involve the audience and not just the author (*Rhet.* 3.14.11).

---

10. See Robbins, "Composition of Eph. 1.3-14," pp. 677-87.
11. Jeal, *Integrating Theology and Ethics*, pp. 82-83.

Much debate has ensued about the change from "we" to "you" in v. 13. Does this simply distinguish the author from the audience, or perhaps the author and his fellow Jewish Christians from the target audience (which is Gentiles)? Or perhaps is the distinction between the first generation of believers, of which Paul is one, and the more recent largely Gentile converts in Asia? The participle in v. 12 does seem to mean "hoping for before" or might be a reference to those who "hoped first." I agree with the many commentators who take this to be a reference to the Jewish Christians such as Paul, and this supports the interpretation that the "saints" referred to in 1.1 are Jewish Christians, a separate group from the Gentile believers (cf. Rom. 1.16; Acts 13.46). This prepares us for the clear reference to the temporal priority involving Israel in 2.11-20, where again Gentiles are explicitly called "you" (see also 3.6). Thus the "we" in 1.13 does indeed refer to those who were Christians before the Gentile audience, Jewish Christians who, as Paul says in Romans 11, are the root, vine, or tree into whom Gentile branches have been grafted.

Some scholars have seen this eulogy as something that might have been used as a part of a baptismal liturgy. This is possible, but not the further conjecture that the "seal" in this eulogy is baptism. Baptism is certainly not the explicit subject of 1.13, any more than it is at 2.5-6.[12] The subject here is the work of the Holy Spirit, not the sacrament of baptism. In the combination of "seal" and "down payment" language both here and in 2 Cor. 1.21-22 the focus is on the Spirit, who is the mark of ownership on or in the believer.

> Unless one could prove that for Paul the imagery *inherently* carried such an allusion — and such proof is currently unavailable — there is nothing that suggests a baptismal motif. All the more so in this letter, where in the Trinitarian formula of 4:4-6 the *one Spirit* is paired with the *one body* (= the church), while the 'one faith' and 'one baptism' are paired with the 'one Lord.' The point to make, of course, is that for Paul, vis-à-vis the later church, the Spirit, not baptism, is the 'seal' of ownership, the primary evidence that one belongs to the new people of God.[13]

What is being praised by Paul are the events of salvation themselves as they transpire in Christ and in the believer, events which are not linked to baptism here.[14]

---

12. See Jeal, *Integrating Theology and Ethics*, p. 92.

13. G. D. Fee, *God's Empowering Presence* (Peabody: Hendrickson, 1994), p. 670; see also J. D. G. Dunn, *Baptism in the Holy Spirit* (Philadelphia: Westminster, 1970), p. 160. For the later practice of sealing as part of the baptismal rite see 2 *Clement* 7.6; 8.6; Hermas, *Similitudes* 8.6.3; 9.16.3-6.

14. On the use of the eulogy form elsewhere in Paul, see Rom. 1.25; 9.5; 2 Cor. 11.31; and especially 2 Cor. 1.3-4; cf. 1 Pet. 1.3-5.

In vv. 3-4 we have three different cognate forms of the word "bless." God, says Paul, has blessed believers with every spiritual blessing "in the heavenlies." This last phrase is key and appears in various forms in this discourse (1.3, 20; 2.6; 3.10; 6.12). It calls for a closer examination.

A Closer Look: For Heaven's Sake

As Lincoln has demonstrated, the phrase "in the heavenlies" has some sort of local sense in every one of these texts (1.3, 20; 2.6; 3.10; 6.12). That is, it refers not to a human condition but to a place.[15] It seems to be little different in sense from "in the heavens" (using *ouranos* rather than the more extended form *epouranos*). It is to be expected in a piece of Asiatic epideictic rhetoric that one would use the more impressive form of the word without implying any real difference in meaning.

Here we may distinguish between three possible meanings of the term: the eternal abode of God; the invisible non-material spiritual realm in general, inhabited by both angels and demons and God and the devil; and a part of the created world, what we call the sky — the upper part of earth's atmosphere. Gen. 1.1 refers to the third of these. There seems to be room for some overlap between these three referents. For instance, the abode of God can sometimes be seen as the extension of the cosmos, namely the uppermost part of it (see Ps. 2.4). But in other texts *shammayim* (heavens, always in the plural in the Hebrew) can be distinguished from God's abode as something God created and put clouds in (Ps. 147.8).

After the OT, however, the term is used in the second sense, not to refer to what believers today would call "heaven," where only God and the good dwell, but rather to the non-material spirit realm which would include good and evil spiritual beings. This world seems coterminous with the material universe and interacts with and influences it in various ways. Paul believes that the created heavens have a place both in this age and the age to come. He seems to see the role of the material heaven as concealing us from the spirit realm. Both of these two senses of heaven are said to undergo change and transformation as a result of the redemptive work of Christ which will culminate in a new heaven and a new earth, renewal, that is, of both the material and the spiritual realms. Apparently this renewal does not affect the eternal abode of God. Paul does not appear to hold to the medieval three-story universe, for he does not assume that Hell, demons, or the like are below. Rather they dwell in the heavens or heavenlies, in the invisible spirit realm, which is coterminous with the material universe. Indeed, it can be argued that Paul only rarely uses the term "heaven" to refer to God's eternal abode. In an apocalyptic passage he speaks of having been taken up into the third heaven, which he calls Paradise (2 Cor. 12.2-4).

---

15. See A. T. Lincoln, *Paradise Now and Not Yet* (Cambridge: Cambridge University Press, 1981), pp. 135-68.

It may be then that Paul's picture of things distinguishes, moving from the top down, the eternal abode of God = Paradise = the third level of heaven, the invisible created spirit world, and the created material heavens. In early Jewish literature as many as seven levels of heaven were spoken of. It should be recognized that Paul is drawing on picture and poetic language from the Psalms and elsewhere. The imagery should not be over-pressed as Paul is not trying to describe a cosmology. "Since Christ has ascended above all the heavens (4:10) and sits at God's right hand in the heavenly places 'above all authority and power' (1:20), the 'principalities and powers' can only be located in the 'lower heavens,' in the realm of the air (cf. 2:2), in the darkness of our world (6:12)."[16]

For Paul, the powers and principalities are in the heavenlies. This makes it difficult to argue that he means human governments or other earthly institutions by such terms.[17] He probably believes that the powers and principalities can influence and use human structures. One could call this the demonizing of the structures. The Book of Revelation seems to present a clear example of this sort of thinking, but the point is that the human structures are not simply identical with the powers and principalities. Paul does not see human government as inherently demonic or evil.[18] Indeed, he stresses in Romans 13 that human authorities derive their authority from God, though they may abuse or misuse it. Had Paul believed government structures and authorities were inherently evil he could never have called them God's servants for good.[19]

Beginning at v. 4 and in several places in this discourse, Paul talks about the concept of election. The key to understanding what he means by this concept is the phrase "in Christ."[20] When Paul says believers were chosen before the foun-

---

16. Schnackenburg, *Ephesians*, p. 51.

17. See especially P. T. O'Brien, "Principalities and Powers and Their Relationship to Structures," *Reformed Theological Review* 40 (1981): 1-10.

18. See B. Witherington and D. Hyatt, *Paul's Letter to the Romans* (Grand Rapids: Eerdmans, 2004), ad loc.

19. An interesting study on these matters is J. E. Wright, *The Early History of Heaven* (Oxford: Oxford University Press, 2000), pp. 139-84.

20. See the summary of usage in Hoehner, *Ephesians*, pp. 173-74. He rightly concludes that we do have the local sense here. The problem with his treatment is that he tries to impose grammatical precision on an epideictic sermon which involves the language of the heart in long effusive sentences. This is like trying to impose mathematical precision on the meter of a poem or song. Hoehner argues that the text must mean God chose "us" before the world began because the grammatical diagram of the sentence suggests such a conclusion. As Hoehner admits, however, even Calvin seems to have agreed that God's choosing "us in Christ" means that Christ is the Elect One chosen before the world began and that believers are "in him." Barth's view is like Calvin's. Hoehner also rejects Chrysostom's suggestion that God chose us through faith in Christ because this would limit or even destroy God's freedom of choice (p. 176). But the NT teaches repeatedly that condescension is the way of the biblical

dation of the world "in him," he does not mean that believers preexisted or even that God's salvation plan preexisted, though the latter is true. He means that Christ preexisted the creation of the universe and that, by God's choosing of him (who is the Elect One), those who would come to be in him were chosen in the person of their agent or redeemer. God, because of his great love, destined those who believe for adoption as sons.[21] This freely given love is stressed in v. 5. This happens only through Christ and according to God's good pleasure. Paul says "we were graced with this grace" (v. 6) in the Beloved, Christ, and for the sake of God's praise.

The concept of election and destining here is corporate. If one is in Christ, one is elect and destined. Paul is not talking about the pre-temporal electing or choosing of individual humans outside of Christ to be in Christ, but rather of the election of Christ and what is destined to happen to those, whoever they may be, who are in Christ.[22] The concept here is not radically different from the concept of the election of Israel. During the OT era, if one was in Israel, one was a part of God's chosen people, and if one had no such connection, one was not elect. Individual persons within Israel could opt out by means of apostasy, and others could be grafted in (see the story of Ruth).[23] These con-

---

God and that God accepts all kinds of limitations in order to have a relationship with human beings. The Incarnation is a clear example of divine self-limiting (see Phil. 2.5-11), as is Christ's death on the cross. There is therefore nothing surprising at all about the notion that an unconditionally loving God might limit his absolute freedom in order to allow humans to respond to his love freely with the aid of divine grace. God treats his people as persons who will be held responsible for their life choices. A loving response to God cannot be coerced or predetermined if it is to be personal and free. Indeed, it is also the case that for any behavior to be truly virtuous or loving it must involve the possibility of contrary choice.

21. See the exposition of Chrysostom in his first homily on Ephesians, who is followed by Cassian and others. A "non-Augustinian" interpretation of this text has a long pedigree, in fact predating the rise of the dominant Augustinian reading of Paul, especially of Romans and Ephesians.

22. Contrast this with what we find at Qumran, where both the righteous who will be elected and the wicked who will be condemned are determined prior to creation of the universe (CD 2.7; 1QS 3.15-17). E. Best aptly observes that predestination is a concept dealing with God's purpose from all eternity rather than with individual salvation. See Best, *Ephesians* (Edinburgh: Clark, 1998), pp. 119-20. P. Perkins, "The Letter to the Ephesians," in *The New Interpreter's Bible* XI (Nashville: Abingdon, 2000), p. 373, also rightly notes the total lack of discussion of the predestination of the wicked here. Ephesians does not depict election as that which divides the human race but as that which unites it in Christ, hence the strong contrast with the Qumran language about the election and salvation of the few righteous in contrast to the majority of the race. See Perkins, "Ephesians," p. 377.

23. See O'Brien, *Ephesians*, p. 98, n. 49: "The idea of the incorporation of many into the representative head (using the preposition *en*) appears in the LXX in relationship to Abraham (Gen. 12:3) and Isaac (Gen. 21:12) as well as in Paul with reference to Adam (1 Cor. 15:22)."

cepts of election were then applied to Christ, who as a divine person could incorporate into himself various others. Christ becomes the locus of election and salvation because in Paul's thinking the story of the people of God is whittled down to the story of Jesus the Anointed One and then built back up in the risen Christ thereafter.[24] When Paul speaks of how a lost person gets "into Christ" he speaks on the more mundane level of preaching, hearing, responding in faith, not of God's pre-choosing of our choices for us.

This doctrine of corporate election in Christ is meant as a comfort for those who already believe,[25] reassuring them that by God's grace and their perseverance in the faith they can and will make the eschatological goal or finish line.[26] This approach to the matter also comports with the ecclesiocentric focus of this document.[27] As Schnackenburg says, the christology found in Col. 1.15-20 is used here in service of an explanation of the benefits believers have in Christ. "The faithful, the members of Christ's body, the Church are included in God's all-embracing plan for and accomplishment of salvation by means of that cosmic christology including Christ's pre-existence."[28]

It is possible that Jesus' baptismal scene is in mind in vv. 6-7, for he is called the Beloved Son, and at Christ's baptism there is also the language of washing away of sins. *Apolytrōsis* (cf. Dan 4.34 LXX) can refer to a buying back or ransoming of a slave. Paul says nothing of a ransom paid to Satan, as God owes Satan nothing. Christ is redeeming the lost persons from the bondage of sin by paying the price for that sin for them. Redemption is only had "in him."[29] This redemption terminology then is metaphorical as is shown by the equation with forgiveness of sins. Here Barth prefers the translation "lapses" because Gentiles were not under the Mosaic Law and transgressions are by definition a willful violation of a known law.[30] However Paul in Romans 2 suggests that

24. See my *Paul's Narrative Thought World* (Louisville: Westminster John Knox, 1994), pp. 245-337.

25. See the influential discussion in M. Barth, *Ephesians 1–3* (Garden City: Doubleday, 1974), pp. 105-9.

26. A very helpful study of Paul's and the other NT authors' conceptions of election and perseverance is found in I. H. Marshall's *Kept by the Power of God* (Minneapolis: Bethany, 1974).

27. See C. C. Newman, "Election and Predestination in Ephesians 1.4-6a: An Exegetical-Theological Study of the Historical, Christological Realization of God's Purpose," *RevExp* 93 (1996): 237-47.

28. Schnackenburg, *Ephesians*, pp. 51-52. He rightly adds that Paul is not talking about the personal preexistence of believers in heaven. What is being discussed is our election in the preexistent Christ, by which it is meant that believers are chosen in him and that believers were in God's plan from the beginning, the plan God enacted in Christ.

29. A. T. Lincoln, *Ephesians* (Waco: Word, 1990), pp. 27-28, does not think the ransom concept is found here, especially since Col. 1.14 seems to be in the background here. He may be correct.

30. Barth, *Ephesians 1–3*, p. 83.

there is a law written on the heart that even the Gentile knows and is required to obey.[31] Thus "lapses" is probably an inadequate translation here.

Forgiveness comes to the believer out of the riches of God's grace, not because she or he merits it. This grace is said to overflow to Gentiles as well as to Jews and comes about by the revelation of the secret, the *mysterion*,[32] which here refers to God's plan to reconcile all things, all peoples, all worlds in Christ.[33] Paul in this discourse favors the use of the verb "made known" found here in v. 9 but also in 3.3, 5, 10 and 6.19. This comports with the epideictic nature of the discourse, which has as one of its main goals making things known, aiding the understanding of fundamental values of the community.

The revelation of the secret comes in preaching, but the preaching only comes about because God has first done something in human history through the death and resurrection of Jesus. It is thus quite unlike other religions that may have had purely other-worldly mysteries in view. This open secret is about what God has accomplished in Christ in space and time. Christ was sent for the administration or ministry[34] in the fullness of time (cf. Gal. 4.4-5; an apocalyptic concept: see *4 Ezra* 4.37; *2 Baruch* 40.3; 1QpHab 7.13-14), summing up under one head all things in himself. The idea of the fullness of time connotes not merely that the right and ripe time has come, thus bringing a long-awaited event or process. It also conveys the notion of the starting of a whole new set of circumstances at the precise time God chose to begin it. *Anakephalaiōsasthai* can simply mean "summing up," but in view of the way Paul will use "head" of Christ in v. 22 it is much more likely that he is playing on the literal meaning of the term: "bringing together under or in one head." This bringing together or summing up in Christ involves both things in heaven and on earth. This would be puzzling were there not things in the heavens that needed this unifying work.

V. 11 reiterates the theme of v. 4 that believers were chosen in Christ. The constant refrain of "in him" must be kept steadily in view throughout the eulogy. Christ carries out the intention of God's good will. V. 12 says that the purpose of redemption is God's glorious praise. This is the ultimate aim of human-

---

31. See Witherington and Hyatt, *Letter to the Romans*, ad loc.

32. Notice that Paul entirely avoids speaking of plural "mysteries," perhaps because he wants to avoid comparison with the mysteries in the mystery cults. Initiation in the Christian sense involved an open secret proclaimed to all, not a hidden revelation given only to those who have been initiated into the cult.

33. See C. C. Caragounis, *The Ephesian Mysterion* (Lund: Gleerup, 1977), pp. 157-58, on incorporation in Christ as the essence of the mystery.

34. *Oikonomia* refers to the management or administration of something or the basis of such administration, namely a plan. Whereas in Col. 1.25 it refers to a plan or stewardship administered by Paul, here God is the one who does the administering and who has a plan. See M. Y. MacDonald, *Colossians, Ephesians* (Collegeville: Liturgical, 2000), p. 202; Lincoln, *Ephesians*, pp. 31-32.

ity — to live for the praise of God, to let all we are and all we do be doxology, a giving of glory to God. The Scottish catechism puts it well in saying that the chief end of humankind is to love God and enjoy God forever.

It was in Christ that the Good News was heard, the word of truth about God's plan, goodwill, and intention. It was also "in him" that believers believed and thus in him were affixed with the seal — the promised Holy Spirit. The seal here is not likely baptism, since Paul nowhere mentions baptism in this passage, but rather the Holy Spirit. "The metaphor of a seal does not imply that the Holy Spirit has stamped us with a seal . . . but that he himself is this seal, a sign characterizing our Christian existence."[35] Seals were used to authenticate documents, but in view of *peripoiēsis* ("ownership" or "acquisition") in v. 14 the seal in view is the brand, the mark of ownership, on a slave. The point is not the protection or "eternal security" of the believer, but rather the identification of who belongs to Christ.

With the change from "we" to "you" in v. 13 Paul gives a sneak preview of the discussion in 2.11–3.6, where the "we" is clearly Jewish Christians.[36] While it is true that the "you" draws the audience into the praise, it also distinguishes them from the author and his fellow Jewish Christians.[37]

The Spirit is also the pledge of our inheritance. The term *arrabōn* means "down payment" or "first installment" or "deposit." It does not simply mean "guarantee" here, though that idea is not excluded. It is the first installment and thus surety that God plans to complete his work of salvation in the believer. The Spirit then is foretaste, not mere foreshadowing, down payment, not mere pledge of the eternal inheritance. "Although Ephesians depicts the gifts of salvation as fully present in the lives of believers, the designation 'pledge' suggests a future perfection to this experience." The benefits Christians already enjoy are but a foreshadowing of the blessings yet to come, a fact which should stimulate even more praise to the ultimate Benefactor. "Despite their minority status in the world of first century CE Asia Minor, Christians found themselves the center of God's cosmic design because they belonged to the risen Lord, who is exalted over all the heavenly powers. Benefits that humans might expect to receive from 'the heavens' have been conferred by God in Christ."[38] Yet still all believers await the acquisition of full redemption or, perhaps better said, they await God's full redemption of his possession, the church.[39] Even in Ephesians, there is a not-yet dimension to salvation.

---

35. Schnackenburg, *Ephesians*, p. 65.
36. So Fee, *God's Empowering Presence*, p. 669. This was also the view of Chrysostom and Ambrosiaster.
37. But see Lincoln, *Ephesians*, p. 38.
38. Perkins, "Ephesians," p. 376.
39. See Best, *Ephesians*, p. 1553.

Thanksgiving Prayer/
Captatio Benevolentiae — 1.15-23

Perhaps the most discussed formal feature of Ephesians 1 is its apparent redundancy, including, as it does, both a eulogy and a thanksgiving section. Some scholars have even taken this apparent redundancy as evidence of the non-Pauline nature of Ephesians. This conclusion, however, not only overlooks the fact that in 1 Thessalonians, another epideictic piece of rhetoric,[1] there is more than one thanksgiving period (cf. 1.2; 2.13; 3.9), and more proximately to the time of and influence on the writing of Ephesians we have two thanksgiving sections in Colossians (1.3-4 and 1.9-13). Furthermore, the rhetorical character of this material has not often been taken into consideration. Asiatic rhetoric, especially in its epideictic form, was well noted for redundancies, intended to create emphasis, and amplification. The thanksgiving prayer in 1.15-23 is not simply a repetition of what we found in the eulogy. Rather, it takes the discourse a step further, repeating and building on what has been said and adding a few new elements. "What emerges in the praising of God in the eulogy is confirmed in the intercession: it is the God who elects and calls who himself guarantees for the faithful the attainment of their heavenly inheritance through the gift of the Holy Spirit."[2]

While it does not introduce any totally new themes, there is in the thanksgiving section some development of themes, for here we have the explicit mention of Christ's resurrection and exaltation, and the relationship between Christ's rule over the cosmos and the church is made clear.[3] In other words, this

---

1. See my *1 and 2 Thessalonians* (Grand Rapids: Eerdmans, 2006).

2. R. Schnackenburg, *The Epistle to the Ephesians: A Commentary* (Edinburgh: Clark, 1991), p. 71.

3. See A. T. Lincoln, *Ephesians* (Waco: Word, 1990), pp. 52-53.

thanksgiving section moves the discourse closer to its major subject, namely the church, which will be treated directly beginning in ch. 2. Some themes then are repeated and further developed, and some things are made explicit as the ecclesiocentric orientation of this discourse becomes more apparent. Paul also makes clear that he has introduced certain themes so that his audience may increase their knowledge of the God of Jesus Christ and of the power, benefits, and hope they have in Christ.[4] In terms of rhetorical intent and effect, Paul is making the audience well-disposed to receive the rest of the discourse in this segment as he establishes good rapport with them by affirming their faith and love and making clear his pastoral concern that they grow in the knowledge of God. He says nothing here about a change in their behavior, only about growth and development of who they already are and what they already have and know. This is an epideictic agenda. As usual with such a section, we also have a preview of what is to be discussed later in the discourse. It is interesting that Quintilian suggests linking praise of a judge to the pursuit of the matter one wants to discourse about (*Inst. Or.* 4.1.16-17), and so here Paul links praise of God in Christ to his usual thanksgiving, which prepares for and previews the discourse which follows. He uses a similar strategy in Rom. 1.8-15.

In terms of structure, the thanksgiving prayer report is found in vv. 15-16, followed by the content of the prayer in vv. 17-19 and a christological and ecclesiological expansion of the prayer in vv. 20-23. There are some reduplication and amplification of the eulogy, as can be seen from a comparison of v. 17 to vv. 8-9 and v. 18 to vv. 12 and 14.[5]

It is also possible to compare 1.20-23 with the peroratio in 6.10-18,[6] which may suggest that we should see these verses as something of a propositio. The proposition that is affirmed is that since God has placed Christ in the position of Lord over the powers, the world, and the church and since Christ is currently ruling all things for the sake of the church, the church is enabled to be the body of Christ in a dark world, fully manifesting the presence of Christ, who dwells in both the church and the world. The body of Christ is possible in a dark and fallen world because of the resurrection and exaltation of Christ and the subjection of the powers under his feet. Indeed, the body is not merely possible, it is a reality manifesting the living presence of God in Christ. Since this is an epideictic discourse, this is not a proposition to be proved but one to be praised and expounded on, revealing or further explaining some of the fundamental values and convictions already held by the Christian communities being addressed.

---

4. Lincoln, *Ephesians*, p. 53.

5. See P. Perkins, "The Letter to the Ephesians," in *The New Interpreter's Bible* XI (Nashville: Abingdon, 2000), pp. 380-81.

6. See Schnackenburg, *Ephesians*, p. 85.

Because of this, I also, hearing of your faith in the Lord Jesus and love which is for all the saints, do not cease to give thanks for you, making mention in my prayers, in order that the God of our Lord Jesus Christ, the Father of glory might give you a spirit of wisdom and revelation in his understanding, having been enlightened in the eyes of your hearts, so that you might know what is the hope of his calling, what is the riches of the glory of his inheritance in the saints, and what is the exceeding greatness of his power unto us who believe according to the work of the might of his power, which is exerted in Christ, whom he raised from the dead and seated at his right hand in the heavens far above all rulers, and powers, and great powers and dominions and all names being named not only in this age but also in the coming one; and all were subjected under his feet and he gave him [to be] head over all for the church, which is his body, the fullness which fills all in all.

Praise turns to prayers of thanksgiving at v. 15, and it may be that the term *hagios* here refers to all Christians, though it may mean all Jewish Christians. Caird argues that the love directed toward "all the saints" is the love that breaks down barriers between Gentiles and Jews as will be discussed at 2.11-22, hence "saints" here refers to Jewish Christians.[7] Paul has only heard of his audience's faith and love, which must surely mean that he has not seen the majority of them face-to-face. If we suppose that this homily circulated in the Lycus Valley before eventually finding its way to Ephesus, this comment is perfectly understandable. The form and content of this thanksgiving period bear some real resemblance to what we find in Philemon (vv. 4-5) and in Colossians (1.3-4; see pp. 119-21 above), which may suggest something about the date when Ephesians was composed, especially if we add to that the obvious literary closeness to Colossians as well.

As Jeal points out, Paul is motivated to give thanks in v. 16[8] both because of all that is said in the eulogy (and in particular how the audience is participating in the blessings mentioned there) and because he has heard of their faith and love.[9] He does not cease to give thanks for them, mentioning them in his prayers (following Col. 1.9),[10] and essentially these prayers are for their contin-

---

7. G. B. Caird's *Paul's Letters from Prison* (Oxford: Oxford University Press, 1976), p. 43.

8. Variation is the rhetorically appropriate approach when one is repeating material previously used, looking for different forms of words or for synonyms. If we compare Col. 1.3 we discover that there the normal verb form *eucharistoumen* is found, but here the less used present participial form *eucharistōn* surfaces. As M. Y. MacDonald, *Colossians, Ephesians* (Collegeville: Liturgical, 2000), p. 216, points out, what is especially striking is that Ephesians offers very little detail about what Paul is giving thanks for in regard to the audience (contrast Col. 1.3-8), but that comports with the character of the document, namely that it is a circular homily.

9. Roy R. Jeal, *Integrating Theology and Ethics in Ephesians: The Ethos of Communication* (Lewiston: Mellen, 2000), p. 94.

10. While *mneia* by itself can mean "remembrance," when coupled with the verb "do/make" the meaning is "to make mention." See Caird, *Paul's Letters*, p. 44.

ued growth and learning. He is sincerely and personally interested in these Christians, but it is also true that his words here have a rhetorical purpose, namely to foster receptivity in them for the rest of the discourse, including the later exhortations.

Paul prays in v. 17 that God will give them both spiritual discernment (wisdom) and revelation of God's understanding of things, having already enlightened them in their innermost being. The reduplication here is very apparent with various different words for knowledge or essential spiritual information used throughout this segment of the prayer, which picks up what Paul has said in vv. 7-8. He is urging the audience to appreciate and take advantage of what they already have, an epideictic theme which does not call for change but rather for growth and development. "The Father of glory" is not a common expression for God in Paul or elsewhere, but it continues the theme of glory from the eulogy (cf. 1 Cor. 2.8: "the Lord of glory," referring to Jesus). The emphasis on God as a strong father figure in this discourse comports with the emphasis on God as the powerful one who calls out and creates a people and rules the world.[11]

The phrase "eyes of the heart" in v. 18 has no biblical precedent,[12] though eyes and heart are associated occasionally in early Jewish literature (Sir. 11.9; cf. Job 31.7; Prov. 15.30). The heart was for the Semitic person the seat of thoughts and will as well as emotion. Thus this inner enlightenment may have both cognitive and affective dimensions. The verb is a perfect passive participle — "having been enlightened" (on enlightening the eyes cf. Pss. 13:3; 19:8; Bar. 1.12; Ezra 9.8). It is this already extant enlightenment that in turn allows God to give the audience even more wisdom and revelation of God's understanding of things. With such enlightenment as they already have they may come to grasp the hope of God's calling, why, that is, God has done as he has and the results he intends.[13] Paul is praying that God will expand and extend what the audience already knows. This is an understandable and appropriate prayer in an epideictic

---

11. On the use of Father language in the NT see B. Witherington and L. Ice, *The Shadow of the Almighty* (Grand Rapids: Eerdmans, 2000).

12. The author of this document is concerned about rhetorical invention, which in Colossians sometimes took the form of coining new words, here it takes the form of coining new phrases. This author is not interested in slavish imitation of the Pauline style, not even of the specific turns of phrase he found in Colossians, which he happily modifies. This bespeaks a creative author drawing on previous material, and Paul fits this bill better than anyone else we know of.

13. The later use of "enlightenment" in a semi-technical sense to refer to the effect of baptism should not be read into this text. See Justin Martyr, *Apologia 1* 61.12; 65.1; *Dialogue* 39.2; 122.1-6. As P. T. O'Brien, *The Letter to the Ephesians* (Grand Rapids: Eerdmans, 1999), p. 134, stresses, the Greek text does not say "the hope of your calling." The calling in question is God's.

discourse meant to remind and reinforce existing realities and values.[14] The audience is not like the Gentiles, who remain in darkness with hardened hearts (4.17-18), for which Paul is thankful.[15] There is similar language from Qumran: "May he illuminate your heart with the discernment of life and grace you with eternal knowledge" (1QS 2.3).

"The saints" in v. 18 may again mean either Jewish Christians or all Christians, but since *hagioi* does not clearly or even probably mean angels elsewhere in Paul's letters, this is probably not the meaning here.[16] The issue in any case is not the believer's inheritance but God's, which is his people.[17] Here as in v. 14 we seem to be dealing with the idea of God acquiring a people for himself. In fact this portion of the verse repeats key terms from vv. 7-14. God's power is extremely great, and he can produce a people from all sorts of diverse ethnic and religious backgrounds. Again we see the definite Asiatic penchant for redundancy (as also in Col. 1:11, for example) with "the might of his power" immediately following the statement about the exceeding greatness of God's power, all of which is followed by a discussion of how Christ has power over the powers. The redundancy is amplified because this is also epideictic rhetoric, and no praise or exulting or glorification is too grand.

In v. 19b Paul shifts from plural "you" to "we," which sets up the parallelism between God's work in the believer and God's work in raising Christ in v. 20.[18] There is interesting aural wordplay with *energeia*, "working" in v. 19 and *enērgēsen*, "he accomplished" in v. 20.[19]

Vv. 20-21 reflect the rhetorical device known as augmentation (*Inst. Or.* 8.4.3-9). The evidence or even proof of God's power is the resurrection of Jesus from the dead. Not only was he raised from the dead, then God sat him at the right hand in the heavenlies, the place of honor as the next in line to the throne. Paul may be drawing here on the creed, which in turn was drawing on the language of Ps. 110.1, one of the OT verses most often used christologically in the

---

14. We are dealing with a mixed metaphor here since hearts do not have eyes, but notice the rhetorically effective use of same endings on three sequential words *pephōtismenous tous opthalmous*. This is a device called homoeoptoton, and the deliberate use of the device explains why we have the accusative case here. Cf. *Rhet. ad Her.* 4.20.28 and Lincoln, *Ephesians*, p. 47. The use of this rhetorical device is in fact found repeatedly in vv. 18-19 (see Jeal, *Integrating Theology and Ethics*, p. 100) and reminds us once more that if we ignore the oral and aural dimensions of this text we have made a mistake.

15. See Jeal, *Integrating Theology and Ethics*, pp. 98-99.

16. The term is used some thirty times in Paul's letters and in all these other instances it refers either to Jewish Christians or to Christians.

17. See O'Brien, *Ephesians*, p. 135.

18. See E. Best, *Ephesians* (Edinburgh: Clark, 1998), p. 169; J. Gnilka, *Der Epheserbrief* (Freiburg: Herder, 1971), p. 91.

19. See Caird, *Paul's Letters*, p. 46.

NT. It may well be that this goes all the way back to Jesus himself, who according to Mark 14.62 applied the same verse to the exaltation of the Son of Man.[20] Not only is Christ said to be seated at right hand of God, he is said to be seated far above the powers and principalities. It needs to be noted that the allusion is not extended to the portion of the Psalm about God making the Anointed One's enemies his footstool, and it cannot be assumed that Paul has that in mind here.[21] Therefore, it cannot be assumed that the powers referred to here are all evil powers. In fact, as the text goes on, the emphasis is placed on Christ having put "all things" under his feet, and all things presumably includes more than malevolent angels. In any case, Paul is not attempting to offer a definitive list of such beings here.

Paul covers his bases by saying Christ is far above any name of any being in the heavenlies which is being named or called on in this age or in the age to come.[22] In other words, Christ rules forever and over all such powers. The text does not indicate whether Paul is thinking here of hostile powers or simply of angels (Heb. 1.3-4), but in light of 6.11 some of them are surely hostile.[23] But nothing is said here about doing battle with such beings or having victory over them, unlike what we find in Col. 2.15. Here the emphasis is on Christ's honor rating or status being higher or on his rule or authority over them.[24] The resurrection and enthronement are only the prelude to the rule of Christ. The "simple assertion about God's action in Christ is expanded in steps that reach a climax in the rule of Christ 'not only in this age but in the age to come.'"[25] The list of terms for the powers (cf. 3.10; 6.12 which make clear that he is referring here to cosmic beings) is another example of amplification, using terms that may or

20. See my *The Christology of Jesus* (Minneapolis: Fortress, 1990), pp. 256-61.

21. C. E. Arnold, *Ephesians: Power and Magic: The Concept of Power in Ephesians in Light of Its Historical Setting* (Cambridge: Cambridge University Press, 1989), p. 56, makes this mistake, but Ps. 110.1 was often used in early Christianity simply to indicate the superior position of Christ, not to assert his specific rule over demons and the like.

22. It is not at all clear that we have here the same idea as found in Phil. 2.9-11, where the focus is on Christ having the divine name "Lord," which is the name above all names. Here "name" seems to refer only to lesser beings who are beneath Christ in power and dignity. Nothing is said here about the power of Christ and his name rendering lesser names used in magic impotent. Pace Arnold, *Ephesians*, pp. 55-56.

23. This is especially likely in view of Col. 2.15 and the heavy dependence of this document on Colossians. Caution is necessary however, since Eph. 2.2 and 6.11 refer to the devil himself, not to his minions, so one cannot just assume that they are solely in view here in 1.21-22.

24. MacDonald, *Colossians, Ephesians*, p. 225, is probably right to see v. 22 as a victory text, but she misreads 6.10-20 as an admonition for believers to engage in spiritual warfare. To the contrary, as we shall see, the believer is urged to put on armor and take a defensive posture in relation to such powers.

25. Jeal, *Integrating Theology and Ethics*, p. 102. I have translated his Greek at the end of the sentence.

may not be exactly synonymous (*Inst. Or.* 8.4.26-27; 9.3.48). The more terms that are listed the more impressive the fact that Christ rules over them all now and forever.[26] It is possible, since there seems to have been a special interest in the cosmic powers in Ephesus and its environs in connection with magic and astrology, that Paul is elaborating here simply to show the superiority of Christ over supernatural powers that some of the audience may have previously been fascinated by or even involved with.[27] However, the generic and passing mention of the powers does not suggest that Paul is dealing with some specific Ephesian problem or audience here.[28] Ephesus was merely representative of the environment in Asia in regard to such matters and Greco-Roman beliefs.[29]

This is the only place in the Pauline corpus where we have the language of the two ages so clearly enunciated (cf. Matt. 12.32). Is he here thinking of a future kingdom, perhaps along the lines found in Colossians 1, which speaks of the kingdom of Christ, to be followed by the kingdom of God (see pp. 125-26 above)? But the language of two ages is not the same as the language of two kingdoms. While there is a clear focus in this piece of epideictic rhetoric on the present, there are nonetheless references to the eschatological future. Hoehner reminds us: "it states that in the future God will, in the fullness of times, unite all things in Christ (1:10), redeem his purchased possession (1:14), demonstrate the riches of his grace in the saints (2:7), redeem those he has sealed (4:30), inherit the kingdom of God (5:5), present his church spotless (5:27), and reward

26. See rightly, Arnold, *Ephesians*, p. 52: "the writer wants to impress indelibly on his readers that no conceivable being can even come close to matching Christ in power and authority. Upon raising Christ from the dead, almighty God exalted him to a position of unrivaled authority from which he exercises his lordship. The significant Christological statements in the prayer are made by the author for their direct ecclesiological relevance — the church now shares in this resurrection power."

27. Paul is certainly not referring to earthly authorities here, not least because he locates these beings in the heavenlies. See P. T. O'Brien, "Principalities and Powers," in *Biblical Interpretation and the Church*, ed. D. A. Carson (Exeter: Paternoster, 1984), pp. 110-50; cf. Lincoln, *Ephesians*, pp. 64-65, critiquing W. Wink *Naming the Powers* (Philadelphia: Fortress, 1984), pp. 117-18, among others whose translation of Eph. 6.12 ("we wrestle not only with flesh and blood but also with principalities and powers . . .") amounts to a misreading of the text; and Arnold, *Ephesians*, pp. 41-56. See also W. Carr, *Angels and Principalities* (Cambridge: Cambridge University Press, 1981), though he misreads texts like Col. 2.15, thinking that it says the same thing as 2 Corinthians 3. Carr globalizes things in the same way as Wink (who says the terminology always refers to both heavenly and earthly powers), except for Carr all the references to the powers in Paul are references to good angels, the heavenly host. This also clearly does not work with a text like Col. 2.15. Only the context can determine the meaning of these terms.

28. Nevertheless, see Arnold, *Ephesians*.

29. On terms for these powers see Schnackenburg, *Ephesians*, p. 77. Cf. Rom. 8.38; Col. 1.16; 1 Cor. 15.24; 1 Pet. 3.22; *1 Enoch* 61.10; *Testament of Levi* 3.8.

believers for their good deeds (6:8)."[30] In any case these beings, whether malevolent or benevolent, are all said to be subjected under Christ's feet.[31]

Christ is over all supernatural beings, but he is also given as head to those natural beings who are collectively called "the church." "To the church" is a dative of advantage, in which case it means "on behalf of" or "for the church."[32] "The rhetorical and practical/pastoral point that the author makes is that Christ rules for the benefit of the church. . . . The church, and therefore the audience . . . , are identified as those for whom Christ reigns."[33] *Ekklēsia* here, as elsewhere in Ephesians (3.10, 21; 5.23-32), surely has a more than local sense since it is Christ's body, but it of course includes the audience of this discourse. This more universal sense of the term is in keeping with the circular nature of the document.

It is not clear at all whether v. 23b means that the church fills out or completes Christ as his body, that it is filled by the same Christ who fills all things, or that it, filled by Christ, fills or penetrates all things (i.e., the world). This last possibility is clearly the least likely since the focus of the passage is not missional. Paul is not speaking of the church spreading throughout the world.[34] The subject here is God, and Christ who is filled with God, just as also Colossians says, and it is the church that is filled with Christ, who has also filled the world or cosmos in the sense that his rule is spread over it all.[35] Rhetorical considerations favor the view that both *plērōma* and *sōma* ("fullness" and "body") refer to the church. We have the repetition of the same sounds, for not only do *plērōma* and *sōma* rhyme, but so also do *autou* and *tou plēroumenou*,[36] and just after *plērōma* we have the alliterative *ta panta en pasin*. This phrase involves paronomasia as well as parechesis (repetition of the same sounds in successive words; see *Rhetorica ad Alexandrum* 1436a.5-13). Again we see the great concern that the words sound right to have a specific effect. Rhetorical considerations are dictating not only word choice but also the particular forms of the

---

30. H. Hoehner, *Ephesians* (Grand Rapids: Baker, 2002), pp. 281-82.

31. Arnold, *Ephesians*, p. 55, insists that evil powers are meant here, but the echo of Ps. 8.6, where it is animals that are in subjection (see vv. 7-8), would not suggest that this is the case. The case for Christ's supremacy over all powers is not made by simply asserting that he is Lord over malevolent powers, and here Paul is trying to globalize things, making evident Christ is Lord of all.

32. See Caird, *Paul's Letters*, p. 48; Lincoln, *Ephesians*, p. 67.

33. Jeal, *Integrating Theology and Ethics*, p. 106.

34. See rightly Perkins, "Ephesians," p. 384.

35. There is the additional point that *plērousthai* does not occur elsewhere with an active sense (i.e., "filling" rather than being filled or completed or the resultant sense of fullness or completeness).

36. If the active form had been used of this word, the rhetorical symmetry would have been lost. See Jeal, *Integrating Theology and Ethics*, p. 108.

words chosen, and the "sound effects" of the passage help the rhetoric to be persuasive.

The grammar favors the second option, that the church is filled by the same Christ who fills all things, but it is just possible that Paul means that the church fills out or completes Christ as his body[37] given the ecclesiocentric character of this discourse. In that case, the point would be that the church is the extension of Christ on earth — being filled with God's presence and Spirit — and thus is where the world can find the divine presence. In either case the cosmic lordship of Christ is exalted and given thanks for here. The real benefit of this reign of Christ is that Christ's power and knowledge are available to the believer to aid his or her growth. "Since the fundamental concern for the audience/church is growth (1:17-19a; 3:14-19) and because the head, body, and growth are bound up together in parenesis (4:12, 15-16), it seems clear that the description of Christ's body in 1:23a has a view toward a growing body that is gaining strength and moving toward maturity (4:13-16)."[38] This being so, the parenesis in chs. 4–6 need not be seen as deliberative rhetoric at all, for a change of behavior is not required. Rather continued growth and maturation in the direction already being pursued is encouraged and lauded.

Since Paul uses the thanksgiving period as a preview of and preparation for what follows, "the thematic images of the resurrection and session of Christ in heaven given in 1:19b-23 are linked directly to the resurrection and session of believers in heaven by 2:1-10. The narration of ideas concerned with salvation in 2:1–3:13 [is] given [its] foundation in the narration of ideas concerned with Christ's resurrection, exaltation and position vis-à-vis the church in 1:19b-23."[39] We have seen here how important christology is for this discourse, bringing the thanksgiving section to a dramatic conclusion. Christology is no less important in Ephesians than it is in Colossians, and dramatic attempts to contrast these two documents on this score are wrongheaded. Christology is not swallowed up by ecclesiology here. Rather, "Ephesians spells out the implications for the life of the church of the christology it shares with Colossians."[40] Indeed, the ecclesiology offered in Ephesians must be seen as result of christology, a result of the work of Christ.

---

37. Against this view O'Brien, *Ephesians*, p. 150, says this notion is foreign to Paul and the rest of the NT.

38. Jeal, *Integrating Theology and Ethics*, p. 106.

39. Jeal, *Integrating Theology and Ethics*, pp. 100-101.

40. MacDonald, *Colossians, Ephesians*, p. 226.

A Closer Look: The Ethos of Community in Ephesians

Should Ephesians be seen as a sectarian tract, addressed to those who feel under attack from their environment, including from the powers of darkness? Does it inculcate an adversarial relationship with the world? Does the author suggest that there are demons under every rock and that Christians must batten down the hatches and live in a defensive mode? The sociological study of this discourse is still in its infancy, and much hinges on how one chooses to read the references to "the world, the flesh, and the devil" in this document. MacDonald is representative of a particular line of approach when she argues that the world is depicted here as dominated by the Evil One (2.1) and that believers are seen as under siege with "the only real defense against it [being] . . . God's armor of ethical and spiritual virtues (6:14-17)." She adds that "Ephesians was in all likelihood composed in an atmosphere of great consciousness of evil and commitment to separation from outsiders. In comparison to the other writings in the Pauline corpus it demonstrates a sectarian identity that is moving in the direction of greater introversion."[41] We need to address this suggestion in several ways.

It needs to be kept in mind that Ephesians is very close to Colossians, literarily and otherwise, including in some of its major theological assumptions. For example, the author of Ephesians, especially if he is Paul, is well aware of the Christus Victor theology of texts like Col. 2.15. These texts reassure the audience that Christ has already triumphed over the powers and principalities and rules over them now. Indeed, Eph. 1.21-22 also says that Christ is already head over all things, including the powers, for the sake of the church. 4.8 adds that when Christ ascended he led captives in his train (presumably referring to wicked powers and principalities). This being so, Christians are charged to live in the light of this knowledge. What exactly does that entail, and what sort of worldview is Paul inculcating in this sermon?

Paul clearly believes that the audience can live in the world in a Christian manner. He does not call for their withdrawal from the world into some sort of commune, conclave, or monastery. He admits that the world has its wicked ways (2.1) and that the ruler of the kingdom of the air, by means of his spirit, is at work in the world in those who are disobedient, those who are not followers of Christ (2.2). However, the power of God in this world is greater than that evil or wicked power. Indeed, in Christ and through his death, resurrection, and exaltation many have been transferred out of the ethos of the world and into the ethos of the redeemed community, and that community need not be fearful about the world any longer, for Christ is ruling the world for the sake of the church. Indeed, so great is the power of God in Christ that a human community in which all kinds of persons and all sorts of barriers, even the Law, have been broken down, has been created right in the midst of the fallen world. This does not sound like escapist literature of a sect focusing on expected participation in another world. But there is more.

41. MacDonald, *Colossians, Ephesians*, p. 226.

Paul speaks clearly of not only his own evangelism (2.6-7), but even speaks of the wisdom of God being revealed now through the church to the powers and principalities (2.10), and he mentions in his list of church functionaries in 4.11 "evangelists," the only such reference in the Pauline corpus. This again does not sound as if the audience is being viewed or even encouraged to be an introversionist sect. Neither does the command to bear witness or speak the truth in love (4.15), which is not said to be limited to discourse with fellow believers.[42] The audience is no longer in darkness, and they are called on to live as children of light in the world (5.8) and to expose publicly the deeds of darkness done by the disobedient (i.e. non-Christians, 5.11-14). This requires engagement with the culture, not withdrawal from it. Again Christians are not only to live in the light but to shed light in the darkness, bearing witness and taking on the role of evangelists. 3.10 does not suggest that the powers are troubling the church.[43] To the contrary it speaks of the wisdom of God being made known to the powers through the church, which may well refer to the church's public proclamation of the truth.

Finally the peroratio in 6.10-18 speaks of preparation for the day of evil so that Christians will be able to remain in the world during that darkest of all days and "stand their ground." The discourse concludes with a request for prayer that Paul will be able to continue fearlessly sharing the gospel with the lost (6.19-20). This discourse is by no means mainly about spiritual warfare, and when such an eschatological battle is referred to the advice given is not "go on the offensive" but "prepare to stand firm, and so withstand the onslaught."[44] Finally, we may note that nothing is said in this discourse about the audience being persecuted, having suffered any martyrdoms, falling afoul of the law, or having bad relationships with their pagan neighbors. Nor is there any exhortation to obey the governing authorities, much less a painting of such authorities in the kind of colors we find in Revelation.[45] Nothing suggests a truly adversarial situation between the Christian community and the social structures that exist around it.

In short, there are no social data in this discourse that suggest a post-Pauline situation or the beginnings of an introversionist sect. In fact, to the contrary, the strong christology of Christ as Lord over all for the sake of the church, the strong belief that God's incomparable power is available and at work in the Christian community, and the inculcation of virtues in individuals and families which will be winsome in the larger culture speak of a community still very much engaging with the culture, challenging its values, and seeking to win people for the gospel. The enemy is not seen as the world, if by world one means lost human beings. The enemy is quite properly

42. See Schnackenburg, *Ephesians*, p. 86.

43. Against MacDonald, *Colossians, Ephesians*, p. 219.

44. One of the things that facilitates this sort of misreading of Ephesians is interpretation of "saints" in 1.18 to refer to angels, which is highly unlikely not only because immediately before in v. 15 Paul uses the term of believers, but also because elsewhere in the Pauline corpus Paul does not use *hagioi* for angels.

45. On which see my *Revelation* (Cambridge: Cambridge University Press, 2003).

seen as the devil and his minions, and so Paul reminds his audience of this in his conclusion at 6.11-12. Neither the world, its lost inhabitants, nor the governing authorities are demonized in this discourse. Rather the supernatural powers themselves are to be resisted directly with the full equipment and arsenal of the believer, always remembering Christ has already triumphed over such powers. Their doom is sure. The gospel of peace has already created the community (2.14-15), and the community is then to put on the footwear of the traveling evangelist who shares this gospel of peace (6.15, echoing Isaiah) and take up the tasks at hand, despite the resistance and presence of evil in the world.

In conclusion we may cite Schnackenburg who comes to a very different conclusion than MacDonald about the nature of the community being inculcated and addressed in Ephesians:

> The border between cosmos and Church is not solid and rigid but is dynamic: the Church should increasingly expand and take possession of the cosmos in an intensive rather than extensive manner. For her growth takes place in inner strengthening, especially in love (4:15) which is the divine principle working against the powers of the ungodly. To the extent that the Church through the Gospel inwardly wins back humanity alienated from God and formerly enslaved by the "powers" she reveals to the ungodly powers God's manifest wisdom (cf. 3.10) and deprivation of their own power. Hence the Church is the representative of the non-violent and yet powerful rule of Christ, but still more: she is a power which pervades and transforms the world — if she convincingly conveys to the world the effective healing-power of Christ within her — i.e. convinces by her own unity and love (cf. 4:12-14). Does the Church thereby become the organ or instrument of Christ's cosmic rule? Only if and only so far as her influence in love is effective (cf. 4:15). In the context of 1:17-23 the view of the Church as the Body and Fulness of Christ is intended to make one thing only clear to the addressees — that, through their incorporation in the Church they have been put under the total beneficent rule of Christ, whose victory over the powers of darkness is certain.[46]

---

46. Schnackenburg, *Ephesians*, p. 84.

Narratio — Gentiles Then and Now and Their Apostle — 2.1-22; 3.2-13

This section consists of several long sentences, some of which have parts missing or delayed until later. For instance, vv. 1-7 form one long sentence in Greek and the main verb "made alive" does not show up until v. 5. The translation thus becomes difficult at various junctures. Basically 2.1-10 goes with what precedes it in 1.19-23, reiterating and amplifying some of what has already been said, and describes the condition of Gentiles then and now vis-à-vis their relationship with God.[1] This is followed by 2.11-22, which deals with the all-encompassing unity believers have in Christ as Jews and Gentiles. 3.2-13 then introduces Paul's story into the mix insofar as it intersects with that of the Gentile audience.

From a rhetorical point of view, a narratio is a statement of pertinent facts relevant to the discourse (Quintilian, *Inst. Or.* 4.2.31; Aristotle, *Rhet.* 3.16.1-11). Jeal suggests that the particular sort of narratio we are dealing with seeks to win the belief of the audience, or I would say, reaffirm what they already know to be true about themselves (see *Rhet. ad Her.* 1.8.12).[2] Ephesians 2 should thus not be seen as the center of the discourse. Rather it is the presupposition and basis of the exhortations that are to come in the second half of the discourse. The reminder of what is already true about the audience prepares them to receive the word about what ought to be true about them.[3] To put it in traditional

---

1. On the "then" and "now" motif, used regularly in the NT see P. Tachau, *"Einst" und "Jetzt" im Neuen Testament* (Göttingen: Vandenhoeck und Ruprecht, 1972).

2. Roy R. Jeal, *Integrating Theology and Ethics in Ephesians: The Ethos of Communication* (Lewiston: Mellen, 2000), pp. 129-30.

3. While it is possible to take 3.2-13 as a digressio which ends the narratio (see A. T. Lincoln, *Ephesians* [Waco: Word, 1990], pp. 171-72, citing Quintilian, *Inst. Or.* 4.3.1, 14), this is not

terms, the ethics is built on a theology of grace, a theology of what God has accomplished in Christ for them and in them through Christ. This moving forward of the discourse is accomplished by the "then-now" contrast — then they were lost and engaged in sinful behavior, now they are saved and have been created in Christ for good works, which works will be specified later in the discourse.

And you, being dead from your transgressions and sins, in which you once walked according to the order of this world, according to the ruler of the domain of the air, [according to] the spirit which is now active in the sons of disobedience, in which we all lived at one time in the desires of our flesh, doing the will of the flesh and of the thoughts, and we were children by nature of wrath as also were the rest; but the God who is rich in mercy, through his great love with which he loved us, made us alive together with Christ, for we also were dead in transgressions (you have been saved by grace), and we were raised and seated in the heavenlies in Christ Jesus, in order to prove in the coming ages the surpassing riches of his grace in goodness upon us in Christ Jesus. For you have been saved by grace through faith, and this not from you, [but rather] the gift of God, not from works lest anyone might have boasted. For you are his handiwork, created in Christ Jesus for good works which God prepared beforehand in order that we might have lived in them.

Therefore remember that at one time you Gentiles in the flesh, who were called the uncircumcision by the ones called the circumcision handwrought in the flesh, because you were at that time without Christ, estranged from the society of Israel, and foreigners to the covenants of promise, having no hope and without God in the world. But now in Christ Jesus you who were once far away have been brought near in the blood of Christ.

For he himself is our peace, the One making both one and destroying the dividing wall of the fence — the hostility — in his flesh, that is, the law of the commandments in decrees he annulled in order that of the two he might create in himself one new person making peace, and might reconcile both in one body to God through the cross, having destroyed the hostility in himself. And coming, he brings Good News of peace to you that were far off, and peace to those near, because through him we both have access in one Spirit to the Father. So then you are no longer foreigners and resident aliens, but you are fellow citizens of the saints and members of the household of God, built on the foundation of the apostles and

---

necessary, and such a conclusion should not be based on the fact that 3.1 is resumed at 3.14. Interlocking structure of the discourse is just as possible. What is decisive in my view is that 3.2-13 builds on what is said in 2.11-22 and brings it to a personal climax in which author and audience are entwined. On interlocking rhetorical structure see B. Longenecker, *Rhetoric at the Boundaries: The Art and Theology of New Testament Chain-Link Transitions* (Waco: Baylor University Press, 2005).

prophets, Christ Jesus himself being the keystone/head of the corner in whom the whole building fit together is growing into a holy temple in the Lord, in whom also you are built together with us into the dwelling of God in the Spirit.[4]

Because of this I, Paul, the prisoner of Christ for you Gentiles. . . .[5] *If surely you have heard about the administration/stewardship of God's grace given to me for your sake according to the revelation made known to me — the mystery, just as I mentioned above in brief, in accordance with which you are able as you read to understand my insight into the mystery of Christ, which to other generations was not made known to the sons of humanity as now it is revealed to his holy apostles and prophets in the Spirit — the Gentiles are inheriting together with [Jews] and are one body and fellow sharers of the promises in Christ Jesus through the gospel, of which I was made a minister according to the gift of God's grace given to me according to the working of his power. To me, to the one who is less than the least of all God's saints, this benefit/grace was given to proclaim to the Gentiles the untraceable riches of Christ and elucidate all*[6] *of what is the nature of the administration*[7] *of the mystery hidden away for ages in the God of all the created in order that it might be made known now to the rulers and authorities in the heavenlies through the assembly — the many-faceted wisdom of God, according to the purpose of the ages which was realized in Christ Jesus our Lord, in whom we have the free speech and free access in confidence through his faithfulness. Therefore I pray you not to lose heart because of my afflictions for you, inasmuch as it is your glory.*

If it was not perfectly clear before, it becomes abundantly evident in this chapter that the author is a Jewish Christian and is writing in the main to Gentiles, which fits the identification of the author as Paul. It is not difficult to believe that Paul, approaching the end of his life with a real sense of concern that the church was becoming mostly Gentile in the west, might write this sort of statement to remind Gentiles of their debt to Israel and to Jewish Christians such as himself. In such a statement it is also hardly surprising that he might look back and speak about the origins of the church and its true foundations as he tries to

---

4. There are no major textual issues in Ephesians 2, but it should be noted that in v. 17 the second occurrence of "peace" should be retained, not only because it is well attested (P46, ℵ, A, B, D, F, G, and others), but because later scribes who created the Textus Receptus tried to simplify the Asiatic style with its redundancies. See Metzger, *TC*, p. 217. As Metzger says, the second reference to peace adds to the force of Paul's statement.

5. This clause actually introduces 3.14ff., but it also serves to introduce Paul into the narratio so that he can discuss his ministry in vv. 2-13.

6. "All" here should probably be retained as original since the universal scope of things is a constant refrain in this sermon and since the textual evidence supports its inclusion. See Metzger, *TC*, p. 534.

7. On the meaning "plan" for *oikonomia* in the papyri see *New Docs* 2, p. 92.

give his audience, who are apparently myopic, a sense of perspective on the church as a whole in regard to its origin, character, and destiny.

2.1 begins with a further discussion of what the Gentiles once were — dead in transgressions and sins (cf. Col. 1.14; 2.13; Rom. 5.12-21; on the notion that the soul that sins dies see Ezek. 18.20; *4 Ezra* 3.25-26; 8.59-60; Bar. 54.15-19). The two terms may be interchangeable and we may chalk this up to the Asiatic style, but if there is a slightly different nuance the first connotes willful sin in violation of known principles.[8] In the Qumran literature we hear of the similar notion of being raised from the "worms of the dead" to "the lot of your holy ones" (1QH 19.10-14), only there the reference is probably to literal resurrection from the dead.

The Gentiles had once lived lives following the present world order.[9] Paul is commenting not on current fashion but on the moral milieu or *Zeitgeist* of the age in which they live.[10] The rhetorical device employed in these verses is antithesis (Quintilian, *Inst. Or.* 9.3.81-86; *Rhet. ad Her.* 4.15.21), contrasting death and life, being lost and being saved, deeds of the flesh and good works. This world order is "according to the ruler of the domain of the air," which is a description of Satan (cf. 4.27; 6.11-12). Paul clearly believed there were powerful dark entities, personal beings who inhabited the realm above and beyond the earth.[11] Satan is seen as the ruler of the evil part of the spirit world, but more importantly he has direct influence on the spirit of the pagan world.[12] Paul then will discuss how the world, the flesh, and the devil all affect human behavior.[13]

But then Paul hastens to add in v. 3 that all Christians, Jew or Gentile, once lived according to the desires of "our flesh," by which he means carrying out in actions one's sinful inclinations. Thus "we," which clearly refers to Jews,

---

8. Hendiadys is the rhetorical device being used here, the nearly synonymous terms reinforcing each other (*Rhet. ad Her.* 4.28.38).

9. The term *aiōn*, "age," does not likely refer here to a spiritual power, not least because everywhere else in the Pauline corpus it has a temporal, not personal, sense. See M. Y. MacDonald, *Colossians, Ephesians* (Collegeville: Liturgical, 2000), p. 229; Lincoln, *Ephesians,* p. 95.

10. See R. Schnackenburg, *The Epistle to the Ephesians: A Commentary* (Edinburgh: Clark, 1991), p. 91; E. Best, *Ephesians* (Edinburgh: Clark, 1998), p. 207.

11. On the air as the intermediate zone between the earthly and heavenly realms inhabited by angels, demons, etc., See Philo, *De Gigantibus* 8-18. See *2 Enoch* 29.4, 5: "And I threw him out from the height with his angels, and he was flying in the air continuously above the abyss."

12. It is possible that Paul believes that just as Christ has sent the Spirit into believers, so there is a spirit or impersonal force that Satan has sent into the lost.

13. See P. T. O'Brien, *The Letter to the Ephesians* (Grand Rapids: Eerdmans, 1999), p. 164; he adds that the three influences (some internal, some external) lead to sin, transgression, and outright disobedience.

were once "children of wrath by nature like everyone else." It should be clear that Paul does not mean that people were destined for wrath, since he is talking about himself and in this case other Jewish Christians. He means that they were acting in a fallen way like those who deserved God's wrath (cf. Wis. 13.1; 1QH 1.25; 1QS 1.10; 3.21). This verse, despite the protest of Barth,[14] does deal with the idea of having a fallen human nature, though it does not say how "we" obtained it.[15] Adam is not discussed in this context.

The care in the rhetorical construction of the discourse may be seen in v. 2 where we have two parallel *kata* clauses that form an isocolon (colons with nearly the same number of syllables), making the sound of the words attractive and forceful and reinforcing the content (see *Rhet. ad Her.* 4.20.27-28; Aristotle, *Rhet.* 3.9.9). Furthermore, vv. 2 and 3 begin with equivalent phrases and constructions *(en hais, en hois)*. It becomes clear that the style is undertaken for its oral effect, not its literary qualities. The first few verses of the chapter bring the audience into the discourse. It is their story as well as Paul's that he is relating here. "Their consequent collaboration with the narrative would tend to the development of the frame of mind the author is attempting to elicit."[16]

V. 4 speaks of "God, who is rich in mercy." God's riches are in fact a major emphasis in chs. 1–2.[17] At 1.7 we heard about the riches of his grace and at 1.18 the riches of his glorious inheritance, and again at 2.7 we will hear of the riches of his grace.[18] The notion of God's abundant compassion and grace dominates the landscape of this discourse.[19]

V. 5 describes not baptism but that which baptism symbolizes — conversion, the change from death to life.[20] Paul does not say that this occurs "in Christ" but "with Christ." With "in Christ" it might be taken to refer only to the objective life made possible by the resurrection of Jesus. Paul is speaking about not only the resurrection of Jesus but also the spiritual transformation of be-

---

14. See M. Barth, *Ephesians 1–3* (Garden City: Doubleday, 1974), pp. 231-32. Notice that both Chrysostom and Jerome in their comments on Ephesians see the notion of original sin referred to here.

15. See Best, *Ephesians,* pp. 211-12.

16. Jeal, *Integrating Theology and Ethics,* p. 136.

17. There is no good reason to see a hymn fragment, much less a baptismal liturgy, included here. The style of vv. 4ff. does not seem to be notably different from what precedes. See the discussion in Lincoln, *Ephesians,* pp. 88-91.

18. See P. Perkins, "The Letter to the Ephesians," in *The New Interpreter's Bible* XI (Nashville: Abingdon, 2000), p. 389.

19. See G. B. Caird, *Paul's Letters from Prison* (Oxford: Oxford University Press, 1976), p. 52: "The ultimate truth about man is to be found neither in his own natural condition nor in the retribution it deserves, but in God's mercy and love."

20. Jeal, *Integrating Theology and Ethics,* p. 137.

lievers. This is clear from the parenthetical remark "you have been saved." The participle "saved" is in the perfect tense, and much has been made of how Paul does not speak in this fashion. But as Barth points out[21] Paul does regularly speak of justification using the aorist tense (Rom. 8.24; 2 Cor. 6.2), which is not so different from what we find here. More to the point, Caird points out how Paul uses the perfect tense quite correctly when he wants to speak of the continuing effects of salvation into the present (Rom. 5.2; 6.7; Gal. 3.8). This is what we find here, not a reference to the past objective fact or completion of salvation.[22] This is why some opt for the translation "you are saved."[23] Comporting with its epideictic character, the emphasis in this discourse is on present or realized eschatology, or what could be called vertical eschatology. "The words 'dead' . . . and 'made alive . . .' are employed as contrasting soteriological terminologies that graphically and therefore rhetorically, persuasively and emotionally, portray the pre-Christian past and the Christian present." This sort of pattern seems to have been characteristic of early Christian preaching.[24] Notice the deliberate paronomasia as Paul in vv. 5-6 begins a series of verbs with the prefix *syn* ("made alive with," "raised with," "seated with") and so by similarity of sound further punctuates the theme of union with Christ.[25]

But in what sense have believers been raised with Christ and seated with him in the heavenlies? In what sense do they reign with him now? One could take this to mean that in Christ, the believer's representative, these things are now true, though they are not yet de facto true in the believer's own life. However, it is more likely that what Paul means is that by the Christian's salvation experience we now have not only new life but power over sin which previously believers did not by nature have. He may also mean that believers have power over the powers and principalities. They can be resisted and will flee upon resistance (see 6.10-18). Thus figuratively Paul can say that "we" are already seated in the seat of power and authority in heaven, which likely means that believers have in part the power and authority "with Christ" that Christ exercises from that locale.[26] This salvation brings light, life, and power into our lives and was given us in order to prove or show now and in the future how great God's grace and goodness is.

Paul is not trying here to promote a new or all-encompassing realized eschatology which eclipses all future eschatology. This is clear from v. 7: we have this exalted place now with Christ in heaven "in order that in the coming ages

---

21. Barth, *Ephesians 1–3*, p. 221.
22. Caird, *Paul's Letters*, p. 52. Cf. Best, *Ephesians*, p. 217.
23. See the discussion in Lincoln, *Ephesians*, pp. 110-11.
24. Jeal, *Integrating Theology and Ethics*, pp. 132-33.
25. Cf. Jeal, *Integrating Theology and Ethics*, p. 141; Schnackenburg, *Ephesians*, p. 88.
26. See the thoughtful discussion in Best, *Ephesians*, pp. 221-23.

he might show the incomparable riches of his grace."[27] Jeal is right that the functional purpose of speaking of salvation as a done deal is to make a deep emotional impact on the audience (pathos: Aristotle, *Rhet.* 1.2.5; Quintilian, *Inst. Or.* 6.1.51; 6.2.2-8) which prepares them to be receptive to the exhortations that follow. The logic is that "since God has already done so much for you, you should respond as follows. . . ." The language of realized eschatology is not meant to describe a fully completed salvation or even one predestined in advance. Paul is using strong language to persuade the audience of how much they have been blessed by God already, so that when he speaks of the not yet and of what they ought to do, he has a solid foundation on which to build.[28] The reference to future ages coupled with the reference to being currently seated in heaven can be reconciled only through the reminder that "we already have our place there 'in Christ Jesus' [not in ourselves] but we do not yet participate fully in his glory because we still live in this world."[29]

V. 8 then picks up the parenthetical remark of v. 5 — "we are saved by grace through faith." Does *touto*, "this," in v. 8b refer to faith or to the whole salvation event? Probably the latter.[30] The work of salvation, including the gift of faith, is all the work and gift of God to the believer, it is not our own doing or striving, though certainly believers must exercise that gift of faith and appropriate its benefit.[31] God will not and does not have or exercise faith for us.

In v. 9 "works" refers to human efforts, not works of the Law. Paul will deal with the latter later in the discourse. Thus there is no reason for the believer to boast as if he has accomplished his own salvation. Rather, saved people are God's handiwork, and they have been saved to serve, created in Christ Jesus for a specific purpose — to do good works. These works are done not to earn God's praise or favor but out of a grateful heart and obedient spirit, responding to the gift of salvation. Believers were not saved simply to revel in the benefits of the salvation experience. Rather God renovates a people so that they will do his will.[32] God pre-

27. Again, there is no good reason not to take "ages" here in a temporal sense, as always elsewhere in Paul's letters. Cf. Lincoln, *Ephesians,* pp. 110-11; MacDonald, *Colossians, Ephesians,* p. 233; Schnackenburg, *Ephesians,* pp. 96-97.

28. Jeal, *Integrating Theology and Ethics,* p. 139.

29. Schnackenburg, *Ephesians,* p. 97. The attempt to deny the future reference here must be seen as special pleading. What this proves is that the "present" focus of epideictic rhetoric in Ephesians should not be taken as an indicator that Paul has abandoned future eschatology. See Best, *Ephesians,* pp. 223-25.

30. See MacDonald, *Colossians, Ephesians,* p. 233.

31. It is noteworthy that Josephus, *Antiquities* 4.193 says that the Law set Jews free from the power of fallen human desire.

32. Schnackenburg, *Ephesians,* p. 92: "The whole way of looking at things is focused on humanity's way of life which for Christians has changed from the compulsion to sin (2:1f.) to the freedom to do good (2:10; cf. 4:1, 17; 5:2, 8)."

pared this result of salvation beforehand so that there was a way believers should live once they were saved if they intended to do what God had in mind when he saved them.[33]

At v. 11 Paul begins to expound on the indebtedness of Gentile Christians not only to God but to their Jewish forebears who were before them in the Lord and who unlike the Gentiles were near to God.[34] The Gentiles are called on in this verse to "remember," and so Paul is not breaking fresh ground but offering a reminder.[35] Deepening awareness of what they have in Christ is intended to make them feel grateful and also receptive to the appeal to continue to grow in the right way and direction. The verse begins with "therefore," indicating that what follows announces the social and personal consequences of the salvation just discussed in 2.1-10.[36]

That the author is a Jewish Christian is quite evident here. Only Jews call Gentiles *ta ethnē* or "the uncircumcision" (cf. Gal. 2.7; Rom. 4.9; Col. 3.11).[37] These were not labels Gentiles used of themselves. This verse also confirms that the audience for this discourse is overwhelmingly if not exclusively Gentile. Thus we may say that Ephesians is Paul's epideictic discourse to Gentiles on the nature and mission of the church. Paul reminds these Gentiles that before they converted they were "without Christ and estranged from the society of Israel."[38] In fact, says Paul, despite all their religiosity, they were *atheos*, without

---

33. We do not really have a summary here of Paul's gospel. Far too much is omitted. But we do have a reiteration of the important theme of salvation by grace through faith. The reference to good works prepared beforehand speaks of God's plan of what he does and would have the saved do once he has a saved people of God. Paul does not say the saved were chosen or prepared in advance. Faith is a gift that must be as freely received as it is freely given. The contrast between the gift of faith and the good works prepared beforehand is notable.

34. The literature on 2.11-22 is enormous, not least because of the way this passage has been perceived to be a key summary of Pauline theology. In particular it has been seen as the best succinct summary of Pauline ecclesiology. See Best, *Ephesians*, pp. 233-34 on the ever-expanding corpus of literature on this passage.

35. Jeal, *Integrating Theology and Ethics*, p. 148: "The anamnesis here in 2:11-22 is not employed simply as a recollection . . . but . . . [is] . . . intended to impress the reality of the past on the mind in such a way that an appreciation of the blessings of the present is instilled in the audience members."

36. MacDonald, *Colossians, Ephesians*, p. 241. I quite agree with O'Brien, *Ephesians*, p. 183, and Lincoln, *Ephesians*, pp. 132-33, that attempts to come up with some particular and presumably local problem between Jewish and Gentile Christians that Paul is addressing here have failed and in any case involve too much mirror-reading of what is a general discourse meant for audiences in several locales.

37. That Jews required circumcision, unlike most others, was widely known; cf. Tacitus, *Historia* 5.5, 2; Josephus, *Antiquities* 1.192.

38. Schnackenburg, *Ephesians*, p. 109, is probably right that there is an echo of Rom. 9.4 in Eph. 2.12, and in both texts "Israel" does not refer to the church.

God. This of course is a Jewish monotheistic perspective which denies that the pagan gods were actually gods. It is ironic that this very term, *atheos,* would later be used of Christians because they refused to worship the pagan gods (cf. *Martyrdom of Polycarp* 3; 9.2; Justin Martyr, *Apologia 1* 6.1; 13.1),[39] a polemic which had also been used against Jews (Josephus, *Contra Apionem* 2.148).

What does Paul mean by "Israel" here? Does he mean non-Christian Israel? Or is he thinking of Jew and Gentile united in Christ? It seems odd that he would call the latter "the commonwealth *(politeia)* of Israel," which suggests a political entity. It is difficult to decide this issue but in light of v. 13 it is reasonably clear that Paul is saying that Gentiles have become a part of the community of God's people through Christ. Yet in v. 12 it is equally clear that "Israel" refers to non-Christian or at least pre-Christian Israel. Paul then does not seem to offer a straightforward replacement theology here, but rather the sort of incorporation theology that one already finds in the discussion of Jew and Gentile in Romans 11.[40] First there was Israel, then Christ, then the Jewish followers of Christ, then Gentile followers of Christ. Gentile believers are connected to the people of God through Christ and through Jewish Christians like Paul. Since both Jews and Gentiles have sinned and fallen short of God's glory it is not accurate to say that Paul's view is simply that the church has been incorporated into historical Israel.[41] But equally Paul does not believe that God has forsaken his first chosen people or reneged on his promises to them. In Romans 9–11 he speaks of non-Christian Jews who have rejected the gospel as being temporarily cut off from the people of God in order that they might be grafted back in on the basis of grace and through Christ. The one new person created in Christ involves believing Jews and Gentiles, and specifically those who believe in Christ. The priority of Jews, however, in the promises and grace of God is to some extent maintained here, as in Romans.

Gentiles were not only estranged from the nation of Israel but also without hope because they were foreigners also in regard to the promises of the various covenants made with Israel.[42] This was true in the past, but now through Christ's blood (i.e., blood shed in death) even Gentiles have been brought near

---

39. See MacDonald, *Colossians, Ephesians,* p. 243.

40. See B. Witherington and D. Hyatt, *Paul's Letter to Romans* (Grand Rapids: Eerdmans, 2004), pp. 266-78.

41. Against, M. Barth, *The Broken Wall: A Study of the Epistle to the Ephesians* (Chicago: Judson, 1959), pp. 122-28.

42. Here and at Rom. 9.4 we have a reference to plural "covenants." Lincoln, *Ephesians,* p. 137, however is wrong that this is the only place we have reference to more than one covenant using this specific Greek term (see Gal. 4.24). In any case, it is clear that Paul is able to distinguish among OT covenants, and in fact he does argue that it is a particular covenant that is obsolete since Christ has come, the Mosaic covenant. See my discussion in *Grace in Galatia* (Grand Rapids: Eerdmans, 1998), pp. 321-57.

to God. 1.7 and its reference to Christ's blood should be compared. Christ's death on the cross is seen as an atoning sacrifice, the chief element of which is the shedding and applying of the blood in the appropriate place and manner. But how does shed blood overcome alienation and produce reconciliation? The answer has to do with ancient covenant rites, in which treaties are enacted, inaugurated, or made valid through blood sacrifices (see Rom. 5.8-11). It is not an accident that the reference to "peace" immediately follows the reference to shed blood.[43]

All this has happened because Christ himself (note the emphatic *autos*) is our peace (v. 14). It does not say that he gives peace but rather that he is our peace, probably echoing Mic. 5.5 (cf. Isa. 9.6).[44] By this Paul means that Christ himself in his own person and death is the destroyer of all hostilities between Jew and Gentile. He has made of the two peoples one new person (v. 15).[45] A unity has been created where previously there had been no such unity. Paul is suggesting that a few Gentile proselytes to Judaism through the years does not constitute the unification of humankind. That unification came in and through Christ. Paul is also saying that Jews as well, such as himself, needed to be redeemed and incorporated into Christ in order to be part of the true people of God.

Christ has accomplished this union by destroying the dividing wall of the hedge.[46] The two words *mesotoichon* and *phragmou*, though they are somewhat different in meaning, are another example of Asiatic repetition with variation. The former refers to a wall between two rooms or houses, and so its purpose is division of space. The second term, however, refers to a fence or hedge (see Isa. 5.2 LXX; Mark 12.1), the purpose of which is to keep something or someone out. Despite the attractiveness of the suggestion that this refers to the wall around the Court of Israel in the Jerusalem Temple with signs warning Gentiles to keep out (see Acts 21.27-31; Josephus, *War* 5.194), it should probably be rejected. Paul is not discussing a particular sign or wall, but that which separated Jew and Gentile, and that is surely the Mosaic Law (cf. Col. 2.14 on decrees of the Mosaic

---

43. On vv. 14-18 Schnackenburg, *Ephesians*, p. 107, stresses: "the whole textual unit has one clear line of thought and the crux of it comes to the fore: Christ, the bringer of peace through the event of the Cross, in his Church."

44. Eph. 2.14-18 has rightly been regarded as the locus classicus on the Pauline concept of peace.

45. Schnackenburg, *Ephesians*, p. 113: "Peace means the overcoming of enmity, the putting aside of differences, the bringing together of separate groups."

46. There are three parallel clauses here (tricola; see *Rhet. ad Her.* 4.19.26) with the third member bringing it to a climax and to clarity. The wall is seen to be the Law and "hostility" describes the effect of the Law on some who were not included. Notice the use of synonyms in the first and third clauses for rhetorical effect. See Jeal, *Integrating Theology and Ethics*, pp. 154-55.

Law).[47] Furthermore, it is doubtful that Gentile Christians in Asia would have recognized such an allusion to the partition wall of the Jerusalem Temple since it is unlikely that more than one or two had ever been in the Temple.[48] *Letter of Aristeas* 139 refers to how Moses "surrounded us with unbroken palisades and iron walls to prevent our mixing with any of the other peoples."[49] The function of Torah was to make Jews a people set apart for God, but also it gave them protection from intruders and interlopers since someone wanting to live as a resident alien in the land would have to live by the rules of Torah.[50] Vv. 14-18 can be said to arise out of the then-now, far-near contrast enunciated in vv. 11-13.[51]

V. 15 offers an expanded description of Torah as the Law of commandments which consists in decrees or regulations.[52] Nothing is said here about only the ceremonial law being the focus. It was the Torah as a whole that separated Jews from Gentiles.[53] This entire Law, says Paul, has been annulled by the death of Christ, and the enmity and distance between peoples that it created has been destroyed by the death of Jesus in his own flesh.[54] The purpose of this

47. See Best, *Ephesians*, pp. 259-61. As Caird, *Paul's Letters*, pp. 57-58, points out, it was the whole Temple, not just the partition wall between the court of the Gentiles and the inner courts that was destroyed in A.D. 70. So even if this document was a post-Pauline creation it is unlikely that that event is alluded to here.

48. See rightly, O'Brien, *Ephesians*, p. 195. There is of course Trophimus from Ephesus mentioned in Acts 21, but he is surely a rare exception.

49. Chrysostom's fifth homily on Ephesians: "Oh amazing loving kindness! He gave us a Law that we should keep it, and when we did not keep it, and ought to have been punished, he even abrogated the Law itself."

50. The tone of this portion of the discourse should be noted. Paul is not really arguing to prove a point here but recalling truths already taught and accepted, which is why there are no polemics here (contrast Galatians) even though he is rehearsing fundamental matters. As Jeal, *Integrating Theology and Ethics*, p. 147, says, "There is no explicit indication of ethnic disunity between Jewish and Gentile Christians" in the audience Paul is addressing. Rather, he is encouraging them to realize and appreciate what is already true in Christ.

51. Jeal, *Integrating Theology and Ethics*, p. 153.

52. Once again, another example of the expansive Asiatic style, piling up words with similar but not identical force to give a sense of comprehensiveness and perhaps clearer delineation.

53. Lincoln, *Ephesians*, p. 142; rightly Best, *Ephesians*, p. 260, also rejects the notion that something less than the entire Mosaic Law is in view.

54. As MacDonald, *Colossians, Ephesians*, pp. 244-45, rightly points out, there is little or no basis in early Jewish literature for not taking the Law as a package deal, as Paul himself also does. This is why he speaks of the Law in the singular and not about "laws." So the attempt to see a reference here or elsewhere in Paul to only the boundary-defining laws as being abolished is not in accord with the evidence from early Judaism and especially also Galatians. See my discussion in *Grace in Galatia*, pp. 341-56. One possible way to put this is that chosen by O'Brien, *Ephesians*, p. 199: What is abolished is the Mosaic law covenant, not the principle of or need for commandments or obedience to God. The Mosaic law covenant is replaced by a new covenant

destruction was creation, creation of a new people of God composed of both Jew and Gentile, which here is called "one new person." Thus both groups could be reconciled to God in one body of believers rather than having separate plans of salvation and reconciliation for Jews and Gentiles. It is "impossible to use Ephesians to support theories of an ongoing covenant with Israel that will bring it to salvation outside of Christ. Ephesians consistently insists that God's plan from the beginning has been a 'new creation' that requires abandoning the barriers that distinguished Jew from Gentile."[55]

V. 16b is even more emphatic: Christ killed the enmity on the cross in himself. The verb *apokatallaxē* is a strengthened form and may be translated "might reconcile thoroughly." V. 17 then suggests that the Good News of peace has been and must be brought to those both far and near, that is, to both Gentiles and Jews, because God is no longer operating under the old economy and plan of salvation.[56] That economy was *pro tempore,* only for a period of time which has now gone by since Christ came. Now "access" to the Father comes through Jesus and the Spirit and not otherwise. The term was used of permission granted for an audience with a king (Xenophon, *Cyropaedia* 1.3.8; 7.5.45) The cognate verb *(prosagō)* is used in the LXX of Lev. 1.3; 3.3; 4.14 to refer to unhindered access to God's presence in the sanctuary.

In v. 19 Paul returns to the theme of what Gentiles no longer are, concluding the narratio as he began it. They are not *xenoi* or *paroikoi.* These terms, again an example of Asiatic variation, refer to those who are foreigners and resident aliens. This could thus refer to pure pagans and then God-fearers or even proselytes, those who were on the fringe of the Jewish community. Paul's point in any case is that Gentiles no longer have any sort of second-class status. They are full equals with Jewish Christians as God's united people.

In v. 19b Paul begins to develop the metaphor of the household, playing on the various meanings of the term *oikos,* "house," "household" (i.e. those who live in the house), or the house or temple of God.[57] Thus Paul says the Gentile Christians are fellow citizens with the saints, which here and in some other places in this discourse means Jewish Christians (see above on 1.1, 18). Those "beside a house" (the literal meaning of *paroikoi*) have become *oikeioi,* those

---

which includes Jews and Gentiles and has some commandments for the new community. See also H. Hoehner, *Ephesians* (Grand Rapids: Baker, 2002), pp. 375-77.

55. Perkins, "Ephesians," pp. 402-3. See A. T. Lincoln, "The Church and Israel in Ephesians 2," *CBQ* 49 (1987): 605-24.

56. Isa. 57.19 may be in the background here, but "those who are far off" are not likely to be Gentiles in that text. See Best, *Ephesians,* p. 270; MacDonald, *Colossians, Ephesians,* p. 243.

57. The most notable rhetorical feature of vv. 19-22 is the elaborate paronomasia on the term "house" and its variants. See Jeal, *Integrating Theology and Ethics,* p. 160; Quintilian, *Inst. Or.* 9.3.66-68 on this rhetorical device.

who belong to a house.[58] The members of God's household are built on a solid foundation of apostles and prophets. The latter are Christian prophets, not OT prophets, since they are mentioned after apostles.[59] In 4.11 apostles and prophets are named again as gifts to the church along with evangelists and teachers. There is no suggestion here that any of these functions had ceased in the church by the time the author was writing. In both 5.18 and 6.18 we hear about various sorts of utterances in the Spirit. There is no suggestion that those sorts of things were a thing of the past either.

It has sometimes been thought that Paul would not speak this way about apostles, but the perspective of this sermon is that it presents God's view, not Paul's, of how the plan of salvation has worked out creating the church. Thus, this is not so much a retrospective comment as it is a comment on what is now true both in the sight of God and in the Christian communities. In epideictic rhetoric the focus is on present realities, and so we have not only realized eschatology but also realized ecclesiology. As such this reference to the apostles could certainly have been made by Paul, if he really did believe that the work of the apostles was foundational to the church, especially to the church of both Jews and Gentiles united. The perspective is intentionally universal and cosmic in scope.

There is much debate about the term *akrogōniaiou* in v. 20. Does it mean "cornerstone," "head of the corner" (i.e., the stone that joins two walls together at the top rather than at the bottom like a cornerstone), or keystone? J. Jeremias has championed the last suggestion and it fits well with this letter, for Christ is said to be above in the heavenlies, the head of the body ruling and holding things together from above.[60] There is plenty of evidence from the second to fourth centuries A.D. for this meaning of the term. In the LXX of 2 Kgs. 25.17 the word is used of the head of a pillar, and thus of something above ground, as also in *Testament of Solomon* 22.7–23.3. Furthermore, the archaeological evidence of ornamented keystones is considerable, as opposed to cornerstones, of which Best says there is no archaeological evidence in the Greco-Roman world and which elsewhere were usually not decorated and were simply a part of the foundation.[61]

On the other hand, in the LXX of Isa. 28.16 this Greek term seems clearly to refer to a foundation stone. But one must ask if Paul would suggest that Christ was one stone among many in the foundation even if it was the first stone laid in the foundation?[62] In 1 Corinthians 3 Paul suggests that Christ is the

---

58. See T. K. Abbott, *The Epistles to the Ephesians and to the Colossians* (Edinburgh: Clark, 1897), p. 69.

59. See rightly, Caird, *Paul's Letters*, p. 61; Schnackenburg, *Ephesians*, p. 122.

60. See J. Jeremias, "Eckstein-Schlußstein," *ZNW* 36 (1937): 154-57; Perkins, "Ephesians," p. 402; Lincoln, *Ephesians*, pp. 154-55.

61. See Best, *Ephesians*, pp. 284-86.

62. Hoehner, *Ephesians*, pp. 404-7, tries to make the case that this was the first stone

whole foundation, using the building metaphor rather differently.[63] If Ps. 118.22 is any clue the reference here is to the head of the corner which binds two walls together (cf. Mark 12.10; Acts 4.11; 1 Pet. 2.7). This view makes sense of the imagery and is perhaps to be preferred to either the idea of the simple capstone of an arch, which seals the arch but does not bind two walls together, or the cornerstone, which is only one among many foundation stones.[64] What is certain is that Paul wants to accord to Christ a more important place than that of prophets and apostles in the sustaining of the church.

In this *narratio* Paul has stressed the contrast between what the Gentile audience was and what it is, making clear that they have a great deal to be thankful and praise God for and a great deal at stake if they choose not to continue going and growing in the direction of being God's dwelling place. The rhetorical force of remembering this and realizing its significance is intended to build momentum for the exhortations that follow. Not to obey would be to renounce who they are and what God had done for them already. The present Christian condition is seen as so far superior to life outside Christ that there hardly seems to be a choice to make since Paul's rhetorical aim is simply to encourage the audience to continue to be and do what they already are and are doing, perhaps now with greater awareness of their fundamental values and of how God should be praised all the more.[65]

In v. 21 Paul makes clear that it is Christ in whom the whole building is fit together. He is the key and the glue that binds it together. The building is growing into a holy temple of God. The *naos* was the inner sanctuary of the Temple where it was believed God dwelled. Obviously Paul can mix metaphors since he is talking about buildings that grow, which was perfectly appropriate in Asiatic epideictic rhetoric. Gentiles and Jews are added like bricks to the walls of the temple. In v. 22 Paul says that Gentiles "are being built together with" Jewish Christians into "a dwelling of God in the Spirit." The implication is that God is doing the building and fitting together into Christ. Believers are not presented here as builders. They are depicted as growing more numerous and also more holy and so closer and closer to God.

3.2-14 brings Paul himself into the discussion and concludes the narration of pertinent facts.[66] It is of course true that Paul was a Spirit-inspired Christian

---

laid which established the orientation of the building. But where is the archaeological evidence for this suggestion?

63. See my *Conflict and Community in Corinth* (Grand Rapids: Eerdmans, 1995), pp. 130-35.

64. See the discussion in Schnackenburg, *Ephesians*, pp. 123-24.

65. See Jeal, *Integrating Theology and Ethics*, p. 162.

66. This section seems to be very closely related to Col. 1.23-29. Both start with the same "if indeed" formula followed by "you have heard," then in Col. 1.25 we have the term *oikonomia*, which is also found here. Eph. 3.3 has similar terminology to what we find in Col. 1.26-27 and

who frequently when contemplating the great mercy and grace of God got carried away with expansive praise of God involving many adjectives, clauses, and inclusive terms like "all" (cf. the conclusions of Romans 8 and 11). Yet it is also the case here as throughout Ephesians that Paul is following the dictates of an Asiatic epideictic style which necessarily involves effusiveness, redundancy, amplification, and long periods. For example, vv. 3-6 amplify what has been said in v. 2, and vv. 2-7 and vv. 8-12 are single sentences. The use of rhetorical devices or forms makes Paul's words not less than sincere but more rhetorically effective for the audience he is addressing. He is able to identify with these Gentiles precisely because he realizes that his own coming to Christ was a matter of pure grace since he was a persecutor of the church. Not only was he given grace to be saved, but in the bargain he was given the daunting task of being apostle to the Gentiles. Here he reflects on all of this. Just as the previous two sections of the narratio were walks down memory lane for the audience, so this section is such for Paul, but its rhetorical function is to apprise or remind the audience of Paul's relationship to and similarities to his audience, which is important since many if not most of them do not know him personally. He can still administer the grace of God to this audience while in chains through a document such as this one.

V. 2 begins with a conditional remark, "if indeed you have heard." The phrase here as in 4.21 signals a possible reminder.[67] The truth is, Paul may assume that some of his audience have heard some of his story, but he also assumes that many have not, hence the rehearsal here. *Oikonomia* here (cf. Col. 1.25) refers to the plan of God's grace, but since the term literally means "household rules" (see pp. 261-62 above), it may recall the discussion of God's household in 2.19-22 and prepare for what follows in chs. 5-6. God has a plan to build a house composed of people — both Jews and Gentiles — and the household codes may reveal something of the blueprints, but the theological and ethical reflections here reveal as much or more.

In vv. 3-6 Paul will describe the content of his message to Gentiles augmenting what he said in v. 2 (see Quintilian, *Inst. Or.* 8.4.1-9). He gained knowledge of "the mystery" from a revelation from God (v. 3; cf. 1.9). This may well allude to the experience described in Gal. 1.15-17,[68] where Paul says that he did

---

Eph. 3.5 follows the wording of Col. 1.26 closely. At Eph. 3.7 Paul calls himself a *diakonos*, as at Col. 1.23-25. A similar sense of the term is found at 1 Cor. 3.5. Here I think the case for the priority of Colossians and its use by the author of Ephesians is quite strong. See the chart in Lincoln, *Ephesians*, pp. 169-70. Not just the common language but the same sequencing of thought points to this conclusion. See the discussions in MacDonald, *Colossians, Ephesians*, pp. 260-62; Schnackenburg, *Ephesians*, p. 128; O'Brien, *Ephesians*, p. 238. One noteworthy difference is the presence of the reference to the Spirit in Ephesians but not in Colossians.

67. See Schnackenburg, *Ephesians*, p. 132, n. 309.

68. On which see my *Grace in Galatia*, ad loc.

not derive his calling or the essence of his message from anyone other than God in Christ. In an epideictic discourse such as this one, persuasion happens not by direct argumentation or proofs but by the effective and emotive presentation of certain facts (as here). If the audience accepts Paul's claims about his authority arising out of his Christian experience, then they are apt to accept his take on the "mystery," which involves and incorporates them. *Proegrapsa* ("written before" or "written above") is perhaps most naturally taken to refer to what Paul has said earlier in this letter,[69] though in view of the parallels with Colossians 1 he might be referring to that other letter. But "briefly" means that this does not refer to other letters which cannot be described thus, and "when you read this" (v. 4) makes this "a hidden exhortation to read the letter aloud in the congregation and reflect on it carefully."[70]

Paul is hoping that as the audience reads or hears this discourse they will come to understand his insight into "the mystery of Christ," that is, the mystery of God's inclusion of Gentiles with Jews in Christ, in the new people of God. Previous generations have not had this mystery made clear to them, and no doubt it came as a surprise to Paul as well, but now it has been "revealed to the holy apostles and prophets in the Spirit" and is being passed along to the audience.[71] Here Paul makes clear that while this revelation was given to him personally it was not given to him alone, for other apostles and prophets came to share this understanding and vision, and some even came to share in his ministry (see 1 Corinthians 1–3). Here then we have the idea conveyed that Paul was one apostle among many and that his message was not that of a maverick but a truth shared by other leaders as well.

No one who has read Galatians or 2 Corinthians carefully will doubt that Paul had a very high view of the authority and revelation granted to an apos-

69. This is how Thucydides uses it in his histories (1.23), referring to an earlier part of the same work. See Best, *Ephesians*, p. 302; Hoehner, *Ephesians*, p. 428; Jeal, *Integrating Theology and Ethics*, p. 168.

70. Schnackenburg, *Ephesians*, p. 132.

71. Would Paul himself have referred to the "holy apostles" (notice also the qualification of the prophets by reference to the Spirit)? This form of expression has given some pause in regard to Pauline authorship, but two considerations need to be kept in view. First, this is a circular document praising the foundations and foundational work in Christ and through his emissaries that created a unified people of God. It is natural for there to be a somewhat idealized or even retrospective flavor to this sort of epideictic rhetoric which offers a review of fundamental truths and values. Secondly, as G. D. Fee, *God's Empowering Presence* (Peabody: Hendrickson, 1994), p. 692, n. 113, says: "it is equally difficult to understand how a pseudepigrapher could have made such a gaffe and then written in v. 8 that Paul is the least of all the saints. One can at least explain Paul's own detachment in v. 5 in light of v. 3; but it is especially difficult to understand why someone writing in Paul's name, who has caught all the subtleties of his thought and language, would not have written "to *us* apostles and prophets."

tle.[72] He is not strictly egalitarian in his view of church leadership if by that one means non-hierarchical. He is quite clearly over many Gentiles, but he prefers to set an example, to lead by love and persuasion rather than by demand and command.

Gentiles are now co-inheritors, sharing one body with, being fellow sharers of the promises with Jewish Christians, promises that are fulfilled in Christ (v. 6).[73] The three *syn-* compounds in v. 6 are intended to give a reinforcing effect on those who heard the cadence of it, representing as it does the use of the rhetorical device known as parechesis.[74] *Syssōma* is not found elsewhere in Greek literature and seems to have been coined by Paul himself. Some have suggested the translation "con-corporate." Invention of this sort was an important rhetorical feature of such discourses, especially Asiatic ones (see pp. 4-11 above). The piling up of *syn-* compounds is a regular feature of Paul's rhetoric (see Rom. 6.4-8; 8.17, 22; 1 Cor. 12.26).[75]

V. 7 takes up what has been said in v. 2. The parallel *kata* phrases have the rhetorical effect of emphasizing the source and power of the gift given to Paul. Stringing together a series of genitives and near synonyms intensifies the sense. This is redundancy not just for its own sake but for the sake of emphasis and impressing the point on the audience — a frequently used technique in epideictic rhetoric, especially of the Asiatic sort.[76] Paul calls himself a "minister," which here means an intermediary or agent of some high ranking person. It does not have its later sense of "deacon."[77]

In v. 8 we have another newly-coined term which means literally "leaster" *(elachistoterō)*, that is "less than the least." Paul's sense of unworthiness was profound, because, even while he was persecuting the followers of Jesus, Jesus' grace was extended to him.[78] This is not false modesty but rather

---

72. On which see my *Conflict and Community in Corinth*, pp. 398-401.

73. MacDonald, *Colossians, Ephesians*, p. 263, says that this is the most concise expression of the Christian message in Ephesians, but it would be better to say it is the most concise expression of what the revealed mystery is.

74. See Jeal, *Integrating Theology and Ethics*, p. 169. By now it should be clear that the evidence of the primary oral and aural character of this discourse is so overwhelming that one must question those who simply persist in evaluating it only from a literary point of view as a written communication, whether a letter or a sermon.

75. Which is another small pointer toward the conclusion that Paul wrote this. If he did not, someone has imbibed his rhetorical finesse and abilities to coin a phrase.

76. See Jeal, *Integrating Theology and Ethics*, p. 169.

77. See MacDonald, *Colossians, Ephesians*, p. 264. This should be taken as yet another piece of evidence of the fact that Ephesians is not a post-Pauline document.

78. The rhetorical device here is notatio (Quintilian, *Inst. Or.* 9.2.58-63), in which character delineation is meant to persuade the audience to accept the word of the speaker. See Jeal, *Integrating Theology and Ethics*, p. 170.

profound gratitude, indicating how Paul really felt about the matter, as a text like 1 Cor. 15.9 shows. This sort of language falls under the ancient rhetorical rules for inoffensive self-praise.[79] The rhetorical aim of such statements is to create a deep emotional response (pathos) in the audience, but it also makes it difficult to reject for if Paul is giving all the credit to God, to object to what he says is to object to what God has done. Humility, while not considered a virtue in the larger Greco-Roman world, was seen as a virtue in the Christian community and so could be referred to in a persuasive manner.[80] The remarks also have a leveling effect, placing Paul in the same situation as the Gentile converts. Paul then very aptly says that the riches of Christ are fathomless, inscrutable, incomprehensible, untraceable.[81] They can be announced but never fully explained. But whatever and whenever true revelation is announced, it comes into effective operation.[82]

This mystery was hidden in God until the time when God chose to reveal it. *Apo tōn aiōnōn* has nothing to do with powers and principalities here. It is rather a temporal term and is part of the then-now contrast (note *nyn,* "now," in v. 10a).[83] But Paul does go on to say that the mystery is now being made known to the powers and principalities through the church, which reveals the many-faceted nature of God's wisdom in this matter.[84] But how does the church accomplish this task? Paul probably thinks this is accomplished through preaching. Even the powers were kept in the dark about these matters until the present time, when the secret was revealed.[85]

This secret's revelation spells the doom of all the plans of the powers of darkness to divide the cosmos on the basis of racial or ethnic prejudices. The overcoming of the barrier between Jews and Gentiles betokens the overcoming of all such human and cosmic barriers in this universe. Christ will reconcile and pacify all. The existence of the church heralds the victory of Christ over the cosmic powers.[86]

---

79. See my discussion in *Conflict and Community in Corinth*, pp. 432-41.

80. See Jeal, *Integrating Theology and Ethics*, p. 170.

81. The adjective here (cf. Rom. 11.33) comes from the noun for footprint or track. Thus what is meant is that which cannot be tracked down or traced back to its source. See O'Brien, *Ephesians*, pp. 242-43.

82. See Caird, *Paul's Letters*, p. 66.

83. See Schnackenburg, *Ephesians*, p. 138.

84. Note here again the rhetorical device of amplification. Paul does not use *poikilos,* which would mean "manifold," but rather the reinforced form *polypoikilos,* which literally and redundantly means "much manifold" or "many-many-faceted."

85. One may compare 1 Pet. 1.12, where we hear of angels longing to look into the apocalyptic secrets and meanings of prophecies that are now being fulfilled in the church age.

86. It is in fact possible that Paul is just referring to the existence of the church as a proclamation to the powers. See Best, *Ephesians*, pp. 323-26.

Paul conceives of these hostile powers as part of the spirit world which he calls the heavenlies, which includes both good and bad powers as well as Christ and even deceased believers. These powers are in a realm that intersects with, interacts with, and influences the material world and its inhabitants. Paul even seems to think that these beings come in family groupings, to judge from v. 15, though that could be referring to family groupings of Christians in heaven. Paul believes in the two-age structure of early Jewish eschatology, and in both ages heaven and earth participate.

According to v. 11 God had this plan or purpose in mind for ages but has only revealed or unveiled it in Christ and through his congregation. The resulting benefit for believers is that believers have "free speech" with direct access to God. "Free speech" is what *parrhēsia* literally means and it has a long history of being connected with the Greek ideals of free speech and democratic procedures, but here the focus is on speaking openly and candidly with God. It also connotes boldness or, in a derived sense, assurance. The rendering "free speech" is to be preferred since Paul will also mention the "all-access" pass into the presence of God one has in Christ. Through Christ the clear channel of communication and the relationship with the Father have been opened up, even to Gentiles. In fact these two nouns about speech and access are governed by one definite article ("the free speech and access . . ."), two dimensions of the same reality.[87]

In v. 12b the *dia* phrase could mean "because of faith in him," but more likely it means "because of his faithfulness" as elsewhere in Paul,[88] as the end of v. 11 suggests, which says this was realized "in Christ." It is due to the finished work of Christ that the prayer lines and access to the throne room have been made available. Notice the alliteration involved here in the Greek words for free speech, open access, and the verb *pepoithēsei*.

V. 13 makes a rhetorically effective transition into the concluding prayer which takes up the remainder of ch. 3. It bears some close resemblances to what is said in Col. 1.23-29. Paul will put into practice immediately the theological truth he has just enunciated. Here in v. 13 he encourages his audience by saying that he prays that they do not lose heart because of his sufferings. His suffering is actually their glory, by which he may mean that it will work for their ultimate good in glory (cf. 2 Cor. 4.12, 15; 2 Tim. 2.10) or just possibly that it should be a source of pride for them since it is an honor to suffer for the cause of Christ. This is also rhetorically effective because it makes clear that what Paul has just said about himself is not intended to be a personal sympathy plea but rather an example of how God continues to work through him even in his humble and

87. See O'Brien, *Ephesians,* p. 250.
88. On the *pistis Christou* issue see my *Paul's Narrative Thought World* (Louisville: Westminster John Knox, 1994), pp. 268-72.

humbled condition. "Paul's ministry has been for their personal benefit."[89] They are to embrace who they already are as Christians and embrace the gospel, which embraced both Paul and them. The generating of understanding and a deep embrace of a set of values is what an epideictic speech is supposed to accomplish. Here the mystery is explicated, assurance is given of the status of the audience as true Christians, the authority and ethos of Paul are undergirded, and empathy between audience and author is generated by the reference to the sufferings and similar faith journeys dependent on pure grace. "The result of the author's statement of these concerns is, rhetorically speaking, that the audience members will be persuaded to accept the authority of Paul to speak, and consequently, will be encouraged to practice the behaviour to which he . . . exhorts them in the paraenesis."[90]

89. Jeal, *Integrating Theology and Ethics*, p. 174.
90. Jeal, *Integrating Theology and Ethics*, p. 175.

Concluding Prayer and Doxology — 3.1, 14-21

The end of the first half of the sermon we call Ephesians is found in the latter half of ch. 3, and since it ends in a doxology, it may be possible to conclude that chs. 1–3 originally stood on its own as a homily. But Paul has a tendency to conclude major portions of a discourse with such liturgical elements (see Rom. 11.36), and this may be the case here as well. There seem to be some echoes of the diction of Col. 2.2-10 in this section, particularly in 3.17-19, but as Schnackenburg says, the author of Ephesians is not attempting to ward off false teaching here.[1]

From a rhetorical point of view, since an epideictic piece of rhetoric is all about praise, it is not a surprise that we have a larger quotient of praise in this discourse than in other Pauline discourses. The prayers Paul offers in Ephesians are acts of praise and adoration, even though they include petitions on behalf of the audience. The language of worship and prayer which began at the outset of the discourse (1.3-14, 15-23) is continued here.

The rhetorical function of this material is to get the audience into a doxological mode, which helps in making them receptive to the exhortations that will follow in chs. 4–6. Epideictic rhetoric focuses often on the arousal of the emotions, especially the deeper ones, and here Paul is indeed trying not only to set up an ethos of adoration for what must be heard next, but also pathos is involved as well (see Aristotle, *Rhet.* 1.2.5; Quintilian, *Inst. Or.* 6.2.8). This is very clear in 3.1, where Paul's status as a prisoner is referred to, as is the fact that he is in this condition "for you Gentiles." They would be an ungrateful lot indeed if they did not hear the following exhortations attentively and openly in

---

1. R. Schnackenburg, *The Epistle to the Ephesians: A Commentary* (Edinburgh: Clark, 1991), p. 146.

light of this fact. "Also by referring to the recipients' ethnicity . . . the author gives further ground for emotional response by pointing out that despite racial differences, Paul, a Jew, would serve them by preaching."[2] Paul is engendering goodwill here.[3] It is also true, as Lincoln points out that this material in ch. 3 serves rhetorically as the transitus between the narratio and the exhortatio. It is in a sense a new exordium which again establishes rapport with the audience and makes them disposed to accept the following exhortations.[4]

Because of this, I Paul, the prisoner of Christ for you Gentiles . . . Because of this, I bend my knee to the Father, from whom every family in heaven and upon earth is named, in order that it might be given to you according to the riches of his glory to be strengthened with power through his Spirit in the inner person, that Christ might dwell through faith in your hearts, caused to take root and founded in love in order that you might be strong enough to grasp with all the saints what [is] the width and length and height and depth, to know the love of Christ surpassing knowledge, in order that you might be filled in all the fullness of God.[5]

But to him who is able to do above all measure which you ask or conceive according to the power which is working in you, to him [be] glory in the church and in Christ Jesus to all generations forever and ever. Amen.

V. 14 begins as did v. 1 with *toutou charin*, "because of this," closely linking what is said here to what precedes in ch. 2, particularly 2.11-22.[6] We find another example of *oratio perpetua* in vv. 14-19, one long sentence involving the usual assortment of *hina* clauses, as is characteristic of the Asiatic style. Jeal makes much of the fact that Paul presents himself as performing a physical act of worship, kneeling in prayer, and so setting both the tone and the example for the audience. This visual image of Paul praying for these Gentiles whom he has not even met creates pathos.[7] Quintilian encourages such physical actions as a way of confronting the audience with the posture and attitude they ought to assume

---

2. Roy R. Jeal, *Integrating Theology and Ethics in Ephesians: The Ethos of Communication* (Lewiston: Mellen, 2000), p. 112.

3. See rightly A. T. Lincoln, *Ephesians* (Waco: Word, 1990), p. 171: "Here at the end, it increases the goodwill of the recipients by reminding them of the suffering apostle's ministry on their behalf. It underlines for the Gentile readers that they owe their participation in the salvation that had been promised . . . to the Gospel that was originally revealed to and proclaimed by Paul."

4. See Lincoln, *Ephesians*, p. 200.

5. In v. 19 instead of the reading given, several good witnesses (P46, B, 462) have "that all the fullness of God may be filled up," This seems to be a dubious later correction. See Metzger, *TC*, pp. 535-36.

6. See M. Y. MacDonald, *Colossians, Ephesians* (Collegeville: Liturgical, 2000), p. 274.

7. See Jeal, *Integrating Theology and Ethics*, pp. 112-113.

(*Inst. Or.* 6.1.30-31). It is possible as well that this effect is enhanced here by the reference to kneeling since that was not the normal posture for prayer in Jewish or Greco-Roman settings (though it was certainly not unprecedented; cf. 1 Kgs. 8.54; Ezra 9.5; Luke 22.14). It perhaps makes clear that the prayer is part of an act of worship or special devotion.[8]

In vv. 14-15 there is a wordplay or paronomasia that is not evident in English involving *patera* (Father) and *patria* (family, clan).[9] Again the aural character of this discourse is clear as Paul relies on the sound of the words to make an impression on the audience (cf. *Rhet. ad Her.* 4.21.29; Quintilian, *Inst. Or.* 9.3.66-68).[10] There is here an emphasis on God as Father of all humans and especially of those who worship and properly serve him. Since we hear of family groupings in heaven, this may be a reference not just to humans but to classes or groupings of angels.[11] It may well be that this way of phrasing things is a deliberate attempt to counter imperial cult rhetoric, for in many inscriptions the emperor would call himself the "father of the fatherland" (i.e., of Italy). Here a greater claim is made for God: he is Father of all such family or ethnic groupings (cf. Acts 3.25), or fatherlands (and even extraterrestrial locations). Here and in 4.6 are the only two places in Paul's letters where we find the concept of God as Father (not just creator) of all.[12] God is Father not just because of the work of creation, but also because of the work of redemption.[13] It is God that

8. See P. T. O'Brien, *The Letter to the Ephesians* (Grand Rapids: Eerdmans, 1999), p. 255.

9. J. Gnilka, *Der Epheserbrief* (Freiburg: Herder, 1971), p. 114. H. Hoehner, *Ephesians* (Grand Rapids: Baker, 2002), p. 474, is right to point out that the translation "fatherhood" does not work because there was a different Greek word for that: *patrotēs*.

10. Jeal, *Integrating Theology and Ethics*, p. 114, n. 200, characterizes this rhetorical device here as adnominatio, the repetition of a word with change in letters and a slight change in sound. This technique was especially used in Asiatic rhetoric, where there was an attempt to pile up words that not only were close in meaning but also sounded alike.

11. See Lincoln, *Ephesians*, p. 202. Schnackenburg, *Ephesians*, p. 147, thinks it must refer to only good angels. He cites later Jewish evidence that speaks of angels being "the upper family" and Israel "the lower family" of God. See Babylonian Talmud *Sanhedrin* 98b. In the LXX the term is used to refer to a family or tribe (Exod. 12.3; Num. 32.28; cf. Judith 8.2). According to 1 Enoch 69.3 the angels are arranged in groups with leaders. Heb. 12.9 probably sheds some light on the matter as it refers to God as "the Father of spirits."

12. The Father language for God is frequently found in Ephesians (1.2, 3, 17; 2.18; here; 4.6; 5.20; 6.23). Father was a term of authority and power in the Greco-Roman world, not always of intimacy, though both overtones are found in its use for God in Ephesians. See O'Brien, *Ephesians*, p. 255.

13. On the use of Father language for God in the NT see B. Witherington and L. Ice, *The Shadow of the Almighty* (Grand Rapids: Eerdmans, 2001). It is not clear, though Paul may have thought this, that Paul is saying here that God is the model of fatherhood, of which human fatherhood is but the derivative. But *patria* does not mean or convey the abstract concept of "fatherhood" in the LXX, for example. See Lincoln, *Ephesians*, p. 203. As

names all families. When God names, he does not simply label but rather creates and constitutes, giving identity (cf. Isa. 40.26; Ps. 147.4; Gen. 25.26; 1 Sam. 25.25).[14] Names often connoted something about the nature of the one named.

Quintilian says that for the sake of force or emphasis one will use the rhetorical device of reduplication, beginning a number of clauses with the same term (*Inst. Or.* 9.3.30; cf. *Rhet. ad Her.* 4.28.38). So Paul has three *hina* clauses in vv. 16-19. Paul prays that the audience may be strengthened according to the riches of God's presence/glory by the Spirit in the inner person.[15] "Riches of his glory" has already occurred in 1.18, and the abundance of God's grace is stressed throughout chs. 1–3. We also see a near redundancy ("strengthen with power") in v. 16.

Vv. 16 and 17 also contain a carefully crafted parallel construction in which two clauses containing the same number of syllables (twenty) both speak of God dwelling in the believer's inner being and thereby strengthening the believer ("strengthened through his Spirit in the inner person" and "Christ dwelling through faith in your hearts"). The parallelism is reinforced by the use in both of initial infinitives having *-ai* endings (homeoteleuton), of *dia* as the first preposition, and of *-on/-ōn* as the last syllable. These parallels count against trying to make something different out of the use of *eis* in one final phrase and *en* in the other: *eis* need not mean "unto" or "into" but can mean "in."[16] Thus "in the inner person" (cf. 2 Cor. 4.16; Rom. 7.22)[17] is the equivalent of "in your hearts," not of the "new person" of 2.15 or 4.24. It is "the base of operations at the center of a person's being where the Spirit does his strengthening and renovating work."[18] This sort of theme and variation or reduplication and amplification we have seen to be characteristic of Asiatic rhetoric.[19]

Lincoln asks, what would the phrase "every fatherhood in heaven" mean, if we translated the text that way?

14. G. B. Caird, *Paul's Letters from Prison* (Oxford: Oxford University Press, 1976), p. 69.

15. Which is certainly not a reference to the whole person viewed from a certain aspect, pace E. Best, *Ephesians* (Edinburgh: Clark, 1998), p. 341.

16. P. Perkins, "The Letter to the Ephesians," in *The New Interpreter's Bible* XI (Nashville: Abingdon, 2000), p. 414; contra M. Barth, *Ephesians 1–3* (Garden City: Doubleday, 1974), p. 369.

17. A phrase found only in Paul in the NT. See G. D. Fee, *God's Empowering Presence* (Peabody: Hendrickson, 1994), pp. 695-96.

18. Lincoln, *Ephesians*, p. 205. See the discussion of the inner self in M. Bouttier, *L'Épître de Saint Paul aux Éphésiens* (Geneva: Labor et Fides, 1991), pp. 157-58, and now by H. D. Betz, "The Concept of the Inner Human Being *(ho esō anthrōpos)* in the Anthropology of Paul," *NTS* 46 (2000): 315-41. Unfortunately our Ephesians text is not discussed as Betz does not think it is by Paul.

19. See Jeal, *Integrating Theology and Ethics*, pp. 119-20, Aristotle, *Rhet.* 3.9.9; *Rhet. ad Her.* 4.20.27.

Paul is not referring here to the initial dwelling of Christ in the new convert's heart. Rather Paul is praying for the continuing presence of Christ within the Christians through faith. The verb *katoikeō* signifies literally to make a home or to settle down and so has in view a more permanent presence. That Paul is praying for this for those who are already Christians means that this is not automatically the case for converts who have already experienced the presence of Christ initially in their lives. Rather this happens through faith. Indeed it is contingent on the exercise of faith, "that is, as they trust him he makes their hearts his home."[20] This shows as clearly as one could want that sanctification and a growing relationship with and presence of Christ in the believer's life is indeed contingent on the believer exercising faith in Christ. It is not a unilateral act or activity of God.[21] "Faith involves a relationship of trust between two parties, and so there can be no implication that the notion of Christ living in the center of a believer's personality means the absorption of that individual personality or the dissolving of its responsibility."[22]

Paul basically believes in humans having two portions to their being — the inner person which involves one's heart, mind, and will and can be called either the human spirit or the inner person, and the outer person, which is identified with the body (cf. 2 Corinthians 4–5).[23] Paul does not affirm the Greek idea of the immortal soul and the body as the two parts of the human being. Often when he uses the term *psychē* he means the physical life or life principle, not the soul (see 1 Cor 15.45, where he quotes Gen. 2.7 and *psychē* clearly refers to one's physical being).

The phrase "in love" in v. 17b (or 18a in some versions) may go either with what precedes or what follows, but it seems better to take it with what follows. Thus it refers to believers being caused to take root and being founded in Christ's love so that they might be equal to the task of grasping "with all the saints" (presumably all Jewish Christians, though it may mean all Christians here) the compass and extent of Christ's love. The participles *errizōmenoi kai tethemeliōmenoi* after "in love" are in the perfect tense: the believers have already been and continue to be well-founded in love.[24] In other words, knowing

20. See O'Brien, *Ephesians*, p. 259.

21. Hoehner, *Ephesians*, p. 481, cannot make sense of this and keeps asking whether Paul would really pray for Christ to dwell in the hearts of believers. The answer is yes, he would and he does, but a certain approach to Reformed theology prevents Hoehner from understanding the significance of this fact.

22. Lincoln, *Ephesians*, p. 207.

23. See my discussion in *Paul's Narrative Thought World* (Louisville: Westminster John Knox, 1994), pp 279-300.

24. Best, *Ephesians*, p. 342. This way of putting things is in keeping with the epideictic character of this discourse, dealing with things that are already true in the present.

and understanding the love of Christ requires being rooted in that love, experiencing it, indeed being grounded in it.[25] One can grasp it only through experience, and even when one experiences it one is left groping for words to describe it. The ultimate goal of being rooted in love and grasping its meaning is to "be filled in all the fullness of God." Grasping and experiencing God's love is the key to receiving the full presence of God into one's life. "As believers are strengthened through the Spirit in the inner person, as they allow Christ to dwell in their hearts through faith, and as they know more of the love of Christ, so the process of being filled up to all the fullness of the life and power of God will take place."[26]

Paul seems to envision a threefold filling: Christ is filled with God, the church is filled with God in Christ, and then, partly directly but perhaps also partly through the church, Christ fills the cosmos. Then, indeed, Christ will be all in all. This is not pantheism but a way of explaining how intimate Christ's relationship will be with all living things when the plan of God is completed. Paul is not suggesting that there will be a little bit of God or Christ in all things at some juncture. He is talking about a historical and cosmic drama that involves a progressive filling — now in the church progressively, then in the cosmos.

Vv. 18 and 19 then continue the epideictic theme of appreciating, enhancing, and strengthening what one already has with the second and third *hina* clauses (after the first in v. 16).[27] The author is concerned about the audience's continued growth and maturing and coming to completion in their faith. N. Dahl is right that difficulties in interpretation in regard to v. 18 could be overcome "if one pays attention to the rhetorical form and asks for the function rather than the precise meaning of the passage."[28] In other words, while these are dimensional terms, Paul is trying to convey a comprehensive understanding of the Christians' faith and their indebtedness to God's riches.[29] The dimen-

---

25. The resultant translation would be "that you, rooted and grounded in love, may have the power to comprehend. . . ." See MacDonald, *Colossians, Ephesians*, p. 276.

26. Lincoln, *Ephesians*, p. 214.

27. See Jeal, *Integrating Theology and Ethics*, p. 121; Schnackenburg, *Ephesians*, p. 150.

28. N. A. Dahl, "Cosmic Dimensions and Religious Knowledge (Eph. 3:18)," in *Jesus und Paulus*, ed. E. E. Ellis and E. Grasser (Göttingen: Vandenhoeck und Ruprecht, 1975), pp. 57-75, here p. 74.

29. Does this use of directional terms reflect a knowledge of magical practices, spells, or prayers which used such terms? See C. E. Arnold, *Ephesians: Power and Magic* (Cambridge: Cambridge University Press, 1989), pp. 89-96. While this is possible there seems to be no direct polemic against such practices here. One could perhaps argue that Paul chose to use these terms with knowledge of such practices, but this positive prayer is focused on inclusion, not exclusion. Certainly counting against Arnold's view is the use of these four terms together in a wide variety of literature — Jewish literature (see Job 11.7-9; Sir. 1.3), Stoic philo-

sional terms should be seen as paralleling the phrase "the knowledge-surpassing love of Christ."[30] The emphasis is on the grandeur and scope and immensity of what is being discussed. "In the *katalabesthai* clause the author wishes the audience members to understand an immensity beyond understanding, while in the *gnōnai* clause they are to know the unknowable."[31] The oxymoronic nature of this is of course clear, but it is characteristic of Asiatic epideictic rhetoric, for which no degree of high praise and hyperbole is too grand when the subject is the work of God and its benefit and blessing to humankind. "The author is so concerned about their Christian growth that he offers the prayer that they will be given strength to perceive the imperceptible."[32] But it is not just the content of the phrases but the sound of the words. The four dimensional terms all end in *-os*, which adds impact and emotional force to the discourse.

The final *hina* clause in v. 19 gives us the ultimate goal of the prayer — that the audience be filled with God to the full. Paul ends the prayer with the rhetorical flourish of alliteration — three words beginning with *p*, two of them cognates from the same stem, *plērōthēte* and *plērōma*. "Concern for the perceived needs of the audience is creatively integrated with the devotional and emotional language of worship."[33] Their growth and development in Christ happens not just through learning but also through worship and prayer and finally through obedience, a subject Paul will dwell on in chs. 4–6. The emotions have been engaged as well as the mind in preparation for the exhortation to the will in the latter half of the discourse.

Vv. 20-21 is Paul's beautiful doxology continuing the tone of worship already inculcated in the prayer. Like many such doxologies it includes a refer-

---

sophical tracts, and Hermetic writings as well as Greek magical papyri, and later church writings and Rom. 8.39 should be kept in mind as well. In other words, it looks to be a stock phrase used in a wide variety of contexts. See Schnackenburg, *Ephesians*, p. 150, and MacDonald, *Colossians, Ephesians*, p. 277: "It seems more likely that the measurements are being used in a more general sense to refer to the vastness of the love of Christ that transforms the universe (3:17, 19) or to the fullness of God (v. 19)." See Barth, *Ephesians 1–3*, pp. 395-97, and O'Brien, *Ephesians*, pp. 261-63, for further critique, and also Hoehner, *Ephesians*, p. 488, who comments that nothing in Ephesians suggests a dependence on or use of magical formulas by the audience, much less by Paul.

30. Jeal, *Integrating Theology and Ethics*, p. 123.

31. Chrysostom, in his seventh homily on Ephesians, says that although the love of Christ lies beyond human comprehension yet it can be known experientially if Christ dwells within a person.

32. Caird, *Paul's Letters*, p. 70: "The attempt to know the unknowable is a paradox which is at the heart of all true religion. *Omnia exeunt in mysteria* ('all things run out into mystery'). Man must know God or perish; but unless he knows him as ultimate mystery, he does not know him at all."

33. Jeal, *Integrating Theology and Ethics*, p. 125.

ence to the one being praised, a praise formula with the word *doxa* (glory), a time or eternity formula, and the word "amen" (cf. Phil. 4.20; Rom. 16.25-27; 2 Tim. 4.18; Heb. 13.21; 1 Pet. 5.11; *1 Clement* 63.1; and especially Rom. 11.36). Only this doxology contains the phrase "in the church" and "in Christ Jesus." "In the church" is significant in that it reflects the ecclesiocentric focus of the discourse.[34] It is God ultimately who is to be and is being praised in this epideictic discourse. *Hyper panta* and *hyperekperissou* are basically synonymous and an example of paronomasia. The latter is a double compound adverb, involving two prefixes ("above" and "out of") that both convey the sense of superabundance.[35] God can always do much more above and beyond whatever we could ever conceive or ask, and the amazing thing is that his power[36] already dwells within the believer, and that is the means by which God is said to accomplish such things. This likely means that by the indwelling Spirit God helps, heals, reveals, strengthens, and causes to grow.

Only in v. 21 do we hear about "glory in the church," which could mean "may he be glorified in the church and in the work of Christ forever," but it may simply refer to God's presence in the church. The church "is his dwelling place in the Spirit. And where he dwells, his glory dwells, as it did in the Temple in Jerusalem."[37] Paul is probably not affirming a sort of *theologia gloriae* of the church, as though it already adequately reflected God's glory or presence. In any case, Paul is affirming that God, not the church, should receive the glory for all these good things that have transpired.

From a rhetorical point of view the sound of the concluding Greek phrase is important — *eis pasas tas geneas tou aiōnos tōn aiōnōn*. Not only the endings of words but also in two cases the beginnings of words have the same sound and this "accentuates the impression of extended time."[38] There should be no end to the praise. The audience is invited not just to agree but to participate in the praise, which is what a rhetorically effective epideictic discourse intended to accomplish.

The first major section of the discourse is concluded with "amen," which again may suggest that originally this discourse stood on its own or was intended to be separable if there was not time for the full proclamation of the Ephesian discourse on one occasion.[39] "The [audience] . . . are left at an intense religious and emotional high point where they may be quite easily influ-

---

34. MacDonald, *Colossians, Ephesians,* p. 280.

35. Schnackenburg, *Ephesians,* p. 158; Hoehner, *Ephesians,* p. 493.

36. Note the play on words between *dynameō* and *dynamin.* Even here in the doxology there is a concern for rhetorically effective speech.

37. Best, *Ephesians,* p. 351.

38. Jeal, *Integrating Theology and Ethics,* p. 128.

39. See Chrysostom's comment on 3.21 in his seventh homily, where he speaks of this as the close of the discourse.

enced to agree with what the author may say subsequently."[40] Nevertheless, Perkins is right that this prayer and doxology section makes a good transition between the two halves of the discourse by disposing the audience to a Christian way of life.[41]

40. Jeal, *Integrating Theology and Ethics*, p. 129.

41. Perkins, "Ephesians," p. 413. She is also right that there is no reason to see Paul reflecting on difficulties in these churches in the petitions of the prayer. This is a general prayer for growth and strengthening that Paul could have prayed for any number of congregations who were already established as Christians but needed to go forward in their faith.

Exhortatio — Reminder of
Community Values and Virtues — 4.1–6.9

Ephesians 4–6 is overwhelmingly parenetic in character, with the theme of unity or the oneness of the community cropping up at various places in various ways.[1] In fact, chs. 4–6 are longer than chs. 1–3, which shows just how concerned Paul was about the issues of behavior in these churches he was addressing. The exhortation begins with the same three words as Rom. 12.1 ("I therefore urge you. . . .") and is given in the form of virtue and vice lists, a household code, creedal material, revisiting of gift lists (cf. 1 Corinthians 12 and Romans 12) and participles that may sometimes be used as imperatives. All of this comes only after the appeal to unity, which is placed first among the ethical exhortations.[2]

Previous parts of this discourse have all prepared for these chapters, reminding the audience of who they are as the church in Christ. "They secure the

---

1. It is worth pointing out, with E. Best, *Ephesians* (Edinburgh: Clark, 1998), p. 353, that secular letters basically did not include parenesis. This leads Best to conclude that Paul may have introduced such material into the letter format. But suppose Paul was not thinking in epistolary terms when this discourse was composed, especially in the middle of the discourse. Suppose, instead, he saw it basically as a transcript of a homily he would have delivered if he were present with these various audiences. In that case there is nothing very innovative about what Paul is doing. Epideictic as well as deliberative speeches might well include such material. I would stress again that it is a mistake to think of Paul's discourses as basically or primarily letters to be evaluated as a literary product on a par with other ancient letters. Epistolary conventions enter into the matter only secondarily at the beginnings and ends of Paul's discourses because they had to be sent in written form.

2. A. T. Lincoln, *Ephesians* (Waco: Word, 1990), p. 229, notes how the sequence Spirit . . . Lord . . . God in 1 Cor. 12.4-6 parallels the one Spirit, one Lord, one God here in Eph. 4.4-6. In my view, Paul is reprising in Ephesians many of the major ethical ideas and themes he had already written about to individual congregations.

audience's goodwill, inspire them, convince them of the rightness of the writer's perspective on their situation and dispose them to carry out the specific injunctions of this *exhortatio*."[3] In an epideictic discourse such as this one, the exhortatio replaces formal arguments. It was a stock feature of Hellenistic ethics, as Dio Chrysostom said, to remind the audience of what they already knew to be the case so that they would act accordingly (*Orations* 17.2).

Some of the parenesis in the first part of this exhortation is direct and some indirect in form, as Paul appeals to the church to more fully become what it already is and ought to be. It is not sufficient simply to talk along the old lines of the ethics being built on the theology of the previous chapters because the exhortations are not grounded in what precedes as if they were simply logical consequences of what has been said. What has gone before is theological prayer and doxology by and large, and so the ethics is grounded in the posture of praise for God for what he has already accomplished in and through Christ. "The particle *oun* in 4:1 does not act as a direct causal connector that introduces conclusions, argumentation or proof, but draws on the rhetorical effect of the 'sermonic' language of chapters 1-3."[4] There is in addition a strong thematic connection between 2.11-22; 3.2-13; and 4.1-6 in the concept of unity. The audience is exhorted to preserve and enhance the unity in the Spirit by its behavior (4.3). But the church unity Paul is talking about here "is not, in the first instance, a task to be achieved or an object of aspiration but a fact, given in the gospel, inherent in the nature of the church and its membership, guaranteed by the one Spirit who inspires it, the one Lord who governs it, the one God who is the source of its life."[5]

Epideictic oratory during the empire, as Quintilian rightly points out, often took a practical turn and was used for more than just entertainment or the display of the "art of speaking well." Quintilian stresses that funeral oratory was one of the main practical uses of epideictic rhetoric in his day (*Inst. Or.* 3.7.1-4), but he also lists other uses such as the stock theme of the praise of the highest deity (in this case he has Jupiter Capitolinus in mind). He stresses that "panegyric applied to practical matters requires proof" (3.7.4), by which he means that practical exhortation requires some substantiation in inartificial proofs such as authoritative documents or logical rationales for the behavior being urged. Paul does both these things in Eph. 4.1-16, not only giving an interesting exposition and application of Psalm 68 but also providing a logical rationale in vv. 4-6 for the first exhortation in vv. 1-3.[6] Quintilian reminds us again, however, that

---

3. Lincoln, *Ephesians*, p. 224.

4. Roy R. Jeal, *Integrating Theology and Ethics in Ephesians: The Ethos of Communication* (Lewiston: Mellen, 2000), p. 178.

5. G. B. Caird, *Paul's Letters from Prison* (Oxford: Oxford University Press, 1976), p. 71.

6. See Jeal, *Integrating Theology and Ethics*, p. 179.

the proper function of panegyric is to "amplify and embellish its themes" (3.7.6), which is what Paul does here by repetition of terms and themes. This is all the more evident when one sees Eph. 4.2-4 as a use of some of the language of Col. 3.12-15 as one way of embellishing his themes.[7]

In his discussion of the praise of human beings Quintilian lists the usual things that are to be praised. It is especially interesting to compare what Paul holds up as virtues to what Quintilian says. For example, Paul immediately lifts up humility and gentleness and the patience to put up with others in love and so preserve unity. Quintilian on the other hand says that fortitude, justice, self-control are the major virtues (3.7.15) and that the chief sources of strength which allow a person to be virtuous in these ways are "wealth, power, and influence, since they are the sources of strength, and the surest tests of character for good or evil" (3.7.14). Paul says that strength comes from being rooted in Christ's love and that emulation of Christ is the order of the day. Quintilian's praise is reserved for the "great man," and the ethic he exhibits is that of patronage and "noblesse oblige," virtues that preserve the existing social order. If, however, the virtues Paul praises were to be practiced, they would lead to a revamping of the existing social order (see pp. 183-87 above). Quintilian is right that epideictic and deliberative oratory are close in that the things usually praised in the former are advised in the latter, and since exhortations can be found in both forms, there is something of a thin line between the two rhetorical species when it comes to ethical exhortations (3.7.28).

Aristotle stressed that the place and subject of panegyric would necessarily differ depending on the character and locale of the audience (*Rhet.* 1.9). Paul must draw on virtues and vices that are already recognized as such in the Christian community in Asia and that distinguish that community in various ways from the virtues of the larger culture. Paul's ethic is an ethic for a subculture. While in the wider culture epideictic rhetoric might primarily focus on what is honorable, Paul focuses on what is loving and produces unity.

The first major exhortation has two parts, 4.1-6 and 7-16. While the theme of how Christians should walk is introduced at 4.1, it is only at 4.17 that Paul returns to that theme as he describes how not to behave. But 4.1-16 can be taken as the more positive side of such a discussion, namely characterizing proper Christian conduct. "If this first part of the Paraclesis-section, 4.1-6, has been given a deliberate rhetorical shape by the author, and the author then places it quite deliberately at the beginning of his admonitions, we can draw certain

---

7. Lincoln, *Ephesians*, p. 228. Lincoln is right of course that the Ephesians version is condensed in comparison to the length of the Colossians material, but the point is that Colossians is only one source of the material here and so we can say that Paul is embellishing his themes and ideas by condensing some material from Colossians and some from elsewhere.

conclusions about his pragmatic objective. There is no doubt he is very concerned about unity in the congregations and the Church in general."[8]

Finally, it is important to ask about the level of moral discourse offered here. Good rhetoricians understood that certain things could be said only to certain audiences. For example, if one was addressing a new and specific audience that did not know the speaker directly, more caution was required in order to gain a hearing and win the audience's heart. If, on the other hand, one was addressing old friends, then one could be much more direct and pointed in one's remarks without fear of losing the audience and rupturing the ongoing relationship. What one says at the start of a relationship, especially in regard to controversial matters, may be a pale shadow of what one will say when one has the full trust, respect, and confidence of the audience, and even their friendship. When Paul addresses the issue of slavery in Philemon, he is direct and was apparently persuasive, or else we would not likely have this letter in our canon. This is third order moral discourse, what can occur among friends who need hold nothing back. But in Colossians we see first order moral discourse, the sort of discourse one has with an audience whom one is addressing and appealing to directly for the first time. Colossians is Paul's opening word and not all that he wanted to say to the Colossian Christians.

Ephesians contains second order moral discourse. That is, Paul is not addressing a particular audience or situation, and so the advice must be of a sort that is generic and can fit a wide audience. The advice he can give is different from what he says in addressing a particular congregation and its distinctive issues. Because this is a circular document he can go a bit beyond what he would say to a particular group of Christians he has not addressed before because he knows that part of the audience may well assume that this or that exhortation is meant primarily for someone else, simply covering the bases. The crucial point for Paul and his rhetorical situation is that he can thus be a bit more direct or free in what he says, even though he will not have directly spoken to some of this audience before. For example, when he speaks about marriage he couches the discussion about submission in marriage within the larger context of mutual submission among all those in Christ (5.21-22). There is certainly more of an attempt to change the structure of the household than there is in Colossians.

There is also the additional factor that Ephesians is a homily, and there would have been a rhetorical expectation of greater boldness and freedom in speech in a homily than in a formal discourse to a particular situation, such as

---

8. R. Schnackenburg, *The Epistle to the Ephesians: A Commentary* (Edinburgh: Clark, 1991), p. 161. Schnackenburg objects to the term parenesis for the material here in Ephesians, but is wrong to do so. What we find here is precisely what M. Dibelius had in mind by the term parenesis: rules and instructions for the current situation but of a generic or general significance.

we find in Colossians. Epideictic oratory was often much bolder than deliberative oratory, and it was part of the pattern of expectation in a rhetorically saturated environment that it would be this way.[9]

The Formation of a More Perfect Union — 4.1-16

*I, the prisoner of the Lord, beseech you then to walk worthily of the calling to which
you were called, with all humility and gentleness, with patience putting up with
one another in love, being eager to keep the unity of the Spirit in the bond of peace;
one bond and one Spirit, just as you were called in one hope of your calling; one
Lord, one faith, one baptism, one God and Father of all, who is above all and
through all and in all.*

    *But to each of us is given the grace according to the measure of the gift of
Christ. Therefore it says "Going up on high, he led a catch of prisoners, he gave gifts
to humans." But the one going up, who is he if not the one that also came down[10] to
the lower parts [of the earth]? The one who came down is himself also the one who
went up far above all the heavens in order that he might fill everything. Also he
himself gave on the one hand the apostles, others to be prophets, others to be evangelists, others to be shepherds and teachers for the equipping of the saints for the
work of ministry, for the building up of the body of Christ until we all might arrive
at the unity of the faith and the knowledge of the Son of God, unto mature manhood, unto the measure of the stature of the fullness of Christ, in order that we
might no longer be minors, tossed about and carried about by every wind of teaching in the trickery of human beings in cunning for the purpose of the scheming of
error, but speaking the truth in love we might grow into him in every way who is
the head, Christ, from whom all the body, fit together and put together through all
the supplying ligaments according to the working in the measure one of each part,
makes growth of the body unto the building up of each in love.*

Eph. 4.1-16 serves as a sort of introduction or overture to what follows in the exhortation portion of the discourse. Major concepts are introduced here which
will be taken up again later, often in more detail. "The unity, stability, growth,
and maturity within the Church, for which it calls, will provide major resources

---

    9. It is precisely when one factors in such rhetorical considerations as these that the
objections to taking Ephesians as a Pauline document because of its differences from
Colossians or Philemon fall by the wayside. The rhetorical situation and the rhetorical character of the address dictate much of what one will or can say to an audience.
    10. ℵ, B, C, K, P, and others add "first" after "came down" to make clear that the refer-
ence is to a prior descent of Christ to earth, not the second coming. This is a later expansion
but nonetheless a correct interpretation. See Metzger, *TC*, p. 536.

for the Church's attempt to live distinctively within society, which is the concern of the ethical exhortations that follow."[11]

Paul, using the language he frequently uses to introduce parenesis, urges his audience to "walk worthily" of their calling (v. 1; cf. Rom. 12.1; 1 Thess. 4.1). He exhorts or appeals to them, trying to persuade them to freely act. He does not lay down the law. The Christian life and lifestyle are said to be a calling.[12] Paul is not thinking here of a call to ministry, though that is included in what he is talking about, but rather their calling simply to be Christians in a non-Christian environment once they have heard the gospel and responded. With this calling came an exhortation to forsake the past ways and take on new ways, which Paul has already emphasized when he spoke of the "then" and "now" of the audience's lives and of their calling in general in 1.18. He will continue this theme here.

Paul again repeats that he is in custody, thus stirring up pathos. This suggests that the audience needs to realize the seriousness and possible consequences of behaving in a Christian manner in a non-Christian world, but it also stirs the deeper emotions of the audience so they will be more ready to receive the wisdom imparted.[13] Prisoners certainly do not normally issue authoritative exhortations to free persons, so we are dealing with an extraordinary person and an extraordinary situation.[14]

Humility (v. 2) was not considered a virtue in the Greco-Roman world but was associated with craven cowering or the obsequiousness of a slave (Epictetus, *Dissertationes* 1.9.10; 3.24.6), was placed first in a list of qualities not to be commended (3.24.56), and was seen as the attribute of a weak person (Josephus, *War* 4.9.2).[15] Gentleness or meekness was occasionally commended in the Greek tradition, but normally only as the behavior of the superior toward an inferior.[16] For example, Aristotle regards it as the mean between excessive anger about everything and failure to be angry about anything (*Nichomachean Ethics* 1.13.20). Paul, however, is not merely commending temperance or a golden mean. He is commending taking on the attitude and roles of a gentle servant as Christ did (see 2 Cor. 10.1; cf. Matt. 11.29), consideration for others,

11. Lincoln, *Ephesians,* p. 232.

12. Notice the Asiatic redundancy: "the calling with which you have been called." It needs to be stressed that even if Paul is using some traditional material in chs. 4–6, he not only makes it his own but also uses it in a way that conforms to the dictates of Asiatic rhetoric.

13. See rightly, P. T. O'Brien, *The Letter to the Ephesians* (Grand Rapids: Eerdmans, 1999), p. 274: "Paul's pastoral appeal is underscored by reference to his own costly commitment."

14. See Best, *Ephesians,* p. 360.

15. Notice the reference to "all" humility, which as Lincoln, *Ephesians,* p. 235, says, is characteristic of Paul's rhetorical style. In fact it is characteristic of the hyperbole or globalizing that one would expect in Asiatic epideictic rhetoric.

16. See *New Docs* 4, pp. 169-70.

and a slow temper — *makrothymia* means a slow fuse.[17] This sort of patience involves putting up with life's irritations and the irritable habits of fellow believers. "For the believer, patience is that cautious endurance that does not abandon hope."[18] Notice that this advice is given to Christians about their relationships with other Christians.

The text says "put up with one another in love." Paul is not a naive idealist and does not assume that everyone in the body of Christ will naturally get along with everyone else. Here love does not amount to being compatible or likeable or warm feelings toward another, but rather tolerating others. "The love Paul requires of us is no common love, but that which cements us together and makes us cleave inseparably to one another, and effects as great and as perfect a union as though it were between limb and limb" (Chrysostom, 11th homily on Ephesians). It is noteworthy that the five virtues listed in Col. 3.12 are reduced to three here, but they keep the same order: humility, gentleness, and patience.[19]

In v. 3 Paul speaks of eagerness to *keep* the unity which has been created by the Spirit of Christ.[20] This is an important emphasis and makes clear that this is indeed an epideictic exhortation, not introducing something new or a change of values, but rather reinforcing the values and course of life already embraced. The Spirit has provided this unity, but believers are responsible for maintaining and fostering it. "Nor is there an exhortation to organize unity because this has been accomplished by the Holy Spirit."[21] In an agonistic culture where honor challenges ruled the day, there was a need for an exhortation to be *eager* to put up with others, to keep the bond of peace, and not to be contentious.[22]

When Paul calls for unity and concord within a particular congregation, as in 1 Corinthians, this implies that there are some factionalism and divisions to be overcome, as in fact that letter states at several points. But the unity referred to here and further inculcated is a unity among congregations in different places. Striving for unity[23] in this situation need imply no strife, only the

17. It can be used even of God; see Rom. 2.4 and 9.22 where "long-suffering" is a common translation.

18. H. Hoehner, *Ephesians* (Grand Rapids: Baker, 2002), p. 508.

19. Schnackenburg, *Ephesians*, p. 163.

20. I like the rendering in M. Barth, *Ephesians 4–6* (Garden City: Doubleday, 1974), p. 428: "Yours is the initiative! Do it now!"

21. Hoehner, *Ephesians*, p. 513.

22. See M. Y. MacDonald, *Colossians, Ephesians* (Collegeville: Liturgical, 2000), p. 287.

23. The Greek term *henotēs* is found in the NT only in Ephesians, here and at 4.13. Ignatius of Antioch, who surely knew this discourse by Paul, later picks up this term and makes it a major theme in his teaching (*Ephesians* 4.2; 5.1; 14.1; *Philippians* 2.2; 3.2; 5.2; 8.1; 9.1; *Smyrneans* 12.2; *Polycarp* 8.3). It would be a useful exercise to compare at length the way Paul speaks here and the way Ignatius addresses converts in a later and ecclesiastically more developed situation but in the same area as Paul's Ephesians was written for.

obstacles of distance and lack of communication and fellowship. The way the theme of unity is handled indirectly supports the contention that this is likely a general discourse meant to circulate through several congregations, seeking to heighten their sense of group unity and loyalty despite separations of space and time.

Possibly citing an early confessional formula,[24] Paul offers up some of the theological and practical bases of that unity in v. 4, with a sevenfold use of the word "one."[25] Father, Son, and Spirit turn out to be the basis for the existence of and the exhortation to unity. A trinitarian structure anchors this statement, with the one Spirit anchoring v. 4, the one Lord anchoring v. 5, and the one God and Father of all anchoring v. 6.[26] The repetition of the terms "one" and "all" and the asyndeton here have rhetorical force, adding weight to the exhortation.[27]

There is but one body of Christ (cf. 2.16, 18). To judge from 1 Corinthians 12, each individual house-church or local gathering was regarded as a full expression of that body.[28] Paul sees one particular local church not as a part of the body of Christ but rather as a miniature full expression of the whole. There is but one Holy Spirit who created or grafted believers into the body (see 1 Cor. 12.1ff.) and one hope that was conveyed to a convert when he was called.[29]

V. 5 may reflect a traditional triad — "one Lord, one faith, one baptism," perhaps one used as part of a baptismal service.[30] There is one Lord, though pagans recognized many (1 Cor. 8.5), and one faith, though presumably with a range of variation and room for some differences on non-essential matters. The "one baptism" is surely water baptism, separated as it is from the reference to the Spirit.[31] This would imply no rebaptisms or repetition of baptism. If one asks why baptism is "one," the simple answer is that a person is only converted

24. The plural "you" in v. 4b, however, counts against this being a preset confessional piece, as does the order of reference to God, for here the Spirit is mentioned first. See the discussion in G. D. Fee, *God's Empowering Presence* (Peabody: Hendrickson, 1994), pp. 702-5.

25. MacDonald, *Colossians, Ephesians*, p. 287, makes the valid point that in light of the echoes of Col. 3.15 and 1 Cor. 12.13 here it is perhaps better to think of liturgical echoes in the text rather than seeing this as a preset liturgical piece inserted here.

26. See Hoehner, *Ephesians*, p. 501.

27. Jeal, *Integrating Theology and Ethics*, p. 180.

28. See Caird, *Paul's Letters*, p. 73, who rightly makes this point. Thus interestingly while Paul is writing to a variety of Asian churches, what he says can be applied to any and all of them at one and the same time.

29. It is simply untrue that Ephesians has no future eschatology. The hope referred to here is more elaborately spoken of in 1.18 (cf. 2.19).

30. See Schnackenburg, *Ephesians*, p. 166.

31. Why no reference to the Lord's Supper? Perhaps either because it is repeated and so could hardly be called "one," or because the focus in these verses is on what creates the unity in the first place, not on what sustains it after the fact. Baptism is an initiatory rite, just as the confession of Jesus is Lord is the initial confession a new believer makes.

to Christ once, and baptism is the symbol of the change from death to life, the putting off of the old and putting on of the new.[32]

There is also, as v. 6 says, but one God and Father of everything and everyone, who is said to be above, through, and in all. The "all" here might be limited to all believers or all congregations, but since it is formulaic we cannot be sure.[33] O'Brien makes a good case, based on the more universal thrust of texts like 3.14-15, that "all" here must refer to all sentient beings or even all things, including all sentient beings.[34]

Each believer is given grace according to the measure of Christ's gift (v. 7). This seems to be rather like what we find in Rom. 12.3, where Paul speaks of the "measure of faith." These texts suggest that God gives different measures of grace and faith to different persons. In practical terms, this means that one must exercise what gifts and faith one has been given, as in the parable of the talents. To whom more is given, more is required, as Paul himself knew all too well. There are those in the body of Christ who have stronger and weaker faith, more gifts and less gifts. But all this giftedness and faith comes in the context of the community for the sake of its mission to the world and its members' ministry to each other. The gifts are given for the common good, as Paul says in 1 Cor. 12, not primarily for the enhancement of the individual's spiritual life, though that is a by-product. Believers must operate within the context of the body of Christ. Only then will they be properly expressing their gifts and be complete.

V. 8 seems to be something of a midrash on a targum (Aramaic paraphrase) of Ps. 68.18.[35] Both the Hebrew and LXX versions of this verse speak of Yahweh in the second person singular ("you went up") and of God receiving gifts, not giving them.[36] Here the third person is used. But Paul may be follow-

---

32. The association of baptism with faith rather than the Holy Spirit is rightly noted by Fee, *God's Empowering Presence*, pp. 704-5, who also adds that a connection between the reception of the Holy Spirit and water baptism was not part of Paul's own experience. According to Acts 9 he received the Spirit through the laying on of hands and afterward received baptism. See my *Troubled Waters: Rethinking the Theology of Baptism* (Waco: Baylor University Press, 2007).

33. See Hoehner, *Ephesians*, pp. 519-20. There were similar sayings from Stoicism and elsewhere. See Marcus Aurelius, *Meditations* 4.23: "all things are from you, all things are in you, all things are to you." It is however much more likely that Eph. 4.6 echoes 1 Cor. 8.5-6, which is itself a modification of the Shema (Deut. 6.4), rather than Stoic teaching. See my *Conflict and Community in Corinth* (Grand Rapids: Eerdmans, 1995), pp. 198-99.

34. O'Brien, *Ephesians*, pp. 284-85.

35. See O'Brien, *Ephesians*, pp. 290-91; Best, *Ephesians*, pp. 378-81, on the form of this quotation.

36. Unlike, for example, Romans 9–11, there are not many explicit Scripture quotations in Ephesians. Besides here there is only 5.31, although there are some allusions. There are in fact far more echoes of earlier Pauline letters, particularly Colossians and Romans, than of the OT. See MacDonald, *Colossians, Ephesians*, p. 290.

ing an Aramaic translation of this Psalm that speaks of giving rather than receiving, specifically of Moses going up on Sinai, receiving the Law from God, and then coming down and giving gifts to humans (cf. *Midrash Tehillin* on Ps. 68.11; *Abot de Rabbi Nathan* 2.2a). This suggests that Paul here is thinking of Christ as the one greater than Moses. It is reasonably clear that Paul has in mind spiritual gifts and character shaped by the Holy Spirit.

A Closer Look: What Goes Up Must Come Down — Pneumatic Exegesis

There is a major debate about when the one who ascended is thought to have descended. Is this a reference to the preexistent Christ's descent in incarnation? Is it Christ's descent into Hades after his death, as is sometimes, though wrongly, thought to be referred to in 1 Peter 3? Or is it the descent of the Holy Spirit after Christ ascended to heaven?[37]

Of these three options the least likely is decidedly the descent into Hades despite the many church fathers who took that view of this text (e.g., Irenaeus, Origen, Tertullian, Chrysostom, Jerome). This very discourse speaks of spiritual beings dwelling in the heavenlies, as is also the point in 1 Peter 3, Jude 6, and 2 Pet. 2.4. Leading a catch of prisoners (v. 8) may well refer to the powers and principalities that have been put in their place as a result of Christ's death and resurrection, but this comes with the ascent, not the descent (cf. Col. 2.15). In any case, the "captives" phrase cannot be taken as referring to initiation rites that involve a descent into Hades.[38] Furthermore, in terms of the structure of vv. 8-9, a descent from earth to somewhere else must be deemed improbable. V. 9b is quite clear: the descent was to the lower parts of the earth. This seems to be a genitive of apposition: "the lower parts, that is, the earth."[39] The air was considered the upper part of earth. Thus we are not talking about parts under or beneath the earth.[40]

Both Caird and Lincoln have made a good case for Paul referring to the coming

---

37. There is now a full-scale monograph that takes this view. See W. H. Harris, *The Descent of Christ: Ephesians 4.7-11 and Traditional Hebrew Imagery* (Leiden: Brill, 1996).

38. See P. Perkins, "The Letter to the Ephesians," in *The New Interpreter's Bible* XI (Nashville: Abingdon, 2000), p. 421, against C. E. Arnold, *Ephesians: Power and Magic* (Cambridge: Cambridge University Press, 1989), p. 57; cf. L. Kreitzer, "The Plutonium of Hierapolis and the Descent of Christ into the 'Lowermost Parts of the Earth' (Ephesians 4, 9)," *Bib* 79 (1998): 381-93, though his view is unlikely not only because he thinks this letter is addressed specifically to Hierapolis (a conjecture without any clear basis in the text of Ephesians) but also because he thinks the myth of Demeter and Persephone lies in the background here, though if so Paul certainly does not make this clear.

39. See MacDonald, *Colossians, Ephesians*, p. 290.

40. Hell, which Paul seldom even alludes to in any case, would not likely have been thought of as in the middle of the earth by an early Jew.

of the Spirit at Pentecost.[41] They draw an analogy with Peter's speech in Acts 2, but there is no clear allusion to Psalm 68 in that speech, which focuses, rather, on Psalm 16 and Joel 2. They also argue that the context in Ephesians 4 supports an allusion to the Spirit coming and giving gifts. But in fact the immediate context (v. 7) speaks of "the gift of Christ," not of the Spirit, and v. 8 associates Christ's gifts with his ascent, not his descent. As Best says, "It is difficult to see Christians interpreting Ps 68 in relation to Pentecost since it has no reference to the Spirit."[42] Only much later in 4.30 do we hear about the work of the Spirit.

Therefore, to identify the descent with the coming of the Spirit one must argue that Christ is identified with the Spirit, for here Paul is surely saying that the very person who ascended is also the one who descended. While it is true that for Paul the Spirit and Christ are closely allied and intertwined in their work, especially when it comes to spiritual gifts and experience, he does not hold to a simple identity of the two, in this discourse or elsewhere. For example he never says that the Spirit died on the cross or sits at the right hand of God. Paul is able to distinguish the existence of the two clearly during and after the lifetime of Jesus. More to the point, in this very discourse the Spirit and Christ are clearly distinguished and indeed even kept apart (cf. 1.3, 13; 2.20-22; 3.16-17; 4.4-5).[43] There is also the further point, made by Schnackenburg, that the sequence of, first, "the lower parts of the earth" and then the filling of the universe must count against the notion that the descent comes after the ascent.[44]

There are three points which strongly favor the view that the descent in question is of the preexistent Christ in the incarnation. First, the focus in vv. 8-9 is on going up, not on coming down, and on the giving of gifts as a result of going up. Second, various early witnesses added the word "first" before "came down" in v. 9 (א, B, C, K, P, Eusebius, Theodoret, Ambrosiaster, John of Damascus, and others). This shows a very widespread and early attempt to make clear that the descent preceded the ascent. "First" is a later explanatory addition, but likely a correct one. Third, the contrast is between going up on high and coming down to earth by the same person. V. 10 makes evident that the ascent occurred so that Christ could fill all things. What Paul means is that only by being on high could Christ accomplish the filling of all things and that only from on high could he give gifts to everyone everywhere at once. Where Christ went was "far above the heavens." Paul does not think the abode of God and Christ is part of the material heavens but rather far above them. It is the spirits that dwell in the heavenlies.

The issues in the quotation of Psalm 68 are complex and show the sort of creative use of OT Scripture that characterizes various early Jewish exegetes, including those at Qumran and Paul and other NT authors. Commenting on the midrash-pesher style of handling this text, Lincoln says "the midrash fulfills a typical function of Haggadah, filling out possible gaps in the meaning of the text. The identity of the

41. See Caird, *Paul's Letters*, pp. 73-76; Lincoln, *Ephesians*, pp. 246-47.
42. See Best, *Ephesians*, p. 385.
43. Best, *Ephesians*, p. 386.
44. Schnackenburg, *Ephesians*, p. 178.

ascender and the descender having been established, vv. 11-16 can then interpret the second line of the citation in v. 8, expanding first on the nature (v. 11) and then on the purpose (vv. 12-16) of the exalted Christ's gifts within the context of the whole Church."[45] The exegesis here is very similar to what we find in John 3.13, which speaks of the ascent and descent of the Son of Man.[46]

It is worth pointing out from a rhetorical point of view that epideictic rhetoric often involved the creative handling of earlier witnesses and documents to add further authority to the exhortation that was given toward the end of the discourse. This was a part of rhetorical "invention" and would add to the persuasive quality of the discourse for the sort of audience Paul is addressing.

In v. 11 we are told that Christ gave the church apostles and prophets.[47] There is no hint here that apostles and prophets are only figures from the past. It is important that they are listed first. Paul sees them as of highest authority. Prophets had considerable authority in the early church, as even a cursory reading of Acts will show.[48] Some were also given to be "evangelists." Here is the only place Paul mentions such a function by the noun *euangelistas* (cf. Acts 21.8; 2 Tim. 4.5). This is clearly not a list of purely local church functionaries, which is appropriate in a circular document such as Ephesians. Paul deals first with those who have a more than local function and may have been involved in the founding of the Christian communities,[49] then turns to figures such as pastors/shepherds and teachers who function locally.[50] It is not clear whether two groups are meant or one, but the grammar suggests two functions by one person — a pastor who is also a teacher, or a teaching pastor, because there is no definite article before "teacher." But against this is the fact that 2.20 lists apostles and prophets under one definite article.[51] Paul does not make clear whether some of these persons are itinerant, as we know apostles were, and some local

---

45. Lincoln, *Ephesians*, p. 226.

46. M. Bouttier, *L'Épître de Saint Paul aux Ephésiens* (Geneva: Labor et Fides, 1991), pp. 183-85.

47. Vv. 11-16 are a single sentence in the Greek, again showing that Paul is maintaining the Asiatic style even if he is using some traditional material. I agree with Schnackenburg, *Ephesians*, p. 180, and Lincoln, *Ephesians*, p. 249, that the proper translation here is probably not "some to be apostles," but rather "he gave the apostles . . . ," though it does look as if we should make something of the *men . . . de* construction here, as does Schnackenburg, *Ephesians*, p. 180: He gave (on the one hand) the apostles, and (on the other) the prophets, the preachers. . . ."

48. On this entire subject see my *Jesus the Seer* (Peabody: Hendrickson, 1999), passim.

49. See Schnackenburg, *Ephesians*, p. 182.

50. Perkins, "Ephesians," p. 422.

51. See Best, *Ephesians*, p. 393.

officials. Pastor-teacher would seem necessarily to be a local function, especially the overseeing portion of the ministry. Paul is quite clear that all such functions and roles and the gifts necessary to carry them out come from Christ, not from the apostles, for Christ is the head of the body and the source of the gifting.

The leadership roles in v. 11 all involve the proclamation of the Word. Of the three prepositional phrases in v. 12 ("for equipping all the saints," "for the work of ministry," "for the building up of the body of Christ") at least the first refers to the work of the leaders. Do the other two describe what "all the saints" do or another task that the apostles and other leaders do?[52] The former seems more likely because it would be innocuous at best to say that the apostles, prophets, evangelists, and teaching pastors were given for the work of ministry. Of course they were. This is obvious from the very terms used to describe them. And could we really think that only the leaders are being said to be responsible for "the building up of the body of Christ"? To judge from the rest of chs. 4–6, surely not. As Best points out 5.19 surely points to non-leaders or non-ministers fulfilling what can be called ministerial functions.[53] There is no clergy-laity distinction in the NT, but there is a leader and follower distinction however, and the leaders are called to equip the followers.[54]

Here Hoehner is quite helpful. He points out that the first prepositional phrase (with *pros*) gives the purpose to the main verb in v. 11, "he gave." The second prepositional phrase (with *eis*) depends on the first, and the third (also with *eis*) on the second, so that we have a chain of prepositional phrases. The "point is that the gifted persons listed in verse 11 serve as the foundational gifts that are used for the immediate purpose of preparing all the saints to minister. Thus every believer must do the work of ministry. This is certainly supported from the context, for in verse 16 edification requires the work of each individual member and not a select group. The final goal evolves from the last, namely that the work of ministry by every believer is to build up the body of Christ."[55] Best is surely correct as well that had v. 12 been about three things that the leaders do for the saints, then we would have expected "all the saints" to come later.[56]

---

52. See the arguments not only by Lincoln, *Ephesians,* p. 253, but also by T. David Gordon, "Equipping Ministry in Ephesians 4?" *JETS* 37 (1994): 69-78; J. J. Davis, "Ephesians 4.12 Once More: Equipping the Saints for the Work of Ministry," *Evangelical Review of Theology* 24 (2000): 161-76; J. C. O'Neill, "The Work of Ministry in Ephesians 4.12 and the New Testament," *ExpT* 112 (2001): 338-40; MacDonald, *Colossians, Ephesians,* p. 292.

53. Best, *Ephesians,* p. 398.

54. See Lincoln, *Ephesians,* p. 253.

55. Hoehner, *Ephesians,* p. 549; see his whole discussion on pp. 547-49 and that of Fee, *God's Empowering Presence,* p. 706, n. 155: the *pros* phrase expresses penultimate purpose, while the *eis* phrases indicate the ultimate goal. Cf. Barth, *Ephesians 4–6,* pp. 478-81.

56. See Best, *Ephesians,* pp. 395-99, especially p. 398, and also O'Brien, *Ephesians,* pp. 302-3.

Katartismos in the first phrase is a rare word, found only here in the NT, but the cognate verb occurs frequently and has the sense of "furnish," "equip," "train," "instruct," or even "perfect" (cf. 1 Thess. 3.10; 1 Cor. 1.10; Heb. 13.21).[57] The sense here seems to be that the leaders train, equip, or instruct all the followers for the purpose of ministry to the end of building up Christ's body.

The unity of the church is spoken of by Paul as both given by the Spirit (v. 3) and also kept and built up by believers (v. 13). Here what is envisioned is teaching and sharing in such a way that the church shares a common faith and understanding, especially of Christ. Paul sees all in one sense as called to some sort of educational ministry, not just the leaders. "Unto the measure of the stature of the fullness of Christ" may well be in apposition to "mature manhood" (cf. Col. 1.28), referring to conformity to the image and moral stature of Christ, hence the male terminology. Moral maturity in the image of Christ is, then, the goal of Christian life and the aim of Christian ministry to those already in Christ. What is less clear is whether Paul is speaking collectively of the church as a body or of each believer as an individual. Is this about the mature congregation?[58] Perhaps v. 13 suggests that since all must become mature, arrive at the unity of faith and the knowledge of the Son, and measure up to the stature of Christ, then all must, like Christ, be involved in the tasks of ministry, for ministry will mold them all. Growth in Christ comes in part through ministerial service for the cause of Christ. Note the future orientation of this verse: "until we all arrive. . . ."

Then by contrast in v. 14 Paul explains what believers are not to do: they are not to act like spiritual juveniles, being tossed about by all sorts of dubious teaching that amounts to hot air (i.e., is overblown).[59] They are not to be deceived by cunning or tricky ideas,[60] or by deceptions[61] of various other sorts. Paul is speaking in general here and so it is probably wrong to envision some

---

57. Those who take the three prepositional phrases as coordinate are more prone to entertain the notion that the phrase reads "for the perfecting of the saints."

58. See Schnackenburg, *Ephesians*, p. 185.

59. Notice that they are asked not to repent and dramatically change their behavior but to continue to grow and grow up, an epideictic theme. Indeed, growth is the agenda in all this long sentence in 4.11-16. See Best, *Ephesians*, p. 404.

60. *Kybeia* means literally dice playing (cf. Plato, *Phaedrus*, 274D; Xenophon, *Memorabilia*, 1.3.2), but since dice were often doctored, it came to mean something like cunning. On corrupt dice playing cf. Mishnah *Sanhedrin* 3.3 to Epictetus 2.19.28. See Hoehner, *Ephesians*, p. 562.

61. *Panourgia* means craftiness or cleverness of some kind, while *plane* means going astray, as opposed to leading astray. *Methodeia*, from which we get the word "method," refers outside Ephesians to a system of tax collection, but in Petronius 36 *methodion* means something like an ingenious surprise or ruse. In Eph. 6.11 it refers to the schemes of the devil. See Caird, *Paul's Letters*, p. 77.

specific opponent that he has in mind, but it is likely that he is talking about using Asiatic rhetoric to impress an audience with some sort of false teaching that is deceptive and cannot deliver what it promises.[62]

The antidote to such false teaching is to "speak the truth in love" and to grow up, growing in Christlikeness, and into Christ in every way, since Christ is the head (v. 15). The verb *alētheuō* (found only elsewhere at Gal. 4.16 in Paul's letters) could be rendered "live out the truth" and a literal rendering would then be something like "truthing in love,"[63] but the LXX use of this verb suggests that the focus is on verbal testimony (see Gen. 20.16; 42.16; Prov. 21.3; Isa. 44.26).

V. 16 is one of the most convoluted verses in the entire discourse. Paul's imagery and redundancies run away with him, but such was permitted in Asiatic and epideictic rhetoric. He speaks of being put together and fitted together by the ligaments, which supply the nutrients one needs to make the body grow, by which he means the building up of each person in love.[64] Here we also have the anomalous idea of the body growing up into the head and in the likeness of the head. Perkins is right to note that in deliberative rhetoric the discussion of unity is brought on by the need to overcome disunity and discord, as in 1 Corinthians. But "Ephesians does not point to a crisis of disunity. Exhortation serves the function of reminding the audience of what has already been true of its experience."[65] In other words, this is an epideictic use of the theme. The focus here is on the body as a whole growing up and maturing, continuing in a positive direction they have already started in. One of the keys to the process is, of course, love. The phrase "in love" is placed last in this long sentence and is thereby emphasized.[66]

New Creatures — 4.17-24; Putting Off and Putting On — 4.25-32

If it was not already clear from the first segment of the parenesis, it becomes very evident here that Paul is addressing a group that has already "learned Christ," that has already been instructed in behavioral and lifestyle issues from a Christian point of view, perhaps in particular having been instructed to emu-

---

62. On the generic character of what is being critiqued here see O'Brien, *Ephesians*, pp. 309-10.

63. O'Brien, *Ephesians*, p. 310.

64. Some have thought that the reference to the ligaments is to specific persons, namely the ministers of the word. See Schnackenburg, *Ephesians*, pp. 189-90; Lincoln, *Ephesians*, p. 315. This is possible, but one might have expected Paul to make the matter clearer if so.

65. Perkins, "Ephesians," p. 423.

66. Best, *Ephesians*, p. 413.

late the behavior of Christ himself. This is, again, exactly what one would expect in an epideictic discourse, where reinforcement of values and virtues already embraced, rather than introduction of changes and new courses of
action, was the order of the day.

There is something of a natural progression in the material in 4.17–5.14
such that one moves from negative description of the Greco-Roman world outside Christ to positive description of Christian life.[67] As Hoehner has pointed
out, one could divide the parenesis in chs. 4–6 into five sections, each beginning
with the verb "walk" and the inferential particle *oun,* "therefore" or "so then"
(4.1, 17; 5.1-2, 7-8, 15).[68] The material here is for the most part traditional material of general applicability which suits the nature of this document — a homily
circulated through various churches.[69]

4.17-24 defines the boundaries that separate insiders from outsiders, with
"Gentiles" here clearly referring to pagans, not Christian Gentiles.[70] It does this
not by discussing baptism or some other ritual, but rather by discussing behavior and spiritual transformation. Vv. 17-19 are about how Gentiles outside
Christ behave, and vv. 20-24 are about how those in Christ should conduct
themselves. Vv. 17-19 are in the typical Asiatic style — participial clauses, prepositional phrases, and relative clauses all strung together in a long sentence.
Again, this is an aural rather than a literary style, and needs to be recognized as
such. There are other aural rhetorical devices in this subsection as well, for example, the paronomasia in v. 28 with *kleptetō* and *kopiatō.*[71] There is also the
sampling or echoing of previous Pauline material, which presumably adds
weight to the discourse at this juncture. Presumably the audience will have
heard some of this material before, such as from Colossians. In 4.17c-19 Rom.
1.21 and 24 are sampled, and in 4.19-24 we find an echo of Col. 3.5, 7-10.[72] It is in
keeping with the epideictic nature of this material that previous material,
drawn on by way of reminder, is used here. "This stress on the tradition which
the readers need to remember provides one of the major links with the preceding pericope of 4:1-16. The significance attached there to the ministers and their
role in passing on the apostolic tradition, and thereby contributing to the
building up and maturing of the body of Christ, can now be seen to be prepar-

---

67. O'Brien, *Ephesians,* p. 318; Schnackenburg, *Ephesians,* p. 193.

68. Hoehner, *Ephesians,* p. 581.

69. Lincoln, *Ephesians,* p. 299.

70. See Perkins, "Ephesians," p. 426; Best, *Ephesians,* p. 417.

71. See Jeal, *Integrating Theology and Ethics,* p. 184 and n. 31.

72. Lincoln, *Ephesians,* p. 273; Perkins, "Ephesians," p. 427. The difference in style from
Romans is, however, noteworthy, for Romans does not reflect the Asiatic style, despite the
similarity in substance. Notice too, how the heavenly-earthly contrast in Colossians becomes
the Gentile outsider, Gentile insider contrast here, so the material is used to a different end.

ing for the reminder of that tradition which will be the vehicle for the writer's paraenesis."[73]

Quintilian remarks that praise or denunciation of certain laws or rules of behavior requires greater powers than ordinary rhetoric and that undertaking such a task "should almost be equal to the most serious tasks of rhetoric" (*Inst. Or.* 2.4.33). He advises that in epideictic rhetoric it is important to periodize the material and talk about the before and the after in the audience's lives, what they once were and what they now are (3.7.10-13). He adds that "at times on the other hand it is well to divide our praises, dealing separately with the various virtues, fortitude, justice, self-control and the rest of them and to assign to each virtue the deeds performed under its influence" (3.7.15). In Eph. 2.11-22 we had something of the before and after approach, and here in ch. 4 we have a list of virtues and vices and the deeds they entail. Quintilian also emphasizes that one needs to praise and denounce in accord with what the audience has already learned if one is to appeal to them to grow and go on in the direction they have already chosen (3.7.23; cf. Aristotle, *Rhet.* 1.9).

The undergirding assumption of Eph. 4.17-32 is that the audience has already "learned Christ" and so learned a particular way of living that is Christ-like, and will readily assent to what Paul is saying here as a familiar and already embraced code of conduct. Some of the themes introduced in this section (darkness, impurity, greed, error, righteousness) will recur later in the discourse.[74] Perhaps more importantly, what we have throughout this section is a reworking of earlier material not only from the Pauline corpus (Romans, Colossians), but also from the OT (Psalms, Isaiah, Zechariah). An audience familiar with any of this material would recognize that Paul was embellishing and amplifying on already received and accepted teaching in the Christian community. This, too, reflects the epideictic nature and strategy of this discourse.[75]

This then I say and testify in the Lord, don't walk any longer just as the Gentiles also walk in the futility of their minds, darkened in thought, being alienated from the life of God through the ignorance which is in them through the hardening of their hearts, which are beyond feeling;[76] they received the debauchery unto the practice of impurity — everything in excess! But you have not so learned Christ, if surely you heard him and were taught in him, just as the truth is in Jesus, you

73. Lincoln, *Ephesians*, p. 274.
74. See Perkins, "Ephesians," p. 428.
75. See Schnackenburg, *Ephesians*, pp. 205-6.
76. Interestingly, several Western witnesses have here *apēlpikotes* (having despaired of one's self) rather than *apēlgēkotes* (having become callous or without feeling). The latter reading is much better supported and is likely right as it describes the condition of the heart, but the substitution comes from an assumption that a scribe simply miscopied some of the letters of the word in question. See Metzger, *TC*, p. 537.

yourselves cast off according to the former way of life the old person destroying himself according to the desire of deceit, but to renew[77] in the spirit of your minds and to clothe yourselves with the new humanity, the one according to God created in righteousness and the holiness of truth.

Therefore cast off "the lie," each one speaking truth with his neighbor, because we are members of one another. "Be angry and do not sin. Do not let the sun set on your anger." Do not give place to the devil. The thief should no longer thieve but rather labor, working the good with hands,[78] in order that he might have something to share with the needy. Every rotten word from your stomach should not go out, but if there is any good for edification in the case of need in order to give benefit to the hearer, and do not grieve the Holy Spirit of God, in whom you were sealed unto the day of redemption. Remove all bitterness, rage, and anger and shouting and cursing from among you with all malice. Be kind to one another, compassionate, being gracious to one another, just as also God in Christ gave grace to you.

V. 17 begins a new paragraph in the discourse, and once again we will have a contrast of the old and new life. There is an urgency to the way this exhortation begins: "I tell you this, and I insist on/testify to it in the Lord. . . ."[79] Vv. 1-16 was simply the overture or prelude to the exhortation which begins to come with full force at this juncture.

The audience is not to walk as they used to as Gentiles.[80] The description here bears some resemblance to Rom. 1.18-32, which also describes life outside Christ.[81] It involves futility of mind,[82] darkened thoughts, alienation from the life of God. This alienation is caused in part by ignorance that has been caused by hardening of the heart, so much so that people become altogether spiritually insensitive. In the OT hardness of heart is associated with or manifested in disobedience (cf. Ps. 95.8; Isa. 6.10; 63.17; Jer. 7.26; 17.23). "Ev-

---

77. On this meaning of the word *ananeoumai* in the papyri see *New Docs* 3, pp. 61-62.

78. Various good manuscripts add "his" before "hands" in v. 28, which may be original in light of its support by **א**, A, D, and G, but the reading without "his" is surely the more difficult reading and was likely emended. Metzger, *TC*, pp. 537-38.

79. See O'Brien, *Ephesians*, p. 319.

80. *Mēketi*, "no longer," implies quite clearly that the audience, or the vast majority of them, were Gentiles and formerly were pagans.

81. On which see B. Witherington and D. Hyatt, *Paul's Letter to the Romans* (Grand Rapids: Eerdmans, 2004), pp. 58-72.

82. The term *mataiotēs* was a stock term in Jewish polemics against paganism. See Caird, *Paul's Letters*, p. 79. It means "emptiness," and was used to translate *hebel* (vanity, emptiness, futility) some thirty-nine times in the LXX of Ecclesiastes. The idea here is not being able to grasp God's revelation due to a fallen mind, and unfortunately the thoughts they do have will not get them anywhere positive and hence are futile. See Hoehner, *Ephesians*, p. 584.

ery surrender to temptation encrusts the heart and narrows the range of its future choice."[83]

> There is such a thing as being in the dark, even when the light is shining, when the eyes are weak. . . . When the strong current of the affairs of this life overwhelms the perceptive power of the understanding, it is thrown into a state of darkness. And in the same way as if we were placed in the depths under water, we should be unable to see the sun through the quantity of water lying, like a sort of barrier, above us, so surely, in the eyes of the understanding also a blindness of the heart takes place, that is, an insensibility, whenever there is no fear [of God] to agitate the soul. (Chrysostom, eighth homily on Ephesians)

Paul seems to be discussing a willful process here, not merely an ignorance of God caused by never hearing or knowing but a willful ignoring of God, as Romans 1 also describes. Clearly enough Paul believes that bad theology or thinking leads to bad practices, that theologies or schools of thought always have ethical consequences. Here Paul discusses debauchery,[84] impurity, and everything done to excess.

Paul then uses a peculiar phrase in v. 20: "but you have not so learned Christ."[85] This could be taken to mean you learned from Christ, you learned about or concerning Christ, or you learned Christ himself.[86] Paul seems to mean that Christ, being the model of the Christian life, of what living really amounts to according to a standard of ethical rectitude, is the model the Christians must follow, and they have presumably learned this model from the missionary preaching. Lincoln suggests that what may also be meant is that they have been shaped by the exalted Christ, the source of a new way of life and a new relationship with God.[87] Hoehner is also surely right that the phrase denotes having a personal knowledge of Christ such that one could actually answer the question What would Jesus do?[88]

V. 21 is not suggesting that they have literally heard Christ in person or been taught by him, but rather that they have heard and met him and learned of him indirectly through the apostles and others who have had contact with the first followers of Jesus and even with Jesus himself.[89] Schnackenburg urges that

---

83. Hoehner, *Ephesians*, p. 584.

84. *Aselgeia* is conduct so scandalous that it would even shock a pagan person.

85. Perkins, "Ephesians," p. 427: "Verses 20-21 are a rhetorical appeal to the audience. They follow an established practice in paraenesis, invoking prior instruction."

86. Jeal, *Integrating Theology and Ethics*, p. 182, n. 25.

87. Lincoln, *Ephesians*, p. 183.

88. Hoehner, *Ephesians*, p. 594.

89. Here is one further clue that we are not dealing with an audience that is two gener-

this alludes to the fact that the early Christian teaching included traditions about and from Jesus.[90] The witnesses taught the truth as it came in the historical person of Jesus, the truth about real life, about the good, about real health. *Ei ge . . .* here has the rhetorical function of reminding the audience of what they surely have already heard before[91] and has the general sense "if you have heard . . . , as I know you have," not expressing doubt.[92] This suggests that teaching about Jesus and his way of life was a regular part of what was taught to Gentile converts.[93] Here only does the name Jesus occur by itself in Ephesians (cf. 1 Thess. 1.10; 4.14; Gal. 6.17; 1 Cor. 12.3; 2 Cor. 4.5, 10-14; 11.4; Rom. 8.11).[94] Best is surely right that this excludes the notion that the instruction was solely about the exalted Christ. "It is not some ideal Christ who is the pattern but the incarnate Jesus."[95]

The old way of life was cast off like an old garment. The old person is not who these Christians are anymore. The old lifestyle was self-destructive, full of wicked desires and deceits. V. 22 refers not just to moral corruption but to a moral corruption that leads to bodily corruption — disease, decay, and death. Instead, they have been renewed in their minds,[96] indeed in the whole tenor or spirit of their minds. Their basic thought patterns and attitudes have changed and they have clothed themselves with the new person which was in accord with the way God intended them to be in the first place when humans were created in righteousness.[97] Probably Paul has the Genesis creation story in mind

---

ations removed from the eyewitnesses. To the contrary, they are in touch with the apostles and others who have seen at least the risen Lord if not also the historical Jesus. This text does not favor the post-Pauline hypothesis about Ephesians.

90. Schnackenburg, *Ephesians,* p. 199. MacDonald, *Colossians, Ephesians,* p. 303, suggests that learning traditions about Christ is certainly involved.

91. Rightly MacDonald, *Colossians, Ephesians,* p. 303.

92. Best, *Ephesians,* p. 427.

93. Lincoln, *Ephesians,* p. 283: "the truth of the Gospel tradition, as summed up in Jesus, was the norm in accord with which the readers had heard of Christ and been taught in Him."

94. Lincoln, *Ephesians,* pp. 280-82, and MacDonald, *Colossians, Ephesians,* p. 304, suggest the alternate translation here "as truth is in Jesus." Best, *Ephesians,* p. 429, suggests "the truth is in Jesus."

95. Best, *Ephesians,* pp. 429-30.

96. Some scholars think "being renewed in the spirit of your mind" could just as well be rendered "being renewed by the Spirit in your mind." In the first of these translations "spirit" means something like "tenor" or "settled disposition" and so would not be an anthropological use of the term. In the second the term refers to the Holy Spirit. See Hoehner, *Ephesians,* p. 608. As Lincoln, *Ephesians,* p. 287, notes, however, the Greek phrase is "of your mind" not "in your mind," which seems to rule out a reference to the Holy Spirit.

97. Caird, *Paul's Letters,* p. 81, is right to point out that Paul is not saying that this is a matter of self-transformation or self-actualization. As 2.5 makes clear, it is God who turns people into new creatures (cf. 2 Cor. 5.17).

here, and so the renewal of the image of God within the believer.[98] "In righteousness and holiness of truth" (v. 24) could refer to a righteousness and holiness that comes from truth.[99] From a rhetorical point of view it is interesting that the virtues being touted here are the same as Quintilian says are some of the major virtues to be praised in epideictic rhetoric (*Inst. Or.* 3.7.15).

So then Christians must cast aside the big lie of pagan culture and speak the truth with their neighbors,[100] and here Paul means the members of the body of Christ since he is talking about the internal building up of the body by each member. He uses scriptural language from Zech. 8.16 and Ps. 4.4 to make his point. But he knows well that there will be anger and trouble even in paradise, so he adds "be angry but sin not," resolve the matter before the day ends. Some have suggested that he must be referring to righteous anger here, because v. 31 forbids anger, and others have suggested that Ps. 4.4 is in the background here, which in essence says "if you do get angry . . . do not sin. . . ."[101] Certainly Paul is, in light of vv. 27 and 31, not legitimizing anger. He simply recognizes anger as an inevitable fact of human existence. The imperative here then is likely to have concessive force, like the Psalm text it draws from.[102] V. 26b may quote a maxim familiar in the Greco-Roman world about the need for reconciliation before sunset after abusing someone with anger (see Plutarch, *Moralia* 488C). The point of the maxim, and the point here, is to deal with matters before they fester, or perhaps before anger turns into sin. It is one thing to be angry and to react properly to it, for there is a place for righteous anger in the faith. (Even so, Paul never exhorts anyone to "be righteously angry.")

But in the passion of the moment, one may say or do something which amounts to sin.[103] To do this is to give the Devil an opportunity to work even among Christians.[104] *Diabolos* is found only here and at 6.11 in Paul's letters but represents the same person as "Satan" or "the prince of the power of the air" (see pp. 244-46 above). Evil in the universe is viewed as having a personal and supernatural face. It has an intentional course and is especially directed against humans. In Christ, however, there are protection against and power over the forces of darkness. Paul believes that when Christ becomes the believer's Lord there is not room for other lordships, or for possession in the believer's life. One

98. See Best, *Ephesians*, pp. 436-37.

99. See Hoehner, *Ephesians*, pp. 612-13.

100. Possibly an allusion to Zech. 8.16, where, as here, the neighbor in question is the fellow believer or member of the believing community.

101. See O'Brien, *Ephesians*, p. 339; cf. D. B. Wallace, "*Orgizesthē* in Eph. 4.26: Command or Condition?" *Criswell Theological Review* 3 (1989): 353-72.

102. Lincoln, *Ephesians*, p. 301.

103. Hoehner, *Ephesians*, p. 620, is probably right that malicious anger is in view in v. 31.

104. *Topos* certainly means "place" though some translate it "foothold." As in Acts 25.16 it means the space or opportunity or chance to do something. See O'Brien, *Ephesians*, p. 340.

cannot become a tool of Satan unless one gives sin place and commits apostasy. Believers have a choice about their course of life in such matters, and certainly more so than unbelievers, who are indeed buffeted about by various forces larger than themselves.

In vv. 28-32 Paul makes clear what sort of changed behavior he has in mind. The thief should no longer steal (cf. 1 Cor. 6.10; 1 Pet. 4.15). Instead he should engage in manual labor so that he can have something to give, helping the needy.[105] Here as regularly elsewhere, Paul does not just give an exhortation but also states the purpose of the exhortation, assuming that sometimes a rationale and a clear intended outcome are required. This is simply a good rhetorical tactic, forestalling possible questions of why or even objections. Paul does not merely say so the thief will have sufficient resources to support himself. He should work and not try to gain something without working.[106]

Paul also says (v. 29) that no rotten words should come out of our mouths, by which he means no slander, no cursing, no abusive speech. Rather, one's speech should be edifying and gracious, benefiting the hearer. Paul is attacking those sins which divide and disrupt the unity of the body of Christ, including sins of speech.

V. 30 speaks of not grieving the Holy Spirit of God.[107] God can be grieved.[108] This is not the same as quenching the Spirit, for stifling spiritual

---

105. This exhortation suggests that a considerable number of the audience came from the lower echelons of society which were regularly faced with hunger and the like. As Caird, *Paul's Letters*, p. 82, says, even the attempt to live at another's expense is a form of theft. The remedy is said to be honest work. It is not impossible that this exhortation was addressed specifically to slaves at some juncture. Slaves were often accused of theft (cf. Tit. 2.10; Phlm. 18), and, as Perkins says, if they were also Christians they had an obligation not to act like such slaves and so be good witnesses for their faith. See Perkins, "Ephesians," p. 429; J. Gnilka, *Der Epheserbrief* (Freiburg: Herder, 1971), p. 271. Against this however, E. Best, "Thieves in the Church: Ephesians 4:28," *Irish Biblical Studies* 14 (1992): 2-9, points out that slaves could hardly contribute to the welfare of the community. This is not necessarily true, since they did have their *peculium*, but he may be right that day laborers and seasonal workers are in view. It is true that outside Rome there was no dole for out-of-work laborers, and so it is not surprising that they resorted to theft. What this verse suggests is that the Christian community was supposed to take care of their own, as Acts 2, 4, and 6 suggest. The Roman elite regarded manual labor as demeaning, but most Jews and Greeks and ordinary Romans did not.

106. Cf. pseudo-Phocylides 153-54: "Work hard so that you can live from your own means; for every idle person lives from what his hands can steal."

107. This verse is linked with v. 29 by *kai*, which may suggest that the sins of speech are specifically what Paul is thinking of as grieving the Holy Spirit. See O'Brien, *Ephesians*, p. 345. Note the amplified version of the Holy Spirit's name here which is not found elsewhere, another Asiatic feature.

108. See *Testament of Isaac* 4.40: "But you shall take care and be alert that you do not grieve the Spirit of the Lord."

gifts is not in view here. Rather sinning in such a way that the Spirit might have to withdraw from the believer is in view. Note the personal nature of the Holy Spirit: "one can only grieve a person."[109] It appears likely that the background of this expression is found in Isa. 63.10: "In his love and mercy he redeemed them; he lifted them up and carried them all the days of old. Yet they rebelled and vexed his Holy Spirit, so he turned and became their enemy and he himself fought against them" (vv. 9b-10). It could hardly be clearer that the subject here is apostasy of the redeemed and God's Spirit being grieved and so responding to their rebellion with judgment. It would appear that Hebrews 6 discusses the same sort of view of sin in the Christian life. When a Christian sins, it most certainly affects his or her spiritual life, doing spiritual damage. If enough damage is done, the Spirit can be grieved.[110] Paul wants his audience to remember that whenever they are acting, the Spirit dwells in them and is affected by their behavior. One must always ask: Is this course of action what the Spirit would lead or prompt me to do?

Though one has been sealed in the Spirit (cf. 2 Cor. 1.21-22 and Eph. 1.13-14) "for the day of redemption," Paul does not rule out something such as willful apostasy breaking that seal. The main concepts conveyed by the metaphor of the seal are authentication and ownership: believers have been marked by and belong to God.[111] There may be a secondary sense of protection, but, as anyone in antiquity knew, a seal could certainly be broken, whether a seal on a vessel or a seal on a document.[112] "Redemption" here is seen as something future, not al-

---

109. Fee, *God's Empowering Presence*, p. 715.

110. An interesting agraphon of Jesus reads: "Do not grieve the Holy Spirit who dwells in you, and do not extinguish the light which shines in you." This version of the saying makes even clearer that the possibility of apostasy is conjured with in the saying. The saying first surfaces in pseudo-Cyprian, *De Aleatoribus* 3, and so its antiquity is uncertain and its connection with Jesus even less secure, but at a minimum it may be a reworking of the saying here in Ephesians, in which case it is its earliest interpretation, an interpretation which indicates that apostasy is certainly a possibility. Further support for interpretation of the Ephesians saying in this way comes from Hermas, *Mandates* 10.2.1-6; 3.2, which speaks of how sadness drives away the Holy Spirit who dwells in Christians. See Schnackenburg, *Ephesians*, p. 210 and nn. 17 and 18.

111. Paul is not referring here to baptism or a ritual of sealing through which one received the Holy Spirit but to the powerful presence of the Holy Spirit within a life as the authentication that one belongs to God. Against Perkins, "Ephesians," p. 430.

112. See Fee, *God's Empowering Presence*, pp. 716-17. MacDonald, *Colossians, Ephesians*, p. 309, confuses the concept of the Spirit as down payment *(arrabōn)* with the sealing by or in the Spirit on the basis of Eph. 1.13-14, but even there sealing and pledging are distinguished. The *arrabōn* does carry the sense of a pledge or first installment which leads to later installments, but the sealing metaphor conveys no such notion of pledge any more than it stresses protection. The mere term or metaphor of the seal does not convey the sense of a "guarantee of [the owner] taking full and final possession of them," pace Lincoln, *Ephesians*, p. 307.

ready fully accomplished. "The reference to 'the day of redemption' reminds the audience that human conduct will be subject to divine judgment."[113] Just so, and that includes Christian conduct, for as Paul says in 2 Cor. 5.10 to Christians: "We must all appear before the judgment seat of Christ so that everyone may receive what is due them for the things done while in the body, whether good or bad."

When it comes even to the people of God, the Scriptures are clear — one is eternally secure only when one is securely in eternity. Short of that, grieving the Spirit, committing apostasy, and facing final judgment are possible for the believer, however unlikely in particular cases. The concept of sealing here then must be balanced by the concept of grieving, and a notion of an unconditional protection or guarantee should not be read into the "sealing" metaphor.

In v. 31 Paul rules out all bitterness, rage, shouting, and cursing that arises from malice. "Malice can take many forms, of which five examples are given: silently harbored grudge, indignant outburst, seething rage, public quarrel, and slanderous taunt."[114] This is perhaps to be seen as a sequence or a description of an anger cycle from start to finish, beginning internally and progressing to full-blown expression.[115] "The rhetorical effect of this accumulation of terms for anger is powerful, and, together with the summarizing phrase 'along with all malice,' indicates that anger in all its forms, together with every form of malice associated with it, is to be removed completely from them."[116] Instead, Christians are to be kind to one another and compassionate. Graciousness toward one another is to be "just as God in Christ was gracious toward you." This suggests that human graciousness is to be no less gracious or charitable but rather commensurate with the divine graciousness one has received. The present participle here, *charizomenoi*, "being gracious," suggests that this activity is to be unceasing. It does include the concept of forgiveness but it is broader than forgiveness and should be translated accordingly (cf. Col. 2.13; 3.12; 2 Cor. 2.7, 10; 12.13).[117]

The Imitation of God, the Image of Holiness — 5.1-21

Most epideictic discourses involve not just praise but also denunciation, in particular denunciation of certain kinds of conduct. In this section of the parenesis

---

113. Perkins, "Ephesians," pp. 430-31. On the day of judgment also entailing redemption see Rom. 2.5, 7; 13.11-12; Phil. 1.6, 10; 2.16.

114. Caird, *Paul's Letters*, p. 83.

115. See Best, *Ephesians*, p. 461.

116. O'Brien, *Ephesians*, p. 350.

117. Hoehner, *Ephesians*, p. 639.

Paul offers not only exhortations (vv. 3a, 4a, 6a, 7, 11) but also short supporting arguments.[118] He seems to be focusing on those pagan sins that the Gentile Christian audience might return to, hence the need to give arguments or rationales for avoiding such behavior and alternatives to such behavior (e.g., don't get drunk with wine and sing bar songs but be filled with the Spirit and sing praises, vv. 18-19). Christians are not to participate with "them" (i.e., non-Christians) in bad behavior. V. 21 is a transitional verse which goes with this section and also introduces the household code by providing the setting or context in which the discussion of submission in Christian marriage should be couched.

The basic pattern of rhetoric when it came to virtues and vices was the praise of famous persons contrasted with the denunciation of the wicked in general, though sometimes a particular example of an evil person was focused on. The goal was the molding of character as much as it was the reinforcing of good behavior (*Inst. Or.* 2.4.20). Here Christ or God in Christ is the pattern that the audience is called to emulate and imitate, and Christ is the one to whom implicit praise is given, while the pagan lifestyle in various of its dimensions is denounced and renounced. Believers are to be light, as Christ is light, and so to act no longer as though they are or they dwell in darkness where no one notices their conduct.

It was of course a help if the vices being denounced were also denounced in the broader cultural setting. Thus, for example, when Paul denounces debauchery, this is no different than when Quintilian sets forth Pleisthenes as an example of debauchery (*Inst. Or.* 3.7.19). Quintilian goes on to say that the mind has as many vices as the body does, and they too need to be denounced (3.7.20). Paul treats both things like insatiable desire ("greed") as well as the behaviors which flesh out the desires as well.

It was of course a harder sell when Paul would denounce behavior that was considered acceptable in the larger Greco-Roman culture, such as certain forms of male sexual and social behavior. Here he would need to provide arguments or rationales such as: if you keep behaving this way you will not enter the dominion of God, or if you need an alternative to getting drunk and carousing, try being filled with the Spirit and singing praises and godly songs instead.

What was most important, according to Aristotle, was to be wise enough to know in advance if the audience was generally in accord with, or knew they ought to be in accord with, the subjects one would praise or blame and the advice one would give before offering one's discourse (*Rhet.* 1.9). "For there can be little doubt as to the attitude of the audience, if that attitude is already determined prior to the delivery of the speech. It will be wise too for him to insert some words of praise for his audience, since this will secure their good will, and

---

118. See Jeal, *Integrating Theology and Ethics*, p. 185.

wherever it is possible this should be done in such manner as to advance his case" (*Inst. Or.* 3.7.23-24).

Paul follows the advice of the rhetoricians. He does not introduce teaching that would be unfamiliar to the Christian audience, but is rather reinforcing what they have heard before, by way of praising and blaming various sorts of attitudes and conduct. He does on occasion amplify, and make more explicitly Christian, exhortations that have been given before, for example in the household codes. This is not a surprise since the epideictic rhetoric in Ephesians is second order moral discourse — discourse offered to those who have heard the initial Pauline treatment of such subjects before (e.g., the sort of material found in Colossians 3–4) and are prepared to receive a more developed or second step of the discussion.

To achieve his rhetorical aims Paul will not only continue to use the "then . . . now" contrast and virtue and vice lists, but also occasionally examples of real Asiatic rhetorical flourish, for example in v. 14, where we have two lines with similar sounding endings and a certain rhythm to the tristich.[119] Paul is undoubtedly quoting or alluding to traditional and familiar material, but he has made it his own, and in particular he has made it suitable for the epideictic character of this discourse. Some of the themes mentioned in regard to the Gentile believer's past and present in 2.1-10 are now brought up again as part of the hortatory section of the discourse.

From a sociological point of view, one can say that in Ephesians in comparison to Colossians, Paul is trying in a more urgent way to firm up the boundaries between the Christian community and the outside world and to make the audience aware of the need to do so. Christian character and relationships in their distinctiveness are given more treatment here than in Colossians. "Compared to other ethical teaching in Pauline literature, including Colossians, the attention given in Ephesians to a distinctive way of life is striking. It seems that the loss of boundary markers associated with Judaism (e.g., circumcision) is being compensated for by detailed attention to ethical boundaries. . . . [One can] sense a fear of forgetting the parameters of identity and ultimately a fear of assimilation. Moreover, it must be remembered that the ethical stance operates in conjunction with religious symbolism that reinforces the idea that believers already inhabit the heavenly realm. They are in the world but not of it."[120] Paul seeks here to provide alternatives not only to pagan behavior but also to pagan worship, as we shall see. The contrast between darkness and light, bad behavior and good, is drawn sharply to emphasize the boundary and the need to think always in a Christian manner about such matters, not to suggest cutting off all contact with those outside the Christian community. In other words, the strin-

---

119. Lincoln, *Ephesians*, p. 318.
120. MacDonald, *Colossians, Ephesians*, p. 322.

gency and stark contrasts here serve a rhetorical purpose — compensation for the blurring of the boundaries that is the experience of a minority community that does not seek to remove itself from social relationships with pagans or from the dominant cultural ethos.

Paul is also concerned about the Christian witness given to the larger culture simply by the Christian community being and appearing to be something distinctive, a city of light set on a hill. The call to wise behavior (5.15-17) is as much outward as inward looking. The ethical exhortation leading up to the peroratio will conclude by dealing with one particular example of Christian social relationship that needed to be exemplary: relationships within the household (5.21–6.9). We may see this material in 5.1-20 as preparing for that discussion, providing its broader foundational context, and then 5.21 serves as the transition into the climax of the hortatory material.

Be imitators then of God, as beloved children, and walk in love, just as also Christ loved us and gave himself for us an offering and a sacrifice to God for a sweet fragrance. But sexual immorality and impurity and all excess should not even be named among you, just as is fitting for saints, and filth and foolish chatter or dirty jokes which are not proper, but rather thanksgiving. For you know this, knowing that every sexually immoral person or impure person or the rapacious, who is an idolater, shall not have an inheritance in the dominion of Christ and God.

Let no one deceive you with empty words, because of this, for the wrath of God comes upon the sons of disobedience. Do not then become fellow sharers with them. For you were once darkness, but now light in the Lord: as children of light walk, for the fruit of all goodness and righteousness and truth, deciding, testing what is pleasing to the Lord. And do not share the works of darkness which are barren, but should you not rather expose them? For the things done in secret by them are shameful even to speak of. But all we speak is revealed by the light, for all that is revealed is light. Therefore it says "Awake, you who are sleeping, and rise from the dead, and Christ will shine on you."[121]

See then carefully how you walk, not as unwise but as wise, redeeming/buying back the time because the days are evil. Because of this do not be foolish but understand what is the will of the Lord. And do not get drunk with wine in which is dissipation, but be filled in/with Spirit, speaking to one another psalms and hymns

---

121. Though textually it has little to commend it, there is an interesting variant in some Western manuscripts: "Christ will touch you," and in others: "you will touch Christ." D* and Jerome have *epipsauseis* instead of *epiphausei*, the former meaning something like "you will attain to" or "have a part in" Christ. This is one more example of an aural variant. Metzger, *TC*, p. 540 suggests the variant may have arisen from the legend that the cross on which Jesus died was erected over the burial place of Adam, who was raised from the dead by the touch of Christ's blood.

and spiritual songs, singing and praising in your hearts to the Lord, giving thanks
always for everything in the name of our Lord Jesus Christ to the God and Father,
submitting oneself to one another in the fear of Christ.

Here at 5.1 is the only place in the Bible where people are called to be imitators
of God, though this was to become a theme in Christian literature in the early
second century (Ignatius, *Ephesians* 1.1; *Trallians* 1.2; *Diognetus* 10.4-6;
Irenaeus, *Adversus Haereses* 3.20.2). In view of 4.32, however, this verse may
simply refer to being imitators of Christ since the author sees Christ as divine
(cf. 1 Thess. 1.6; 1 Cor. 11.1). Here the point is to love as God loves, as is shown
in v. 2. Mimesis or impersonation, as it was called in rhetorical contexts, was
not an uncommon theme in earlier literature. The discussion was often of how
an actor skillfully impersonates someone else (Aristotle, *Problematica* 19.15;
Poetica 24.13).

Philo is one of the few Jewish writers earlier or contemporaneous with
Paul who develops the theme of the imitation of God (*De Fuga et Inventione*
12.63; *De Virtute* 31.168; 32.168; *De Specialibus Legibus* 4.13). He stresses that to
become like God is to become holy, just, and wise, which is not unlike Paul's
exhortation here. In particular, Philo illustrates from the life of Moses what
this mimesis looks like, and he stresses that like God we should be gracious
and kind.[122] Since Paul goes on to use the phrase "as beloved children," there
may be an implication that he is drawing on the idea of children emulating
their parents. Imitation in a rhetorical context is usually a deliberative theme
as it is usually part of a call for a change of behavior, but here it may simply be
a matter of reinforcement, comporting with the epideictic character of this
document.

Christ is said to have given himself as an offering or sacrifice. If the two
words *prosphoran* and *thysian* are not simply stylistic variants or synonyms,
which is typical with Asiatic amplification, the former normally refers to an offering and the latter to sacrifice, but both can be used of either bloody or un-
bloody sacrifices (cf. Phil. 2.17).[123] "Taken together the two words convey that
Christ handed himself over as the offering and sacrifice that would fulfill all the
offerings and sacrifices of the OT."[124] He was given, says Paul, for a sweet fragrance (cf. Phil. 4.18), the point being that the offering was acceptable to God
(cf. Exod. 29.18; Lev. 2.9, 12; Ezek. 20.41).

In v. 3 Paul contrasts what he has just said with certain kinds of behavior.
Porneia is not a technical term for fornication but refers to a wide range of sexual sins, and when used more narrowly seems to mean prostitution or in-

122. See Hoehner, *Ephesians,* pp. 644-45.
123. See Best, *Ephesians,* p. 470.
124. Hoehner, *Ephesians,* p. 649.

cest.[125] Some Greco-Roman writers (Musonius Rufus, for example) banned sexual activity outside marriage, but that was a rare counsel in that world. Normally, the most restrictive of Greco-Roman moralists would allow men to frequent prostitutes, while women had to confine themselves to their husbands. Not surprisingly in a patriarchal culture, women were treated much more strictly. Paul places restrictions on behavior, particularly male behavior, that outside the Jewish realm was basically seen as acceptable. The word *pleonexia* is sometimes translated "greed," but its core meaning is an insatiable acquisitive drive. Paul says that such things should not even be mentioned, never mind done, by Christians. "The expression 'as is fitting among saints' points to the existence of standards: lines separating the pure and holy community from the outside world."[126] The negative counterpart is in v. 4: "which is inappropriate." Appropriate, honorable, and praiseworthy conduct is an epideictic topic (as opposed to what is true or false, which is a forensic topic), and it is notable that we have little phrases signaling this concern in various places in this section (see also 6.1).

The list of evils continues in v. 4 with three words for sins of speech, all of which occur only here in the NT.[127] The first, *aischrotēs,* "obscenity," is similar to *aischrologia,* which occurs in Col. 3.8.[128] The second, *mōrologia,* means literally the words or language of a fool. It refers not to speech that lacks intelligence or education but to speech that lacks wisdom or a godly perspective on life.[129] The third, *eutrapelia,* had both positive and negative connotations. In the former case it means wittiness and pleasantry (see Aristotle, *Nichomachean Ethics* 4.8, 1128a), even facetiousness, but in a negative context such as here it refers to coarse humor, sexual innuendoes, or even dirty jokes.[130] These are not the kind

125. See B. Malina, "Does *Porneia* Mean Fornication?" *NovT* 14 (1972): 10-17; J. Jenson, "Does *Porneia* Mean Fornication? A Critique of Bruce Malina," *NovT* 20 (1978): 161-84.

126. MacDonald, *Colossians, Ephesians,* p. 311.

127. As Best, *Ephesians,* p. 474, says, vv. 3-4 should be taken together as one sentence with the verbs in v. 4 depending on the verb in v. 3.

128. This is another example where it appears that Ephesians is an exercise in rhetorical variation based on Colossians and other Pauline writings such as Romans. This assumes both that the audience is familiar with one or more earlier Pauline letters, especially Colossians, and that the author felt he had the freedom to handle Paul's material in this rhetorical way, which suggests someone with considerable authority. In other words, the evidence suggests that the implied author is likely to be the same as the named author of this document.

129. See Best, *Ephesians,* p. 478.

130. L. Kreitzer, "'Crude Language' and 'Shameful Things Done in Secret (Ephesians 5:4,12)': Allusions to the Cult of Demeter/Cybele in Hierapolis," *JSNT* 71 (1998): 51-77, suggests that ritualized vulgarity or cursing might be in view, but if so Paul does not make this clear, and in any case Kreitzer's case depends on the dubious assumption that Ephesians is not a circular letter or homily, but is rather targeting the specific situation in Hierapolis. See rightly, Lincoln, *Ephesians,* p. 330. It is interesting to compare and contrast the community-

of things which should come out of Christian mouths, which should rather be used to express thanksgiving.[131]

Paul begins v. 5 by noting that the audience already knows all this. "The author is not correcting believers who lack holiness that they ought to have but is reinforcing an established Christian way of life."[132] Just so, this approach is the essence of epideictic hortatory material. Paul warns clearly that the sexually immoral, the insatiable, will have no inheritance in the dominion of God and Christ (cf. 1 Cor. 6.9-10; Gal. 5.19-21).[133] "The apostle is not asserting that the believer who ever falls into these sins is automatically excluded from God's kingdom. Rather what is envisaged here is the person who has given himself or herself up without shame or repentance to this way of life."[134] Paul adds that insatiableness, rapaciousness, and excessive desire to have or to obtain is a form of idolatry. Anything or anyone one desires or loves more than God becomes an idol.

The double referent "of Christ, of God" for "dominion" is found nowhere else in the NT. Barth suggests that "of Christ" is in apposition to "of God."[135] This may well be correct (cf. Rev. 11.15). In any case Paul is talking about a future inheriting of the dominion, showing yet again that Ephesians certainly does have some future eschatological material. It is interesting that the references in the NT to the dominion of Christ tend to be in the later NT letters (cf. 2 Tim. 4.1, 18; 2 Pet. 1.11; Col. 1.13), but the notion is also found in 1 Cor. 15.24 by implication and of course in Revelation 20 as well.[136]

V. 6 indicates that idle words bring the wrath of God on disobedient ones. The verb "comes" is in the present tense here, so the reference is probably not to

---

forming ethical discussion here with that at Qumran. 1QS 7.14-15 says that uncontrolled laughter over a dirty or improper joke is punishable by a thirty-day suspension from the community. Notice the lack of disciplinary sanctions mentioned in Ephesians.

131. Caird, *Paul's Letters*, p. 84, rightly notes the rhetorical wordplay between *eutrapelia* and *eucharistia*.

132. Perkins "Ephesians," p. 436.

133. Notice again the Asiatic redundancy: "know this, knowing. . . ." In Jewish ethics "greed" was sometimes seen as a form of covetousness, in particular of sexual covetousness, and was associated with fornication (*Testament of Levi* 14.5-6; *Testament of Judah* 18.2; 1QS 4.9-10; CD 4.15-18).

134. O'Brien, *Ephesians*, p. 363.

135. Barth, *Ephesians 4–6*, p. 565.

136. Best, *Ephesians*, p. 482 queries: "Certainly unbelievers have no inheritance in this kingdom, but are the elect who have been baptized and become members of the community able to lose their inheritance?" The term "lose" is not appropriate, as if one's salvation could somehow be misplaced, but Paul certainly does affirm the possibility of Christians committing apostasy, a willful rebellion involving wrenching of oneself out of the hold God has on one's life. See pp. 293-302 above, and see Gnilka, *Epheserbrief,* pp. 255-56, who says Paul is warning Christians of the danger of falling back into their pagan way of life.

future or even near future judgment though it could be translated "is coming" with a future reference.[137] Paul believed in partially realized blessing and judgment in the present, as Romans 1 makes evident.

Paul says in v. 7 that believers must not share in this horrible fate by sharing in conveying empty words or acting like the sons of disobedience. He is not urging disassociation from pagans altogether,[138] only disassociation from certain kinds of pagan behavior.[139] He reminds the audience that they were once not merely in darkness, but *were* darkness, but now in Christ are light and so must live as light. Paul does not say that they are light in themselves, but that they are light "in the Lord," through, that is, their connection with Christ.[140] This means living in a way that goodness, righteousness, and truth, which are the fruit of light, characterize one's life. As Schnackenburg puts it, virtue is the result of the divine vitality planted in believers which produces such fruit.[141] This does not rule out moral striving, but it makes clear that the power, energy, inclination, and wisdom for virtuous behavior are not self-generated or created by means of mere exhortation. Calling believers "light" also means that as enlightened people they have God's light within them and so have a guide within themselves in regard to their conduct.

But there is a measure of moral discernment involved: v. 10 speaks about deciding or testing or finding out by experience what pleases the Lord.[142] The Christian life is not all a matter of following preset rules. It also involves using good Christian judgment and character to decide what is and is not "light."[143] The works of darkness do not bear good fruit. They are sterile.

V. 11 adds that it is the believer's job as light to expose such dark deeds. This might be accomplished by prophetic witness or simply by living the kind of life that makes sinners ashamed and reveals them for what they are. "There is no contradiction between the two commands to expose the excesses of paganism and not even to speak of them. The works of darkness are to be exposed by the light i.e. by what Christians are, not by what they say. They are not being licensed to scold."[144] Paul reminds the audience that God's light reveals all that

---

137. See MacDonald, *Colossians, Ephesians*, p. 313.

138. As O'Brien, *Ephesians*, p. 365, says, Paul is urging that believers not become partners with pagans in such behavior.

139. Best, *Ephesians*, p. 486; Hoehner, *Ephesians*, pp. 668-69. It seems therefore somewhat less stringent than what we find in 2 Cor. 6.14–7.1, which is also about unequal partnerships. See my *Conflict and Community in Corinth*, pp. 402-6.

140. Hoehner, *Ephesians*, p. 671.

141. Schnackenburg, *Ephesians*, p. 224.

142. See MacDonald, *Colossians, Ephesians*, p. 314.

143. See Perkins, "Ephesians," p. 437: "This expression implies that believers must determine what is suitable behavior in concrete circumstances."

144. Caird, *Paul's Letters*, p. 85.

we speak or think. Humans cannot hide, even though Paul knows of the kind of unspeakable things that go on in the dark. He was not naive but simply chose not to honor such dark deeds by talking at length about them, unlike modern tabloid journalism.[145]

V. 13 is puzzling. What does "All that is revealed is light" mean?[146] It might mean that all will be made apparent for what it is or that all that can withstand God's searchlight is substantive, that everything else is shadows of darkness or ephemeral.

We do not know where the saying in v. 14b comes from.[147] It may be a Christian saying or a fragment from a Christian hymn, but we cannot be sure.[148] In light of what follows in vv. 18-19 it is probably from a Christian song that draws on Isa. 60.1 and possibly Isa. 26.19.[149] Christian living requires care, diligence, and wisdom (v. 15).[150] Believers are to love, redeeming the time (v. 16; cf. Col. 4.5).[151] This could mean to make up for the time lost when one was a sinner, or to make the most of the time one has to bear witness and live well, probably the latter.[152] We are to do this because the days are already evil. Paul believes that he lives in the eschatological age where good and evil are in a death struggle until the end. Salvation has already broken into history and is snatching people out of this present darkness. It is necessary, therefore, to understand the will of the Lord (v. 17), which requires discernment and effort and wisdom in a dark age. Such understanding is not innate.

---

145. Ironically, Christians would come to be accused of the very sorts of behavior condemned here. For example, Marcus Cornelius Fronto (A.D. 100-166) accused Christians not only of religious sacrilege and secret rites but that "they are a crowd that furtively lurks in hiding places, shunning the light; they are speechless in public but gossip away in corners. . . . They recognize each other by secret marks and signs; hardly have they met when they love each other, throughout the world, uniting in the practice of a veritable religion of lusts" (as quoted by Minucius Felix in the next century in his *Octavius* 8-9).

146. MacDonald, *Colossians, Ephesians*, p. 316, is confused about the reason for the repetition of ideas and terms here, but this is typical of Asiatic rhetoric.

147. Notice the introductory phrase "therefore it says . . . ," which indicates a quotation follows. The same introductory phrase was used in 4.8 to set up the OT quotation there.

148. Best, *Ephesians*, pp. 496-99, notes certain Semitisms in the hymn fragment and takes this to be a sign of the earliness of the composition, which is probably correct. Cf. Schnackenburg, *Ephesians*, pp. 228-29.

149. Caird, *Paul's Letters*, p. 86. See O'Brien, *Ephesians*, pp. 374-75, on the connections with Isaiah 60.

150. Some have seen 5.15-21 as a summary climax of the entire parenesis in chs. 4–6, but this is overstating things. See, however, O'Brien, *Ephesians*, p. 379.

151. See pp. 199-200 above. R. P. Martin, *Ephesians, Colossians, and Philemon* (Atlanta: John Knox, 1991), p. 66, notes that *exagorazomenoi* literally refers to snapping up every chance at a bargain.

152. See Best, *Ephesians*, p. 505; cf. Col. 4.5.

In v. 18 we have a clear contrast: "Do not get drunk with wine" (Paul does not say not to drink wine, but rather not to engage in dissipation),[153] "but rather be filled in Spirit." This contrast is also found in the Pentecost story in Acts 2 and suggests that early Christian worship was often ecstatic and jubilant, involving loud singing. An outsider might have difficulty distinguishing exuberant praise (especially if it involved singing in tongues) and drunken singing and carousing. Paul might be contrasting Christian worship with Bacchic rites, which involved drunkenness and frenzy and orgiastic behavior (cf. Isa. 28.7; Philo, *De Ebrietate* 147-48; *De Vita Contemplativa* 85, 89; Macrobius, *Saturnalia* 1.18.1; Hippolytus, *Refutation* 5.8.6-7).[154]

Paul tells Christians who already have the Spirit to "be filled," and the verb is in the present continual tense. He might be referring to the sort of repeated fillings that happen to Christians who already have the full measure of the Spirit but are inspired in spiritually high moments to speak and sing. In such cases it is a matter of the indwelling Spirit inspiring and lifting up the individual, not a matter of the individual getting more of the Spirit. This is not some second work of grace or of sanctification. "For they who sing psalms are filled with the Holy Spirit, as they who sing satanic songs are filled with an unclean spirit" (Chrysostom, nineteenth homily on Ephesians). There is a difference between mere ecstatic utterance and heartfelt praise, which is an act of adoration. Since early Christian worship took place not only in the context of a home, but also often in the context of a fellowship meal, drunkenness and worship were not unrelated issues, as 1 Corinthians 11 demonstrates.

As Fee points out, what often gets overlooked in the discussion of Eph. 5.18-21 is that we have a series of participles that modify the exhortation to be filled by/with the Spirit — speaking, singing, giving thanks, and submitting.[155] He also rightly notes that the emphasis here is not on the ecstasy-producing potential of the Spirit but on being filled or having the fullness of the Spirit's presence.[156] Nor is the emphasis on being "high" or drunk on the Spirit as opposed to being drunk from wine. Rather the picture is of individuals and a community together totally given over to the Spirit and the Spirit's presence and leading. Philo seems to describe something of what Paul has in mind here: "Now when grace fills the soul, that soul thereby rejoices and smiles and dances, for it is possessed and inspired, so that to many of the unenlightened it may seem to be drunken, crazy, and beside itself. . . . For with those possessed by God not

---

153. This part of the verse possibly draws on Prov. 23.31.

154. See C. L. Rogers, "The Dionysian Background of Eph. 5.18," *Bibliotheca Sacra* 136 (1979): 249-57.

155. Fee, *God's Empowering Presence*, p. 719.

156. See A. J. Köstenberger, "What Does It Mean to Be Filled with the Spirit? A Biblical Investigation," *JETS* 40 (1997): 229-40.

only is the soul wont to be stirred and goaded as it were into ecstasy but the body is also flushed and fiery . . . and thus many of the foolish are deceived and suppose that the sober are drunk" (*De Ebrietate* 146-48). Far from being filled with the Spirit leading to dissipation or drunkenness, Paul affirms that it leads to wisdom and to the spirit of a sound mind and to the proper adoration and singing that all of God's creatures should render back to God. In other words, it is the key to living the Christian life in a manner pleasing to God and edifying to others as well as one's self.

The Spirit is both the means and the substance of the filling, and v. 19 tells what sort of response the Spirit prompts in the believer.[157] Christians sing hymns to Christ and also give thanks to God through the impulse and empowering of the Spirit. Note the implicitly Trinitarian nature of this discussion.[158] The life of the Spirit-filled community is to be characterized by joyful singing, thanksgiving, and submission to one another. "If believers were only filled with wisdom, the influence would be impersonal; however the filling by the Spirit adds God's personal presence, influence, and enablement to walk wisely, all of which are beneficial to believers and pleasing to God. With the indwelling each Christian has all of the Spirit, but the command to be filled by the Spirit enables the Spirit to have all of the believer."[159]

It is possible that the three sorts of songs mentioned in v. 19 had differing forms. *Psalmos* probably means psalms, usually praise songs with accompaniment, since the cognate verb originally meant "pluck a string." *Hymnois* may be more hymn-like liturgical and a cappella pieces which were written out in advance, and "spiritual songs" may mean spontaneous songs from the heart prompted by the Spirit, but we cannot be certain about any of this (cf. Col. 3.16). This could just be another example of Asianism, with the love for piling up near synonyms.[160] "It is likely that in the singing and chanting traditional elements such as Jewish liturgical materials were combined with ecstatic, innovative tendencies."[161] What we can be sure of is that the Christians are to address these songs, surprisingly enough, to each other,[162] rather than just to God! They are to speak to one another in songs of praise. This makes it clear that worship is not just a matter of adoration but also involves edification. V. 19c probably means not "only in your hearts" but rather "in a heartfelt way," understanding that the singing is addressed ultimately to the Lord. Perhaps

157. Barth, *Ephesians 4–6*, pp. 582-83.
158. Fee, *God's Empowering Presence*, pp. 721-23.
159. Hoehner, *Ephesians*, p. 705.
160. See Lincoln, *Ephesians*, p. 346.
161. MacDonald, *Colossians, Ephesians*, p. 318.
162. *Heautois* has the same sense as *allēlois* here. They are not singing or humming each to himself or herself!

what is meant is that the internal praise is to the Lord, but the external praise is to each other.

We are always to do this in the spirit of thanksgiving (cf. 1 Thess. 5.18) and submitting ourselves to one another. Singing in worship is not to be a protracted display of ego, and as 1 Corinthians 14 suggests believers are to defer to each other, taking turns. Here as in 1 Corinthians 14 nothing suggests a clergy-dominated worship service. Everyone is allowed to join in and participate as the Spirit leads them.

If we ask what the relationship is between the material in 5.1-20 and the material in 5.21–6.9, the answer is that a general discussion of sanctified or holy living leads to a particular example of what sanctified living looks like, namely the Christian family. Schnackenburg is right that we find this very same sort of ethical discussion in the earlier Paulines, for example in 1 Thess. 4.3-7 where we find another exhortation to holiness in relationships.[163]

Christians in the House — 5.21–6.9

The final section of the exhortatio applies the more general principles enunciated in 4.1–5.20 to a more specific situation — the Christian home. Unlike what we find in 1 Corinthians 7, Paul does not here address the situation of a religiously mixed marriage, and so all members of the household are addressed directly in this climax of the parenesis. As we have already noted (see pp. 279-83 above), what we are dealing with here is second order moral discourse, a form of discourse that goes beyond what one would say to an audience of Christians on a first occasion when one addresses them. Many of the differences between the household code in Colossians 3–4 and what we find here can largely be explained on that basis. The sort of discourse found in Col. 3–4 is presumed to be already familiar to the audience of Ephesians, and so here the discussion of ethics within the Christian family is taken a step further.

This becomes apparent especially when one considers not only the detailed analogy between the married couple and Christ and the church, but also the way that Paul contextualizes the code by introducing it with 5.21, which give a whole different look to the exhortation to submission within marriage and make the code here "more thoroughly Christian than that of Colossians."[164] In Colossians the husband is told to not be embittered with his spouse, but here that exhortation is replaced by the analogy of Christ and the church. If the audience was already familiar with Colossians, this change would have been

163. Schnackenburg, *Ephesians*, p. 218.
164. Lincoln, *Ephesians*, p. 355.

readily apparent and striking. As we have said previously, the trajectory and contextualizing of the argument are as important as the details of what Paul says. What we see here is an attempt to provide a significant equalizing of relationships within Christian marriage, altering the usual character and direction of a patriarchal marriage situation.

Another factor that shapes the Ephesian version of the household code is that the theme of the unity of the church and unity in the church comes into play and helps shape the discussion of household relationships, mainly by the suggestion that following the Christ-church models will bring harmony to the household, which then becomes an example of the unity of the house-church. It is asking the wrong question to ponder whether Paul is mainly concerned with the husband and wife relationship here or the Christ and the Church relationship. The latter relationship is the context for understanding and norming the former relationship when one is dealing with the Christian family. So Paul is concerned with both relationships, and in particular he is concerned with how the Christ-Church relationship provides a pattern for behavior within the marriage.[165] Marriage is seen as such a fundamental relationship that it in fact terminates or at least relativizes the relationship husband and wife had previously had with their parents.

The rhetorical force of this argument depends on several factors, not all of which are usually recognized, including, first, the audience's familiarity with the material. Paul offers some new rhetorical rationales and builds on what has been assented to in the past. Such is the nature of epideictic rhetoric which appeals to already received values and virtues, and of second order moral discourse as well. Second, Paul offers supplementary motivations and arguments of such a self-explanatory and uncontroversial character (e.g., everyone takes care of his own body, we should love in analogous fashion to the way Christ loves) that will produce ready assent.[166] Third, the emphasis on the modified behavior required of the head of the household (who receives the bulk of the exhortations, as husband, parent, and master), especially in loving and acting in a Christian manner with family members, has the rhetorical effect of setting up a trajectory or momentum in a direction of a more egalitarian approach to the marital situation. This trajectory can be seen not only by comparing what we find in Eph. 5.21–6.9 with what we find in Colossians 3–4, but even more by comparing what we find here with other household codes of the era (e.g., Hierocles, *On Duties*). And fourth, here the concentration is on the husband-wife relationship whereas in Colossians it is on the master-slave relationship. This may be because of the circular nature of this document, so that the relationship most commonly in evidence in the audience is given the most atten-

---

165. See the discussion in Martin, *Ephesians, Colossians, and Philemon*, pp. 68-70.
166. See Jeal, *Integrating Theology and Ethics*, pp. 192-95.

tion. The rhetorical effect of this however is to focus on the constituting unit of the household (husband and wife) and especially on the way the husband's actions are to mirror Christ's.

There is no reason to assume that Paul is drawing on any sources other than Colossians in this treatment of the household code, whatever sources he may have relied on in composing the Colossian code, and so we are dealing with rhetorical amplification of a known source (the 117 words in Colossians become 324 in Ephesians; see pp. 319-25 below).

Submitting to one another in the fear of Christ.[167] *Wives to their own husbands as to the Lord, because the husband is head of the wife as also Christ is head of the church, himself the Savior of the body. But as the church submits to Christ, thus also wives to husbands in all things. Husbands, love your wives, just as also Christ loved the church and gave himself for her, in order that he might sanctify her, cleansing through the cleansing of water through the word, in order to present the church to himself glorious, without a spot or a wrinkle or any such thing, in order that she be holy and without blemish/faultless. Thus husbands ought to love their own wives as their own bodies. The one loving his own wife loves himself. For no one ever hates his own flesh, but feeds it and takes care of it, just as also Christ [does] the church, because we are members of his body — "because of this a person leaves his father and mother and is united to his wife and the two are into one flesh." The mystery of this is great, but I myself am speaking about Christ and about the church, but also you, let each one of you so love his own wife as yourself, but wives, fear your husbands.*

Children, obey your parents [in the Lord],[168] *for this is right. "Honor your father and mother" (this is the first commandment with a promise) "in order that it may go well for you and so that you may live long upon the earth." And fathers, do not anger your children, but bring them up in the training and admonition of the Lord.*

Slaves, obey your masters according to the flesh with fear and trembling in the singleness of your hearts, as to Christ, not to catch their eye as man pleasers but as slaves of the Lord doing the will of God from your hearts, with enthusiasm serving as to the Lord and not to humans, knowing that each one, if he does something good, will be recompensed by the Lord, whether he is a slave or free. And masters,

---

167. P46, B, Clement, Origen, and various other Greek witnesses have no verb here, so it must be carried over from v. 21. This is in all likelihood the correct reading here (see Metzger, *TC*, p. 541), although many manuscripts (including ℵ, A, and K) have one or another form of *hypotassō* here. The omission is surely the more difficult, and correct, reading.

168. This phrase is omitted in B, D*, G, and a few other witnesses. If it were an addition we might expect it to take the same form as the phrase in v. 22 or Col. 3.20, so it is probably original. See Metzger, *TC*, pp. 541-42.

do the same to them, abandoning the threats, knowing that his and your Lord is in heaven, and there is no partiality with him.

Wives and Husbands — 5.21-33   Eph. 5.21 is a transitional verse[169] directed to all members of the audience, as is shown by the use of the masculine participle *hypotassomenoi*.[170] The participle could be taken as an imperative, but since it is dependent on the preceding verb "be filled" it should probably not be taken in this fashion; or one could say that it has an imperatival sense like the verb to be supplied in v. 22, but serves as a participle in v. 21. This verb *hypotassō* appears in Greek literature rather late and in the active sense refers to arranging or placing someone under something else and in the middle, as here, to order or arrange oneself under something or someone. Most often in earlier literature it refers to submitting to or surrendering to or humbling oneself before God (Pss. 36.7; 61.2, 6; 2 Macc. 9.12).[171] In Paul, the verb is used to refer to the subordination of Christ to God, of believers to one another, of prophetic gifts to the prophets, and of wives, children, and slaves to the head of the household (cf. 1 Cor. 15.28; 14.32; Col. 3.18). The term does usually carry an overtone of authority and of the submission of oneself to authority.[172]

This verse calls for mutual submission of all Christians to each other and is not specifically directed to marital partners, but certainly includes them. Humble serving of each other is what is in mind (cf. Phil. 2.1-5).[173] It builds on

---

169. See R. D. Balge, "Exegetical Brief: Ephesians 5.21 — A Transitional Verse," *Wisconsin Lutheran Quarterly* 95 (1998): 41-43.

170. It is interesting that a number of significant manuscripts transpose vv. 20 and 21 (P46, D*, F, G, and others), not recognizing the connection between the two verses or possibly trying to distance v. 21 from v. 22 lest the radical implications of v. 21 for what follows be noticed. See Schnackenburg, *Ephesians*, p. 244, n. 5.

171. *Hypotassō* was used of the subordinate partner in a marital relationship in the papyri. See *New Docs* 1, p. 36. As Horsley notes, this subordination however is exclusive in nature, to be rendered only to one's mate.

172. See the discussion by O'Brien, *Ephesians*, p. 399, and the notes there.

173. Hoehner, *Ephesians*, p. 717, tries to suggest that 5.21 might mean that one should submit to those one ought to submit to, i.e., to those in authority. But this is surely wrong. Paul could easily have said to submit to those in charge in the congregation, but he does not do so. He says "submit yourselves" (no limitation as to who is involved) "to one another" (no limitation as to who is involved). Barth, *Ephesians 4–6*, pp. 609, 708-15, points out how the concept of mutual subordination within a hierarchical set of relationships is not a contradiction in terms. He points to situations where citizens both rule and are ruled or where husband and wife honor and serve and so submit to one another while there is still a hierarchical structure in place (cf. Aristotle, *Politics* 1259B; Plutarch *Moralia* 143B; 144F). Here O'Brien, *Ephesians*, pp. 402-3, also engages in special pleading. He argues that *hypotassō* could not possibly refer to mutual submission, but must always refer to submission within preset ordered relationships, and that "to one another" is not always fully reciprocal. He is

Eph. 4.2-3, which spoke of bearing with one another in love, which demonstrates the mutuality involved. More importantly, since v. 22 is elliptical, whatever "submission" means in v. 21, it also means in v. 22, by which I mean, it is not a gender-specific activity. Indeed it would be better to take v. 21 as the heading for what follows in the exhortations to wife and husband, in which case

---

right however that the meaning of these words must be determined by their use in context, and the context here is that "to one another" qualifies "submit" and does not suggest that anyone is exempt from the submitting or that anyone is not a proper person to submit to. Already in 4.25 we have a clear example of "to one another" used of full reciprocity. But most of all O'Brien fails to come to grips with the fact that this participle is dependent on "be filled." All the actions from singing to giving thanks to submitting are called for by Paul of all the audience, not just some. The submitting to one another is to be undertaken by all those who are filled with the Spirit, which is to say by all Christians in the audience. Chrysostom realized quite clearly the radical notion Paul is dealing with here because he indicates that it deconstructs traditional hierarchical understandings of submission and relationships. "Let there be an interchange of service and submission. . . . Let no one sit down in the rank of freeman and the other in the rank of a slave; rather it were better that both masters and slaves be servants of one another" (nineteenth homily). Paul could use *hypotassō* in a less familiar sense than usual, but in fact does not do so. The verb here still means to order oneself under another, and it is simply predicated of all Christians. Paul is not rejecting the concept of hierarchical order in authority relationships here. For example, as an apostle he exercised such a role over his converts. What he is rejecting is the notion of a gender-specific hierarchical order, such that one set of adult persons in the audience should do the submitting and others the ordering or leading. Furthermore, it will not do to say that v. 21 is explained by vv. 22ff., because v. 22 has no verb. V. 21 sets the tone for what follows and defines who are the participants in the submission here. The audience who heard this would have heard it in the order it is presented here. They would not have been able to leap ahead in the discourse and come to the conclusion that what follows changes or severely qualifies the meaning of v. 21. The detailed discussion of this matter by G. W Dawes, *The Body in Question: Metaphor and Meaning in the Interpretation of Ephesians 5.21-33* (Leiden: Brill, 1998), pp. 206-17, should be consulted. As he says, the context of 5.21, namely what precedes it and is connected to it, does not at all favor the notion that Paul means "let some submit to others where appropriate." See also the discussion in K. Snodgrass, *Ephesians* (Grand Rapids: Zondervan, 1996), pp. 292-96.

It should also be noted that the ordering of parent-child or master-slave relationships is of course hierarchical, but the crucial points about this are: 1) The hierarchy is not gender-generated or gender-specific in character and so provides no analogy with a male-dominated relationship. Indeed, it is probable that both parents are seen as over the children here, which makes it clear that the submission of children does not have to do with gender. 2) In Philemon Paul has begun to deconstruct the very notion of brothers or sisters being kept or treated as slaves. He sees that hierarchy in the same way he does the male-female hierarchy — as something to be transformed in the home and not determinative of roles in the church service. But then Paul also sees the hierarchical relationship between parents and children, while continuing to exist, taking on a different character in Christ than in the world. The leaven of the gospel is being put into all these relationships by Paul.

what is described in vv. 22ff. is how, given their differing roles, nonetheless the husband and wife will each submit to and serve one another.[174]

If we are puzzling about how mutual submission and hierarchically arranged relationships can be compatible, Lincoln provides some helpful remarks:

> There is an interesting parallel in 1 Pet. 5:5 where the exhortation "you that are younger be subject to the elders" is followed immediately by the further appeal "clothe yourselves, all of you, with humility toward one another." The latter admonition was not meant to cancel out the former. Rather, the writer holds that there is a general sense in which elders are to serve their flock, including its younger element, in a submissive attitude, but that mutuality goes along with a hierarchical view of roles.[175]

Just so, and it may be added that throwing the Spirit and Christ as exemplars into the mix changes the very nature and character of such hierarchical relationships.

The phrase "in the fear of Christ" in v. 21 bears witness to the connection with what follows as well since immediately in v. 22 we hear about the wife fearing, a note repeated in v. 33, and of slaves fearing at 6.5. The phrase in v. 21 should probably be compared to 2 Cor. 5.11, in which case what is meant is that one's present conduct will be reviewed one day by Christ when he sits for final judgment. In other words, we likely have an eschatological sanction applied in several places in this household code, including in its heading in v. 21. This does not remove but rather adds to the notion that what is meant is a proper respect and reverence for Christ.

Sampley is on the right track when he suggests that v. 21 is meant to qualify and indeed prevent a reading of the material in vv. 22ff. as if some sort of absolute unilateral submission were intended.[176] Paul, by placing this verse here, is critiquing the normal understanding of household relationships where only certain members of the household are doing the submitting or serving.[177] "Not in

---

174. That Paul in what follows will only deal with a representative sampling of relationships in regard to what submission looks like is clear enough. For example, he does not deal with any relationships outside the household structure (e.g., the submission of soldiers to officers or citizens to rulers), and even within the household he does not discuss, for example, relationships in the extended family, such as the widowed mother of the family head to her son. In other words, the household code is not meant to be comprehensive in scope, only providing representative examples.

175. Lincoln, *Ephesians*, p. 366.

176. J. P. Sampley, *And the Two Shall Become One Flesh: A Study of Traditions in Ephesians 5.21-33* (Cambridge: Cambridge University Press, 1971), p. 117.

177. I agree with Lincoln, *Ephesians*, p. 366, however, that Sampley goes too far in saying that the author did not agree with the household code. If he had that much disagreement with it, why cite it in the first place when one was under no obligation to do so?

the Christian church," says Paul, where everyone should submit to and serve everyone else out of reverence for Christ.[178] But Best is right to note that since v. 21 is dependent on v. 18 what is suggested is not that mutual submission is a natural thing but rather that it is something that can and does happen when someone is filled with the Spirit and so led by God in his or her behavior.[179] "What he does is to require that the code of subordination shall be properly baptized with the spirit of Christ. The whole passage is an excellent illustration of the general ethical principle . . . that the Spirit-filled man must and can discern the will of God within the limitations imposed by a defective social order."[180]

As in Colossians, Paul addresses each subordinate member of the household first, and then the head of the household.[181] Furthermore, he gives the head of the household much more exhortation, at least in his discussion of husband and wife relationships, than he does the subordinate member in the relationship. This suggests that he is not merely repeating previous advice. It will be well to take a more detailed look at this household code in general here, before we begin to address individual verses beginning with 5.22.

A Closer Look: The Christian Household Code Revisited

I have elsewhere dealt at length with the Pauline household codes and their social setting.[182] Here a few things need to be revisited, and further dialogue with the commentators since the mid-1980s needs to be undertaken. Let us say first that the Christian modification of the household code in this discourse makes clear that Paul is not interested in modifications meant to mollify the concerns of outsiders about Christianity and its house-church meetings. There is no evidence of an apologetic motif or character to this material, for even the quotations from the OT do not stand alone but are set in the context of the more explicitly Christian terms of the discussion. There was in any case no OT discussion about husbands and wives such as we find here.

Second, there is still no evidence of a fixed household code in the Greco-

---

178. Best, *Ephesians*, p. 517, speaks of an unresolved tension between mutuality and the authority of some in the Pauline churches, but this does not exist if leaders are servant leaders, taking the lead in humbling themselves and serving others and so setting an example as Christ did (cf. Phil. 2.4-11).

179. Best, *Ephesians*, p. 518.

180. Caird, *Paul's Letters*, p. 88.

181. See Schnackenburg, *Ephesians*, p. 243.

182. Witherington, *Women in the Earliest Churches* (Cambridge: Cambridge University Press, 1988), pp. 42-61 and the notes. The most recent helpful overview and comparison of all the NT household codes is J. Woyke, *Die neutestamentliche Haustafeln. Ein kritischer und konstruktiver Forschungsüberblick* (Stuttgart: Katholisches Bibelwerk, 2000). Also very helpful and up to date is the survey in English by Hoehner, *Ephesians*, pp. 720-29.

Roman or Jewish world that might have been adopted and adapted by Paul. There are certainly ethical discussions of household duties and relationships, but still no evidence of a fixed table. As I have said before, it is not that important that various authors before, during, and after NT times discussed the patriarchal household and in particular the duties of its subordinate members to the head of the household. That they did is neither surprising nor does it establish some sort of evidence of literary dependence of the NT material on what came before.[183] The patriarchal family structure was pervasive and often included extended family such as domestic servants. The earlier writings do demonstrate the stability and continuity of the patriarchal family structure from the time of Aristotle until well after NT times. C. Osiek is right to point out that the Greco-Roman discussion is about how the master of the house should manage and exercise authority in his household — he is to rule his slaves like a despot, his children like a king, and his wife treating her as a rational being but one without inherent authority (Aristotle, *Politics* 1259a37, 1260a9).[184] But the Christian household codes "are not about how *he* should act authoritatively but benevolently and how *he* should require everyone to treat him with respect."[185] Notice also there is no discussion in the NT about how the *pater familias* should manage his finances, quite unlike the discussions in Aristotle and elsewhere. In short, the Christian code is about everyone in the household and treats everyone as moral agents, even the children. It is not all about the head of the household any more.

What the Greco-Roman evidence shows is a more restrictive approach, especially to women's roles, than what we find here in Ephesians. This is also true of the early Jewish evidence. Philo, for example, says that wives must be in servitude to their husbands, as if they were slaves (*Hypothetica* 7.3, 6). Josephus speaks of the need for the wife to be obedient (*Contra Apionem* 2.199) but does not use the term *hypotassō*. In fact use of *hypotassō* as Paul uses it here of all believers in relationship to each other as well as of the relationship of wife to husband seems to have no precedent in the literature.[186] Pseudo-Callisthenes, *History of Alexander* 1.22.4 does use this term of the wife submitting to her husband, but the earliest manuscript of that document dates to A.D. 300 and in any case is unlikely to have influenced Paul. Paul's near contempo-

---

183. See *Women in the Earliest Churches,* p. 44. It is also to be kept in mind that a list of whom one has duties to, especially if the duties are not explicated (as they are not in Epictetus), is not the same thing as a table of exhortations and duties.

184. See the discussion of R. Dudrey, "'Submit Yourselves to One Another': A Socio-Historical Look at the Household Code of Ephesians 5.15–6.9," *Restoration Quarterly* 41 (1999): 27-44.

185. C. Osiek, "The Ephesian Household Code," *The Bible Today* 36 (1998): 360-64, here p. 361.

186. Martin, *Ephesians, Colossians, Philemon,* p. 70: "If we permit the word's etymology to add its weight, it is clear that submit/submissiveness cannot carry the sense of degrading servility, since 1 Cor. 15:28 shows how submission characterizes the relationship between Christ and the Father, and the elements of voluntary consent and agreement are found in other places where the term is employed (1 Cor. 14:32; 16:16) as well as Eph. 5:24."

rary Plutarch uses this term in his *Advice to Bride and Groom* 33, but this also could not have influenced Paul's discussion, since it was written later. Especially noteworthy is the absence in all such discussions of imperatives or lists of social duties in reciprocal pairs, much less of an exhortation to husbands to love their wives. Furthermore, the Christian code appears to be distinguished by this sequence in each of the exhortations: address to a particular social group within the household, an imperative, often with an appropriate object, an amplification of the imperative usually in the form of a prepositional phrase, and a reason clause providing theological warrant or sanction or motivation.[187]

What of the suggestion of G. E. Cannon that the household codes reflect a sort of retrenchment and backing off from the gospel of freedom that Paul preached (Gal. 3.28), an attempt to restrict overly liberated women, slaves, or minors? This explanation certainly does not make much sense of the character and trajectory of the Ephesian household code in particular, set as it is in the context of a call for mutual submission and a call for loving self-sacrifice by the husband/father/master not characteristic of the advice given in the Greco-Roman setting. Perkins puts it this way: "this ethic describes the well-ordered Christian household independent of the views or actions of outsiders."[188]

While I do not think that Ephesians manifests the life of an introversionist sect, I do agree that this code is not conditioned by what might be thought to be acceptable to pagan outsiders who were neighbors. There is far too much evidence in Ephesians of drawing a strong line between pagan immorality and Christian behavior to think that this code was trying to be particularly sensitive to the world's reaction to the Christian household. Rather Paul is trying to model household relationships on the servant-like and self-sacrificial relationship of Christ to his church. The advice given here would certainly not make the believers invisible in the midst of the larger culture. Rather, it would make Christian homes stand out as witnesses to Christ and his love and self-sacrifice. The husband would probably have been seen as somewhat restricted or compromised by the advice given here.[189] The code does not reflect a defensive or apologetic quality, as though the church were trying either to blend in with the existing cultural standards or to defend its distinctiveness.[190] Rather the code is a bold and positive attempt to modify the existing structure.

There seems to be reasonably clear evidence that the Ephesian code is an amplification of the Colossian code, not a critique of it. The two codes share some 70 words

---

187. D. C. Verner, *The Household of God: The Social World of the Pastoral Epistles* (Chico: Scholars, 1983), pp. 86-87. The clearest of the distinctives is the series of exhortations to various groups. See Lincoln, *Ephesians,* p. 361.

188. Perkins, "Ephesians," p. 140.

189. Against MacDonald, *Colossians, Ephesians,* p. 338.

190. So Best, *Ephesians,* p. 524. He is wrong, however, in saying that it has no missionary potential, because early Christians believed that as they simply were themselves, some aspects of their lives and lifestyles would appear winsome to a world weary of rancorous and dysfunctional relationships, divisions, honor challenges, and the like.

in common, even though the Ephesian code has 207 more words than Colossians' 117! In other words, only 47 words from the Colossian code do not recur in Ephesians. The two codes have the same order: wives, husbands, children, fathers, slaves, masters. The only clear evidence of a major source is Colossians.[191] There is of course also evidence of the use of such traditional material as quotations from the OT and perhaps commonplaces as well.[192] It cannot be said that this code simply arises out of earlier Hellenistic Jewish discussions about the household because it is christologically shaped: the christological element is not just added on, and because the code not only seeks to ameliorate the harsher effects of patriarchy but also sets a different course by setting the discussion in a more egalitarian context and then stressing the Christian duties of the head of the household. This is nothing like what we find in Philo or Josephus or Sirach.

Since the material in this household code attempts to regulate and Christianize an existing institution, we should not see this material as an implicit critique of asceticism or the validity of remaining single in Christ. Such a suggestion forgets in any case that the very chapter which makes the case for the "charisma" of singleness (1 Corinthians 7) also argues that each man should have his own wife and vice versa. MacDonald is wrong then to radically distinguish what is said there from what is said here. Nothing here suggests that Paul would not still prefer singleness for some of his converts.[193] Nor does anything here suggest that we should read this text as part of a later Christian attempt to develop endogamy rules which would in effect turn the Christian community into an introversionist sect with very rigid boundaries. We have not reached here what we find in Ignatius of Antioch where the bishop must approve a Christian's choice of mate (*Polycarp* 5.1-2)!

No, this discourse is still about exposing the deeds of darkness and being light to those around who might be watching. If these imperatives in Ephesians were enacted it would not only be noticeable to the neighbors but might well be appealing, especially to the subordinate members of other families, who would recognize the ethos of love that characterizes the relationships, in particular the actions of the head of the household. As MacDonald herself points out, the advice here is not significantly different from the earliest advice found in the Pauline letters about marriage (1 Thess. 4.4-5) in regard to the issue of the way Christian practices should be distinctive from pagan practices.[194] The emphasis on holiness in that text is echoed here.

It is especially a misreading of the trajectory of this passage to say that the "primary purpose of Eph. 5:21–6:9 is to provide theological justification and motivation for the subordination of wives, children and slaves to the head of the household."[195] Nor, against Verner, is the household code here an attempt to correct the liberationist

191. So Lincoln, *Ephesians*, pp. 354-55.
192. See Sampley, *And the Two.*
193. Against MacDonald, *Colossians, Ephesians,* pp. 338-39.
194. MacDonald, p. 339.
195. MacDonald, p. 341.

thrust of Gal. 3.28.[196] It is of course quite true that Paul does not appear here in the guise of a modern feminist. He still speaks of the headship of the man in the family. But that headship has been transformed by the model of Christ. It is precisely the Christian aspects added to this code in a more dramatic way than in the Colossian code that show where the argument is leading, as does the setting of the discussion in the context of v. 21 where all are submitting to one another. In other words, if anything is the primary purpose of this code, it is to both ameliorate the harsher effects of patriarchy and to guide the head of the household into a new conception of his roles that Christianizes his conduct in various ways and so turns marriage into more of a partnership and household management more into a matter of actualizing biblical principles about love of neighbor and honoring others.

Schnackenburg is much nearer the mark than MacDonald when he says, "Because of the way in which Christ exercises his position as 'head' in relationship to the Church any unworthy 'subordination' is excluded. . . . [Paul] lays stress upon Christ . . . in his capacity as Saviour, which is then described as a loving self-offering for the Church. A one-sided 'domineering' understanding of the 'Head' is excluded by this attribute."[197] If the code is set in the context of mutual submission and Christ is given as the example of loving self-sacrifice, and if nowhere in this code is the head of the household told to subordinate or command subordination of the other household members and so "order" his house (contrast *1 Clement* 1.3; 21.6-9; Polycarp, *Philippians* 4.2), then it cannot be said that this code simply repristinizes the existing patriarchal order of things with gender-specific subordination of the female but no similar expectations of the male head of the household. Clearly, the loving self-sacrifice of the husband is depicted as the same sort of subordination, the same sort of stepping down and serving others, that Christ engaged in, and if Christ is the model of subordination and service, not only in his relationship to the Father but in the way he chooses to serve his church, then there is nothing particularly patriarchal about the concept here. Rather subordination has been broadened to describe the relationship of all Christians to each other, including all relationships within the Christian household. In fact, what this household code suggests is that all members of the household are also members of the church and are expected to behave according to Christian standards.[198]

---

196. Verner, *Household*, p. 109. See rightly the comment of Best, *Ephesians*, p. 523, who points out that Gal. 3.28 says nothing about parents or children.

197. Schnackenburg, *Ephesians*, pp. 246-47.

198. See rightly Dudrey, "Submit Yourselves," pp. 40-41:

I am convinced that the primary purpose of the household passages of the NT is *not* to repress the socially downtrodden, but to transform spiritually all who are in Christ — husbands, fathers, and masters included. This in turn transforms all their relationships. Rather than deconstructing the submission of Christian wives to their husbands, we should pay renewed attention to the constructing of mutual submission and reciprocal self-sacrifice that is the major force of the household codes. . . . That Paul upholds the existing social order is not primary, but secondary: it is his opening

It is also noteworthy that Paul does not, either here or elsewhere, connect his discussions of the household with discussions about a Christian's relationships with external authority figures such as rulers and emperors (contrast 1 Pet. 2.13–3.7). For Paul, the household is dealt with as an "in-house" matter, not as part of the larger agenda of the ordering of society in general. In fact this household code has very modest aims and functions. Not only is it confined to relationships within the Christian family, it does not even discuss all of those relationships. For example, nothing is said about relationships among children or among slaves. Nothing is said about relationships with extended family members who may dwell in the household (e.g., the widowed mother of the husband or the freedman living on the estate). Nothing is said of relationships among Christian households either. There is nothing here about the hospitality the household should offer to strangers or even to fellow believers. Nor does the code deal with problematic situations such as that of the battered wife or the beaten slave or the problems caused by masters selling off one member of a slave family.[199]

This code does not seek to be all things to all situations. It has rather a rhetorical purpose of setting the Christian tone for the household by commenting on a representative sampling of the relationships in the household, and showing what a more Christian model of domestic life might and should look like. Schnackenburg is right when he says that whatever sources Paul uses here, he has made them his own. "In his enrichment of the existent exhortation for husband and wife in their marriage by the ecclesiological motif, and his inclusion of Christian spouses in the relationship between Christ and the Church, he has created instruction on Christian marriage which, in spite of possible external influences, must be regarded as his own work and consequently must first be declared to be such and appreciated as such."[200]

The analogy drawn between the relationship of husband and wife and the relationship of Christ and the church[201] is not, of course, an identity statement, so not everything predicated of Christ and the Church can also be predicated of husband and wife and vice versa. One of the clearest signs we are dealing with a somewhat loose analogy is the fact that Christ and the church are seen as bridegroom and bride, but they are compared to those who are already married. Accordingly, one must not press the analogy beyond its obvious points of contact — love of Christ and love of the husband for the wife which entails self-sacrifice and self-giving; submission of the wife and of the church; headship of the husband and of Christ; provision and care for

---

gambit, his communication bridge to his audience which he crosses over with the new and transforming perspective of Christ. In Christ each of these relationships is transformed: What is new is the perspective of Christ, which charges husbands, fathers, and slave owners also to submit [them]selves to one another out of reverence for Christ.

He adds that by changing all three relationships into relationships of reciprocity, even including heads of households viewing themselves as fellow slaves of Christ with their own slaves, Paul is indeed working social change from within the Christian household.

199. See Best, *Ephesians*, pp. 524-25, and indeed his whole excursus, pp. 519-27.
200. Schnackenburg, *Ephesians* p. 244.
201. On which see further my *Women in the Earliest Churches*, pp. 54-56.

the wife like Christ's provision and care for the church. This means that the material in vv. 26-27 on Christ's sanctifying work and effect on the church is probably not meant to be pressed to suggest that this is the effect of the Christian husband on the wife, although in light of 1 Cor. 7.14, this is not impossible, though there the influence flows from the Christian wife to the non-Christian husband as well as from the Christian husband to the non-Christian wife. In other words, the sanctifying role, if it can be called that, is not gender-specific.

The flow of thought is from husband and wife to a more detailed reflection on Christ and the church and then back again. The husband is not called or seen as the savior of the wife, so what is said in vv. 23c, 26a-27c seems to be comments reserved for only the Christ-church relationship. It should also be said that the direction of influence between these two pairs of relationships does not flow one way. The language and even the imagery of betrothal in Paul's day influence the description of Christ's relationship to the church, but it is also clear from v. 25c that Christ's action for the church affects the way Paul describes the role of the husband's headship. Furthermore, the submissive and reverent response of the church to Christ conditions how Paul describes the relationship of wife to husband. Though v. 31a shows that Paul is well aware of the story of Adam and Eve, nonetheless his advice here draws more from the pattern of the relationship of Christ and the church. If in Colossians we see first order moral discourse in the form of a first attempt to give a Christian shape to the Christian family relationships, here we see the discussion and effort taken a step further.

A good deal of debate has raged over the structure of Eph. 5.22-33 and where the emphasis lies. One plausible reading of the structure is that there is something of a chiasm, and also a dual focus on both husband and wife and Christ and the church. This latter fact is why there is a dual conclusion, in v. 32 in regard to Christ and the church and in v. 33 in respect to marriage. The chiasm is seen in the way that wives are addressed in vv. 22-24 and v. 33b and husbands in vv. 25-29 and v. 33a, so that the discussion alternates back and forth not only between husbands and wives but also between marriage and Christ and the church.[202]

The wife is called upon first and is called upon to be subordinating herself (carrying over the middle passive participle from v. 21).[203] Nothing is said about the husband demanding subordination or being given instructions to pass on to his wife, unlike what we find in 1 Clement 1.3; 21.6. Rather, each mem-

---

202. See Best, *Ephesians*, p. 530; J. Cambier, "Le grande mystère concernant le Christ et son Église. Ephésiens 5,22-33," *Bib* 47 (1966): 43-90, 223-42; S. F. Miletic, *"One Flesh": Eph. 5:21-22, 31: Marriage and the New Creation* (Rome: Pontifical Biblical Institute, 1988).

203. Notice that the exhortation to the wife has forty-one words here, which makes it four times the length of what we find in the Colossian household code. See Hoehner, *Ephesians*, p. 729.

ber of the household, even children and slaves, is addressed as a responsible moral agent capable of hearing and heeding these exhortations. This is not then advice given to the head of the household to use. Each person is addressed in turn. The word *idiois* is important here because it indicates that husbands and wives, not men and women in general, are in view here, and it indicates that the subject here is family behavior, not the submission of women to men or church leaders in worship.[204] Neither worship nor the relationship of women to male church leaders is discussed here. Of course "her own" also implies a clear endorsement of monogamy, which becomes even more clear when Paul cites Gen. 2.24 in v. 31.

The phrase "as to the Lord" should be compared to that in Col. 3.18: "as is fitting in the Lord." The analogy in the two relationships is stressed by the way things are worded. It is possible that the phrase could even be read to mean "as to a lord," in which case an analogy with Christ is not in view (cf. 1 Pet. 3.6), but we would have expected *hōs tois kyriois* were that the case. Probably all that is meant is that the subordination of wife to husband is in some ways like the subordination she offers to Christ. Since only Christ is her Savior, it is not in all respects like her relationship to Christ. Possibly we should see v. 24b as giving clearer explanation: the wife should submit in "all things" to her husband just as she does to Christ.[205] Of course what is assumed is that the husband will act as he should, modeling himself on Christ, and that he would not ask of his wife anything that Christ would not want him to ask. The context is clearly assumed to be not just superficially Christian, but one where actual Christian behavior is being practiced. R. W. Wall says too much in claiming that spiritual hierarchy involving Christ dismantles the social hierarchy, but what Paul says does reconfigure and revise that social hierarchy and put it under Christian constraints.[206] Best is nearer the mark when he says that the wife's relationship to her husband is set within the context of her relationship with the Lord, which also means that the marriage relationship has a vertical component since Christ is involved there as well as in individual Christians' lives.[207]

204. Hoehner, *Ephesians*, p. 732: "If Paul had meant that all females are to be submissive to all males, he would have used the adjectives *thēlys* 'female' and *arsēn* 'male,' as he does in Gal. 3:28, rather than the nouns *gynē* 'woman, wife' and *anēr* 'man, husband.'"

205. This seems to mean in every area of the relationship. See O'Brien, *Ephesians*, p. 417, but O'Brien rightly goes on to add (p. 418) that it goes without saying that this does not involve being complicit in sin or anything contrary to God's commands. Cf. Acts 5.29. Again, Paul is envisioning the ideal situation here, not addressing particular problems that could and do arise. This is the nature of praise and wisdom in an epideictic piece of rhetoric in any case.

206. R. W. Wall, "Wifely Submission in the Context of Ephesians," *Christian Scholars Review* 17 (1988): 272-85.

207. Best, *Ephesians*, p. 533.

Paul does not envision or deal with a situation in which the husband might ask something not in accord with Christian love, faith, or ethics.[208] Paul is clearly dealing in general terms and with broad strokes, but then this is what one would expect in a circular homily of an epideictic sort. The point of comparison with the relationship of Christ and church has to do with roles voluntarily assumed, not with a comparison of natures. Headship or subordination is a role one assumes in relationship to another and is to be characterized in both cases by loving and self-sacrificial behavior, which is in any case a form of submission.[209] As O'Brien says, proper exercise of authority should not be seen as tyranny, nor should proper submission be seen as an indication of inferiority of any sort.[210] "Christ is not depicted as a supreme example of male superiority over women. Rather the 'husband's' function as 'head' is modeled after (and limited by) the measure of Christ's headship. Thus, not an absolute, but only a very qualified role as 'head' is attributed to man. 1 Cor. 11:3 makes this explicit by the sequence in which Christ's and the husband's headship are given: the 'head of every husband is Christ, the head of a wife is her husband.'"[211] And Paul never commands the husband to exercise his headship.[212] This section of the discourse has nothing to do with cracking the whip in order to enforce the subordination of women, as there is no indication in this discourse of any particular problems in the ordering of Christian relationships.

The crucial term in v. 23a is *kephalē*, which has been applied to Christ in 1.22-23 and 4.15. The term is used here to say something about the character of an ongoing relationship. The origin of women is not at issue here, and so the translation "source" is not appropriate in this context.[213] It is possible that Paul

---

208. Notice, too, as Caird, *Paul's Letters*, p. 88, does that Paul does not appeal to the natural order of things or to prevailing social custom or cultural values. He appeals to the model of how one relates to Christ. "In this way the demands of social custom can be transformed by being treated as service *to the Lord*." Cf. Lincoln, *Ephesians*, p. 373, who notes that this is an ideal picture and the possibility of a conflict between submitting to Christ and to the husband is not even considered. "So in this writer's vision of Christian marriage what is called for from wives is complete subordination to complete love."

209. Barth, *Ephesians 4–6*, p. 610: "the subordination of wives is an example of the same mutual subordination which is also shown by the husband's love, the children's obedience, the parents' responsibility for their offspring, the slave's and master's attitude toward one another." He pushes things too far however when he tries to make some sort of clear distinction between *hypotassō* and *hypakouō* ("obey"). But he is right that the object of female submission is limited to one particular male in the household — her husband. Lincoln, *Ephesians*, p. 368, is right that there is little difference between voluntary obedience and voluntary submission, for the former is just a particular form of the latter.

210. O'Brien, *Ephesians*, p. 412.

211. Barth, *Ephesians 4–6*, p. 614.

212. O'Brien, *Ephesians*, p. 419.

213. See rightly, Best, *Ephesians*, p. 535.

has taken the phrase "head of the household" (cf. Aristotle, *Politics* 1255B) and applied it specifically to the husband's relationship with his wife, but it is also possible that he derives the usage from his application of the term to Christ in various contexts. There is no clear evidence from the Greco-Roman literature of the period that the husband was seen as the head of the wife and the wife as the husband's body. The conjecture of a christological source for the use of "head" for the husband gains legs from the fact that Paul only mentions the headship of the husband in contexts where he also mentions the headship of Christ (1 Cor. 11.3ff. and here). Christ then is said to have authority over his bride, to which the church responds by submitting to that authority.[214] Here the rationale (*hoti* = because) for submission of the wife is given: because her husband is her head.

The *hōs* in v. 23 probably suggests an analogous view of the husband's headship. The imagery itself however does not indicate how this headship is to be exercised. Barth is probably right that v. 25 suggests that it means that the husband is to "go ahead" or take the lead or initiative in active loving and self-sacrificial service as Christ has done in relationship to the church.[215] "Head" then means head servant, and refers to a sort of servant leadership (cf. Luke 22.25ff.). If Christ, the one who lovingly offered himself as a sacrifice, is the model of headship, then general patriarchy and the assumptions of a patriarchal culture are not providing the model or the way it is to be enacted.[216] The last clause of v. 23, "and he himself is its Savior," makes evident that the analogy should not be pressed and does not include many aspects of the two relationships. The emphatic "he himself" and the adversative *alla* that begins the next verse make clear that Christ alone is in view.[217] The husband is not being called the wife's savior.[218] This is the only place in the NT where we find the phrase "Savior of the body."[219] The meaning of this phrase seems to be that Christ is the protector, sanctifier, healer, even rescuer of the

214. It is interesting that the term *ekklēsia* occurs some nine times in the whole of Ephesians, six times right here in 5.22-33. In fact no other NT paragraph has such a preponderance of uses of the term. It is clear enough that the "church" is emphasized in this passage.

215. Barth, *Ephesians 4–6*, pp. 618-19.

216. Caird, *Paul's Letters*, p. 88, suggests that Paul might be doing a midrash on Gen. 2.18-25, but that text does not speak specifically of the headship of the husband, though it does indicate that Adam was the source of Eve. See Schnackenburg, *Ephesians*, p. 247, who rightly says that the model of Christ rules out a domineering or dominating sense being implied by the term "head."

217. See O'Brien, *Ephesians*, pp. 414-15; Caird, *Paul's Letters*, p. 89.

218. See Lincoln, *Ephesians*, pp. 370-71.

219. It is very unlikely that this reflects Gnostic notions, which in fact rather seem to be dependent on Ephesians. See Lincoln, *Ephesians*, pp. 362-71; Perkins, "Ephesians," p. 133; MacDonald, *Colossians, Ephesians*, p. 327.

body.[220] This is different from the notion of Christ as Savior of the world, which has to do with conversion and the initial change into a new person.

Submission is applied to the church's relationship to Christ in v. 24, and it involves a submission in all things, a free giving and ordering of oneself in relationship to Christ.[221] Paul is not talking about Christ's relationship with individual Christians but with his body as a corporate entity. This becomes important in what follows in vv. 25-30 as we shall see, for example, in v. 26. The background to these verses, even though the church is never directly called Christ's bride here, is probably the OT material about the sacred relationship or marriage between Yahweh and Israel (Hos. 2.16; Isa. 54.4-5; 62.4-5; Ezek. 16.7-8). Paul's near contemporary Philo waxes eloquent about the covenant of marriage between God and his people made at Sinai (*De Cherubim* 13). Paul seems to have seen his own role as that of leading the bride to the groom (2 Cor. 11.2).

The husband must love the wife in analogous fashion to the way Christ loves the church (v. 25, the only place in the NT where Christ is directly said to love the church).[222] Hoehner notes that Paul uses only 41 words to exhort the wife, but some 116 to exhort the husband about his duties, and rightly adds that this exhortation does not really have a precedent in the OT or in the household codes of the Greco-Roman era.[223] But then no non-Christian household code has the example of Christ norming the relationships. In a world of arranged marriages, the exhortation to love is not at all surprising. But loving one's wife is not optional but rather obligatory and so is stressed here. The wife is not exhorted to love her husband, a gap that was noticed and filled in later by Clement of Alexandria (*Paedagogus* 3.95.1). Clearly enough, by "love" here Paul is not referring primarily or solely to a feeling which cannot be commanded, but rather to decisions of the will and commitments which can be commanded and instructed.[224]

Christ did not love the church because it was lovely or loveable. Indeed,

---

220. There is no evidence that the author of this document thought in terms of a preexistent church/body. See Lincoln, *Ephesians*, p. 374.

221. Caird, *Paul's Letters*, p. 89: "The Church's submission to Christ, as Paul never tired of pointing out, is not obedience to his dictation, but faith; and faith is the acceptance of his free and unconditioned grace and of the constraints of love which that grace entails (e.g. 2 Cor. 5:14)." Or Lincoln, *Ephesians*, p. 372: "The Church's subordination, then, means looking to its head for his beneficial rule, living by his norms, experiencing his presence and love, receiving from him gifts that will enable growth to maturity, and responding to him in gratitude and awe."

222. Barth, *Ephesians 4–6*, p. 623: "Instead of a love principle, the Prince of Love is set forth."

223. Hoehner, *Ephesians*, pp. 746, 748.

224. The term *agapē* is not used in the Hellenistic literature in relationship to households. See my *Women in the Earliest Churches*, p. 51.

what Paul goes on to suggest in v. 26 is that the love of Christ cleanses the church, in effect gives the church a spiritual makeover so that it is spiritually without spot, wrinkle, or blemish. The love of Christ makes the bride lovely. It would appear, since the marriage of Christ and the church is not spoken of directly but only the preparation for it, that Paul, as elsewhere in the NT, sees the wedding as still in the future.[225] Paul is speaking here of the process of sanctification that takes place when the Word is proclaimed, heard, and applied to the life of the church by means of the Holy Spirit. The goal is nothing less than the church becoming holy and without fault, going on to perfection. Cleansing, consecration, sanctifying, perfecting is the process Paul has been engaging in throughout this discourse by means of his words, and particularly in the exhortatio. "Anthropologists have noted the tendency in Mediterranean societies for social groups (e.g. households, villages) to be viewed as symbolically female. Just as the purity of the woman must be guarded, so too must the boundaries of the community be protected. The idea of a woman-church reflects such values."[226]

Paul is not talking here about the baptism of individual Christians but rather the sanctifying of the body of Christ as a whole by means of the Word.[227] "Having cleansed her by the washing of water with the word" does not mean, as the New Living Translation has it, "to make her holy and clean, washed by baptism and God's word." As in 6.17, the "word" here is the preached word of the gospel, not some baptismal confession or formula. Furthermore, the order of the Greek sentence, with the participle following the main verb, suggests that the cleansing is coincidental with the making holy or sanctifying, and the aorist tenses indicate that the process is viewed as a complete whole, not as temporally already completed.[228] Christ died in order to cleanse the church and make her holy. That process is still ongoing and will not be completed until he comes again, at which time the bride will be truly and fully glorious, having been made like Christ.[229]

It is probable, too, that Paul draws on the notion of the bridal bath or shower, which was a part of Jewish marriage customs. In Ezek. 16.9 Yahweh is said to have bathed his bride Israel with water and washed off the blood from

---

225. Against Schnackenburg, *Ephesians*, p. 251, who has trouble accepting that there is any future eschatology in this document, on which see pp. 244-45 and 300-302 above. See rightly, Barth, *Ephesians 4–6*, p. 628.

226. MacDonald, *Colossians, Ephesians*, p. 329.

227. The Church is nowhere in the NT said to be baptized, much less baptized by Christ with water. O'Brien is right to stress this, and see Hoehner, *Ephesians*, pp. 753-55.

228. See rightly O'Brien, *Ephesians*, p. 422; Best, *Ephesians*, p. 542.

229. O'Brien, *Ephesians*, pp. 424-25. He rightly notes that the theme of the "presentation" of God's people is connected with the final day. Cf. 2 Cor. 4.14; Rom. 14.10; 1 Cor. 8.8; Col. 1.22, 28. The term "glorious" points in the same direction.

her. "The operative and link term is 'join' (v. 31) which the LXX uses of Israel's covenant with Yahweh (Deut. 10:20; II Kings 18:6)."[230] There is some possibility of echoes from the Song of Solomon here as well in its discussion of the bride (5.1).[231]

V. 28 begins with a comparison, "in the same manner also" referring back to the example of Christ and the church. The husband's responsibility to love his wife is compared to Christ's love for the church, not with the man's love for his own body. The wife is to be considered and loved as his own *sōma* just as the church is Christ's body. Lest we accuse Paul of a degrading view of the wife as merely a "body,"[232] Sampley rightly points out that vv. 28-29 have to be read in light of Gen. 2.24, which is cited in v. 31.[233] The change to *sarx* from *sōma* in v. 29 is surely because of the influence of this text.[234] The reference to "no one" hating their own body shows clearly how far Paul is from being ascetic.[235] It is important, then, in comparing this text to 1 Corinthians 7 to say that there Paul is not an advocate of asceticism within marriage and that advocating singleness is not the same thing as advocating various sorts of extreme asceticism, including forms that treat physicality and sexuality as something inherently evil or wicked. Paul was not a Gnostic before his time in regard to these matters.[236]

The point then is not that the wife is a mere body for the husband but that there is an organic unity between husband and wife making them one flesh. It does not say that the two simply become one, or one person, but rather "one flesh." In other words they become different parts of a third entity — a couple. This may also explain why Paul does not use the headship-subordination concept of men and women in general. Only those who are united in a one-flesh union become the head and body of each other, just as the spiritual union between Christ and the church makes the headship-subordination relationship

230. Martin, *Ephesians, Colossians, and Philemon,* p. 70.

231. See Bouttier, *Ephésiens,* p. 245; Sampley, *And the Two,* pp. 45-51.

232. On which compare the analogy in Plutarch, *Advice to the Bride and Groom* 142: a husband should rule his wife not the way a master rules his property but the way a soul rules the body. MacDonald, p. 329, is right, however, that Paul does not share Plutarch's interest or belief in the soul-body dichotomy.

233. See also Jeal, *Integrating Theology and Ethics,* pp. 194-95.

234. Sampley, *And the Two,* pp. 139-45.

235. Cf. Lincoln, *Ephesians,* p. 379; M. Y. MacDonald, *The Pauline Churches: A Socio-Historical Study of Institutionalization in the Pauline and Deutero-Pauline Churches* (Cambridge: Cambridge University Press, 1988), p. 119. This hyperbolic statement is of course one more example of the fact that we need to take into account that this discourse is both Asiatic and epideictic in character and that such hyperbole to make a point is characteristic of such rhetoric.

236. See my *Women in the Earliest Churches,* pp. 54-61.

possible and real.[237] This leads to a further point: subordination presupposes a relationship of identification and union in the first place.[238] V. 33 makes even clearer that what Paul has in mind is loving one's wife as one's nearest neighbor, indeed as oneself, not merely as a part of oneself. Thus vv. 28-30 are not comments on a woman's nature or purpose but deal, rather, with the one-flesh union imagery. V. 29 exhorts the husband to feed and take tender care for his other self.[239] The language of nourishing and cherishing is found in ancient marriage contracts in the Greco-Roman world and so would be familiar to the audience as ways of talking about the marriage relationship.[240] "The lover is so closely united with his beloved that his love of her can be called love of himself."[241]

In v. 30 Paul introduces the first person plural: "because we are members of his body." The audience is drawn into the exhortation, because even if one or another of them is not married, nonetheless they are part of Christ's body. Some manuscripts offer a longer reading here, adding "from his flesh and from his bones" (ℵ, D, G, P, Chrysostom, Jerome, and various others). Besides the fact that the shorter reading has good external support and geographical spread (P46, ℵ*, A, B, etc.) there is also the question of what it would mean to say one is a member of Christ's bones. Probably the longer ending reflects the influence of the quotation in v. 31. It is possible that anti-Docetic concerns are reflected in the longer text.[242] More certainly, it needs to be remembered that already in 4.15-16 we heard about the organic relationship between the body and the Head.[243]

The quotation of Gen. 2.24 in v. 31 explains that marriage was part of God's original plan for humankind and thus also how marriage is a relationship that God uses as part of his salvation plan for humankind.[244] Except for

---

237. Caird, *Paul's Letters*, p. 89, makes the helpful point that since marriage is the only voluntary union (compared, for instance, to the sort of solidarity that is created by physical relationships and natural descent in families, clans, ethnic groups and the like), it is not an accident that marriage is the point of comparison with the relationship between the church and Christ, which also is a voluntary matter, not something derived by birth.

238. This is a very different sort of subordination than that called for in, for instance, 1 Cor. 14.34 or 1 Timothy 2, where the issue is silence and subordination or submission to the teaching, prophesying, or order of worship, not subordination to another person. The Law, referred to in 1 Corinthians 14, says nothing about submission of women to men, but it certainly does speak of the proper silence and submission when God speaks through one person or another. See my discussion in *Women in the Earliest Churches*, pp. 90-104.

239. On the verb connoting tender care cf. 1 Thess. 2.7 and see Hoehner, *Ephesians*, p. 767.

240. See Gnilka, *Epheserbrief*, p. 264.

241. Barth, *Ephesians 4–6*, p. 636.

242. See Lincoln, *Ephesians*, p. 351; Metzger, *TC*, p. 541.

243. See Perkins, "Ephesians," p. 452.

244. MacDonald, *Colossians, Ephesians*, p. 330.

inconsequential minor differences the quotation corresponds to the LXX. This text of course was important in the Jesus tradition as well (Mark 10.7-8 par.; 1 Cor. 6.16), and it seems it was important in other early Jewish discussions as well (cf. Philo, *Legum Allegoriae* 2.49).[245] It is interesting how seamlessly the quotation is enfolded into the argument without an introductory formula (cf. also 4.25-26 and 6.2 in comparison to 4.8 and 5.14 where there are introductory formulas).

There seems little doubt that Paul interprets Gen. 2.24 to refer to some sort of spiritual as well as physical union of husband and wife. In 1 Cor. 6.16 he even daringly uses the same text to talk about the physical bonding when a man has intercourse with a prostitute. For Paul intercourse is no mere momentary sexual encounter or moment of pleasure. It is an act which creates a bond between two people. From 1 Cor. 7.10 and Rom. 7.1-4 we can see that Paul thought that only death dissolved such a bond between two Christians. Possibly a reason Paul would talk about Christian husband and wife in such exalted terms, comparing their relationship to that of Christ and the church, is that he saw both relationships as meant to be indissoluble and irrevocable. More certainly, the verb *kollaō* means to glue or cement something to something else and so refers to a very strong bond (sometimes translated "cleaving"). Its expanded form *proskollaō* has the same sense and can be used to refer to people clinging to each other (Plato, *Leges* 5.728b). Here and in Mark 10.7 this verb is used in quoting Gen. 2.24. It seems likely that here it is a euphemism for or at least includes the idea of sexual intercourse, a bonding that creates a union.[246] "Each personality is enlarged by the inclusion of the other, ideally effecting the perfect blending of two separate lives into one. Continuity with the old personality is not broken, but the radical transformation resulting from the intimate personal encounter creates a new self."[247]

The great "mystery" in v. 32, as elsewhere in Ephesians, has to do with God's salvation plan for creating a people or a body of Christ, but more particularly here it has to do with the nature of the mysterious spiritual union between the two that results from the saving act, a union which neither divinizes the church nor dissolves the separate identity of either Christ or Christians.

What is the "mystery" referred to in v. 32?[248] Is it the mystery of the hidden meaning of the cited text, the mystery of Christian marriage, the mystery of the relationship of Christ and the church, or the mystery of the analogy of the

---

245. See Schnackenburg, *Ephesians*, pp. 254-55.

246. See Hoehner, *Ephesians*, p. 773.

247. R. Batey, "The *mia sarx* Union of Christ and the Church," *NTS* 13 (1967): 270-81, here p. 279.

248. See the detailed study by C. Caragounis, *The Ephesian Mysterion: Meaning and Content* (Lund: Gleerup, 1977).

two relationships? In later Christian tradition, for example in the *Gospel of Philip* 64-71, the subject of the mystery is said to be Christian marriage. But Paul tells us rather plainly that he is speaking about Christ and the church. The mystery, as elsewhere in Ephesians, has to do with God's salvation plan for creating a people or a body of Christ, but more particularly here it has to do with the nature of the mysterious spiritual union between the two that results from the saving act, a union which neither divinizes the church nor dissolves the separate identity of either Christ or Christians. The mystery is called "great" not because of its obscurity but precisely because of its significance and magnitude.[249] The emphatic "but I say to you" marks a contrast. It is found only here in Paul's letters, and elsewhere in the NT only in the adversative statements of Jesus in the Sermon on the Mount (Matt. 5.22, 28, 32, 34, 39, 44). It appears that this is Paul's way of signaling that he will allegorize the text (cf. Gal. 4.24), offering a new and different interpretation that goes beyond the usual discussion of marriage.[250]

V. 33 then must be seen as a return to the initial topic of husband and wife by way of counterpoint to what has just been said about Christ and the church. *Plēn* then should be seen as resumptive of the original topic stating what is essential after a digression — "now at any rate. . . ."[251] Only here in the household codes does the NT address husband or wife in the singular ("each of you").[252] Paul seeks thus to get the attention of each person in the audience, stressing individual responsibility. Again he stresses the husband's duty to love. By contrast, the wife is called upon, not again to submit, but to fear her husband, or, perhaps better said, respect him.[253] The respect presumably is given due to the role God has assigned him, not based on circumstances or performance, any more than reverence for Christ depends on circumstances or performance. It would seem that in both v. 28 and 33 the references to "himself" and "as himself" echo Lev. 19.18, in which case Paul is saying the wife is the nearest neighbor

---

249. Schnackenburg, *Ephesians,* p. 255.

250. See rightly, Hoehner, *Ephesians,* pp. 779-80.

251. Schnackenburg, *Ephesians,* pp. 256-57.

252. See Best, *Ephesians,* p. 558. No husband in the audience is exempt from these exhortations for any reasons. Notice, as Best also points out, that there is no element of polemic in Paul's rhetoric here. He is not combating other notions of marriage but rather offering a positive Christian exposition of marriage, which comports well with the epideictic nature of this document.

253. Some ancient philosophers taught that wives should literally fear their husbands (cf. Xenophon, *Concerning Household Management* 7.25; pseudo-Aristotle, *Concerning Household Management* 3.144.2; cf. also 1 Pet. 3.2). Here, however, the reverence or respect comes under the general heading of submitting out of reverence or holy fear of Christ. See Barth, *Ephesians 4–6,* pp. 649-50, who stresses that the fear and trembling meant here involves both respect and anticipation of the love the husband has to share.

and that the Great Commandment's second part applies to marriage.[254] Barth puts it this way: "the special form of *agapē* between husband and wife flourishes within the framework of the general love for neighbors and enemies, is the school and test case of the latter, and publicizes its reality and power. The wife is the husband's primary and exemplary neighbor."[255]

In this discussion of Christian marriage Paul has combined the theological and ethical concerns of this discourse about unity with a typological discussion of the parallels between the Christ-church and husband-wife relationships. The tone of the whole discussion is positive and without polemics, highlighting and praising the mystery that is great of a union which binds together God and God's people, and also binds believers to each other, including even in the household. No part of life, and no human relationship is beyond the grasp of the loving God who came and gave himself in Christ, so modeling self-sacrificial, servant-like, and submissive behavior, for it was Jesus who said "nevertheless, not my will but thine be done," submitting to the will of another.[256]

Children and Parents — 6.1-4 The form of exhortation to children and parents is much more precise than what precedes it — the party in question is addressed, the imperative is stated and amplified, and the motivation is presented.[257] We have 35 words addressed here to children, but only 13 in Colossians, and 16 addressed to fathers here, compared to only 10 in Colossians. Again we see that the code in Ephesians seems to be an expansion on what we find in Colossians.

Children are exhorted to obey their parents in 6.1-3. The term *tekna* here can include adult children, but it certainly is not limited to them, who in any case would not necessarily be living in the household any more.[258] As Lincoln says, "the children in view here have to be old enough to be conscious of a relationship to their Lord and to be appealed to on the basis of it, but young enough still to be in the process of being brought up (cf. 6:4)."[259] Though *hypotassō* in 5.21 is broader than *hypakouō* here, it is hardly plausible that Paul demanded a less stringent or less all-encompassing form of submission of children than of wives. Indeed, if anything "obey" may suggest a more strict standard of response and what makes this especially clear is the active imperative

---

254. See Lincoln, "The Use of the OT in Ephesians," *JSNT* 14 (1982): 16-57. Cf. P. Qualls and J. D. W. Watts, "Isaiah in Ephesians," *Review and Expositor* 93 (1996): 249-57. There is a strong case to be made for many of the ideas as well as allusions in this homily coming from Isaiah, which is in any case the most used portion of the OT in the NT.

255. Barth, *Ephesians 4–6*, p. 719.

256. See O'Brien, *Ephesians*, p. 438; Lincoln, *Ephesians*, p. 388.

257. Hoehner, *Ephesians*, p. 785.

258. O'Brien, *Ephesians*, pp. 440-41, who rightly adds that the admonition about instruction suggests Paul has particularly in mind non-adult children.

259. Lincoln, *Ephesians*, p. 403.

form of the verb here. One can conceive of situations where a spouse might disagree and so not obey a direct imperative but nonetheless submit to the consequences of such an act of "civil disobedience," showing one's respect for the head of the household. Children, on the other hand, are simply called on to obey. It is the parents they are to obey (tois goneusin). Notice that both parents are to be obeyed, though only fathers are exhorted in the next clause.

The ground or rationale for the imperative is "because this is right," or more literally "for this is righteous." In Rom. 1.29-31 Paul identifies the disobedience of children as an all too common Gentile sin, but he is on common ground with the wider culture in that no one argued against children obeying their parents (cf. Philo, De Specialibus Legibus 2.225-36; Dionysius of Halicarnassus, Roman Antiquities 2.2.26.1-4; Plutarch, Moralia 479-80). Indeed, in the Greco-Roman world a child was under the control of his or her father until he died (the Greek custom) or until he was sixty (the Roman custom). Thus it was sufficient to use the pragmatic appeal to what was generally recognized to be right.[260] But Paul also applies the sanction of Scripture by quoting the fifth commandment (Exod. 20.12; cf. Deut. 5.16), which he says is the first among the ten that comes with an accompanying promise. "First" here may refer to first in significance since this commandment is certainly not first in the Decalogue (but see below).[261] In other words, there is a divine sanction for obedience to parents that further confirms that this is the right sort of conduct. The promise provides a further motivation for the children to respond appropriately (cf. 1 Tim. 4.8).

Several things are puzzling about this. It seems on first blush, that an earlier commandment, the one about graven images, also has a promise (Exod. 20.4-6). On closer inspection however the promise there is not attached to the commandment but is part of the explanation of a jealous God and is in any case a general promise applicable to all the commandments. Thus one could say that the commandment to obey parents is the first to have a specific promise attached to it.[262] The Hebrew and LXX text speaks of living long in the (promised) land, but in Paul's quotation this is broadened to "on the earth," and "which the Lord God is giving you" is omitted.

The phrase "in the Lord" is probably original (see p. 315 n. 168 above) and shows that Paul is continuing the discussion in a Christian vein, not commenting on households of mixed religion. It is interesting, as MacDonald says, that Christian children are here addressed directly, which presupposes that they would be in the listening audience.[263] Schnackenburg is surely right that since the promise here has to do with being well and living long on earth, it is not a

---

260. Jeal, Integrating Theology, p. 195.

261. See Best, Ephesians, p. 567.

262. See Hoehner, Ephesians, pp. 790-91.

263. MacDonald, Colossians, Ephesians, p. 332.

promise about eternal benefits, and since such concepts of "shalom" or well-being are common from early Judaism there is no good reason to see this verse as evidence of a loss of a sense of future eschatology or the possible imminence of Christ's return.[264] Since Paul never speaks or speculates about the timing of that return, he expects his converts to go on with Christian life as it should be lived, whether Christ comes sooner or later, always of course having one eye on the horizon.[265] Deut. 4.4 and 5.33 provide the background here where a promise of long life is connected with obedience to the Law. It is important to note that Paul makes children, as well as wives and slaves, as responsible for the good ordering of the household as he does the head of the household. This distinguishes what he says from some of the contemporary discussions of the matter.[266] Since Paul in all likelihood is not addressing converts who lived in Roman colony cities in Asia, it is not at all clear that the audience was directly under Roman laws about the *patria potestas,* and since we know so little about Asian Greek laws about such matters, it is hard to judge how different Paul's exhortations are from the prevailing views among his audience.[267]

The parallel exhortation in 6.4 is probably addressed to fathers in particular. *Pateres* could on occasion refer to parents in general (Heb. 11.23), especially in light of the reference to discipline or admonition, which was traditionally the father's role.[268] This focus on the father is not entirely a surprise since, as we have seen, the children in view here must be old enough to educate, and since in the Greco-Roman world, after age seven and until about age sixteen the father ostensibly had charge of a son's education (cf. Plutarch, *Cato Major* 20; Prudentius, *Contra Symmachum* 1.197-214), though a pedagogue and a tutor were normally enlisted to aid in the task. The education, besides learning to read and write, included training in ethics, religion, household management, philosophy, public service (liturgies), and the early exercises which would lead to a knowledge of rhetoric (pseudo-Plutarch, *Education of Children* 7DE).

---

264. Schnackenburg, *Ephesians,* p. 262.

265. Against Lincoln, *Ephesians,* pp. 405-6. Hoehner, *Ephesians,* p. 794, is right in noting: "The English term 'imminent' can connote nearness of time but the NT idea of imminency, especially in connection with the parousia, is not so concerned with the nearness of time, but rather the possibility of its occurrence at any time."

266. See Barth, *Ephesians 4–6,* p. 757: "When Paul places major emphasis on the contributions of the 'weaker' members, in actuality he takes a revolutionary step. *They* above all shall and will be the carriers of responsibility, changes, and progress!"

267. Lincoln, *Ephesians,* pp. 398-402, gives a helpful survey of Roman and Jewish discussions but does not take adequately into consideration the Greek factor in Asia.

268. There are several good reasons for this conclusion here: 1) the change in terminology from "parents" to "fathers"; 2) the previous reference to obeying mothers does not find a parallel reference to mothers here; 3) the fact that Paul in this household code is stressing the responsibilities of the head of the household. See MacDonald, *Colossians, Ephesians,* p. 333.

Best rightly notes that the father is in as much need of exhortation about proper behavior in relation to his children as the children are.[269] The exhortation involves one remark about what is wrong for a father to do and one about what is right to do, set off by *mē . . . alla* to indicate a contrast.[270] The father is not to make his children angry (cf. Col. 3.21 and see pp. 192-93 above). "Fathers are made responsible for ensuring that they do not provoke anger in their children. This involves avoiding attitudes, words, and actions which would drive a child to angry exasperation or resentment and thus rules out excessively severe discipline, unreasonably harsh demands, abuse of authority, arbitrariness, unfairness, constant nagging and condemnation, subjecting a child to humiliation, and all forms of gross insensitivity to a child's needs and sensibilities."[271] While Paul was not the only advocate of such moderation (cf. pseudo-Phocylides 207; Seneca, *De Ira* 2.21.1-3; Plutarch *Moralia, De liberis educandis* 12a), it is noteworthy that he insists on children not being treated as mere property. Rather, they deserve respect. We see an Asiatic flavor in the second half of this verse, which literally reads "bringing up your children in the upbringing. . . ." *Paideia* can have the sense of "discipline," but it is probably used more broadly here to refer to training or upbringing or even instruction (cf. Sir. 1.27, where it is coupled with "wisdom"). *Nouthesia,* translated "admonition," involves verbal correction. In the earlier Jewish wisdom literature this was seen as an essential part of a father's role in relationship to his children (cf. Wis. 11.10; 12.25-26; Philo, *De Specialibus Legibus* 2.229-32 says discipline was especially the father's task; cf. 1 Cor. 10.11; Tit. 3.10).

Paul's use of *tekna,* "children," here may suggest the education of both male and female children, which was practiced to some degree in the Greco-Roman world and in early Judaism, though it seems to have been rare or exceptional.[272] "Your children" also limits the field of focus and authority to one's own children.[273] It is not just any sort of education that is referred to here. It is Christian education — the training and admonition of the Lord. "Of the Lord" could mean either with the Lord in view or with the Lord using the father as the instructor, probably the former.[274] The exhortation to the father then suggests that a gentle and generous approach is in keeping with this education being done in a Christian way as well as having Christian content. This is strikingly different from what we hear in Sir. 30.1-13, which stresses strict discipline including constant correction and beating so that the son will become like his fa-

---

269. Best, *Ephesians,* p. 568.
270. See Jeal, *Integrating Theology and Ethics,* p. 195.
271. Lincoln, *Ephesians,* p. 406.
272. See my *Women in the Earliest Churches,* pp. 5-23.
273. O'Brien, *Ephesians,* p. 446.
274. See Best, *Ephesians,* p. 569.

ther. Here the father is to model Christlike behavior and pedagogy as part of the way the Christian child learns.[275] Fathers modeling virtues or behavior were seen as part of good Greek praxis of managing the home and educating one's offspring (Plato, *Leges* 5.729B; *Protagoras* 324b-25a).

Slaves and Masters — 6.5-9   This material is a perfect example, if taken in the wrong way (not recognizing the context and trajectory), of how a superficial treatment of the material will lead to conclusions opposite to what is intended. Paul is not endorsing slavery or providing a Christian rationale to bolster and undergird the institution.[276] On the contrary, he is trying to reform an existing institution within the context of the Christian household. The argument here is a further step along the way toward what Paul will say in Philemon, and it is probably an adaptation and expansion of Col. 3.22-25.[277] It is only a little longer than the parallel text (here 28 words are addressed to the master, in Colossians only 18). It is second order moral discourse — an address to those who have already heard the opening salvo such as we find in Colossians on this subject, but also an address to those with whom Paul does not have the intimacy of relationship that we find between Paul and Philemon.[278]

Just how Christian the rhetoric is here is nicely indicated by Jeal's summary: "The argument, succinctly, is that Christ is lord of all, and every action in the master/slave relationship should be done with the connection of both parties to Christ fully in mind."[279] The slave's service is ultimately to the Lord, and the master's supervision is to be done with full cognizance that he is accountable to the Lord for what he says and does. In other words, the slave's actions cease to be mere servitude to a human master, and the master's actions cease to be those of one who has absolute authority over another human being. Both parties are called on to be proactive, not reactive to their situations. In both cases their eyes must be on the Lord and on how to please him, not on mundane or merely human considerations and factors. In 6.5, as in 5.22, 25, 29, the argument is based on the relationship to Christ. In v. 8 the argument is based on eschatology. "The Christological argument has the strongest and the determinative position. It implies that both the supposedly high and the supposedly low are subordinated to the same highest authority. Therefore, before the Lord *and* before one another, parents and children, masters and slaves occupy the same position: all must obey (6.1, 4-7, 9). In this they are equals. . . . To the Christological basis of the exhorta-

---

275. See Schnackenburg, *Ephesians*, pp. 262-63.

276. Against Perkins, "Ephesians," p. 454; MacDonald, *Colossians, Ephesians*, p. 341.

277. See Perkins, "Ephesians," pp. 451-53.

278. See Martin, *Ephesians, Colossians, Philemon*, p. 74: "The local situation at Colossae is not reflected in Ephesians which transposes the teaching into a more general ethical rubric." This is because Paul is addressing a general audience of wider scope and nature.

279. Jeal, *Integrating Theology*, p. 196.

tion belongs its eschatological foundation. . . . Sweating slaves and threatening masters alike are to live now as people determined by the future."[280]

Exhorting slaves directly as moral agents is remarkable since normal Greco-Roman household counsel was directed only to the master.[281] "Fear and trembling" are the typical reactions to God of a Christian as they work out their Christian lives (cf. Phil. 2.12; Col. 3.22; also on this phrase 1 Cor. 2.3; 2 Cor. 7.15). Paul is the only NT writer to use the phrase. He is not advising false humility or cringing before a human master. Rather he is redirecting the slaves' service to God with God becoming the ultimate authority figure in their lives.[282] They are to do this "in singleness of heart," which means without duplicity, hypocrisy, or ulterior motives (cf. Tit 2.9-10 on the temptations to which they were prey). "Masters according to the flesh" (cf. Col. 3.22) implies a contrast or comparison with the slaves' Master in heaven, namely Christ. "For Christian slaves there was ultimately one *kyrios,* and reminding them of this by calling their masters *kata sarka* in distinction from the Master in heaven immediately sets the social structures of the household in a Christian perspective and limits their significance."[283] Even the slave is called to stop living a lie and instead to do his life work with integrity in a way that glorifies God and genuinely serves others.[284] Lincoln is right that, unlike *Didache* 4.11, the earthly master is not said here to stand in the stead of the heavenly Master as his representative.[285] Rather the earthly master is placed under and is answerable to the heavenly Master.

What is especially being critiqued in v. 6 is work done only when the human master is watching, work done to curry favor with the human master. Rather, since they are now Christ's slaves, the slaves are to look to please him. *Opthalmodoulia* occurs only here and in Col. 3.22 in ancient literature and is probably a Pauline coinage, once again demonstrating Paul's adeptness at rhetorical invention. It is not certain whether it means service rendered only while the master is watching or service meant to get his attention.[286] Hoehner sug-

---

280. Barth, *Ephesians 4–6,* p. 756. "The content of the *Haustafel* (5:21–6:9) is thoroughly permeated by references to the Lord. Step by step it is totally dependent upon the reality and validity of Christ's work and his presence." He is right, in my judgment, that we are not dealing with a mere Christian sugar-coating of an existing institution. Paul is rewriting the nature of the institutions, renovating them from the inside out with christological and eschatological modifications and sanctions.

281. See O'Brien, *Ephesians,* pp. 448-49.

282. See rightly, Caird, *Paul's Letters,* p. 90.

283. Lincoln, *Ephesians,* p. 420.

284. Schnackenburg, *Ephesians,* p. 263.

285. Lincoln, *Ephesians,* p. 421.

286. See MacDonald, *Colossians, Ephesians,* p. 334. C. F. D. Moule, "A Note on *opthalmodoulia,*" *ExpT* 59 (1947-48): 250, suggests that it refers to someone doing only what the master can see and so cutting corners.

gests that it means outward service not matched by inward dedication, but this goes beyond the plain sense of the word.[287]

Another proof of the close connection between the Colossian code and what we find here is that *anthrōpareskoi* is also only found here and in Col. 3.22 in the NT. It refers to people-pleasers as opposed to "slaves of Christ." The latter concept norms the rest of the discussion. The idea here is that the Christian slave in fact belongs to Christ and is in the first place accountable for his or her behavior to Christ. Such a slave is only on loan, so to speak, to the human master, and so the human master's authority is attenuated and indeed is restricted by what God requires of the Christian master. "Slave of Christ" is even applied to a free person in 1 Cor. 7.20-22, and the same is implied here because masters are said to have a heavenly Master. The slaves in question are to carry out the will of God from their very inner selves (*ek psychēs*). Enthusiasm was seen not only as a virtue in a slave (Lucian, *Bis Accusatus* 16) but in POxy 494.6 a slave is freed because of his enthusiasm and affection in serving his master. Paul may then be inculcating virtues here that lead to emancipation.

V. 7 makes evident just how radical Paul's advice really is. The slave is to serve with enthusiasm (literally "with goodwill," *met' eunoias*), doing it as if for the Lord, not for humans. Now of course the basic posture of a slave in antiquity is of one who has no choice about matters. The master's wish is the slave's command. But here Paul is saying that this is no longer the case in a Christian household. Here the will that must be done even by the slave is the will of God, and the slave is not to consider himself to be serving human masters, which is of course what every ancient slave normally did assume he was doing. The full force of the contrast "as to the Lord and not as to humans" must be felt to appreciate Paul's argument.

V. 8 brings in a reference to eschatological reward. Paul in good epideictic fashion relies in both v. 8 and v. 9 on what the audience already knows about their Lord and their faith (*eidotes hoti* in both verses).[288] Regardless of social station or status one will be rewarded, each one for whatever good she or he has done.[289] The divine arithmetic is done differently than human arithmetic, for God plays no favorites. The verb *komizō* means "receive back" or "be requited" (see Col. 3.25; pp. 194-95 above). "The heavenly Lord overlooks nothing and nobody and treats slaves no differently from free people. Thus the addition 'be he slave or free,' which is at first surprising, makes sense: the heavenly Lord does

---

287. Hoehner, *Ephesians*, p. 808.

288. See Jeal, *Integrating Theology and Ethics*, p. 196.

289. Martin, *Ephesians, Colossians, Philemon*, p. 74. The future eschatological stress here should be noted. It is characteristic of Paul to talk about future scrutiny of human, including Christian, endeavors (cf. 1 Cor. 4.5; 2 Cor. 5.10; Rom. 14.12).

not differentiate."[290] But this raises a pressing question: Should human beings then be partial and make such distinctions between slaves and free persons, for do we not have a call here to be like our heavenly Master?

V. 9 begins with a reference to "their Master and yours." Here Paul, in not so subtle a way, indicates that the real Master of these slaves is Christ, just as he is the real Master of the owners. Masters are said to share the same motivation and attitude and consideration for doing things in a Christian way as slaves. "Do the same" demands "a corresponding behavior on the part of masters."[291] But Chrysostom (twenty-second homily on Ephesians) took this to mean that masters, since they are Christians and among those who must respond to the exhortation in 5.21, are actually to serve their slaves.[292] He even adds "for the master himself is a servant." This calling of all Christians to servanthood, and so to submitting to one another comports with the teaching of Jesus about himself being a servant of others and his exhortation to his disciples to be the same way (Mark 10.45; Luke 22.24-29). Chrysostom's understanding is a possible reading of "do the same" and would certainly make the discourse even more radical.[293] There was the precedent in the larger culture of the celebration of Saturnalia, during which masters and slaves exchanged roles for a day. But here Paul is referring to an ongoing Christian way of slaves and masters relating to each other and to the Lord.[294]

Masters are on the one hand to stop threatening and should reward good behavior. Masters and slaves have equal status before God, and he will judge both as adult Christian moral agents. There is no partiality with the Lord in heaven, but then this implies that there should also be none with earthly lords either, not least because the lord has a Lord in heaven whom he must answer to.[295] *Prosōpolēmpsia*, "partiality," seems to have appeared for the first time in

---

290. Schnackenburg, *Ephesians*, pp. 264-65.

291. Schnackenburg, *Ephesians*, p. 265.

292. O'Brien, *Ephesians*, p. 454, too quickly dismisses this possibility.

293. All of Chrysostom's twenty-second homily on Ephesians should be read. He argues that the Bible recognizes that slavery is in the world because of sin. He calls it "the fruit of covetousness, of degradation, of savagery." He recognizes that Paul is trying to reform a fallen situation with his exhortations here. Above all, he makes it clear that it is nonsense to say that Eph. 5.21 could not apply to each and every Christian rather than just to those already subordinate in society. If masters can become servants, then those who exercise authority over others have learned to submit and serve.

294. This is second order moral discourse, and Paul is not yet ready to discuss manumission and the like in such a context. He reserves this for the third order discourse in Philemon. See pp. 68-73 above. It was clearly a topic of regular Christian discussion by the end of the first century and in fact was seen as something of a Christian duty. Cf. *1 Clement* 55.2; Ignatius, *Polycarp* 4.3; Hermas, *Similitude* 1.8; Best, *Ephesians*, p. 580.

295. MacDonald, *Colossians, Ephesians*, p. 336.

Greek literature in the NT (cf. Rom. 2.11; Col. 3.25; Jas. 2.1). It might have some background in the Hebrew concept of "lifting the face" indicating an elevation of someone's status and honor, and so a way of giving another more respect (Lev. 19.15; Deut. 1.27; 16.19).[296] Lincoln suggests that the Greek word is a short form of *prosōpon lambanein,* which literally means to take or judge at face value.[297] J. M. Bassler points out that this notion of the impartiality of God is what undergirds Paul's statement in Gal. 3.28 about the equality of slave and free (as well as Jew and Gentile and male and female) in Christ.[298] But strictly speaking what Gal. 3.28 says is that in Christ there is neither slave nor free, which explains why here and in the parallel sections in Colossians and Philemon Paul has been in the process of deconstructing various aspects of the social relationship of masters and slaves, bit by bit.

As Best points out, there are many relationships within the household Paul does not discuss (slaves relating to slaves, children relating to children, masters relating to their freedmen and freedwomen, and so on).[299] Paul only seeks to treat a representative sampling of such relationships, showing how they can be lived out in a Christian manner. Again however it is crucial to remember the trajectory of the argument and not just its position. We are one step closer to Philemon here than we were in Colossians. Recognizing this fact allows us to evaluate this material more fairly and in its context as second order moral discourse.

296. See O'Brien, *Ephesians,* p. 455.

297. Lincoln, *Ephesians,* p. 424.

298. J. M. Bassler, *Divine Impartiality: Paul and a Theological Axiom* (Chico: Scholars, 1982), pp. 178-83.

299. Best, *Ephesians,* p. 582.

Peroratio — Standing notwithstanding the Opposition — 6.10-20

In any oral discourse, the final salvo needs to be memorable as it is probably what the audience will most remember about the speech or proclamation. From a rhetorical point of view the final exhortation is in the emphatic position, and one may conclude that this is what Paul has been working toward all along as a climax to his discourse.[1] The peroratio in an epideictic piece of rhetoric should emphasize behavior in the present which will reflect the values and virtues of the community addressed and help them to live out those values. It is no accident that this peroratio emphasizes "standing" rather than advancing or retreating, which would involve a change in behavior. Even the previous emphasis on "walking" was an exhortation to continue walking in the way the audience has begun to behave (4.1, 17; 5.2, 8, 15).

It is interesting that Paul here returns to the more full blown Asiatic and epideictic style that was only to some degree in evidence in 4.1–6.9 but was clearly manifest in chs. 1–3. This suggests that he has been using traditional material in 4.1–6.9 that he has not fully transformed for this epideictic discourse, particularly in the household codes, but it also reflects that Paul is well aware of the conventions that applied to the peroratio, which, as Quintilian says, is where one should give free rein to the torrent of one's emotions and eloquence (*Inst. Or.* 4.1.28; 6.1.51; cf. 6.1.9-10).[2] For "while the chief task of the peroration

---

1. See G. D. Fee, *God's Empowering Presence* (Peabody: Hendrickson, 1994), p. 723.

2. It is interesting that Chrysostom saw clearly what many modern commentators have not been able to see, namely that Eph. 6.10-20 is a carefully composed and rhetorically adept peroration. He devotes two whole sermons and part of a third (his twenty-second through twenty-fourth homilies on Ephesians) to expounding Paul's rhetoric here, and he emphasizes the parallels with the Roman military. For example, he stresses that the soldier's

consists of amplification, we may legitimately make free use of words and reflections that are magnificent and ornate. It is at the close of our drama that we must really stir the theater . . ." (6.1.52). "For it is in its power over the emotions that the life and soul of oratory is to be found" (6.2.7).

The two major functions of the peroratio were to offer something of a recapitulation of major themes and also to exhibit pathos, appealing to the deeper emotions of the audience (particularly anger, fear, and pity; see *Inst. Or.* 6.2.20). On this latter matter, it is especially important to have a rhetorically informed view of what Paul is doing here, or else one may take the "sturm und drang" of Paul's emotive rhetoric here as a sign that there were major concerns about the cosmic powers, astrology, magic, and the like among Paul's audience.[3] To the contrary, Paul is following the proper rhetorical conventions here, seeking to refresh the memory as well as arouse the deeper emotions with a stirring call to arms (cf. Aristotle, *Rhet.* 3.19.1-6; Quintilian, *Inst. Or.* 6.1.1). There need not have been specific issues in this audience for Paul to have spoken this way since the worldview enunciated here was widely shared by early Christians. What is clear is that we have a helpful recapitulation especially of concepts and ideas from the eulogy and the thanksgiving (cf. 1.3-14, 16-23). Christians are called here to preserve and hold on to their core values against the attacks of the dark powers. They are to stand on that which they have petitioned God about and praised him for in the beginning of the discourse.[4]

As Jeal points out, this peroratio develops nicely out of the parenesis which preceded in 4.1–6.9 in that previously the discussion has been about behavior in relationship to other Christians and to a lesser extent non-Christians, but now the discussion is about behavior in relationship to the devil and the cosmic powers.[5] But this peroration also does a fine job of meeting the require-

---

ability to stand firmly on solid ground is crucial to his ability to defend himself, and he stresses the devil's stratagems and ability to deceive the opposition. He likens the rhetorical elements of enumeration and emotional appeal to "drawing up this army and arousing their zeal" (beginning of the twenty-third homily).

3. Cf. for instance what happens with C. E. Arnold, *Ephesians: Power and Magic* (Cambridge: Cambridge University Press, 1989), pp. 103-21, who takes this material at face value, not taking into account the deliberate upping of the emotional ante and the rhetorical hyperbole involved here. Another sort of false conclusion would be to take this peroratio as some sort of an appeal to go on the offensive against the powers of darkness, when in fact Paul's exhortation is to stand and withstand the onslaught of the fiery darts. The posture urged here is defensive, not a call to a deliverance ministry.

4. See P. T. O'Brien, *The Letter to the Ephesians* (Grand Rapids: Eerdmans, 1999), p. 459.

5. R. R. Jeal, *Integrating Theology and Ethics in Ephesians: The Ethos of Communication* (Lewiston: Mellen, 2000), p. 197.

ments of appealing to authority as a form of amplification and making the discourse's conclusion more compelling. Thus for example, Paul draws on a number of passages from the LXX version of Isaiah (11.4, 5; 49.2; 52.7; 59.17) as well as Wis. 5.17-20 in presenting the armor of God image (cf. Cicero, *De Inventione* 1.53.101; *Rhet. ad Her.* 2.30.48).[6]

Lincoln has now presented us with a compelling analysis of how this peroratio not only recapitulates major themes from earlier in Ephesians (prayer, the mystery, etc.) but involves striking rhetorical invention in that it is modeled on the exhortation of a commander to his troops before they go into battle.[7] Such speeches fell into the category of epideictic rhetoric,[8] and one thing that certainly characterizes such speeches can be summarized as "nothing succeeds (rhetorically speaking) like excess." The troops had to be galvanized and steeled for battle. Effusive speech and amplification were the order of the day (e.g., Thucydides 2.89; Xenophon, *Cyropaedia* 1.4; Polybius 3.63; Dionysius of Halicarnassus 6.6; Diodorus Siculus 18.15; Dio Cassius 38.36-46). No form of rhetoric so suited such harangues as epideictic Asiatic rhetoric for it was already full of emotion and the use of repetition and redundancy.

In this particular peroratio we have first the recapitulation and amplification followed by the pathos in the reference to prayer for Paul the ambassador in chains.[9] In fact we see the appeal to several emotions in this peroration — both fear and courage are aroused, followed in the end by an appeal to empathy or pity, which Quintilian says is the chief emotion one ought to arouse at the end of a peroration (6.1.27, 46). Paul's peroratio has three parts: 6.10-13 provides the opening salvo and exhortation to take up the armor of God, vv. 14-17 provide the rhetorical invention, linking the parts of the armor to various virtues and divine gifts, and vv. 18-20 return to the theme of prayer so stressed in chs. 1–3 with a final effort at pathos with the reference to Paul in chains needing

---

6. See A. T. Lincoln, "'Stand, Therefore . . .': Ephesians 6:10-20 as Peroratio," *Biblical Interpretation* 3 (1995): 99-114. Where I would differ from Lincoln is that I would not see 4.1–6.9 as deliberative in form, and thus this peroratio develops quite nicely out of the epideictic reaffirmation of values already held and being observed in that section of Ephesians. See pp. 279-83 above.

7. See especially Lincoln, "Stand, Therefore."

8. See T. C. Burgess, "Epideictic Literature," *Studies in Classical Philology* 3 (1902): 209-14, 231-33.

9. Since I do not see this discourse as pseudonymous, I disagree with Lincoln about the rhetorical technique of "personification" being used here. No, Paul is simply being himself as in Phlm. 9-10; Gal. 6.17; and elsewhere. Paul is not reluctant to use his own suffering or detention as a tool to invoke empathy in the audience and compliance with his exhortations. Quintilian says it is appropriate and often necessary to mention one's own wounds and suffering in the peroration to arouse the audience to action (*Inst. Or.* 6.1.21).

prayer.[10] We move from the call to preparation for battle and assuming a defensive posture to encouragement by a description of the armor available to a reference to the human commander or leader being in chains and needing prayer. This last would only reinforce the exhortation to protect oneself and stand firm. There is a striking partial parallel to what we find here in Wis. 5.1-2: "Then the righteous person with much boldness and freedom . . . will stand and confront his persecutors and those who thought nothing of his labors. Seeing this, they will be shaken with a dreadful fear and will be utterly amazed at the incredibleness of his deliverance."[11]

Cicero says that amplification should above all include metaphors or dramatic imagery to conclude and cinch an act of persuasion (*De Partitionibus Oratoriae* 15.53). Quintilian urges a use of a variety of figures of speech in a recapitulation, even though he adds "this final recapitulation must be as brief as possible. . . . On the other hand the points selected for enumeration must be treated with weight and dignity, enlivened by apt reflections and diversified by suitable figures" (*Inst. Or.* 6.1.2). He goes on to emphasize that one must touch on large themes and touchstones of the community, appealing to truth, justice, and the community's larger interests (6.1.7). It is then no accident that Paul refers to truth, righteousness, and the like as he enumerates the parts of the armor. Quintilian also adds that the appeal to fear and discussion of the danger the adversary presents should come in the peroration rather than in the exordium (6.1.12-13). Again it is not accidental that Paul refers to the devil and his minions in the peroratio. It is also no accident that Paul so strongly appeals to the audience at this juncture to stand. He believes, at the end of the day, that the church has a crucial role to play in the cosmic drama, as it must bear witness, not least by its very existence, that the powers are doomed (3.10). Its members will stand and withstand the onslaught, but only if they actively put on the full armor of God, God's own armor, and equip themselves with the traits and gifts of God listed here.[12] "These concluding verses serve as an effective peroration to Ephesians because they focus Christian attention and behavior on the crucial and emotional struggle against the forces that had formerly led the recipients to sin and ensuing death (2:1-3)."[13] Such a discourse would be apt for an audience composed overwhelmingly of Gentile converts, as this one was. It was also apt because it was penned by the apostle to the Gentiles concerned that his audience continue to hold on to the truths and virtues previously taught them.

---

10. See the analysis by P. Perkins, "Ephesians," *New Interpreter's Bible* XI (Nashville: Abingdon, 2000), p. 458.

11. See the discussion in R. A. Wild, "Put on the Armor of God," *The Bible Today* 36 (1998): 365-70, here p. 370.

12. Lincoln, "Stand, Therefore," p. 102.

13. Jeal, *Integrating Theology and Ethics,* p. 198.

Finally, be strong in the Lord and in the might of his strength. Put on the full armor of God in order for you to be able to stand firm against the stratagems of the devil, because we are not wrestling with blood and flesh, but with the rulers and authorities, with the world rulers of this darkness, with the spiritual forces of evil in the heavenlies. Because of this take up the full armor of God in order that you might be able to stand in the day of evil and, having won through everything, to stand. Stand then, girding your loins in truth, and putting on the breastplate of righteousness, and shoeing the feet in the readiness of the gospel of peace, in everything taking up the shield of faith with which you will be able to quench all the flaming darts of evil, and take the helmet of salvation and the sword of the Spirit, which is the word of God, through every prayer and petition praying on every occasion in the Spirit and for this being alert in all perseverance and prayers for all the saints and for me in order that a word be given to be with the opening of my mouth in freedom of speech to make known the mystery of the gospel, for which I am ambassador in chains, in order for me to speak freely in it, as it is necessary for me to speak.

Here one of Paul's typical extended military metaphors (cf. 1 Thess. 5.8; Rom. 13.12; 2 Cor. 6.7; 10.3-4; 2 Tim. 2.3) serves as a final emotional appeal (the peroratio). It describes how Christians are in the midst of spiritual warfare and should put on the very armor of God, which is always complete and adequate. Perseverance in the long run requires strength and being adequately equipped with such things as faith, the gospel message, righteousness, and hope. The exhortation here is similar to what we find in a shorter form at the conclusion of another Pauline discourse (1 Cor. 16.13), and it should be noted that Paul sometimes also makes a final remark about the demise of the powers of darkness (Rom. 16.20).

The peroration probably begins in v. 10 with *to loipon* ("finally"), though *tou loipou* ("from now on") also has good textual support. As Hoehner points out, however, the former reading has better geographical spread as well as early and strong witnesses and should be preferred here, since "from now on" is only supported by manuscripts of the Alexandrian text type.[14] A further reason to support this conclusion is that "finally" is the appropriate way to begin the peroration in a rhetorical discourse such as this one. Not surprisingly, there is no similar exhortation to "stand" in Colossians precisely because it is not an example of epideictic rhetoric but is deliberative in character and does want to urge a change in behavior.[15] The exhortation

14. H. Hoehner, *Ephesians* (Grand Rapids: Baker, 2002), p. 819 and n. 1.

15. One of the best ways to explain most of the differences between Colossians and Ephesians is by rhetorical analysis. Each document confines itself to material appropriate to its respective type of rhetoric, and even many of the alterations made in the Ephesian han-

here could be either "be strong" or if taken as passive "be strengthened," probably the former (cf. Josh. 1.6-9).[16]

The Christian is urged in v. 11 to put on the *panoplia*, the full armor of God, by which is meant not merely the armor that God gives but the armor God wears. The image here is of the fully-armed foot soldier. There seem to be two primary sources of the imagery: the description of Yahweh as a warrior in Isa. 59.17 and elsewhere, which refers to armor God is not merely the maker of but also the wearer of when he is attacked by his foes, and the armor worn by Roman soldiers, all the more so since Paul is under house arrest and could likely examine such armor on a regular basis (cf. Polybius 6.23; Judith 14.3). The description is not intended to be complete, just representative and evocative. Standing firm requires effort. It does not automatically happen. Effort must be made to equip oneself with these protective attributes, qualities, or resources.

The devil is said to have his methods or wiles.[17] Here *methodeias* probably means "schemes" or "strategems" since the imagery is military (see 4.14).[18] The idea is that Satan plots and attacks believers. "Mention of the schemes of the devil reminds us of the trickery and subterfuge by which evil and temptation present themselves in our lives. Evil rarely looks evil until it accomplishes its goal; it gains entrance by appearing attractive, desirable, and perfectly legitimate. It is a baited and camouflaged trap."[19]

The armor here is for protection against attack, not for going on the offensive against Satan.[20] This is made clear by the main verb, which emphasizes standing and withstanding, not advancing or attacking. The other main verbs suggest the same: resist, pray, be alert, watch. One is to stand and protect one's turf, not attempt to take over Satan's turf. Arnold is correct that this part of the

---

dling of material shared in common with Colossians are made with the difference in rhetorical approach under consideration. The style (Asiatic) is shared in common, but the rhetorical species differs.

16. See O'Brien, *Ephesians*, p. 460. The middle sense of "be strong" makes better sense in light of the verbal sense of what follows the imperative to "receive."

17. R. Schnackenburg, *The Epistle to the Ephesians*, trans. H. Heron (Edinburgh: Clark, 1991), p. 272, rightly points out that Paul uses here the less Semitic term *diabolos* rather than "the Satan," which may relate to the fact that the audience is overwhelmingly Gentile. This may also explain use of *diabolos* in Luke-Acts and 1 John 3.8, 10, but the term is also found in documents directed to Jewish Christians (Jas. 4.7; 1 Pet. 5.8; Jude 9).

18. G. B. Caird, *Paul's Letters from Prison* (Oxford: Oxford University Press, 1976), p. 92.

19. K. Snodgrass, *Ephesians* (Grand Rapids: Zondervan, 1996), p. 339.

20. Against T. R. Yoder-Neufeld, *'Put on the Armour of God': The Divine Warrior from Isaiah to Ephesians* (Sheffield: Sheffield Academic, 1997), who argues that Paul portrays the believer as the Divine Warrior going on the offensive against Satan. See the critique in Hoehner, *Ephesians*, p. 818.

discourse, picking up on a theme in 1.10, places a heavy emphasis on power words (vv. 10, 11, 13, 16).[21]

Paul is as clear as he can be in v. 12 that the real enemies are not human beings or human institutions but Satan and his spiritual forces (pneumatika), though humans can be tempted, deceived, and even used by the dark powers (cf. 2.2; 4.14).[22] It is all too easy to mistake the human vessel of evil for evil itself. Palē originally referred to a wrestling match, but could also connote a "fight." If the former image is in view here, then we are to imagine close combat, hand to hand.[23] But, as Lincoln points out, this term simply stands for any contest or battle and was often used of military battles (cf. Euripides, Heracles 159; Philo, De Abrahamo 243; 2 Macc. 10.28; 14.18).[24]

V. 12 then speaks of the spiritual forces of darkness. Notice again that there is evil in the heavenlies (see pp. 243-45 above on the prince of the power of the air). Again, Paul is referring to the spirit world, not the dwelling place of God. A new term comes up — kosmokratōr. This literally means "world ruler." It was originally an astrological term used of the planets and stars with the belief that they were gods and had control over human destinies. Thus we have here a combination of familiar terms ("rulers," "authorities") with forms found only here, and Schnackenburg suggests that what we have here is rhetorical amplification rather than a real delineation of four separate groups of supernatural evil beings.[25] This is particularly clear from the last term, pneumatika, which is a general term for all such dark powers.[26] The amplification indicates the dangerous nature of these beings. Jewish apocalyptic literature used such terms to refer to pagan deities, demoting them to the level of lesser demonic beings (cf. Jubilees 10.3-13; 1 Enoch 15.8-12; Testament of Simeon 4.9), as does Paul himself (1 Cor. 10.20).

V. 13 speaks of being able to stand in the evil day, the climactic day of tribulation which precedes the end of the world (cf. 1 Cor. 7.26; 1 Thess. 5.2-4; 1 Enoch 50.2; 55.3; 63.8; Jubilees 23.11-13; Assumption of Moses 1.18; Testament of Levi 5.5; 1QM 15.12).[27] As is characteristic of Asiatic rhetoric we have a good

---

21. Arnold, Ephesians: Power and Magic, pp. 107-12.

22. Here W. Carr, Angels and Principalities: The Background, Meaning, and Development of the Pauline Phrase hai archai kai hai exousiai (Cambridge: Cambridge University Press, 1981), pp. 104-10, resorts to special pleading without textual evidence that this text is a later interpolation into Ephesians because of its reference to malevolent spirits. See the refutation of Carr in C. E. Arnold, "The Exorcism of Ephesians 6.12 in Recent Research," JSNT 30 (1987): 71-87.

23. See M. E. Gudorf, "The Use of palē in Ephesians 6:12," JBL 117 (1998): 334.

24. See A. T. Lincoln, Ephesians (Waco: Word, 1990), p. 444.

25. Schnackenburg, Ephesians, p. 268.

26. Lincoln, Ephesians, p. 445.

27. Hoehner, Ephesians, p. 834, resorts to special pleading to deny this refers to the final great evil day.

deal of repetition here from the material in vv. 10-11.[28] Nothing is said about the believer being absent in the evil day. Already Paul has said that the days are evil, but now he is speaking of the climax of such times.[29] He is quite convinced that Christians must be prepared to go through and stand up under the great tribulation.[30] This is not about victory or defeat in that day but about "holding fast to territory already won by Christ,"[31] namely the spiritual life of the believer.

V. 14 suggests that Paul also believes that the protection God's armor provides will be sufficient, but all of it must be put on.[32] What this amounts to is embracing and embodying the virtues spoken of as well as accepting the divine gifts offered. The key verb in this portion of the peroration is *katergazomai*, which refers sometimes to combat that leads to victory[33] but in Paul does not have the sense of "conquer" or "subdue" but rather either "prepare" (2 Cor. 5.5) or "accomplish," "bring about" (Rom. 7.15-20; 2 Cor. 9.11; Phil. 2.12),[34] and this is true elsewhere in the NT as well.[35] The sense here is that victory comes by holding one's ground and not giving in an inch to the forces of evil ("resist the devil and he will flee from you"). "The items listed are taken from the model of the soldier at the place of duty and ready for battle. The belt is a sign of this preparedness as the Romans spoke of *miles accinctus,* meaning a soldier on parade, with his belt (Latin *cingulum*) fastened in position."[36]

The Christian does not have just a few assets here and there but rather the weapons of God revealed in Scripture (see 2 Cor. 10.4).[37] But he or she must appropriate these assets and qualities and gifts from God, must put them on and then stand fast. There is some debate as to whether we should see "truth" here as the objective truth of the gospel or as subjective truth, namely the believer's integrity and faithfulness (so Chrysostom and many

---

28. See M. Y. MacDonald, *Colossians, Ephesians* (Collegeville: Liturgical, 2000), p. 345.

29. See rightly J. Gnilka, *Der Epheserbrief* (Freiburg: Herder, 1971), p. 308; Lincoln, *Ephesians*, p. 446; cf. M. Barth, *Ephesians 4–6* (Garden City: Doubleday, 1974), pp. 804-5.

30. It is interesting in light of the imagery about to be used that Polybius 6.24 says that a centurion was supposed to be the kind of person who could be relied on under pressure to stand fast and not to give way.

31. Hoehner, *Ephesians*, p. 836.

32. It is possible to take Eph. 6.14-20 as all one long sentence (the eighth and last such sentence in Ephesians). See Hoehner, *Ephesians*, p. 837. However, it is possible to see something of a new sentence beginning with the imperative "receive, take" in v. 17.

33. Cf. Barth, *Ephesians 4–6*, p. 765; Herodotus 1.123; Thucydides 6.11.1; Josephus, *Antiquities* 2.44.

34. See Barth, *Ephesians 4–6*, p. 766.

35. See O'Brien, *Ephesians*, p. 472.

36. R. P. Martin, *Ephesians, Colossians, and Philemon* (Atlanta: John Knox, 1991), p. 76.

37. Schnackenburg, *Ephesians*, p. 277.

modern commentators). Since Paul says this is something one girds oneself with, the image suggests it is something objective to start with but becomes an intimate part of one's own protection and so subjective. The truth leads to truthfulness, integrity and faithfulness.[38] In view of Isa. 11.5, it would seem that the reference to righteousness must refer to the subjective virtue or attribute of the believer (cf. Rom. 10.3; Matt. 5.20). Sanctifying righteous living guards the life of the believer (cf. Rom. 6.13; 14.17).[39] In any case, "the picture presented is of a soldier waiting attentively, not of a soldier provoking aggression."[40]

The imagery here also suggests that while the evil age lasts there are still powerful forces of evil that can pester and persecute Christians and that Christians must be equipped to fend off. Believers fight from a position of strength since they are standing on the high ground, but they must never underestimate the power of the enemy. *Hetoimasia* in v. 15 means "readiness" and suggests a state of combat readiness, having put on the leather sandals or short boot (the *caliga*) needed by the soldier for battle.[41] Obviously one cannot stand firm without the proper footgear. It is striking that this warrior that Paul describes is equipped with "the gospel of peace."[42] Isa. 52.7, which refers to the feet of the messengers who bring news of peace, is alluded to here. This contrasts dramatically with the warrior in Isaiah 59, who clothes himself with vengeance and fury. Similarly, in Wis. 5.20 the divine warrior carries stern wrath for a sword. In Wis. 5.18 it is the helmet of doom that God puts on, but here "the helmet of salvation." Prayer and proclamation of the gospel of peace are the believer's two great offensive weapons against Satan. Nothing is said about deliverance or exorcism rituals. "It is not for believers to attack them in an attempt to inflict another defeat, for believers have not been equipped with the javelins necessary for attack: instead they need to stand where they are; if they hold their line, that itself will be another defeat for the powers."[43] It is knowledge of the gospel of peace that makes the believer ready to stand.[44]

In v. 16 Paul speaks of the *thyreos,* a full-length shield covered with leather

---

38. See Hoehner, *Ephesians,* pp. 839-40. The parallel in Isa. 11.5 suggests a subjective interpretation of both truth and righteousness here.

39. See Hoehner, p. 841.

40. MacDonald, *Colossians, Ephesians,* p. 343.

41. MacDonald, *Colossians, Ephesians,* p. 345; Lincoln, *Ephesians,* p. 449.

42. Probably the imagery of shoes is used because of the prophecy in Isaiah 52: "How wonderful are the feet of those who come across the mountains bringing the good news, news of peace."

43. E. Best, *Ephesians* (Edinburgh: Clark, 1998), p. 610.

44. Cf., for example, the means by which Jesus withstands the devil — by quoting Scripture (Matt. 4.1-11; Luke 4.1-13).

soaked in water or other substances to extinguish burning arrows.[45] Paul says that *all* the darts are quenched. The shield is Christian faith, which is "capable ... not only of blocking the threatening arrows but even of putting them out."[46] Particular stress is placed on faith by the phrase "besides all these." Here, as at various points in this peroration Paul says "you will be able" *(dynēsesthe)* or the like. He does not say that Christians will inevitably resist and stand. Rather, they are enabled to do so. Whether they do so or not depends on whether they draw on the resources they have been given and put their Christian virtues into practice.

V. 17 begins a new sentence with a verb rather than a participle ("receive") and speaks of "the helmet of salvation" and "the sword of the Spirit." R. Wild is probably correct that the reason for this break in the structure is that what has come before involves the believer actively doing something, but salvation and the Word of God are pure gifts to be received.[47] But this description also comports with what we know of Roman practice. Normally the attendant would place the helmet on the soldier and hand him his sword.[48] It is the Christian who receives salvation and the Word. This is then not likely a reference to initial salvation or justification (cf. 1 Thess. 5.8: the helmet of the hope of salvation). In fact "salvation" here might have its more generic sense of rescue or deliverance from harm in light of the background in Isa. 59.17. This is especially likely in view of the fact that we have here the neuter adjective *sōtērion* (rather than the noun *sōtēria*), which is not found elsewhere in Paul's writings (only at Luke 2.30; 3.6; Acts 28.28 elsewhere in the NT).

The sword referred to is the Roman short sword, the *machaira*, not the *romphaia,* which was the broad sword. Paul likely means by it the means by which the Spirit pierces the hardheartedness of others and the darkness, which is the Word of God. On God's Word as the only weapon God needs see Hos 6.5; Isa. 11.4; Rev. 1.16; 19.11. Perhaps Isa. 11.4, where word and breath stand in parallel, lies in the background of the juxtaposing of Word and Spirit here. It is telling that the usual image is of God speaking judgment and so striking down his foes (Rev. 1.16; 2.12, 16; 19.13, 15), but here the word in mind is the gospel of peace, the message about Christ's death and resurrection reconciling all into one body. The well-equipped soldier, the secure believer,[49] has only one offensive weapon to use against the darkness and its powers, the proclamation of the

---

45. On the use of flaming arrows in ancient warfare see Herodotus 8.52; Thucydides 2.75; Livy 21.8.

46. Schnackenburg, *Ephesians,* p. 279.

47. R. Wild, "The Warrior and the Prisoner: Some Reflections on Ephesians 6.10-20," *CBQ* 46 (1984): 284-98, here p. 297.

48. See MacDonald, *Colossians, Ephesians,* p. 346.

49. See Perkins, "Ephesians," p. 463.

Good News of peace through Christ. Notice Paul calls his audience to such activities just as he solicits their prayers for his own continuance of spreading the Good News despite being under house arrest.[50]

In v. 18 Paul says that believers must also be equipped with prayer.[51] It is not enough to have faith, righteousness, or truth. One must also continue to rely on God for aid day after day. Prayer is not said to be one of the believer's weapons and no part of the soldier's armor is used as a point of analogy with it.[52] Paul speaks of prayer "at all times" or occasions and with all kinds of prayer.[53] It is possible, to judge from Rom. 8.26-27 and 1 Cor. 14.1-5, that Paul is referring here with "in the Spirit" to what we call charismatic prayer, praying in the Spirit.[54] On the other hand, it is equally possible that he may just be referring to Spirit-filled or Spirit-prompted ordinary prayer.[55] Notice again the Asiatic redundancy here with "prayer" mentioned no less than four times (using *proseuchē* and *deēsis*). It appears we have returned to the use of Colossians material here (see Col. 4.3-4).

Paul also speaks here of vigilance or diligence in prayer, which suggests persistence despite opposition or impediments. *Proskarterēsis* occurs only here in the NT and is rare in the Greek of the period, but its cognate verb has the sense of persisting obstinately or adhering fiercely.[56] Perhaps the imagery of the soldier on watch is also alluded to here.[57] Believers must pray for all the saints

50. This text and its climax make quite clear that the author is not addressing an isolated or isolationist sect, nor is he inculcating such an attitude or approach to Christian community. Against MacDonald, *Colossians, Ephesians,* p. 350, this text calls for resistance to the powers and principalities *while* sharing the gospel with other people.

51. As Schnackenburg, *Ephesians,* p. 267, points out, the syntax here must count against the notion that 6.18-20 should be separated from 6.10-17. This verse begins with a prepositional phrase followed by two participles.

52. See Lincoln, *Ephesians,* p. 451.

53. Paul is not really doing a taxonomy of prayer here, distinguishing various types. This is more a matter of Asiatic rhetoric, using repetition (four references to prayer) for strong emphasis.

54. See the discussion in Fee, *God's Empowering Presence,* pp. 731-32. The reason for hesitation is that this prayer is for the saints and for Paul, and so has a specific intercessory content and does not seem to be the same as the Abba or praise language that glossolalia entails. At the very least Paul is speaking about a form of prayer especially aided by the Spirit.

55. See Best, *Ephesians,* p. 605. P. T. O'Brien, "Romans 8:26, 27: A Revolutionary Approach to Prayer?" *RTR* 46 (1987): 65-73. I think O'Brien is likely right about our text here, but probably wrong about Romans 8. See Lincoln, *Ephesians,* p. 452.

56. Barth, *Ephesians 4–6,* p. 778.

57. See Best, *Ephesians,* p. 597: "The weapons are primarily defensive since a position has to be held; any direct attack on the powers is left to Christ and is conceived as already having taken place."

and for Paul himself as they all do battle.[58] Prayer is not the whole armor, but it is an important part. One must be in prayer to face the foe. Paul asks for prayer that he might be given the words and the liberty in the Spirit to say what needs to be said to those around him. He wishes to proclaim the mystery of the gospel openly, which is to say the miracle of reconciliation of all sorts of people in Christ (on the "mystery" see pp. 236-37 above).

Paul calls himself an "ambassador" as in 2 Cor. 5.20 (cf. Phlm. 9), an ambassador for Christ, in chains because he serves another ruler. There is deliberate irony in the phrase "ambassador in chains." It connotes both an honorable status and a shameful state or condition. Normally an ambassador had diplomatic immunity, but not Paul the ambassador of Christ. In the Roman Empire the imprisonment of an ambassador would be seen as a direct affront to the one who sent him.[59] Thus in a sense Paul inverts the usual understanding of status, considering it an honor to be in chains for such a king. Yet still he asks prayer that he might have freedom and boldness and powerful rhetoric inspired by the Spirit to speak the truth in love to those with whom he comes in contact.

58. "All the saints" seems to refer to every believer, whereas "saints" seems to refer more specifically to Jewish Christians. See pp. 225-26 above.

Those who see Ephesians as pseudonymous have a difficult time explaining the request for prayer for Paul the ambassador in chains, especially since this passage draws on the parallel in Colossians, which mentions prayer for Paul *and others*. It does not really make sense to think of an author of Ephesians eliminating the reference to others, thus leaving the audience with a request to pray for the now deceased Paul alone. To suggest that this comports with regular epistolary practice of the age is an inadequate response because in this very passage the audience is asked to gird themselves with truth, and to beware deception, the stratagems of the powers of darkness. If the author is deliberately attempting to deceive the audience here about the matter of authorship, this raises an ethical dilemma in the context of early Christianity. Nor is it convincing to argue that the later Pauline representative is asking for such prayer. Was he also in prison? This is a very specific request for prayer for someone who was in chains, someone named Paul. See rightly Hoehner, *Ephesians,* pp. 861-62, 66.

59. O'Brien, *Ephesians,* pp. 488-89.

Epistolary Postscript —
The End of the Matter — 6.21-24

Though there is no mention of Paul's coworkers here in the postscript, this material is so dependent on Col. 4.7-8 that in v. 22 he says "how *we* are" *(ta peri hēmōn).*[1] Two more pointers to the encyclical nature of this document are the absence of personal greetings here at the end of the document[2] and the blessing in v. 24 "with *all* who love our Lord Jesus."[3] The assumption here is that Tychicus will not merely take this document part of the way to the audience and then hand it off to another messenger, but rather will go the entire way and be able to give further oral explanations about Paul's situation and the like. This was in keeping with the newer method of Roman postal delivery since the time of Augustus, whereas before his time it had always involved a relay system. Augustus found it better at both ends to have someone take a document the entire way, someone who could interpret it to the receiver and come back and report to the sender.[4]

But in order that you also might know the things concerning me, what I do, Tychicus, the beloved brother and faithful minister in the Lord, will make known to you everything, whom I have sent to you for this very thing in order that you might know the things concerning me and be encouraged in your hearts. Peace to the brothers and sisters and love with faithfulness from God the Father and the

---

1. R. P. Martin, *Ephesians, Colossians, and Philemon* (Atlanta: John Knox, 1991), p. 78.
2. R. Schnackenburg, *The Epistle to the Ephesians: A Commentary* (Edinburgh: Clark, 1991), p. 288.
3. Rightly, Schnackenburg, p. 292: "probably is directed to a circle of congregations not far from Ephesus, possibly including that town."
4. See *New Docs* 7, p. 56.

Lord Jesus Christ. Grace be with all who love the Lord Jesus Christ in incorruption/ immortality.[5]

Paul is sending Tychicus, the only other individual mentioned by name in this discourse, with the document. "You also" in v. 21 suggests that this document is sent along with another to a different or more specific audience, presumably Colossians. We have here thirty-two consecutive words copied directly from Colossians, which means that the scribe had Colossians before him while composing Ephesians. This in itself suggests that Ephesians is some kind of homily meant to circulate in the same territory as Colossians. But, unlike Colossians, Onesimus is not mentioned here as a companion to Tychicus. This may suggest that Ephesians was not destined for the household of Philemon, whatever other congregations in or around Colossae it may have gone to.[6]

Tychicus seems clearly to have been important to Paul during the latter stages of his ministry. A native of the province of Asia (Acts 20.4), he was with Paul in Greece and at the end of the so-called third missionary journey went with Paul to Troas and then on to Jerusalem, helping carry the Collection. 2 Tim. 4.12 indicates that he was still working with Paul even later, being sent for some purpose to Ephesus, and Tit. 3.12 may even suggest that he sent to Crete to replace Titus.[7] Tychicus is to report on Paul's situation to the audience. "Send" here is in the form of an epistolary aorist ("sent," but from Paul's point of view meaning "am sending"). Tychicus is a "faithful minister" (*diakonos;* see pp. 264-69 above on this term).

The final benediction in vv. 23-24 is in the third person, probably because the document was intended to be an encyclical.[8] Here alone is the audience

---

5. There are no theologically significant textual variants in this passage. It is however interesting to note the subscripts appended here in various manuscripts. ℵ, A, B, and others have "to Ephesus." B and P have "to Ephesus from Rome." L adds that it was written through Tychicus from that locale, as does the Textus Receptus. These are of course traditional guesses based on the text itself and perhaps on church tradition.

6. On the issue of pseudonymity in the case of this particular document see H. Hoehner, *Ephesians* (Grand Rapids: Baker, 2002), pp. 871-72: "Verses 21-22 . . . if Tychicus was the author . . . , make no sense at all. Why would the congregation want to know of Paul's situation when he was already dead? Were they to pray for the dead? It is incongruous for a pseudonymous author to ask the Ephesian believers to pray for Paul when he knew Paul was no longer living. It is even more preposterous to think that Tychicus would report about Paul's situation if the letter were not by Paul himself. It would mean that Tychicus would be part of a fraud. If the author was pseudonymous, then the Ephesians would not have known who he was, and if they knew who he was, the letter is not pseudonymous!" Contrast this with the discussion in A. T. Lincoln, *Ephesians* (Waco: Word, 1990), pp. 461-64.

7. See P. T. O'Brien, *The Letter to the Ephesians* (Grand Rapids: Eerdmans, 1999), p. 492.

8. See G. B. Caird, *Paul's Letters from Prison* (Oxford: Oxford University Press, 1976), p. 93. It is interesting that the same conclusion can be reached by someone who sees this as a

called "brothers."[9] The document began with "grace and peace" and ends with these two now in reverse order. It also began with a reference to "God the Father and the Lord Jesus Christ" (1.2) and ends in the same fashion. There is then some rhetorical concern for symmetry. Only here in this discourse do we hear about believers' love for Christ, though love has been a frequent topic in Ephesians.

The discourse ends with the interesting phrase "in incorruption" or "in immortality." This would seem to qualify "grace," in which case Paul is wishing grace unalloyed upon his audience. But it may be suggesting where this grace leads us: unto and into eternity. Chrysostom in his twenty-fourth homily on Ephesians suggests that the phrase means either "in purity" or "for the sake of the incorruptible things."[10] If so, the document ends where it began with the eternal God and his eternal plan to give believers grace so that they might have eternal life.[11] Since, however, Paul does use the same term of the resurrection body (1 Cor. 15.42-54), that, rather than life in heaven, may well be referred to here. The translation "immortality" leaves one's options open since it does not specify in what form immortality comes (disembodiment or resurrection body). 2 Tim. 1.10 associates incorruptibility with Christ's abolition of death and bringing of life to light, which again may suggest a connection with resurrection.[12] Nevertheless, the phrase may modify "love," in which case we should translate "in undying/unceasing love."[13]

In any case, as Schnackenburg points out, we have two final blessings, one in v. 23, one in v. 24, one looking to the present, one to the future,[14] just as at the beginning of the document we had both the eulogy and the thanksgiving. Amplification of this sort is typical of Asiatic rhetoric, and our author is faithful to follow the conventions right to the end of the document. Having begun the discourse with God's love and grace and the believer's faith, Paul ends the discourse in the same manner.

---

post-Pauline letter. See M. Y. MacDonald, *Colossians, Ephesians* (Collegeville: Liturgical, 2000), p. 353, who recognizes that the third person plural "gives the impression of a greater distance between the author and the recipients of the letter and thus suggests a wider audience."

9. The impersonal way this is phrased, "peace to the brothers" not "peace to you brothers," also supports the idea of an encyclical.

10. The term first appears in the biblical tradition in Wis. 2.23; 6.18-19; cf. *4 Maccabees* 9.22; 17.12. See E. Best, *Ephesians* (Edinburgh: Clark, 1998), p. 620.

11. Caird, *Paul's Letters*, p. 94; M. Barth, *Ephesians 4–6* (Garden City: Doubleday, 1974), p. 814.

12. See P. Perkins, "Ephesians," *New Interpreter's Bible* XI (Nashville: Abingdon, 2000), p. 406.

13. See Hoehner, *Ephesians*, pp. 876-77.

14. Schnackenburg, *Ephesians*, p. 291.

Bridging the Horizons — Ephesians

> The salvation of man is not to be conceived as the rescue of favored individuals out of a doomed world to participate in an otherworldly existence totally unrelated to life on earth. Man's personality is so intimately linked with his environment that he must be saved in the context of all the corporate relationships and loyalties, achievements and aspirations, which constitute a genuinely human existence.[1]

Sometimes when the soteriology of Ephesians is discussed it has been suggested that the author is so heavenly minded that he has given up on the eschatological dimensions of salvation, particularly the resurrection of the bodies of believers. This is a mistake, and partly it comes from the failure to recognize that this is a sermon in epideictic form and as such is supposed to focus on things that are true in the present and worth affirming and valuing. The rhetorical species and function of this discourse effects the mode of the eschatological teaching in it. This is too seldom noticed. But Ephesians does have a few references to the fact that salvation has three tenses — past, present, and future. In fact, it can be argued that in Ephesians the term "salvation" primarily if not exclusively refers to final salvation, not conversion, which is spoken of using the language of redemption and adoption as children (see ch. 1).

It is of course difficult to maintain the right balance between language such as the sealing and down payment language in reference to the Spirit in ch. 1 and the discussions about moral danger and apostasy elsewhere in the discourse. It is sometimes assumed that since one has been sealed by the Holy Spirit, one is spiritually bullet-proof and eternally secure. Alas, this is not Paul's point. The

---

1. G. B. Caird, *Paul's Letters from Prison* (Oxford: Oxford University Press, 1976), p. 40.

metaphor of the seal was well known and commonly used, and it was equally well known that seals could be broken. But the language of down payment or deposit in the form of the Spirit clearly implies that salvation has only just begun at conversion. There will need to be future "deposits." The house has not been bought or guaranteed just because the down payment has been made. Failure to think through the implications of the metaphorical language in Ephesians 1 has led to all sorts of distorted views of Pauline soteriology.

And this of course brings us to the whole language of incorporation, of being in Christ, of being elect. According to ch. 1, election takes place in Christ, and not elsewhere. He is the Elect One chosen from before the foundations of the world and destined to be our Savior. Believers are only chosen "in him," as the eulogy repeats over and over again. This corporate concept of election really does not differ much from that applied to Israel in the OT. Being part of the elect group depended on a variety of factors, including faith and faithfulness, and one could be in the group at one juncture and then out later, broken off from the people of God as Paul describes it in Romans 11. There is nothing in Ephesians 1 that suggests that certain individuals were predetermined to be in Christ. There is, however, the clear language that Christ himself was chosen in advance to be the agent of and locus in which all salvation happens. That is a very different matter.

This balance between divine action in Christ and human response can be seen at the end of the discourse as well, in the wonderful peroratio. Here the believer is equipped for spiritual battle by being given the very armor of God himself. It is interesting how some of the verbs refer to something simply given to the believer (the helmet, the sword) and some refer to the action that the believer himself must take once these gifts are in place — standing, praying, resisting, speaking, and the like. Salvation and faith are gifts, but they are gifts that do not work automatically. They are gifts that must be embraced, used, and expressed. Ephesians then gives no succor to either a hard-line Calvinist theology or to a Pelagian theology that suggests salvation is somehow a human self-help program. No indeed. Paul insists that salvation, like the helmet, is a gift — but the believer must receive it, wear it, use it to be protected. Spiritual protection does not happen by divine fiat alone any more than perseverance in the faith is simply the work of God in the believer alone. It is rather the working by God of salvation into the community of believers which the believers must then work out with fear and trembling as Paul makes so very clear in Phil. 2.12-13. What this means is that while our working out of our salvation as a group (for the "you" in Philippians 2 is plural) is essential to the completion of sanctification in our lives, salvation remains a gift. We are not saved either by means of our own efforts, or without our own efforts. There is a paradox here in regard to salvation which Paul would have us embrace without trying to resolve it on either the divine or the human side of the equation.

Robert Frost wrote a remarkable poem entitled "Mending Wall" which he recited at the inauguration of John F. Kennedy. In this poem there is the perspective given by one interlocutor that "good fences make good neighbors," but Frost's response in the poem is that "something there is that does not love a wall." Paul in Eph. 2.14 holds the latter view and even goes so far as to say that the wall known as the Law creates hostility, presumably because it shuts some people out from God. Christ has broken down the wall which separated Jew and Gentile. That is, the Mosaic Law was abolished or annulled through the death and resurrection of Jesus, which inaugurated the new age and the new covenant. Indeed, one could say that Christ came to break down all the ethnic, social, sexual, and even religious barriers that stand in the way of creating one unified people of God. This is the significance of a statement like Gal. 3.28 of course, but the matter is made all the more clear in Ephesians where we even hear that God's salvation plan is "to bring all things in heaven and on earth together under the one head, even Christ." In other words, there is universalism to the scope of this salvation plan within the context of the particularism that is Jesus Christ. All must come to the Father through Jesus the Son, and this is so because only the Son has provided the redemption and salvation which can transform both the world of humans and the cosmic realm and forces as well. The worldwide church inclusive of all human groups then becomes the visible image and microcosm of God's plan. "As the community of the redeemed, both Jews and Gentiles, the church is the masterpiece of God's grace (cf. 2:7). It is a realm of his presence and authority (1:22, 23; 2:22), the instrument through which his wisdom is made known to the spiritual powers in the heavenly realm (3:10)."[2]

Sometimes our view of salvation becomes too cramped and small. We think of it as in essence something that happens in the human heart but hardly affects the rest of the world or the rest of life. It is important then to note that while "Christ in your heart" often occurs in modern Christian literature, it appears in the NT only in Eph. 3.17, and there it has the plural "your hearts." It is not referring to an isolated individual experience of Christ. Each member individually and all together as a community have Christ within them. This experience is that of all Christians, not just the elite super-spiritual ones.

But if all theology is of grace, as Ephesians 1–3 suggests, what is the basis of all ethics? The essential answer is gratitude — the response of a grateful heart to what God has done in one's life. E. Best makes the important point that when Christ's love and not fear rules people's lives, they can face up to their moral obligations.[3] Indeed, they are enabled and empowered to do so by the love of God shed abroad in their hearts (see Romans 5). Grace is what empow-

---

2. P. T. O'Brien, *The Letter to the Ephesians* (Grand Rapids: Eerdmans, 1999), p. 268.
3. E. Best, *Ephesians* (Edinburgh: Clark, 1998), p. 347.

ers obedience and willing submission to God's will, and the motivation for being ethical is in part gratitude, in part a desire to be like Christ and emulate
Christ, as the analogy between husband and wife and Christ and the church
suggests in Ephesians 5, and in part because one wants to please one's Lord.

Chrysostom, in his twentieth homily on Ephesians, has these things to say
about Christian marriage and subordination in marriage:

> There is no relationship between [human] and [human] so close as that be-
> tween man and wife, if they be joined together as they should be. . . . For in-
> deed, in very deed, this love is more despotic than any despotism: for others
> indeed may be strong, but this passion is not only strong, but unfading. For
> there is a certain love, deeply seated in our nature, which imperceptibly to
> ourselves knits together these bodies of ours. Thus even from the very be-
> ginning woman sprang from man, and afterwards from man and woman
> sprang both man and woman. Do you perceive the close bond and connec-
> tion? . . . [God] permitted the man to marry . . . even his own flesh. And
> thus the whole he framed from one beginning, gathering all together like
> stones in a building, into one. For neither on the one hand did he form her
> from without, and this was so that the man might not feel towards her as
> towards an alien, nor again did he confine her to her own kind, that she
> might not, by contracting herself, and making all center in herself, be cut
> off from the rest.

We have stressed in our treatment of the household code of Ephesians that it
assumes the existence of a Christian one-flesh union between husband and wife
such that these exhortations can actually be worked out in such a context. If
there is no such union, then these commandments cannot be obeyed. Indeed, if
the relationship is not a Christian one in regard to both parties' orientation and
behavior, they probably should not be obeyed as they lead to abuse of the subordinate partner in the relationship. If there is not mutual submission, service
and love in the relationship, then the relationship is violated and its reciprocity
deformed. It is no accident that Paul here stresses that mutual submission is
something that all Christians should be involved in toward all other Christians,
just as he says singing is something we should all do in relationship to each
other. It is only in the context of a community of submission that the submission of wife to husband and the loving self-sacrifice of husband to wife can be
encouraged, nurtured, and sustained. In other words, by the umbilical verbal
connection of 5.21 to what follows it is made perfectly clear that this ethics of
married life can only be played out and lived out in a functioning Christian
community. Then the husband and wife's relationship simply becomes a particular example and model of what mutual submission ought to look like. In
Eph. 5.21ff. we reach the apex of canonical discussion of Christian marriage,
and it is no accident that Paul treats the subject as a high and holy one that is at

the heart of all human relationships. He treats it as a deeply personal matter, but not as a private matter that is simply between the marital partners. Indeed not. If they are modeling their behavior on the interpersonal behavior of Christ and the church, then they must be constantly looking to the church, just as the church will be looking to them for their cues as to how this relationship should be played out.

When a Christian marriage fails, which does indeed happen, it is also a failure of the Christian community to support and nurture and guide that relationship. It is not a private failure. All the Christian ethics in Paul's letters are community ethics, ethics for Christians to wrestle with together and help each other obey. Our modern individualistic culture neither understands the primacy of community as it is enunciated in Ephesians, nor knows how to respond to such ethical enjoinders because of its radical individualism. There desperately needs to be a rebirth of understanding of community, of the body of Christ, of life together as the family of faith if one is to make sense of what Paul says here. Otherwise, what we are being taught here becomes an unrealizable ethical ideal, not a description of what by the grace of God and the help of the community can be real. And we need to understand clearly that God's grace, his sanctifying power, is ministered to us primarily through and in cooperation with the body of Christ. If we long to have more holy marriages, we must together become a less dysfunctional and more holy people working out our salvation together with fear and trembling as God works in the midst of the community to will and to do.

There is, in some portions of the church today, a rather extreme and morbid curiosity about or fascination with the powers of darkness. This can be seen from the popularity of the various novels of Frank Peretti (e.g., *This Present Darkness*) as well as the more recent best-selling series by Timothy LaHaye and friends called the "Left Behind" series. As Gordon Fee points out, it appears that we have one extreme or another when it comes to texts like Eph. 6.10-20: a tendency to relegate demons to the dustbin by calling them a part of the mythology of an earlier more primitive time, or a tendency to recognize the existence of such spiritual beings and attribute to them an importance out of all proportion to what the Scriptures assign them. Fee adds that

> as in most such matters, Paul's position lies in the "radical middle" — to take them with dead seriousness, but also to recognize that they are a tethered foe, restrained by Christ's victory over them in the cross and resurrection (Col. 2:15; Eph. 2:6-7). In our present existence as "already but not yet," one would be foolhardy indeed to deny the presence of such "spiritual forces of evil" or understand them in some kind of "demythologized" way as mere "forces" and not true spirit beings. But we need also to recognize that the thrust of this passage is not for us to become enamored with them,

but to withstand them through the armor provided by Christ in the gospel and through the weapons of the Spirit.[4]

It needs to be said as well that nothing in Ephesians 6 encourages Christians to go on the offensive against the powers of darkness by any other means than the proclamation of the gospel of peace and light. The armor described in the peroration is meant to equip the saint for adequately "standing" and "withstanding" the spiritual powers that bewitch, bother, and bewilder us all. There is nothing here that warrants or encourages either deliverance ministries or the demonizing of all human dilemmas, as if there were a demon under every rock along the path of life. There is absolutely nothing in the NT that warrants "the devil made me do it" or talk of demons of colds, of warts, of lust, or the like. The NT, including Ephesians, is persistent and clear in stressing that human beings have responsibility for their own behavior, especially Christian human beings empowered and enabled by God's Spirit. There can be no justification, particularly for Christians, for sloughing off responsibility for sin onto the Nefarious One or the powers of darkness. Why? Because the Lordship of Christ, so ably expounded in Ephesians, is greater than any other source or sort of spiritual power. "Greater is he who is in us" than any of these lesser powers that pester us from without. Put another way, if Christ dwells in a believer, there is no room for other sorts of lordships in the Christian life. Christ cannot be forced out of the Christian heart by a lesser spiritual force. Demonic possession only transpires when someone willingly submits to such a power. It does not happen by accident any more than apostasy happens by accident. Indeed, one could say that real apostasy, real grieving of the Holy Spirit, would have to happen before a Christian could then embrace or be enveloped by the powers of darkness. Even in this scenario, human choice is involved before demonic possession can happen.

Thus, at every turn in Ephesians and elsewhere in the NT, responsibility for human ills and misbehavior is laid at the door of the humans in question, including Christian humans. Christians are not exempt from ethical behavior just because they are saved. Indeed, it is a required part of their working out their salvation, a part of their progressive sanctification. In fact, "to whom more is given more is required." Christians are enabled and called to a higher standard of rectitude and love than anyone else on earth.

Ephesians, like Colossians, is emphatic that Christ has already fought and won the battle of D-Day against the powers and principalities and has led them off in a Roman-style triumph. All that is left is rearguard action, for they know their doom is sure. They are on a short leash, or better said, a chain, which is in the hands of the one who defeated them on the cross, stripping himself of their

---

4. G. D. Fee, *God's Empowering Presence* (Peabody: Hendrickson, 1994), p. 726.

malevolent powers and thereby equipping us against them as well by the same act. This theology desperately needs to permeate the conservative church more adequately. At the same time, the warning of C. S. Lewis in his classic *The Screwtape Letters* should be engraved on the lintel of the doors of the liberal church that tries to say that the powers of darkness are just a part of pure primitive mythology, not modern reality. Lewis pointed out that it is the chief tactic or smokescreen of the devil to convince intelligent people that he does not exist! Obviously this tactic is working in some quarters of the church. That extreme approach to the powers of darkness is no more grounded in the NT than the "demon under every rock approach" of some conservative churches. Just as we should not give the devil too much credit (much less give him "his due"), at the same time we should not lightly dismiss or underestimate the fact that our struggle is not, as Paul reminds us, just against flesh and blood, but rather also against the prince of the power of the air and his minions. But still and all, as Luther says in the great Reformation hymn "Ein' feste Burg":

> A mighty fortress is our God, a bulwark never failing;
> Our helper He, amid the flood of mortal ills prevailing:
> For still our ancient foe doth seek to work us woe;
> His craft and power are great, and, armed with cruel hate,
> On earth is not his equal.

> Did we in our own strength confide, our striving would be losing;
> Were not the right Man on our side, the Man of God's own choosing:
> Dost ask who that may be? Christ Jesus, it is He;
> Lord Sabaoth, His Name, from age to age the same,
> And He must win the battle.

> And though this world, with devils filled, should threaten to undo us,
> We will not fear, for God hath willed His truth to triumph through us:
> The Prince of Darkness grim, we tremble not for him;
> His rage we can endure, for lo, his doom is sure,
> One little word shall fell him.

> That word above all earthly powers, no thanks to them, abideth;
> The Spirit and the gifts are ours through Him Who with us sideth:
> Let goods and kindred go, this mortal life also;
> The body they may kill: God's truth abideth still,
> His kingdom is forever.

Index of Authors

Index of Scripture and Other Ancient Writings